CLYMER® MANUALS

KAWASAKI
KLR650 • 2008-2017

WHAT'S IN YOUR TOOLBOX?

More information available at Clymer.com
Phone: 805-498-6703

Haynes Publishing Group
Sparkford Nr Yeovil
Somerset BA22 7JJ England

Haynes North America, Inc
859 Lawrence Drive
Newbury Park
California 91320 USA

ISBN 10: 1-62092-274-6
ISBN-13: 978-1-62092-274-3
Library of Congress: 2016955152

Author: 2013 through 2017 information by Ed Scott
Technical Illustrations: Mitzi McCarthy
Cover: Mark Clifford Photography at www.markclifford.com

AUG 3 0 2017
© **Haynes North America, Inc. 2009, 2011, 2016**
With permission from J.H. Haynes & Co. Ltd.

Clymer is a registered trademark of Haynes North America, Inc.

Printed in the U.S.A.

All rights reserved. No part of this book may be reproduced or transmitted in any form or by any means, electronic or mechanical, including photocopying, recording or by any information storage or retrieval system, without permission in writing from the copyright holder.

While every attempt is made to ensure that the information in this manual is correct, no liability can be accepted by the authors or publishers for loss, damage or injury caused by any errors in, or omissions from, the information given.

M240-2, 11U2, 16-312   ABCDEFGHIJKLMNOPQRS

Chapter One General Information	1
Chapter Two Troubleshooting	2
Chapter Three Lubrication, Maintenance and Tune-up	3
Chapter Four Engine Top End	4
Chapter Five Engine Lower End	5
Chapter Six Clutch, Gearshift Mechanism and Lubrication System	6
Chapter Seven Transmission and Shift Mechanism	7
Chapter Eight Fuel System	8
Chapter Nine Electrical System	9
Chapter Ten Cooling System	10
Chapter Eleven Wheels, Tires and Drive Chain	11
Chapter Twelve Front Suspension and Steering	12
Chapter Thirteen Rear Suspension	13
Chapter Fourteen Brakes	14
Chapter Fifteen Body	15
Index	16
Wiring Diagram	17

Common spark plug conditions

NORMAL
Symptoms: Brown to grayish-tan color and slight electrode wear. Correct heat range for engine and operating conditions.
Recommendation: When new spark plugs are installed, replace with plugs of the same heat range.

WORN
Symptoms: Rounded electrodes with a small amount of deposits on the firing end. Normal color. Causes hard starting in damp or cold weather and poor fuel economy.
Recommendation: Plugs have been left in the engine too long. Replace with new plugs of the same heat range. Follow the recommended maintenance schedule.

TOO HOT
Symptoms: Blistered, white insulator, eroded electrode and absence of deposits. Results in shortened plug life.
Recommendation: Check for the correct plug heat range, over-advanced ignition timing, lean fuel mixture, intake manifold vacuum leaks, sticking valves and insufficient engine cooling.

CARBON DEPOSITS
Symptoms: Dry sooty deposits indicate a rich mixture or weak ignition. Causes misfiring, hard starting and hesitation.
Recommendation: Make sure the plug has the correct heat range. Check for a clogged air filter or problem in the fuel system or engine management system. Also check for ignition system problems.

PREIGNITION
Symptoms: Melted electrodes. Insulators are white, but may be dirty due to misfiring or flying debris in the combustion chamber. Can lead to engine damage.
Recommendation: Check for the correct plug heat range, over-advanced ignition timing, lean fuel mixture, insufficient engine cooling and lack of lubrication.

ASH DEPOSITS
Symptoms: Light brown deposits encrusted on the side or center electrodes or both. Derived from oil and/or fuel additives. Excessive amounts may mask the spark, causing misfiring and hesitation during acceleration.
Recommendation: If excessive deposits accumulate over a short time or low mileage, install new valve guide seals to prevent seepage of oil into the combustion chambers. Also try changing gasoline brands.

HIGH SPEED GLAZING
Symptoms: Insulator has yellowish, glazed appearance. Indicates that combustion chamber temperatures have risen suddenly during hard acceleration. Normal deposits melt to form a conductive coating. Causes misfiring at high speeds.
Recommendation: Install new plugs. Consider using a colder plug if driving habits warrant.

OIL DEPOSITS
Symptoms: Oily coating caused by poor oil control. Oil is leaking past worn valve guides or piston rings into the combustion chamber. Causes hard starting, misfiring and hesitation.
Recommendation: Correct the mechanical condition with necessary repairs and install new plugs.

DETONATION
Symptoms: Insulators may be cracked or chipped. Improper gap setting techniques can also result in a fractured insulator tip. Can lead to piston damage.
Recommendation: Make sure the fuel anti-knock values meet engine requirements. Use care when setting the gaps on new plugs. Avoid lugging the engine.

GAP BRIDGING
Symptoms: Combustion deposits lodge between the electrodes. Heavy deposits accumulate and bridge the electrode gap. The plug ceases to fire, resulting in a dead cylinder.
Recommendation: Locate the faulty plug and remove the deposits from between the electrodes.

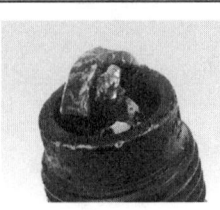

MECHANICAL DAMAGE
Symptoms: May be caused by a foreign object in the combustion chamber or the piston striking an incorrect reach (too long) plug. Causes a dead cylinder and could result in piston damage.
Recommendation: Repair the mechanical damage. Remove the foreign object from the engine and/or install the correct reach plug.

CONTENTS

QUICK REFERENCE DATA IX

CHAPTER ONE
GENERAL INFORMATION 1
- Manual organization
- Warnings, cautions and notes
- Safety
- Serial numbers
- Fasteners
- Shop supplies
- Tools
- Measuring tools
- Electrical system fundamentals
- Service methods
- Storage
- Specifications

CHAPTER TWO
TROUBLESHOOTING 29
- Starting the engine
- Engine spark test
- Engine performance
- Electrical testing
- Starting system
- Engine noise
- Motorcycle noise
- Engine lubrication
- Engine leakdown test
- Clutch
- Gear shift linkage and transmission
- Brakes
- Steering and handling
- Specifications

CHAPTER THREE
LUBRICATION, MAINTENANCE AND TUNE-UP 39

    Pre-ride inspection
    Tune-up and service intervals
    Fuel and lubricants
    Periodic lubrication

    Maintenance and inspection
    Engine tune-up
    Spark plugs
    Specifications

CHAPTER FOUR
ENGINE TOP END 70

    Exhaust system
    Cylinder head cover
    Camshafts and cam chain tensioner
    Cylinder head

    Valves
    Cylinder
    Piston and piston rings
    Specifications

CHAPTER FIVE
ENGINE LOWER END 103

    Engine
    Cam chain and lower guide
    Left crankcase cover
    Engine balancer
    Crankcase

    Seal replacement
    Crankcase bearings
    Crankshaft
    Engine break-in
    Specifications

CHAPTER SIX
CLUTCH, GEARSHIFT MECHANISM AND LUBRICATION SYSTEM. 123

    Right crankcase cover
    Clutch
    External gearshift linkage
    Oil pump

    Primary drive gear
    Clutch cable replacement
    Specifications

CHAPTER SEVEN
TRANSMISSION AND SHIFT MECHANISM 140

    Transmission
    Input shaft
    Output shaft

    Transmission inspection
    Shift drum and forks
    Specifications

CHAPTER EIGHT
FUEL SYSTEM 151

    Carburetor
    Carburetor operation
    Fuel valve
    Evaporative emissions control system
      (California models only)

    Throttle cable
    Choke cable
    Air filter housing
    Specifications

CHAPTER NINE
ELECTRICAL SYSTEM... 169

Electrical component replacement
Continuity testing guidelines
Electrical connectors
Negative battery terminal
Battery
Charging system
Alternator cover
Stator
Rotor and starter clutch
Regulator/rectifier
Starting system
Starter
Starter relay
Starter circuit relay
Ignition system
Fan system
Coolant temperature gauge and sending unit
Meter unit
Lighting system
Switches
Fuses
Specifications

CHAPTER TEN
COOLING SYSTEM... 203

Safety precautions
Radiator and fan
Thermostat
Coolant temperature sending unit
Water pump
Coolant reserve tank
Specifications

CHAPTER ELEVEN
WHEELS, TIRES AND DRIVE CHAIN... 210

Front wheel and speedometer drive unit
Rear wheel
Front and rear hubs
Rim and spoke service
Drive chain
Sprockets
Tire changing
Specifications

CHAPTER TWELVE
FRONT SUSPENSION AND STEERING... 230

Handlebar
Handlebar left hand grip replacement
Balancer weights
Fork service
Front fork
Steering stem and head
Specifications

CHAPTER THIRTEEN
REAR SUSPENSION... 248

Shock absorber
Shock absorber linkage
Swing arm
Shock absorber adjustment
Specifications

CHAPTER FOURTEEN
BRAKES 261

    Brake fluid selection
    Brake service
    Front brake pads
    Front brake caliper
    Front master cylinder
    Rear brake pads
    Rear brake caliper
    Rear master cylinder
    Rear brake pedal
    Brake system draining
    Brake system bleeding
    Brake disc
    Specifications

CHAPTER FIFTEEN
BODY 285

    Side covers
    Seat
    Fuel tank
    Lower fairing
    Upper fairing
    Front fender
    Rear carrier
    Rear fender
    Subframe
    Skid plate
    Specifications

INDEX 291

WIRING DIAGRAM 296

QUICK REFERENCE DATA

```
MODEL: _____  YEAR: _____
VIN NUMBER: _____
ENGINE SERIAL NUMBER: _____
CARBURETOR SERIAL NUMBER OR I.D. MARK: _____
```

FUEL, LUBRICANTS AND FLUIDS

Fuel type	Unleaded gasoline; 87 octane minimum
Fuel tank capacity	22 liters (5.8 gal.)
Engine oil	SG, four-stroke engine oil*
	SAE 10W-30, 10W-40, 20W-40, 10W-50 or 20W-50
Engine oil capacity	
Without filter change	2.2 liters (2.3 quarts)
With filter change	2.5 liters (2.6 quarts)
Cooling system capacity	1.55 liters (1.64 quarts)
Coolant mixture	50:50 (distilled water/antifreeze)
Coolant type	Ethylene glycol containing anti-corrosion inhibitors for aluminum engines
Drive chain	O-ring type chain lubricant
Fork oil grade	Kayaba G-10 or equivalent 10-weight fork oil
Brake fluid type	DOT 4
Control cables	Cable lube
Air filter	Foam air filter oil

*API SH, SJ or SL with JASO MA certification.

ROUTINE CHECKS AND ADJUSTMENTS

Brake pad lining minimum thickness	1.0 mm (0.040 in.)
Brake pedal pushrod length	69-71 mm (2.72-2.80 in.)
Choke lever free play	2-3 mm (0.08-0.12 in.) at tip
Clutch lever free play	8-12 mm (0.31-0.47 in.)
Drive chain play	35-45 mm (1.38-1.77 in.)
Drive chain length service limit (20 links/21 pins)	323 mm (12.72 in.)
Radiator cap relief pressure	93-123 kPa (13.5-17.8 psi)
Wheel rim runout (radial and lateral)	2.0 mm (0.08 in.)
Throttle grip free play	2-3 mm (0.08-0.12 in.)
Tire pressure	
Front	150 kPa (22 psi)
Rear	
Load up to 97.5 kg (215 lb.)	150 kPa (22 psi)
Load 97.5-182 kg (215-401 lb.)	200 kPa (29 psi)

TUNE-UP SPECIFICATIONS

Battery	12 volt, 14 amp-hour
Compression	529-853 kPa (77-124 psi)
Idle speed	1200-1400 rpm
Ignition timing*	
Idle	10° BTDC at 1300 rpm
Advanced	30° BTDC at 4000 rpm

(continued)

TUNE-UP SPECIFICATIONS (continued)

Pilot mixture screw	1 5/8 turns out
Spark plug type	NGK DPR8EA-9 or ND X24EPR-U9
Spark plug gap	0.8-0.9 mm (0.031-0.035 in.)
Valve clearance (engine cold)	
Exhaust	0.15-0.25 mm (0.006-0.010 in.)
Intake	0.10-0.20 mm (0.004-0.008 in.)

*Not adjustable (set by igniter).

MAINTENANCE TORQUE SPECIFICATIONS

Item	N•m	in.-lb.	ft.-lb.
Balancer chain tensioner bolt	8.8	78	—
Coolant drain plug	8.8	78	—
Oil drain plug	29	—	21
Oil filter cover bolts	8.8	78	—
Rear axle nut	98	—	72
Rotor bolt plug	2.5	22	—
Spark plug	14	—	10
Timing plug	2.5	22	—

CHAPTER ONE

GENERAL INFORMATION

This detailed and comprehensive manual covers 2008-on Kawasaki KLR650. Models with a L suffix were manufactured to meet California requirements.

The text provides complete information on maintenance, tune-up, repair and overhaul. Hundreds of photos and drawings guide the reader through every job. All procedures are in step-by-step format and designed for the reader who may be working on the motorcycle for the first time.

MANUAL ORGANIZATION

A shop manual is a reference tool and, as in all Clymer manuals, the chapters are thumb-tabbed for easy reference. Important items are indexed at the end of the manual. Frequently used specifications and capacities from individual chapters are summarized in the *Quick Reference Data* at the front of the manual.

During some of the procedures there will be references to headings in other chapters or sections of the manual. When a specific heading is called out in a step, it is *italicized* as it appears in the manual. If a sub-heading is indicated as being "in this section," it is located within the same main heading. For example, the sub-heading *Handling Gasoline Safely* is located within the main heading *SAFETY*.

This chapter provides general information on shop safety, tool use, service fundamentals and shop supplies. **Tables 1-6** at the end of the chapter provide general motorcycle, mechanical and shop information.

Chapter Two provides methods for quick and accurate diagnoses of problems. Troubleshooting procedures present typical symptoms and logical methods to pinpoint and repair a problem.

Chapter Three explains all routine maintenance.

Subsequent chapters describe specific systems such as engine, clutch, transmission, fuel system, electrical system, wheels, tires, drive chain, suspension, brakes and body components.

Specification tables, when applicable, are located at the end of each chapter.

WARNINGS, CAUTIONS AND NOTES

The terms WARNING, CAUTION and NOTE have specific meanings in this manual.

A WARNING emphasizes areas where injury or even death could result from negligence. Mechanical damage may also occur. WARNINGS *are to be taken seriously.*

A CAUTION emphasizes areas where equipment damage could result. Disregarding a CAUTION could cause permanent mechanical damage, though injury is unlikely.

A NOTE provides additional information to make a step or procedure easier or clearer. Disregarding a NOTE could cause inconvenience, but would not cause equipment damage or injury.

SAFETY

Professional mechanics can work for years and never sustain a serious injury or mishap. Follow these guidelines and practice common sense to safely service the motorcycle:
1. Do not operate the motorcycle in an enclosed area. The exhaust gasses contain carbon monoxide, an odorless, colorless and tasteless poisonous gas. Carbon monoxide levels build quickly in small enclosed areas and can cause unconsciousness and death in a short time. Make sure the work area is properly ventilated, or operate the motorcycle outside.
2. *Never* use gasoline or any flammable liquid to clean parts. Refer to *Handling Gasoline Safely* and *Cleaning Parts* in this section.
3. *Never* smoke or use a torch in the vicinity of flammable liquids, such as gasoline or cleaning solvent.
4. Do not remove the radiator cap or any cooling system hose while the engine is hot. The cooling system is pressurized and the high temperature coolant may cause injury.
5. Dispose of and store coolant in a safe manner. Do not allow children or pets access to open containers of coolant. Animals are attracted to antifreeze.
6. Avoid contact with engine oil and other chemicals. Most are known carcinogens. Wash your hands thoroughly after coming in contact with engine oil. If possible, wear a pair of disposable gloves.
7. If welding or brazing on the motorcycle, remove the fuel tank and shocks to a safe distance at least 15 m (50 ft.) away.
8. Use the correct types and sizes of tools to avoid damaging fasteners.
9. Keep tools clean and in good condition. Replace or repair worn or damaged equipment.
10. When loosening a tight fastener, be guided by what would happen if the tool slips.
11. When replacing fasteners, make sure the new fasteners are the same size and strength as the originals.
12. Keep the work area clean and organized.
13. Wear eye protection *any time* the safety of your eyes is in question. This includes procedures involving drilling, grinding, hammering, compressed air and chemicals.
14. Wear the correct clothing for the job. Tie up or cover long hair so it can not catch in moving equipment.
15. Do not carry sharp tools in clothing pockets.
16. Always have an approved fire extinguisher available. Make sure it is rated for gasoline (Class B) and electrical (Class C) fires.
17. Do not use compressed air to clean clothes, the motorcycle or the work area. Debris may be blown

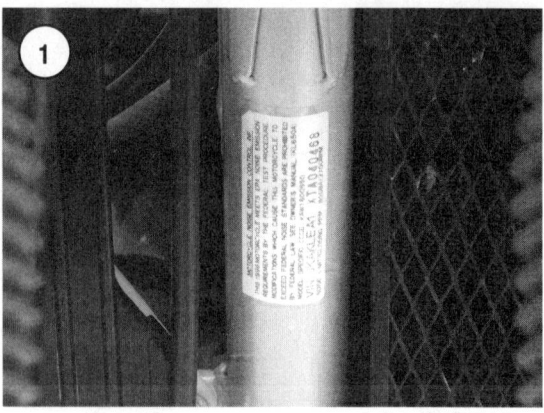

into the eyes or skin. *Never* direct compressed air at anyone. Do not allow children to use or play with any compressed air equipment.
18. When using compressed air to dry rotating parts, hold the part so it cannot rotate. Do not allow the force of the air to spin the part. The air jet is capable of rotating parts at extreme speeds. The part may be damaged or disintegrate, causing serious injury.
19. Do not inhale the dust created by brake pad and clutch wear. These particles may contain asbestos. In addition, some types of insulating materials and gaskets may contain asbestos. Inhaling asbestos particles is hazardous to health.
20. Never work on the motorcycle while someone is working under it.
21. When placing the motorcycle on a stand or overhead lift, make sure it is secure before walking away.

Handling Gasoline Safely

Gasoline is a volatile flammable liquid and is one of the most dangerous items in the shop. Because gasoline is used so often, many people forget that it is hazardous. Only use gasoline as fuel for internal combustion gasoline engines. Keep in mind when working on a motorcycle, gasoline is always present in the fuel tank, fuel line and fuel body. To avoid an accident when working around the fuel system, carefully observe the following precautions:
1. *Never* use gasoline to clean parts. Refer to *Cleaning Parts* in this section.
2. When working on the fuel system, work outside or in a well-ventilated area.
3. Do not add fuel to the fuel tank or service the fuel system while the motorcycle is near open flames, sparks or where someone is smoking. Gasoline vapor is heavier than air, collects in low areas and is more easily ignited than liquid gasoline.
4. Allow the engine to cool completely before working on any fuel system component.

GENERAL INFORMATION

chemical is being used and whether it is poisonous and/or flammable.

2. Do not use more than one type of cleaning solvent at a time. If mixing chemicals is required, measure the proper amounts according to the manufacturer.

3. Work in a well-ventilated area.
4. Wear chemical-resistant gloves.
5. Wear safety glasses.
6. Wear a vapor respirator if the instructions call for it.
7. Wash hands and arms thoroughly after cleaning parts.
8. Keep chemicals away from children and pets, especially coolant. Animals are attracted to antifreeze.
9. Thoroughly clean all oil, grease and cleaner residue from any part that must be heated.
10. Use a nylon brush when cleaning parts. Metal brushes may cause a spark.
11. When using a parts washer, only use the solvent recommended by the manufacturer. Make sure the parts washer is equipped with a metal lid that will lower in case of fire.

Warning Labels

Most manufacturers attach information and warning labels to the motorcycle. These labels contain instructions that are important to safety when operating, servicing, transporting and storing the motorcycle. Refer to the owner's manual for the description and location of labels. Order replacement labels from the manufacturer if they are missing or damaged.

SERIAL NUMBERS

Serial numbers are stamped on various locations on the frame, engine and carburetor. Record these numbers in the *Quick Reference Data* section in the front of this manual. Have these numbers available when ordering parts.

The frame serial number is stamped on the right side of the steering head.

The VIN number label (**Figure 1**) is located on the right side of the frame adjacent to the steering head.

The engine serial number is stamped on the right, upper surface of the crankcase (**Figure 2**).

The carburetor serial number is located on the right side of the carburetor body above the float bowl (**Figure 3**).

5. Do not store gasoline in glass containers. If the glass breaks, an explosion or fire may occur.
6. Immediately wipe up spilled gasoline with rags. Store the rags in a metal container with a lid until they can be properly disposed, or place them outside in a safe place for the fuel to evaporate.
7. Do not pour water onto a gasoline fire. Water spreads the fire and makes it more difficult to put out. Use a class B, BC or ABC fire extinguisher to extinguish the fire.
8. Always turn off the engine before refueling. Do not spill fuel onto the engine or exhaust system. Do not overfill the fuel tank. Leave an air space at the top of the tank to allow room for the fuel to expand due to temperature fluctuations.

Cleaning Parts

Cleaning parts is one of the more tedious and difficult service jobs performed in the home garage. Many types of chemical cleaners and solvents are available for shop use. Most are poisonous and extremely flammable. To prevent chemical exposure, vapor buildup, fire and injury, observe each product's warning label and note the following:

1. Read and observe the entire product label before using any chemical. Always know what type of

CHAPTER ONE

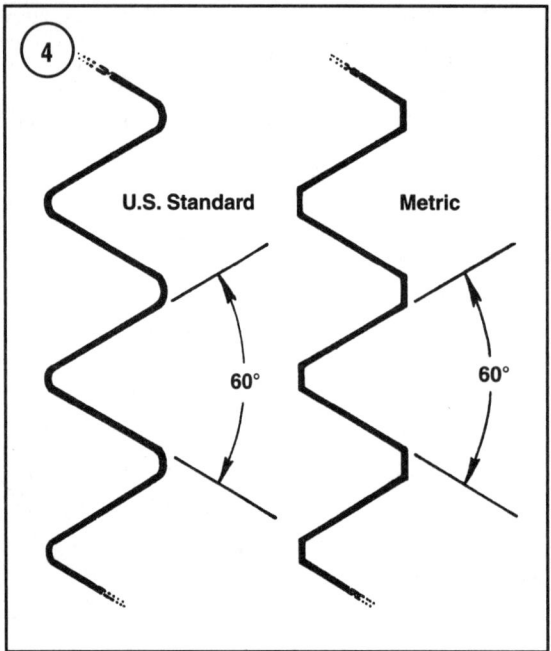

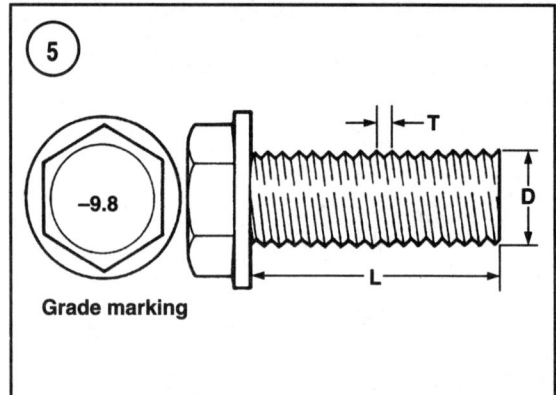

FASTENERS

WARNING
Do not install fasteners with a strength classification lower than what was originally installed by the manufacturer. Doing so may cause equipment failure and/or damage.

Proper fastener selection and installation is important to ensure the motorcycle operates as designed and can be serviced efficiently. Make sure replacement fasteners meet the requirements.

Threaded Fasteners

Threaded fasteners secure most of the components on the motorcycle. Most are tightened by turning them clockwise (right-hand threads). If the normal rotation of the component being tightened would loosen the fastener, it may have left-hand threads. If a left-hand threaded fastener is used, it is noted in the text.

Two dimensions are required to match the thread size of the fastener: the number of threads in a given distance and the outside diameter of the threads.

Two systems are currently used to specify threaded fastener dimensions: the U.S. Standard system and the metric system (**Figure 4**). Pay particular attention when working with unidentified fasteners; mismatching thread types can damage threads.

To ensure the fastener threads are not mismatched or cross-threaded, start all fasteners by hand. If a fastener is difficult to start or turn, determine the cause before tightening with a wrench.

Match fasteners by their length (L, **Figure 5**), diameter (D) and distance between thread crests (pitch, T). A typical metric bolt may be identified by the numbers, 8—1.25 × 130. This indicates the bolt has a diameter of 8 mm, the distance between thread crests is 1.25 mm and the length is 130 mm. Always measure bolt length as shown in L, **Figure 5** to avoid installing replacements of the wrong lengths.

If a number is located on the top of a metric fastener (**Figure 5**), this indicates the strength. The higher the number, the stronger the fastener. Typically, unnumbered fasteners are the weakest.

Many screws, bolts and studs are combined with nuts to secure particular components. To indicate the size of a nut, manufacturers specify the internal diameter and thread pitch.

The measurement across two flats on a nut or bolt indicates the wrench size.

Torque Specifications

The materials used in the manufacture of the motorcycle may be subjected to uneven stresses if fasteners are not installed and tightened correctly. Improperly installed fasteners or ones that worked

GENERAL INFORMATION

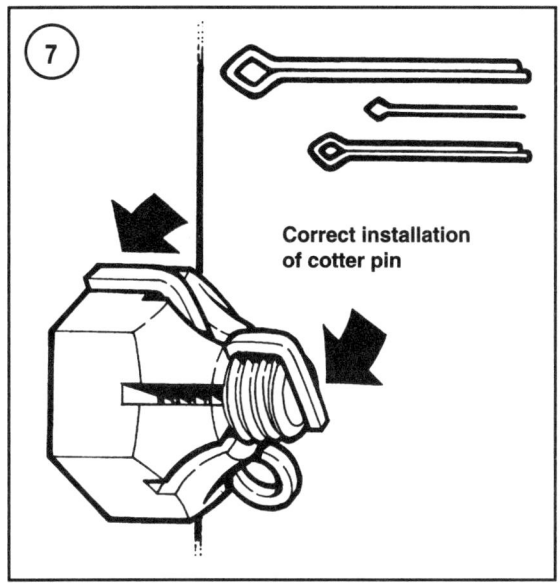

Correct installation of cotter pin

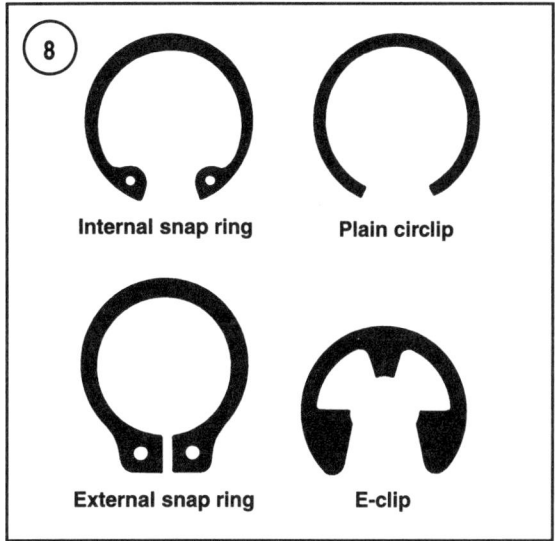

Internal snap ring — Plain circlip
External snap ring — E-clip

loose can cause extensive damage. It is essential to use an accurate torque wrench (as described in this chapter), with the torque specifications in this manual.

Specifications for torque are provided in Newton-meters (N•m), foot-pounds (ft.-lb.) and inch-pounds (in.-lb.). Refer to **Table 4** for general torque recommendations. To use **Table 4**, first determine the size of the fastener as described in *Threaded Fasteners* (this section). Torque specifications for specific components are at the end of the appropriate chapters. Torque wrenches are covered in *Tools* (this chapter).

Self-Locking Fasteners

Several types of bolts, screws and nuts incorporate a system that creates interference between the two fasteners. Interference is achieved in various ways. The most common types used are the nylon insert nut, or a dry adhesive coating on the threads of a bolt.

Self-locking fasteners offer greater holding strength than standard fasteners, which improves their resistance to vibration. Self-locking fasteners cannot be reused. The materials used to form the lock become distorted after the initial installation and removal. Do not replace self-locking fasteners with standard fasteners.

Some fasteners are equipped with a threadlock preapplied to the fastener threads (**Figure 6**). When it is necessary to reuse one of these fasteners, remove all threadlock residue from the threads. Then apply the threadlock specified in the text.

Washers

The two basic types of washers are flat washers and lockwashers. Flat washers are simple discs with a hole to fit a screw or bolt. Lockwashers are used to prevent a fastener from working loose. Washers can be used as spacers and seals or to help distribute fastener load and prevent the fastener from damaging the component.

As with fasteners, when replacing washers make sure the replacements meet the original specifications.

Cotter Pins

A cotter pin is a split metal pin inserted into a hole or slot to prevent a fastener from loosening. In certain applications, such as the rear axle, the fastener must be secured in this way. For these applications, a cotter pin and castellated (slotted) nut is used.

To use a cotter pin, first make sure the diameter is correct for the hole in the fastener. After correctly tightening the fastener and aligning the holes, insert the cotter pin through the hole and bend the ends over the fastener (**Figure 7**). Unless instructed to do so, never loosen a tightened fastener to align the holes. If the holes do not align, tighten the fastener just enough to achieve alignment.

Cotter pins are available in various diameters and lengths. Measure length from the bottom of the head to the tip of the shortest pin.

Snap Rings and E-clips

Snap rings (**Figure 8**) are circular-shaped metal retaining clips. They are required to secure parts and gears in place on parts such as shafts, pins or rods. External type snap rings are used to retain items on shafts. Internal type snap rings secure parts within housing bores. In some applications, in addition to securing the component(s), snap rings of varying thicknesses also determine endplay. These are usually called selective snap rings.

The two basic types of snap rings are machined and stamped snap rings. Machined snap rings (**Figure 9**) can be installed in either direction because both faces have sharp edges. Stamped snap rings (**Figure 10**) are manufactured with a sharp edge and round edge. When installing a stamped snap ring in a thrust application, install the sharp edge facing away from the part producing the thrust.

E-clips are used when it is not practical to use a snap ring. Remove E-clips with a flat blade screwdriver by prying between the shaft and E-clip. To install an E-clip, center it over the shaft groove and push or tap it into place.

Observe the following when installing snap rings:
1. Remove and install snap rings with snap ring pliers. Refer to *Tools* in this chapter.
2. In some applications, it may be necessary to replace snap rings after removing them.
3. Compress or expand snap rings only enough to install them. If overly expanded, they lose their retaining ability.
4. After installing a snap ring, make sure it seats completely.
5. Wear eye protection when removing and installing snap rings.

SHOP SUPPLIES

Lubricants and Fluids

Periodic lubrication helps ensure a long service life for any type of equipment. Using the correct type of lubricant is as important as performing the lubrication service, although in an emergency the wrong type is better than not using one. The following section describes the types of lubricants most often required. Make sure to follow the manufacturer's recommendations.

Engine oils

Engine oil for a four-stroke motorcycle engine use is classified by three standards: the American Petroleum Institute (API) service classification, the Society of Automotive Engineers (SAE) viscosity rating and the Japanese Automobile Standards Organization (JASO) T 903 certification standard.

The JASO certification specifies the oil has passed requirements specified by Japanese motorcycle manufacturers.

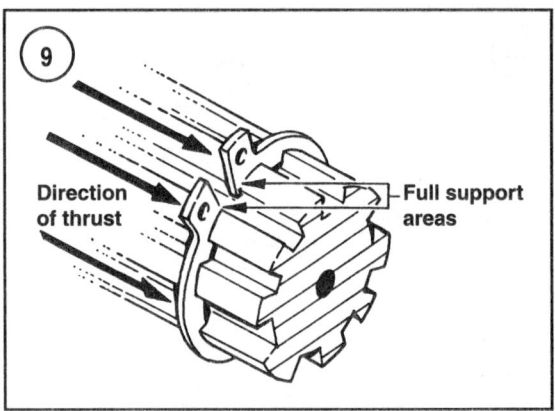

The API and SAE information is on all oil container labels. The JASO information is found on oil containers sold by the oil manufacturer specifically for motorcycle use. Two letters indicate the API service classification. The number or sequence of numbers and letter (10W-40 for example) is the oil's viscosity rating. The API service classification and the SAE viscosity index are not indications of oil quality. The JASO certification label identifies two separate oil classifications and a registration number to ensure the oil has passed all JASO certification standards for use in four-stroke motorcycle engines.

The API service classification indicates that the oil meets specific lubrication standards and is not an indication of oil quality. The first letter in the classification *S* indicates that the oil is for gasoline engines. The second letter indicates the standard the oil satisfies.

The JASO certification label identifies two separate oil classifications and includes a registration number to ensure the oil has passed all JASO certification standards for use in four-stroke motorcycle engines. The classifications are: MA (high friction applications) and MB (low friction applications).

Viscosity is an indication of the oil's thickness. Thin oils have a lower number while thick oils have a higher number. Engine oils fall into the 5- to 50-weight range for single-grade oils.

Most manufacturers recommend multi-grade oil. These oils perform efficiently across a wide range of operating conditions. Multi-grade oils are identified by a W after the first number, which indicates the low-temperature viscosity.

Engine oils are most commonly mineral (petroleum) based; however, synthetic and semi-synthetic types are being used more frequently. Always use oil with a classification recommended by the manufacturer (Chapter Three). Using oil with a different classification can cause engine damage.

GENERAL INFORMATION

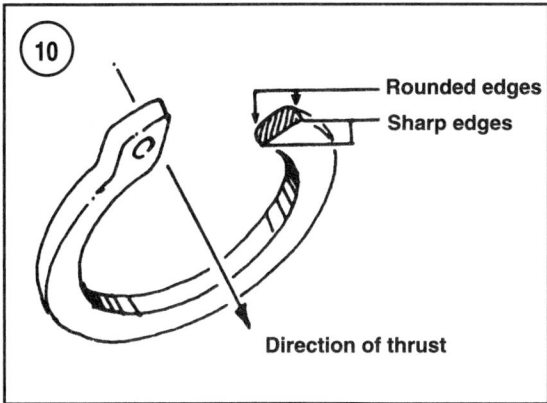

Greases

Grease is lubricating oil with thickening agents added to it. The National Lubricating Grease Institute (NLGI) grades grease. Grades range from No. 000 to No. 6, with No. 6 being the thickest. Typical multipurpose grease is NLGI No. 2. For specific applications, manufacturers may recommend a water-resistant type grease or one with an additive, such as molybdenum disulfide (MoS^2).

Brake fluid

WARNING
Never put a mineral-based (petroleum) oil into the brake system. Mineral oil causes rubber parts in the system to swell and break apart, resulting in complete brake failure.

Brake fluid is the hydraulic fluid used to transmit hydraulic pressure (force) to the wheel brakes. Brake fluid is classified by the Department of Transportation (DOT). Current designations for brake fluid are DOT 3, DOT 4 and DOT 5. This classification appears on the fluid container. The models covered in this manual require DOT 4 brake fluid.

Each type of brake fluid has its own definite characteristics. Do not intermix different types of brake fluid; this may cause brake system failure. DOT 5 brake fluid is silicone-based. DOT 5 is not compatible with other brake fluids or in systems for which it was not designed. Mixing DOT 5 fluid with other fluids may cause brake system failure. When adding brake fluid, *only* use DOT 4 brake fluid.

Brake fluid damages any plastic, painted or plated surface it contacts. Use extreme care when working with brake fluid, and remove any spills immediately with soap and water.

Hydraulic brake systems require clean and moisture-free brake fluid. Never reuse brake fluid. Keep containers and reservoirs properly sealed.

Cleaners, Degreasers and Solvents

Many chemicals are available to remove oil, grease and other residue from the motorcycle. Before using cleaning solvents, consider their uses and disposal methods, particularly if they are not water-soluble. Local ordinances may require special procedures for the disposal of many types of cleaning chemicals. Refer to *Safety* and *Cleaning Parts* in this chapter for more information on their uses.

Use brake parts cleaner to clean brake system components when contact with petroleum-based products will damage seals. Brake parts cleaner leaves no residue. Use electrical contact cleaner to clean electrical connections and components without leaving any residue. Carburetor cleaner is a powerful solvent used to remove fuel deposits and varnish from fuel system components. Use this cleaner carefully; it may damage finishes.

Generally, degreasers are strong cleaners used to remove heavy accumulations of grease from engine and frame components.

Most solvents are designed to be used with a parts washing cabinet for individual component cleaning. For safety, use only nonflammable or high flash point solvents.

Gasket Sealant

Sealants are used in combination with a gasket or seal or occasionally used alone. Use extreme care when choosing a sealant different from the type originally recommended. Choose sealants based on their resistance to heat, various fluids and their sealing capabilities.

One of the most common sealants is RTV, or room temperature vulcanizing, sealant. This sealant cures at room temperature over a specific time period. This allows the repositioning of components without damaging gaskets.

Moisture in the air causes the RTV sealant to cure. Always install the tube cap as soon as possible after applying RTV sealant. RTV sealant has a limited shelf life and will not cure properly if the shelf life has expired. Keep partial tubes sealed and discard them if they have surpassed the expiration date. If there is no expiration date on a sealant tube, use a permanent marker and write the date on the tube when it is first opened. Manufacturers usually specify a shelf life of one year after a container is opened, though it is recommended to contact the sealant manufacturer to confirm shelf life.

Removing RTV sealant

Silicone sealant is used on many engine gasket surfaces. When cleaning parts after disassembly, a razor blade or gasket scraper is required to remove the silicone residue that cannot be pulled off by hand from the gasket surfaces. To avoid damaging gasket surfaces, use Permatex Silicone Stripper (part No. 80647) to help soften the residue before scraping.

Applying RTV sealant

Clean all old sealer residue from the mating surfaces. Then inspect the mating surfaces for damage. Remove all sealer material from blind threaded holes; it can cause inaccurate bolt torque. Spray the mating surfaces with aerosol parts cleaner, and then wipe with a lint-free cloth. Because gasket surfaces must be dry and oil-free for the sealant to adhere, be thorough when cleaning and drying the parts.

Apply RTV sealant in a continuous bead 2-3 mm (0.08-0.12 in.) thick. Circle all the fastener holes unless otherwise specified. Do not allow any sealant to enter these holes. Drawings in specific chapters show how to apply the sealer to specific gasket surfaces. Assemble and tighten the fasteners to the specified torque within the time frame recommended by the RTV sealant manufacturer.

Gasket Remover

Aerosol gasket remover can help remove stubborn gaskets. This product can speed up the removal process and prevent damage to the mating surface that may be caused by using a scraping tool. Most of these types of products are very caustic. Follow the gasket remover manufacturer's instructions for use.

Threadlock

> *CAUTION*
> *Threadlock is anaerobic and damages most plastic parts and surfaces. Use caution when using these products in areas where plastic components are located.*

A threadlock is a fluid applied to the threads of fasteners. After tightening the fastener, the fluid dries and becomes a solid filler between the threads. This

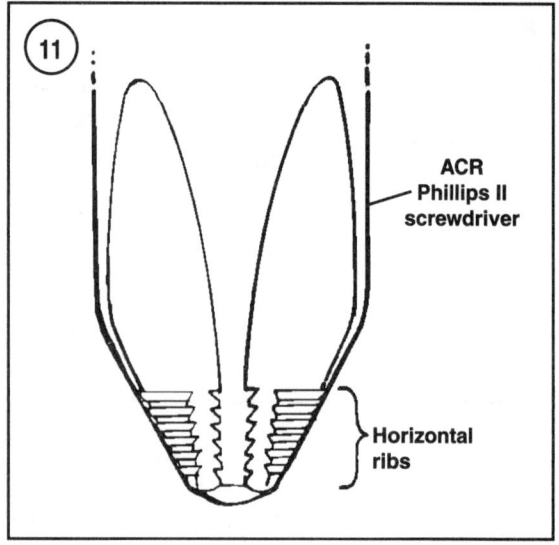

makes it difficult for the fastener to work loose from vibration or heat expansion and contraction. Some threadlock formulas also provide a seal against fluid leaks.

Before applying threadlock, remove any residue from both thread areas and clean them with aerosol parts cleaner. Use the threadlock sparingly. Excess fluid can run into adjoining parts.

Threadlock is available in various strengths, temperatures and repair applications.

TOOLS

Most of the procedures in this manual can be carried out with hand tools and test equipment familiar to the home mechanic. Always use the correct tools for the job. Keep tools organized and clean and store them in a tool chest with related tools organized together.

Quality tools are essential. The best are constructed of high-strength alloy steel. These tools are light, easy-to-use and resistant to wear. Their working surfaces are devoid of sharp edges and the tools are carefully polished. They have an easy-to-clean finish and are comfortable to use. Quality tools are a good investment.

When purchasing tools to perform the procedures covered in this manual, consider the tool's potential frequency of use. If a tool kit is just now being started, consider purchasing a tool set from a quality tool supplier. These sets are available in many tool combinations and offer substantial savings when compared to individually purchased tools. As work experience grows and tasks become more complicated, specialized tools can be added.

Some of the procedures in this manual specify special tools. In most cases, the tool is illustrated in use.

GENERAL INFORMATION

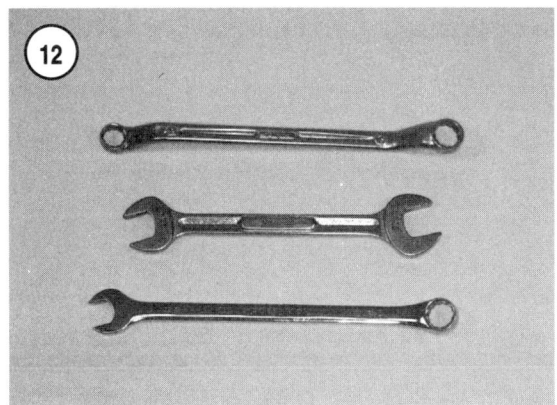

In some case it may be possible to substitute similar tools or fabricate a suitable replacement. However, at times, the specialized equipment or expertise may make it impractical for the home mechanic to perform the procedure. When necessary, such operations are identified in the text with the recommendation to have a dealership or specialist perform the task.

Screwdrivers

The two basic types of screwdrivers are the slotted tip (flat blade) and the Phillips tip. These are available in sets that often include an assortment of tip sizes and shaft lengths.

As with all tools, use the correct screwdriver. Make sure the size of the tip conforms to the size and shape of the fastener. Use them only for driving screws. Never use a screwdriver for prying or chiseling. Repair or replace worn or damaged screwdrivers. A worn tip may damage the fastener, making it difficult to remove.

Phillips-head screws are often damaged by incorrectly fitting screwdrivers. Quality Phillips screwdrivers are manufactured with their crosshead tip machined to Phillips Screw Company specifications. Poor quality or damaged Phillips screwdrivers can back out and round over the screw head (camout).

Compounding the problem of using poor quality screwdrivers are Phillips-head screws made from weak or soft materials and screws initially installed with air tools.

An effective screwdriver for Phillips screws is the ACR Phillips II screwdriver. Horizontal anti-camout ribs (ACR) on the driving faces or flutes of the screwdriver's tip (**Figure 12**) improve the driver-to-fastener grip. While designed for ACR Phillips II screws, ACR Phillips II screwdrivers also work well on all common Phillips screws. ACR screwdrivers are availabe in different tip sizes and interchangeable bits to fit screwdriver bit holders.

Another way to prevent camout and increase the grip of a Phillips screwdriver is to apply valve grinding compound or Permatex Screw & Socket Gripper onto the screwdriver tip. After loosening/tightening the screw, clean the screw recess to prevent possible contamination.

Wrenches

Box-end, open-end, and combination wrenches (**Figure 12**) are available in a variety of types and sizes.

The number stamped on the wrench refers to the distance between the work areas. This size must match the size of the fastener head.

The box-end wrench is an excellent tool because it grips the fastener on all sides. This reduces the chance of the tool slipping. The box-end wrench is designed with either a 6- or 12-point opening. For stubborn or damaged fasteners, the 6-point provides superior holding ability by contacting the fastener across a wider area at all six edges. For general use, the 12-point works well. It allows the wrench to be removed and reinstalled without moving the handle over such a wide arc.

An open-end wrench is fast and works best in areas with limited overhead access. It contacts the fastener at only two points, and is subject to slipping under heavy force or if the tool or fastener is worn. A box-end wrench is preferred in most instances, especially when breaking loose and applying the final tightness to a fastener.

The combination wrench has a box-end on one end, and an open-end on the other. This combination makes it a convenient tool.

Adjustable Wrenches

An adjustable wrench (**Figure 13**) can fit nearly any nut or bolt head that has clear access around its entire perimeter.

However, adjustable wrenches contact the fastener at only two points, which makes them more subject

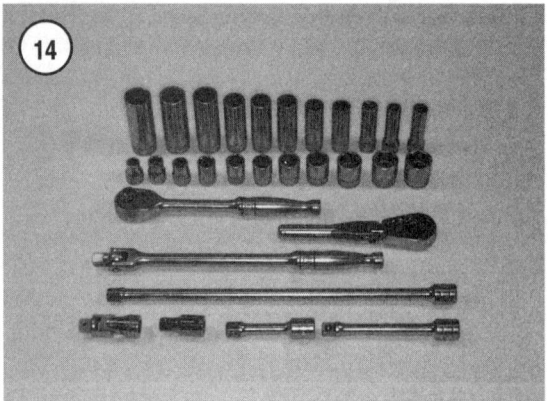

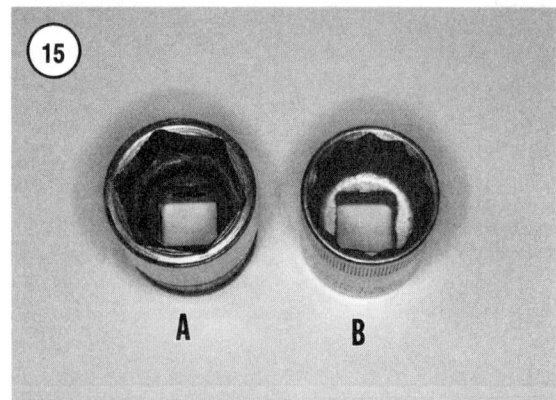

to slipping off the fastener. One jaw is adjustable and may loosen, which increases this possibility. Make certain the solid jaw is the one transmitting the force.

However, adjustable wrenches are typically used to prevent a large nut or bolt from turning while the other end is being loosened or tightened with a box-end or socket wrench.

Socket Wrenches, Ratchets and Handles

WARNING
Do not use hand sockets with air or impact tools; they may shatter and cause injury. Always wear eye protection when using impact or air tools.

Sockets that attach to a ratchet handle (**Figure 14**) are available with 6-point (A, **Figure 15**) or 12-point (B) openings and different drive sizes. The drive size indicates the size of the square hole that accepts the ratchet handle. The number stamped on the socket is the size of the work area and must match the fastener head.

As with wrenches, a 6-point socket provides superior-holding ability, while a 12-point socket needs to be moved only half as far to reposition it on the fastener.

Sockets are designated for either hand or impact use. Impact sockets are made of a thicker material for more durability. Compare the size and wall thickness of a 19-mm hand socket (A, **Figure 16**) and the 19-mm impact socket (B). Use impact sockets when using an impact driver or air tool. Use hand sockets with hand-driven attachments.

Various handles are available for sockets. The speed handle is used for fast operation. Flexible ratchet heads in varying lengths allow the socket to be turned with varying force and at odd angles. Extension bars allow the socket setup to reach difficult areas. The ratchet is the most versatile. It allows

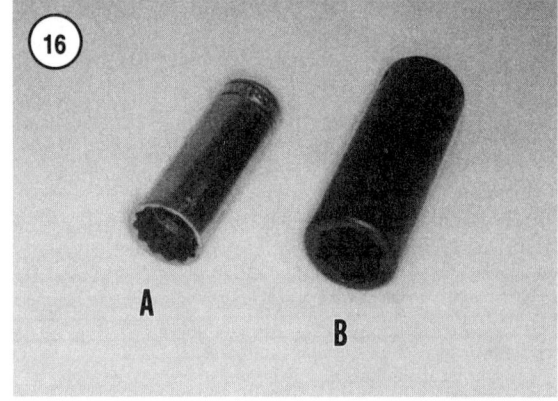

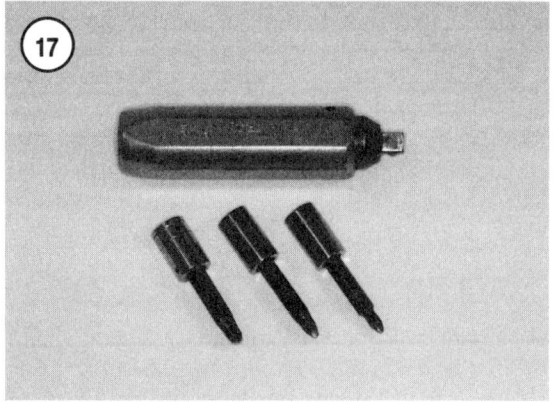

the user to install or remove the nut without removing the socket.

Sockets combined with any number of drivers make them undoubtedly the fastest, safest and most convenient tool for fastener removal and installation.

Impact Driver

WARNING
Do not use hand sockets with air or impact tools because they may shatter

GENERAL INFORMATION

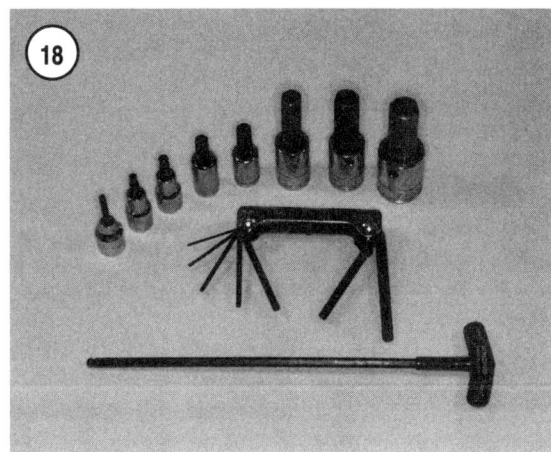

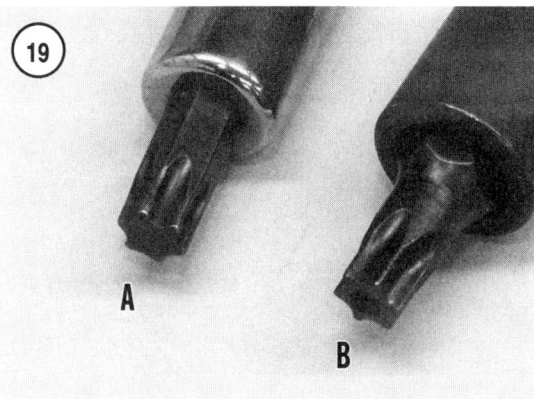

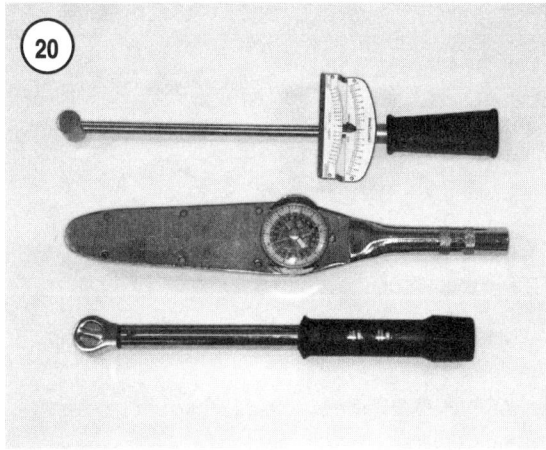

designed for impact use. Refer to *Socket Wrenches, Ratchets and Handles* in this section.

Allen Wrenches

Allen, or setscrew wrenches (**Figure 18**), are used on fasteners with hexagonal recesses in the fastener head. These wrenches are available in a L-shaped bar, socket and T-handle types. Allen bolts are sometimes called socket bolts.

Torx Fasteners

A Torx fastener head is a 6-point star-shaped pattern (A, **Figure 19**). Torx fasteners are identified with a T and a number indicating their drive size: for example, T25. Torx drivers are available in L-shaped bars, sockets and T-handles. Tamper-resistant Torx fasteners are also used and have a round shaft in the center of the fastener head. Tamper-resistant Torx fasteners require a Torx bit with a hole in the center of the bit (B, **Figure 19**).

Torque Wrenches

A torque wrench (**Figure 20**) is used with a socket, torque adapter or similar extension to tighten a fastener to a measured torque. Torque wrenches come in several drive sizes (1/4, 3/8, 1/2 and 3/4) and have various methods of reading the torque value. The drive size indicates the size of the square drive that accepts the socket, adapter or extension. Common methods of reading the torque value are the reflecting beam, the dial indicator and the audible click.

When choosing a torque wrench, consider the torque range, drive size and accuracy. The torque specifications in this manual provide an indication of the range required. A torque wrench is a precision tool that must be properly cared for to remain accurate. Store torque wrenches in cases or separate padded drawers within a toolbox. Follow the manufacturer's instructions for their care and calibration.

Torque Adapters

Torque adapters (**Figure 21**), or extensions, extend or reduce the reach of a torque wrench. Specific adapters are required to perform some of the procedures in this manual. These are available from the motorcycle manufacturer or can be fabricated by welding a socket (A, **Figure 22**) that matches the fastener onto a metal plate (B). Use another socket or extension (C, **Figure 22**) welded to the plate to

and cause injury. Always wear eye protection when using impact or air tools.

An impact driver provides extra force for removing fasteners by converting the impact of a hammer into a turning motion. This makes it possible to remove stubborn fasteners without damaging them. Impact drivers and interchangeable bits (**Figure 17**) are available from most tool suppliers. When using a socket with an impact driver make sure the socket is attach to the torque wrench drive (**Figure 23**). The adapter shown (**Figure 24**) is used to tighten a fastener while preventing another fastener on the same shaft from turning.

If a torque adapter changes the effective lever length, the torque reading on the wrench will not equal the actual torque applied to the fastener. It is necessary to recalibrate the torque setting on the wrench to compensate for the change of lever length. When a torque adapter is used at a right angle to the drive head, calibration is not required because the lever length has not changed.

To recalculate a torque reading when using a torque adapter, use the following formula, and refer to **Figure 25**.

$$TW = \frac{TA \times L}{L + A}$$

TW is the torque setting or dial reading on the wrench.

TA is the torque specification and the actual amount of torque that will be applied to the fastener.

A is the amount the adapter increases (or in some cases reduces) the effective lever length as measured along the centerline of the torque wrench.

L is the lever length of the wrench as measured from the center of the drive to the center of the grip.

The effective lever length is the sum of *L* and *A*.

Example:

TA = 20 ft.-lb.
A = 3 in.
L = 14 in.
$$TW = \frac{20 \times 14}{14 + 3} = \frac{280}{17} = 16.5 \text{ ft.-lb.}$$

In this example, the torque wrench would be set to the recalculated torque value (TW = 16.5 ft.-lb.). When using a beam-type wrench, tighten the fastener until the pointer aligns with 16.5 ft.-lb. In this example, although the torque wrench is pre set to 16.5 ft.-lb., the actual torque is 20 ft.-lb.

Pliers

Pliers come in a wide range of types and sizes. Pliers are useful for holding, cutting, bending, and crimping. Do not use them to turn fasteners unless they are designed to do so. **Figure 26** and **Figure 27** show several types of pliers. Each design has a specialized function. Slip-joint pliers are general-purpose pliers used for gripping and bending. Diagonal cutting pliers are needed to cut wire and can be used to remove cotter pins. Needlenose pliers are used to hold or bend small objects. Locking pliers (**Figure 27**), sometimes called Vise Grips, hold objects tight-

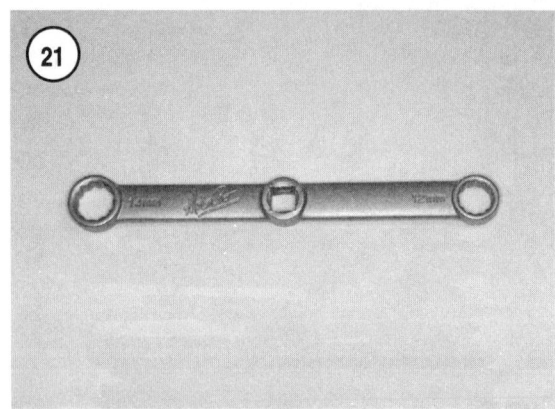

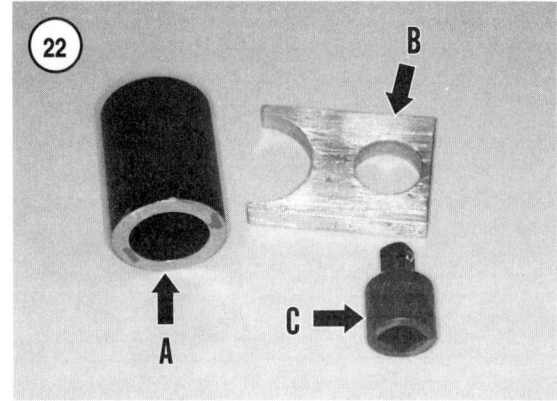

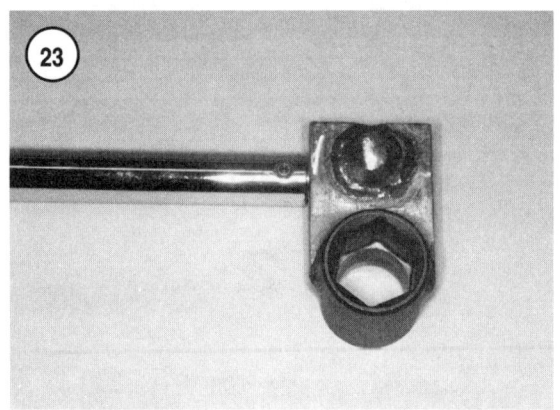

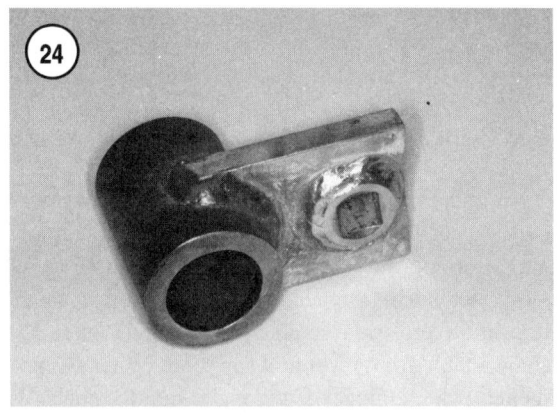

GENERAL INFORMATION

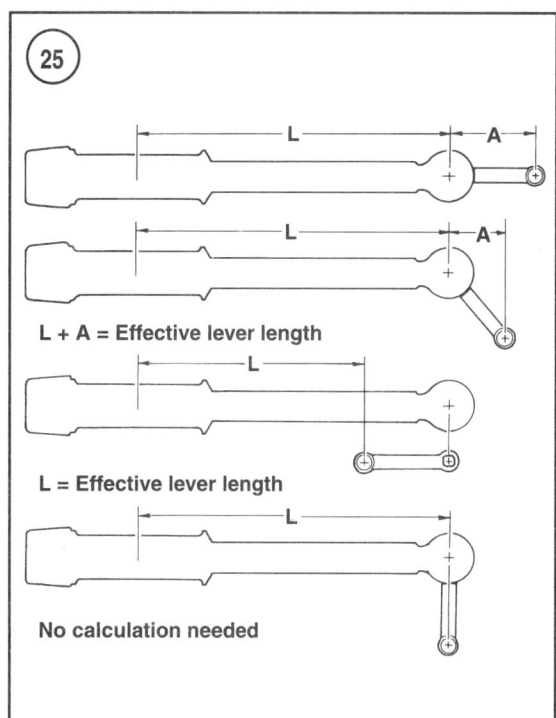

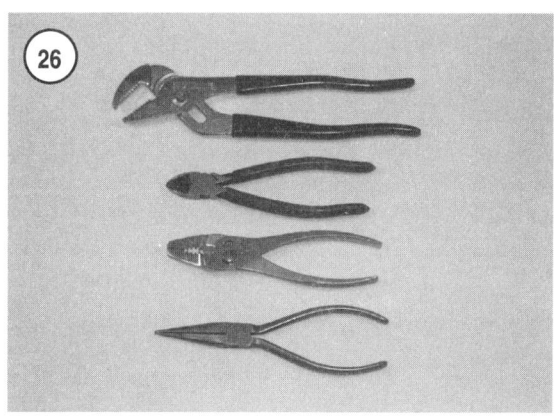

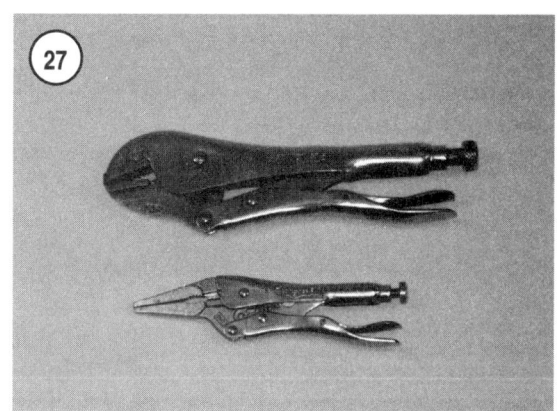

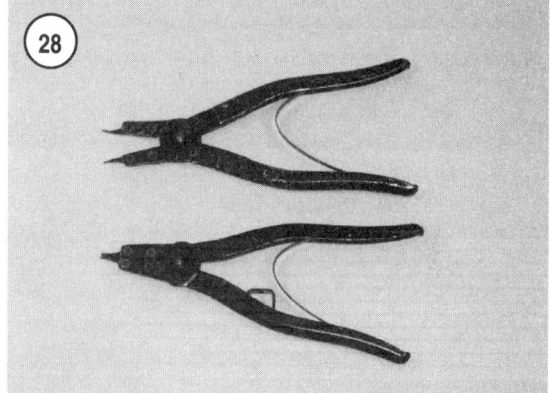

ly. They have many uses ranging from holding two parts together, to gripping the end of a broken stud. Use caution when using locking pliers; the sharp jaws will damage the objects they hold.

Snap Ring Pliers

WARNING
Snap rings can slip and fly off when removing and installing them. In addition, the snap ring pliers tips may break. Always wear eye protection when using snap ring pliers.

Snap ring pliers are specialized pliers with tips that fit into the ends of snap rings to remove and install them.

Snap ring pliers (**Figure 28**) are available with a fixed action (either internal or external) or are convertible (one tool works on both internal and external snap rings). They may have fixed tips or interchangeable ones of various sizes and angles. For general use, select convertible type pliers with interchangeable tips.

Hammers

WARNING
Always wear eye protection when using hammers. Make sure the hammer face is in good condition and the handle is not cracked. Select the correct hammer for the job and make sure to strike the object squarely. Do not use the handle or the side of the hammer to strike an object.

Various types of hammers are available to fit a number of applications. A ball-peen hammer is used to strike another tool, such as a punch or chisel. Soft-faced hammers are required when a metal object must be struck without damaging it. *Never* use a metal-faced hammer on engine and suspension components; damage will occur in most cases.

Ignition Grounding Tool

Some test procedures in this manual require turning the engine over without starting it. Do not remove the spark plug cap(s) and crank the engine without grounding the plug cap(s). Doing so will damage the ignition system.

An effective way to ground the system is to fabricate the tool shown in **Figure 29** from a No. 6 screw, two washers and a length of wire with an alligator clip soldered on one end. To use the tool, insert it into the spark plug cap and attach the alligator clip to a known engine ground. A separate grounding tool is required for each spark plug cap.

This tool is safer than a spark plug or spark tester because there is no spark firing across the end of the plug/tester to potentially ignite fuel vapor spraying from an open spark plug hole or leaking fuel component.

MEASURING TOOLS

The ability to accurately measure components is essential to successfully service many components. Equipment is manufactured to close tolerances, and obtaining consistently accurate measurements is essential.

Each type of measuring instrument is designed to measure a dimension with a certain degree of accuracy and within a certain range. When selecting the measuring tool, make sure it is applicable to the task.

As with all tools, measuring tools provide the best results if cared for properly. Improper use can damage the tool and cause inaccurate results. If any measurement is questionable, verify the measurement using another tool. A standard gauge is usually provided with measuring tools to check accuracy and calibrate the tool if necessary.

Accurate measurements are only possible if the mechanic possesses a feel for using the tool. Heavy-handed use of measuring tools produces less accurate results. Hold the tool gently by the fingertips so the point at which the tool contacts the object is easily felt. This feel for the equipment will produce more accurate measurements and reduce the risk of damaging the tool or component. Refer to the following sections for specific measuring tools.

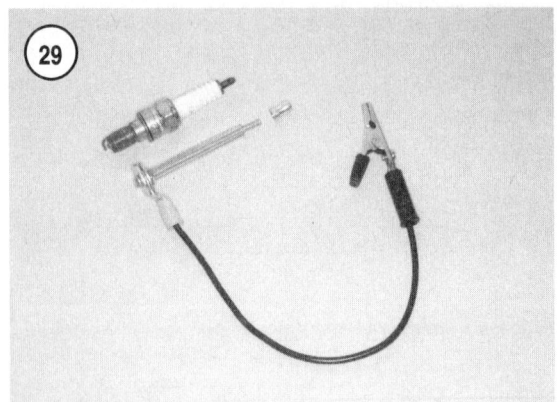

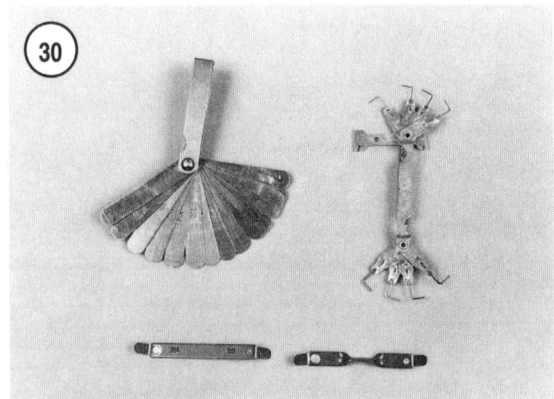

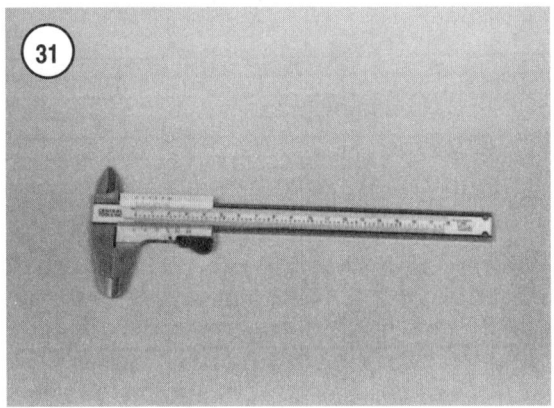

marked with its thickness. Blades can be of various lengths and angles for different procedures.

A common use for a feeler gauge is to measure valve clearance. Wire (round) type gauges are used to measure spark plug gap.

Feeler Gauge

The feeler, or thickness gauge (**Figure 30**), is used for measuring the distance between two surfaces.

A feeler gauge set consists of an assortment of steel strips of graduated thicknesses. Each blade is

Calipers

Calipers (**Figure 31**) are excellent tools for obtaining inside, outside and depth measurements. Although not as precise as a micrometer, they allow reasonable precision, typically to within 0.05 mm

GENERAL INFORMATION

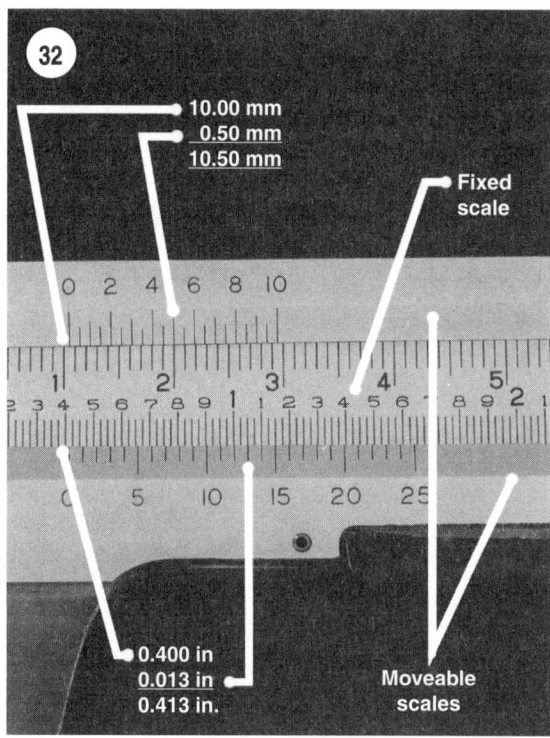

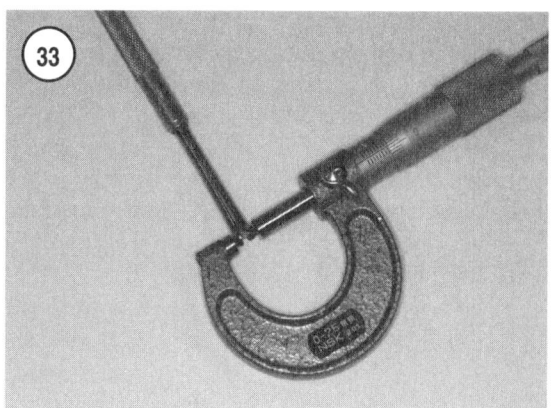

(0.001 in.). Most calipers have a range up to 150 mm (6 in.).

Calipers are available in dial, vernier or digital versions. Dial calipers have a dial readout that provides convenient reading. Vernier calipers have marked scales that must be compared to determine the measurement. The digital caliper uses a LCD to show the measurement.

Properly maintain the measuring surfaces of the caliper. There must not be any dirt or burrs between the tool and the object being measured. Never force the caliper closed around an object; close the caliper around the highest point so it can be removed with a slight drag. Some calipers require calibration. Always refer to the manufacturer's instructions when using a new or unfamiliar caliper.

To read a vernier caliper refer to **Figure 32**. The fixed scale is marked in 1 mm increments. Ten individual lines on the fixed scale equal 1 cm. The moveable scale is marked in 0.05 mm (hundredth) increments. To obtain a reading, establish the first number by the location of the 0 line on the moveable scale in relation to the first line to the left on the fixed scale. In this example, the number is 10 mm. To determine the next number, note which of the lines on the movable scale align with a mark on the fixed scale. A number of lines will seem close, but only one will align exactly. In this case, 0.50 mm is the reading to add to the first number. The result of adding 10 mm and 0.50 mm is a measurement of 10.50 mm.

Micrometers

A micrometer (**Figure 33**) is an instrument designed for linear measurement using the decimal divisions of the inch or meter. While there are many types and styles of micrometers, most of the procedures in this manual call for an outside micrometer. The outside micrometer is used to measure the outside diameter of cylindrical forms and the thicknesses of materials.

A micrometer's size indicates the minimum and maximum size of a part that it can measure. The usual sizes are 0-25 mm (0-1 in.), 25-50 mm (1-2 in.), 50-75 mm (2-3 in.) and 75-100 mm (3-4 in.).

Micrometers that cover a wider range of measurements are available. These use a large frame with interchangeable anvils of various lengths. This type of micrometer offers a cost savings; however, its overall size may make it less convenient.

Adjustment

Before using a micrometer, check its adjustment as follows.
1. Clean the anvil and spindle faces.
2A. To check a 0-1 in. or 0-25 mm micrometer:
   a. Turn the thimble until the spindle contacts the anvil. If the micrometer has a ratchet stop, use it to ensure the proper amount of pressure is applied.
   b. If the adjustment is correct, the 0 mark on the thimble will align exactly with the 0 mark on the sleeve line. If the marks do not align, the micrometer is out of adjustment.
   c. Follow the manufacturer's instructions to adjust the micrometer.
2B. To check a micrometer larger than 1 in. or 25 mm, use the standard gauge supplied by the manufacturer. A standard gauge is a steel block, disc or rod that is machined to an exact size.

a. Place the standard gauge between the spindle and anvil and measure its outside diameter or length. If the micrometer has a ratchet stop, use it to ensure the proper amount of pressure is applied.
b. If the adjustment is correct, the 0 mark on the thimble will align exactly with the 0 mark on the sleeve line. If the marks do not align, the micrometer is out of adjustment.
c. Follow the manufacturer's instructions to adjust the micrometer.

Care

Micrometers are precision instruments. They must be used and maintained with great care. Note the following:
1. Store micrometers in protective cases or separate padded drawers in a toolbox.
2. When in storage, make sure the spindle and anvil faces do not contact each other or another object. If they do, temperature changes and corrosion may damage the contact faces.
3. Do not clean a micrometer with compressed air. Dirt forced into the tool causes wear.
4. Lubricate micrometers to prevent corrosion.

Reading

When reading a micrometer, numbers are taken from different scales and added together.

For accurate results, properly maintain the measuring surfaces of the micrometer. There cannot be any dirt or burrs between the tool and the measured object. Never force the micrometer closed around an object. Close the micrometer around the highest point so it can be removed with a slight drag.

The standard metric micrometer is accurate to one one-hundredth of a millimeter (0.01 mm). The sleeve line is graduated in millimeter and half millimeter increments. The marks on the upper half of the sleeve line equal 1.00 mm. Each fifth mark above the sleeve line is identified with a number. The number sequence depends on the size of the micrometer. A 0-25 mm micrometer, for example, will have sleeve marks numbered 0 through 25 in 5 mm increments. This numbering sequence continues with larger micrometers. On all metric micrometers, each mark on the lower half of the sleeve equals 0.50 mm.

The tapered end of the thimble has 50 lines marked around it. Each mark equals 0.01 mm. One complete turn of the thimble aligns its 0 mark with the first line on the lower half of the sleeve line, or 0.50 mm.

When reading a metric micrometer, add the number of millimeters and half-millimeters on the sleeve line to the number of one one-hundredth millimeters on the thimble. Perform the following steps while referring to **Figure 34**.

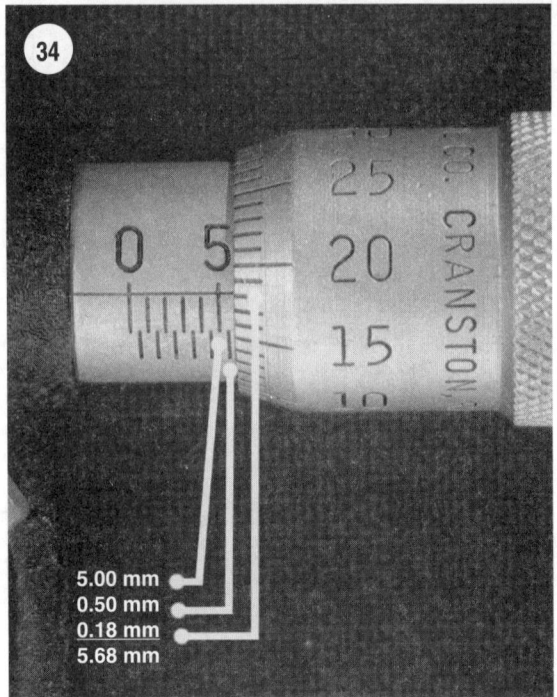

5.00 mm
0.50 mm
0.18 mm
5.68 mm

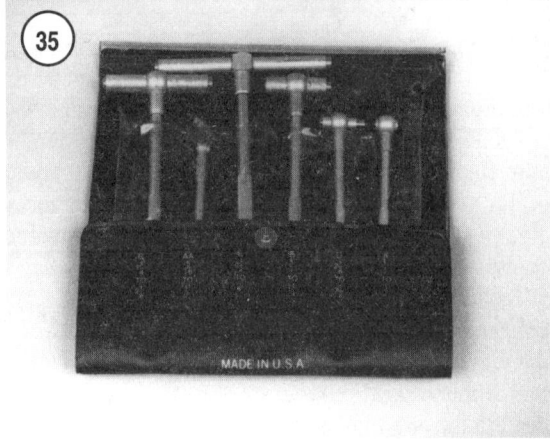

1. Read the upper half of the sleeve line and count the number of lines visible. Each upper line equals 1 mm.
2. See if the half-millimeter line is visible on the lower sleeve line. If so, add 0.50 mm to the reading in Step 1.
3. Read the thimble mark that aligns with the sleeve line. Each thimble mark equals 0.01 mm.
4. If a thimble mark does not align exactly with the sleeve line, estimate the amount between the lines. For accurate readings in two-thousandths of a millimeter (0.002 mm), use a metric vernier micrometer.
5. Add the readings from Steps 1-4.

GENERAL INFORMATION

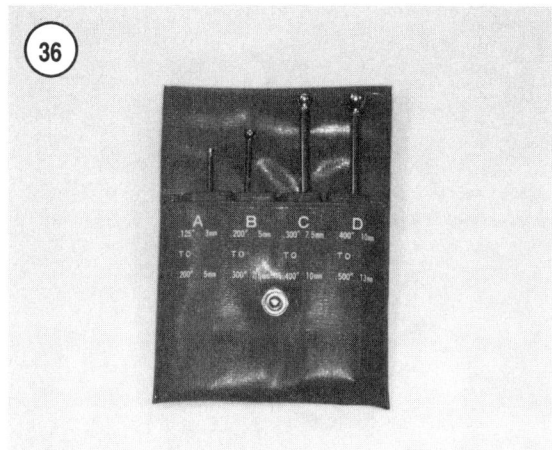

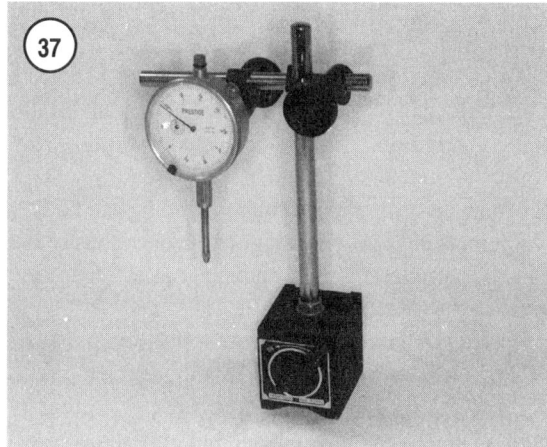

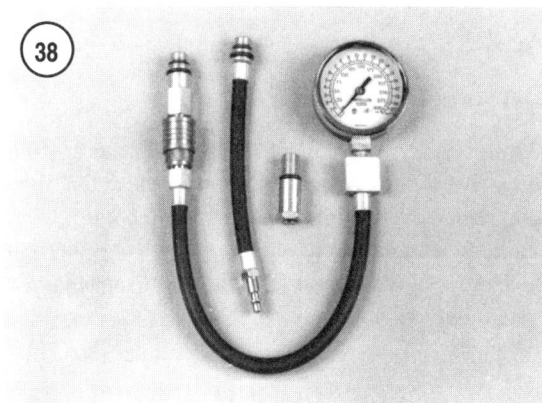

Telescoping and Small Hole Gauges

Use telescoping gauges (**Figure 35**) and small hole gauges (**Figure 36**) to measure bores. Neither gauge has a scale for direct readings. An outside micrometer must be used to determine the reading.

To use a telescoping gauge, select the correct size gauge for the bore. Compress the moveable post and carefully insert the gauge into the bore. Carefully move the gauge in the bore to make sure it is cen-

tered. Tighten the knurled end of the gauge to hold the moveable post in position. Remove the gauge and measure the length of the posts. Telescoping gauges are typically used to measure cylinder bores.

To use a small hole gauge, select the correct size gauge for the bore. Carefully insert the gauge into the bore. Tighten the knurled end of the gauge to carefully expand the gauge fingers to the limit within the bore. Do not overtighten the gauge; there is no built-in release. Excessive tightening can damage the bore surface and tool. Remove the gauge and measure the outside dimension with a micrometer (**Figure 33**). Small hole gauges are typically used to measure valve guides.

Dial Indicator

A dial indicator (**Figure 37**) is a gauge with a dial face and needle used to measure variations in dimensions and movements. Measuring brake rotor runout is a typical use for a dial indicator.

Dial indicators are available in various ranges and graduations and with three types of mounting bases: magnetic, clamp or screw-in stud.

Cylinder Bore Gauge

A cylinder bore gauge is similar to a dial indicator. These typically consist of a dial indicator, handle and different length adapters (anvils) to fit the gauge to various bore sizes. The bore gauge is used to measure bore size, taper and out-of-round. When using a bore gauge, follow the manufacturer's instructions.

Compression Gauge

A compression gauge (**Figure 38**) measures combustion chamber (cylinder) pressure, usually in psi or kg/cm^2. The gauge adapter is either inserted and held in place or screwed into the spark plug hole to obtain the reading. Disable the engine so it will not start and hold the throttle in the wide-open position when performing a compression test. An engine that does not have adequate compression cannot be properly tuned. Refer to Chapter Three when performing a *Compression Test*.

Multimeter

A multimeter (**Figure 39**) is an essential tool for electrical system diagnosis. The voltage function indicates the voltage applied or available to various electrical components. The ohmmeter function tests circuits for continuity, or lack of continuity, and measures the resistance of a circuit.

Some manufacturers' specifications for electrical components are based on results using a specific test meter. Results may vary if using a meter not recommend by the manufacturer. Such requirements are noted when applicable.

Ohmmeter (analog) calibration

Each time an analog ohmmeter is used or the scale is changed, the ohmmeter must be calibrated.

Digital ohmmeters do not require calibration.

1. Make sure the meter battery is in good condition.
2. Make sure the meter probes are in good condition.
3. Touch the two probes together and observe the needle location on the ohms scale. The needle must align with the 0 mark to obtain accurate measurements.
4. If necessary, rotate the meter ohms adjust knob until the needle and 0 mark align.

ELECTRICAL SYSTEM FUNDAMENTALS

A thorough study of the many types of electrical systems used in today's motorcycles is beyond the scope of this manual. However, a basic understanding of voltage, resistance and amerage is necessary to perform diagnostic tests.

Refer to Chapter Two for troubleshooting.

Voltage

Voltage is the electrical potential or pressure in an electrical circuit and is expressed in volts. The more pressure (voltage) in a circuit, the more work can be performed.

Direct current (DC) voltage means the electricity flows in one direction. All circuits powered by a battery are DC circuits.

Alternating current (AC) means the electricity flows in one direction momentarily and then switches to the opposite direction. Alternator output is an example of AC voltage. This voltage must be changed or rectified to direct current to operate in a battery-powered system.

Resistance

Resistance is the opposition to the flow of electricity within a circuit or component and is measured in ohms. Resistance causes a reduction in available current and voltage.

Resistance is measured in an inactive circuit with an ohmmeter. The ohmmeter sends a small amount

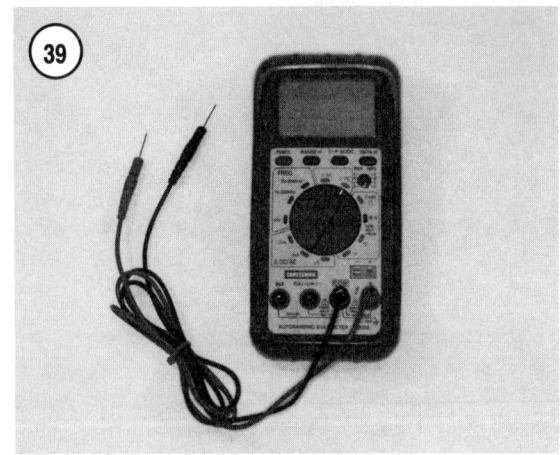

of current into the circuit and measures how difficult it is to push the current through the circuit.

An ohmmeter, although useful, is not always a good indicator of a circuit's actual ability under operating conditions. This is due to the low voltage (6-9 volts) that the meter uses to test the circuit. The voltage in an ignition coil secondary winding can be several thousand volts. Such high voltage can cause the coil to malfunction, even though it tests acceptable during a resistance test.

Resistance generally increases with temperature. Perform all testing with the component or circuit at room temperature. Resistance tests performed at high temperatures may indicate false resistance readings and cause the unnecessary replacement of a component.

Amperage

Amperage is the unit of measure for the amount of current within a circuit. Current is the actual flow of electricity. The higher the current, the more work can be performed up to a given point. If the current flow exceeds the circuit or component capacity, the system will be damaged.

SERVICE METHODS

Many of the procedures in this manual are straightforward and can be performed by anyone reasonably competent with tools. However, consider previous experience carefully before performing any operation involving complicated procedures.

1. Front, in this manual, refers to the front of the motorcycle. The front of any component is the end closest to the front of the motorcycle. The left and right sides refer to the position of the parts as viewed by the rider sitting on the seat facing forward.

GENERAL INFORMATION

2. When servicing the motorcycle, secure it in a safe manner.
3. Label all similar parts for location and mark all mating parts for position. If possible, photograph or draw the number and thickness of any shim as it is removed. Identify parts by placing them in sealed and labeled plastic bags. It is possible for carefully laid out parts to become disturbed, making it difficult to reassemble the components correctly without a diagram.
4. Label disconnected wires and connectors with masking tape and a marking pen. Do not rely on memory alone.
5. Protect finished surfaces from physical damage or corrosion. Keep gasoline and other chemicals off painted surfaces.
6. Use penetrating oil on frozen or tight bolts. Avoid using heat where possible. Heat can warp, melt or affect the temper of parts. Heat also damages the finish of paint and plastics. Refer to *Heating Components* in this section.
7. When a part is a press fit or requires a special tool for removal, the information or type of tool is identified in the text. Otherwise, if a part is difficult to remove or install, determine the cause before proceeding.
8. To prevent objects or debris from falling into the engine, cover all openings.
9. Read each procedure thoroughly and compare the figures to the actual components before starting the procedure. Perform the procedure in sequence.
10. Recommendations are occasionally made to refer service to a dealership or specialist. In these cases, the work can be performed more economically by the specialist than by the home mechanic.
11. The term replace means to discard a defective part and replace it with a new part. Overhaul means to remove, disassemble, inspect, measure, repair and/or replace parts as required to recondition an assembly.
12. Some operations require the use of a hydraulic press. If a press is not available, have these operations performed by a shop equipped with the necessary equipment. Do not use makeshift equipment that may damage the motorcycle. Do not direct high-pressure water at steering bearings, fuel body hoses, wheel bearings, suspension and electrical components. The water forces the grease out of the bearings and could damage the seals.
13. Repairs are much faster and easier if the motorcycle is clean before starting work. Degrease the motorcycle with a commercial degreaser; follow the directions on the container for the best results. Clean all parts with cleaning solvent.
14. If special tools are required, have them available before starting the procedure. When special tools are required, they will be described at the beginning of the procedure.
15. Make sure all shims and washers are reinstalled in the same location and position.
16. Whenever rotating parts contact a stationary part, look for a shim or washer.
17. Use new gaskets if there is any doubt about the condition of old ones.
18. If self-locking fasteners are used, replace them. Do not install standard fasteners in place of self-locking ones.
19. Use grease to hold small parts in place if they tend to fall out during assembly. Do not apply grease to electrical or brake components.

Heating Components

WARNING
Wear protective gloves to prevent burns and injury when heating parts.

CAUTION
Do not use a welding torch when heating parts. A welding torch applies excessive heat to a small area very quickly, which can damage parts.

A heat gun or propane torch is required to disassemble, assemble, remove and install many parts and components in this manual. Read the safety and operating information supplied by the manufacturer of the heat gun or propane torch while also noting the following:
1. The work area should be clean and dry. Remove all combustible components and materials from the work area. Wipe up all grease, oil and other fluids from parts. Check for leaking or damaged fuel system components. Repair or remove these parts before beginning work.
2. Never use a flame near the battery, fuel tank, fuel lines or other flammable materials.
3. When using a heat gun, remember that the temperature can be in excess of 540° C (1000° F).
4. Have a fire extinguisher near the job.
5. Always wear protective goggles and gloves when heating parts.
6. Before heating a part installed on the motorcycle, check areas around the part and those hidden that could be damaged or possibly ignite. Do not heat surfaces than can be damaged by heat. Shield materials near the part or area to be heated: for example, cables and wiring harnesses.
7. Before heating a part, read the entire procedure to make sure the required tools are available. This

allows quick work while the part is at its optimum temperature.

8. The amount of heat recommended to remove or install a part is typically listed in the procedure. However, before heating parts without a specific recommendation, consider the possible effects. To avoid damaging a part, monitor the temperature with heat sticks or an infrared thermometer, if possible. Another way, though not as accurate, is to place tiny drops of water on the part. When the water starts to sizzle, the part is hot enough. Keep the heat in motion to prevent overheating.

Removing Frozen Fasteners

If a fastener cannot be removed, several methods may be used to loosen it. First, liberally apply penetrating oil, and let it penetrate for 10-15 minutes. Rap the fastener several times with a small hammer. Do not hit it hard enough to cause damage. Reapply the penetrating oil if necessary.

For frozen screws, apply penetrating oil as described, and then insert a screwdriver in the slot and rap the top of the screwdriver with a hammer. This loosens the rust so the screw can be removed in the normal way. If the screw head is too damaged to use this method, grip the head with locking pliers and twist it out.

If heat is required, refer to *Heating Components* in this section.

Removing Broken Fasteners

If the head breaks off a screw or bolt, several methods are available for removing the remaining portion. If a large portion of the remainder projects out, try gripping it with locking pliers. If the projecting portion is too small, file it to fit a wrench or cut a slot in it to fit a screwdriver (**Figure 40**).

If the head breaks off flush, use a screw extractor. To do this, center punch the exact center of the screw or bolt (A, **Figure 41**), and then drill a small hole in the screw (B) and tap the extractor into the hole (C). Back the screw out with a wrench on the extractor (D, **Figure 41**).

Repairing Damaged Threads

Occasionally, threads are stripped through carelessness or impact damage. Often the threads can be repaired by running a tap (for internal threads on nuts) or die (for external threads on bolts) through the threads (**Figure 42**). To clean or repair spark plug threads, use a spark plug tap.

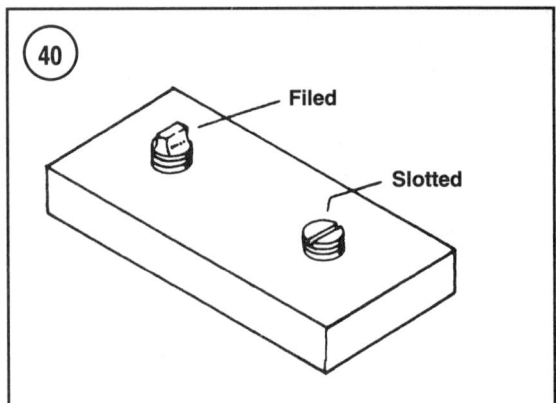

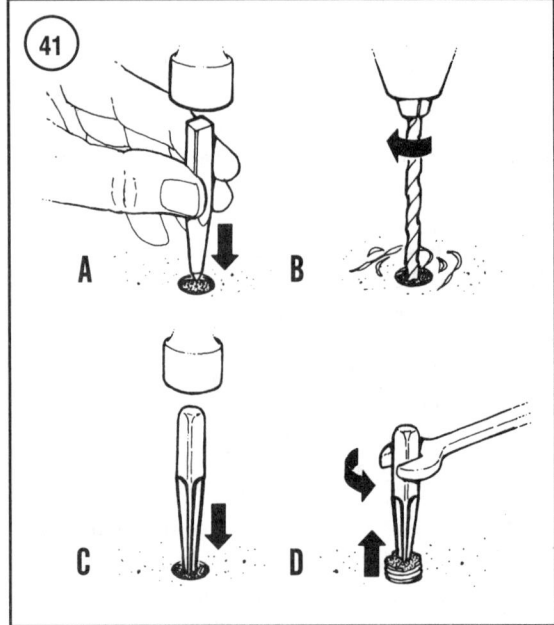

If an internal thread is damaged, it may be necessary to install a Helicoil or some other type of thread insert. Follow the manufacturer's instructions when installing its insert.

If it is necessary to drill and tap a hole, refer to **Table 6** for metric tap and drill sizes.

Stud Removal/Installation

A stud removal tool (**Figure 43**) is available from most tool suppliers. This tool makes the removal and installation of studs easier. If one is not available and the threads on the stud are not damaged, thread two nuts onto the stud and tighten them against each other. Remove the stud by turning the lower nut.

1. Measure the height of the stud above the surface.
2. Thread the stud removal tool onto the stud and tighten it, or thread two nuts onto the stud.

GENERAL INFORMATION

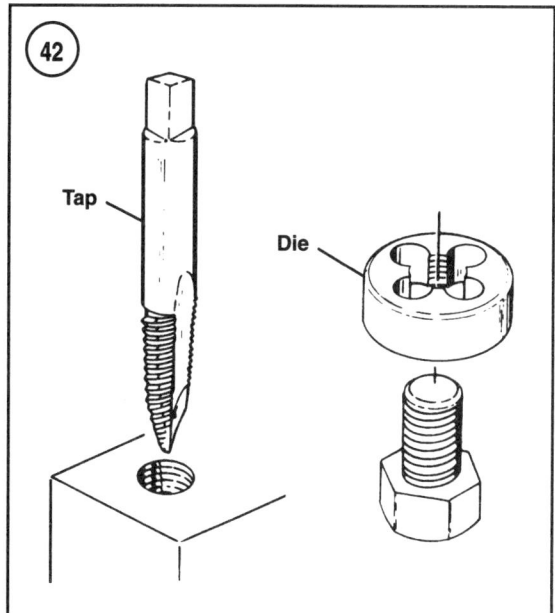

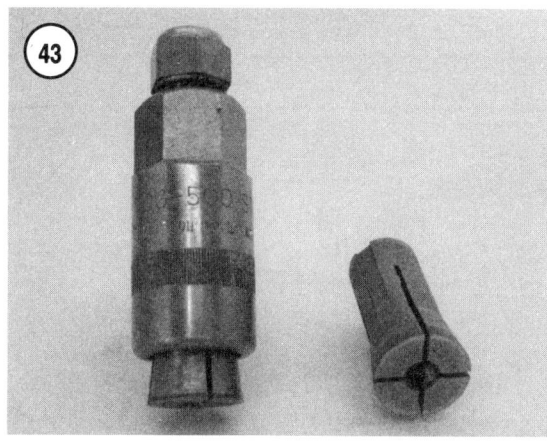

3. Remove the stud by turning the stud remover or the lower nut.
4. Remove any threadlock residue from the threaded hole. Clean the threads with an aerosol parts cleaner.
5. Install the stud removal tool onto the new stud, or thread two nuts onto the stud.
6. Apply threadlock to the threads of the stud.
7. Install the stud and tighten with the stud removal tool or the top nut.
8. Install the stud to the height noted in Step 1 or its torque specification.
9. Remove the stud removal tool or the two nuts.

Removing Hoses

When removing stubborn hoses, do not exert excessive force on the hose or fitting. Remove the hose clamp and carefully insert a small screwdriver or similar blunt nose tool between the fitting and hose. Apply a spray lubricant under the hose and carefully twist the hose off the fitting. Clean the fitting of any corrosion or rubber hose material with a wire brush. Clean the inside of the hose thoroughly. Do not use any lubricant when installing the hose (new or old). The lubricant may allow the hose to come off the fitting, even with the clamp secure.

Bearings

Bearings are precision parts; they must be maintained with proper lubrication and maintenance. If a bearing is damaged, replace it immediately. When installing a new bearing, make sure to prevent damaging it. Bearing replacement procedures are included in the individual chapters where applicable; however, use the following sections as a guideline.

Unless otherwise specified, install bearings with the manufacturer's mark or number facing outward.

Removal

While bearings are normally removed only when damaged, there may be times when it is necessary to remove a bearing that is in good condition. However, improper bearing removal will damage the bearing and maybe the shaft or case half. Note the following when removing bearings:
1. Before removing the bearings, note the following:
   a. Refer to the bearing replacement procedure in the appropriate chapter for any special instructions.
   b. Remove any seals that interfere with bearing removal. Refer to *Seal Replacement* in this section.
   c. When removing more than one bearing, identify the bearings before removing them. Refer to the bearing manufacturer's numbers on the bearing.
   d. Note and record the direction in which the bearing numbers face for proper installation.
   e. Remove any set plates or bearing retainers before removing the bearings.
2. When using a puller to remove a bearing from a shaft, make sure the shaft is not damaged. Always place a piece of metal between the end of the shaft and the puller screw. In addition, place the puller arms next to the inner bearing race. Refer to **Figure 44**.
3. When using a hammer to remove a bearing from a shaft, do not strike the hammer directly against the shaft. Instead, use a brass or aluminum rod between the hammer and shaft (**Figure 45**) and make sure to

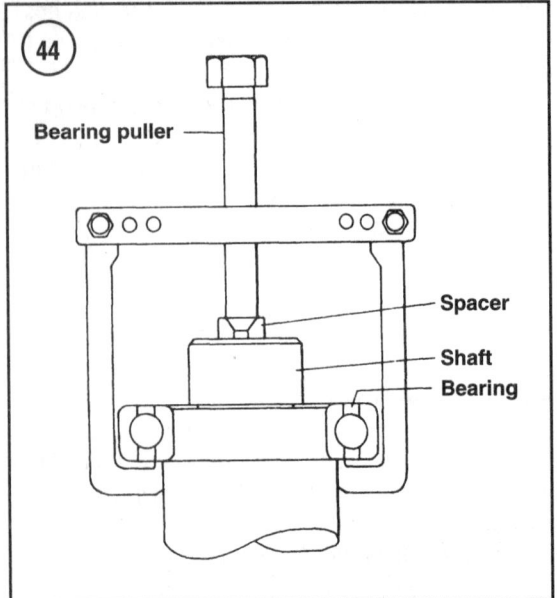

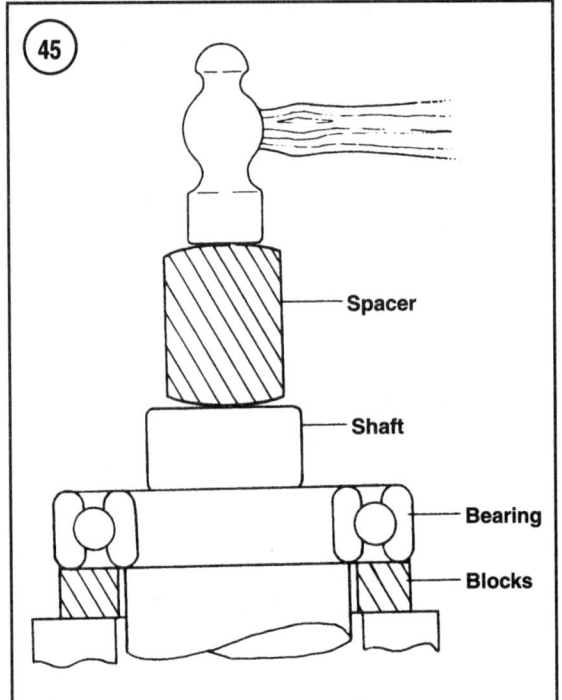

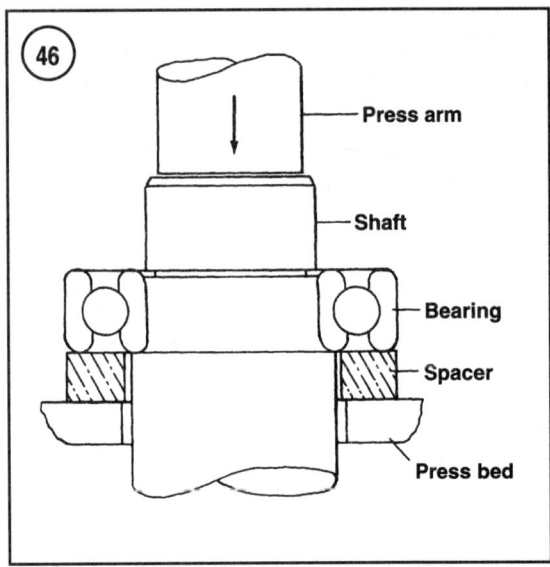

support both bearing races with wooden blocks as shown.

4. The ideal method of bearing removal is with a hydraulic press. Note the following when using a press:
   a. Always support the inner and outer bearing races with a suitable size wooden or aluminum ring (**Figure 46**). If only the outer race is supported, pressure applied against the balls and/or the inner race will damage them.
   b. Always make sure the press arm (**Figure 46**) aligns with the center of the shaft. If the arm is not centered, it may damage the bearing and/or shaft.
   c. The moment the shaft is free of the bearing, it will drop to the floor. Secure or hold the shaft to prevent it from falling.
   d. When removing bearings from a housing, support the housing with 4 × 4 in. wooden blocks to prevent damage to gasket surfaces.

5. Use a blind bearing puller to remove bearings installed in blind holes (**Figure 47**).

Installation

1. When installing a bearing in a housing, apply pressure to the *outer* bearing race (**Figure 48**). When installing a bearing on a shaft, apply pressure to the *inner* bearing race (**Figure 49**).

2. When installing a bearing as described in Step 1, a driver is required. Never strike the bearing directly with a hammer or the bearing will be damaged. When installing a bearing, use a piece of pipe or a driver with a diameter that matches the bearing race.

Figure 50 shows the correct way to use a driver and hammer to install a bearing on a shaft.

3. Step 1 describes how to install a bearing in a housing or over a shaft. However, when installing a bearing over a shaft and into the housing at the *same time,* a tight fit will be required for both outer and inner bearing races. In this situation, install a spacer underneath the driver tool so pressure is applied evenly across both races. Refer to **Figure 51**. If the outer race is not supported, the balls push against the outer bearing race and damage it.

GENERAL INFORMATION

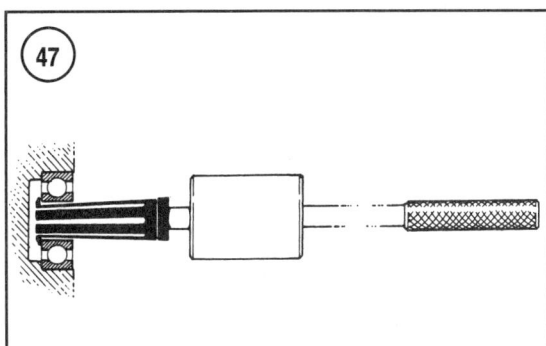

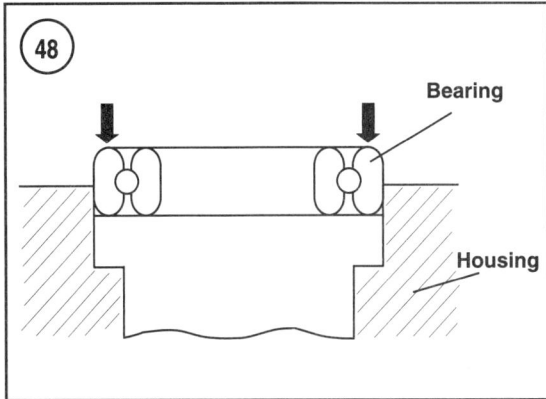

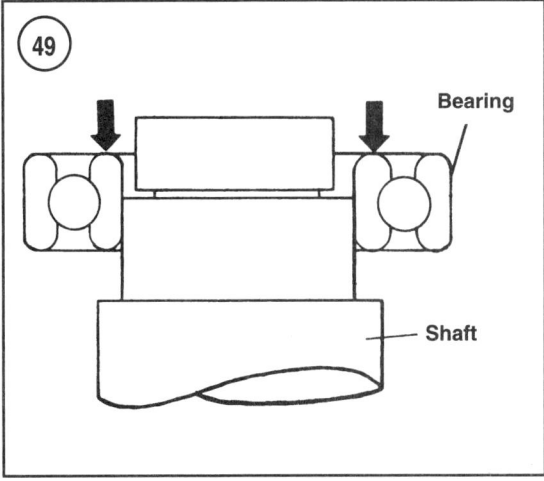

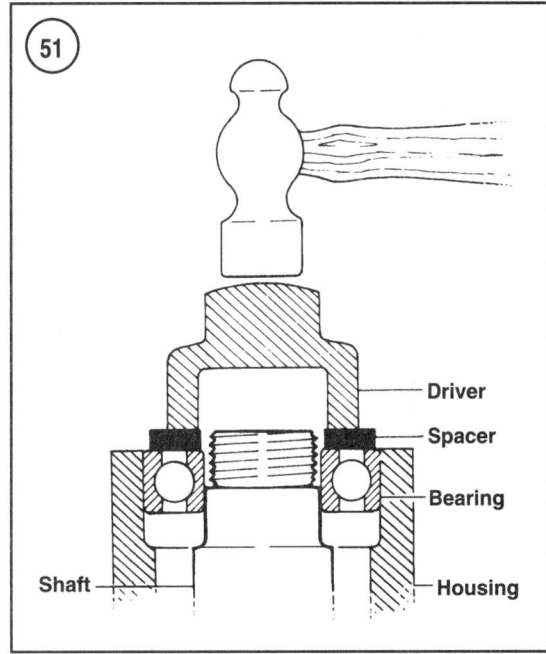

Interference fit

1. Follow this procedure when installing a bearing over a shaft. When a tight fit is required, the bearing inside diameter will be smaller than the shaft. In this case, driving the bearing on the shaft using normal methods may cause bearing damage. Instead, heat the bearing before installation. Note the following:

    a. Secure the shaft so it is ready for bearing installation.

    b. Clean all residues from the bearing surface of the shaft. Remove burrs with a file.

    c. Fill a suitable pot or beaker with clean mineral oil. Place a thermometer rated above 120° C (248° F) in the oil. Support the thermometer so it does not rest on the bottom or side of the pot.

    d. Remove the bearing from its wrapper and secure it with a piece of heavy wire bent to hold it in the pot. Hang the bearing in the pot so it does not touch the bottom or sides of the pot.

    e. Turn the heat on and monitor the thermometer. When the oil temperature rises to approximately 120° C (248° F), remove the bearing from the pot and quickly install it. If necessary, place a socket on the inner bearing race and tap the bearing into place. As the bearing chills, it tightens on the shaft, so installation must be done quickly. Make sure the bearing is installed completely.

2. Follow this step when installing a bearing in a housing. Bearings are generally installed in a housing with a slight interference fit. Driving the bearing into the housing using normal methods may damage the housing or cause bearing damage. Instead, heat the housing before the bearing is installed. Note the following:
   a. Before heating the housing in this procedure, wash the housing thoroughly with detergent and water. Rinse and rewash the housing as required to remove all oil and chemicals.
   b. Heat the housing to approximately 100° C (212° F) with a heat gun or on a hot plate. Monitor temperature with an infrared thermometer, heat sticks or place tiny drops of water on the housing; if they sizzle and evaporate immediately, the temperature is correct. Heat only one housing at a time.
   c. If a hot plate is used, remove the housing and place it on wooden blocks.
   d. Hold the housing with the bearing side down and tap the bearing out with a suitable size socket and extension. Repeat for all bearings in the housing.
   e. Before heating the bearing housing, place the new bearing in a freezer, if possible. Chilling a bearing slightly reduces its outside diameter while the heated bearing housing assembly is slightly larger due to heat expansion. This makes bearing installation easier.
   f. While the housing is still hot, install the new bearing(s) into the housing. Install the bearings by hand, if possible. If necessary, lightly tap the bearing(s) into the housing with a socket placed on the outer bearing race (**Figure 48**). Do not install bearings by driving on the inner bearing race. Install the bearing(s) until it seats completely.

Seal Replacement

Seals are used to contain oil, water, grease or combustion gasses in a housing or shaft. Improper removal of a seal can damage the housing or shaft. Improper installation of the seal can damage the seal.

Before replacing a seal, identify it as a rubber or Teflon seal. Both types are used on the models covered in this manual. On a rubber seal (**Figure 52**), the body and sealing element will be made of the same

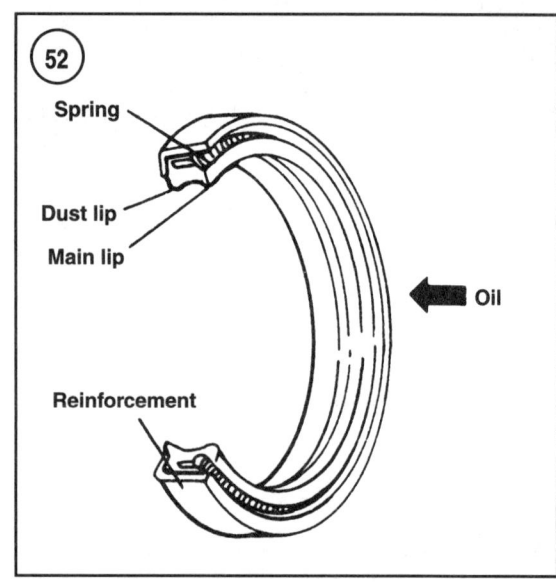

material. The seal lip (element) will also be equipped with a garter spring. On a Teflon seal, the body and seal lip will be noticeably different. The outer part is normally made of rubber and the sealing lip, placed in the middle of the seal, is Teflon. A garter spring is not used.

Rubber seals

1. Prying is generally the easiest and most effective method of removing a seal from the housing. However, always place a rag under the pry tool (**Figure 53**) to prevent damage to the housing.
2. Before installing a typical rubber seal, pack waterproof grease in the seal lips.
3. In most cases, install seals with the manufacturer's numbers or marks face out.
4. Install seals either by hand or with tools. Center the seal in its bore and attempt to install it by hand. If necessary, install the seal with a socket or bearing driver placed on the outside of the seal as shown in **Figure 54**. Drive the seal squarely into the housing until it is flush with its mounting bore. Never install a seal by hitting against the top of the seal with a hammer.

STORAGE

Several months of non-use can cause a general deterioration of the motorcycle. This is especially true in areas of extreme temperature variations. This deterioration can be minimized with careful preparation for storage. A properly stored motorcycle is much easier to return to service.

GENERAL INFORMATION

Storage Area Selection

When selecting a storage area, consider the following:
1. The storage area must be dry. A heated area is best, but not necessary. It should be insulated to minimize extreme temperature variations.
2. If the building has large window areas, mask them to keep sunlight off the motorcycle.
3. Avoid storage areas close to saltwater.
4. Consider the area's risk of fire, theft or vandalism. Check with your insurer regarding motorcycle coverage while in storage.

Preparing the Motorcycle for Storage

The amount of preparation a motorcycle should undergo before storage depends on the expected length of non-use, storage area conditions and personal preference. Consider the following list the minimum requirement:
1. Wash the motorcycle thoroughly. Make sure all dirt, mud and road debris are removed.
2. Start the engine and allow it to reach operating temperature. Drain the engine oil regardless of the riding time since the last service. Fill the engine with the recommended type and quantity of oil.
3. Fill the fuel tank completely.
4. Remove the spark plug from the cylinder head. Ground the spark plug cap to the engine. Refer to *Ignition Ground Tool* in this chapter. Pour a teaspoon of engine oil into the cylinders. Place a rag over the openings and slowly turn the engine over to distribute the oil. Reinstall the spark plug.
5. Remove the battery. Store it in a cool, dry location. Charge the battery once a month. Refer to *Battery* in Chapter Nine for service.
6. Cover the exhaust and intake openings.
7. Apply a protective substance to the plastic and rubber components, including the tires. Make sure to follow the manufacturer's instructions for each type of product being used.
8. Rotate the front tire periodically to prevent a flat spot from developing and damaging the tire.
9. Cover the motorcycle with old bed sheets or something similar. Do not cover it with any plastic material that will trap moisture.

Returning the Motorcycle to Service

The amount of service required when returning a motorcycle to service after storage depends on the length of non-use and storage conditions. In addition to performing the reverse of the above procedure, make sure the brakes, clutch, throttle and engine stop switch work properly before operating the motorcycle. Refer to Chapter Three and evaluate the service intervals to determine which areas require service.

Tables 1-6 are on the following pages.

Table 1 GENERAL DIMENSIONS AND WEIGHT

Ground clearance	210 mm (8.3 in.)
Overall height	1350 mm (53.2 in.)
Overall length	2295 mm (90.4 in.)
Overall width	960 mm (37.8 in.)
Seat height	890 mm (35.0 in.)
Wheel base	1480 mm (58.3 in.)
Dry weight	175 kg (386 lb.)
Curb weight	196 kg (432 lb.)

Table 2 TECHNICAL ABBREVIATIONS

A	Ampere
AC	Alternating current
A.h	Ampere hour
C	Celsius
cc	Cubic centimeter
CDI	Capacitor discharge ignition
cid	Cubic inch displacement
CKP	Crankshaft position sensor
cm	Centimeter
cu. in.	Cubic inch and cubic inches
cyl.	Cylinder
DC	Direct current
ECM	Electronic control module
ECU	Electronic control unit
F	Fahrenheit
fl. oz.	Fluid ounces
ft.	Foot or Feet
ft.-lb.	Foot pounds
gal.	Gallon and gallons
H/A	High altitude
hp	Horsepower
Hz	Hertz
ID	Inside diameter
in.	Inch and inches
in.-lb.	Inch-pounds
in. Hg	Inches of mercury
k	One-thousand ohms (2k = 2000 ohms)
kg	Kilogram
kg/cm2	Kilogram per square centimeter
kgm	Kilogram meter
km	Kilometer
km/h	Kilometer per hour
kPa	Kilopascals
kW	Kilowatt
L	Liter and liters
L/m	Liters per minute
lb.	Pound and pounds
m	Meter
mL	Milliliter
mm	Millimeter
N•m	Newton meter
O^2	Oxygen
OD	Outside diameter
oz.	Ounce and ounces
psi	Pounds per square inch
pt.	Pint and pints
qt.	Quart and quarts
rpm	Revolution per minute
TDC	Top dead center
V	Volt
W	Watt

*Add model/manual specific abbreviations as needed.

GENERAL INFORMATION

Table 3 GENERAL TORQUE RECOMMENDATIONS

Thread diameter (mm)	N•m	in.-lb.	ft.-lb.
5	5	42	–
6	8	72	–
8	19	–	14
10	34	–	25
12	55	–	40
14	85	–	63
16	135	–	100
18	190	–	140
20	275	–	203

Table 4 CONVERSION FORMULAS

Multiply:	By:	To get the equivalent of:
Length		
Inches	25.4	Millimeter
Inches	2.54	Centimeter
Miles	1.609	Kilometer
Feet	0.3048	Meter
Millimeter	0.03937	Inches
Centimeter	0.3937	Inches
Kilometer	0.6214	Mile
Meter	3.281	Feet
Fluid volume		
U.S. quarts	0.9463	Liters
U.S. gallons	3.785	Liters
U.S. ounces	29.573529	Milliliters
Imperial gallons	4.54609	Liters
Imperial quarts	1.1365	Liters
Liters	0.2641721	U.S. gallons
Liters	1.0566882	U.S. quarts
Liters	33.814023	U.S. ounces
Liters	0.22	Imperial gallons
Liters	0.8799	Imperial quarts
Milliliters	0.033814	U.S. ounces
Fluid volume (continued)		
Milliliters	1.0	Cubic centimeters
Milliliters	0.001	Liters
Torque		
Foot-pounds	1.3558	Newton-meters
Foot-pounds	0.138255	Meters-kilograms
Inch-pounds	0.11299	Newton-meters
Newton-meters	0.7375622	Foot-pounds
Newton-meters	8.8507	Inch-pounds
Meters-kilograms	7.2330139	Foot-pounds
Volume		
Cubic inches	16.387064	Cubic centimeters
Cubic centimeters	0.0610237	Cubic inches
Temperature		
Fahrenheit	(°F – 32) × 0.556	Centigrade
Centigrade	(°C × 1.8) + 32	Fahrenheit
Weight		
Ounces	28.3495	Grams
Pounds	0.4535924	Kilograms
Grams	0.035274	Ounces
Kilograms	2.2046224	Pounds
Pressure		
Pounds per square inch	0.070307	Kilograms per square centimeter
Kilograms per square centimeter	14.223343	Pounds per square inch
Kilopascals	0.1450	Pounds per square inch
Pounds per square inch	6.895	Kilopascals
Speed		
Miles per hour	1.609344	Kilometers per hour
Kilometers per hour	0.6213712	Miles per hour

Table 5 METRIC TAP DRILL SIZE

Metric size	Drill equivalent	Decimal fraction	Nearest fraction
3 x 0.50	No. 39	0.0995	3/32
3 x 0.60	3/32	0.0937	3/32
4 x 0.70	No. 30	0.1285	1/8
4 x 0.75	1/8	0.125	1/8
5 x 0.80	No. 19	0.166	11/64
5 x 0.90	No. 20	0.161	5/32
6 x 1.00	No. 9	0.196	13/64
7 x 1.00	16/64	0.234	15-64
8 x 1.00	J	0.277	9/32
8 x 1.25	17/64	0.265	17/64
9 x 1.00	5/16	0.3125	5/16
9 x 1.25	5/16	0.3125	5/16
10 x 1.25	R	0.339	11/32
11 x 1.50	3/8	0.375	3/8
12 x 1.50	13/32	0.406	13/32
12 x 1.75	13/32	0.406	13/32

Table 6 METRIC, DECIMAL AND FRACTIONAL EQUIVALENTS

mm	in.	Nearest fraction	mm	in.	Nearest fraction
1	0.0394	1/32	26	1.0236	1 1/32
2	0.0787	3/32	27	1.0630	1 1/16
3	0.1181	1/8	28	1.1024	1 3/32
4	0.1575	5/32	29	1.1417	1 5/32
5	0.1969	3/16	30	1.1811	1 3/16
6	0.2362	1/4	31	1.2205	1 7/32
7	0.2756	9/32	32	1.2598	1 1/4
8	0.3150	5/16	33	1.2992	1 5/16
9	0.3543	11/32	34	1.3386	1 11/32
10	0.3937	13/32	35	1.3780	1 3/8
11	0.4331	7/16	36	1.4173	1 13/32
12	0.4724	15/32	37	1.4567	1 15/32
13	0.5118	1/2	38	1.4961	1 1/2
14	0.5512	9/16	39	1.5354	1 17/32
15	0.5906	19/32	40	1.5748	1 9/16
16	0.6299	5/8	41	1.6142	1 5/8
17	0.6693	21/32	42	1.6535	1 21/32
18	0.7087	23/32	43	1.6929	1 11/16
19	0.7480	3/4	44	1.7323	1 23/32
20	0.7874	25/32	45	1.7717	1 25/32
21	0.8268	13/16	46	1.8110	1 13/16
22	0.8661	7/8	47	1.8504	1 27/32
23	0.9055	29/32	48	1.8898	1 7/8
24	0.9449	15/16	49	1.9291	1 15/16
25	0.9843	31/32	50	1.9685	1 31/32

CHAPTER TWO

TROUBLESHOOTING

The troubleshooting procedures described in this chapter provide typical symptoms and logical methods for isolating the cause(s). There may be several ways to solve a problem, but only a systematic approach will be successful in avoiding wasted time and possibly unnecessary parts replacement. Gather as much information as possible to aid in diagnosis. Never assume anything and do not overlook the obvious. Make sure the engine stop switch is in the run position and there is fuel in the tank.

An engine needs three basics to run properly: correct air/fuel mixture, compression and a spark at the correct time. If one of these is missing, the engine will not run.

Learning to recognize symptoms makes troubleshooting easier. In most cases, expensive and complicated test equipment is not needed to determine whether repairs can be performed at home. On the other hand, be realistic and do not start procedures that are beyond your experience and equipment available. If the motorcycle requires the attention of a professional, describe symptoms and conditions accurately and fully. The more information a technician has available, the easier it is to diagnose the problem.

STARTING THE ENGINE

Before starting the engine, always perform a pre-ride inspection of the motorcycle, as described in Chapter Three.

Safety Switches

The motorcycle is equipped with safety switches that prevent the engine from starting or running if certain conditions occur. The following describes each switch and when it prevents the engine from running:
1. Neutral switch. With the transmission in any position except neutral, with the clutch engaged (clutch lever out), the engine will not start.
2. Starter lockout switch (located in clutch lever assembly). With the transmission in gear, the engine will not start if the clutch is engaged (clutch lever out). If the clutch is disengaged with the transmission in gear, the engine will start.
3. Side stand switch. If the side stand is down with the engine in gear and running, the engine will stop when the clutch lever is released.
4. Engine stop switch (A, **Figure 1**). When moved to the off position the switch will prevent the engine from starting, or, will stop the engine when it is running. The engine will start and run only when the switch is in the run position.

Engine Is Cold

1. Shift the transmission into neutral.
2. Check that the engine stop switch is in the run position.

3. Turn the fuel valve lever from the off position (**Figure 2**) to the on (vertical) position. An arrow on the fuel valve points to the lever position.
4. Move the choke lever (**Figure 3**) fully rearward to richen the air/fuel mixture.
5. Turn on the ignition switch (A, **Figure 4**).
6. Check that the neutral light (B, **Figure 4**) comes on.
7. Press the starter button (B, **Figure 1**) while keeping the throttle closed.

NOTE
The type of choke system used on the KLR is most effective if the throttle remains completely closed during start-up.

8. When the engine starts, gradually move the choke lever forward as the engine warms up. Allow the engine to warm up at an idle for 1 minute, or until the engine responds smoothly and does not require the choke.

CAUTION
Do not race the engine during the warm-up period. Excessive wear and potential engine damage can occur when the engine is not up to operating temperature.

Engine Is Warm or Hot

1. Shift the transmission into neutral.
2. Check that the engine stop switch is in the run position.
3. Turn the fuel valve lever from the off position (**Figure 2**) to the on (vertical) position. An arrow on the fuel valve points to the lever position.
4. Turn on the ignition switch (A, **Figure 4**).
5. Check that the neutral light (B, **Figure 4**) comes on.
6. Press the starter button (B, **Figure 1**) while keeping the throttle closed.

Engine Is Flooded

If the engine fails to start after several tries (particularly if the choke has been used), it is probably flooded. This occurs when too much fuel is drawn into the engine and the spark plug fails to ignite the air/fuel mixture. The smell of gasoline is often evident when the engine is flooded. If there are no obvious signs of fuel overflow from the carburetor, try starting the engine by fully opening the throttle (no choke) and operating the starter. If the engine starts,

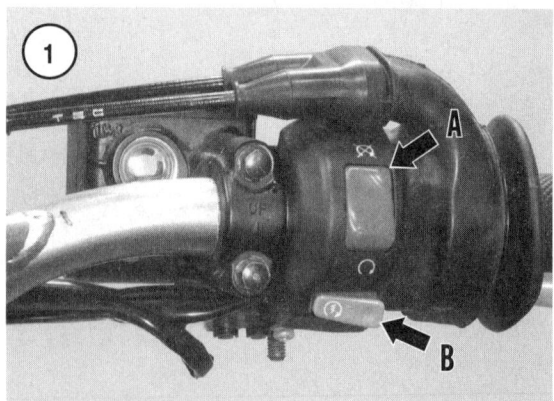

keep the engine running at a fast idle until it has burned the excess fuel from the engine.

If the engine does not start, perform the following troubleshooting steps before making other checks:
1. Check that the choke lever is fully to the front.
2. Look for gasoline overflowing from the carburetor or overflow hose.
   a. If gasoline is evident, the float in the carburetor bowl is stuck or adjusted too high.
   b. Remove and repair the float assembly or adjust it as described in Chapter Eight.
3. Check the air filter for excessive buildup.

TROUBLESHOOTING 31

4. Remove the spark plug and dry the electrodes. Reinstall the plug and try starting the engine as described.
5. Perform an engine spark test.

ENGINE SPARK TEST

An engine spark test indicates whether the ignition system is providing adequate power to the spark plug. It is a quick way to determine if a problem is in the electrical system or fuel system.

CAUTION
*When performing this test, the spark plug lead must be grounded before cranking the engine. If it is not, it is possible to damage the CDI circuitry. A spark plug can be used for this test, but a spark tester (**Figure 5**) will clearly show if spark is occurring, as well as the strength of the spark. This tester can be purchased at parts supply stores or suppliers of ignition test equipment.*

1. Remove the spark plug. Inspect the spark plug by comparing its condition to the plugs shown in Chapter Three.
2. Connect the spark plug lead to the spark plug or to a spark tester.
3. Ground the plug/tester to bare metal on the engine. Position the plug/tester so the firing end can be viewed (**Figure 6**).
4. Crank the engine and observe the spark. A fat, blue spark should appear at the firing end. The spark should fire consistently as the engine is cranked.
5. If the spark appears weak, or fires inconsistently, check the following areas for the possible cause:
  a. Fouled/improperly gapped spark plug.
  b. Damaged/shorted spark plug lead and cap.
  c. Loose connection in ignition system.
  d. Damaged coil.
  e. Damaged ignition switch.
  f. Dirty/shorted engine stop switch.
  g. Damaged exciter coil or crankshaft position sensor (check ignition timing).
  h. Damaged CDI unit.

ENGINE PERFORMANCE

If the engine does not operate at peak performance, the following lists of possible causes may help isolate the problem. The most common causes of poor engine performance are listed first for each area. These are the easiest to check.

Review Chapter Eight (*Fuel System*) and Chapter Nine (*Electrical System*) to gain a working knowledge of each of these systems. Throughout the chapters, explanations, photos and diagrams are provided to aid in learning the function of the major components that make up each system.

Engine Will Not Start or Starts and Dies

1. Fuel system:

NOTE
For California models, if the fuel tank is overfilled, heat can cause the fuel to expand and overflow into the evapora-

tive emission control unit lines, located near the filler neck. This can cause hard starting and engine hesitation until the fuel is cleared from the system.

a. Fuel valve off.
b. Fuel tank near empty.
c. Improper operation of choke lever.
d. Choke plunger stuck open.
e. Idle speed too low.
f. Engine flooded.
g. Clogged fuel tank cap vent.
h. Contaminated fuel.
i. Clogged fuel valve, fuel line or carburetor.
j. Clogged air filter.
k. Fuel tank diaphragm-valve vacuum hose disconnected or leaking.
l. Malfunctioning fuel tank diaphragm valve.
m. Pilot mixture screw misadjusted.
n. Float valve clogged or sticking.
o. Air leaks at intake duct.
p. Wrong pilot jet for altitude.
q. Damaged vacuum hose(s).

2. Ignition:
   a. Fouled/improperly gapped spark plug.
   b. Damaged/shorted spark plug lead and cap.
   c. Loose connection in ignition system.
   d. Damaged coil.
   e. Damaged ignition switch.
   f. Dirty/shorted engine stop switch.
   g. Damaged exciter coil or crankshaft position sensor (check ignition timing).
   h. Damaged CDI unit.
3. Engine:
   a. Compression release malfunctioning.
   b. Improper valve clearance.
   c. Leaking cylinder head gasket.
   d. Stuck/seized valve.
   e. Worn piston and/or cylinder.

Poor Idle and Low Speed Performance

1. Fuel system:
   a. Improper operation of choke lever.
   b. Choke plunger stuck open.
   c. Idle speed too low.
   d. Engine flooded.
   e. Clogged fuel tank cap vent.
   f. Contaminated fuel.
   g. Clogged fuel valve, fuel line or carburetor.
   h. Clogged air filter.
   i. Fuel tank diaphragm-valve vacuum hose disconnected or leaking.
   j. Malfunctioning fuel tank diaphragm valve.
   k. Pilot mixture screw misadjusted.
   l. Float valve clogged or sticking.
   m. Air leaks at intake duct.
   n. Loose carburetor diaphragm cover.
   o. Torn or damaged slide diaphragm.
   p. Dragging carburetor slide.
   q. Wrong pilot jet for altitude.
   r. Clogged muffler.
2. Ignition:
   a. Fouled/improperly gapped spark plug.
   b. Damaged/shorted spark plug lead and cap.
   c. Loose connection in ignition system.
   d. Damaged coil.
   e. Damaged ignition switch.
   f. Dirty/shorted engine stop switch.
   g. Damaged exciter coil or crankshaft position sensor (check ignition timing).
   h. Damaged CDI unit.
3. Engine:
   a. Compression release malfunctioning.
   b. Improper valve clearance.
   c. Low compression.
   d. Improper valve/camshaft timing.

Engine Lacks Power and Acceleration

1. Fuel system:
   a. Improper operation of choke lever.
   b. Choke plunger stuck open.
   c. Contaminated fuel.
   d. Clogged fuel valve, fuel line or carburetor jets.
   e. Clogged air filter.
   f. Fuel tank diaphragm-valve vacuum hose disconnected or leaking.
   g. Malfunctioning fuel tank diaphragm valve.
   h. Float valve clogged or sticking.
   i. Air leaks at intake duct.
   j. Loose carburetor diaphragm cover.
   k. Torn or damaged slide diaphragm.
   l. Dragging carburetor slide.
   m. Wrong pilot or main jet for altitude.
   n. Clogged muffler.
2. Ignition:
   a. Fouled/improperly gapped spark plug.
   b. Damaged/shorted spark plug lead and cap.
   c. Loose connection in ignition system.
   d. Damaged coil.
   e. Damaged exciter coil or crankshaft position sensor (check ignition timing).
   f. Damaged CDI unit.
3. Engine:
   a. Compression release malfunctioning.
   b. Improper valve clearance.
   c. Low compression.
   d. Improper valve/camshaft timing.
4. Brakes and wheels:
   a. Brake pads dragging on brake disc.

TROUBLESHOOTING

  b. Worn/seized wheel bearings.
  c. Drive chain too tight.
5. Clutch:
  a. Clutch incorrectly adjusted.
  b. Weak clutch springs.
  c. Worn clutch plates and discs.

Poor High Speed Performance

1. Fuel system:
  a. Improper operation of choke lever.
  b. Choke plunger stuck open.
  c. Contaminated fuel.
  d. Clogged fuel valve, fuel line or carburetor jets.
  e. Clogged air filter.
  f. Air leaks at intake duct.
  g. Float valve too high.
  h. Loose carburetor diaphragm cover.
  i. Torn or damaged slide diaphragm.
  j. Dragging carburetor slide.
  k. Worn needle and jet.
  l. Wrong main jet for altitude.
  m. Clogged muffler.
2. Ignition:
  a. Damaged exciter coil or crankshaft position sensor (check ignition timing).
  b. Damaged CDI unit.
3. Engine:
  a. Engine oil level too high.
  b. Improper valve clearance.
  c. Weak/broken valve spring(s).

Engine Backfires

1. Pilot mixture screw adjusted too lean.
2. Air leaks into exhaust system.
3. Inoperative air cut-off valve (backfiring during deceleration).
4. Damaged exciter coil or crankshaft position sensor (check ignition timing).

Engine Overheating

CAUTION
Engine overheating can occur when the motorcycle is operated at slow speed at high rpm. This can occur in severe off-road riding conditions. Even though the fan turns on, excessive heat buildup can cause the engine to overheat. When this occurs, stop and allow the engine to cool. If overheating continues after the motorcycle is ridden at moderate speeds and lower rpm, check the motorcycle and determine the cause of overheating.

1. Cooling system:
  a. Coolant level low.
  b. Water in system; no coolant mix.
  c. Air in system.
  d. Radiator clogged.
  e. Radiator cap damaged.
  f. Thermostat damaged.
  g. Fan fuse blown.
  h. Fan relay or switch faulty.
  i. Fan shaft seized.
  j. Water pump impeller loose.
  k. Water pump impeller damaged.
  l. Water temperature sending unit faulty.
  m. Water temperature gauge faulty.
2. Engine:
  a. Excessive idling.
  b. Insufficient oil level or viscosity.
  c. Incorrect spark plug heat range.
  d. Clogged crankcase oil strainer.
  e. Excessive carbon buildup on piston/cylinder head.
3. Fuel system (causing lean fuel mixture):
  a. Clogged/pinched fuel tank cap vent hose.
  b. Air leaks at intake duct.
  c. Wrong pilot or main jet for altitude.
  d. Clogged carburetor jets.
  e. Float level too low.
4. Ignition:
  a. Improper spark plug heat range.
  b. Damaged exciter coil or crankshaft position sensor (check ignition timing).

ELECTRICAL TESTING

Refer to Chapter Nine for testing the starting system, ignition system, charging system, fan system and switches. Refer to *Starting System* (this chapter) for initial troubleshooting procedures. These inspections should be made before disassembling and bench testing components. When doing any electrical tests, refer to the diagrams in the chapter and at the back of the manual.

Before testing a component, check the electrical connections related to that component. Check for corrosion and bent or loose connectors. Most of the connectors have a lock mechanism. If these are not fully locked, a connection may not be made. If there are connectors that are not locked, pull the connector apart and clean the fittings before reassembling.

STARTING SYSTEM

Starter Turns Slowly

1. Weak battery.
2. Poorly connected/corroded battery terminals and cables.
3. Loose starter motor cable.
4. Worn or damaged starter.

Starter Turns, But Does Not Crank Engine

1. Worn or damaged starter clutch.
2. Damaged teeth on starter motor shaft or starter gears.

Starter Does Not Operate

When the starter does not operate, refer to *Starting System* in Chapter Nine for the system diagram and component testing procedures. Begin testing at the starter relay.

ENGINE NOISE

Noise is often the first indicator that something is wrong with the engine. In many cases, damage can be avoided or minimized if the rider immediately stops the motorcycle and diagnoses the source of the noise. Anytime engine noise is ignored, even when the motorcycle seems to be running correctly, the rider risks causing more damage and injury.

Pinging During Acceleration

1. Poor quality or contaminated fuel.
2. Lean fuel mixture.
3. Excessive carbon buildup in combustion chamber.
4. Damaged exciter coil or crankshaft position sensor (check ignition timing).

Knocks, Ticks or Rattles

1. Engine top end:
    a. Improper valve clearance.
    b. Broken or weak valve spring.
    c. Damaged compression release.
    d. Loose cam chain/damaged tensioner.
    e. Worn piston pin or piston pin bore.
    f. Worn connecting rod small end.
    g. Worn piston, rings and/or cylinder.
2. Engine bottom end:
    a. Loose balancer chain.
    b. Worn connecting rod bearing.
    c. Worn crankshaft bearings.
    d. Worn balancer bearings.
    e. Worn transmission bearings.
    f. Worn or damaged transmission gears.
    g. Incorrect installation of balancer.

MOTORCYCLE NOISE

The following possible causes of noise will likely occur only when the motorcycle is in motion.
1. Excessively loose drive chain.
2. Worn chain sliders.
3. Loose exhaust system.
4. Loose/missing body fasteners.
5. Loose skid plate.
6. Loose shock absorber.
7. Loose engine mounting bolts.
8. Brake pads dragging on brake disc.
9. Worn/seized wheel bearings.

ENGINE LUBRICATION

An improperly operating engine lubrication system will quickly lead to engine seizure. Check the engine oil level before each ride, and top off as described in Chapter Three. Refer to Chapter Six for oil pump service.

High Oil Consumption or Excessive Exhaust Smoke

1. Worn valve guides.
2. Worn or damaged piston rings.

Oil Leaks

1. Clogged air box breather hose.
2. Loose engine parts.
3. Damaged gasket sealing surfaces.

TROUBLESHOOTING

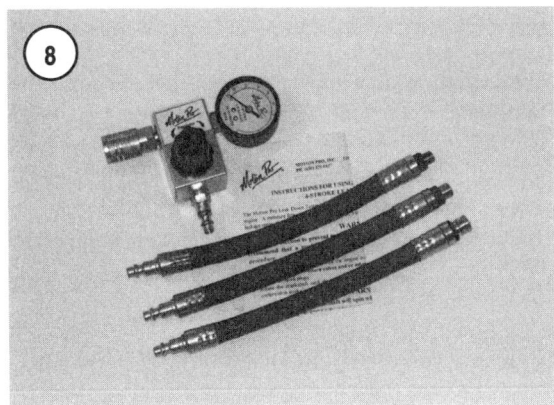

High Oil Pressure

1. Incorrect type of engine oil.
2. Clogged oil filter.
3. Clogged oil gallery or oil jets.

Low Oil Pressure

1. Low oil level.
2. Incorrect type of engine oil.
3. Worn or damaged oil pump.
4. Clogged oil strainer screen.
5. Clogged oil filter.
6. Internal oil leaks.

No Oil Pressure

1. Low oil level.
2. Damaged oil pump.
3. Damaged oil pump drive shaft.
4. Damaged oil pump drive gear.
5. Incorrect oil pump installation.

Oil Contamination

1. Blown head gasket allowing coolant to leak into the engine.
2. Water contamination.
3. Oil and filter not changed at specified intervals or when operating conditions demand more frequent changes.

Engine Oil Pressure Test

Check engine oil pressure after installing a new oil pump, reassembling the engine or when troubleshooting the lubrication system.

To perform this test, use an oil pressure gauge (part No. 57001-164, or equivalent) and adapter (part No. 57001-1182).

1. Make sure the engine oil level is correct as described in Chapter Three.
2. Remove the skid plate as described in Chapter Fifteen.
3. Place a drain pan under the oil passage plug (**Figure 7**) on the right crankcase cover to catch any oil leaks.
4. Unscrew the oil passage plug.
5. Install the adapter, then thread the gauge into the oil passage switch hole. Make sure the fitting is tight to avoid oil leaks.
6. Start the engine and allow it to reach normal operating temperature.
7. Maintain the engine speed at 4000 rpm and note the gauge reading. Oil pressure must be between 78-147 kPa (11-21 psi). If the oil pressure is lower than specified, check the following:
    a. Defective relief valve.
    b. Oil leak from oil passageway or external oil line.
    c. Plugged oil screen.
    d. Defective oil pump.
    e. Combination of the above.
8. If the oil pressure is higher than specified, check the following:
    a. Plugged oil filter.
    b. Oil viscosity too heavy (drain oil and install lighter weight oil).
    c. Plugged oil passageway or external oil line.
    d. Combination of the above.
9. Shut off the engine and remove the test equipment.
10. Install a new O-ring onto the oil passage plug.
11. Apply a light coat of grease to the O-ring and install the oil passage plug.
12. Tighten the oil passage plug to 25 N•m (18 ft.-lb.).
13. Run the engine and check for leaks.

ENGINE LEAKDOWN TEST

The condition of the piston rings and valves can be checked with a leakdown tester. With all valves in the closed position, the tester is screwed into the spark plug hole and air pressure is applied to the combustion chamber. The gauge on the tester is then observed to determine the rate of leak from the combustion chamber. An air compressor is required to use the leakdown tester (**Figure 8**).

1. Start the engine and allow it to warm up.
2. Shut off the engine and remove the carburetor and exhaust pipe.
3. Remove the spark plug.
4. Set the piston to TDC on the compression stroke.

5. Install the leakdown tester following the manufacturer's instructions. The tester must not leak around the spark plug threads.
6. Make the test following the manufacturer's instructions for the tester. When pressure is applied to the cylinder, check that the engine remains at TDC. If necessary, put the transmission in gear.
7. While the cylinder is under pressure, listen for air leaking at the following areas.
   a. Exhaust port. If there are leaks, the exhaust valves are leaking.
   b. Intake port. If there are leaks, the intake valves are leaking.
   c. Crankcase breather tube. If there are leaks, the piston rings are leaking.
8. A cylinder with a leakdown of 5 percent or less is ideal. A cylinder with more than 10 percent leakdown should be inspected to determine if leaking is caused by normal wear or damage. Inspection of the parts will indicate what action should be taken.

CLUTCH

The two main clutch problems are clutch slip (clutch does not fully engage) and clutch drag (clutch does not fully disengage). These problems are often caused by incorrect clutch adjustment or a damaged/unlubricated cable. Perform the following checks before removing the right crankcase cover to troubleshoot the clutch:
1. Check the clutch cable routing from the handlebar to the engine. Check that the cable is free when the handlebar is turned lock to lock, and that the cable ends are installed correctly.
2. With the engine off, pull and release the clutch lever. If the lever is hard to pull, or the action is rough, check for the following:
   a. Damaged/kinked cable.
   b. Incorrect cable routing.
   c. Cable not lubricated.
   d. Worn/unlubricated lever at the handlebar.
   e. Damaged release lever at the engine.
3. If no damage was detected in the previous steps, and the lever moves without excessive roughness or binding, check the clutch adjustment as described in Chapter Three. Note the following:
   a. If the clutch cannot be adjusted to the specifications in Chapter Three, the clutch cable is stretched or damaged.
   b. If the clutch cable is in good condition and adjustment is correct, the clutch plates may be worn or warped.

Slipping

When the clutch slips, the engine accelerates faster than what the actual forward speed indicates. When continuous slipping occurs between the clutch plates, excessive heat quickly builds up in the assembly. This causes plate wear, warp and spring fatigue.

One or more of the following can cause the clutch to slip:
1. Clutch wear or damage:
   a. Incorrect clutch adjustment.
   b. Weak or damaged clutch springs.
   c. Loose clutch springs.
   d. Worn friction plates.
   e. Warped clutch (steel) plates.
   f. Worn/damaged release lever assembly.
   g. Damaged pressure plate.
   h. Clutch housing and hub unevenly worn.
2. Clutch/engine oil:
   a. Excessive oil in crankcase.
   b. Incorrect oil viscosity.
   c. Oil additives.

Dragging

When the clutch drags, the plates are not completely separating. This causes the motorcycle to creep or lurch forward when the transmission is put into gear. Once underway, shifting is difficult. If this condition is not corrected, it can cause transmission gear and shift fork damage, due to the abnormal grinding and impacts on the parts. One or more of the following can cause the clutch to drag:
1. Clutch wear or damage:
   a. Worn/damaged release lever assembly.
   b. Warped clutch (steel) plates.
   c. Swollen friction plates.
   d. Warped pressure plate.
   e. Incorrect clutch spring tension.
   f. Galled clutch housing bushing.
   g. Uneven wear on clutch housing grooves or clutch hub splines.
   h. Incorrectly assembled clutch.
2. Clutch/engine oil:
   a. Low oil level.
   b. Incorrect viscosity oil.
   c. Oil additives.

Noise

Clutch noise is usually caused by worn or damaged parts, and is more noticeable at idle or low engine speeds. Clutch noise can be caused by the following conditions:
1. Wear in the clutch lifter bearing and/or lifter.

TROUBLESHOOTING

2. Excessive axial play in the clutch housing.
3. Excessive friction plate to clutch housing clearance.
4. Excessive wear between the clutch housing and primary drive gear.
5. Worn or damaged clutch housing and primary drive gear teeth.

GEAR SHIFT LINKAGE AND TRANSMISSION

Transmission problems are often difficult to distinguish from problems with the clutch and gear shift linkage. Often, the problem is symptomatic of one area, while the actual problem is in another area. For example, if the gears grind during shifting, the problem may be caused by a dragging clutch or a component of the shift linkage, not a damaged transmission.

Of course, if the damaged part is not repaired, the transmission eventually becomes damaged, too. Therefore, evaluate all the variables that exist when the problem occurs, and always start with the easiest checks before disassembling the engine.

When the transmission exhibits abnormal noise or operation, drain the engine oil and check it for contamination or metal particles. Examine a small quantity of oil under bright light. If a metallic cast or pieces of metal are seen, excessive wear and/or part failure is occurring.

Difficult Shifting

1. Clutch:
   a. Improper clutch operation.
   b. Incorrect clutch adjustment.
   c. Incorrect oil viscosity.
2. Shift shaft:
   a. Loose/stripped shift lever.
   b. Bent/damaged shift shaft.
   c. Worn pawl plate engagement points.
   d. Damaged pawl plate or pawl spring.
   e. Damaged return spring or loose spring post.
3. Lever:
   a. Damaged lever.
   b. Broken lever spring.
   c. Loose lever bolt.
4. Shift drum and shift forks:
   a. Worn/loose shift cam.
   b. Worn shift drum grooves.
   c. Worn shift forks/guide pins.
   d. Worn shift drum bearings.

Gears Do Not Stay Engaged

1. Lever:
   a. Damaged lever.
   b. Broken lever spring.
2. Shift drum and shift forks:
   a. Worn/loose shift cam.
   b. Worn shift drum grooves.
   c. Worn shift forks/guide pins.
3. Transmission:
   a. Worn gear dogs and mating recesses.
   b. Worn gear grooves for shift forks.
   c. Worn/damaged shaft snap rings or thrust washers.

BRAKES

The brake system is critical to riding performance and safety. Inspect the brakes frequently and replace worn or damaged parts immediately. The brake system on this motorcycle uses DOT 4 brake fluid. Always use new fluid from a sealed container. The troubleshooting checks in **Figure 9** can assist in isolating brake problems.

When checking brake pad wear, check that the pads in each caliper squarely contact the disc. Uneven pad wear on one side of the disc can indicate a warped or bent disc, damaged caliper or pad pins.

STEERING AND HANDLING

Correct poor steering and handling immediately after it is detected, since loss of control is possible. Check the following areas:

1. Excessive handlebar vibration:
   a. Incorrect tire pressure.
   b. Unbalanced tire and rim.
   c. Loose/broken spokes.
   d. Damaged rim.
   e. Loose or damaged handlebar clamps.
   f. Loose steering stem nut.
   g. Worn or damaged front wheel bearings.
   h. Bent or loose axle.
   i. Cracked frame or steering head.
2. Handlebar is hard to turn:
   a. Tire pressure too low.
   b. Incorrect cable routing.
   c. Steering stem adjustment too tight.
   d. Bent steering stem.
   e. Improperly lubricated or damaged steering bearings.
3. Handlebar pulls to one side:
   a. Bent fork leg.
   b. Fork oil levels uneven.
   c. Bent steering stem.
   d. Bent frame or swing arm.
4. Shock absorption too soft:

38 CHAPTER TWO

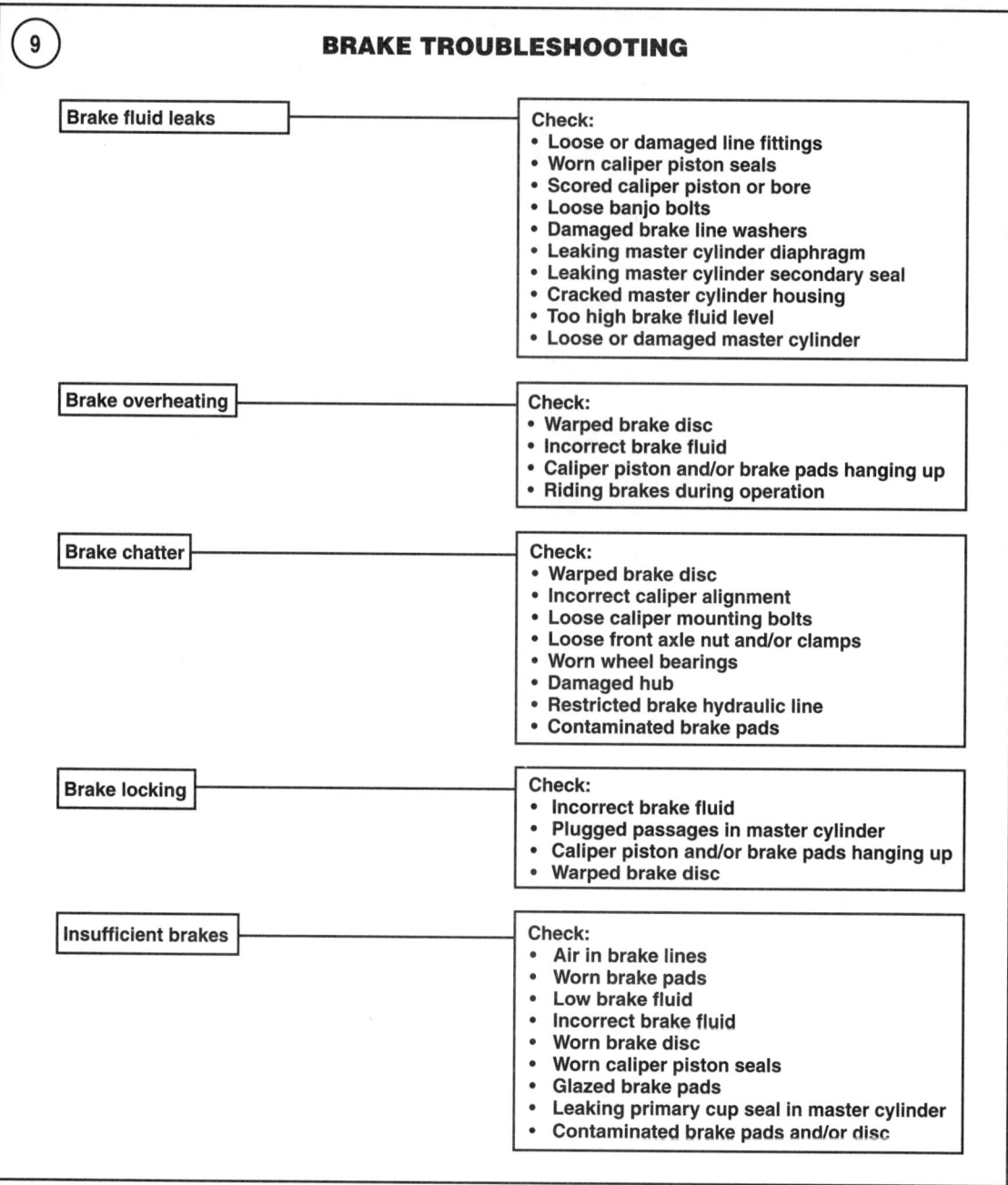

⑨ **BRAKE TROUBLESHOOTING**

Brake fluid leaks — Check:
- Loose or damaged line fittings
- Worn caliper piston seals
- Scored caliper piston or bore
- Loose banjo bolts
- Damaged brake line washers
- Leaking master cylinder diaphragm
- Leaking master cylinder secondary seal
- Cracked master cylinder housing
- Too high brake fluid level
- Loose or damaged master cylinder

Brake overheating — Check:
- Warped brake disc
- Incorrect brake fluid
- Caliper piston and/or brake pads hanging up
- Riding brakes during operation

Brake chatter — Check:
- Warped brake disc
- Incorrect caliper alignment
- Loose caliper mounting bolts
- Loose front axle nut and/or clamps
- Worn wheel bearings
- Damaged hub
- Restricted brake hydraulic line
- Contaminated brake pads

Brake locking — Check:
- Incorrect brake fluid
- Plugged passages in master cylinder
- Caliper piston and/or brake pads hanging up
- Warped brake disc

Insufficient brakes — Check:
- Air in brake lines
- Worn brake pads
- Low brake fluid
- Incorrect brake fluid
- Worn brake disc
- Worn caliper piston seals
- Glazed brake pads
- Leaking primary cup seal in master cylinder
- Contaminated brake pads and/or disc

    a. Low fork oil level.
    b. Fork oil viscosity too low.
    c. Shock absorber rebound damping too low.
    d. Shock absorber spring preload too low.
    e. Shock absorber spring weak.
5. Shock absorption too hard:

    a. High tire pressure.
    b. High fork oil level.
    c. Fork oil viscosity too high.
    d. Bent fork.
    e. Shock absorber rebound damping too high.
    f. Shock absorber spring preload too high.

Table 1 OIL PRESSURE TEST SPECIFICATIONS

Oil pump pressure at 4000 rpm	78-147 kPa (11-21 psi)
Oil passage plug torque specification	25 N•m (18 ft.-lb.)

CHAPTER THREE

LUBRICATION, MAINTENANCE AND TUNE-UP

This chapter describes lubrication, maintenance and tune-up procedures. Specifications are listed in **Tables 1-4** located at the end of this chapter.

To maximize the service life of the motorcycle and gain the utmost in safety and performance, it is necessary to perform periodic inspections and maintenance. Minor problems found during routine service can be corrected before they develop into major ones. A neglected motorcycle is unreliable and may be dangerous to ride.

Table 1 lists the recommended lubrication, maintenance and tune-up intervals. If the motorcycle is operated in extreme conditions, it may be appropriate to reduce the interval between some maintenance tasks.

Before servicing the motorcycle, make sure the procedures and the required skills are thoroughly understood. If experience and equipment are limited, start by performing basic procedures, and perform more involved tasks after gaining further experience and acquiring the necessary tools.

PRE-RIDE INSPECTION

Routinely perform the following inspections before riding the motorcycle. When riding the motorcycle on extended travel and over rough terrain, perform these inspections at least once daily. Perform the inspections when the engine is cold. Refer to the procedures and tables in this chapter for information concerning fuel, lubricants, tire pressure and component adjustments. Start the motorcycle as described in *Starting the Engine* (Chapter Two).

1. Check fuel lines and fittings for leaks.
2. Check fuel level.
3. Check engine oil level.
4. Check coolant level.
5. Check brake operation and lever/pedal free play.
6. Check throttle operation and free play.
7. Check clutch operation and free play.
8. Check steering for smooth operation and no cable binding.
9. Check tire condition and air pressure.
10. Check wheel condition and spoke tightness.
11. Check axle nut tightness.
12. Check for loose nuts and bolts.
13. Check exhaust system for tightness.
14. Check drive chain condition and adjustment.
15. Check rear sprocket for tightness.
16. Check air filter for dirt/debris buildup.
17. Check suspension for leaks and proper settings for riding conditions.
18. Check engine stop switch for proper operation.
19. Check lights and signals for proper operation.

TUNE-UP AND SERVICE INTERVALS

The maintenance and lubrication intervals in **Table 1** are based on equal use of the motorcycle, both on and off the road. If the motorcycle is regularly operated in extreme weather conditions, or subjected to water or sand, perform the service procedures more frequently.

Record when each service is performed in a maintenance log.

FUEL AND LUBRICANTS

Fuel Requirements

The engine is designed to operate on unleaded pump-grade gasoline, with a pump octane rating of 87. Gasoline containing more than 15% ethanol or 5% methanol is not recommended.

NOTE
On California models, do not fill the tank up to the neck of the fuel tank. Heat can cause the fuel to expand and overflow into the evaporative emission control unit lines, located near the filler neck. This can cause hard starting and engine hesitation until the fuel is cleared from the system.

Engine Oil Selection

Regular oil and filter changes contribute more to engine longevity than any other maintenance. **Table 1** lists the recommended oil and filter change intervals. The time interval is more important than the mileage interval because combustion acid, formed by gasoline and water vapor, contaminates the oil even if the motorcycle is not run for several months. If a motorcycle is operated under dusty conditions, the oil gets dirty quicker and should be changed more frequently than recommended.

Oil requirements for motorcycle engines are more demanding than for automobile engines. Oils specifically designed for motorcycles contain special additives to prevent premature viscosity breakdown, protect the engine from oil oxidation resulting from higher engine operating temperatures and provide lubrication qualities designed for engines operating at higher rpm. Consider the following when selecting engine oil:

1. Do not use oil with oil additives or oil with graphite or molybdenum additives. These may adversely affect clutch operation.
2. Do not use vegetable, non-detergent or castor-based racing oils.
3. The Japanese Automobile Standards Organization (JASO) has established an oil classification for motorcycle engines. JASO motorcycle specific oils are identified by the JASO T 903 Standard. The JASO label (**Figure 1**) appears on the oil container and identifies

① JASO CERTIFICATION LABEL

Sales company oil code number

M001XXXXX

MA

OIL CLASSIFICATION
MA: Designed for high-friction applications
MB: Designed for low-friction applications

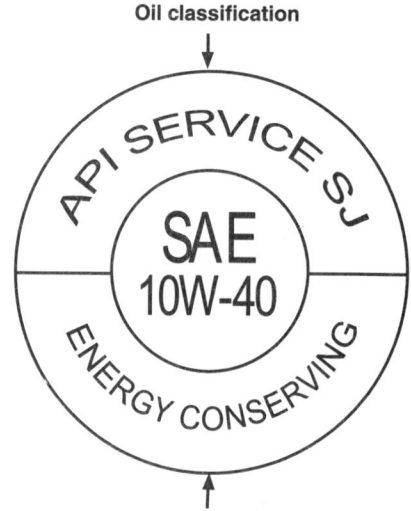

② API SERVICE SYMBOL

Oil classification

SAE 10W-40
API SERVICE SJ
ENERGY CONSERVING

When ENERGY CONSERVING is listed in this part of the label, the oil has demonstrated energy-conserving properties in standard tests. Do not use ENERGY CONSERVING classified oil in motorcycle engines. Instead, look for this API service symbol.

SAE 10W-40
API SERVICE SJ

Oil viscosity

LUBRICATION, MAINTENANCE AND TUNE-UP

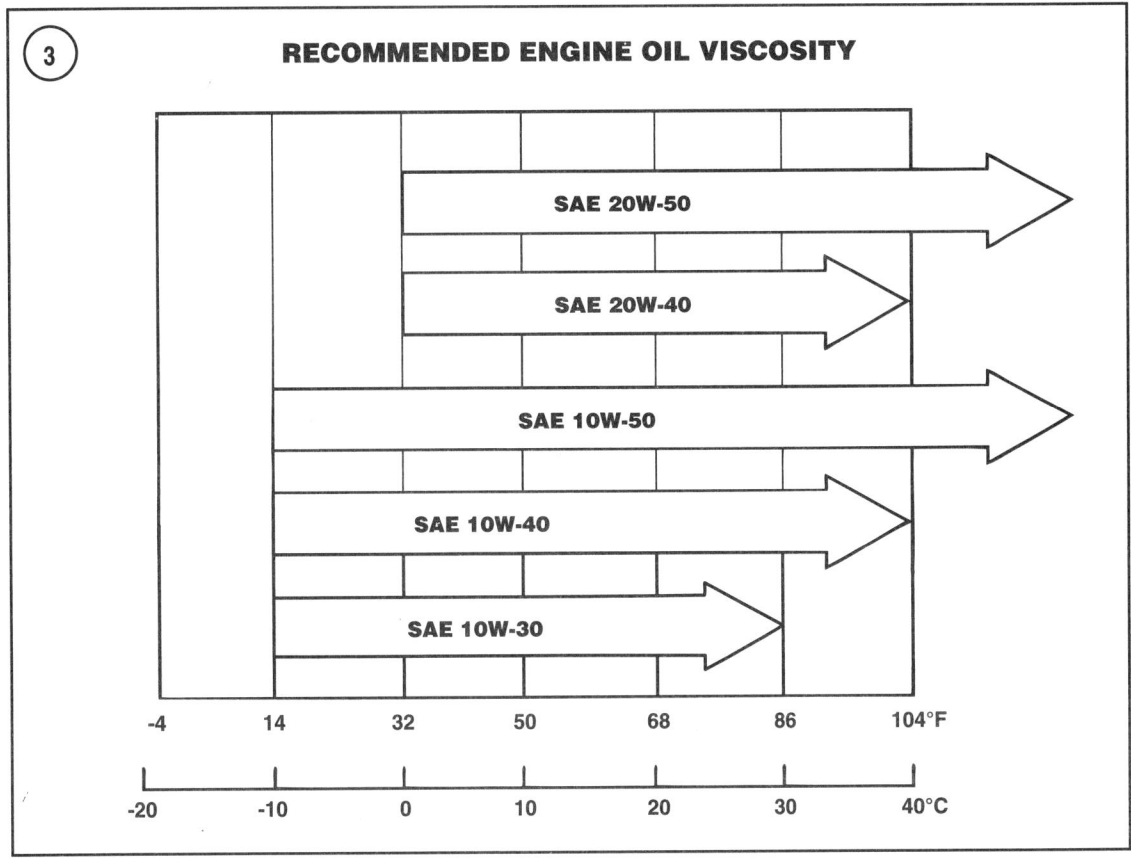

3. RECOMMENDED ENGINE OIL VISCOSITY

the two separate motorcycle oil classifications—MA and MB. Kawasaki recommends the MA classification. JASO classified oil also uses the Society of Automotive Engineers (SAE) viscosity ratings.

4. When selecting an American Petroleum Institute (API) classified oil, use only a high-quality motorcycle oil. Kawasaki recommends two classifications of oil:
   a. Oil with API classification SE, SF or SG of the correct viscosity.
   b. Oil with API classification SH, SJ or SL and JASO MA classification of the correct viscosity.

NOTE
Do not use SG or higher classification oils that display the term Energy Conserving on the oil container circular API service label (Figure 2).

5. **Figure 3** indicates when different viscosity oils should be used, based on the ambient temperature.

Fork Oil

The fork uses 10-weight fork oil in the fork legs. Refer to **Table 2** for the recommended fork oil.

Grease

Use a good quality, lithium-base grease to lubricate components requiring grease. Some components require the extreme-pressure qualities of molybdenum disulfide grease, or the protective qualities of waterproof grease. When these greases are required, it is indicated in the procedures in this manual. Grease components frequently, as this purges water and grit from the component and extends its life.

Chain Lubricant

Use a good-quality chain lubricant that is compatible with the type of chain installed on the motorcycle. An O-ring chain was standard equipment for the years covered by this manual. If an O-ring chain is installed, use chain lubricant designed specifically for O-ring chains. Since the links of an O-ring chain are permanently lubricated and sealed, O-ring chain lubricant is formulated to prevent exterior corrosion of the chain and to condition the O-rings. It is not tacky and resists the adhesion of dirt. Avoid lubricants that are tacky or designed for conventional chains. These lubricants attract dirt and subject the O-rings to unnecessary abrasion.

CHAPTER THREE

Control Cable Lubricant

Use lithium grease to lubricate the control cable pivots. Lubricate the cable with light oil or a commercial cable lubricant.

Air Filter Oil

Use a commercial air filter oil, designed specifically for foam filters. This type of oil adheres to the foam and effectively traps dust.

PERIODIC LUBRICATION

Engine Oil Level Check

Check the oil level in the sight glass (**Figure 4**). Add oil through the oil fill hole after removing the oil fill cap (**Figure 5**) located on the right crankcase cover.
1. When checking the oil level, note the following:
    a. To achieve an accurate measurement, check the oil after the engine has been allowed to stand. This test is best performed on a cold engine.
    b. If the engine has been running, allow the engine to stand for several minutes so the oil can drain to the crankcase.
    c. If the oil was changed prior to this check, start the engine and allow the oil to circulate throughout the engine. Failure to run the engine prior to checking the oil level causes an inaccurate reading.
2. Park the motorcycle on level ground.
3. Hold the motorcycle upright (off the sidestand) so the engine is level.
4. Check the oil level in the sight glass (**Figure 4**).
    a. The oil level should be between the upper (A, **Figure 6**) and lower (B) level marks that are to each side of the sight glass. Read the oil level at the center of the sight glass (C, **Figure 6**), not at the edges.
    b. Preferably, keep the oil level near the upper mark.
5. If the oil level is too low, remove the oil fill cap (**Figure 5**) on the right crankcase cover and add the appropriate type of oil to bring the level to the upper mark. Add oil in small quantities and check the level often. Do not overfill the crankcase.
6. Screw the oil fill cap into place. If oil leaks are evident around the cap, replace the O-ring on the cap.

Engine Oil and Filter Change

Change the oil and filter at the intervals recommended in **Table 1**. If the motorcycle is used in extreme conditions (hot, cold, wet or dusty) change the oil more often using the type of oil recommended in *Engine Oil Selection* (this chapter).

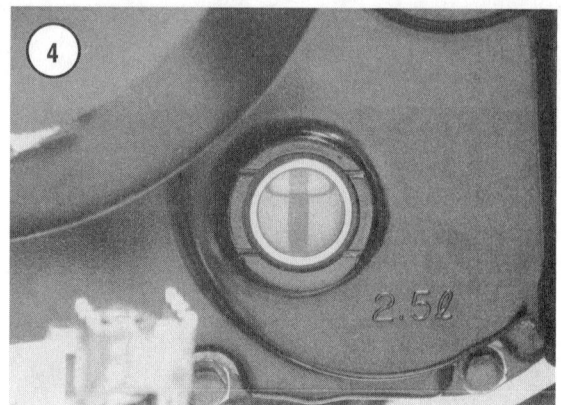

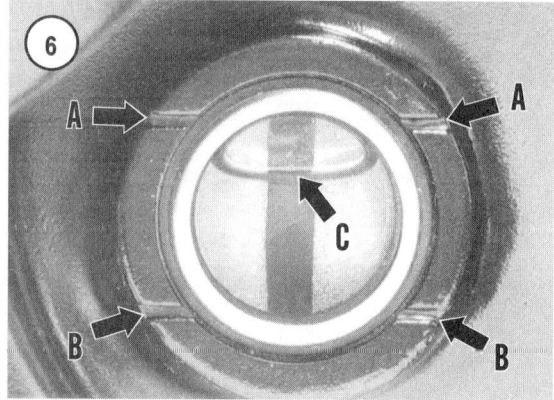

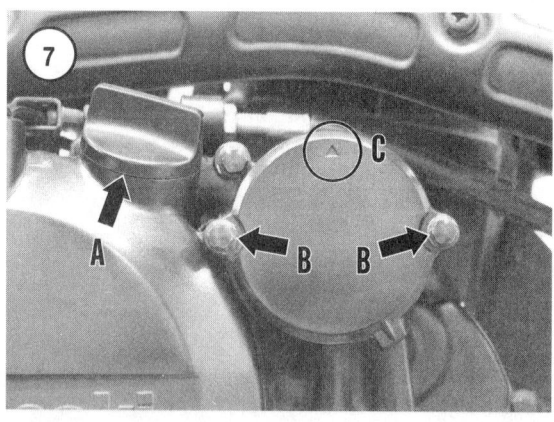

LUBRICATION, MAINTENANCE AND TUNE-UP

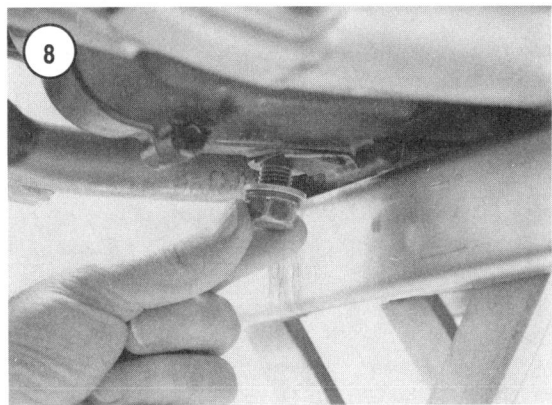

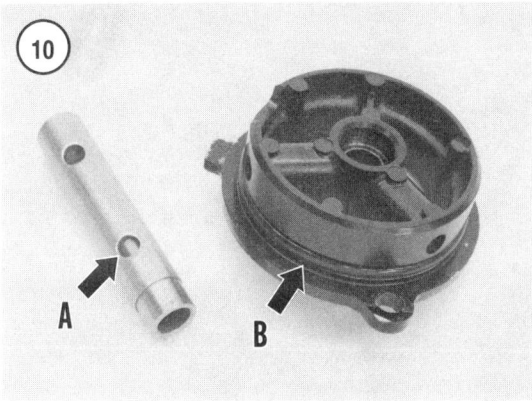

Always change the oil when the engine is warm. Contaminants will remain suspended in the oil and it will drain more completely and quickly.

> **WARNING**
> *Prolonged contact with used engine oil may cause skin cancer. Minimize contact with the engine oil.*

1. Support the motorcycle so it is level and secure.
2. Wipe the area around the oil fill cap. Remove the cap from the engine (A, **Figure 7**).
3. Place a drain pan below the engine drain plug. Then, remove the drain plug (**Figure 8**) and allow the oil to drain from the engine completely.
4. Reposition the drain pan underneath the oil filter cover.

> **NOTE**
> *An O-ring seals the filter cover to the engine. When removing the cover, grasp the tab on the cover and work the cover straight out. Avoid binding, or using tools to pry off the cover.*

5. Remove the bolts from the oil filter cover (B, **Figure 7**). Remove the cover carefully to avoid disturbing the filter.
6. Remove the filter (**Figure 9**) and mounting pin.
7. Clean and inspect the filter housing and parts.
   a. The oil filter bypass valve is inside the mounting pin (A, **Figure 10**). When cleaning the pin, check that the spring-loaded valve is clean and free to open. Press the valve open from the narrow (stepped) end of the mounting pin to check.
   b. Install a new seal washer on the drain plug. Replace the drain plug if the threads are damaged or excessively worn.
   c. Install a new, lubricated O-ring onto the filter cover (B, **Figure 10**).
   d. If leaks are evident around the oil fill plug, replace the O-ring on the plug.
8. Wipe dirt and oil from around the drain plug hole. Install the drain plug and tighten to 29 N•m (21 ft.-lb.).
9. Install the mounting pin and new oil filter as follows:

> **CAUTION**
> *The mounting pin must be installed in the correct direction or engine failure may occur.*

   a. Lubricate the grommets at both ends of the filter, then insert the mounting pin into the filter. The filter grommets must rest on the wide part of the mounting pin and not on the narrow end (**Figure 11**).

b. Insert the filter and mounting pin into the filter housing. The narrow end of the pin (**Figure 12**) must be inserted first. Fully seat the pin into the collar at the back of the filter housing.
c. Align and install the oil filter cover squarely against the engine cover. Check that the arrow on the cover (C, **Figure 7**) points up and that the O-ring is not pinched.
d. Finger-tighten the mounting bolts. Tighten the bolts to 8.8 N•m (78 in.-lb.), making several passes to avoid binding the cover.

10. Fill the crankcase with the required quantity and type of engine oil.
    a. Refer to **Table 2** for engine oil capacity.
    b. Note that oil capacity is greater when the filter is changed.
11. Screw the fill cap into place.
12. Check the engine oil level as described in *Engine Oil Level Check* (this section).
13. Check all fittings for leaks.

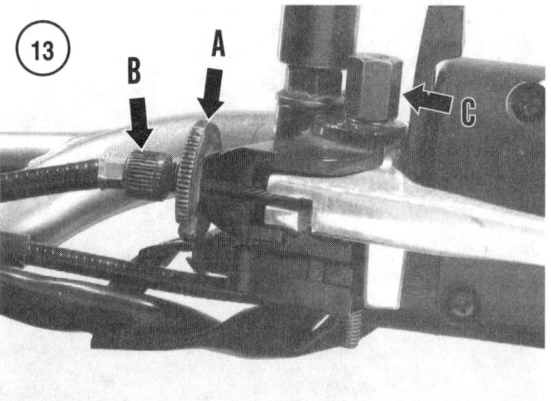

NOTE
There are a number of ways to discard used oil safely. The easiest way is to pour it from the drain pan into a gallon plastic bleach, juice or milk container for disposal. Some service stations and oil retailers will accept used oil for recycling. Do not discard oil in household trash or pour it onto the ground. Never add other fluids to any engine oil to be recycled. To locate a recycler, contact the American Petroleum Institute (API) at www.recycleoil.org.

14. Dispose of the used engine oil in an environmentally safe manner.

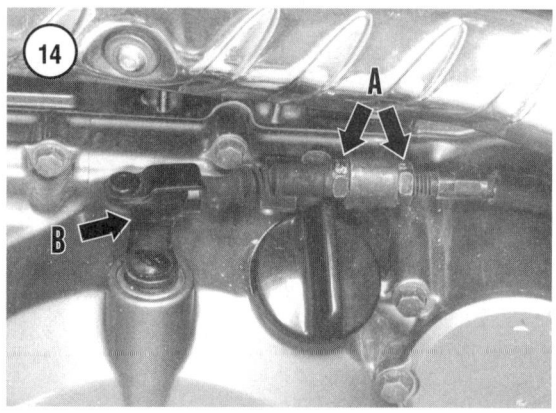

Fork Oil Replacement

Each fork leg must be removed to drain and refill the fork oil. Refer to Chapter Twelve.

Cable Lubrication

If there is binding or drag in the throttle or clutch, this can indicate a lack of cable lubrication or worn parts. Since the throttle uses two cables, also check the adjustment. Use lithium grease to lubricate the control cable pivots. Lubricate the cables with light oil or cable lubricant. If the clutch or throttle cables continue to operate poorly after lubrication, disconnect the cable(s) at both ends and check for binding or drag. Replace the cable(s) if necessary. If the cable(s) is in good condition, check for binding or drag in the carburetor or clutch.

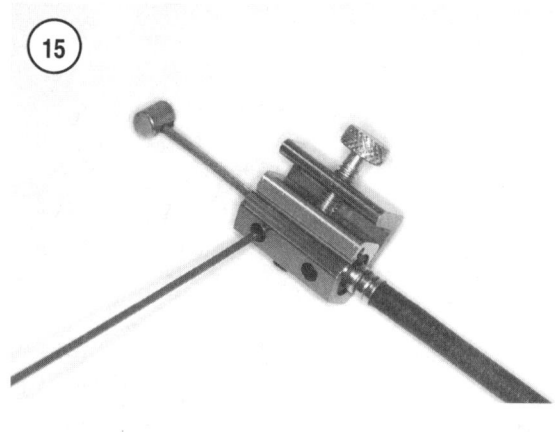

LUBRICATION, MAINTENANCE AND TUNE-UP

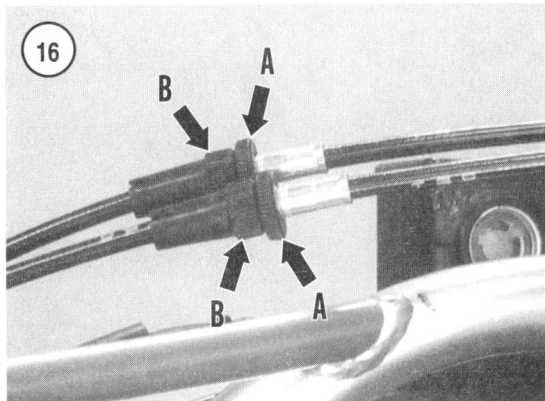

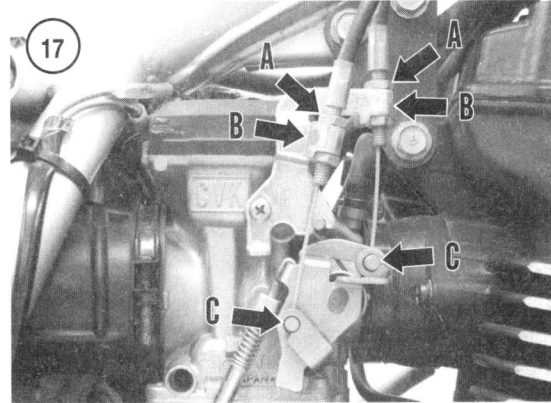

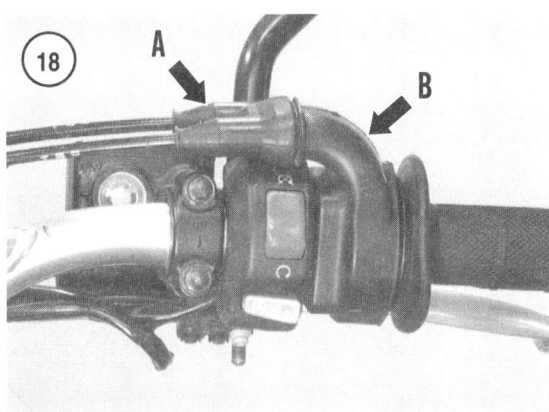

Clutch cable and starter lockout switch

1. Remove the clutch lever hand guard.
2. Loosen the clutch cable locknut (A, **Figure 13**). Then, turn the adjuster (B, **Figure 13**) in to increase cable slack.
3. Align the slots on the nut and adjuster, and detach the cable from the cable lever.

NOTE
It may be necessary to turn the adjustment nuts (A, Figure 14) at the lower end of the clutch cable to obtain suf-

ficient cable slack to detach the cable from the hand lever.

4. Remove the cable end from the release lever (B, **Figure 14**) at the lower end of the cable.
5. Attach a cable lubricator (**Figure 15**), and lubricate the cable with an aerosol cable lubricant. Keep the cable in a vertical position so the lubricant can pass to the opposite end. Move the cable in the housing to help distribute the oil. Stop lubrication when oil is seen at the opposite end of the cable.
6. Remove the clutch lever pivot bolt (C, **Figure 13**). Then, remove the clutch lever.
7. Clean the lever pivot hole and the pivot bolt. Lubricate the lever and pivot bolt with lithium grease.
8. Install the clutch lever and pivot bolt. Tighten the pivot bolt securely.
9. Reattach the clutch cable ends to the hand lever and clutch release lever.
10. Adjust the clutch lever as described in this chapter.

Throttle cables

The throttle uses two cables. One cable pulls the throttle open during acceleration, while the other pulls the throttle closed during deceleration. In operation, the cables always move in opposite directions to one another. Use the following procedure to disassemble, clean and lubricate the cables and throttle assembly.

1. Remove the right hand guard.
2. At the handlebar, loosen the locknuts (A, **Figure 16**). Loosen the adjuster (B) on each cable.
3. At the carburetor, loosen the locknuts (A, **Figure 17**) and detach the cables from the holders (B) and throttle pulley (C). The left cable is the accelerator cable.
4. Slide the rubber cable cover (A, **Figure 18**) off the throttle housing.
5. Move the rubber throttle housing cover (B, **Figure 18**) off the throttle housing by pushing it toward the cables. The cover must be pushed off the housing to allow housing disassembly.
6. Remove the screws (**Figure 19**) from the throttle housing. Separate and remove the housing halves.
7. Separate each cable guide (A, **Figure 20**) from its housing half (B). Note that each cable guide will only fit into its corresponding housing half.
8. Remove the cable ends from the throttle drum (**Figure 21**).

NOTE
The curved cable guides around the upper ends of the throttle cables are not removable.

9. Clean the throttle assembly and cable ends.

10. Attach a cable lubricator (**Figure 15**), and lubricate each cable with an aerosol cable lubricant. Keep the cable in a vertical position so the lubricant can pass to the opposite end. Move the cable in the housing to help distribute the oil. Stop lubrication when oil is seen at the opposite end of the cable.

11. Lubricate the throttle drum, cable ends and throttle housing with lithium grease.

12. Install the cables by reversing the removal procedure while noting the following:
   a. Pull all slack out of the cables, then check that they move in the correct direction when the throttle is operated.
   b. Adjust throttle free play as described in this chapter.

Drive Chain Cleaning and Lubrication

The motorcycle is equipped with an O-ring chain that requires routine cleaning and lubrication. If the chain has been replaced with a standard chain, it too requires regular cleaning, lubrication and adjustment for long life. Although O-ring chains are internally lubricated and sealed, the O-rings must be kept clean and lubricated to prevent them from drying out and disintegrating.

Never clean chains with high-pressure water sprays or strong solvents. This is particularly true for O-ring chains. If water is forced past the O-rings, water will be trapped inside the links. Strong solvents can soften the O-rings so they tear or damage easily.

Although chains are often lubricated while they are installed on the motorcycle, the chain should periodically be removed from the motorcycle and thoroughly cleaned. The following procedure describes the preferred method for cleaning and lubricating the chain.

1. Refer to *Drive Chain, Removal and Installation* in Chapter Eleven to remove the chain.
2. Immerse the chain in kerosene and work the links so dirt is loosened.

CAUTION
Brushes with coarse or wire bristles can damage O-rings.

3. Lightly scrub the chain with a soft-bristle brush.
4. Rinse the chain with clean kerosene and wipe dry.

NOTE
*While the chain is removed, check that it is still within the wear limit as described in **Drive Chain and Sprockets Inspection** (this chapter).*

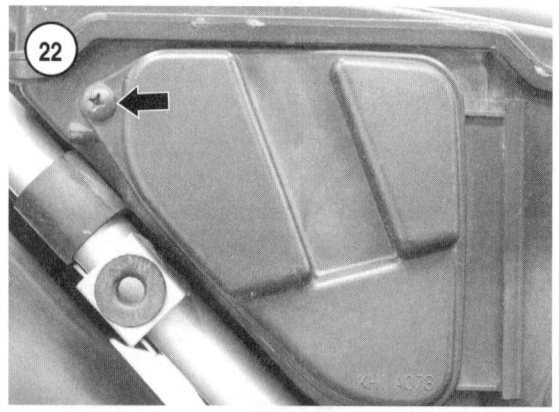

LUBRICATION, MAINTENANCE AND TUNE-UP

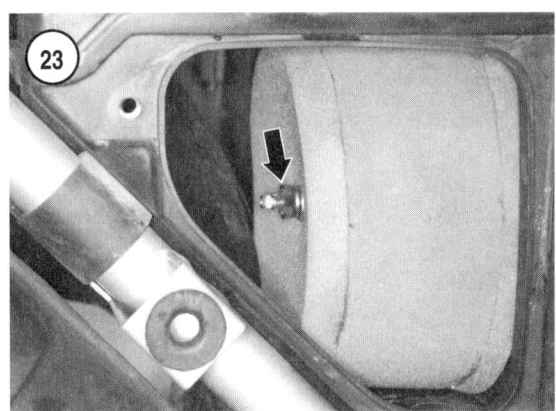

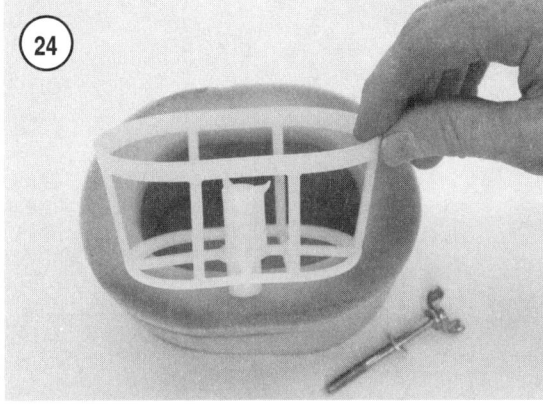

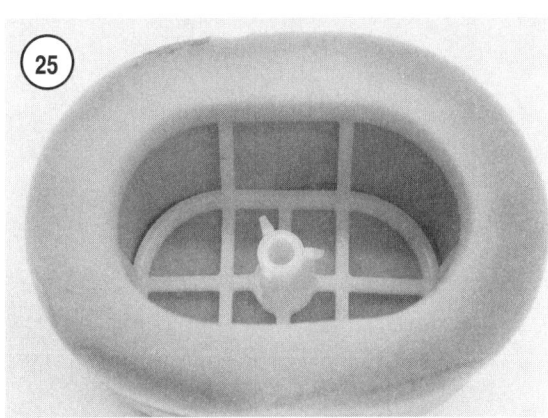

5. Lubricate the chain with chain lubricant. Lubricate an O-ring chain with lubricant intended for O-ring chains.

CAUTION
Because the links of an O-ring chain are permanently lubricated and sealed, O-ring chain lubricant is formulated to prevent exterior corrosion of the chain and to condition the O-rings. It is not tacky and resists the adhesion of dirt. Avoid lubricants that are tacky or designed for conventional chains. These lubricants attract dirt and subject the O-rings to unnecessary abrasion.

6. Install the chain as described in Chapter Eleven.
7. Adjust the chain as described in this chapter.

Air Filter Cleaning and Lubrication

The engine is equipped with a reusable, foam air filter. Do not operate the motorcycle without the air filter, or with a damaged air filter. Dust that enters the engine can cause severe engine wear and clog carburetor passages.

Service the air filter at the interval listed in **Table 1**. Clean the air filter more often when riding in sand or in wet or muddy conditions.

1. Remove the right side cover as described in Chapter Fifteen.
2. Remove the screw and cover (**Figure 22**) from the air filter housing.
3. Remove the retaining bolt and washer (**Figure 23**) from the air filter assembly. Then, remove the assembly from the engine.
4. Remove the frame from the air filter (**Figure 24**).
5. Wash all parts in solvent (kerosene), a commercial filter wash, or hot soapy water. Squeeze the cleaner from the filter. Do not wring the filter, as tearing may occur. Shake off any particles that may remain on the filter.
6. Allow the filter to completely dry.

CAUTION
Use oil specifically formulated for foam filters. This type of oil adheres to the foam and effectively traps dust.

7. Apply filter oil to the filter, squeezing the filter so the oil is distributed evenly. Squeeze out the excess oil. When performing this step, handle the filter with disposable gloves, or put the filter in a plastic bag to squeeze and distribute the oil. Follow the manufacturer's instructions when oiling the filter.
8. Install the frame into the filter, seating it under the foam lip (**Figure 25**).
9. Apply lithium grease around the perimeter of the filter lip. This helps seal the filter against the housing.
10. Clean the housing and filter sealing surface. Check that the drain in the bottom of the housing is open.
11. Clean the housing cover and inspect the gasket (**Figure 26**).
12. Install the filter, checking that it seats against the filter housing. Install the washer and retaining bolt.
13. Align and fit the filter assembly into the air filter housing. Check that the filter is completely seated against the housing, then tighten the bolt.

48

14. Install the cover, fitting the tab on the right side into the housing.
15. Screw the cover into place.
16. Reinstall the right side cover as described in Chapter Fifteen.

Air Filter Housing Drain Hose

Whenever the air filter is inspected, check the air filter housing drain hose (**Figure 27**) for excess oil that has drained from the filter. This hose is located behind the rear brake pedal. If oil is in the hose reservoir, remove the plug from the drain hose and allow the oil to drain. The drain hose is not attached to the water drain hole that is visible in the air filter housing. The drain hose attaches to a fitting in the housing duct, near the air filter.

MAINTENANCE AND INSPECTION

Evaporative Emissions Control System Inspection (California Models Only)

No adjustments are required for the evaporative emissions system. Visually inspect the hoses and connections as recommended in **Table 1**. Refer to Chapter Eight for a schematic view of the system and its components.

Fastener Inspection

Inspect all fasteners on the motorcycle. Verify tightness and check them for damage.
1. Retorque nuts, bolts and screws as specified in the tables at the end of each chapter. Refer to **Table 3** in Chapter One when a torque value is not specified.
2. Check that all cotter pins are secure and undamaged.
3. Check that tie straps, used to secure cables and electrical wiring, are not broken or missing.

Muffler Cleaning

The muffler is approved by the U.S. Forest Service for spark arresting. The muffler also limits exhaust noise to 80 decibels. This information is stamped into the muffler near the rear heat shield. In order for the muffler to perform correctly and not affect engine performance, the internal baffle should regularly be purged of carbon buildup. This is particularly important if the engine has been running too rich.

WARNING
Do not spray solvents or other combustible liquids into the muffler to aid in

CHAPTER THREE

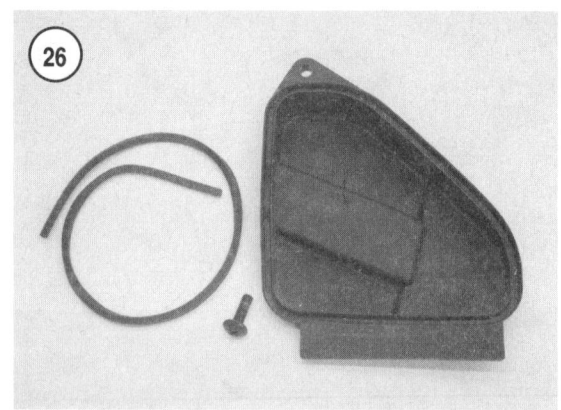

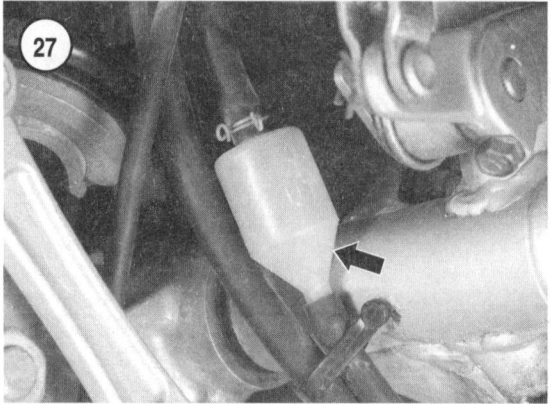

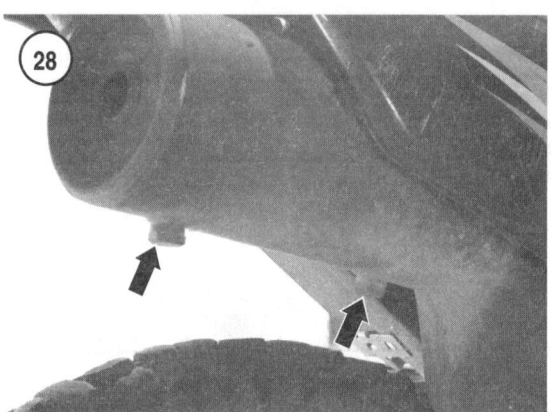

removing buildup. This can result in an explosion and/or fire.

1. Park the motorcycle in an open area, away from any combustible materials.
2. Remove the two plugs at the rear end (**Figure 28**) of the muffler and the front end (**Figure 29**) of the muffler.
3. Start the engine.
4. Wearing gloves, use a rubber mallet to tap on the surface of the muffler as the engine speed is raised and lowered. Also, momentarily place a folded shop

LUBRICATION, MAINTENANCE AND TUNE-UP

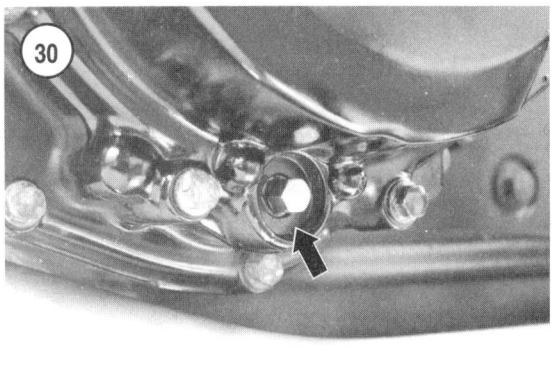

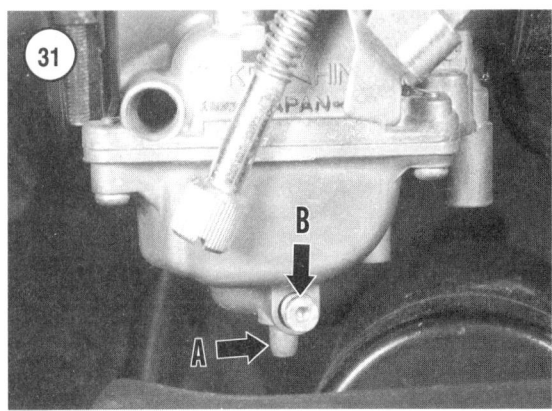

cloth over the end of the muffler to force exhaust pressure out of the plug openings.
5. When no more carbon particles are purged, stop the engine and install the plugs.

Balancer Chain Tensioner Adjustment

As the balancer chain and guide wear, the tensioner assembly takes excess slack out of the chain. Since the tensioner assembly is spring-loaded, it automatically tightens the chain when the tensioner bolt is loosened. When the bolt is tightened, it locks the tensioner into place until the bolt is again loosened, usually at the next scheduled maintenance.

1. If desired, remove the skid plate for easier access to the tensioner bolt. The bolt is located below the alternator cover (left side of engine), near the frame (**Figure 30**).
2. Remove the rubber plug.
3. Loosen the tensioner bolt by turning it no more than two turns counterclockwise.
4. Retighten the tensioner bolt to 8.8 N•m (78 in.-lb.).
5. Install the rubber plug.
6. Install the skid plate, if removed.

CAUTION
When starting the engine after performing the tensioner adjustment, listen for any abnormal engine noise coming from the balancer chain assembly. Do not race the engine. If noise is heard, immediately shut off the engine and inspect the condition of the tensioner assembly. It is possible for the shaft lever or the tensioner spring to break, prior to the adjustment. The tensioner bolt will hold the tensioner assembly in place, although the part is broken. At the scheduled maintenance interval, when the tensioner bolt is loosened, the untensioned assembly is free to create chain slack or fall apart. This slack could cause the chain to derail, causing engine damage.

7. Start engine and verify tensioner adjustment.

Carburetor Float Chamber Drain

The carburetor float chamber is equipped with a drain so moisture and sediment can be flushed from the chamber. Moisture and sediment can clog carburetor jets and cause poor engine performance. If the motorcycle is stored or not started for an extended period, drain the float chamber.

WARNING
Do not drain the float chamber while the engine is hot or running.

1. Support the motorcycle so it is vertical and level.
2. Connect a length of 6 mm (1/4 in.) ID hose onto the drain (A, **Figure 31**). Route the end of the hose into a suitable container.
3. Turn the drain screw (B, **Figure 31**) out two turns and allow all fuel in the chamber to flow into the container.
4. Close the drain screw.
5. Disconnect the drain hose.

Coolant Level Inspection

> *WARNING*
> *Inspect the cooling system when the engine and coolant are cold. Severe injury could occur if the system is checked while it is hot. If the radiator cap must be removed while the coolant is still warm, cover the cap with a towel and open it slowly. Do not remove the cap until all pressure is relieved. Also, when the engine is hot, the cooling fan can operate even though the key is in the off position. Do not touch the fan or use tools near it until the engine has cooled.*

Refer to **Table 2** for the recommended coolant and mixing ratio.

1. Support the motorcycle so it is vertical and level.
2. At the reserve tank cover, check the coolant level in the window (**Figure 32**). The level should be between the low and full marks shown on the cover. If the level is too low, do the following:
    a. Remove the right, lower fairing as described in Chapter Fifteen.
    b. Remove the two screws securing the reserve tank cover.
    c. Remove the cap (**Figure 33**) from the reserve tank and fill it to the full mark embossed on the reserve tank. Do not allow the tank level to fall below the low mark, which is also embossed on the tank.
    d. Check for leaks at the hoses and reserve tank.
    e. Install the reserve tank cover.
    f. If the reserve tank is empty, check the level in the radiator. The coolant level should be at the bottom of the filler neck on the radiator (**Figure 34**).
    g. If the coolant level is below the filler neck, add coolant mixture to raise the level.
    h. Install the radiator cap.
    i. Start the engine and inspect for leaks. If there is water leaking from the drain hole at the bottom of the water pump (A, **Figure 35**), this indicates that the leak is occurring at the mechanical seal in the water pump. Repair the water pump as described in Chapter Ten. If engine oil is leaking from the hole, the oil seal in the right crankcase cover is leaking. Replace the seal as described in Chapter Six.

> *CAUTION*
> *If the coolant level continues to drop, pressure test the cooling system. Severe engine damage can occur if the engine is allowed to overheat.*

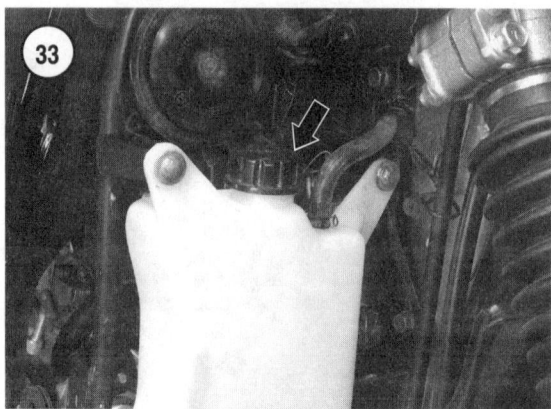

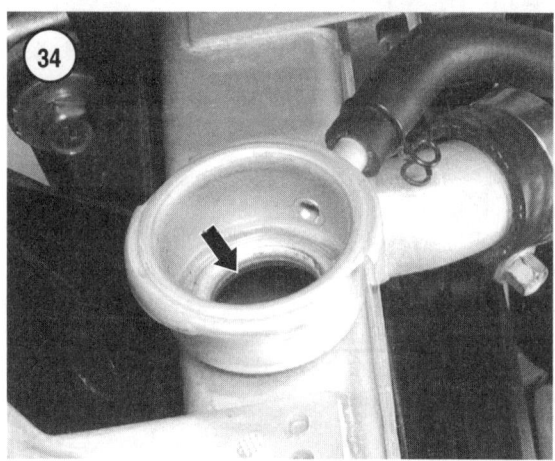

Cooling System Inspection

Annually check the condition of the cooling system, or whenever it is suspected that overheating is occurring. The radiator cap and cooling system are checked individually with a cooling system tester. This tester applies the required pressure to the cooling system and cap. A pressure gauge attached to the tester is observed and leaks can be detected. A Kawasaki dealership can perform this inspection, or a tester can be purchased at an automotive parts

LUBRICATION, MAINTENANCE AND TUNE-UP

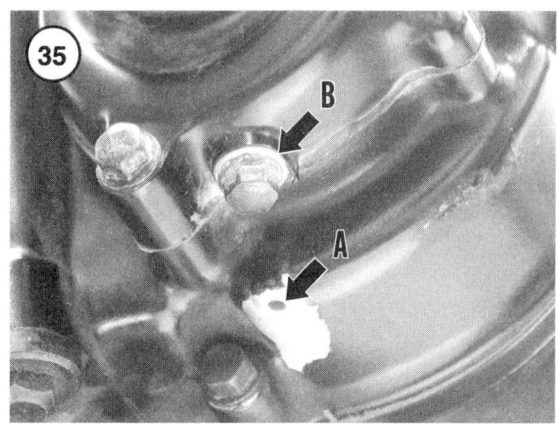

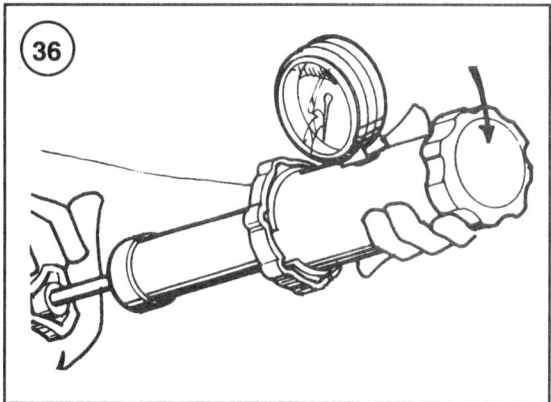

supplier. Test the radiator cap and cooling system as follows:

WARNING
Test the cooling system when the engine and coolant are cold. Severe injury could occur if the system is checked while it is hot.

1. Support the motorcycle so it is vertical and level.
2. Remove the radiator cap and check the following:
   a. Rubber seals. Check for cracks, compression and pliability. Replace the cap if damage is evident.
   b. Relief valve. Check for damage. Replace the cap if damage is evident.
3. Determine the cap relief pressure. Wet the seal on the radiator cap, then attach the cap to the tester (**Figure 36**). Apply pressure to the cap. Relief pressure for the cap is as follows:
   a. 2008-2014 models: 93-123 kPa (13.5-17.8 psi).
   b. 2015-on models: 107.9-1.37.3 kPa (15.6-19.9 psi).
   c. If the gauge holds pressure up to the relief pressure range, the cap is good.
   d. If the gauge does not hold pressure, or the relief pressure is too high or low, replace the cap.

CAUTION
Do not exceed 137 kPa (20 psi). Excessive pressure can damage the cooling system components.

4. Check that the radiator is filled to the bottom of the filler neck (**Figure 34**). Attach the tester to the radiator, then pump the tester to 137 kPa (20 psi). Observe the pressure gauge and note the following:
   a. If the gauge holds the required pressure, the cooling system is in good condition.
   b. If the gauge does not hold the required pressure, check for leaks at the radiator and all fittings. If the pressure lowers and then stabilizes, check for swollen radiator hoses. Replace or repair the cooling system so it maintains the test pressure.

Coolant Draining and Replacement

WARNING
Replace the coolant in the cooling system when the engine and coolant are cold. Severe injury can occur if the system is drained while it is hot.

CAUTION
Do not allow coolant to contact painted surfaces. If contact does occur, immediately wash the surface with water.

1. Remove the skid plate as described in Chapter Fifteen.
2. Support the motorcycle so it is vertical and level.
3. Remove the right, lower fairing as described in Chapter Fifteen.
4. Place a drain pan under the right side of the engine, below the water pump. Remove the drain plug (B, **Figure 35**) from the bottom of the water pump.
5. As coolant begins to drain from the engine, slowly loosen and remove the radiator cap so the flow from the engine increases. Be ready to reposition the drain pan, if necessary.
6. Remove the reserve tank cover.
7. Detach the overflow hose (A, **Figure 37**) from the tank.
8. Remove the bolts from the corners of the reserve tank (B, **Figure 37**). Invert the tank and pour out the contents.
9. Flush the cooling system and reserve tank with clean water. Check that all water drains from the system.
10. Inspect the condition of:
    a. Radiator hoses. Check for leaks, cracks and loose clamps.

b. Radiator core. Check for leaks, debris and tightness of mounting bolts.

c. Radiator fan. Check for damaged wiring and tight connections.

11. Install a new seal washer on the coolant drain plug. Install and tighten the drain plug to 8.8 N•m (78 in.-lb.).
12. Install the tank and connect the overflow hose.
13. Refill the radiator with a coolant mixture as specified in **Table 2**.
    a. Tip the motorcycle from side to side to allow the coolant to flow through the engine, and to purge air from the water jackets.
    b. Refill the radiator as the coolant level goes down.
    c. When the coolant level no longer goes down, fill the radiator to the bottom of the filler neck (**Figure 34**). Install the radiator cap.
    d. Fill the reserve tank to the full mark.
14. Install the fuel tank.
15. Start the engine and allow the coolant to circulate for about 30 seconds. Shut off the engine and do the following:

> *WARNING*
> *Cover the cap with shop cloths and open it slowly. Do not remove the cap until all pressure is relieved.*

    a. Remove the radiator cap and check the level. If necessary, add coolant to bring the level to the bottom of the filler neck. Install the radiator cap.
    b. Check the level in the reserve tank. If necessary, remove the cap from the reserve tank and fill it to the full mark.
16. Rinse and dry the frame and engine where coolant was splashed.
17. Start the engine and allow it to reach operating temperature.
18. Check for leaks at the drain plug, hoses and reserve tank.
19. Install the reserve tank cover and removed body parts.
20. Dispose of the old coolant in an environmentally-safe manner.

Drive Chain and Sprockets Inspection

Riding with a worn drive chain and sprockets is both unreliable and potentially dangerous. Inspect the chain and rear sprocket for wear and replace if necessary. If there is wear, replace both sprockets and the chain. Mixing old and new parts will prematurely wear the new parts.

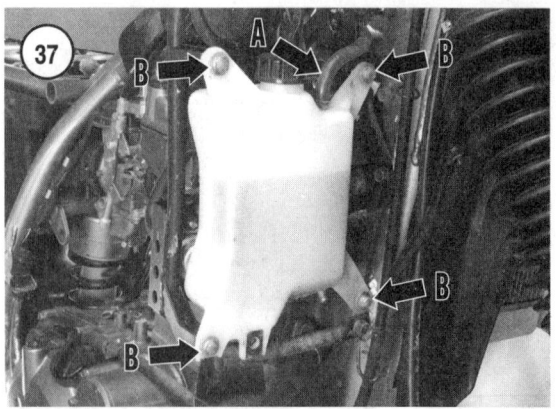

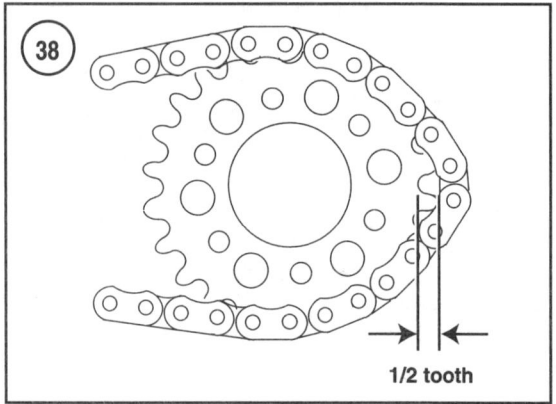

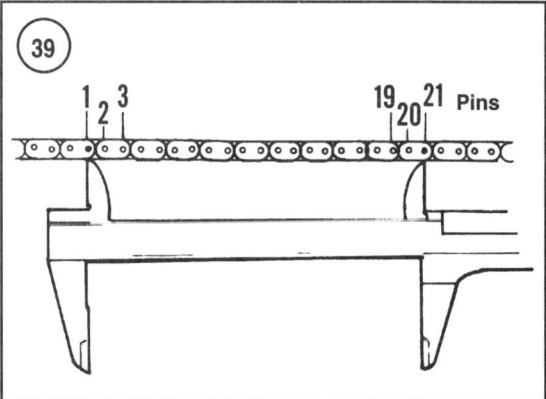

Determine if the chain should be measured for wear by pulling one chain link away from the sprocket. Generally, if more than half the height of the sprocket tooth is visible (**Figure 38**), measure the chain for wear. Refer to the following procedure to accurately measure chain wear and inspect the rear sprocket.

1A. If the chain is not removed from the sprockets, loosen the axle nut and turn the chain adjusters equally to take all play out of the chain along its top run.

1B. If the chain is removed from the sprockets, lay the chain on a flat surface and pull the ends of the chain to remove the slack.

LUBRICATION, MAINTENANCE AND TUNE-UP

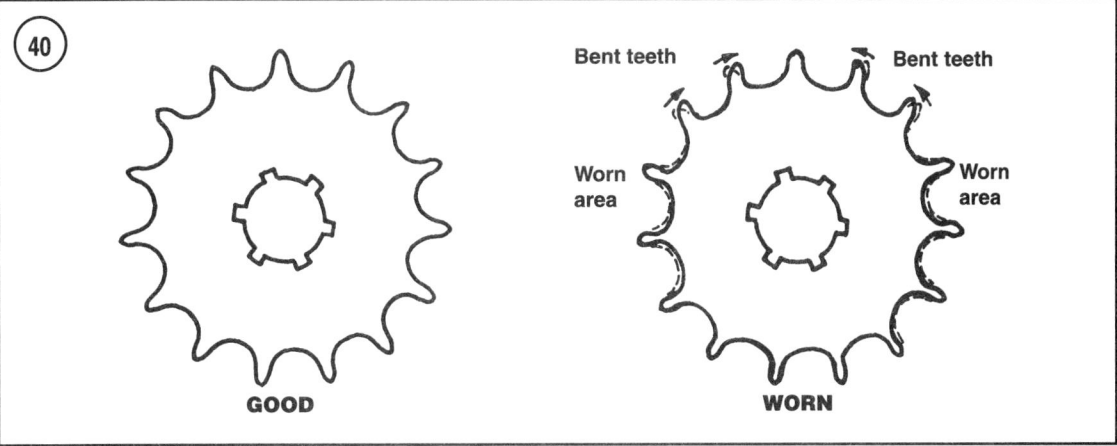

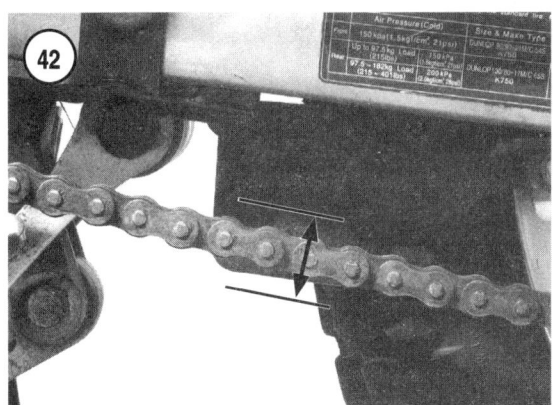

causes premature wear of the rollers and pins. Replace the chain if there is abnormal wear.

3. Inspect the teeth on the front and rear sprockets. Compare the sprockets to **Figure 40**. A new sprocket will have symmetrical and uniform teeth. A used sprocket will wear on the back side of each tooth (**Figure 41**). The sprocket shown has some usable life, but should be replaced if other damage is evident, or if a new chain is being installed. If either sprocket is worn out, replace both sprockets together.

Drive Chain Adjustment

The drive chain must have adequate play so it can adjust to the actions of the swing arm when the motorcycle is in use. Too little play can cause the chain to become excessively tight and cause unnecessary wear to the driveline components. Too much play can cause excessive looseness and possibly cause the chain to jump off the sprockets.

1. Support the motorcycle so the rear wheel is off the ground.
2. Rotate the rear wheel and determine where the chain is tightest along its bottom length (least amount of play).
3. Make a small mark on the swing arm, indicating the midpoint between the sprockets.
4. Measure the play in the bottom length of chain (**Figure 42**) as follows:
   a. Place a tape measure so it is stable and vertical, below the swing arm midpoint.
   b. Press the chain down and note where a chain link-pin aligns with the tape measure. Note the measurement.
   c. Push the chain up and note where the same link pin aligns with the tape measure. Note the measurement.
   d. The difference between the two measurements is the chain play.

2. Measure the length of any 20-link (21 pin) span (**Figure 39**). Measure center-to-center from the pins.
   a. The service limit for the chain is 323 mm (12.72 in.). If the measured distance meets or exceeds the service limit, replace the chain.
   b. If the chain is within the service limit, inspect the inside surfaces of the link plates. The plates should be shiny at both ends of the chain roller. If one side of the chain is worn, the chain has been running out of alignment. This also

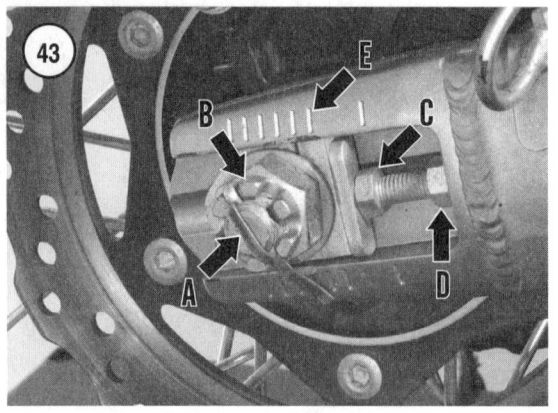

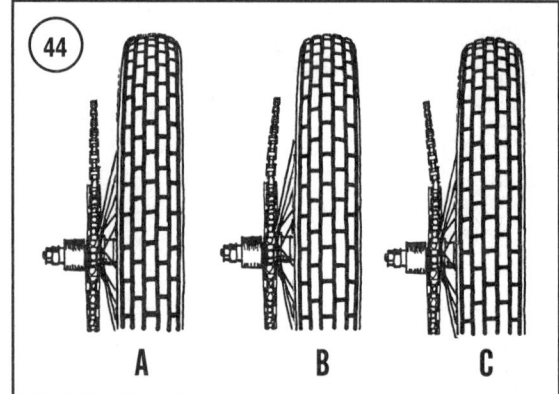

e. Refer to **Table 4** for the required amount of play.
5. If necessary, adjust the chain play as follows:
   a. Remove the cotter pin (A, **Figure 43**) from the axle nut, then loosen the nut (B).
   b. Loosen the chain adjuster locknuts (C, **Figure 43**) on both sides of the wheel.
   c. Equally turn the chain adjusters (D, **Figure 43**) on each side of the swing arm until the chain play is correct. Use the index marks on the swing arm and axle plate (E, **Figure 43**) to equally adjust the chain. If increasing chain play, push the wheel forward to take the play out of the adjusters.

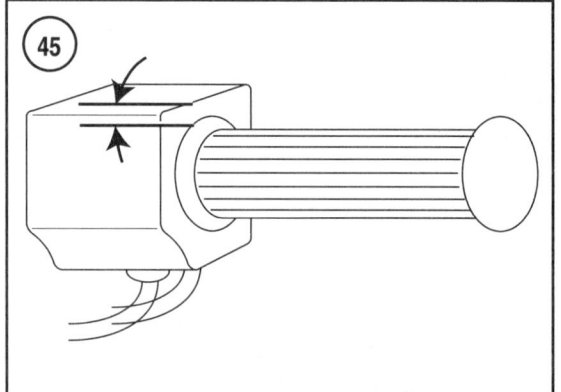

NOTE
If free play cannot be adjusted within the limits of the adjusters, the chain is excessively worn and should be replaced.

   d. When free play is correct, check that the wheel is aligned (A, **Figure 44**). If the chain curves in (B, **Figure 44**) or out (C) readjust the chain so the wheel is aligned with the rest of the motorcycle.
   e. Tighten the axle nut to lock the setting. Then, tighten the axle nut to a final torque of 98 N•m (72 ft.-lb.).
   f. Recheck the chain play. Adjust, if necessary.
   g. Tighten the adjuster locknuts securely.
   h. Install a new cotter pin.

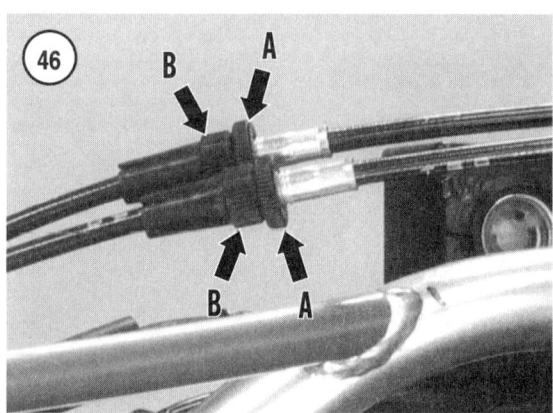

Throttle Free Play Adjustment

Before adjusting the throttle cables, check that they are in good condition. To achieve accurate cable adjustment, the cables must not bind or drag. Engine idle speed should also be correct before adjusting the cables.
1. Measure the amount of free play at the throttle grip (**Figure 45**). Correct free play is 2-3 mm (0.08-0.12 in.). If free play is incorrect, adjust the cable as follows.
2. At the handlebar, pull back the rubber boots from the throttle cable adjusters.
3. Loosen the locknuts (A, **Figure 46**), then turn the cable adjusters (B) completely in.
4. Turn the front adjuster (decelerator cable) out only far enough to eliminate play when the throttle is closed. At the carburetor, the decelerator cable is on the right (A, **Figure 47**). Feel the cable for tightness. Do not make the cable excessively tight.
5. Turn the rear adjuster (accelerator cable) out until free play is 2-3 mm (0.08-0.12 in.) at the throttle

LUBRICATION, MAINTENANCE AND TUNE-UP

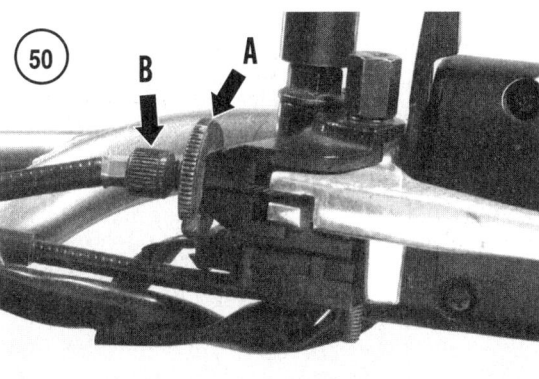

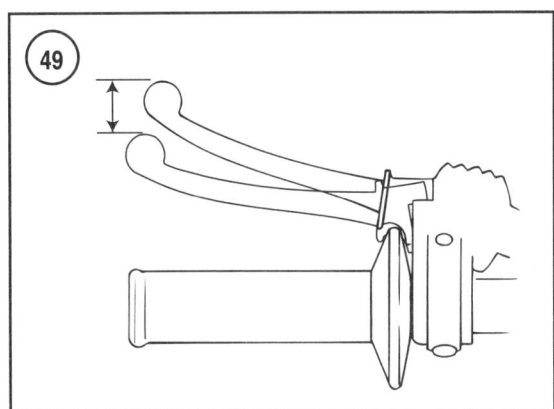

grip. At the carburetor, the accelerator cable is on the left (B, **Figure 47**). Feel the cable for play when the carburetor is closed.

6. Operate the throttle and watch the action of the cables and throttle pulley on the carburetor. The throttle pulley should rotate through its full range.

7. If correct play cannot be achieved at the handlebar adjusters, adjust the cables at the carburetor as follows:

    a. Loosen the locknuts (**Figure 48**) and reposition the cables so the threads are approximately centered in the holders.

    b. Tighten the locknuts.

    c. Repeat the cable adjustment procedure.

8. When adjustment is correct, tighten the locknuts (A, **Figure 46**) on the upper adjusters.

9. Install the rubber boots over the adjusters.

10. At engine startup, turn the handlebar from side to side as the engine idles. If engine speed varies, check for proper cable adjustment and cable routing.

Clutch Lever Adjustment

The clutch lever free play is continually changing due to the clutch cable wearing and stretching over time, as well as clutch plate wear. Maintain the clutch lever free play within the specification listed in this procedure. Insufficient free play causes clutch slippage and premature clutch plate wear. Excessive free play causes clutch drag and rough shift pedal operation.

NOTE
Clutch cable adjustment is possible at the handlebar clutch lever or at the release lever on the engine. Make minor adjustments at the clutch lever. Make major adjustments at the release lever.

1. Remove the left hand guard.
2. Determine the clutch lever free play at the end of the clutch lever as shown in **Figure 49**. If the free play is more or less than 8-12 mm (0.31-0.47 in.), adjust the cable as described in the following steps.
3. Loosen the locknut (A, **Figure 50**) then turn the clutch lever cable end adjuster (B) as required to obtain the specified amount of free play.
4. If the proper amount of free play cannot be achieved with the clutch lever adjuster, the position of the lower cable housing end must be changed. Perform the following:

    a. Turn the clutch lever adjuster (B, **Figure 50**) in all the way.

b. Loosen the locknuts (**Figure 51**) at the lower adjuster and reposition the cable so the threads are approximately centered in the holder.
   c. Tighten the locknuts.
   d. Repeat the cable adjustment procedure.
5. When adjustment is correct, tighten the locknut (A, **Figure 50**) at the handlebar.
6. Install the left hand guard.
7. At engine startup, check for proper clutch operation.

Choke Cable Adjustment

The choke cable must be properly adjusted to ensure that it fully opens and closes.
1. Move the choke lever (**Figure 52**) fully to the rear (start position), then move it fully to the front (run position) and check that the cable moves freely. If the cable binds, inspect the cable and where it attaches to the carburetor.
2. With the choke lever fully to the front, check for free play at the tip of the lever. The free play should be 2-3 mm (0.08-0.12 in.). If free play is incorrect, adjust the cable as follows:
   a. Remove the fuel tank as described in Chapter Fifteen.
   b. Loosen the locknut (A, **Figure 53**) and turn the cable adjuster (B) to increase/decrease play in the housing.
   c. When adjustment is correct, tighten the locknut.
   d. Install the fuel tank as described in Chapter Fifteen.

Front Brake Lever Adjustment

There is no routine adjustment required for the front brake lever. If the master cylinder is in good condition and properly bled, the lever is automatically adjusted. If the brake drags, or brake lever play is unacceptable, inspect for worn or damaged parts in the master cylinder and brake caliper.

Rear Brake Pedal Adjustment

Brake pedal position and free play will be correct if the master cylinder is in good condition, properly installed and adjusted. Also, the pedal must be installed in the correct position on the pedal shaft. Inspect and adjust the pedal and linkage as follows:
1. Check that the pedal is at, or near level with the footpeg (**Figure 54**). If the pedal is not near level, inspect the pedal assembly for:
   a. Alignment of the marks on the pedal and pivot shaft (**Figure 55**). If the marks are not aligned,

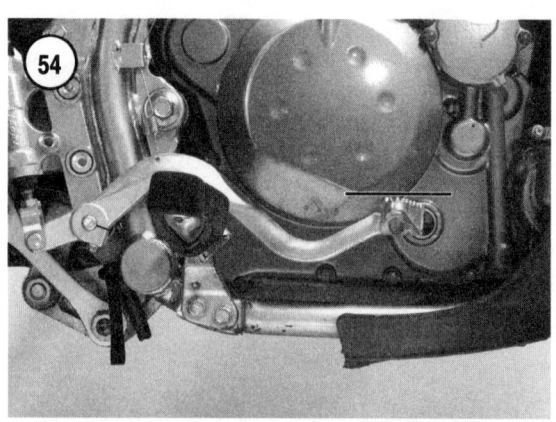

LUBRICATION, MAINTENANCE AND TUNE-UP

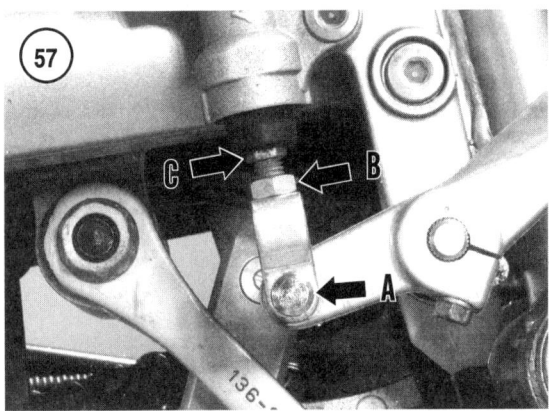

remove, inspect and install the pedal assembly (Chapter Fourteen).
  b. A broken or missing pedal shaft spring.
  c. A bent brake pedal.
2. Measure the pushrod length, from the center of the bottom master cylinder mounting bolt to the center of the clevis pin, as shown in **Figure 56**. The correct pushrod length is 69-71 mm (2.72-2.80 in.). If it is out of specification, adjust as follows:
  a. Remove the cotter pin, washer and clevis pin (A, **Figure 57**).
  b. Loosen the pushrod locknut (B, **Figure 57**).
  c. Turn the pushrod nut (C, **Figure 57**) as required to obtain the correct pushrod length measurement.
  d. Tighten the pushrod locknut. Install the clevis pin (A, **Figure 57**) and washer. Secure with a new cotter pin. Bend the cotter pin arms over to lock it.
3. Check the brake pedal adjustment from the riding position. If brake action continues to be incorrect, bleed the brake.
4. With the rear wheel off the ground, turn the wheel and operate the pedal to ensure the brake can be fully engaged and disengaged. If the brake drags, or if brake pedal height and free play cannot be achieved using the specified adjustments, inspect for worn or damaged parts in the master cylinder and caliper.
5. Check brake light operation. If necessary, adjust the switch as described in this section.

Rear Brake Light Switch Adjustment

The rear brake light should turn on when the brake pedal is depressed. When checking operation of the light, the ignition switch must be in the on position. Adjust the brake light switch position by turning the nut on the switch (**Figure 58**) as follows:

1. If the light comes on too late (too much pedal travel), turn the switch adjustment nut and raise the switch position.
2. If the light comes on too early (too little pedal travel), turn the switch adjustment nut and lower the switch position.

NOTE
If the light does not come on after adjustment, check the bulb condition. If necessary, disconnect the switch wires and use an ohmmeter to check for continuity. The switch is in the on position when the switch plunger is extended.

Brake Fluid Level Inspection

1. Support the motorcycle so the brake fluid reservoir being checked (front or back) is level.

NOTE
If the brake fluid is not clear to slightly yellow, the fluid is contaminated and should be replaced. Drain and bleed the brake system (Chapter Fourteen).

2. Inspect the front reservoir as follows:
   a. The fluid level should be above the mark (**Figure 59**) adjacent to the sight glass.
   b. If the fluid level is below the low mark, remove the cover and diaphragm. Then, add DOT 4 brake fluid. Replace the diaphragm and cap.
   c. Check for master cylinder leaks and worn brake pads.
3. Inspect the rear reservoir (**Figure 60**) as follows:
   a. The fluid level should be between the upper and lower level marks, embossed on the reservoir.
   b. If the fluid level is below the low mark, remove the guard assembly to access the reservoir (**Figure 61**).
   c. Remove the cap, diaphragm plate and diaphragm. Then, add DOT 4 brake fluid.
   d. Replace the diaphragm, diaphragm plate and cap. Then, screw the guard assembly into place.
   e. Check for master cylinder leaks and worn brake pads.

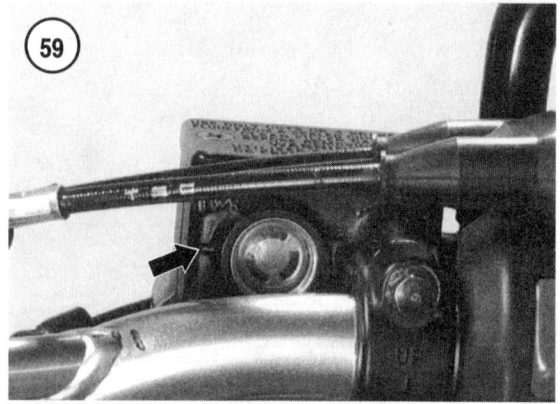

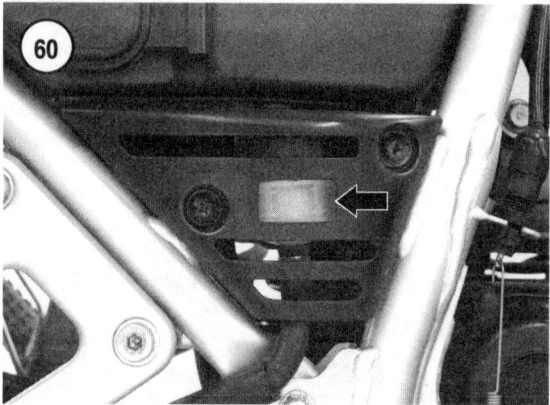

Brake Pads and Disc Inspection

Check the brake discs and pads regularly to ensure they are in good condition. During severe riding conditions, the scoring of a disc can occur rapidly if the brake pads are damaged or have debris lodged in the pad material. If damage is evident for any of the following inspections, refer to Chapter Fourteen for brake pad replacement, disc specifications and service limits.

1. Support the motorcycle so the wheels are off the ground.
2. Visually inspect the front and rear discs for the following:
   a. Scoring. The disc should be smooth in the friction area.
   b. Runout. Spin the wheel and visually check for lateral movement of the disc. Runout should not be evident.
   c. Disc thickness. If the disc shows wear in the friction area, measure the thickness of both discs.
3. Inspect the brake pads. The pads are visible by looking into the caliper, on both sides of the disc. If the front or rear pad material (**Figure 62**) is less than 1 mm (0.04 in.) thick, replace the pad set for that wheel. Some pad sets have a wear indicator, which can be a groove or step at the edge of the pad.

Steering Head Bearing Inspection

The steering head is fitted with tapered roller bearings and should be inspected whenever the steering feels loose or uncontrollable. The bearings must be greased regularly and torqued properly in order to prevent wear and to maintain proper handling characteristics.

LUBRICATION, MAINTENANCE AND TUNE-UP

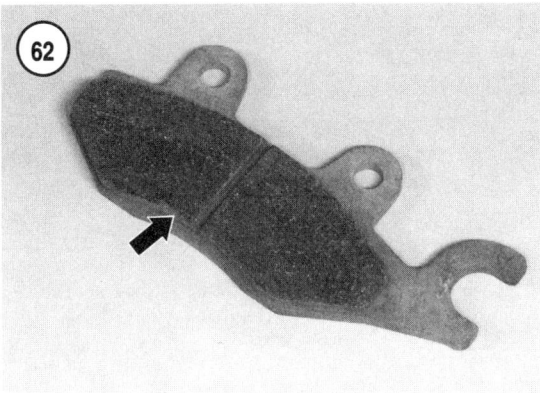

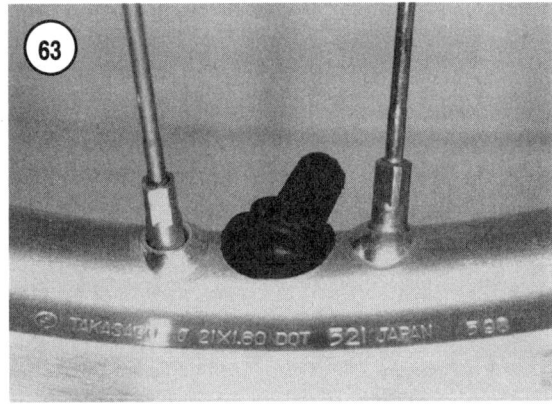

1. Support the motorcycle so the front wheel is off the ground.
2. Inspect the steering head as follows:
   a. Turn the handlebar in both directions and feel for roughness or binding.
   b. Grasp the fork legs near the axle and check for front-to-back play.
3. If there is roughness, binding or play in the steering head, refer to *Steering Play Check and Adjustment* in Chapter Twelve to adjust the steering head.

Swing Arm Bearing Inspection

A general lateral inspection of the swing arm bearings can be made in the following procedure. To perform a more thorough inspection, refer to *Swing Arm, Bearing Inspection* in Chapter Thirteen. The procedure inspects for lateral and vertical wear in the swing arm bearings and pivots.

1. Support the motorcycle so the rear wheel is off the ground.
2. Have an assistant steady the motorcycle, then grasp the ends of the swing arm and leverage it from side to side. There should be no detectable play. If play is evident, refer to Chapter Thirteen for servicing the swing arm.

Rear Suspension Adjustment

The rear shock absorber is adjustable to meet the requirements of the riding conditions. Refer to *Shock Absorber Adjustment* in Chapter Thirteen to adjust the rear shock absorber.

Tire Pressure

The tires must be inflated to meet the demands of the riding conditions. The standard air pressure recommendation is listed in **Table 4**. Slight over- or under-inflation is permissible if the riding conditions justify the change. However, do not exceed the inflation range embossed on the tire sidewall. Since inner tubes are used in the tires, too low of air pressure for the riding conditions can cause the tire to slip on the rim. This can bend the valve stem, as shown in **Figure 63**. Running with the valve stem bent can sever the valve stem and deflate the tire. Correct the condition by adjusting the tire and inner tube positions as described in this section.

Tube Alignment

When the tube valve stem is bent, as shown in **Figure 63**, the tube must be realigned to prevent valve stem damage. A bent valve stem can sever and deflate the tire. Align the tube as follows:
1. Wash the tire and rim.
2. Remove the valve stem core and deflate the tire.
3. With an assistant steadying the motorcycle, break the tire-to-rim seal completely around both sides of the tire.
4. Support the motorcycle so the wheel is off the ground.
5. Check that the valve stem is loose.
6. Lubricate both tire beads by spraying with soapy water.
7. Have the assistant apply the brake for the wheel being aligned.
8. Grasp the tire, then turn it and the tube until the valve stem is straight.

WARNING
Do not over inflate the tire to seat the beads. If the beads do not seat, deflate the tire and relubricate the beads.

9. When the tube is correctly positioned, install the valve stem and inflate the tire. If necessary, reapply the soap solution to the beads to help seat the tire on the rim. Check that the beads uniformly seat around the rim.

Spoke Tension

Spoke tension should be checked regularly and whenever the wheel has been respoked. During the break-in period, check spoke tension often. Refer to *Rim and Spoke Service* in Chapter Eleven for inspecting and properly tightening the spokes.

ENGINE TUNE-UP

Refer to *Carburetor Systems* in Chapter Eight for information concerning the function of the carburetor jets and jet needle.

Valve Clearance

The engine is designed with two intake valves and two exhaust valves. Valves must be adjusted correctly so they will completely open and close during the combustion cycle. Valves that are out of adjustment can cause poor performance and engine damage. Valve clearance is adjusted by placing the correct size of shim (A, **Figure 64**) on top of each valve lifter, which rests under the camshaft. Whenever the valve clearance is incorrect, the camshafts must be removed and correctly-sized shims inserted to bring the clearance within specification.

Typically, when valve clearance is near the smallest acceptable clearance, the clearance is increased, even though the valve is technically within specification. Valves more often lose clearance than gain clearance between inspections, and therefore are adjusted toward the larger clearance specification. A small, marginally-acceptable clearance may be out of specification by the next inspection interval. However, do not increase clearance beyond the largest specification.

Check the valve clearance when the engine temperature is below 35° C (95° F). Read the entire procedure and understand the skill and equipment required. Refer to **Table 3** for valve clearance specifications and check/adjust the valve clearances as follows:

1. Support the motorcycle so it is stable and secure.
2. Remove the cylinder head cover as described in Chapter Four.
3. Remove the timing plug (A, **Figure 65**) and the rotor bolt plug (B).
4. Set the engine at TDC as follows:
   a. Fit a socket onto the rotor bolt (**Figure 66**) and turn the crankshaft counterclockwise until the T mark on the rotor is aligned with the index mark in the timing hole (**Figure 67**).
   b. Verify the engine is at TDC by checking the camshaft lobes. If properly set, all cam lobes

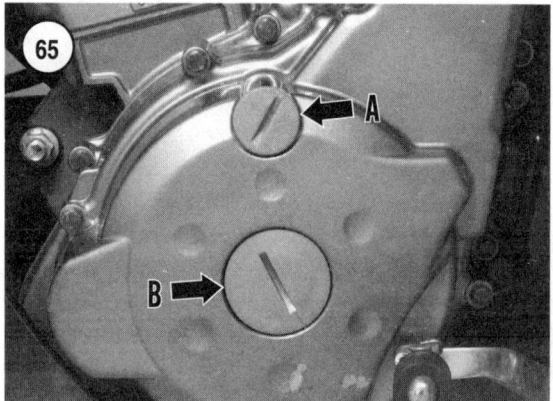

LUBRICATION, MAINTENANCE AND TUNE-UP

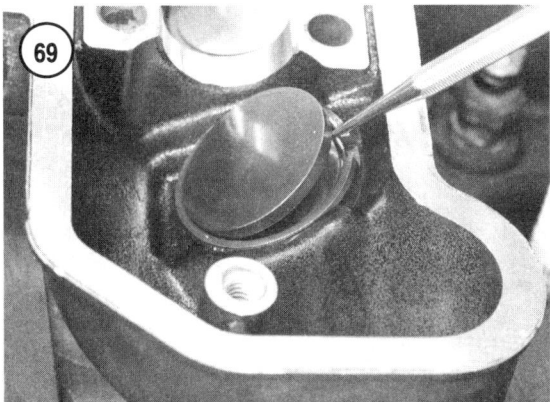

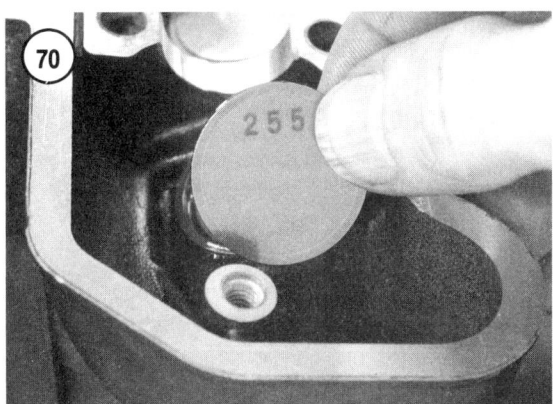

(B, **Figure 64**) will be facing away from the center of the engine. If the lobes point toward the center of the engine, rotate the crankshaft one full turn counterclockwise and realign the T mark on the rotor with the index mark in the timing hole.

5. For each valve, use a flat feeler gauge to determine the clearance between the valve shim and cam lobe (**Figure 68**). Clearance is correct if slight resistance is felt when the gauge is inserted and withdrawn. Record the measurement and valve location. This information will be necessary to determine the correct size shim to install, if out of specification.

6. If adjustment is required, refer to Chapter Four for camshaft removal.

7. Remove the shim from the valve lifter(s) (**Figure 69**) that needs adjustment as follows:
   a. Rotate the valve lifter so the notch in the edge of the lifter is accessible.
   b. Wedge a small-tipped tool between the shim and lifter, then tilt the tool back to break the oil adhesion between the parts.
   c. Remove the shim and note its location in the cylinder head.

8. Determine the size of the shim to install on the valve lifter as follows:

NOTE
*Shims are available in increments of 0.05 mm (0.002 in.). Shim thickness ranges from 2.0 mm (a No. 200 shim) to 3.2 mm (a No. 320 shim). The number on the shim surface is the original thickness of the shim. For example, if the removed shim is marked 255 (**Figure 70**), the shim is 2.55 mm thick. The next larger shim size is 2.60 mm thick and the next smaller size is 2.50 mm thick. The replacement shim should make clearance fall within the valve clearance range. If possible, when removing and installing shims, measure the shims with a caliper to determine their actual thickness.*

   a. Refer to **Table 3** for the intake and exhaust valve clearances.
   b. Find the difference between the specified clearance and the existing clearance. This difference is the amount that must be added (loose valve) or subtracted (tight valve) from the value of the shim removed in Step 7.
   c. For example: If the existing clearance for an exhaust valve is 0.14 mm, and the specified clearance is 0.15-0.25 mm, the difference is 0.01-0.11 mm. In this example, the replacement shim should be this much smaller than the removed shim. If the removed shim is 2.55 mm thick (a No. 255 shim), the replacement shim should be 2.45 mm thick (a No. 245 shim). This would increase clearance by 0.10 mm and make clearance 0.24 mm, which is within the specification.

9. Lubricate the replacement shim with engine oil, then install the shim onto the valve lifter. Place the shim number down so it does not get worn away by the camshaft lobe.

10. Repeat the procedure for the remaining valves that are out of specification.

11. Install the camshaft(s) as described in Chapter Four.
12. Check valve clearance. If clearance is not correct, remove the camshaft(s) and adjust the valves that are out of specification.
13. Install the cylinder head cover as described in Chapter Four.
14. Install the timing plug (A, **Figure 65**) and the rotor bolt plug (B). Tighten both plugs to 2.5 N•m (22 in.-lb.).

Carburetor Idle Speed and Mixture Adjustment

The carburetor must be adjusted so the idle speed keeps the engine running, but is also low enough to provide compression braking. Additionally, the pilot mixture screw must be adjusted so throttle response is good from idle to 1/4 throttle.

Use the following procedure to adjust the idle speed and pilot mixture screw for the standard jets. Jet needle position is not adjustable.
1. Check the throttle cables for proper adjustment.
2. Check the air filter for cleanliness.

NOTE
Unless already removed, the pilot mixture screw will be blocked by a plug. To remove the plug, it is necessary to remove the carburetor from the engine and drill a hole in the plug so it can be pried out. Follow the steps in the carburetor disassembly procedure in Chapter Eight. Also, if the mixture screw is accessible, there is minimal clearance between the pilot screw bore and starter. A special tool (Kawasaki part No. 57001-1240 or an equivalent) is necessary for access.

3. Set the pilot mixture screw (A, **Figure 71**) as follows:
   a. Lightly seat the screw, then turn it out 1 5/8 turns. This is a starting point for adjustment.
   b. Start the engine and allow it to warm up.
   c. Set the engine idle speed to 1200-1400 rpm. Set the idle speed by turning the throttle stop screw (B, **Figure 71**). Raise and lower the engine speed a few times with the throttle to ensure that it returns to the set idle speed.
   d. Mark the position of the pilot air screw or tool. From its initial setting, turn the pilot air screw in and out in small increments to find the points where the engine speed begins to decrease. Set the pilot screw between the two points.
   e. Reset the idle speed to bring it within its required setting.

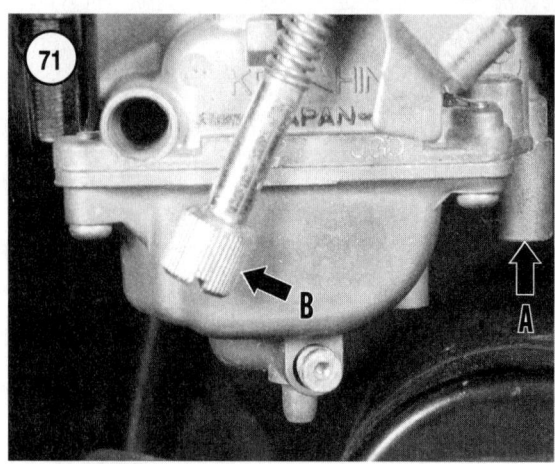

4. Test ride the motorcycle and check throttle response. If throttle response is poor from an idle, adjust the pilot mixture screw out (richer) or in (leaner) by 1/8 turn increments until the engine accelerates smoothly.
5. If necessary, adjust the throttle cables for proper play.

Engine Timing

The ignition timing is electronically controlled by the CDI unit. No adjustment is possible to the timing. The timing is checked to verify the CDI unit is functioning properly. If ignition timing operation needs to be verified, perform the procedure as described in *Ignition Timing* in Chapter Nine.

Compression Test

A cylinder compression test can help verify the condition of the piston, rings and cylinder head assembly without disassembling the engine. By keeping a record of the compression reading at each tune-up, readings can be compared to determine if normal wear is occurring.

This engine typically has 529-853 kPa (77-124 psi) of compression when broken in properly. Since the compression release opens the right exhaust valve slightly during engine cranking, compression can vary. It is recommended that the owner perform regular compression tests and record the readings. If a current reading is extremely different from a previous reading, troubleshooting can begin to correct the problem. The condition of the compression release should be inspected first. Operating the engine when compression readings are abnormal can lead to severe engine damage.

1. Warm the engine to operating temperature.

LUBRICATION, MAINTENANCE AND TUNE-UP

CAUTION
The spark plug must be grounded in order to prevent possible damage to the CDI unit.

2. Remove the spark plug. Insert the spark plug into the cap, then ground the plug to the cylinder.
3. Thread or insert a compression gauge into the spark plug hole. The gauge must be fitted airtight in the hole for an accurate reading.
4. Hold or secure the throttle fully open.
5. Operate the starter and turn the engine over until the highest gauge reading is achieved.
6. Record the reading. Compare the reading with previous readings, if available. Under normal operating conditions, compression will slowly lower from the original specification, due to wear of the piston rings and/or valve seats.
   a. If the reading is higher than normal, this can be caused by a broken or jammed compression release spring. If the spring cannot retract the compression release weights, no compression will be released when the engine is cranking. Commonly, carbon buildup in the combustion chamber is another cause of high compression. This can cause high combustion chamber temperatures and potential engine damage.
   b. If the reading is lower than normal, this can be caused by worn piston rings, worn valves, a damaged piston, leaking head gasket, or a combination of these parts. The compression release is less likely to be the problem in this case since the release weights are probably not spinning fast enough to stop the release of compression as it would when the engine fired and camshaft speed increased.
   c. To help pinpoint the source of the leak, pour 15 cc (1/2 oz.) of four-stroke engine oil through the spark plug hole and into the cylinder. Turn the engine over to distribute and clear excess

oil. Recheck compression. If compression increases, the piston rings are worn or damaged. If compression is the same, the piston, head gasket, valves or compression release are worn or damaged.

SPARK PLUGS

Spark Plug Removal

Careful removal of the spark plug is important in preventing grit from entering the combustion chamber. It is also important to know how to remove a plug that is seized, or is resistant to removal. Forcing a seized plug can damage the threads in the cylinder head.
1. Remove the fuel tank (Chapter Fifteen).
2. Grasp the spark plug cap (**Figure 72**) and twist it loose from the spark plug. There may be a slight suction and resistance while removing the cap.
3. Clean dirt from the well around the spark plug, preferably with compressed air.
4. Fit a spark plug wrench onto the spark plug, then remove it by turning the wrench counterclockwise. If the plug is seized or drags excessively during removal, stop and try the following techniques:
   a. Apply a penetrating lubricant such as Liquid Wrench or WD-40 and allow it to stand for 15 minutes.
   b. If the plug is completely seized, apply moderate pressure in both directions with the wrench. Only attempt to break the seal so lubricant can penetrate under the spark plug and into the threads. If this does not work, and the motorcycle is still operable, install the spark plug cap and fuel tank, then start the engine. Allow it to completely warm up. The heat of the engine may be enough to expand the parts and allow the plug to be removed.
   c. When a spark plug has been loosened, but drags excessively during its removal, apply penetrating lubricant around the spark plug threads. Turn the plug in (clockwise) to help distribute the lubricant onto the threads. Slowly remove the plug, working it in and out of the cylinder head as lubricant is added.
   d. Inspect the threads in the cylinder head for damage. Clean and true the threads with a spark plug thread-chaser.
5. Inspect the removed plug to determine if the engine is operating properly.
6. A spark plug that is in good condition and will be reused after inspection should be cleaned with electrical contact cleaner and a shop cloth. Do not use abrasives or wire brushes to clean the plugs.

Spark Plug Gap and Installation

Proper adjustment of the electrode gap is important for reliable and consistent spark. Also, the proper preparation of the spark plug threads will ensure that the plug can be removed easily in the future, without damage to the cylinder head threads.

1. Refer to **Table 3** for the required spark plug gap.
2. Insert a wire feeler gauge (the size of the required gap) between the center electrode and the ground electrode.
3. Pull the gauge through the gap. If there is slight drag, the setting is correct. If the gap is too large or small, adjust the gap by bending the ground electrode (**Figure 73**) to achieve the required gap. Use an adjusting tool (**Figure 74**) to bend the electrode. Do not pry the electrode with a screwdriver or other tool. Damage to the center electrode and insulator is possible.
4. Inspect the spark plug to ensure it is fitted with a crush washer.
5. Wipe a small amount of antiseize compound onto the spark plug threads. Do not allow the compound to get on the electrodes.
6. Finger-tighten the spark plug into the cylinder head. This will ensure the plug is not cross-threading.
7. Tighten the spark plug to 14 N•m (124 in.-lb.). If a torque wrench is not available, turn a new spark plug 1/4-1/2 turn from the seated position; a used spark plug 1/8-1/4 turn from the seated position.
8. To help prevent water from migrating under the spark plug cap, wipe a small amount of dielectric grease around the interior of the cap. Press and twist the cap onto the spark plug.

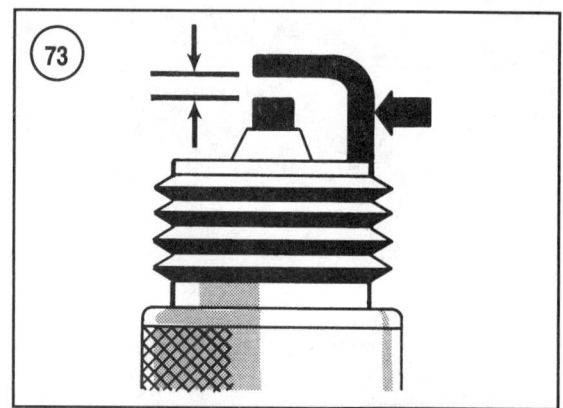

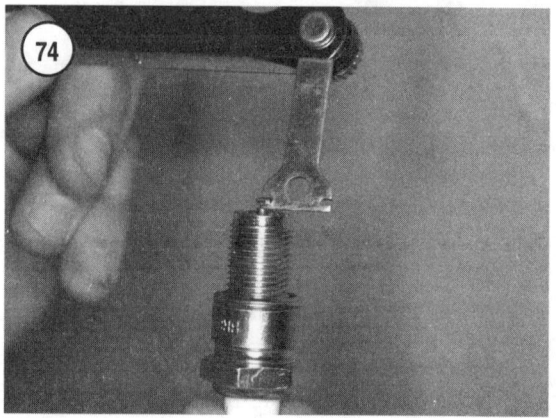

Spark Plug Selection

Refer to **Table 3** for the recommended standard or resistor-type spark plug and gap.

> **CAUTION**
> *The following paragraphs provide general information and operation fundamentals that apply to all spark plugs. However, before changing to a plug other than what is recommended by Kawasaki, check with the spark plug manufacturer for specific part numbers and equivalents that apply to this motorcycle. Poor performance or engine damage can occur by installing a spark plug that is not compatible with this engine.*

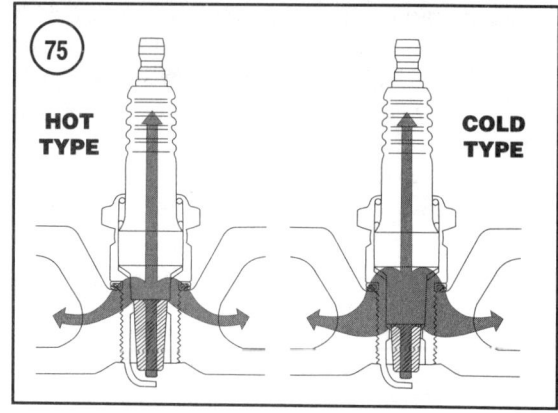

Heat range

Spark plugs are available in several heat ranges to accommodate the load and performance demands put on the engine. The standard spark plug recommended by manufacturers is usually a medium heat-range plug that operates well over a wide range of engine speeds. As long as engine speeds vary, these plugs will stay relatively clean and perform well.

If the engine is run in hot climates, at high speed or under heavy loads for prolonged periods, a spark plug with a colder heat range is recommended. A colder plug quickly transfers heat away from its fir-

LUBRICATION, MAINTENANCE AND TUNE-UP

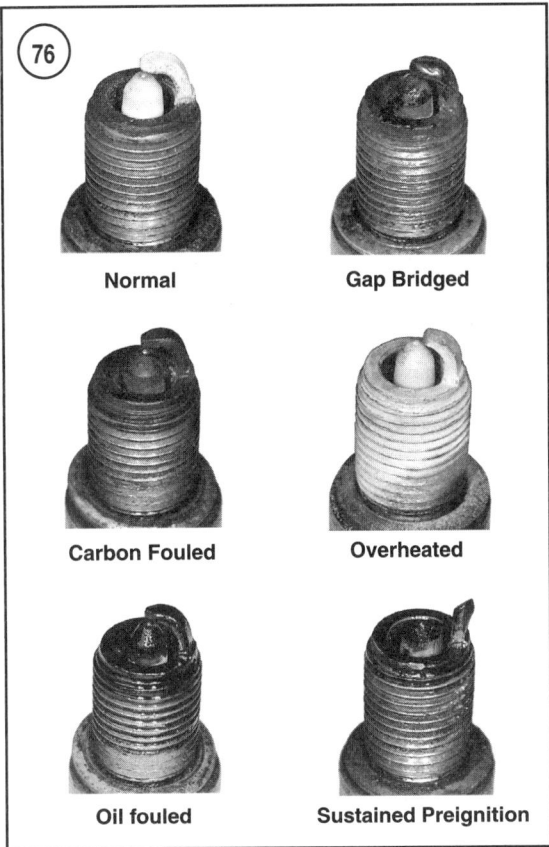

76 Normal / Gap Bridged / Carbon Fouled / Overheated / Oil fouled / Sustained Preignition

ing tip and to the cylinder head (**Figure 75**). This is accomplished by a short path up the ceramic insulator and into the body of the spark plug. By transferring heat quickly, the plug remains cool enough to avoid overheating and preignition problems. If the engine is run slowly for prolonged periods, this type of plug may foul and cause poor performance.

If the engine is run in cold climates or at slow speed for prolonged periods, a spark plug with a hotter heat range is recommended. A hotter plug slowly transfers heat away from its firing tip and to the cylinder head. This is accomplished by a long path up the ceramic insulator and into the body of the spark plug (**Figure 75**). By transferring heat slowly, the plug remains hot enough to avoid fouling and buildup. If the engine is run in hot climates or fast for prolonged periods, this type of plug may overheat, cause preignition problems and possibly melt the electrode. Damage to the piston and cylinder assembly is possible.

If choosing to change a spark plug to a different heat range, go one step hotter or colder from the recommended plug. Do not try to correct poor carburetor or ignition problems by using different spark plugs. This can only compound the existing problems and possibly lead lo severe engine damage.

Reach

Reach is the length of the threaded portion of the plug. Always use a spark plug that is the correct reach. Too short of a reach can lead to deposits or burning of the exposed threads in the cylinder head. Misfiring can also occur since the tip of the plug is shrouded and not exposed to the fuel mixture. If the reach is too long, the exposed plug threads can burn, causing preignition. It is also possible that the piston may contact the plug on the upstroke, causing severe engine damage.

Spark Plug Reading

The spark plug is an excellent indicator of how the engine is operating. By correctly evaluating the condition of the plug, you can diagnose and pinpoint problems, or potential problems. When removing the spark plug, compare the firing tip with the ones shown in **Figure 76**. The following paragraphs provide a description, as well as common causes for each of the conditions.

> *CAUTION*
> *In all cases, when the spark plug does not read normal, find the cause of the problem before continuing engine operation. Severe engine damage is possible when abnormal plug readings are ignored.*

Normal

The plug has light tan or gray deposits on the tip. No erosion of the electrodes or abnormal gap is evident. This indicates an engine that has properly adjusted carburetion, ignition timing, and proper fuel. This heat range of the plug is appropriate for the conditions in which the engine has been operated. The plug can be cleaned and reused.

Carbon-fouled

The plug is black with a dry, sooty deposit on the entire plug surface. This dry sooty deposit is conductive and can create electrical paths that bypass the electrode gap. This often causes misfiring of the plug.
1. Fuel mixture too rich.
2. Spark plug range too cold.
3. Faulty ignition component.
4. Prolonged idling.
5. Clogged air filter.
6. Poor compression.

Oil-fouled

The plug is wet with black, oily deposits on the electrodes and insulator. The electrodes do not show wear.
1. Prolonged idling or low idle speed.
2. Spark plug range too cold.
3. Worn valve guides.
4. Worn piston rings.
5. Ignition component failure.

Gap-bridged

The plug is clogged with deposits between the electrodes. The electrodes do not show wear.
1. Incorrect oil being used.
2. Incorrect fuel or fuel contamination.
3. Carbon deposits in combustion chamber.
4. High-speed operation after excessive idling.

Overheated

The plug is dry and the insulator has a white or light gray cast. The insulator may also appear blistered. The electrodes may have a bluish-burnt appearance.
1. Fuel mixture too lean.
2. Spark plug range too hot.
3. Air leak into intake system.
4. No washer on spark plug.
5. Plug improperly tightened.
6. Faulty ignition component.

Preignition

The plug electrodes are severely eroded or melted. This condition can lead to severe engine damage.
1. Faulty ignition component.
2. Spark plug range too hot.
3. Air leak into intake system.
4. Carbon deposits in combustion chamber.

Worn out

The plug electrodes are rounded from normal combustion. There is no indication of abnormal combustion or engine conditions. Replace the plug.

Spark Plug Cap

The spark plug cap should fit tight on the spark plug and be in good condition. A cap that does not seal and insulate the spark plug terminal can lead to flashover (shorting down the side of the plug), particularly when the motorcycle is operated in wet conditions.

To help prevent water from migrating under the cap, wipe a small amount of dielectric grease around the interior of the cap before installing it onto the plug.

Table 1 MAINTENANCE SCHEDULE*

Pre-ride	Check tire pressure cold; adjust to suit load
	Check brakes for a solid feel
	Check rear brake pedal play; adjust if necessary
	Check throttle grip for smooth operation and return
	Check for smooth, but not loose, steering
	Check axles, all suspension nuts, bolts, and fasteners; tighten if necessary
	Check engine oil level; add oil if necessary
	Check lights and horn operation, especially brake light
	Check for any abnormal engine noise and leaks
	Check engine stop switch operation
	Check front and rear brake fluid levels; add fluid if necessary
	Check tire wear
Every 400 miles (600 km)	Lubricate drive chain
Every 600 miles (1000 km)	Check drive chain slack (adjust if necessary), chain wear and guide wear
	(continued)

LUBRICATION, MAINTENANCE AND TUNE-UP

Table 1 MAINTENANCE SCHEDULE* (continued)

Initial 600 miles (1000 km)	Check throttle free play; adjust if necessary
	Check idle speed; adjust if necessary
	Check choke operation, adjust if necessary
	Check fuel system for leaks
	Check coolant level
	Change engine oil and replace filter
	Check evaporative emission control system (California models)
	Check radiator and coolant hoses
	Check front and rear brake fluid levels; add fluid if necessary
	Check brake light operation; adjust rear switch if necessary
	Check steering play; adjust if necessary
	Check and tighten all nuts, bolts and fasteners
	Check spoke tightness and wheel runout
4000 miles (6000 km)	Check spark plugs; replace if necessary
	Check all fasteners
	Check control cables; lubricate as necessary
	Check evaporative emission control system (California models)
	Check front and rear brake fluid levels; add fluid if necessary (or every month, whichever occurs first)
	Check brake light operation; adjust rear switch if necessary
	Check spoke tightness and wheel runout
	Check tire wear
	Check brake pad wear
7500 miles (12,000 km)	Check spark plugs; replace if necessary
	Check throttle free play; adjust if necessary
	Check clutch operation; adjust lever free play if necessary
	Check steering play; adjust if necessary
	Clean air filter*
	Check idle speed; adjust if necessary
	Check choke operation; adjust if necessary
	Check fuel system for leaks
	Check coolant level
	Check coolant hoses
	Change engine oil (or annually, whichever occurs first) and oil filter*
	Check rear shock absorber for oil leaks
	Check rear suspension
	Check fork for leaks
	Check air suction valve and vacuum hoses
	Check tire and wheel for damage
	Check wheel bearings
	Check balancer chain tension; adjust if necessary
	Check emissions system (California models)
	Check all fasteners
	Perform all general lubrication
	Check control cables; lubricate as necessary
12,000 miles (18,000 km)	Check spark plugs; replace if necessary
	Check control cables; lubricate as necessary
	Check emissions system (California models)
	Check spoke tightness and wheel runout
15,000 miles (24,000 km)	Check spark plugs; replace if necessary
	Clean air filter*
	Check throttle free play; adjust if necessary
	Check clutch operation; adjust lever free play if necessary
	Check idle speed; adjust if necessary
	Check choke operation; adjust if necessary
	Check fuel system for leaks
	Check coolant level
	Check coolant hoses
	(continued)

Table 1 MAINTENANCE SCHEDULE* (continued)

15,000 miles (24,000 km) (cont.)	Change engine oil (or annually, whichever occurs first) and oil filter* Change brake fluid Lubricate steering stem bearing Check rear shock absorber for oil leaks Lubricate swing arm pivot bolt and bearing Lubricate rear suspension Check valve clearance (U.S. and Canada models only) Check balancer chain tension; adjust if necessary Check emissions system (California models) Check air suction valve and vacuum hoses Check tire and wheel for damage Check spoke tightness and wheel runout Check wheel bearings Perform all general lubrication Check all fasteners Check control cables; lubricate as necessary
20,000 miles (30,000 km)	Check spark plugs; replace if necessary Check control cables; lubricate as necessary Check emissions system (California models) Check spoke tightness and wheel runout
24,000 miles (36,000 km)	Check spark plugs; replace if necessary Check throttle free play; adjust if necessary Check clutch operation; adjust lever free play if necessary Check idle speed; adjust if necessary Check choke operation; adjust if necessary Check fuel system for leaks Clean air filter* Change engine oil (or annually, whichever occurs first) and oil filter* Change coolant (or every 3 years, whichever occurs first) Check rear shock absorber for oil leaks Check fork for oil leaks Check balancer chain tension; adjust if necessary Check emissions system (California models) Check air suction valve and vacuum hoses Check tire and wheel for damage Check spoke tightness and wheel runout Check wheel bearings Perform all general lubrication Check all fasteners Check control cables; lubricate as necessary
26,000 miles (42,000 km)	Check valve clearance (All models except U.S. and Canada)
30,000 miles (48,000 km)	Change engine oil (or annually, whichever occurs first) and oil filter* Replace fuel hose (or every 4 years, whichever occurs first) Change brake fluid
Every two years	Change air filter element* Change brake fluid
Every three years	Change coolant Replace coolant hoses
Every four years	Replace brake master cylinder cup and dust seal Replace brake caliper piston seal and dust seal Replace fuel hose Replace brake hose

*Manufacturer's recommendation. More frequent service may extend engine life, particularly in severe operating conditions.

LUBRICATION, MAINTENANCE AND TUNE-UP

Table 2 FUEL, LUBRICANTS AND FLUIDS

Fuel type	Unleaded gasoline; 87 octane minimum
Fuel tank capacity	22 liters (5.8 gal.)
Engine oil	SG, four-stroke engine oil*
	SAE 10W-30, 10W-40, 20W-40, 10W-50 or 20W-50
Engine oil capacity	
Without filter change	2.2 liters (2.3 quarts)
With filter change	2.5 liters (2.6 quarts)
Cooling system capacity	1.55 liters (1.64 quarts)
Coolant mixture	50:50 (distilled water/antifreeze)
Coolant type	Ethylene glycol containing anti-corrosion inhibitors for aluminum engines
Drive chain	O-ring type chain lubricant
Fork oil grade	Kayaba G-10 or equivalent 10-weight fork oil
Brake fluid type	DOT 4
Control cables	Cable lube
Air filter	Foam air filter oil

*API SH, SJ or SL with JASO MA certification.

Table 3 ROUTINE CHECKS AND ADJUSTMENTS

Brake pad lining minimum thickness	1.0 mm (0.040 in.)
Brake pedal pushrod length	69-71 mm (2.72-2.80 in.)
Choke lever free play	2-3 mm (0.08-0.12 in.) at tip
Clutch lever free play	8-12 mm (0.31-0.47 in.)
Drive chain play	35-45 mm (1.38-1.77 in.)
Drive chain length service limit (20 links/21 pins)	317.5-318.2 mm (12.50-12.53 in.)
Radiator cap relief pressure	
2008-2014 models	93-123 kPa (13.5-17.8 psi)
2015-on models	107.9-137.3 kPa (15.6-19.9 psi)
Wheel rim runout (radial and lateral)	2.0 mm (0.08 in.)
Throttle grip free play	2-3 mm (0.08-0.12 in.)
Tire pressure	
Front	150 kPa (22 psi)
Rear	
Load up to 97.5 kg (215 lb.)	150 kPa (22 psi)
Load 97.5-182 kg (215-401 lb.)	200 kPa (29 psi)

Table 4 TUNE-UP SPECIFICATIONS

Battery	12 volt, 14 amp-hour
Compression	529-853 kPa (77-124 psi)
Idle speed	1200-1400 rpm
Ignition timing*	
Idle	10° BTDC at 1300 rpm
Advanced	30° BTDC at 4000 rpm
Pilot mixture screw	1 5/8 turns out
Spark plug type	NGK DPR8EA-9 or ND X24EPR-U9
Spark plug gap	0.8-0.9 mm (0.031-0.035 in.)
Valve clearance (engine cold)	
Exhaust	0.15-0.25 mm (0.006-0.010 in.)
Intake	0.10-0.20 mm (0.004-0.008 in.)

*Not adjustable (set by igniter).

Table 5 MAINTENANCE TORQUE SPECIFICATIONS

Item	N•m	in.-lb.	ft.-lb.
Balancer chain tensioner bolt	8.8	78	–
Coolant drain plug	8.8	78	–
Oil drain plug	29	–	21
Oil filter cover bolts	8.8	78	–
Rear axle nut	98	–	72
Rotor bolt plug	2.5	22	–
Spark plug	14	–	10
Timing plug	2.5	22	–

CHAPTER FOUR

ENGINE TOP END

This chapter provides information for removal, inspection and installation of the engine top end components. These include the exhaust system, cylinder head, valves, cylinder, piston, piston rings and camshafts. All parts can be removed with the engine in the frame.

Tables 1-3 are located at the end of this chapter. **Table 1** lists general engine specifications and **Table 2** lists engine service specifications.

EXHAUST SYSTEM

WARNING
Do not remove the exhaust pipe or muffler while they are hot.

Muffler Removal/Installation

1. Support the motorcycle so it is stable and secure.
2. Remove the right side cover as described in Chapter Fifteen.
3. Remove the rear brake reservoir cover (**Figure 1**).
4. Loosen the exhaust pipe clamp bolt (**Figure 2**).
5. Support the muffler. Then remove the muffler mounting bolts (**Figure 3**) and remove the muffler.
6. Inspect the gasket in the end of the exhaust pipe. If necessary, replace it.
7. Reverse the removal steps to install the muffler. Tighten the exhaust pipe clamp bolt and muffler bolts to 21 N•m (15.5 ft.-lb.). Retighten the bolts after running the engine and allowing it to cool.

Exhaust Pipe Removal/Installation

1. Support the motorcycle so it is stable and secure.
2. Remove the right lower fairing as described in Chapter Fifteen.
3. Remove the right side cover as described in Chapter Fifteen.
4. Remove the rear brake reservoir cover (**Figure 1**).
5. Loosen the exhaust pipe clamp bolt (**Figure 2**).
6. Remove the exhaust pipe bracket bolt (**Figure 4**).

NOTE
The exhaust pipe retaining nuts may be corroded. To prevent thread damage, apply pentrating oil and work the nuts off by turning them back and forth in small increments to break loose the corrosion.

ENGINE TOP END

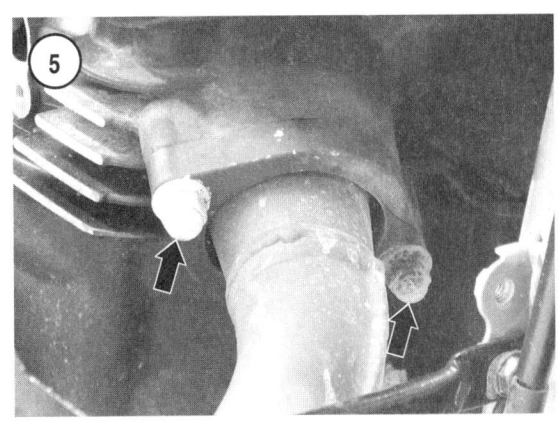

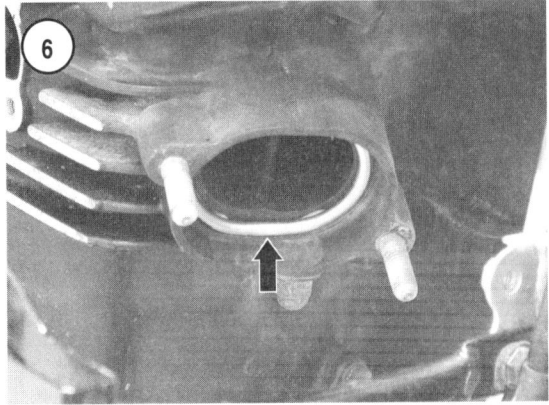

7. Remove the exhaust pipe retaining nuts (**Figure 5**).
8. Remove the exhaust gasket (**Figure 6**) in the cylinder head.
9. Reverse the removal procedure to install the exhaust pipe while noting the following:
    a. Inspect the gasket in the rear end of the exhaust pipe. If necessary, replace it.
    b. Install a new gasket into the cylinder head exhaust port with the round side out.
    c. Apply anti-seize compound to the threads.
    d. Tighten the exhaust pipe nuts and bolts to 21 N•m (15.5 ft.-lb.). Retighten the bolts after running the engine and allowing it to cool.

CYLINDER HEAD COVER

Removal/Installation

Refer to **Figure 7**.
1. Support the motorcycle so it is stable and secure.
2. Remove the fuel tank and lower fairings (Chapter Fifteen).
3. Remove the fan assembly as follows:
    a. Disconnect the fan switch connector (**Figure 8**).

CHAPTER FOUR

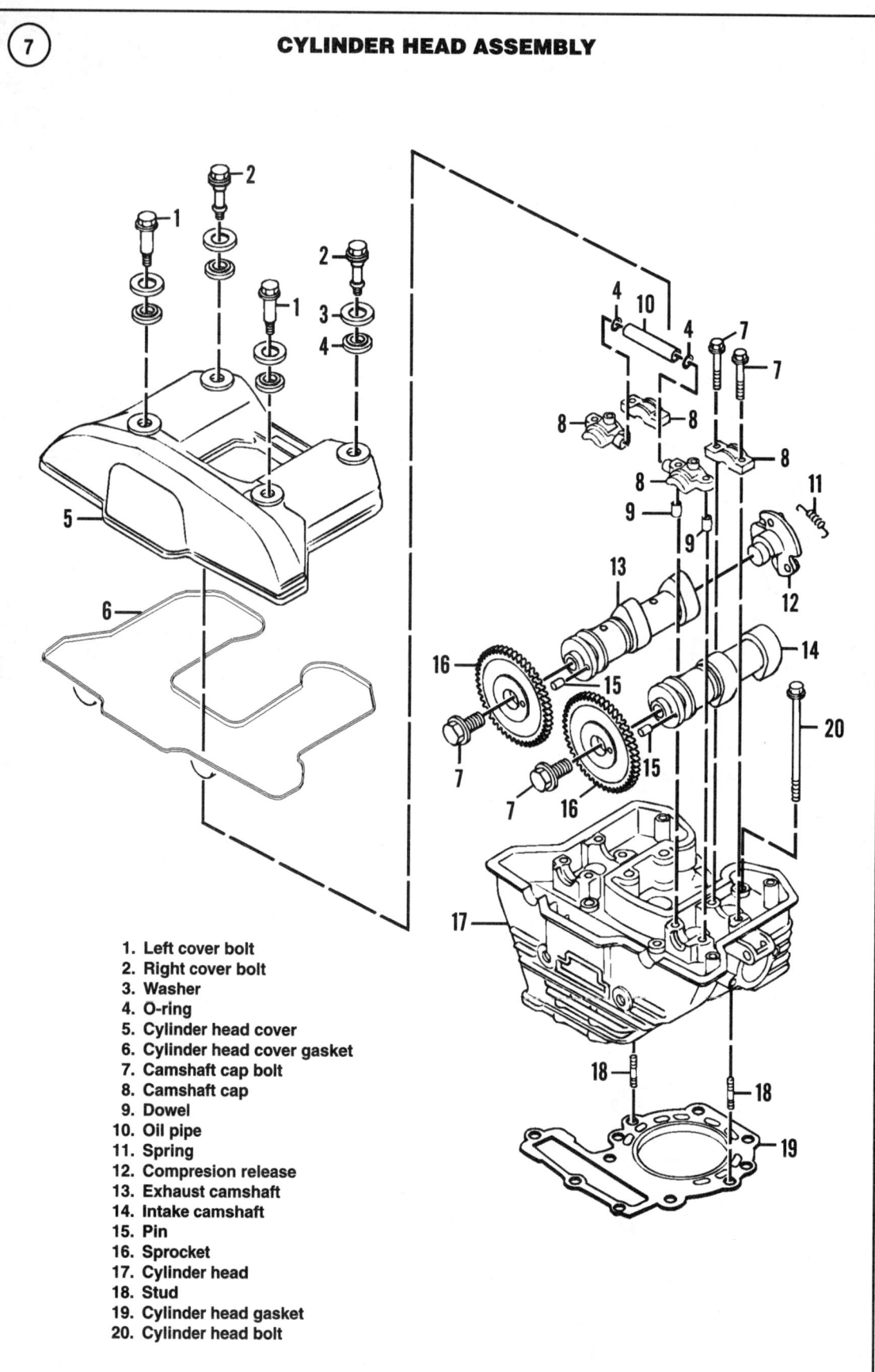

CYLINDER HEAD ASSEMBLY

1. Left cover bolt
2. Right cover bolt
3. Washer
4. O-ring
5. Cylinder head cover
6. Cylinder head cover gasket
7. Camshaft cap bolt
8. Camshaft cap
9. Dowel
10. Oil pipe
11. Spring
12. Compresion release
13. Exhaust camshaft
14. Intake camshaft
15. Pin
16. Sprocket
17. Cylinder head
18. Stud
19. Cylinder head gasket
20. Cylinder head bolt

ENGINE TOP END

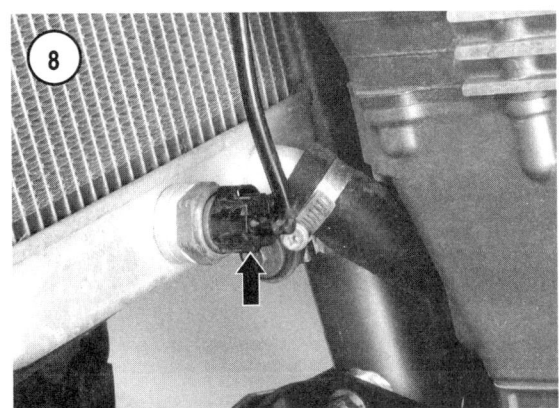

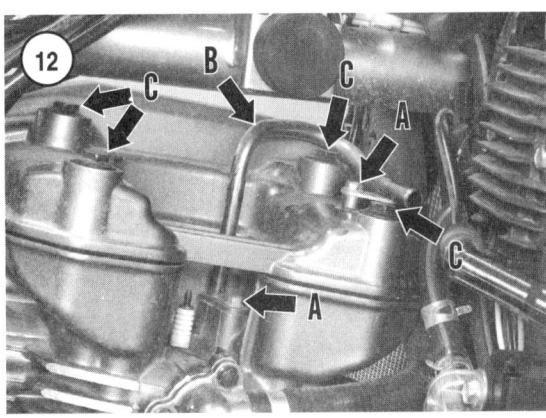

b. Remove the wires from the retainers, then remove the fan mounting bolts (**Figure 9**).

c. Secure the fan out of the way.

4. Disconnect the spark plug cap (A, **Figure 10**) from the spark plug.

5. Disconnect the coolant temperature sending unit connector (B, **Figure 10**).

6. Disconect the intake hose (A, **Figure 11**) from the Clean Air System (CAS) vacuum switch.

7. Disconnect the vacuum hose (B, **Figure 11**) from the vacuum pipe.

8. Remove the mounting bolts (A, **Figure 12**), then remove the vacuum pipe (B).

9. Remove the four cover bolts (C, **Figure 12**).

10. Remove the left fuel tank rubber mounting pad from the frame.

NOTE
Additional clearance in Step 11 may be obtained by separating the gasket from the cover.

11. Tilt the left side of the cover up, then remove the cover out the left side of the engine, passing the cover over the cam chain, chain guide and sprockets.

12. If necessary, refer to Chapter Three for performing the valve clearance inspection and adjustment. If valve adjustment is required, refer to this chapter for camshaft removal.

13. Reverse the removal procedure to install the cover. Note the following:

a. Clean the gasket and the gasket surfaces on the cylinder head and cover. Apply RTV silicone sealant to the gasket surface (A, **Figure 13**) on the left side of the cylinder head. This will help seal the plugs that are part of the gasket.

b. Check that the O-rings on the cover bolts are in good condition. Replace if necessary.

c. Install the cylinder head cover bolts and tighten them to 8 N•m (71 in.-lb.). Do not overtighten the bolts. The left cover bolts are threaded into the camshaft caps.

d. Replace the O-ring on the vacuum pipe (**Figure 14**) if deteriorated or damaged.
e. Tighten the M5 vacuum pipe mounting bolt to 5.9 N•m (52 in.-lb.).
f. Tighten the M6 vacuum pipe mounting bolt to 9.8 N•m (87 in.-lb.).

CAMSHAFTS AND CAM CHAIN TENSIONER

Camshaft and Cam Chain Tensioner Removal

The camshafts and cam chain tensioner can be removed with the engine mounted in the frame. If performing the valve clearance inspection and adjustment procedure (Chapter Three), the camshafts must be removed only when valve clearance is incorrect.

Refer to **Figure 7**.

1. Remove the cylinder head cover as described in this chapter.
2. Remove the timing plug (A, **Figure 15**) and the rotor bolt plug (B).
3. Set the engine at TDC (top dead center) as follows:
   a. Fit a socket onto the rotor bolt and turn the crankshaft counterclockwise until the T mark on the rotor is aligned with the index mark in the timing hole (**Figure 16**).
   b. Verify the engine is at TDC by checking the camshaft lobes. If properly set, all camshaft lobes (A, **Figure 17**) will point away from the center of the engine. If the lobes point toward the center of the engine, rotate the crankshaft counterclockwise one full turn and realign the TDC T-mark.

NOTE
Before further disassembly, measure and record the valve clearance (refer to Chapter Three for valve clearance inspection and adjustment procedures) for all valves. Incorrect clearances can be adjusted during the reassembly process, preventing removal of the camshafts a second time.

4. Remove the cam chain tensioner (A, **Figure 18**) from the cam chain tunnel as follows:
   a. Loosen, but do not remove the center bolt (B, **Figure 18**).
   b. Remove the top and bottom bolts (C, **Figure 18**).

CAUTION
Anytime the tensioner mounting bolts are loosened, the tensioner must be completely removed and reset. Do not partially remove, then retighten the

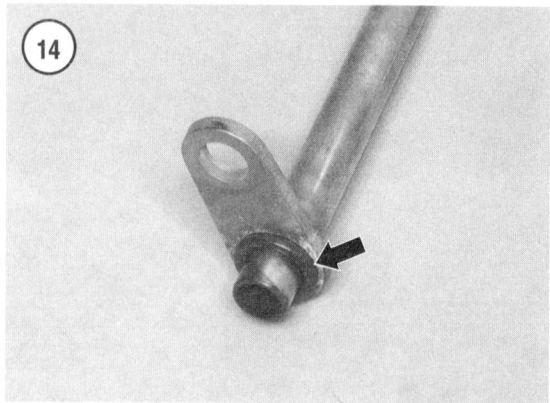

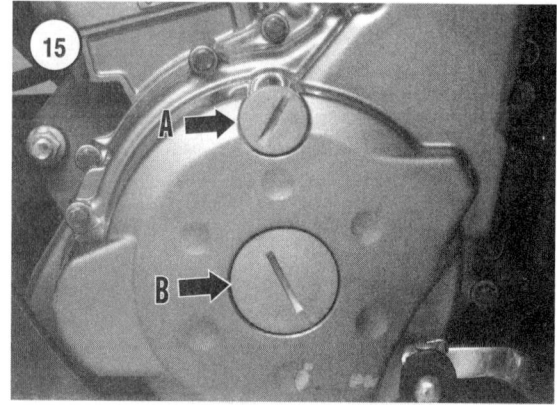

ENGINE TOP END

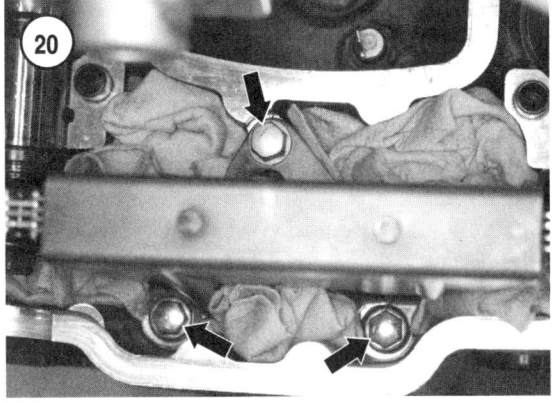

bolts. The ratchet-type plunger will have extended and locked itself. Retightening the bolts causes the cam chain and tensioner to be too tight, possibly causing engine damage if the engine is operated. Also, do not turn the crankshaft when the tensioner is removed from the engine. Camshaft timing could be altered because of the excess slack in the cam chain. This also could cause engine damage if the engine is operated.

   c. Remove the tensioner and gasket.

5. Remove the camshaft caps (B, **Figure 17**) as follows:

   a. Stuff clean shop cloths around the cam chain and in the cam chain tunnel to prevent parts or debris from entering the engine. This way, if parts do fall into the tunnel, they will not enter the crankcase. The cam chain tunnel leads to the left end of the crankshaft, in the left crankcase cover.

   b. Loosen the eight camshaft cap bolts. Loosen the bolts equally in several steps.

   c. Remove the bolt and cap sets from the right intake and exhaust valves. Raise the caps straight up and slowly. Account for the two dowels (**Figure 19**) under each cap. The dowels may be loose and fall from the cap. If the dowels fit securely in either the cap or cylinder head, they may be left in place. Keep all sets of parts identified and together.

CAUTION
If the caps are tight, light tapping with a small, soft mallet can be used to loosen the caps. Do not pry on the caps or the machined surfaces may be damaged. Check that all caps are marked with their cylinder head position.

   d. Remove the bolt and cap sets from the left intake and exhaust valves. Since these caps are joined by the oil supply pipe, slowly raise both caps straight up. Account for the two dowels under each cap. The dowels may be loose and fall from the cap. If the dowels fit securely in either the cap or cylinder head, they may be left in place. Inspect the oil pipe and O-rings during inspection of the camshaft caps. Keep all sets of parts identified and together.

6. Remove the upper cam chain guide (B, **Figure 13**) as follows:

   a. Check that the cam chain tunnel is stuffed with clean shop cloths.

   b. Loosen the three bolts securing the guide (**Figure 20**).

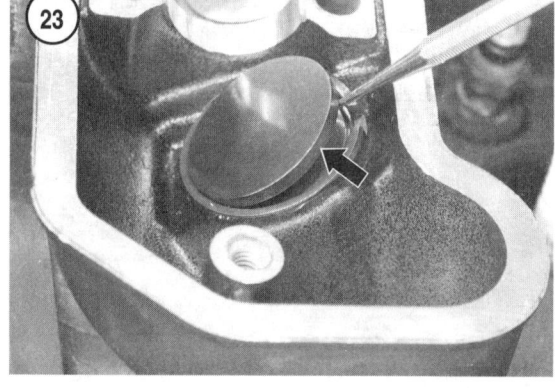

    c. Remove the single bolt to the inside of the guide.
    d. Raise the guide and remaining two bolts from the engine (**Figure 21**).

7. Attach a length of wire to the cam chain. Secure the wire so the chain (**Figure 22**) cannot fall into the engine when the camshafts are removed.

NOTE
If the crankshaft must be turned while the cam chain is loose, keep tension on the chain while turning the crankshaft. This prevents possible chain binding at the crankshaft sprocket.

8. Lift both camshafts out of the cylinder head. It is not necessary to remove the shims (**Figure 23**) or valve lifters.
9. Check that the cylinder head openings are properly covered to prevent parts or debris from entering the engine.
10. Inspect the camshafts, caps and cam chain tensioner as described in this section.
11. If necessary, refer to Chapter Five for cam chain inspection. Although the chain cannot be removed from the engine, a partial inspection can be performed.

Camshaft and Cam Chain Tensioner Installation

Refer to **Figure 7**.
1. Prior to installing the camshafts and cam chain tensioner, note the following:
    a. Adjust any valves that are out of specification as described in Chapter Three. If the valves were reconditioned, install their original shims at this time. Valve clearance will need to be rechecked after the camshafts are installed. It is possible that the camshafts will have to be removed a second time to correctly set the valves.
    b. Check that the cam chain tensioner is disassembled and reset, as described in the inspection procedure. The tensioner must be reset before installation.
    c. Lubricate parts with engine oil during assembly.

2. Inspect the cylinder head and ensure that all surfaces are clean. Remove any shop cloths from the cam chain tunnel.
3. Check that the engine is at TDC and is held in this position. If it is not at TDC, turn the crankshaft counterclockwise until the T mark on the rotor is aligned with the index mark in the timing hole (**Figure 16**). The engine must remain at TDC when installing and timing the camshafts.
4. Install and time the camshafts. Refer to **Figure 24** as needed. The camshafts are properly installed when the arrow on both sprockets point to the front of the engine, and the arrows and marks are parallel to the top edge of the cylinder head. All cam chain slack on the tension side of the chain and across the top of the sprockets must also be eliminated.
    a. Identify the alignment marks on the exhaust camshaft sprocket (**Figure 25**).
    b. Pull up on the tension side (front side) of the cam chain and install the exhaust camshaft (with compression release). Check that the

ENGINE TOP END

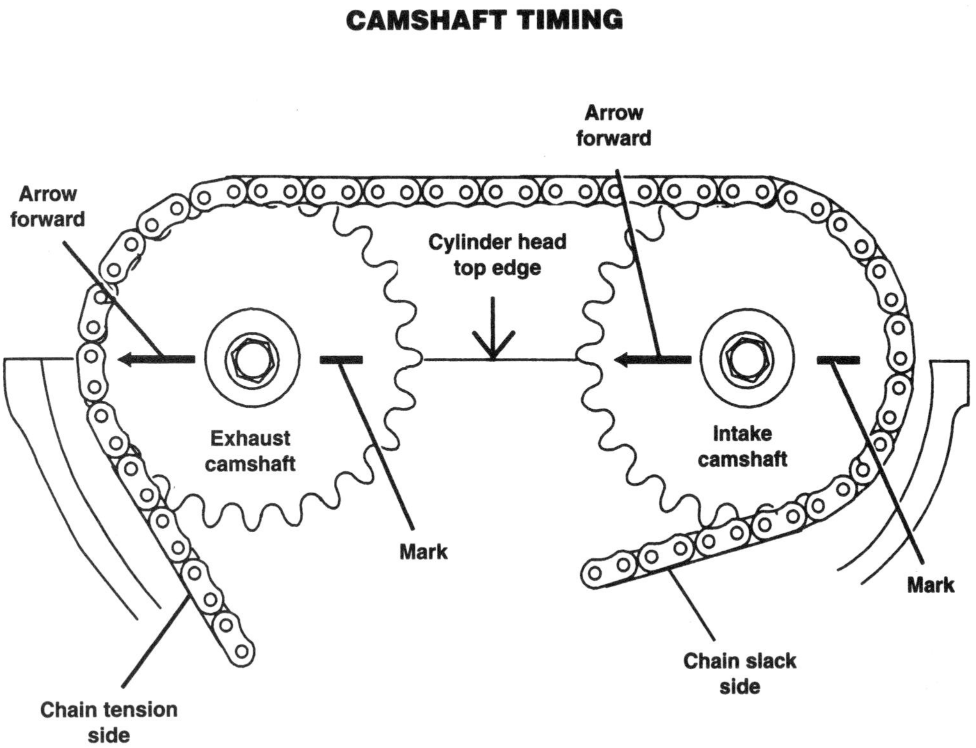

CAMSHAFT TIMING

(Figure 24: Camshaft timing diagram showing exhaust camshaft and intake camshaft with chain, arrows forward, cylinder head top edge, marks, chain tension side, and chain slack side)

shoulder at the left end of the camshaft, seats into the head, then seat the taut chain onto the sprocket. Check that the cam lobes point away from the center of the engine.

c. Check that the engine is still at TDC when the sprocket marks are aligned. If necessary, reposition the assembly.

d. Identify the alignment marks on the intake camshaft sprocket (**Figure 25**).

e. Keeping the chain taut, but seated on the exhaust cam sprocket, install the intake camshaft. Check that the shoulder at the left end of the camshaft, seats into the head, then seat the taut chain onto the sprocket. Check that the cam lobes point away from the center of the engine.

5. With the engine at TDC, inspect the installation (**Figure 26**).

   a. The cam chain should be taut at the front and across the cam sprockets. The excess chain slack at the rear, between the intake camshaft and crankshaft sprocket, will be taken up by the cam chain tensioner.

   b. The arrows on both sprockets must point forward.

c. The arrows and alignment marks on both sprockets must be parallel to the top edge of the cylinder head.
6. Install the upper cam chain guide as follows:

NOTE
The guide must be installed before the camshaft caps. The oil pipe between the left caps will block installation of the guide.

a. Install the two long bolts into the outside holes in the guide (**Figure 21**).
b. Lower the upper cam chain guide into the cam chain tunnel just far enough to start the bolts into their holes. Tighten the bolts with a socket and extension. Check that the socket and extension fit together tightly and cannot separate when lowered into the tunnel. Tighten the outer bolts (**Figure 20**) to 10 N•m (89 in.-lb.).
c. Stuff the cam chain tunnel with clean shop cloths to prevent parts from falling into the engine.
d. Apply threadlock to the remaining guide bolt. Tighten the inner bolt (**Figure 20**) to 8.8 N•m (78 in.-lb.).

7. Install the camshaft caps (B, **Figure 17**) and dowels (**Figure 19**) as follows:
a. Install the dowel and cap sets for the left intake and exhaust valves. Since the caps are joined by the oil pipe, lower both caps into position equally. Install and finger-tighten the bolts.
b. Install the dowel and cap sets for the right intake and exhaust valves. The arrows on the caps must point forward. Install and finger-tighten the bolts.
c. Seat the camshafts by first lightly tightening the bolts in a crossing pattern (**Figure 27**).

CAUTION
Failure to evenly tighten the camshaft cap bolts could cause damage to the cylinder head, camshafts or caps.

d. Tighten the cap bolts evenly, in several steps, to 12 N•m (106 in.-lb.).
e. Remove all shop cloths from the cylinder head.

CAUTION
If for any reason the tensioner mounting bolts are loosened, the tensioner must be completely removed and reset. Do not partially remove, then retighten the bolts. The ratchet-type plunger will have extended and locked itself. Retightening the bolts will cause the cam chain and tensioner to be too tight, possibly causing engine damage if the engine is operated.

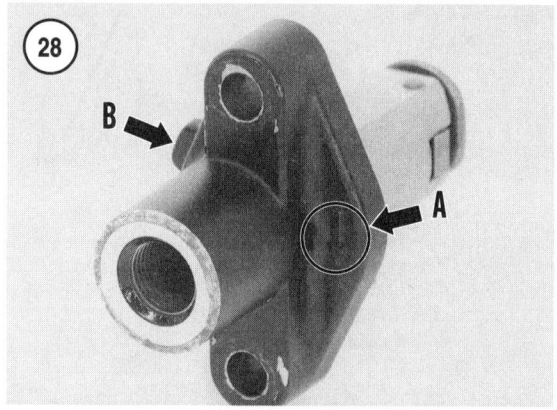

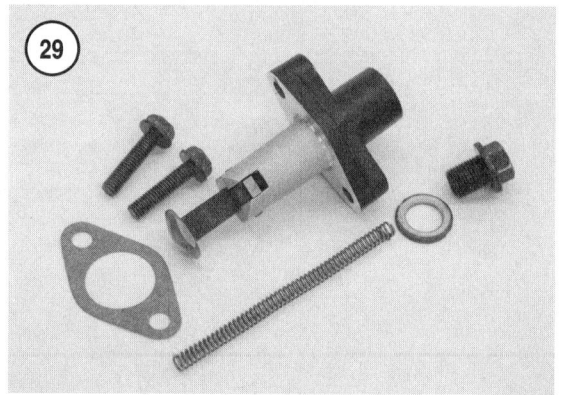

8. Install the cam chain tensioner as follows:
a. Orient the tensioner housing so the arrow (A, **Figure 28**) on the housing points down when installed. Also note the position of the boss (B, **Figure 28**) on the housing.
b. Install a new gasket, the housing and the top and bottom bolts (B, **Figure 18**).
c. Insert the spring and washer, then install and tighten the center bolt (A, **Figure 18**). For 2012 models, engage the spring with the rod.

CAUTION
If abnormal resistance is felt when turning the crankshaft, stop and re-

ENGINE TOP END

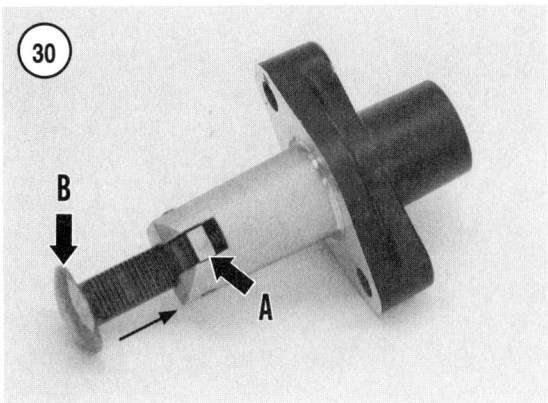

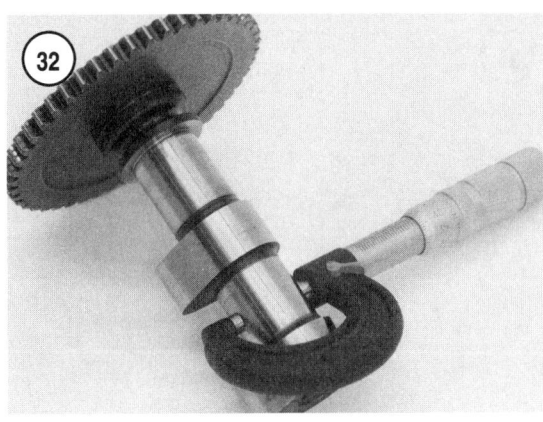

check the alignments. Improper alignment can cause engine damage.

9. Turn the crankshaft slowly counterclockwise several times, then place it at TDC.
   a. Check that the camshaft sprocket arrows point forward and are parallel with the top edge of the cylinder head. If the camshafts are not properly aligned, disassemble the head and re-align the camshaft(s).
   b. Check valve clearances (Chapter Three). If necessary, remove the camshafts and install the proper size valve lifter shim(s).

10. Install the timing plug and the rotor bolt plug. Tighten the plugs to 2.5 N•m (22 in.-lbs.).
11. Install the cylinder head cover as described in this chapter.

Cam Chain Tensioner Inspection

The tensioner assembly is a spring-loaded, ratcheting-type tensioner. As the cam chain wears and develops slack, the spring-loaded plunger extends and locks itself against the back of the lower chain guide. The guide then pivots forward and retightens the chain.

Since the tensioner is self-adjusting, there is no routine maintenance required. However, anytime the tensioner is loosened or removed the tensioner must be reset. Do not partially remove, then retighten the bolts. The plunger will have extended and locked itself. Retightening the bolts will cause the cam chain and tensioner to be too tight, possibly causing engine damage if the engine is operated.

1. Remove the center bolt and disassemble the tensioner (**Figure 29**).
   a. Inspect the parts for visible damage.
   b. Install a new gasket during installation.
2. Reset the plunger as follows:
   a. Press and hold the ratchet release (A, **Figure 30**).
   b. Press and seat the plunger (B, **Figure 30**) into the tensioner housing.
   c. Do not install the spring, washer and center bolt until the tensioner housing has been mounted and the camshafts and chain have been installed and timed.

Camshaft and Compression Release Inspection

The compression release is located on the right end of the exhaust camshaft. The release slightly opens the right exhaust valve during engine cranking. The reduction in compression makes starting easier. When the engine starts, the release is centrifugally disengaged.

In the following procedure, replace parts that are visibly damaged or not within the specifications in **Table 2**.

1. Clean the camshafts in solvent and dry thoroughly.
2. Inspect the camshafts for scoring or other visible damage.
3. For each camshaft, do the following:
   a. Measure the cam lobe heights (**Figure 31**) with a micrometer.
   b. Measure the camshaft journal outside diameter (**Figure 32**) where the cap fits over the cam.

c. Inspect the camshaft sprocket teeth for wear or other damage. The profile of each tooth should be symmetrical. If the sprocket is worn, replace both cam sprockets and the cam chain as a set. When this type of damage occurs, also inspect the crankshaft sprocket, cam chain tensioner and chain guides.
4. Inspect the automatic compression release (**Figure 33**), located on the exhaust camshaft.
   a. Inspect the spring for visible damage.
   b. Pivot the weights outward and check for smooth operation. When the weights are pivoted and released, the spring should fully retract the weights. Replace the spring if it is fatigued.

Camshaft Cap Inspection

1. Clean the camshaft caps in solvent and dry with compressed air. For the left intake and exhaust valve caps, pull the oil pipe out of the caps. Prevent damage to the bearing surface of the caps when handling and inspecting them.
2. For each camshaft cap do the following:
   a. Check all oil passages (A, **Figure 34**) for cleanliness.
   b. Inspect the bearing surface (B, **Figure 34**) in the cap and the mating bearing in the cylinder head for scoring or other visible damage. If either part is damaged, replace the caps and cylinder head as a set. The parts are only available as a single part number. The caps are machined with the cylinder head, so their dimensions and alignments are unique to that cylinder head.

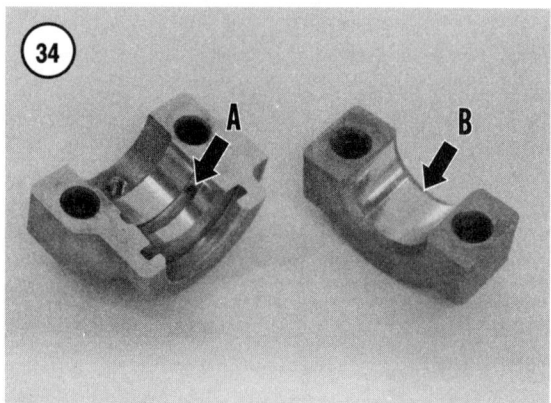

3. For the left intake and exhaust valve caps, inspect the oil pipe and O-rings (**Figure 35**). The oil pipe is held and sealed by the O-ring in each cap. Since the actual condition of the O-rings cannot be determined without removing them from the caps, periodically replace the O-rings to ensure a good seal around the oil pipe. Leakage past the O-rings will reduce the amount of oil reaching the exhaust camshaft. A convenient time to replace the O-rings is during a valve adjustment procedure, when the camshafts must be removed.
   a. Lubricate the ends of the oil pipe and twist it into the caps. If the pipe is firm in both caps, the O-rings can be reused.
   b. If the pipe is loose in the caps, or if the O-rings are visibly damaged, replace the O-rings. Use a small, curved pick to remove the O-rings from the caps. Lubricate the new O-rings before installation. Always lubricate and twist the oil pipe into the caps. Pushing the pipe straight in may cause the O-rings to distort and roll out of the grooves.

4. To determine the bearing oil clearance between the camshaft and cap bearing surface, use a Plastigage kit. To use the kit, the parts must be temporarily installed in the head, placing a small strand of the Plastigage under each cap. After the parts have been torqued, they are disassembled and the width of the compressed Plastigage is measured with a scale. **Figure 36** shows a typical view of the material being measured with the Plastigage scale. The measured width corresponds to a specific clearance between the parts. Perform the clearance check as follows:
   a. Stuff clean shop cloths in the cam chain tunnel to prevent parts from entering the engine.

ENGINE TOP END

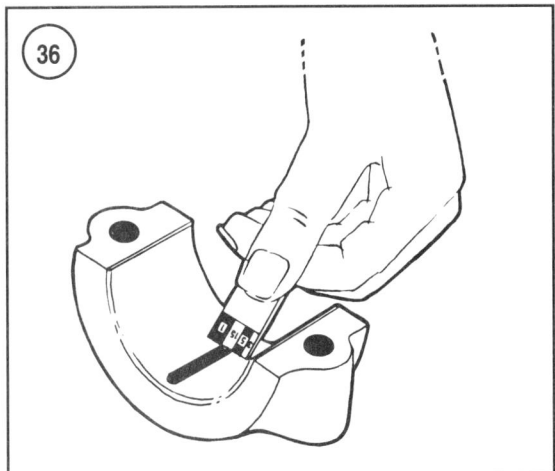

b. Install the camshafts into the cylinder head. The compression release is on the exhaust camshaft. Check that the shoulder at the left end of each camshaft seats into the head. Position the camshafts so the cam lobes are horizontal and not contacting the valve lifters. It is not necessary to install the chain onto the camshafts.

c. Place a strip of Plastigage onto each camshaft journal, parallel to the camshaft. Install the cap and dowels at that location. On the left journals, align the Plastigage so it contacts a flat surface on the inside of the cap. Finger-tighten the cap bolts.

d. Seat the camshafts by first lightly tightening the bolts in a crossing pattern.

CAUTION
Failure to evenly tighten the camshaft cap bolts could cause damage to the cylinder head, camshafts or caps.

e. Tighten the cap bolts evenly, in several steps, to 12 N•m (106 in.-lb.).

NOTE
Do not allow the camshaft to turn while the Plastigage is fitted between the parts.

f. After achieving the proper torque, loosen the cap bolts. Loosen the bolts equally in several steps. Carefully remove the caps, dowels and Plastigage strips. Keep all strips with their respective cap.

g. Using the scale included with the Plastigage kit, measure the width of the Plastigage to determine if clearance is within the specification. If oil clearance is not within specification, measure the camshaft journal to determine which part(s) are worn. Replace the camshaft, cylinder head, or if necessary, both parts.

CYLINDER HEAD

Removal

The cylinder head can be removed with the engine mounted in the frame. Refer to **Figure 7**.

1. Drain the engine coolant as described in Chapter Three.

NOTE
If cylinder head removal is necessary for access to other engine parts and not for service, detach the coolant hose and leave the housing and thermostat in place in Step 2.

2. Remove the coolant hose, thermostat and housing (**Figure 37**) as described in Chapter Ten.
3. Remove the carburetor as described in Chapter Eight.
4. Remove the exhaust pipe as described in this chapter.
5. Remove the cylinder head cover, camshafts and cam chain tensioner as described in this chapter.
6. Remove the shims (**Figure 23**) from the valve lifters as follows:
   a. Rotate the valve lifter so the notch in the edge of the lifter is accessible.
   b. Wedge a small-tipped tool between the shim and lifter, then tilt the tool back to break the oil adhesion between the parts.
   c. Remove the shim and mark its location in the cylinder head. The shims must be identified, since they can vary in thickness. Make a drawing of the cylinder head so all parts from each location can be placed in the appropriate position on the guide.
7. Remove the engine mounting bolt (A, **Figure 38**).

8. Remove the engine mounting bracket bolts (B, **Figure 38**), then remove the mounting brackets (C).

9. Remove the banjo bolt and seal washers from the oil pipe (A, **Figure 39**).

10. Remove the nut from the rear of the cylinder head (B, **Figure 39**).

11. Remove the nut and bolt from the front of the cylinder head (**Figure 40**).

12. Stuff the cam chain tunnel with clean shop cloths to prevent parts from entering the engine.

CAUTION
Do not remove the four cylinder head bolts before removing the nuts and bolt in the previous steps. Doing so will overstress the smaller fasteners.

13. Remove the four cylinder head bolts located in the cylinder head (**Figure 41** and **Figure 42**). Loosen the bolts in a crossing pattern and in several passes.

14. Loosen the cylinder head by lightly tapping around its base with a soft mallet. Lift the head out the left side of the engine while routing the cam chain out of the head. Secure the chain so it does not fall into the engine.

15. Stuff clean shop cloths into the cam chain tunnel, then remove the head gasket, two dowels, front chain guide and rubber damper that are fitted in the cylinder (**Figure 43**).

16. At the workbench, remove the spark plug, coolant temperature sending unit, carburetor intake duct and rear cam chain guide.

17. Remove the valve lifters (**Figure 44**). Note their location in the head and store them with the shims. If necessary, remove and inspect the valve assembly as described in this chapter.

18. Wash all parts in solvent and dry with compressed air. Note the following:
   a. Remove all gasket residue from the cylinder head and cylinder. Do not scratch or gouge the surfaces.
   b. Remove all carbon deposits from the combustion chamber. Use solvent and a soft brush or hardwood scraper. Do not use sharp-edged tools that could scratch the valves or combustion chamber. If the piston crown is cleaned, keep solvent and carbon deposits out of the gap between the piston and cylinder.

CAUTION
If the valves are removed from the head, the valve seats are exposed and can be damaged from careless cleaning. A scratched or gouged valve seat does not seal properly.

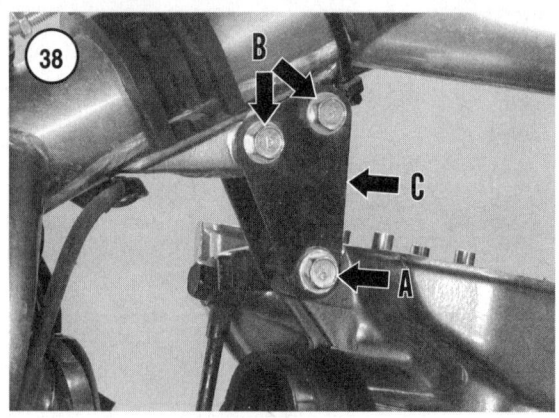

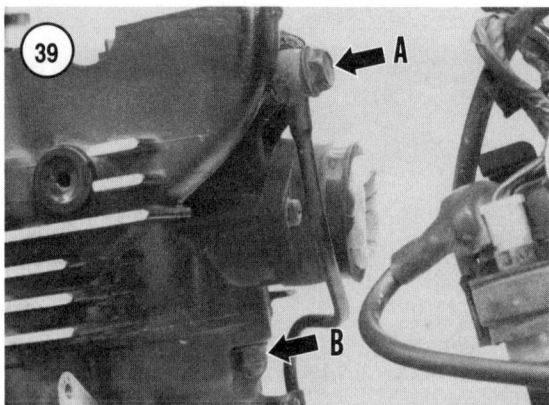

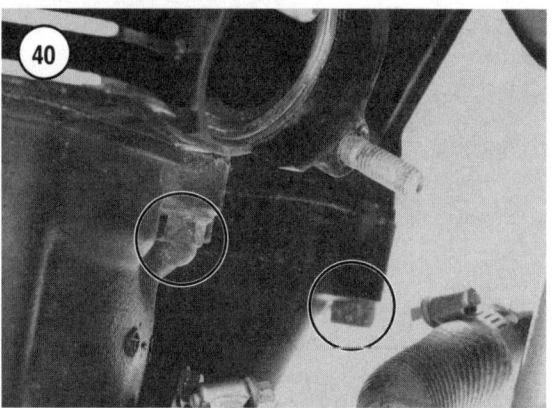

ENGINE TOP END

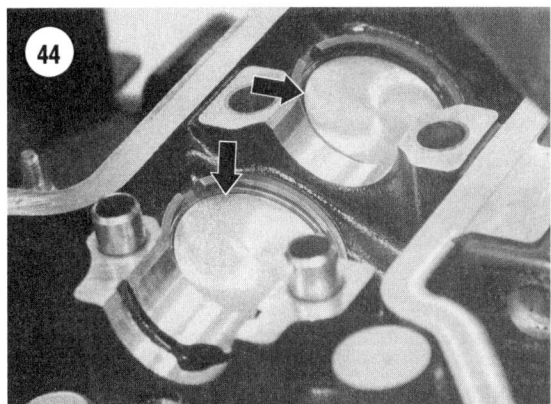

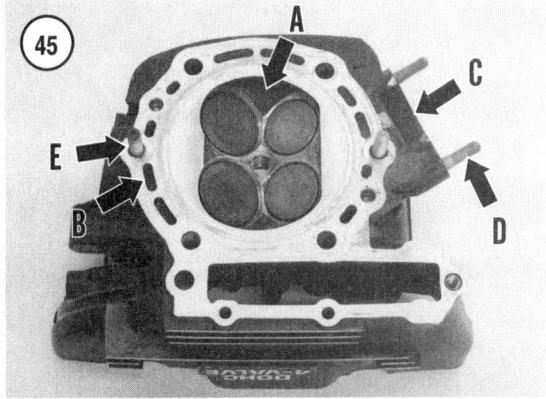

c. If the cylinder head has been bead-blasted, wash the entire assembly in hot, soapy water after it has been reconditioned. This will remove blasting grit that is lodged in crevices and threads. Clean and chase all threads to ensure no grit remains. Blasting grit that remains in the head will be picked up by the engine oil and circulated throughout the engine. This will damage the bearings, piston and rings.
d. Check all oil passages for debris or blockage.
e. Check all parts for visible wear or damage.

19. Inspect the cylinder head as described in this section.

Inspection

Anytime the cylinder head is removed, the valves should be tested for leakage with a solvent test. This test is quick and easy to perform and helps identify problems in the valve train. Refer to *Valves* in this chapter for the solvent test.

NOTE
If the spark plug hole threads are galled, stripped or cross-threaded, the cylinder head should be fitted with a steel thread insert, such as a HeliCoil. Thread damage can be minimized by applying antiseize compound to the spark plug threads before installation. Do not overtighten the spark plug.

1. Inspect the spark plug hole threads. If the threads are dirty or mildly damaged, use a spark plug thread tap to clean and straighten the threads. Keep the tap lubricated while cleaning the threads.
2. If necessary, clean the entire cylinder head after thread repair.
3. Inspect the inside of the cylinder head.
    a. Inspect for cracks or damage in the combustion chamber (A, **Figure 45**), water jackets (B) and exhaust port (C).
    b. Inspect the studs (D, **Figure 45**) and dowels (E) for damage or looseness.
4. Inspect the outside of the cylinder head.
    a. Inspect for cracks or damage around the holes for the spark plug and coolant temperature sending unit.
    b. Inspect the camshaft bearing surfaces and mating caps for obvious scoring or damage. If either part is damaged, replace the caps and cylinder head as a set. The parts are only available as a single part number. The caps are machined with the cylinder head, so their dimensions and alignments are unique to that cylinder head.

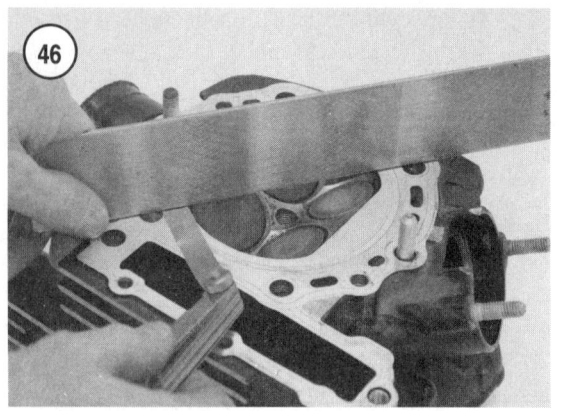

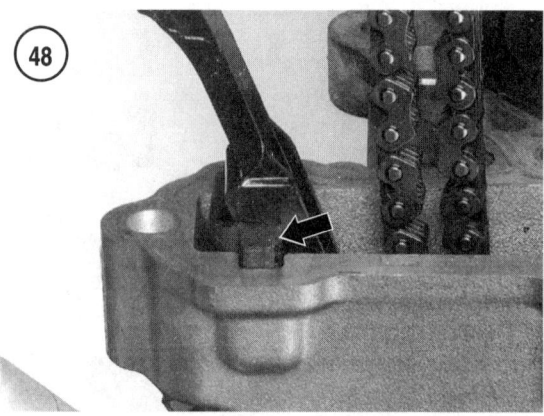

c. If cracks are found anywhere in the cylinder head, take the head to a dealership or machine shop to see if the head can be repaired. If not, replace the head and camshaft cap set.

5. Inspect the cylinder head for warp as follows:
   a. Lay a machinist's straightedge across the cylinder head as shown in **Figure 46**.
   b. Try to insert a flat feeler gauge between the straightedge and the machined surface of the head. If clearance exists, record the maximum measurement.
   c. Repeat the measurement several times, laying the straightedge both across and diagonally on the head in several places.
   d. Compare the measurements to the warp service limit listed in **Table 2**. If the clearance is not within the service limit, take the cylinder head to a dealership or machine shop for further inspection and possible resurfacing.

6. Inspect the front and rear cam chain guides (**Figure 47**) for wear and damage.

7. Inspect the cylinder fasteners for damaged threads and heads. Replace rusted fasteners.

8. Assemble and install the cylinder head as described in this section.

Installation

Refer to **Figure 7**.

1. Note the following:
   a. Check that any gasket residue is removed from all mating surfaces. All cylinder head surfaces must be clean and dry.
   b. The valve lifters and shims can be installed after the cylinder head is installed.

2. Install the rear cam chain guide into the cam chain tunnel.

3. Install the front cam chain guide and rubber damper. Seat the guide in the notch. Make sure the rubber damper (**Figure 48**) sits on top of the chain guide locating pin. The cylinder head gasket fits over the damper.

NOTE
*Make sure the rubber damper on the rear cam chain guide (**Figure 48**) is not dislodged when installing the head gasket or cylinder head.*

4. Install the dowels and a new cylinder head gasket onto the cylinder (**Figure 49**).

5. Lower the cylinder head onto the engine, routing the cam chain up through the head.
   a. Keep adequate tension on the cam chain so it does not bind at the crankshaft sprocket.

ENGINE TOP END

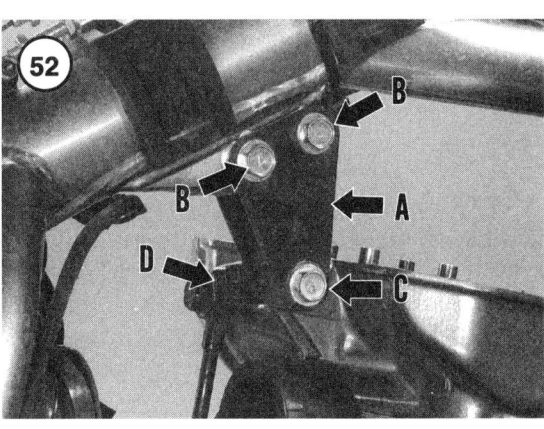

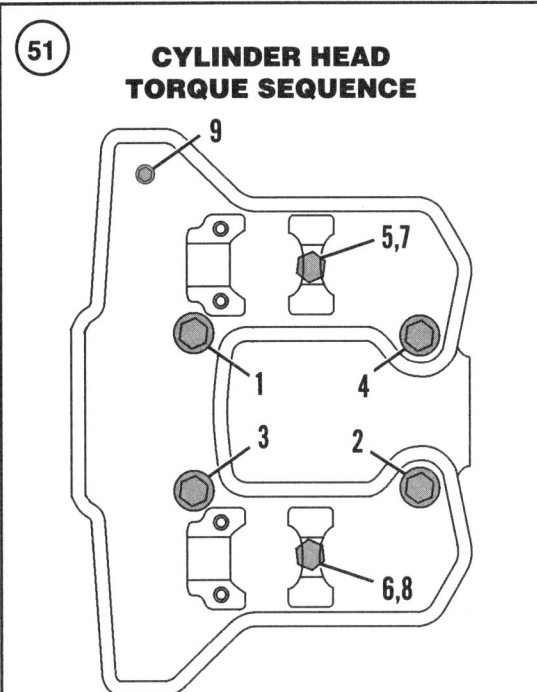

Secure the cam chain when the cylinder head is seated.
  b. Be careful to not dislodge the dowels as the head is positioned.
  c. Cover engine openings as needed.
6. Install and tighten the four cylinder head bolts (**Figure 50**) as follows:
  a. Apply molybdenum disulfide grease to the bolt threads and to the seating surface on the heads.
  b. Refer to the tightening sequence in **Figure 51**.
  c. Tighten the cylinder head bolts in two steps. In the first step, tighten the bolts to 31 N•m (23 ft.-lb.). In the second step, tighten the bolts to 62 N•m (46 ft.-lb.).
7. Install and finger-tighten the nut at the rear of the cylinder head (B, **Figure 39**) and the nut and bolt at the front of the cylinder head (**Figure 40**).

NOTE
The nuts and bolt in this step should be retorqued after the engine has been started, warmed up and allowed to completely cool.

  a. Refer to the tightening sequence in **Figure 51**. Note that the nuts are tightened twice before tightening the bolt.
  b. Tighten the cylinder head nuts to 25 N•m (18.5 ft.-lb.). A 12-mm crowfoot wrench may be preferred. If necessary, fit a torque adapter onto the torque wrench to improve access to the nuts. Refer to Chapter One for adjusting torque readings when adapters are used.
  c. Tighten the front bolt (8 mm) to 18 N•m (13 ft.-lb.).
8. Install the oil pipe (A, **Figure 39**). Use new seal washers and install the banjo bolt. Tighten the bolt to 20 N•m (15 ft.-lb.).
  a. If the complete oil pipe assembly was removed from the crankcase, align and finger-tighten all banjo bolts and the retainer bolt before torquing.
  b. Tighten the retainer bolt to 8 N•m (71 in.-lb.).
9. Install the upper engine mounting brackets and fasteners using the following procedure:
  a. Install the brackets (A, **Figure 52**), frame bolts (B) and nuts. Tighten finger-tight.
  b. Apply threadlock to the engine mounting bolt (C, **Figure 52**) threads. Install the bolt and bracket nut (D, **Figure 52**). Install the bracket nut so the curved end is toward the mounting bracket. The bracket nut will rotate and stop when it contacts the mounting bracket.
  c. Tighten the front frame bolt to 25 N•m (18.5 ft.-lb.). Tighten the rear frame bolt to 25 N•m (18.5 ft.-lb.).
  d. Tighten the engine mounting bolt (C, **Figure 52**) to 25 N•m (18.5 ft.-lb.).

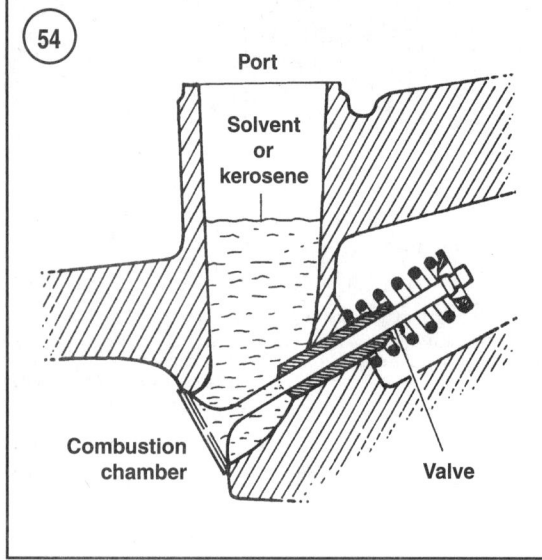

NOTE
If the valve assembly was not reconditioned or disturbed when the cylinder head was removed, reinstall the original shim. If clearance was incorrect before the head was removed, refer to the valve adjustment procedure in Chapter Three to determine the correct size of shim to install. If the valves were reconditioned, install the original shim at this time. Recheck valve clearance after the camshafts are installed. Camshaft removal may be necessary a second time to correctly adjust the valves.

10. Install the valve lifter and shim sets in their appropriate locations as follows:
   a. Lubricate the valve lifters (**Figure 44**) with engine oil, then insert them into their bores.
   b. Seat the shims into the valve lifters. If the shim size is stamped on the shim and is visible

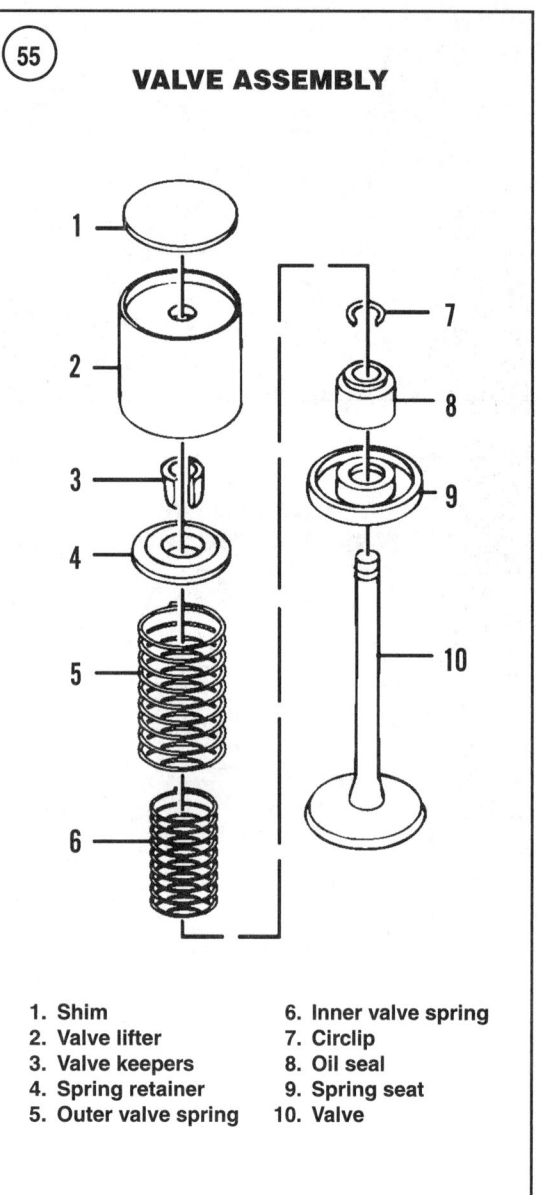

1. Shim
2. Valve lifter
3. Valve keepers
4. Spring retainer
5. Outer valve spring
6. Inner valve spring
7. Circlip
8. Oil seal
9. Spring seat
10. Valve

(**Figure 53**), place the number down, so it is not worn away by the cam lobe.

11. Install the cam chain tensioner, camshafts and cylinder head cover as described in this chapter.
12. Install the spark plug as described in Chapter Three.
13. Install the coolant temperature sending unit, thermostat and coolant hose as described in Chapter Ten.
14. Fill the engine with coolant as described in Chapter Three.
15. Install the carburetor as described in Chapter Eight.
16. Install the exhaust pipe as described in this chapter.

ENGINE TOP END

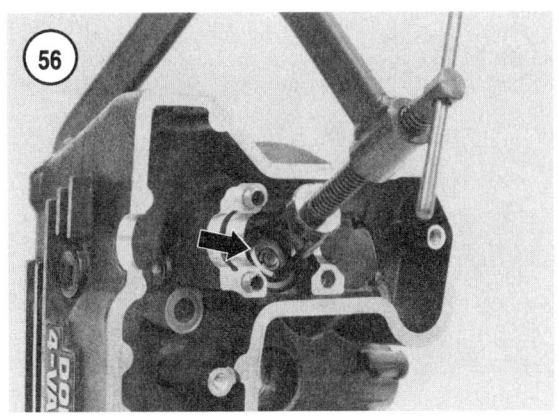

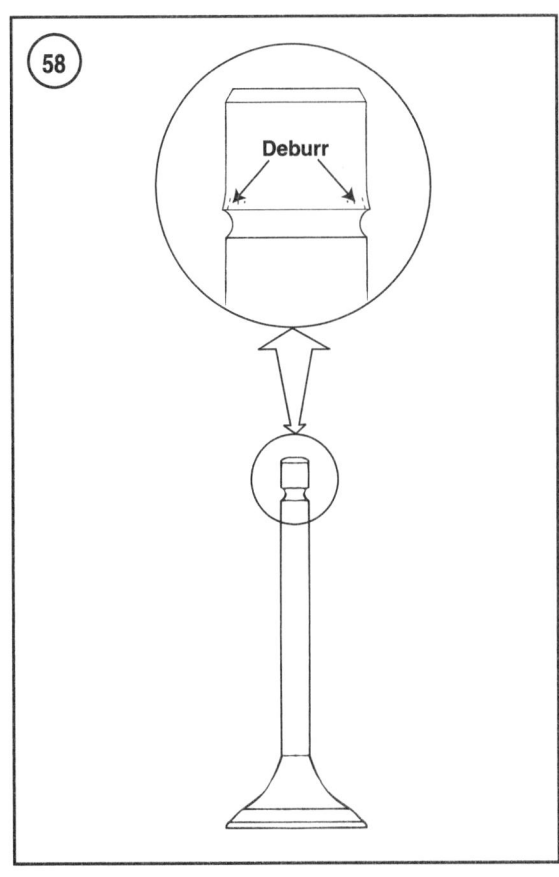

VALVES

Solvent Test

Perform the solvent test with the valve assembly in the cylinder head. This test can reveal if valves are fully seating, as well as expose undetected cracks in the cylinder head.

1. Remove the cylinder head as described in this chapter.
2. Check that the combustion chamber is dry and the valves are seated.
3. Support the cylinder head so the port faces up (**Figure 54**).
4. Pour solvent or kerosene into the port.
5. Inspect the combustion chamber for leakage around the valve.
6. Repeat the process for the other valves.
7. If there is any leaking, it can be caused by:
    a. A worn or damaged valve face.
    b. A worn or damaged valve seat (in the cylinder head).
    c. A bent valve stem.
    d. A crack in the combustion chamber.

Valve Removal

Refer to **Figure 55**.

1. Remove the cylinder head, shims, and valve lifters as described in this chapter.
2. Perform the solvent test on the intake and exhaust valves as described in this section.
3. Install a valve spring compressor (Kawasaki part No. 57001-241 or equivalent) and adapter (Kawasaki part No. 57001-1078 or equivalent) onto the valve assembly. Fit the stationary end of the tool squarely onto the valve head. Fit the other end of the tool squarely on the spring retainer (**Figure 56**).

CAUTION
Do not overtighten and compress the valve springs. This can result in loss of valve spring tension.

4. Tighten the compressor until the spring retainer no longer holds the valve keepers in position. Lift the keepers from the valve stem. A magnetic tool (**Figure 57**) works well.
5. Slowly relieve the pressure on the valve springs and remove the compressor from the head.
6. Remove the spring retainer and valve springs.
7. Slide the circlip on the oil seal down, then remove the oil seal, circlip and spring seat.
8. Inspect the valve stem for sharp and flared metal (**Figure 58**) around the groove for the keepers. If necessary, deburr the valve stem before removing

the valve from the head. Burrs on the valve stem can damage the valve guides.

9. Remove the valve from the cylinder head.
10. After removing each valve assembly, store the parts with the shim and valve lifter for that location (**Figure 59**).
11. Repeat Steps 3-10 for the remaining valves.

Valve Component Inspection

During the cleaning and inspection of the valve assemblies, do not allow the sets of parts to get intermixed. Work with one set of parts at a time, repeating the procedure until all parts are inspected. After inspecting each set of parts, return them to their storage container. Refer to **Table 2** for specifications.

NOTE
In the following procedure, whenever the valves, valve guides and valve seats must be replaced or reconditioned, it is recommended that the work be done by a dealership. These parts should be replaced or reconditioned as a set. Replacing and servicing of these parts require special equipment, as well as experience in replacing and fitting the parts.

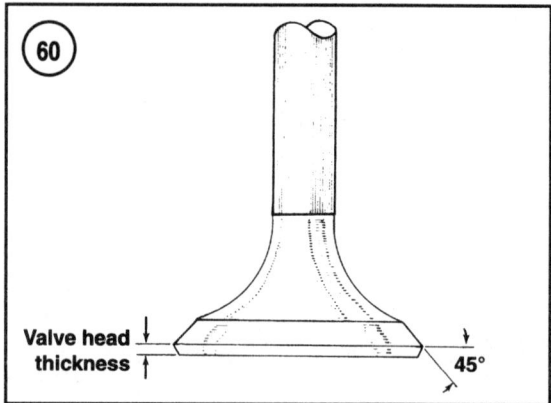

1. Clean the valve assembly in solvent.

CAUTION
The valve seating surface is a critical surface and must not be damaged. Do not scrape on the seating surface or place the valve where it could roll off the work surface.

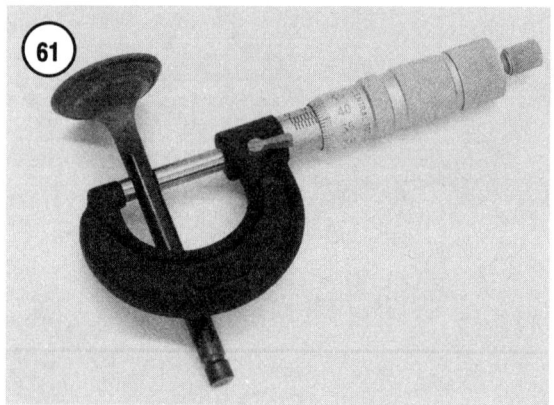

2. Inspect the valve head as follows:
   a. Inspect the top and perimeter of each valve. Check for burning or other damage on the top and seating surface. Replace the valve if damage is evident. If the valve head appears uniform, with only minor wear, the valve can be lapped (described in this section) and reused if the other valve measurements are acceptable.
   b. Measure the thickness (**Figure 60**). Record the measurement.
3. Inspect the valve stem as follows:
   a. Inspect the stem for visible wear and scoring. Also check the end of the valve stem for flare.
   b. Measure the valve stem diameter (**Figure 61**). Record the measurement (margin above seat).
   c. Check the valve stem for runout. Place the valve in a V-block and measure runout with a dial indicator (**Figure 62**). Record the measurement.

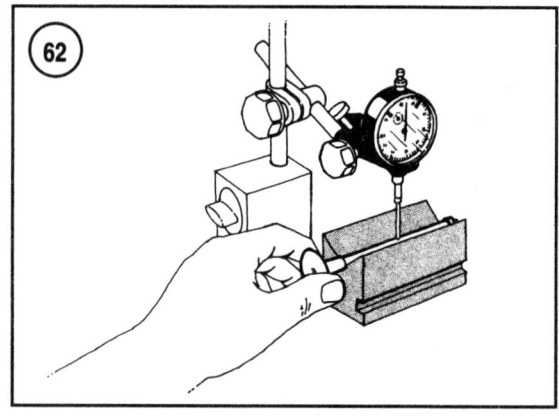

ENGINE TOP END

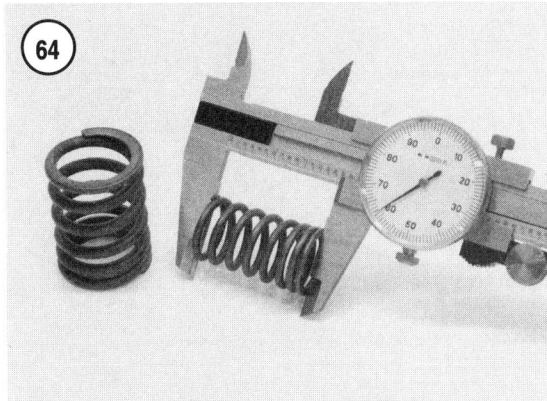

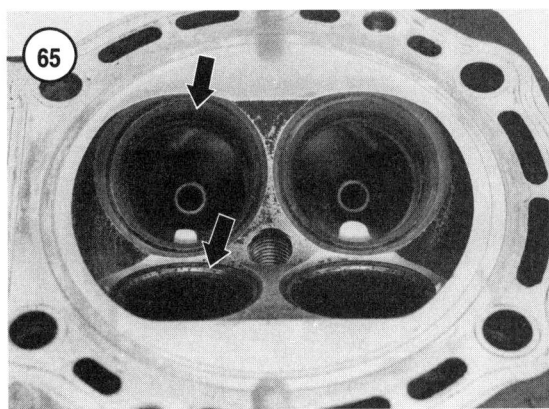

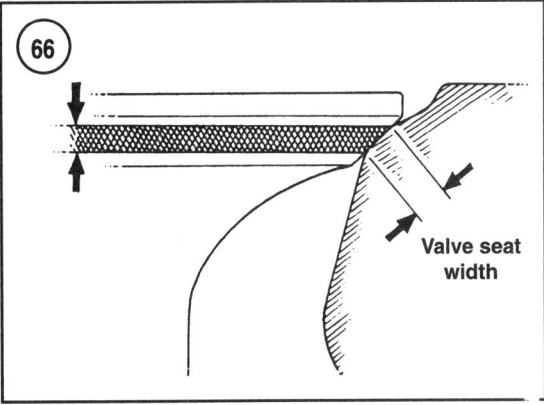

4A. If a small hole gauge and micrometer are available, inspect the valve guides as follows:
   a. Clean the valve guides (**Figure 63**) so they are free of all carbon and varnish. Use solvent and a stiff, narrow brush.
   b. Measure each valve guide hole at the top, center and bottom. Use a small hole gauge and micrometer to make the measurements. Record the measurements.

4B. If a small hole gauge and micrometer are not available, inspect the valve guides as follows:
   a. Insert the appropriate valve into the guide.
   b. With the valve head off the seat, move the valve stem side to side in the valve guide. Move the valve in several directions, checking for perceptible play. If movement is easily detected, the valve guide and/or valve is worn. Take the valves and cylinder head to a dealership and have the parts accurately measured to determine the extent of wear.

5. Check the inner and outer valve springs as follows:
   a. Visually check the springs for damage.
   b. Measure the length of each valve spring (**Figure 64**). Record the measurements.

6. Inspect the valve spring seat, spring retainer, keepers and valve lifter for visible wear or damage.

7. Inspect the valve seats (**Figure 65**) in the cylinder head to determine if they must be reconditioned.
   a. Clean and dry the valve seat and valve mating area with contact cleaner.
   b. Coat the valve seat with machinist's marking fluid.
   c. Install the appropriate valve into the guide, then lightly tap the valve against the seat so the fluid transfers to the valve contact area. Do not rotate the valve.
   d. Remove the valve from the guide and measure the imprinted valve seat width (**Figure 66**) at several locations.
   e. Clean all marking fluid from the valves and seats.

Valve Installation

Perform the following procedure for each set of valve components. All components should be clean and dry. Refer to **Figure 55** as needed.

CAUTION
Install valve components that are within specification in their original positions. Replace the oil seal and circlip.

1. Coat the valve stem and interior of the oil seal with molybdenum disulfide grease.

2. Install the spring seat into the head.
3. Install a new oil seal onto the valve guide, checking that the circlip seats onto the seal and valve guide.
4. Insert the appropriate valve into the cylinder head. Rotate the valve stem as it enters and passes through the seal. Check that the seal remains seated, then hold the valve in place.
5. Install the inner and outer valve springs with the small coil pitch, facing down (**Figure 67**).
6. Install the spring retainer.
7. Install a valve spring compressor over the valve assembly. Fit the tool squarely onto the spring retainer and the valve face.

CAUTION
Do not overtighten and compress the valve springs. This can result in loss of valve spring tension.

8. Tighten the compressor until the spring retainer is compressed enough to install the valve keepers.
9. Insert the keepers around the groove in the valve stem (**Figure 68**).
10. Slowly relieve the pressure on the spring retainer, then remove the compressor from the head.
11. Tap the end of the valve stem with a soft mallet to ensure that the keepers are seated in the valve stem groove.
12. After all valves are installed, perform the solvent test as described in this chapter.
13. Install the cylinder head as described in this chapter.

Valve Lapping

Valve lapping restores accurate sealing between the valve seat and valve contact area, without machining. Lapping should be performed on valves and valve seats that have been inspected and are within specifications. Lapping should also be performed on valves and valve seats that have been reconditioned.
1. Lightly coat the valve face with fine-grade lapping compound.
2. Lubricate the valve stem, then insert the valve into the head.
3. Wet the suction cup on the lapping tool and press it onto the head of the valve (**Figure 69**).
4. Spin the tool back and forth between your hands to lap the valve to the seat. Every 5 to 10 seconds, rotate the valve 180° and continue to lap the valve into the seat.
5. Frequently inspect the valve seat. Stop lapping the valve when the valve seating area (**Figure 70**) is smooth, even and polished. Keep each lapped valve

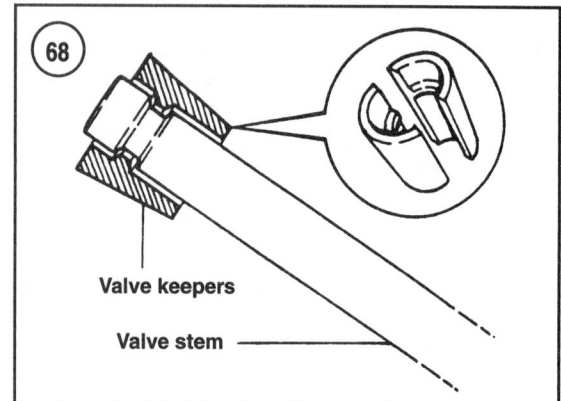

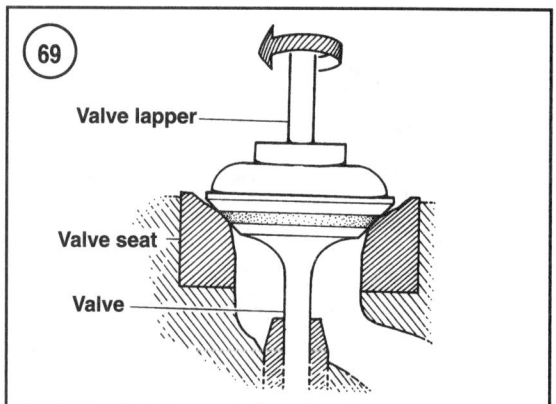

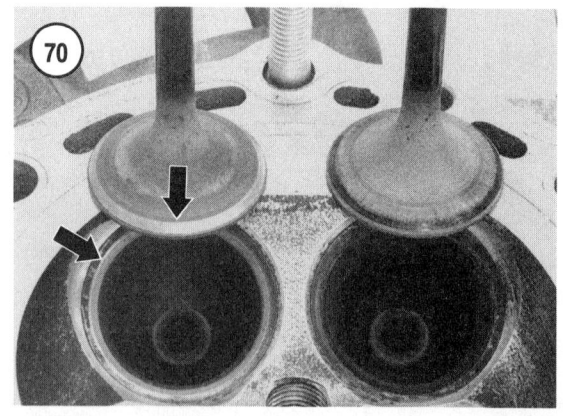

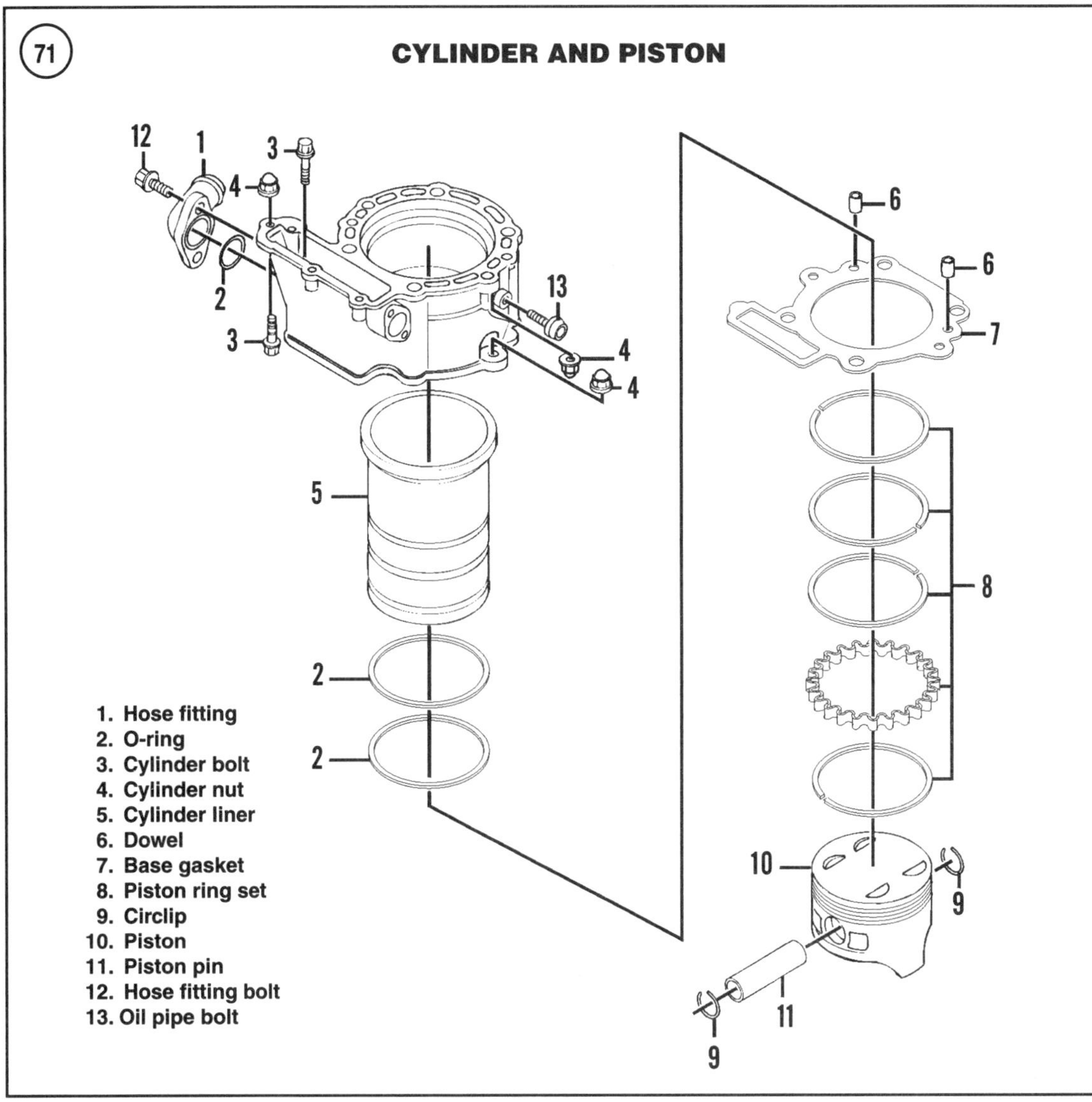

ENGINE TOP END

CYLINDER AND PISTON

71

1. Hose fitting
2. O-ring
3. Cylinder bolt
4. Cylinder nut
5. Cylinder liner
6. Dowel
7. Base gasket
8. Piston ring set
9. Circlip
10. Piston
11. Piston pin
12. Hose fitting bolt
13. Oil pipe bolt

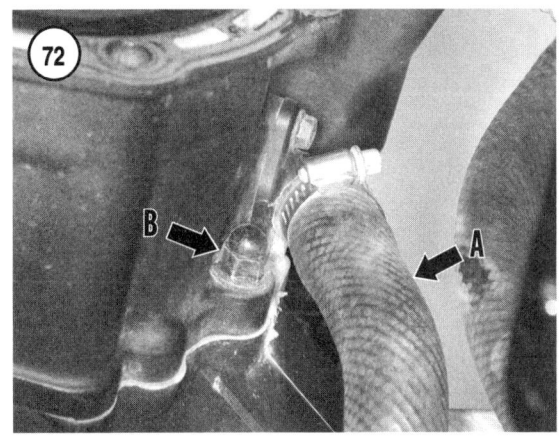

72

identified so it can be installed in the correct seat during assembly.

6. Clean the valves and cylinder head in solvent to remove all lapping compound. Any abrasive allowed to remain in the head will cause premature wear and damage to other engine parts.

7. After the valves are installed in the head, perform the *Solvent Test* described in this section. If there are any leaks, remove that valve and repeat the lapping process.

CYLINDER

Removal

The cylinder and piston can be removed with the engine mounted in the frame. Read all procedures completely before attempting a repair. Refer to **Figure 71**.

1. Remove the cylinder head as described in this chapter.
2. Remove the coolant hose (A, **Figure 72**) at the front of the cylinder.

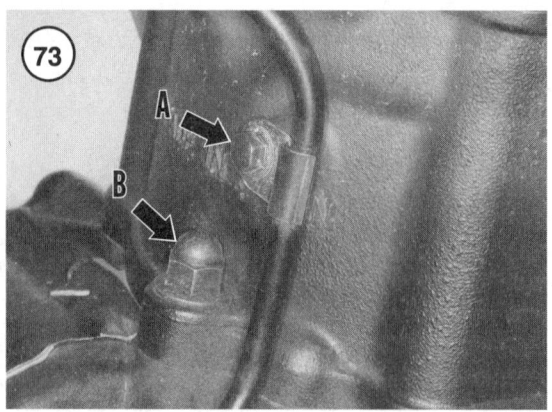

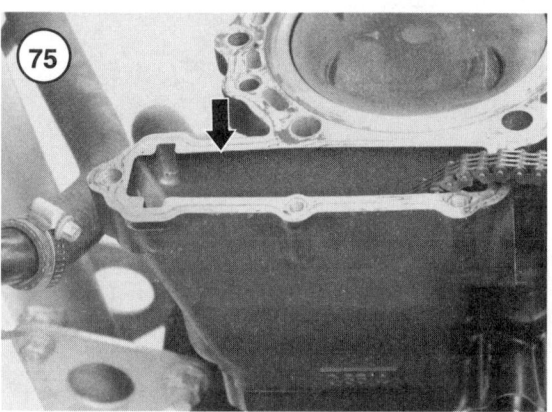

3. Remove the oil pipe retainer and bolt (A, **Figure 73**) at the rear of the cylinder.
4. If the engine crankcases will be split, remove the remaining banjo bolts and seal washers (**Figure 74**) securing the oil pipe.
5. Remove the cylinder 6 mm mounting bolt located in the cam chain tunnel (**Figure 75**). Stuff clean shop cloths into the tunnel to prevent parts from entering the engine.
6. Remove the cylinder mounting nuts at the front (B, **Figure 72**) and rear (B, **Figure 73**) of the cylinder.
7. Loosen the cylinder by tapping around the base. If necessary, apply penetrating oil to the joint.
8. Slowly lift the cylinder from the crankcase.
   a. Account for the two dowels (**Figure 76**) under the cylinder. If loose, remove the dowels to prevent them from possibly falling into the engine.
   b. Route the cam chain out of the cylinder and secure.
9. Remove the base gasket.
10. Stuff clean shop cloths into the cam chain tunnel and around the piston. Support the piston and rod so it does not contact the crankcase or studs (**Figure 77**).
11. Inspect the cylinder as described in this section.

Inspection

1. Remove all gasket residue from the top and bottom cylinder block surfaces.
2. Wash the cylinder in solvent and dry with compressed air.
3. Inspect the overall condition of the cylinder for obvious wear or damage.
   a. Inspect the cylinder bore (A, **Figure 78**) for scoring or gouges. If damaged, overbore the cylinder.
   b. Inspect the water jackets, (B, **Figure 78**) for deposits.

ENGINE TOP END

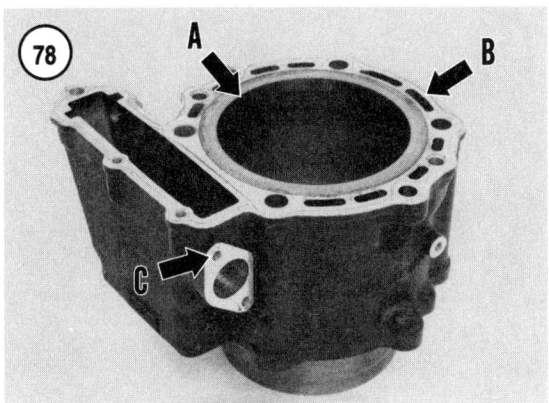

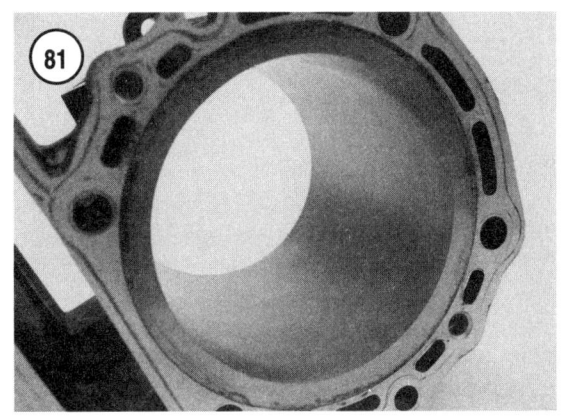

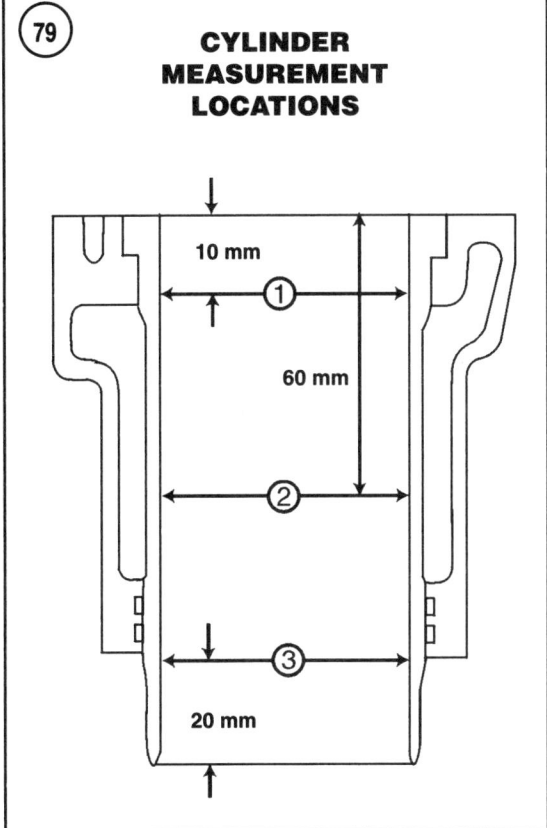

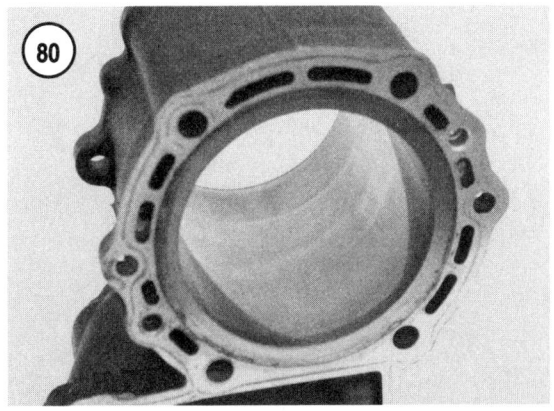

c. Inspect all threads (C, **Figure 78**) for condition and cleanliness.

4. Measure and check the cylinder for wear. Measure the inside diameter of the cylinder with a bore gauge or inside micrometer as follows:

   a. Measure the cylinder along the bore axis at the three points shown in (**Figure 79**). At each point, measure the cylinder front to back (measurement X) and side to side (measurement Y). Record the measurements for each location.

   b. Compare the largest X or Y cylinder bore measurement recorded to the specifications and service limit listed in **Table 2**. If the cylinder bore is not within the service limit, rebore and hone the cylinder. The rebored cylinder diameter should not vary more than 0.01 mm (0.0004 in.) at any point.

NOTE
Oversize pistons and ring sets are available in a 0.5 mm (0.020 in.) and 1.0 mm (0.040 in.) increase. The new service limit for the cylinder is 0.1 mm (0.004 in.) more than the actual diameter of the cylinder after boring. The new service limit for the piston is 0.15 mm (0.006 in.) less than the actual diameter of the piston. If wear exceeds the replacement piston sizes, replace the cylinder liner and use a standard piston and ring set.

5. If cylinder boring is necessary, take the cylinder to a dealership or machine shop to have any machine work performed. If the cylinder is to be overbored and fitted with the next size piston and rings, take the new piston to the shop so the cylinder can be accurately bored and honed to accommodate the actual piston size.

6. If the cylinder is within all service limits, and a new piston and rings will be installed (see *Piston Inspection* in this chapter), deglaze the cylinder, preferably with a 240-grit hone. Cylinder glaze appears as a hard, shiny surface (**Figure 80**). After deglazing,

the crosshatching in the cylinder provides a uniform surface capable of retaining oil and mating with the rings (**Figure 81**).

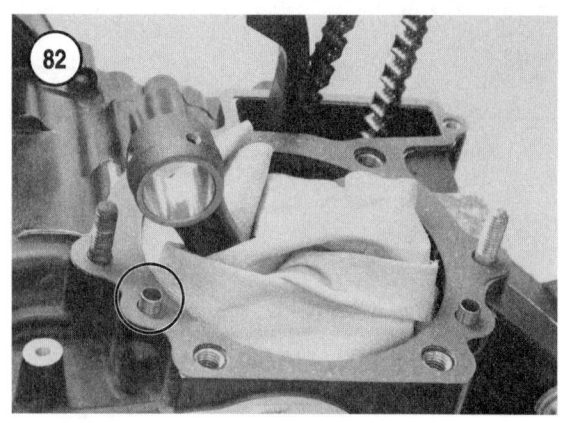

CAUTION
Wash the cylinder in hot, soapy water. Solvents do not remove the fine grit left in the cylinder. This grit causes premature wear of the rings and cylinder.

7. Thoroughly wash and scrub the cylinder in hot, soapy water after inspection and service, to remove all fine grit and material/residue left from machine operations. Check cleanliness by rubbing a clean, white cloth over the bore. No residue should be evident. When the cylinder is thoroughly clean and dry, immediately coat the cylinder bore with oil to prevent corrosion. Wrap the cylinder until engine reassembly.
8. Perform any service to the piston assembly before installing the cylinder.

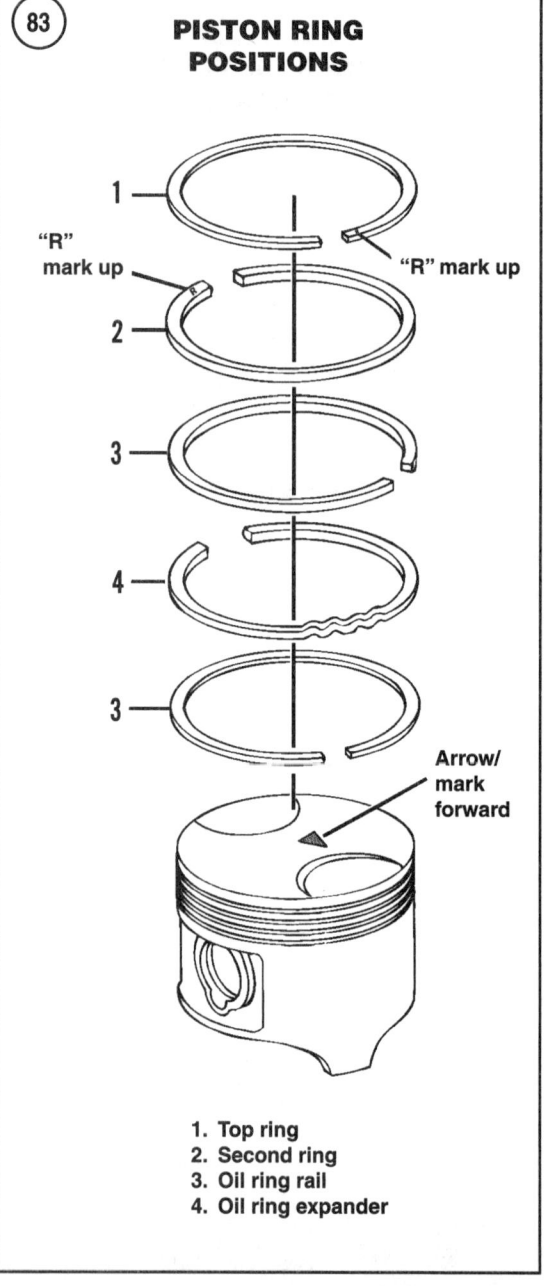

Installation

Refer to **Figure 71**.
1. Check that any gasket residue is removed from all mating surfaces.
2. Install the dowels and a new base gasket onto the crankcase. **Figure 82** shows the gasket and dowels installed before the piston is installed. Whenever the piston is removed, it is easier to install the gasket before the piston, since the cam chain must also be handled and routed through the gasket. Gasket bending or other damage is less likely to occur.
3. Lubricate the following components with engine oil:
   a. Piston and rings.
   b. Piston pin and connecting rod.
   c. Cylinder bore.
4. Support the piston so the cylinder can be lowered into place.
5. Stagger the piston ring gaps around the piston as shown in **Figure 83**. Note that the top and second ring gaps are opposite one another, pointing to the front and back of the piston. The oil ring rail gaps are about 30° apart, pointing to the sides.
6. Lower the cylinder onto the crankcase.
   a. Route the cam chain and guide through the chain tunnel. Secure the cam chain so it cannot fall into the engine.
   b. As the piston enters the cylinder, compress each ring so it can enter the cylinder. A ring compressor can also be used. When the bottom ring is in the cylinder, remove any holding fixture and shop cloths from the crankcase.

ENGINE TOP END

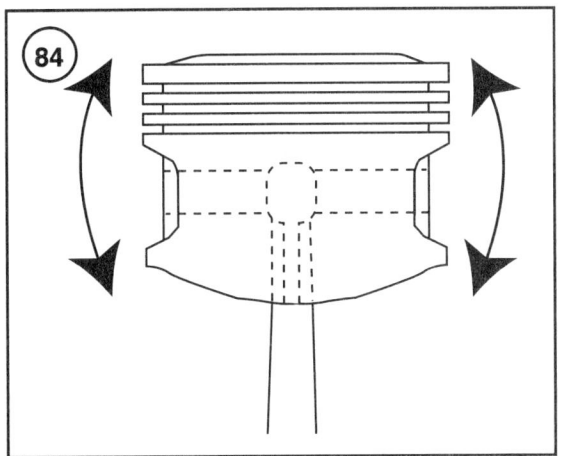

84

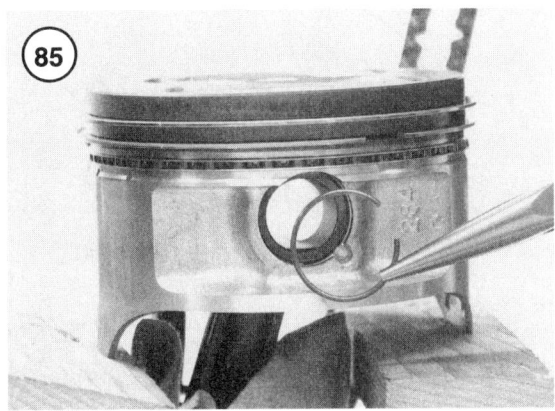

85

86

b. Tighten the bolt to 10 N•m (89 in.-lb.).
9. Install the oil pipe retainer and bolt (A, **Figure 73**) at the rear of the cylinder. Tighten the bolt to 8 N•m (71 in.-lb.).
   a. If the entire oil pipe was removed, install new seal washers on the banjo bolts, then finger-tighten the bolts (**Figure 74**).
   b. After installing the cylinder head, tighten all the oil pipe banjo bolts and the retainer bolt to the specifications in **Table 3**.
10. Install the coolant hose (A, **Figure 72**) at the front of the cylinder.
11. Install the cylinder head as described in this chapter.

PISTON AND PISTON RINGS

The piston is made of aluminum alloy and fitted with three rings. The piston is held on the small end of the connecting rod by a chrome-plated, steel piston pin. The pin is a precision fit in the piston and rod, and is held in place by circlips. As each component of the piston assembly is cleaned and measured, record and identify all measurements. Refer to the measurements when checking the specification and service limits in **Table 2**.

Piston Removal

1. Remove the cylinder as described in this chapter.
2. Before removing the piston, check the piston and piston pin for obvious play. Hold the rod and try to tilt the piston side to side (**Figure 84**). If a tilting (not sliding) motion is detected, there is wear on either the piston pin, pin bore or connecting rod. Wear could be on any combination of the three parts. Careful inspection is required to determine which parts should be replaced.
3. Stuff clean shop cloths around the connecting rod and in the cam chain tunnel to prevent parts from entering the crankcase.

NOTE
New circlips must be installed during assembly.

4. Rotate the ends of the circlips to the removal gaps, then remove the circlips (**Figure 85**) from the piston pin bore. Discard the circlips.

CAUTION
Do not attempt to drive out the pin with a hammer and drift. The piston and connecting rod assembly will likely be damaged.

5. Press the piston pin (**Figure 86**) out of the piston by hand. If the pin is tight, a pin puller (Kawasaki

7. Install and tighten the cylinder mounting nuts at the front (B, **Figure 72**) and rear (B, **Figure 73**) of the cylinder.
   a. If necessary, remove the coolant hose fitting in order to tighten the front nut.
   b. Tighten the nuts evenly, in several steps, to 25 N•m (18.5 ft.-lb.).
8. Install and tighten the 6 mm cylinder mounting bolt located in the cam chain tunnel (**Figure 75**).
   a. Stuff clean shop cloths into the tunnel to prevent parts from entering the engine.

part No. 57001-910) and adapter (Kawasaki part No. 57001-1211) are available from a dealership. A simple removal tool can be made as shown in **Figure 87**. The end of the padded pipe rests against the piston, not the piston pin. The hole in the pipe must be larger than the diameter of the piston pin. As the nut on the end of the rod is tightened, the nut and washer at the opposite end drive the piston pin into the pipe.

6. Lift the piston off the connecting rod.
7. Inspect the piston and piston pin as described in this section.

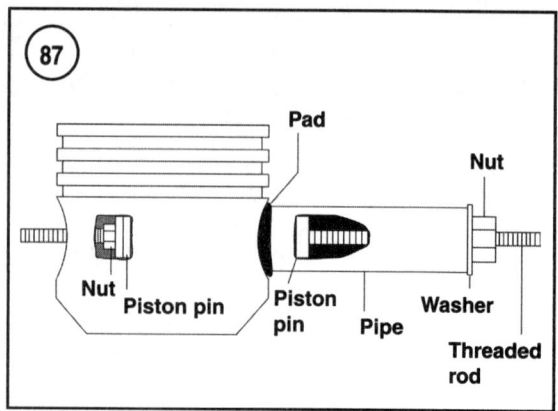

Piston Inspection

1. Remove the piston rings as described in this section.
2. Clean the piston.
    a. Clean the carbon from the piston crown. Use a soft scraper, brushes and solvent. Do not use tools that can gouge or scratch the surface. This type of damage can cause hot spots on the piston during engine operation.
    b. Clean the piston pin bore, ring grooves and piston skirt. Clean the ring grooves with a soft brush, or use a broken piston ring (**Figure 88**) to remove carbon and oil residue. Mild galling or discoloration can be polished off the piston skirt with fine emery cloth and oil.
3. Inspect the piston. Replace the piston if damage is evident.
    a. Inspect the piston crown (A, **Figure 89**) for wear or damage. If the piston is pitted, overheating is likely occurring. This can be caused by a lean fuel mixture and/or preignition.
    b. Inspect the ring grooves (B, **Figure 89**) for dents, nicks, cracks or other damage. The grooves should be square and uniform for the circumference of the piston. Particularly inspect the top compression ring groove. It is lubricated the least and is subject to the highest combustion temperatures. If the oil ring was difficult to remove, the piston has likely overheated and distorted.
    c. Inspect the piston skirt (C, **Figure 89**). If the skirt shows signs of severe galling or partial seizure (bits of metal embedded in the skirt), replace the piston.
    d. Inspect the interior of the piston. Check the crown (A, **Figure 90**), skirt, piston pin bores (B) and bosses for cracks or other damage. Check the oil holes (C, **Figure 90**) and circlip grooves for cleanliness and damage.
4. Measure the width of all ring grooves. Replace the piston if any measurement exceeds the service limit listed **Table 2**.

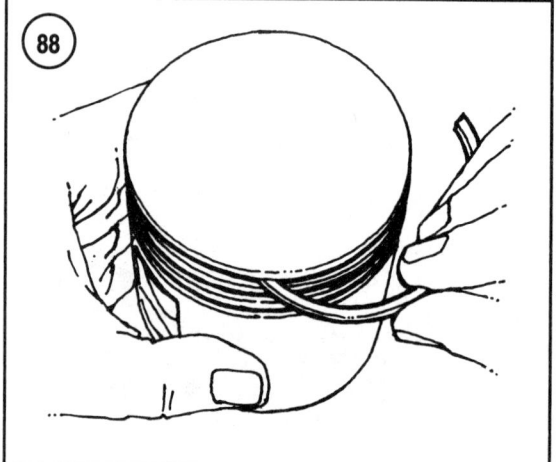

5. Inspect the piston ring-to-ring groove clearance as described in *Piston Ring Inspection/Removal* (this section).

Piston-to-Cylinder Clearance Inspection

Measure the clearance between the piston and cylinder to determine if the parts can be reused. If parts do not fall within specification, the cylinder should be bored oversize to match an oversize piston assem-

ENGINE TOP END

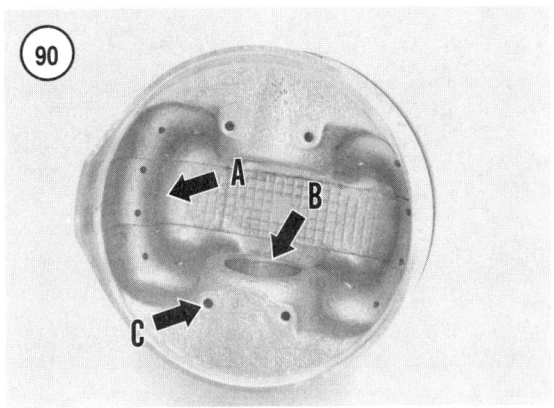

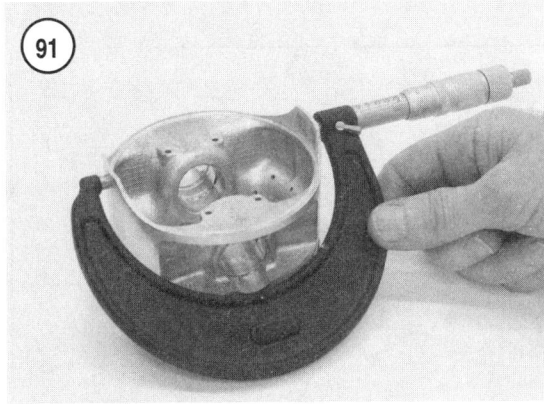

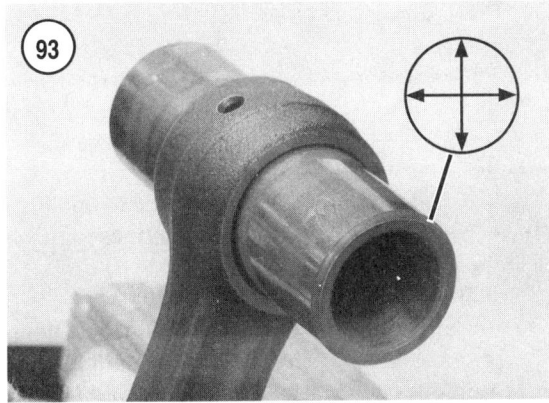

bly. Clean the piston and cylinder with solvent and dry before measuring.

1. Measure the outside diameter of the piston. Measure 5 mm (0.2 in.) up from the bottom edge of the piston skirt (**Figure 91**) and 90° to the direction of the piston pin. Record the measurement.

2. Determine clearance by subtracting the piston measurement from the largest cylinder measurement. If cylinder bore measurements are not yet known, the procedure is described under *Cylinder Inspection* in this chapter. If the piston-to-cylinder clearance exceeds the specifications in **Table 2**, the cylinder must be overbored and fitted with an oversize piston assembly.

Piston Pin Inspection

1. Clean the piston pin.
2. Inspect the pin for chrome flaking, wear or discoloration from overheating.
3. Inspect the bore in the small end of the connecting rod (**Figure 92**). Check for scoring, uneven wear, and discoloration from overheating.
4. Lubricate the piston pin and slide it into the connecting rod. Slowly rotate the pin and check for radial play (**Figure 93**). If play is detectable, one or both of the parts are worn. Kawasaki does not provide specifications for the pin diameter or connecting rod bore. Therefore, if neither part has obvious wear, have the pin diameter compared to the diameter of a new pin. If the pin is worn, replace the pin and recheck for play in the connecting rod. If play still exists, replace the rod.
5. Lubricate the piston pin and slide it into the piston bores. Slowly rotate the pin and check for radial play. If play is detectable, one or both of the parts are worn. Kawasaki does not provide specifications for the pin diameter or piston pin bore. Therefore, if neither part has obvious wear, have the pin and piston pin bore dimensions compared to the dimensions of new parts. Replace worn parts.

Piston Ring Inspection/Removal

The piston is fitted with two compression rings and an oil control ring assembly. The oil ring assembly consists of two side rails and an expander ring.

1. Check the piston ring-to-ring groove clearance as follows:
   a. Clean the rings and grooves so accurate measurements can be made with a flat feeler gauge.
   b. Press the top ring into the piston groove.
   c. Insert a flat feeler gauge between the ring and groove (**Figure 94**). Record the measurement.

Repeat this step at other points around the piston. Replace the rings if any measurement exceeds the service limit in **Table 2**. If excessive clearance remains after new rings are installed, replace the piston.

  d. Repeat substeps b and c for the second compression ring. The oil control ring is not measured.

2. Remove the top and second rings with a ring expander (**Figure 95**) or by hand (**Figure 96**).

  a. Spread the rings only enough to clear the piston.

  b. As each ring is removed, check that the top mark is visible. The top ring and the second ring should be marked with R. If necessary, mark the rings on their top surface if they will be reinstalled. The oil control ring rails are not marked.

3. Remove the oil ring assembly by first removing the top rail, followed by the bottom rail. Remove (by hand) the expander ring last.

4. Clean and inspect the piston as described in *Piston Inspection* (this section).

5. Measure the thickness of the top and second rings (**Figure 97**). Replace all the rings if any measurement exceeds the service limit listed in **Table 2**.

6. Inspect the end gap of the top and second rings as follows:

  a. Insert a ring into the bottom of the cylinder. Use the piston to square the ring to the cylinder wall. Push the ring about 10 mm (0.4 in.) into the cylinder.

  b. Measure the end gap with a feeler gauge (**Figure 98**). Replace all the rings if any measurement exceeds the service limit listed in **Table 2**. Always replace rings as a set. If new rings are to be installed, gap the new rings after the cylinder has been serviced. If the new ring gap is too narrow, carefully widen the gap using a fine-cut file as shown in **Figure 99**. Work slow and measure often.

7. Roll each ring around its piston groove (**Figure 100**) and check for binding or snags. Repair minor damage with a fine-cut file.

Piston Ring Installation

If new piston rings will be installed, the cylinder must be honed. This is necessary to deglaze and crosshatch the cylinder surface. The newly honed surface is important in providing lubrication pockets for the new rings, helping them seat and seal against the cylinder. A dealership or machine shop can hone the cylinder for a minimal cost. Refer to *Cylinder Inspection* in this chapter to determine if the cylinder should be honed and reused. If the cylinder needs to be overbored, a larger piston and rings have to be installed.

1. Check that the piston and rings are clean and dry. When installing, spread the rings only enough to clear the piston.

2. Install the rings as follows:

  a. Install the oil ring expander in the bottom groove, followed by the bottom rail and top rail. The ends of the expander must of overlap.

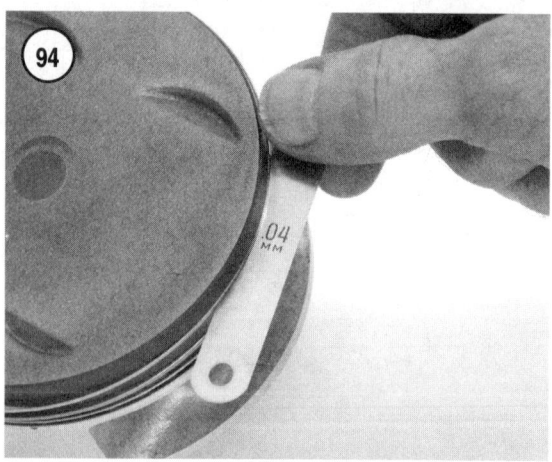

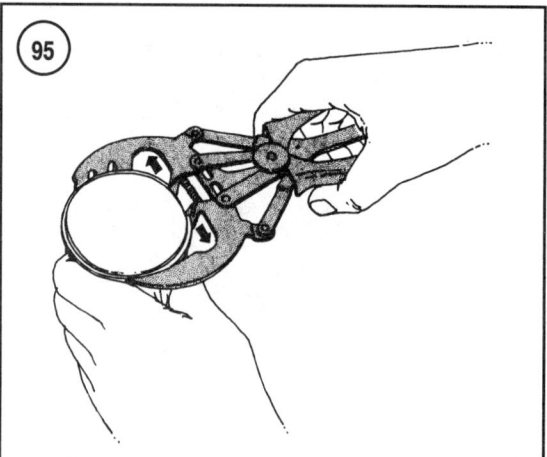

ENGINE TOP END

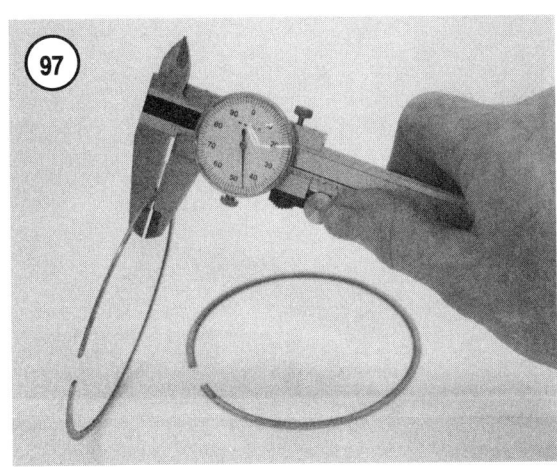

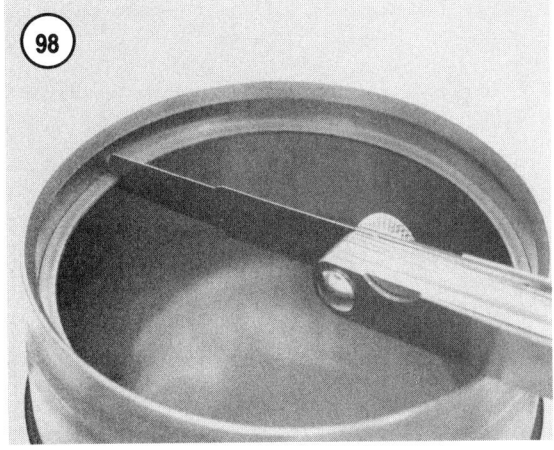

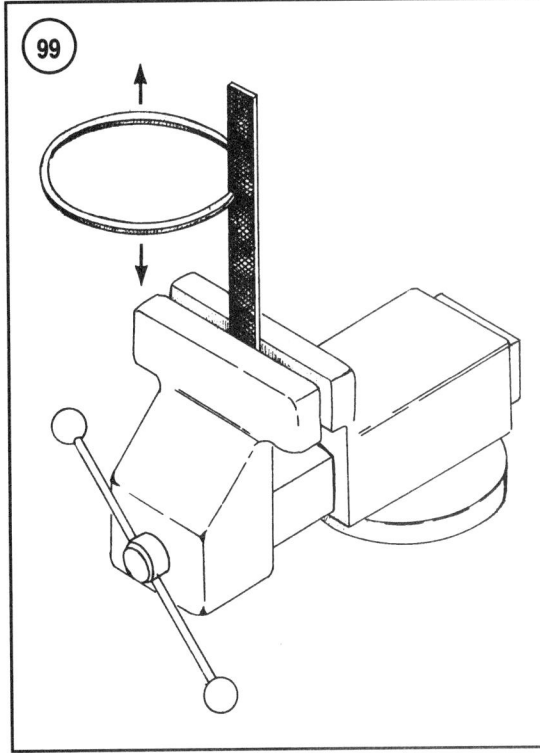

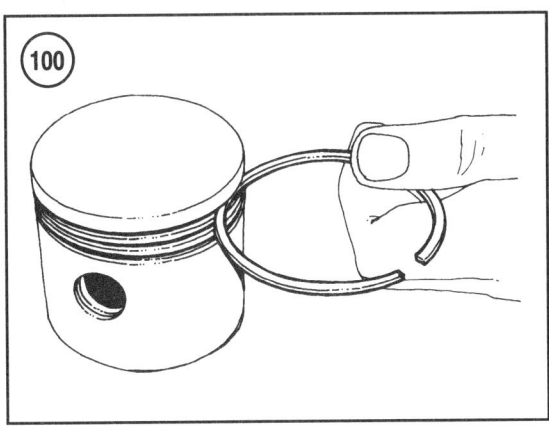

The rails can be installed in either position and direction.

b. Install the second ring. Check that the R mark faces up.
c. Install the top ring. Check that the R mark faces up.

3. Check that all rings rotate freely in their grooves.

Piston Installation

1. Install the piston rings onto the piston as described in this section.
2. Check that all parts are clean and ready to be installed. Always use new circlips when installing the piston.

CAUTION
Never install used circlips. Severe engine damage could occur. Circlips fatigue and distort when they are removed, even though they appear reusable.

3. Install a new circlip into the left piston pin boss. Rotate the ends of the circlip away from the gap. By installing the circlip in the left boss first, the remaining circlip can be installed at the right side of the engine, where work space is better.
4. Lubricate the following components with engine oil:
   a. Piston pin.
   b. Piston pin bores.
   c. Connecting rod bore.

CAUTION
The piston must be installed correctly. Failure to install the piston correctly can lead to severe engine damage.

5. Start the piston pin into the open pin bore, then place the piston over the connecting rod. The arrow/mark stamped on the piston crown (**Figure 101**) must point forward.

6. Align the piston with the rod, then slide the pin through the rod and into the other piston bore.

7. Install a new circlip into the right piston pin boss. Rotate the ends of the circlip away from the gap.

8. Stagger the piston ring gaps on the piston as shown in **Figure 83**. Note that the top and second ring gaps are opposite one another, pointing to the front and back of the piston. The oil ring rails are about 30° apart, pointing to the sides.

9. Install the cylinder as described in this chapter.

10. Refer to Chapter Five for break-in procedures.

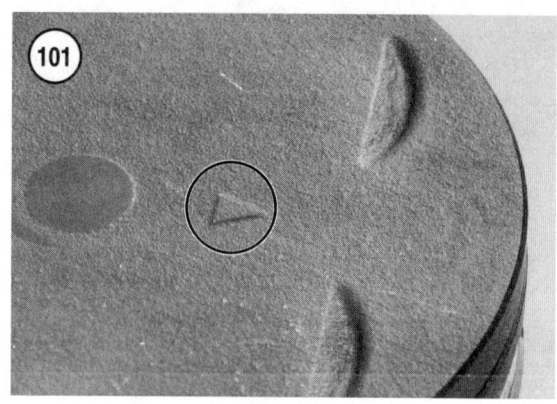

Table 1 GENERAL ENGINE SPECIFICATIONS

Engine type	Four-stroke, single-cylinder
Valve system	Chain-driven DOHC 4-valve
Cooling system	Liquid cooled
Lubrication system	Forced pressure, wet sump
Engine displacement	651 cc (39.7 cu. in.)
Bore and stroke	100.0 x 83.0 mm (3.94 x 3.27 in.)
Compression ratio	9.8:1
Valve timing	
Intake valve opens	19° BTDC
Intake valve closes	69° ABDC
Intake valve duration	268°
Exhaust valve opens	57° BBDC
Exhaust valve closes	37° ATDC
Exhaust valve duration	274°

Table 2 ENGINE TOP END SERVICE SPECIFICATIONS

Item	Standard mm (in.)	Service Limit mm (in.)
Camshaft		
Chain length (20 links/21 pins)	127.0-127.4 (5.0-5.02)	128.9 (5.07)
Bearing oil clearance	0.020-0.062 (0.0008-0.0024)	0.15 (0.0059)
Bearing inside diameter	23.000-23.021 (0.9055-0.9063)	23.08 (0.9086)
Journal outside diameter	22.959-22.980 (0.9039-0.9047)	22.93 (0.9027)
Lobe height		
Intake	36.742-36.856 (1.4465-1.4510)	36.64 (1.443)
Exhaust	36.243-36.357 (1.4269-1.4314)	36.14 (1.423)
Cylinder compression	529-853 kPa (77-124 psi)	–
Cylinder head warp limit	–	0.05 (0.002)
(continued)		

ENGINE TOP END

Table 2 ENGINE TOP END SERVICE SPECIFICATIONS (continued)

Item	Standard mm (in.)	Service Limit mm (in.)
Cylinder bore		
Inside diameter	100.000-100.012 (3.9370-3.9375)	100.10 (3.9409)
Piston-to-cylinder clearance	0.043-0.070 (0.0017-0.0028)	– –
Piston		
Mark direction	Arrow facing forward	
Outside diameter measurement point	5.0 (0.2) from bottom	–
Outside diameter	99.942-99.957 (3.9347-3.9353)	99.79 (3.9290)
Ring groove width		
Top ring	1.22-1.24 (0.0480-0.0488)	1.32 (0.0520)
Second ring	1.21-1.23 (0.0476-0.0484)	1.31 (0.0520)
Piston rings		
Thickness (top and second)	1.17-1.19 (0.0461-0.0469)	1.10 (0.0433)
Ring-to-groove clearance		
Top ring	0.03-0.07 (0.0012-0.0028)	0.17 (0.0067)
Second ring	0.02-0.06 (0.0008-0.0024)	0.16 (0.0063)
End gap		
Top ring		
Early 2008	0.20-0.35 (0.0079-0.0138)	0.7 (0.0276)
Late 2008-on	0.30-0.40 mm (0.012-0.016 in.)	0.7 mm (0.0276 in.)
Second ring	0.40-0.55 (0.0158-0.0217)	0.9 (0.0354)
Valve clearance		
Intake	0.10-0.20 (0.004-0.008)	
Exhaust	0.15-0.25 (0.006-0.010)	
Valve head thickness (margin above seat)		
Intake	1.0 (0.040)	0.5 (0.020)
Exhaust	1.0 (0.040)	0.7 (0.028)
Valve seat		
Angle	45°	
Width	0.8-1.2 (0.031-0.047)	
Intake outside diameter	36.9-37.1 (1.453-1.461)	
Exhaust outside diameter	31.9-32.1 (1.256-1.264)	
Valve stem		
Intake outside diameter	6.965-6.980 (0.2742-0.2748)	6.95 (0.2736)
Exhaust outside diameter	6.955-6.970 (0.2738-0.2744)	6.94 (0.2732)
Runout (total indicator reading)	0.0-0.01 (0.0-0.0004)	0.05 (0.0020)
Valve guide inside diameter		
Intake and exhaust	7.000-7.015 (0.2756-0.2762)	7.08 (0.2787)
Valve spring free length		
Inner intake and exhaust	37.6 (1.48)	36.2 (1.43)
Outer intake and exhaust	40.5 (1.59)	39.0 (1.54)

Table 3 ENGINE TOP END TORQUE SPECIFICATIONS

	N•m	in.-lb.	ft.-lb.
Camshaft cap bolts	12	106	–
Camshaft sprocket bolts	49	–	36
Coolant temperature sending unit	15	–	11
Cylinder head bolts*			
10 mm			
First step	31	–	23
Second step	62	–	46
Cylinder head cover bolts	8	71	–
Cylinder 6 mm mounting bolt	10	89	–
Cylinder mounting nuts	25	–	18.5
Exhaust pipe nuts	21	–	15.5
Exhaust pipe mounting bolt	21	–	15.5
Muffler bolts	21	–	15.5
Oil pipe			
Banjo bolts	20	–	15
Retainer bolt	8.8	78	–
Rotor bolt plug	2.5	22	–
Spark plug	14	–	10
Timing plug	2.5	22	–
Upper cam chain guide			
Inner bolt	8.8	78	–
Outer bolts	10	89	–
Upper engine mounting bolts	25	–	18.5
Vacuum pipe mounting bolt			
5 mm	5.9	52	–
6 mm	9.8	87	–

*Refer to text for sequence.

CHAPTER FIVE

ENGINE LOWER END

This chapter provides procedures for servicing or removing the following lower end components:
1. Cam chain and lower guide.
2. Left crankcase cover.
3. Engine balancer.
4. Crankcase, bearings and seals.
5. Crankshaft and connecting rod.

To access and service some of these components, the engine must be removed from the frame, and all assemblies attached to the crankcase taken off.

ENGINE

The following removal and installation procedure outlines the basic steps necessary to remove the engine from the frame. Depending on the planned level of disassembly, consider removing top end components, and those located in the crankcase covers, while the engine remains in the frame. Since the frame keeps the engine stabilized, tight nuts and bolts are easier to remove if the engine is held steady. Also, if the actual engine problem is unknown, it may be discovered in an assembly other than the crankcase.

During engine removal, make note of mounting bolt directions and how cables and wire harnesses are routed. Refer to the appropriate chapters for removal, inspection and installation procedures for the various components in the engine top end and crankcase covers.

Removal and Installation

1. Support the motorcycle so it is stable and level with the rear wheel off the ground.
2. If possible, perform a compression test (Chapter Three) and leakdown test (Chapter Two) before dismantling the engine.
3. Drain the engine oil (Chapter Three).
4. Remove the skid plate, side covers, seat and fuel tank (Chapter Fifteen).
5. Disconnect the battery leads (Chapter Nine).
6. Remove the radiator (Chapter Ten).
7. Remove the coolant reserve tank (Chapter Ten).
8. Remove the front footpegs.
9. Remove the shift lever.
10. Remove the rear brake pedal (Chapter Fourteen).
11. Disconnect the clutch cable at the engine (Chapter Six).
12. Remove the exhaust pipe (Chapter Four).
13. Remove the starter relay and mounting bracket (Chapter Nine).
14. Remove the starter (Chapter Nine).
15. Remove the carburetor (Chapter Eight).
16. Remove the spark plug lead and water temperature sending unit lead.

17. Detach the vacuum switch valve hose (A, **Figure 1**).
18. Detach the vacuum switch valve hose (B, **Figure 1**) from the cylinder head cover pipe.
19. Disconnect the regulator/recitifier connector (C, **Figure 1**).
20. Open any main wiring harness clamps that obstruct engine removal.
21. Remove the ignition coil (Chapter Nine) and mounting bracket.
22. Disconnect the horn connectors.
23. Remove the right, lower fairing mounting bracket.
24. Remove the sprocket guard and drive chain (Chapter Eleven).
25. Disconnect the stator, crankshaft position sensor and neutral switch wiring harness connectors (Chapter Nine).
26. Remove the crankcase breather hose.
27. Inspect the engine and verify that it is ready for removal. If desired, remove any additional components that will make engine removal and handling easier.
28. Remove the engine mounting bolts and brackets as follows:

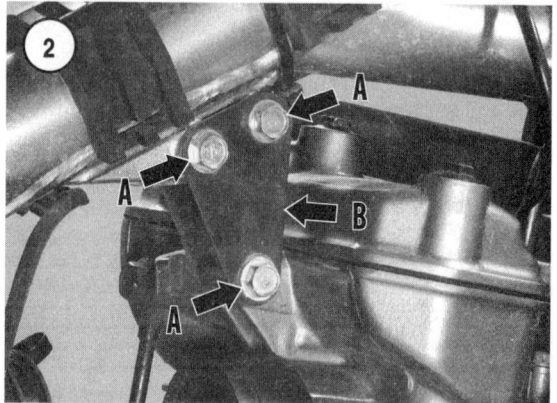

WARNING
When removing the bolts, be aware that the engine may shift in the frame. Keep hands protected and check the stability of the motorcycle and engine after removing each set of bolts. Get assistance when removing the engine from the frame.

a. Remove the bolts (A, **Figure 2**) and upper mounting brackets (B).
b. Remove the bolts (A, **Figure 3**) and lower mounting brackets (B).
c. Remove the rear mounting bolt (A, **Figure 4**).
d. Remove the swing arm pivot nut (B, **Figure 4**). Do not remove the pivot bolt at this time.

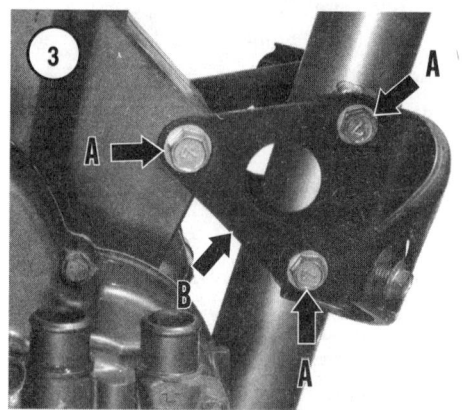

WARNING
*In the following step, do not completely remove the swing arm pivot bolt from the frame. Pull the bolt (**Figure 5**) out just far enough to remove the engine. Complete removal allows the swing arm to fall.*

e. Pull the swing arm pivot bolt out so it clears the engine, then remove the engine from the frame.
f. Push the swing arm pivot bolt back into the frame.
g. Clean and inspect the frame surrounding the engine. Check for cracks and damage, particularly at welded joints.

ENGINE LOWER END

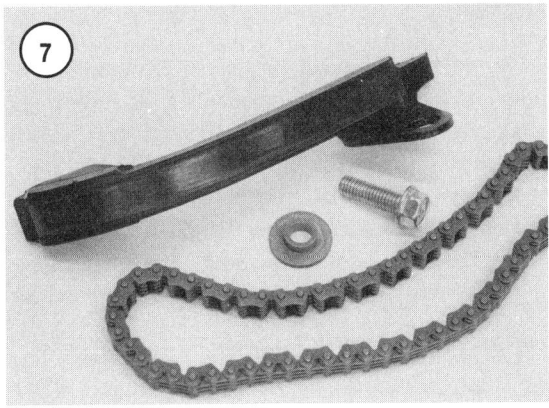

29. Refer to the procedures in this chapter for servicing the crankcase assembly.

30. Reverse this procedure to install the engine. Note the following:
   a. If the chain is endless (no master link), check that it is routed over the swing arm pivot before installing the swing arm pivot bolt.

NOTE
If the engine top end is not installed when the engine is mounted in the frame, do not tighten any mounting nuts until the upper mounting brackets have been installed and aligned with their mounting points.

   b. Install the engine mounting brackets, bolts and nuts. Finger-tighten all nuts before applying final torque. Note the original direction of the bolts during installation. Tighten all 8-mm mounting bolts first. Then, tighten the 10-mm mounting bolts. Finally, torque the swing arm pivot bolt. Refer to **Table 2** for the torque specifications.
   c. Carefully route electrical wires so they are not pinched or in contact with surfaces that get hot.
   d. Apply dielectric grease to electrical connections before reconnecting.
   e. If assemblies have been removed from the top end or crankcase covers, install those components. Refer to the appropriate chapters for inspection and installation procedures.
   f. Fill the engine with engine oil (Chapter Three).
   g. Fill the cooling system with coolant (Chapter Three).
   h. Adjust the clutch free play (Chapter Three).
   i. Tighten the front footpeg mounting bolts to 25 N•m (18 ft.-lb.).
   j. Check throttle cable adjustment (Chapter Three).
   k. Check rear brake pedal height. (Chapter Three).
   l. Check chain adjustment (Chapter Three).
   m. Start the engine and check for leaks.
   n. Check throttle and clutch operation.
   o. If the engine top end has been rebuilt, perform a compression check. Record the result and compare it to future checks.
   p. Read the *Engine Break-In* procedure in this chapter.

CAM CHAIN AND LOWER GUIDE

If the engine balancer assembly will be removed, the cam chain and lower guide can be removed during that procedure. Use the following procedure when only the cam chain and lower guide need to be removed.

Removal/Inspection/Installation

1. Remove the camshafts, and lift the cam chain off the camshaft sprockets (Chapter Four).
2. Remove the alternator cover and rotor (Chapter Nine).
3. Remove the rear cam chain guide (A, **Figure 6**) and the lower cam chain guide (B). If necessary, rotate the crankshaft to access the bolt behind the front left balancer weight.

4. Remove the cam chain from the sprocket.
5. Inspect the cam chain and guide (**Figure 7**).
   a. Pull the cam chain tight and measure a 20-link span (21 pins). Refer to **Table 1** for specifications. Check several lengths of the chain.
   b. Inspect the chain guide for wear on its face.
6. Reverse the removal procedure to install the cam chain and guides. Note the following:
   a. Check that the shouldered spacer seats in the cam chain guide. The guide should pivot on the spacer.
   b. Apply threadlock to the guide bolt threads.
   c. Tighten the rear cam chain and lower cam chain guide bolts to the specifications listed in **Table 2**.

LEFT CRANKCASE COVER

Removal/Installation

The left crankcase cover is located between the alternator cover and left crankcase.

1. Remove the alternator cover, starter drive gears and rotor (Chapter Nine). If the crankcase halves will be disassembled, also remove the starter (Chapter Nine).
2. Remove the tensioner bolt and shaft lever from the balancer tensioner shaft (**Figure 8**).
3. Remove the nine bolts (**Figure 9**) from the perimeter of the crankcase cover.
4. Remove the gasket and two dowels behind the cover.
5. Inspect the parts for damage. To inspect the tensioner bolt and balancer tensioner shaft lever, refer to the inspection procedures in *Engine Balancer* (this chapter).
6. Reverse this procedure to install the left crankcase cover, tensioner bolt and shaft lever. Note the following:
   a. Install the lever so the weld joint faces in.
   b. Using a crossing pattern, evenly tighten the left crankcase cover bolts in several steps to 8.8 N•m (78 in.-lb.).

ENGINE BALANCER

The engine uses a rotating balancer assembly to dampen the vibration that is inherent to a single-cylinder engine. The three balancer weights are shaft-mounted and synchronized with the crankshaft. The balancer shaft at the front of the engine has a weight at each end of the shaft, while the rear balancer shaft has a single weight located between the crankcase halves. Both balancer shafts are chain-driven by a sprocket on the left end of the crankshaft.

Removal

The following procedure details the complete removal of the balancer components from the engine crankcase. Refer to **Figure 10**.
1. Remove the right crankcase cover (Chapter Six).
2. Remove the alternator cover (Chapter Nine).
3. Remove the right balancer weight as follows:
   a. Flatten the bent lockwasher (A, **Figure 11**) so the nut (B) can be removed from the balancer shaft.
   b. Hold the rotor with a rotor holder tool. The tool can be braced against the bottom of the left footpeg. Remove the nut and lockwasher securing the right balancer weight (C, **Figure 11**). Remove the weight and spacer from the shaft.
4. Remove the left crankcase cover, tensioner bolt and shaft lever as described in this chapter.
5. Remove the balancer chain tensioner assembly as follows:
   a. Remove the tensioner spring (**Figure 12**). If the spring must be used again, do not score, scratch or bend the spring ends. Fracturing can occur.
   b. Rotate the spring lever counterclockwise to relieve chain tension, then carefully pull the

ENGINE LOWER END

ENGINE BALANCER

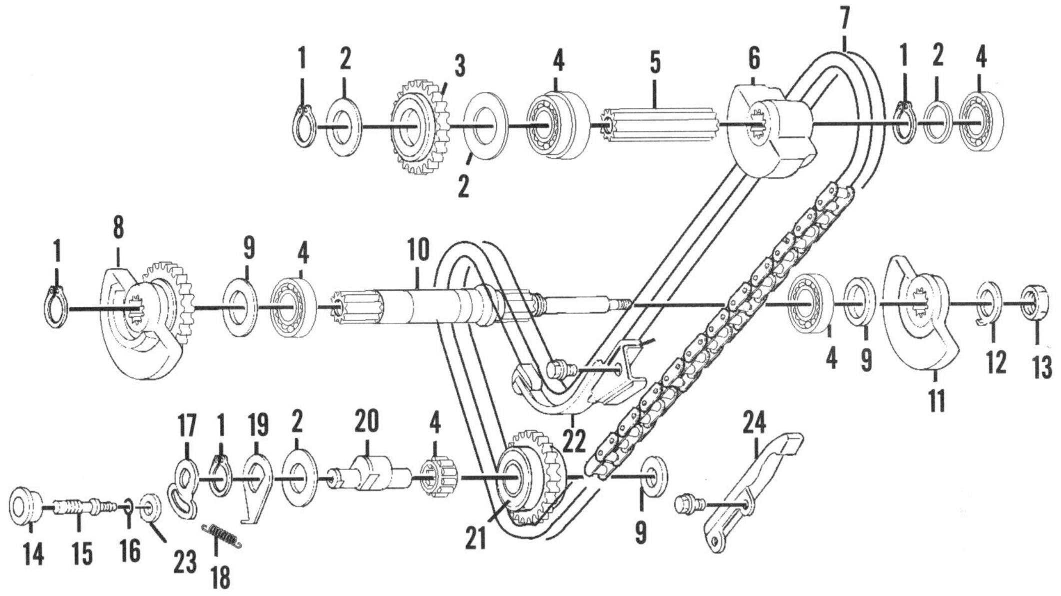

1. Snap ring
2. Washer
3. Rear balancer sprocket
4. Bearing
5. Rear balancer shaft
6. Rear balancer weight
7. Balancer chain
8. Left balancer weight/sprocket
9. Spacer
10. Front balancer shaft
11. Right balancer weight
12. Lockwasher
13. Nut
14. Plug
15. Tensioner bolt
16. O-ring
17. Shaft lever
18. Tensioner spring
19. Spring lever
20. Tensioner shaft
21. Tensioner sprocket
22. Lower cam chain guide
23. Washer (2012)
24. Balancer chain guide

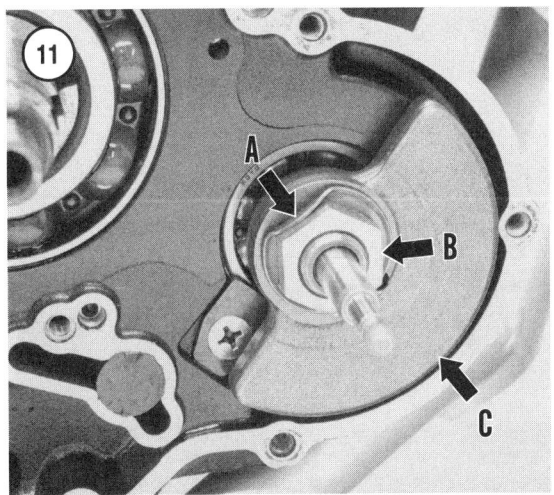

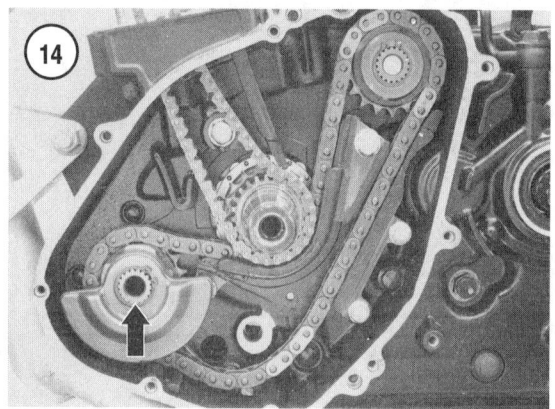

tensioner shaft assembly (A, **Figure 13**) from the crankcase.

CAUTION
If the spacer falls, it can roll into the crankcase opening located below the tensioner shaft bore. If this occurs, use a magnetic tool or wire to retrieve the part.

  c. Keep the opposite end of the shaft tilted up, to prevent dropping the spacer (B, **Figure 13**), located behind the sprocket.

6. Remove the snap ring (**Figure 14**) from the left end of the front balancer shaft. Remove the weight/sprocket and spacer.
7. Remove the five bolts (**Figure 15**) securing the lower cam chain guide and balancer chain guides.
8. Remove the cam chain (A, **Figure 16**).
9. Remove the snap ring (B, **Figure 16**), washer(s) (C), rear balancer sprocket (D) and balancer chain (E).
10. Refer to *Crankcase* in this chapter to remove the balancer shafts (**Figure 17**) located between the crankcase halves.
11. Inspect the complete balancer assembly as described in this section.

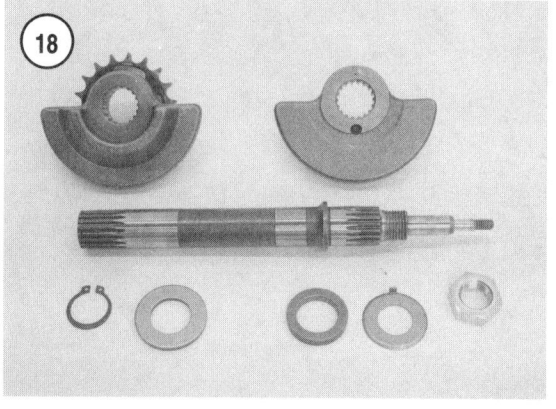

ENGINE LOWER END

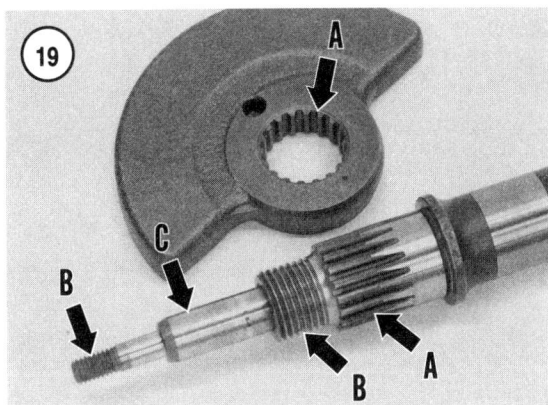

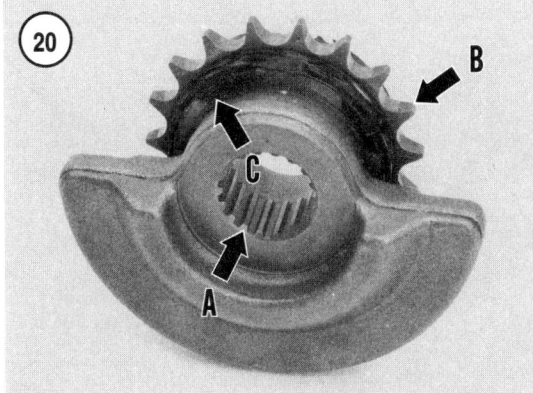

Inspection

During inspection, replace any parts that are visibly damaged or worn. Refer to **Figure 10**.

1. Inspect the front balancer shaft assembly (**Figure 18**).
    a. Inspect the spacers and locknut.
    b. Inspect the splines (A, **Figure 19**), threads (B), snap ring groove and polished surfaces (C) on the shaft and right weight.
    c. Inspect the splines (A, **Figure 20**), sprocket teeth (B) and rubber mounting (C) on the left sprocket. Replace parts that are fatigued, worn or missing.
    d. Install a new snap ring and lockwasher during assembly.
2. Inspect the rear balancer shaft assembly (**Figure 21**).
    a. Inspect the spacers.
    b. Inspect the splines, snap ring grooves and polished surface on the shaft.
    c. Inspect the splines in the weight.
    d. Inspect the splines, sprocket teeth and rubber mounting on the sprocket. Replace parts that are fatigued, worn or missing.
    e. Install a new snap ring at the left end of the shaft during assembly.
    f. Install a new snap ring on the right end of the shaft at this time. Install the snap ring so the sharp edge faces in (toward balancer weight).
3. Inspect the tensioner assembly (**Figure 22**).
    a. Inspect the spacer and washer(s).
    b. Install a new O-ring onto the tensioner bolt.
    c. Inspect the fit of the bearing (A, **Figure 23**) in the sprocket (B) and on the tensioner shaft (C). The shaft and sprocket bore should be smooth, and the bearing should fit firmly between the parts. The sprocket teeth and rubber mounting must be in good condition.
    d. Assemble the tensioner shaft, bearing, sprocket and spring lever (**Figure 24**). The lever should fit flat and firmly to the shaft. The shaft should

CHAPTER FIVE

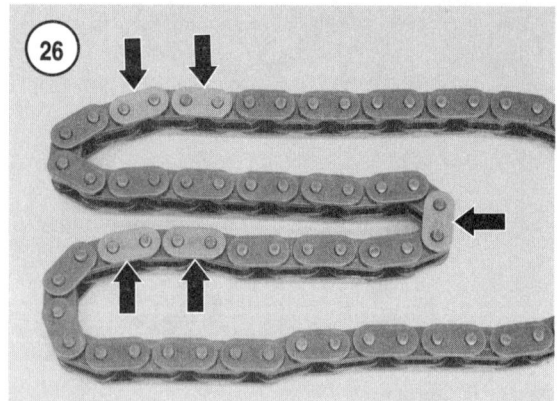

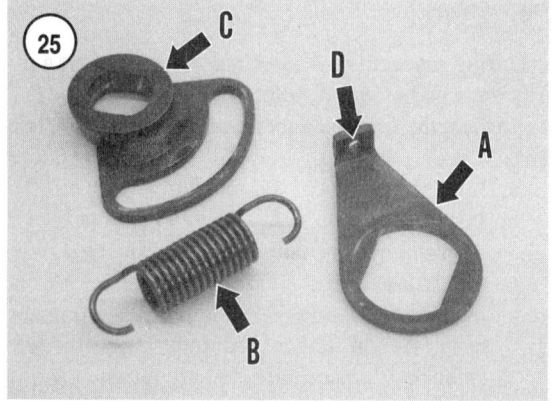

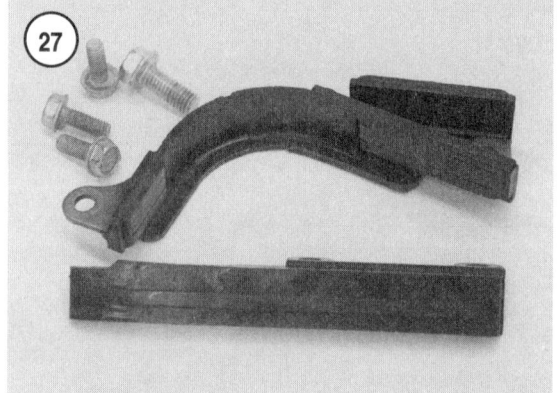

rotate freely and smoothly when the lever is operated. The sprocket should spin freely and smoothly on the shaft.

4. Inspect the spring lever (A, **Figure 25**), spring (B) and shaft lever (C) for the following specific damage.
   a. Inspect the weld on the shaft lever for breakage.
   b. Inspect the spring hole (D, **Figure 25**) in the spring lever. The hole should be smooth with no sharp edges that could damage the spring ends.
   c. Inspect the spring ends and coils for damage. Any scratches, scoring or abnormal bends of the spring wire could weaken the spring, causing it to break. Preferably, install a new spring whenever the tensioner assembly is removed.
   d. If other damage is evident, replace the damaged part(s).

5. Inspect the balancer chain.
   a. Pull the chain tight and measure a 20-link span (21 pins). Refer to **Table 1** for balancer chain specifications. Repeat the check on several lengths of the chain.
   b. Note the positions of the silver chain links (**Figure 26**). These links are used to position and synchronize the balancer shaft assemblies

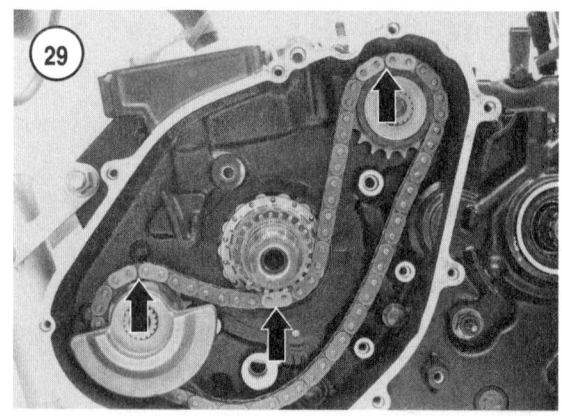

ENGINE LOWER END

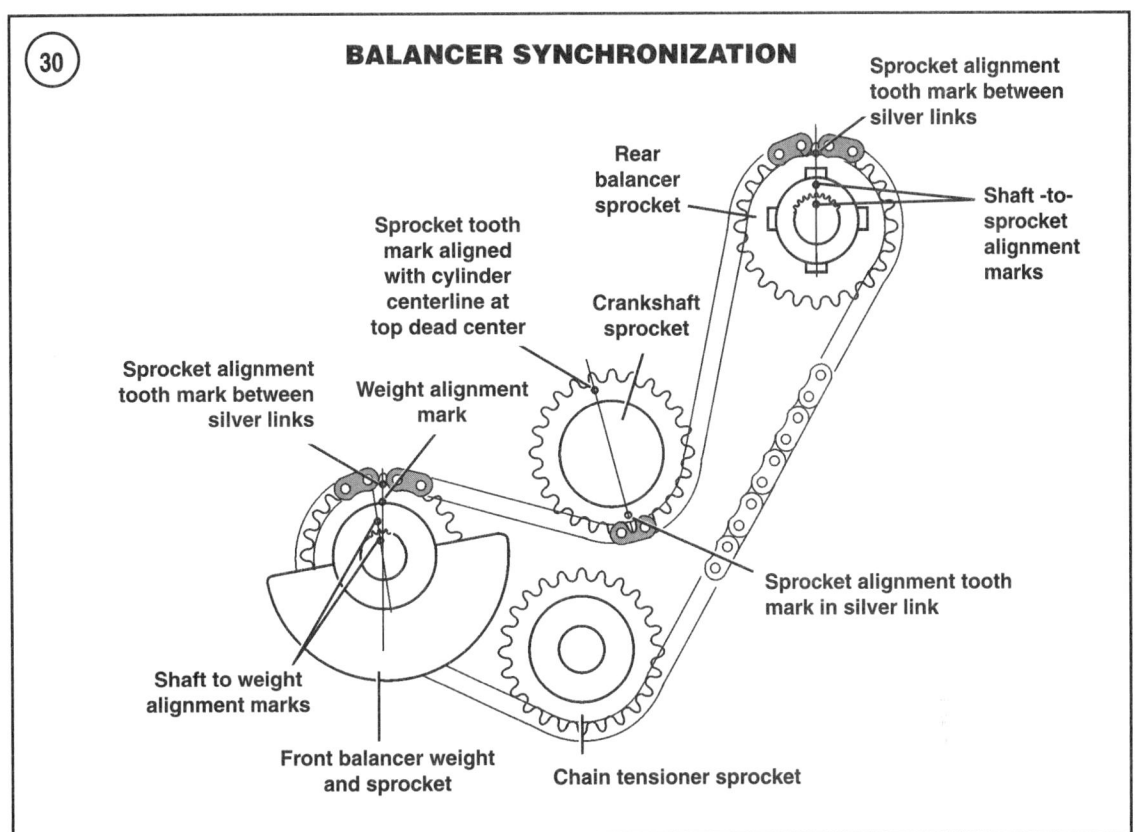

with the crankshaft. The silver links must face out when the chain is installed.
6. Inspect the chain guides (**Figure 27**) for wear.

Installation/Synchronization

During assembly, the sprockets and weights must be properly aligned on their respective shafts (**Figure 28**). In addition, the crankshaft and sprocket/shaft assemblies must be aligned and engaged with the proper silver links of the balancer chain (**Figure 29**). Follow the procedure closely and check all alignments often as the balancer is assembled. During assembly, lubricate all components with engine oil. Refer to **Figure 10** as needed.

1. Assemble the crankcase halves as described in *Crankcase* in this chapter.
2. Install the following component(s):
   a. Install the spacer on the left end of the front shaft.
   b. Install the washer on the rear shaft.
3. Position the crankshaft at top dead center. The alignment mark(s) on the crankshaft sprocket should be parallel to the cylinder centerline.
4. Orient the balancer chain and identify the silver links (**Figure 26**). There are two pairs of silver links, with a single silver link placed between the pairs. The silver links are used to position and synchronize the balancer shaft assemblies with the crankshaft. The silver links must face out when the chain is installed.
5. Position and align the balancer chain on the sprockets as follows. Refer to **Figure 30** to verify proper installation.
   a. Identify the pair of silver links to the right of the single silver link. These links will be engaged with the rear sprocket.
   b. Identify the alignment tooth mark on the rear sprocket.
   c. Align and engage the rear sprocket alignment tooth mark with the chain, then install the sprocket onto the shaft. The sprocket alignment tooth mark must be between the silver links. If installed correctly, the shaft-to-sprocket alignment marks will also be aligned between the silver links (**Figure 31**).

NOTE
During chain routing and alignment with the crankshaft and front balancer shaft, the shafts may rotate slightly. As long as the chain remains seated in the aligned sprocket(s), overall alignment is not affected.

d. Route the chain under the crankshaft, engaging the single silver link with the alignment tooth mark on the crankshaft sprocket (**Figure 32**).

e. Align and engage the front sprocket alignment tooth mark with the chain. The mark must be between the silver links. If installed correctly, the weight alignment mark on top of the weight will also be aligned between the silver links (**Figure 33**). Do not refer to the marks aligning the shaft and weight.

6. If necessary, slowly rotate the crankshaft and balancer shafts back into the top dead center position.

7. Check that all sprocket alignments are correct. If necessary, reposition any sprockets that are not aligned at top dead center.

8. Install the washer and a new snap ring onto the rear balancer shaft. Install the snap ring with the sharp edge facing out.

9. Install a new snap ring onto the front balancer shaft. Install the snap ring with the sharp edge facing in.

10. Engage the cam chain with the crankshaft sprocket, then route the chain toward the top of the engine. Use wire to secure the chain and to minimize slack.

11. Install the lower cam chain guide and balancer chain guides. Note the following:

   a. Check that the shouldered spacer seats in the cam chain guide. The guide should pivot on the spacer.

   b. If the front balancer weight must be rotated to install the chain guide and bolt at the crankshaft, apply tension to the lower part of the balancer chain. If the chain does not remain seated on the sprockets, balancer alignments may be lost. Recheck balancer alignments after installing the guides.

   c. Apply threadlock to the bolt threads.

   d. Tighten the bolts to the specifications in **Table 2**.

12. Install the balancer chain tensioner assembly (**Figure 34**). Note the following:

   a. Install the sprocket with the wide shoulder facing out.

   b. Install the spring lever with the tensioner spring hole facing out.

   c. If possible, install the spring by hand. If pliers must be used, avoid excessive stretching, scoring or damage to the ends of the spring.

   d. Recheck balancer alignments after installing the tensioner.

13. Install the right balancer weight as follows:

   a. Temporarily install the rotor and finger-tighten the rotor nut.

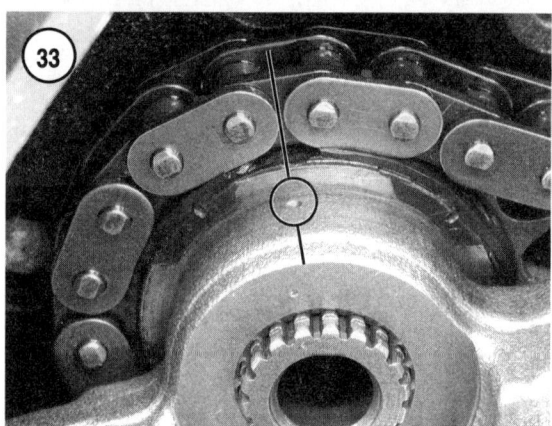

   b. Install the spacer and weight onto the shaft. Check that the marks on the weight and shaft are aligned (**Figure 35**).

   c. Install a new lockwasher, engaging the tab on the washer with the weight.

   d. Hold the rotor with the rotor holder tool. The holder tool can be braced against the top of the left footpeg. Install the locknut and tighten to 44 N•m (32 ft.-lb.).

   e. Bend one side of the washer (A, **Figure 11**) against the nut.

   f. Remove the rotor and continue assembly.

ENGINE LOWER END

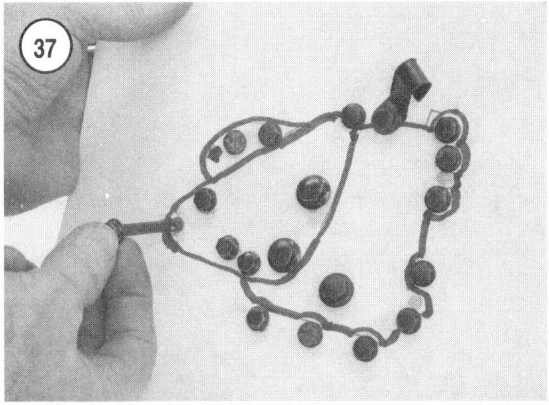

14. Install the left crankcase cover, tensioner bolt and shaft lever as described in this chapter.
15. Install the rotor, starter drive gears and alternator cover (Chapter Nine). If the crankcase halves were disassembled, also install the starter (Chapter Nine).
16. Install the right crankcase cover (Chapter Six).

CRANKCASE

The following procedures detail the disassembly and reassembly of the crankcase. When the two halves of the crankcase are disassembled, or split, the crankshaft, balancer shafts and transmission assemblies can be removed for inspection and repair. Before proceeding with this procedure, remove the engine from the frame as described in this chapter. All assemblies located in the crankcase covers must be removed. It may be easier to remove these assemblies with the engine in the frame. The engine will remain steady during the disassembly process.

The crankcase halves are made of cast aluminum alloy. Do not hammer or pry on the cases. The cases will fracture or break. The cases are aligned at the joint by dowels, and joined with liquid sealant.

The crankshaft is made of two full-circle flywheels, press-fitted to the crankpin. The assembly is supported at the left end by a roller bearing, and at the right end by a ball bearing. A needle bearing fitted at the large end supports the connecting rod.

Disassembly

Any reference to the left or right side of the engine refers to the side of the engine as it is mounted in the frame-not on the workbench. As components are removed, keep the parts organized and clean. Leave the right case half facing down until all assemblies have been removed from the crankcase.

1. Place the engine on wooden blocks with the left side facing up (**Figure 36**).
2. Loosen the 13 bolts at the perimeter of the crankcase and the six bolts within the left crankcase cover area. Loosen each bolt 1/4 turn, working in a crossing pattern. Loosen the bolts until they can be removed by hand.

> *NOTE*
> *Since the bolt lengths vary, make a drawing of the crankcase shape on a piece of cardboard. Punch holes in the cardboard at the bolt locations. Insert each removed bolt into the corresponding hole in the template (**Figure 37**).*

3. Separate the crankcase halves as follows:

CAUTION
Pry the crankcase only at the notch. Do not pry the case halves on the mating surfaces. Damage to the crankcase halves will likely occur.

a. With the left side of the engine facing up, lightly pry the crankcase halves at the notch located at the back of the engine. The notch is between the bores for the swing arm bolt and rear engine mounting bolt. Pry slowly and only enough to break the seal between the crankcase halves. If necessary, use a heat gun to soften the joint sealant, making separation easier.
b. When the case seal breaks, raise and lower the left case half until it is fully released. Evenly lift the left case half from the right half (**Figure 38**).
c. Account for the two dowels between the case halves when the case halves are separated (**Figure 39**).

4. Remove the front balancer shaft (**Figure 40**).
5. Remove the rear balancer shaft and weight (**Figure 41**). Account for the shaft washer between the bearing and weight. Inspect the complete balancer assembly as described in this chapter.

CAUTION
Take extreme care when removing, handling and storing the crankshaft. Striking or dropping the crankshaft may cause misalignment or damage.

6. Remove the crankshaft assembly (**Figure 42**) from the crankcase. The crankshaft should free itself from the right bearing without the use of tools. Do not lift the crankshaft by the connecting rod. Inspect the crankshaft assembly and crankcase halves as described in this chapter.

CAUTION
Take extreme care when removing, handling and storing the transmission. Wrap and store the assembly until it is inspected. Do not expose the assembly to dirt or place it in an area where it could roll and fall to the floor.

7. Remove the transmission assembly from the crankcase as follows:
   a. Remove the two shift fork shafts (A, **Figure 43**).
   b. Remove the shift drum (**Figure 44**), disengaging it from the shift forks. If necessary, raise the transmission shafts slightly to disengage the forks from the shift drum.
   c. Remove the No. 1, No. 2 and No. 3 shift forks (**Figure 45**).

ENGINE LOWER END

42

43

44

45

d. Remove the input shaft (A, **Figure 46**) and output shaft (B) assemblies as a unit, keeping the gears meshed and the shafts upright.

e. Disassemble and inspect the transmission (Chapter Seven).

Assembly

1. Read the entire procedure to ensure that all tools, parts and supplies are on hand, as well as proper preparation of the crankcase halves. Follow these practices when assembling the crankcase:

   a. Check that all mating surfaces are smooth, clean and dry. Minor irregularities can be repaired with an oil stone. After thorough removal of the old sealant, clean all mating surfaces with a highly evaporative solvent, such as brake cleaner or electrical contact cleaner. The new sealant will not adhere to any oily surfaces.

   b. Lubricate the crankshaft, bearings and transmission assembly with engine oil.

   c. Lubricate seal lips with grease.

   d. To install the crankshaft, use the crankshaft installation jig (Kawasaki part No. 57001-1174). The tool can be ordered from a dealership. The tool (**Figure 47**) is adjusted to fit snugly between the flywheels, opposite the crankpin. As the crankcase halves are seated together, the tool prevents the flywheels from flexing or binding, causing misalignment of the flywheels.

   e. A liquid gasket sealant is required to seal the crankcase halves. Use Kawabond 5 or Yamabond 4; both are available at dealerships. These sealants are durable and can be submerged in oil. Kawabond 5 is thinner than Yamabond 4, and may be considerably more difficult to apply evenly.

   CAUTION
   Do not attempt to seal the cases with RTV silicone sealant, commonly found at auto parts stores. The sealant is inadequate for this application. Oil leakage and possible engine damage is likely to occur.

2. Place the right crankcase half on wooden blocks, with the open side of the case half facing up.

3. Install the transmission as follows:

   a. Mesh the input shaft and output shaft assemblies. Keeping the gears meshed and the shafts upright, insert the assembly into the case (**Figure 46**).

   b. Identify the shift forks (**Figure 45**). Shift forks No. 1 and No. 2 can be identified by the casting around the guide pins (**Figure 48**). These forks mate with the output shaft gears. Shift fork No. 1 mates with fourth gear and shift fork No. 2 mates with fifth gear. Shift fork No. 3 has a smaller claw diameter and only mates with third gear on the input shaft.

c. Install the shift forks, engaging them with the appropriate gears. Check that the guide pin on each fork points toward the shift drum area.

d. Install the shift drum (**Figure 44**), engaging it with the shift forks. If necessary, raise the transmission shafts slightly to engage the forks with the shift drum. Note that shift fork No. 1 and No. 3 share the same groove in the shift drum.

e. Align the bores in the shift forks, then insert the shift fork shafts (A, **Figure 43**) through the forks and into the case. Check that the shafts are fully seated in the case.

f. Check transmission operation. While turning the shafts and shift drum, observe the action of the shift drum and forks. The shift drum should move through its complete rotation and the forks should operate smoothly. Also check that both shafts turn freely when the shift drum is in the neutral position. The neutral position can be identified by the neutral switch indentation on the shift drum (B, **Figure 43**). When the indentation is at the 8 o'clock position, the transmission should be in neutral. Leave the transmission in neutral during engine assembly.

4. Install the crankshaft as follows:
   a. Insert the crankshaft installation jig between the crankshaft flywheels (**Figure 49**). Install the jig so it is opposite the crankpin and straddles the rod.
   b. Lubricate the crankshaft and case bearing.
   c. Position the crankshaft so the installation tool is aligned between the cylinder studs.
   d. Insert the crankshaft into the case bearing and hand-press the crankshaft into place. If the crankshaft does not fully seat, place supports under the right case half and around the bearing before applying additional pressure.
   e. After the crankshaft is seated, check that it moves freely. Temporarily remove the installation jig, then hold the connecting rod while rotating the crankshaft. After proper installation is verified, re-install the jig.

5. Install the rear balancer shaft and weight (**Figure 41**). Install the shaft with the splined end facing out. At the smooth end of the shaft, check that a new snap ring is installed and the washer is on the shaft. The washer is placed between the snap ring and bearing. If necessary, refer to **Figure 10** for proper orientation of the parts.

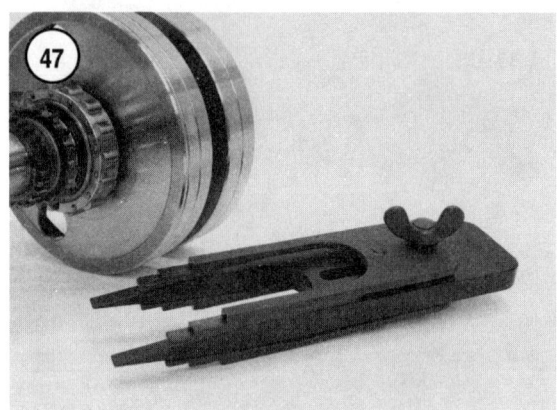

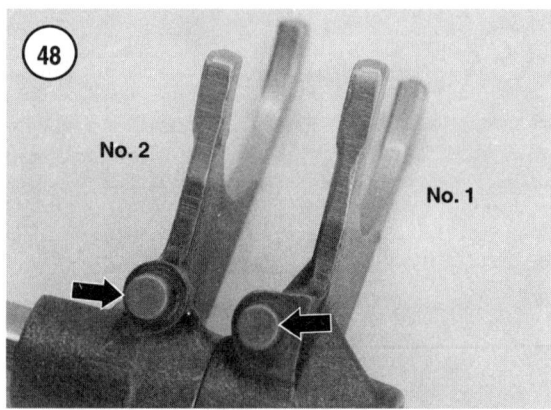

6. Install the front balancer shaft (**Figure 40**).
7. Install the left crankcase half onto the right half as follows:
   a. Check that all mating surfaces are clean and dry.
   b. On the right crankcase half, insert the two dowels and secure the crankshaft installation jig between the cylinder studs (**Figure 50**). Strong rubber bands work well.
   c. Apply liquid gasket sealant, such as Kawabond 5 or Yamabond 4, to all mating surfaces. This includes applying the sealant around all bolt holes. Use enough sealant to fill voids and pro-

ENGINE LOWER END

vide a continuous seal on the entire joint. Do not use excessive amounts of sealant.

d. Check that all shafts are aligned vertically, then fit the left case half squarely onto the right half.
e. If necessary tap the left case half with a mallet to evenly seat the case halves. Do not force the case halves. If the case halves are not seating, a shaft is probably misaligned with its bore. Lift the left case half and slightly move it side to side until the shaft(s) are properly guided.

8. Remove each crankcase bolt from the template and insert the bolts into the appropriate holes. Finger-tighten the bolts.
9. Using a crossing pattern, tighten the bolts equally in several passes to 8.8 N•m (78 in.-lb.).
10. Rotate the crankshaft and transmission shafts and check for smooth operation. If binding is evident, separate the case halves and correct the problem.
11. Allow the sealant to set for at least an hour before handling the crankcase.
12. Remove the installation jig from the crankshaft. If desired, leave the connecting rod supported by the rubber bands until they must be removed. Cover the cylinder opening to prevent the entry of parts or debris.
13. The crankcase assembly is ready for installation into the frame. If desired, top end components and those located in the side covers can be installed at this time. Refer to the appropriate chapters for inspection and installation procedures for the components in the engine top end and crankcase covers.

Inspection

1. From the left crankcase half, remove the oil seals from the output shaft bearing (A, **Figure 51**) and shift shaft bore (B). Remove the seals as described in this chapter.
2. Remove the neutral switch (C, **Figure 51**).
3. In the right crankcase half, remove the oil pickup tube (A, **Figure 52**) and breather tube (B). Do not remove the plugs (**Figure 53**) from the oil passages. The plugs should remain seated in the case.
4. Remove all sealant from the gasket surfaces. Avoid gouging or scratching the surfaces.
5. Clean the crankcase halves with solvent. Flush all bearings last, using clean solvent.

WARNING
Do not spin the bearings with compressed air. Damage could occur.

6. Dry the crankcase halves with compressed air.
7. Flush all passages with compressed air.

8. Inspect the bearings for roughness, pitting, galling and play. Replace any bearing that is not in good condition, or is loose in the crankcase bore. Always replace the opposing bearing at the same time.
9. Inspect the case halves for fractures around all mounting and bearing bosses, stiffening ribs and threaded holes. If repair is required, the crankcase should be taken to a dealership or machine shop that repairs precision aluminum castings.
10. Check all threaded holes for damage or sealant buildup. Clean threads with the correct size metric tap. Lubricate the tap with oil or aluminum cutting fluid.
11. After the seals and any bearings are replaced:
    a. Insert a new O-ring (C, **Figure 52**) into the groove on the oil pickup tub (A) and install the tube.
    b. Apply threadlock to the oil pickup tube bolts. Then, install and tighten the bolts to 8.8 N•m (78 in.-lb.).
    c. Install the breather tube (B, **Figure 52**).
    d. Install a new seal washer onto the neutral switch, then install and tighten the switch to 15 N•m (11 ft.-lb.).

SEAL REPLACEMENT

Output Shaft

> *CAUTION*
> *When prying out a seal, do not allow the end of the tool to touch the seal bore or snag the oil hole in the bore. Scratches in the bore will cause leakage and excessive prying can break the casting.*

1. Pry out the old seal (A, **Figure 51**). If necessary, place a block of wood on the case to improve leverage and protect the case from damage.
2. If a new bearing will be installed, replace the bearing before installing the new seal.
3. Clean the oil seal bore.
4. Apply grease to the lip and sides of the new seal.
5. To help prevent the new seal from being driven too deep, pass a wire tie (**Figure 54**) or similar object through the oil hole and leave it there until the new seal is installed.
6. Place the seal in the bore, with the closed side of the seal facing out. The seal must be square to the bore.
7. Drive or press the seal into place. Use a driver that fits at the perimeter of the seal.
8. Move the object placed in the oil hole and verify that the hole is uncovered. Remove the object from the oil hole.

Shift Shaft

> *CAUTION*
> *When prying out a seal, do not allow the end of the tool to touch the seal bore. Scratches in the bore will cause leakage.*

1. Pry out the old seal (B, **Figure 51**). If necessary, place a block of wood on the case to improve leverage and protect the case from damage.
2. Clean the oil seal bore.
3. Apply grease to the lip and sides of the new seal.

> *NOTE*
> *This seal is commonly replaced when the engine is assembled. If the shift shaft is passing through the bore, cover the shaft splines with plastic wrap, to prevent tearing the seal lip when it passes over the shaft.*

4. Place the seal in the bore, with the closed side of the seal facing out. The seal must be square to the bore.
5. Press the seal into place by hand. If necessary, use a driver that fits at the perimeter of the seal.

ENGINE LOWER END

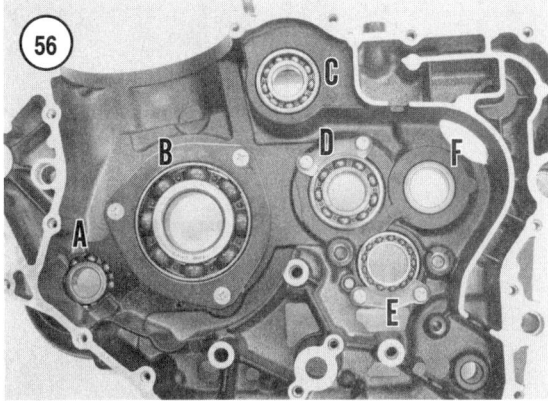

CRANKCASE BEARINGS

Refer to Chapter One for additional removal and installation techniques for bearings. Also refer to *Interference Fit* (Chapter One) if heat application is recommended for the removal and installation of the bearings in the housings.

Drivers and Pullers

Preferably, remove crankcase bearings with a press. Pressure can be controlled and applied more evenly. If bearing drivers and pullers must be used, the manufacturer recommends the following tools.

1. Bearing driver set (Kawasaki part No. 570011-1129), or an equivalent. The set can be ordered from a dealership.
2. Blind bearing puller. Used for transmission shaft bushings.

Identification

1. When replacing crankcase bearings, note the following:
   a. Where used, remove bearing retainers (**Figure 55**) before attempting bearing removal. When installing retainers, clean the screw threads and install the screws using threadlock.
   b. Identify and record the size code of each bearing before removing it from the case. This eliminates confusion when installing the bearings in their correct bores.
   c. Record the orientation of each bearing in its bore. Note if the size code faces toward the inside or outside of the crankcase. Commonly, the markings should face up when installing the bearing.
   d. Use a hydraulic press or a set of bearing drivers to remove and install bearings. All bearings in the crankcases are an interference-fit. Removing and installing the bearings is eased by using heat, as described in *Interference Fit* in Chapter One.
   e. Bearings that are only accessible from one side of the case can be removed with a blind bearing puller.
2. The following substeps identify the right crankcase half bearings. The direction of the manufacturer's marks on each bearing is also indicated. When the marks are facing in, this indicates they face the inside of the crankcase. When the marks are facing out, this indicates they face the outside of the crankcase.
   a. Front balancer shaft bearing (A, **Figure 56**). Manufacturer's marks facing out.
   b. Crankshaft bearing (B, **Figure 56**). Manufacturer's marks facing in.
   c. Rear balancer shaft bearing (C, **Figure 56**). Manufacturer's marks facing in.
   d. Input shaft bearing (D, **Figure 56**). Manufacturer's marks facing in.
   e. Shift drum bearing (E, **Figure 56**). Manufacturer's marks facing in.
   f. Output shaft bushing (F, **Figure 56**).
3. The following substeps identify the left crankcase half bearings. The direction of the manufacturer's marks on each bearing is also indicated. When the marks are facing in, this indicates they face the inside of the crankcase. When the marks are facing out, this indicates they face the outside of the crankcase.
   a. Output shaft bearing (A, **Figure 57**). Manufacturer's marks facing out.
   b. Input shaft bushing (B, **Figure 57**).
   c. Shift drum bushing (C. **Figure 57**).
   d. Rear balancer shaft bearing (D, **Figure 57**). Manufacturer's marks facing in.
   e. Crankshaft bearing race (E, **Figure 57**). Manufacturer's marks facing in. The roller bearing is mounted on the crankshaft.
   f. Front balancer shaft bearing (F, **Figure 57**). Manufacturer's marks facing out.

Replacement

All crankcase bearings can be removed and installed using the following steps. Read the entire procedure before replacing any bearing.

CAUTION
*Before performing this procedure, refer to Steps 1-3 in the **Crankcase Bearings, Identification** section to determine if there is specific information related to the bearing being installed. Do not install a bearing until any specific information is known.*

1. Remove the seal from the bearing, if applicable.
2. Make note of which side of the bearing is facing up.

CAUTION
Do not heat the housing or bearing with a propane or acetylene torch. The direct heat will destroy the case hardening of the bearing and will likely warp the housing.

3. Heat the crankcase as described in *Interference Fit* (Chapter One). Observe all safety and handling procedures when the case is heated.
4. Support the heated crankcase on wooden blocks, allowing space for the bearing to fall from the bore.
5. Remove the damaged bearing from the bore, using a press, hand-driver set or bearing puller.
6. Clean and inspect the bore. Check that all oil holes (where applicable) are clean.
7. Place the new bearing in a freezer and chill for at least one hour.
8. When the bearing is chilled, reheat the crankcase.
9. Support the heated crankcase on wooden blocks, then lubricate the mating surface of the bore and bearing. Place the bearing squarely over the bore and check that it is properly oriented.
   a. If the correct orientation of a bearing is not known, generally, bearings that are not sealed on either side should be installed with the manufacturer's marks (stamped on the side of the bearing) facing up.
   b. Generally, bearings with one side sealed should have the sealed side facing down.

CAUTION
If a press is not available, the bearing can be seated by hand, using a driver and hammer. Place the driver squarely over the bearing, then drive the bearing into the crankcase. Avoid using excessive force when driving the bearing.

Bearing and crankcase damage could occur.

10. Press the new bearing into place using a driver that fits onto the outer bearing race.
11. Install the seal (if applicable) as described in this chapter.

CRANKSHAFT

Inspection

Handle the crankshaft assembly carefully during inspection. Do not place the crankshaft where it could accidentally roll off the workbench. The crankshaft is an assembly-type, with its two halves joined by a crankpin. The crankpin is hydraulically pressed into the flywheels and aligned, both vertically and horizontally, with calibrated equipment.

If any part of the crankshaft assembly is worn or damaged, have a dealership evaluate all the parts to determine the practicality of repair.

1. Clean the crankshaft with clean solvent and dry with compressed air. Lubricate the rod bearing and shaft bearing with engine oil.
2. Inspect the right end of the crankshaft.

ENGINE LOWER END

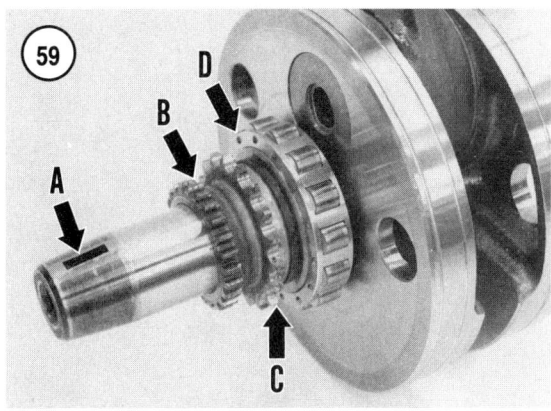

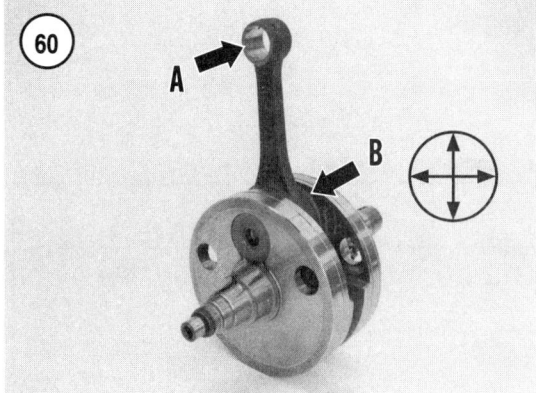

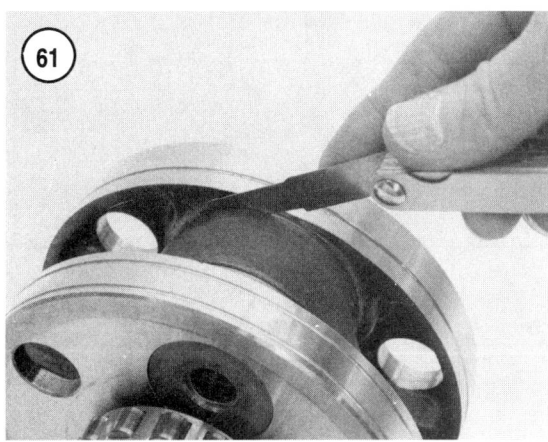

a. Inspect the keyway (A, **Figure 59**) and seating surface for the rotor. Burnishing can be removed with 320-grit carborundum cloth.
b. Inspect the cam chain sprocket (B, **Figure 59**) and balancer sprocket (C) for wear and broken teeth.
c. Inspect the bearing (D, **Figure 59**) for heat discoloration or other damage. Check that the rollers turn freely and are firmly in the bearing race.

NOTE
The left crankshaft bearing and cam chain/balancer sprocket assembly are only available as part of the left crankshaft half.

4. Inspect the connecting rod.
    a. Inspect the rod small end (A, **Figure 60**) for scoring, galling or heat damage. Refer to Chapter Four for additional inspections of the rod bore, piston pin and piston.
    b. Inspect the rod big end and bearing for visible scoring, galling or heat damage.
    c. Inspect the rod for radial clearance (B, **Figure 60**). Mount the crankshaft in a set of V-blocks and accurately measure play. An acceptable method is to grasp the rod and feel for radial play in all directions. There should be no perceptible play. Refer to **Table 1** for specifications.
    d. Measure the connecting rod side clearance (**Figure 61**). Refer to **Table 1** for specifications.
5. Place the crankshaft in a flywheel alignment jig and measure crankshaft runout with a dial indicator. The jig centers should be inserted into the ends of the crankshaft. Measure at the two points shown in **Figure 62**. The maximum difference in gauge readings is the total runout. If the runout exceeds the specifications listed in **Table 1**, have a dealership evaluate and possibly retrue the crankshaft.

NOTE
If the crankshaft was dropped or damaged, or if the engine exhibited abnormal vibration, have the crankshaft alignment checked before assembling the engine.

a. Inspect the shaft threads (A, **Figure 58**. The primary drive-gear nut is torqued to these threads. Light damage can be corrected with a thread file.
b. Inspect the keyway (B, **Figure 58**) and seating surfaces for the primary drive gear and oil pump drive gear.
c. Inspect the bearing surface (C, **Figure 58**) for scoring, heat discoloration or other damage. Burnishing can be removed with 320-grit carborundum cloth.
3. Inspect the left end of the crankshaft.

ENGINE BREAK-IN

If the rings were replaced, a new piston was installed, the cylinder block was rebored or honed, or if major lower end work was performed, the engine should be broken in just as though it were new. The performance and service life of the engine depends greatly on a careful and sensible break-in.

During break-in, oil consumption will be higher than normal. It is therefore important to check and correct the oil level frequently (Chapter Three). At no time should the oil level be allowed to drop below the minimum level. If the oil level is low, the oil will overheat resulting in insufficient lubrication and increased wear.

For the first 0-500 miles (0-800 km), do not operate the engine above 4000 rpm.

At 500-1000 miles (800-1600 km), do not operate the engine above 6000 rpm.

Avoid hard acceleration immediately after starting the engine, even if warm. Allow a couple of minutes for engine oil to circulate.

Perform the maintenance procedures described in **Table 1** of Chapter Three.

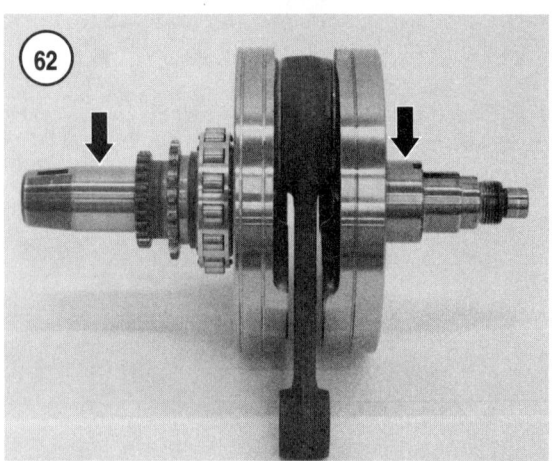

Table 1 ENGINE LOWER END SPECIFICATIONS

Item	Standard mm (in.)	Service limit mm (in.)
Balancer chain length (20 links/ 21 pins)	190.0-190.5 (7.48-7.50)	193.4 (7.61)
Camshaft chain length (20 links/21 pins)	127.0-127.4 (5.0-5.02)	128.9 (5.07)
Connecting rod		
Side clearance	0.25-0.35 (0.010-0.014)	0.60 (0.024)
Radial clearance	0.008-0.020 (0.0003-0.0008)	0.07 (0.003)
Crankshaft runout (total indicated reading)		
Left half	0.03 (0.0012)	0.08 (0.003)
Right half	0.04 (0.0016)	0.10 (0.004)

Table 2 ENGINE LOWER END TORQUE SPECIFICATIONS

Item	N•m	in.-lb.	ft.-lb.
Balancer shaft weight lock nut (right side)	44	–	32
Crankcase bolts	8.8	78	–
Engine mounting bolts			
8 mm	25	–	18
10 mm	44	–	32
Front footpeg mounting bolts	25	–	18
Left crankcase cover bolts	8.8	78	–
Lower chain guide bolts			
6 mm	12	106	–
8 mm	18	–	18
Neutral switch	15	–	11
Oil pickup tube mounting bolts	8.8	78	–
Oil pressure relief valve	15	–	11
Primary drive gear nut	155	–	114
Rear balancer chain guide bolts	8.8	78	–
Rear cam chain guide bolt	19	–	14
Swing arm pivot bolt	88	–	65

CHAPTER SIX

CLUTCH, GEARSHIFT MECHANISM AND LUBRICATION SYSTEM

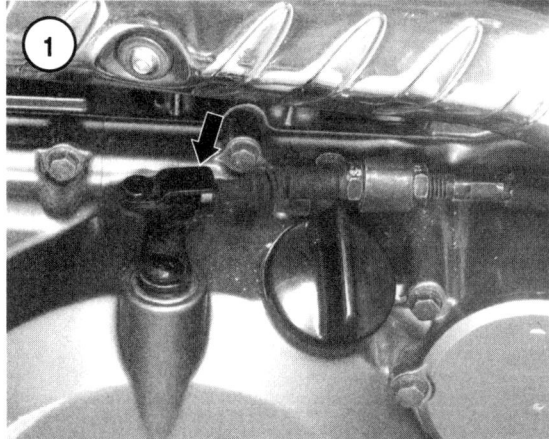

This chapter provides service procedures for the following components:
1. Right crankcase cover.
2. Clutch.
3. External gearshift linkage.
4. Oil pump.
5. Primary drive gear.
6. Clutch cable replacement.

RIGHT CRANKCASE COVER

Removal/Installation

1. Remove the skid plate (Chapter Fifteen).
2. Drain the engine oil and remove the oil filter (Chapter Three).
3. Drain the cooling system (Chapter Three).
4. Remove the rear brake pedal (Chapter Fourteen).
5. Remove the right front footpeg.
6. Remove the clutch cable holder, then detach the clutch cable from the release lever (**Figure 1**). The cable does not have to be removed from the cable holder.
7. Remove the water pump cover and impeller assembly (Chapter Ten).
8. Remove the 15 bolts from the perimeter of the crankcase cover (**Figure 2**).
9. Turn the clutch release lever so it points to the back. This disengages it from the clutch lifter, located behind the cover.

10. Hold the release lever in position and remove the cover. If necessary, lightly tap the cover to help loosen it from the engine.
11. Account for the two dowels that fit between the crankcase and cover (A, **Figure 3**).
12. Remove the O-ring at the oil filter housing (B, **Figure 3**).
13. Remove the cover gasket.
14. Remove the crankcase oil strainer (**Figure 4**).
15. Inspect the cover assembly as described in this section.
16. Reverse the removal steps to install the right crankcase cover assembly. Note the following:
    a. Install a new, lubricated O-ring on the oil filter housing.
    b. Clean all residue and oil from the cover and engine gasket surfaces.
    c. Check that the crankcase oil strainer (A, **Figure 5**) is installed and seated.
    d. Apply molybdenum disulfide grease to the end of the crankshaft (B, **Figure 5**) and impeller shaft (C). Do not plug the oil hole in the crankshaft with grease.
    e. Install a new cover gasket on the crankcase dowels.
    f. Apply molybdenum disulfide grease to the contact points of the clutch release lever and clutch lifter.
    g. Turn the clutch release lever so it points to the rear. Then, install the cover. When the cover is installed, turn the release lever forward to engage it with the clutch lifter.
    h. Tighten the front footpeg mounting bolts to 25 N•m (18 ft.-lb.).
    i. Install a new oil filter and fill the engine with oil (Chapter Three).
    j. Fill the engine with coolant (Chapter Three).
    k. Check clutch operation. If necessary, adjust the clutch (Chapter Three).

Inspection/Disassembly

1. Wipe the cover clean. Do not submerge the cover in solvent unless all bearing and seal assemblies are removed.
2. Inspect the crankshaft oil seal in the crankcase cover (**Figure 6**). This seal fits over the end of the crankshaft and must be in good condition. Oil under pressure passes from the oil filter housing and into the end of the crankshaft, where it then goes to the crankpin and connecting rod. If this seal leaks, oil pressure will be reduced to these parts. Replace the seal as follows:
    a. Remove the bolt and seal retainer plate.
    b. Pry the seal from its bore (**Figure 7**).
    c. Lubricate the new seal with grease.

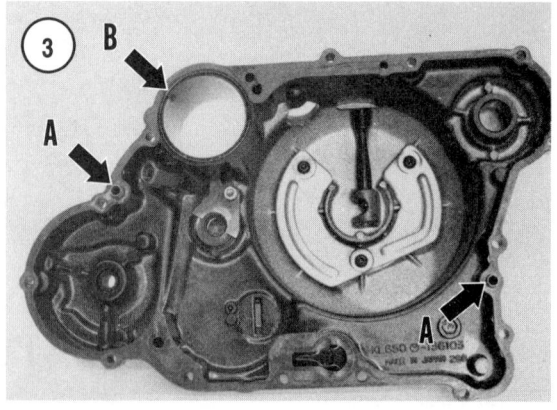
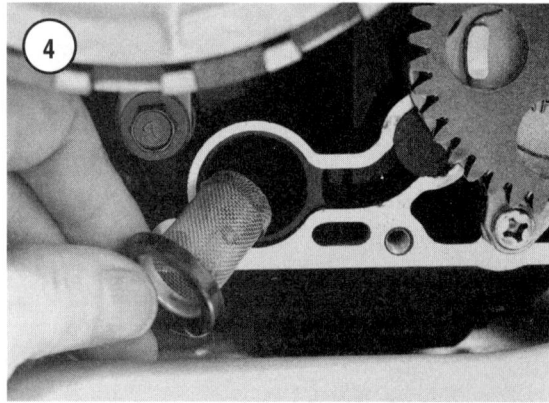

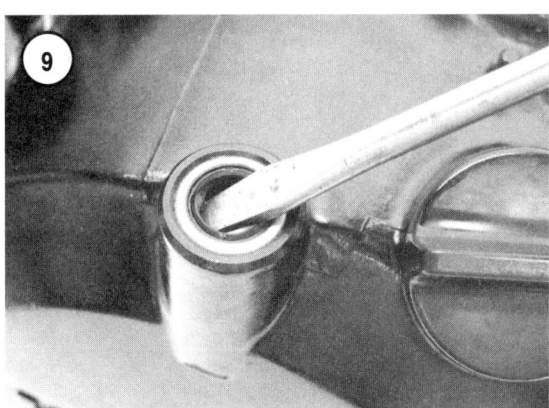

   d. Place the seal over the bore, with the closed side facing up.
   e. Place a driver or socket (**Figure 8**) over the seal that is sized to fit the perimeter of the seal.
   f. Drive the seal into place.
   g. Install the seal retainer plate and bolt. Note the correct orientation of the plate (**Figure 6**).
   h. Tighten the seal retainer bolt to 12.5 N•m (111 in.-lb.).

3. Inspect the clutch release lever, seal and bearing.
   a. Inspect the lever for shaft wear and fit it in the bearing.
   b. Inspect the seal. If oil leakage is evident, replace the seal. Pry the seal from its bore (**Figure 9**), then apply grease to the new seal. Seat the seal using a driver that fits on the perimeter of the seal. The wear ring on the seal should rest slightly above the case. The wear ring prevents the clutch release lever from contacting the case.
   c. Inspect the bearing (**Figure 10**). If damaged or worn, remove the seal and drive the bearing out of the bore. Lubricate the new bearing, then drive it into the bore. Use a driver that fits on the perimeter of the bearing. Install the bearing with the manufacturers marks facing up. Drive the bearing no deeper than flush with the inside of the case. Install a new seal.

4. Inspect the oil pressure relief valve (**Figure 11**). If engine or oil pump damage has occurred, remove the valve from the crankcase cover. Remove the snap ring from the valve, then disassemble and clean the parts. Also clean the oil passage in the cover. When installing, apply threadlock to the relief valve threads. Tighten the oil pressure relief valve to 15 N•m (11 ft.-lb.).

5. Inspect and clean the crankcase oil strainer (**Figure 4**) whenever the crankcase cover is removed. Oil passes from this screen to the oil pump. A plugged, damaged or missing screen could cause engine damage. If the screen or grommet is distorted or damaged, replace the parts. Inspect and clean the passage where the strainer seats.

CLUTCH ASSEMBLY

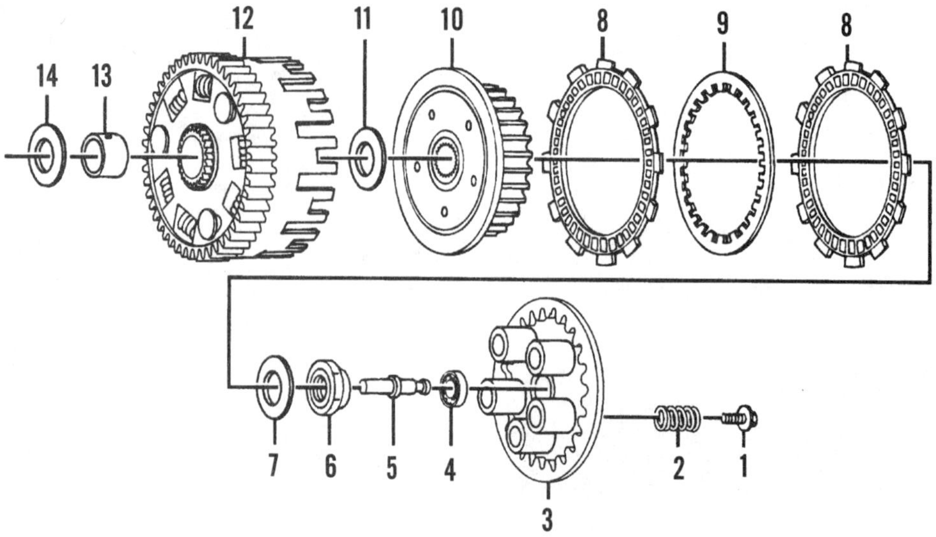

1. Bolt
2. Spring
3. Pressure plate
4. Lifter bearing
5. Lifter
6. Locknut
7. Lockwasher
8. Friction plate
9. Clutch plate
10. Clutch hub
11. Washer
12. Clutch housing
13. Collar
14. Spacer

CLUTCH

The clutch assembly consists of an outer housing and a clutch hub. A set of clutch plates and friction plates are alternately locked to the two parts. The gear-driven clutch housing is mounted on the transmission input shaft and can rotate freely. The housing receives power from the primary drive gear mounted on the crankshaft. As the clutch is engaged, the housing and friction plates transfer the power to the clutch plates, locked to the clutch hub. The clutch hub is splined to the input shaft and powers the transmission. The plate assembly is engaged by springs and disengaged by a cable-actuated release lever and lift assembly.

The clutch operates immersed in the engine oil supply. Oil additives should not be added to the oil supply, since these can cause poor clutch operation. The friction plates can also become contaminated.

Removal

Refer to **Figure 12**.

1. Remove the right crankcase cover as described in this chapter.

CLUTCH, GEARSHIFT MECHANISM AND LUBRICATION SYSTEM

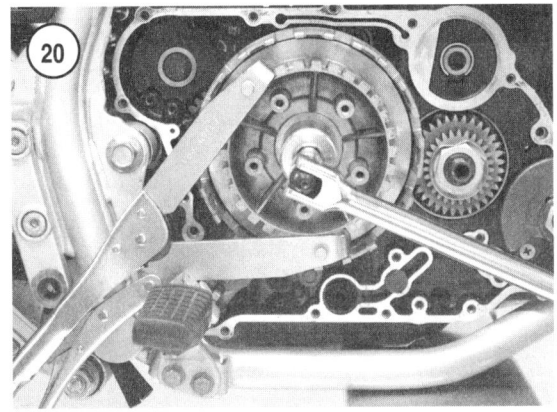

2. Remove the five bolts (**Figure 13**) compressing the clutch springs. Make several passes to relieve the pressure equally on the bolts.

3. Remove the bolts and springs (**Figure 14**) from the clutch.

4. Remove the pressure plate. When removing, keep the plate tilted up so the lifter bearing (**Figure 15**) in the back of the plate does not fall out.

5. Remove the clutch lifter (**Figure 16**).

6. Remove the plates from the clutch housing and clutch hub (**Figure 17**). Note that the outer friction plate seats into the shallow slots (**Figure 18**) of the outer housing.

7. Remove the clutch locknut (**Figure 19**) as follows:

   a. Temporarily install the right front footpeg.

CAUTION
Do not attempt to prevent gear rotation by using screwdrivers or other tools. This can cause gear breakage.

   b. Attach a clutch holder tool (**Figure 20**) to the clutch hub and rest it on the footpeg.
   c. Loosen the locknut.
   d. Remove the clutch locknut and lockwasher.

8. Remove the clutch hub (**Figure 21**).

9. Remove the washer (**Figure 22**).

10. Remove the clutch housing (**Figure 23**).
11. Remove the clutch housing collar (**Figure 24**).
12. Remove the spacer (**Figure 25**).
13. Inspect the clutch assembly as described in this section.

Inspection

Always replace clutch plates, friction plates or springs as a set if they do not meet specifications. If any part shows signs of wear or damage, replace it, regardless of its specification. Refer to the specifications listed in **Table 1** for component service limits, when applicable.

1. Clean the parts in solvent and dry with compressed air. Also clean the transmission shaft.
2. Measure the thickness (**Figure 26**) of each friction plate. Measure at several locations around the perimeter.
3. Inspect the tabs (**Figure 27**) on the friction plates. The tabs must not be damaged. Check that each plate slides smoothly in the clutch housing.
4. Measure each clutch plate (**Figure 28**) for warp. Lay each plate on a surface plate, or thick piece of glass, and measure any gap around the perimeter of the plate.

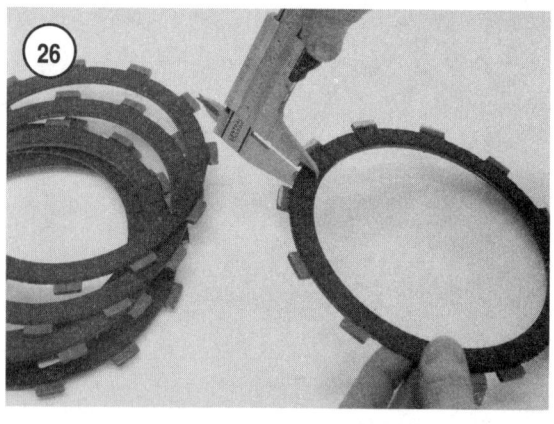

CLUTCH, GEARSHIFT MECHANISM AND LUBRICATION SYSTEM

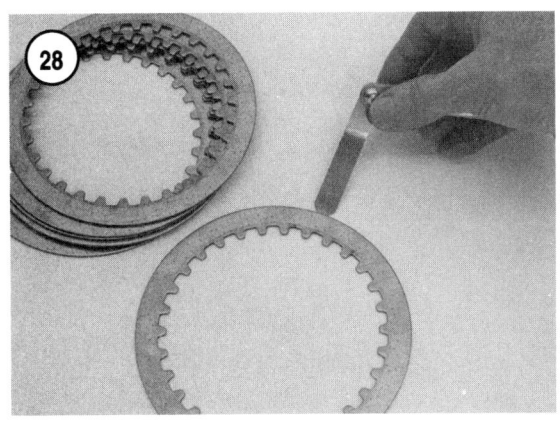

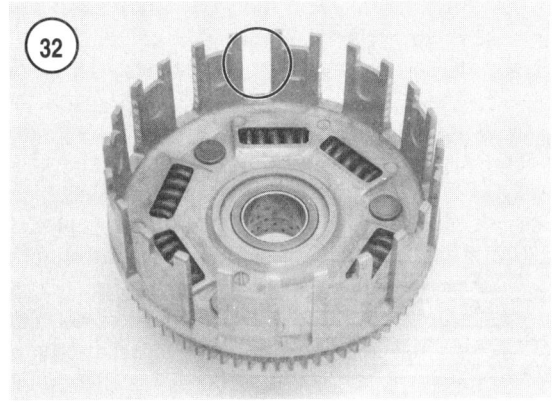

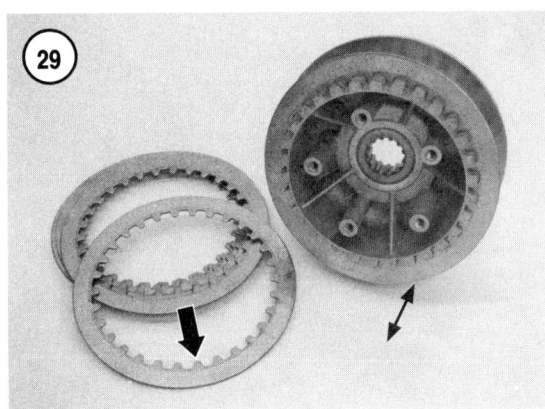

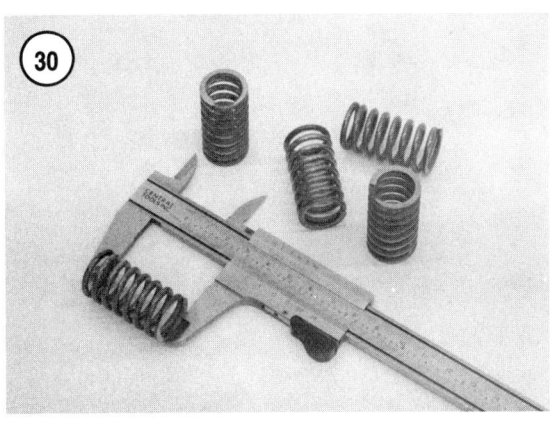

5. Inspect the inner teeth on the plates (**Figure 29**). The teeth must not be damaged. Check that each plate slides smoothly on the clutch hub.

6. Measure the free length (**Figure 30**) of each clutch spring.

7. Inspect the clutch housing and collar (A, **Figure 31**).

    a. Inspect the surface of the collar and housing bore for wear and damage. Check the fit of the collar in the bore and on the transmission shaft. The collar should move freely, but have no obvious play.

    b. Inspect the oil pockets in the housing bore for cleanliness.

    c. Inspect the gear teeth (B, **Figure 31**) for wear or damage.

    d. Inspect the damper springs (C, **Figure 31**) and rivets (D) on both sides of the housing for looseness or damage.

    e. Inspect the slots (**Figure 32**) for nicks, wear and damage. The slots must be smooth and free of defects so the friction plates smoothly engage and disengage. If chatter marks are evident (**Figure 33**), light damage can be smoothed using a fine-cut file or oilstone.

8. Inspect the clutch hub.

a. Inspect the shaft splines (A, **Figure 34**). The hub should fit on the transmission shaft with no obvious play.
b. Inspect the perimeter of the hub (B, **Figure 34**) for wear and damage on the contact area.
c. Inspect the bosses (C, **Figure 34**) for damage.
d. Inspect the outer splines (D, **Figure 34**) for nicks, wear and damage. The splines must be smooth and free of defects so the clutch plates smoothly engage and disengage. If chatter marks are evident, light damage can be smoothed using a fine-cut file or oilstone.

9. Inspect the pressure plate, lifter and bearing.
   a. Inspect the pressure plate for cracks, particularly around the bosses (A, **Figure 35**) and bearing seat (B).
   b. Inspect the perimeter (C, **Figure 35**) of the pressure plate for wear and damage on the contact area.
   c. Inspect the bearing for radial and axial play. The bearing should fit in the pressure plate with minimal play. If the bearing is replaced, install the bearing with the manufacturer's marks facing up.
   d. Inspect the lifter for wear at the contact area with the bearing. The lifter is a loose-fit in the bearing. When the lifter is installed in the transmission shaft, and the bearing is installed in the pressure plate, the parts self-center.
   e. Inspect the lifter for fit with the release lever (**Figure 36**). Replace both parts if either part is damaged.
10. Inspect the bolts, washers and spacer for visible damage.
11. Inspect the splines, threads and polished surfaces on the transmission shaft for damage.
12. Install the clutch assembly as described in this section.

Installation

During assembly, lubricate the parts and transmission shaft with engine oil, unless specified otherwise.
1. Install the spacer.
2. Install the clutch housing collar.
3. Install the clutch housing onto the collar.
4. Install the washer.
5. Install the clutch hub.

CAUTION
If the lockwasher is no longer cupped, replace the lockwasher.

6. Install the lockwasher, with the words OUT SIDE (**Figure 37**) facing out.

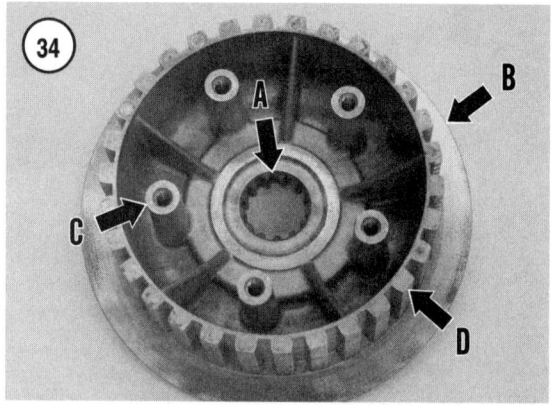

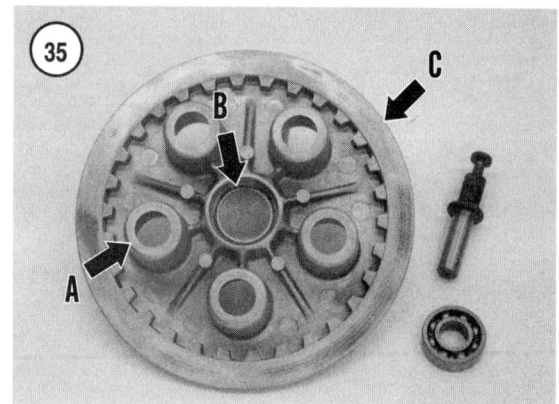

CLUTCH, GEARSHIFT MECHANISM AND LUBRICATION SYSTEM

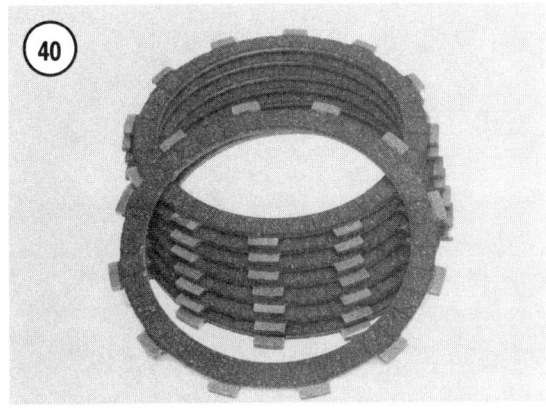

CAUTION
Do not reuse the locknut.

7. Install a new locknut, with the wide side of the nut (**Figure 38**) in contact with the lockwasher.
8. Tighten the clutch locknut as follows:
   a. Temporarily install the right footpeg.
   b. Attach a clutch holder tool (**Figure 39**) to the clutch hub and rest it against the footpeg.
   c. Tighten the clutch locknut to 135 N•m (100 ft.-lb.).
9. Install the plates into the clutch housing and clutch hub as follows:
   a. Lubricate the plates with engine oil. To prevent possible seizure, particularly with new friction plates, it is important that the face of the friction plates (**Figure 40**) be completely coated with oil. If possible, allow the plates to soak in engine oil before installing.
   b. Beginning with a friction plate, alternately install friction plates and clutch plates into the clutch housing and clutch hub (**Figure 41**). Note that the outer friction plate seats into the shallow slots (**Figure 18**) of the outer housing.
10. Install the clutch lifter. Apply molybdenum disulfide grease to the lifter, particularly at the bearing contact point.
11. Install the pressure plate and bearing.
12. Lock the pressure plate to the clutch hub as follows:
    a. Install the clutch springs on the hub bosses.
    b. Finger-tighten the five bolts (**Figure 42**).
    c. Using a crossing pattern, evenly tighten the clutch spring bolts in several steps to 9.8 N•m (87 in.-lb.).
13. Install the right crankcase cover as described in this chapter.
14. Install the right front footpeg and tighten the mounting bolts to 45 N•m (33 ft.-lb.).

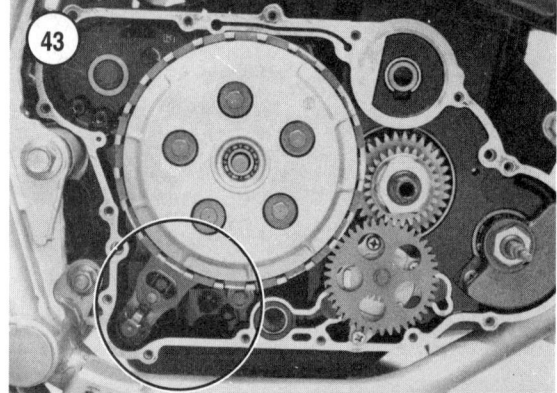

EXTERNAL GEARSHIFT LINKAGE

Removal

The external gearshift linkage is located behind the right side cover and is partially covered by the clutch (**Figure 43**). Visual inspection of the shift shaft assembly is possible without removing the clutch. To completely remove the external gearshift linkage, perform the following:

1. Remove the right crankcase cover as described in this chapter.
2. Remove the clutch as described in this chapter.
3. Put the transmission in neutral. This can be verified by the position of the lever on the shift cam. The roller should rest in the neutral detent on the shift cam (**Figure 44**).
4. Remove the shift lever from the left side of the engine. Mark where the lever is located on the shaft splines, so the lever can be installed in the same position.
5. Pull the shift shaft assembly from the engine (**Figure 45**).
6. Remove the gear positioning lever (A, **Figure 46**) and torsion spring.
7. Remove the shift cam (B, **Figure 46**).
8. Remove the pin (**Figure 47**) from the end of the shift drum.
9. If visibly damaged or loose, remove the return spring post (C, **Figure 46**).
10. Inspect the parts as described in this section.

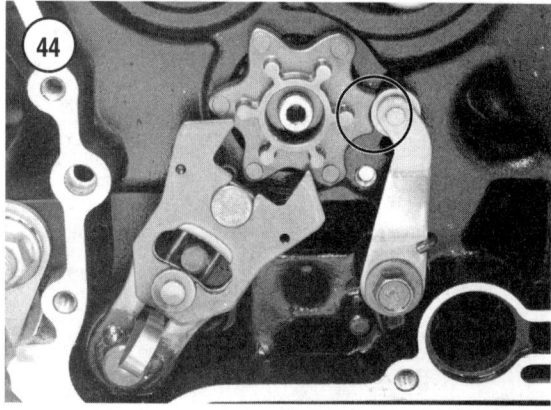

Inspection

Inspect the components of the gearshift linkage and replace parts that are worn, damaged or fatigued. Inspect as follows:

1. Clean the parts in solvent.
2. Inspect the shift shaft assembly (**Figure 48**).
   a. Inspect the return spring for fatigue or damage.
   b. Inspect the pawl tips for wear.

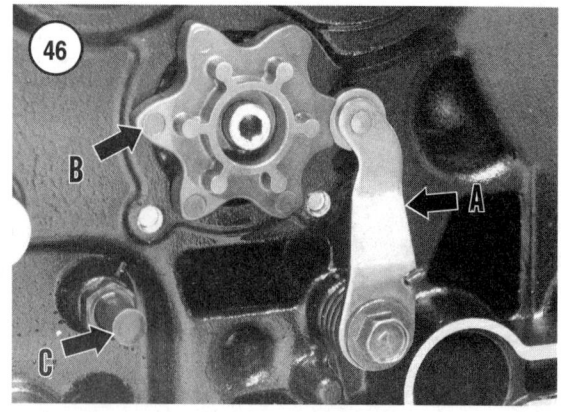

CLUTCH, GEARSHIFT MECHANISM AND LUBRICATION SYSTEM

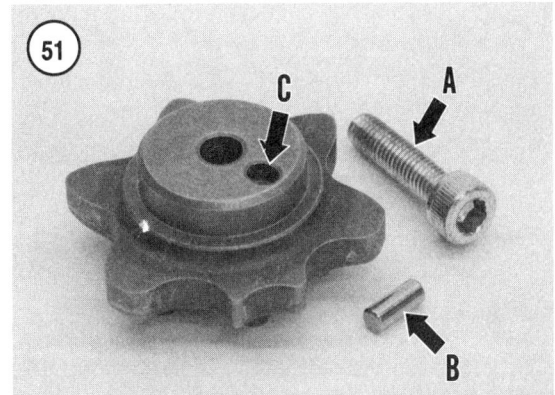

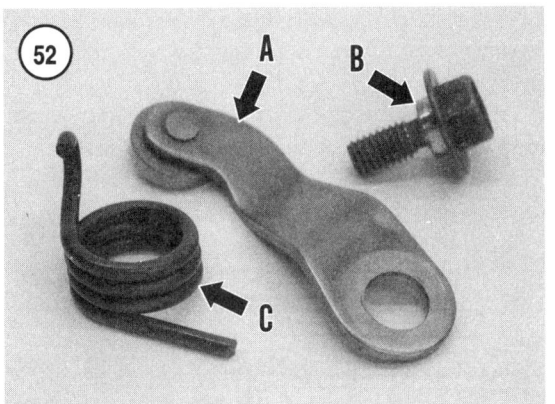

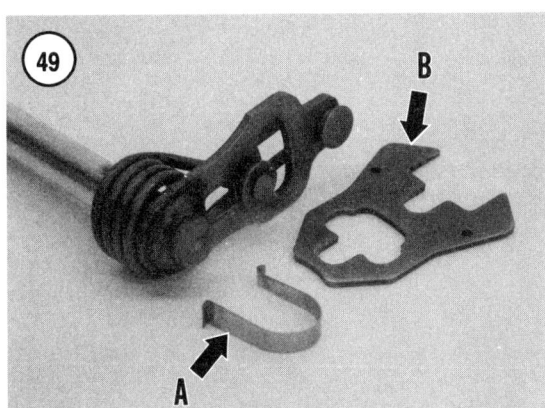

  c. Check that the pawl slides freely and returns to the extended position. If the pawl jams or drags, remove the band spring (A, **Figure 49**) and pawl (B) from the shift shaft. Then, determine which part(s) are damaged. When installing the band spring, engage the narrow end with the pawl.
  d. Inspect the condition of the splines on the shaft and in the shift lever.
3. Inspect the shift cam.
  a. Inspect the pawl engagement points (A, **Figure 50**) for wear.
  b. Inspect the lever engagement points (B, **Figure 50**) for wear in the high and low areas. The neutral detent should not be worn away and should allow the lever roller to rest in the detent.
  c. Inspect the shift cam bolt (A, **Figure 51**), pin (B) and pin bore (C). The pin and bore should not be worn. It is normal for the pin bore to be elongated.
  d. Inspect the fit of the pin in the shift drum. The pin should fit with minimal perceptible play.
  e. Inspect the bolt thread condition and cleanliness. All threadlock residue must be removed before tightening the bolt.
4. Inspect the gear positioning lever (A, **Figure 52**), bolt (B) and spring (C). 2011-on models also include a washer.

a. The lever roller should be round, turn freely and have no play in its pivot.
b. The shoulder on the bolt should fit into the lever with minimal, or no play. If either part is loose, replace both parts.
c. Inspect the ends of the spring for wear.
5. Inspect the return spring post (C, **Figure 46**) for wear and tightness.

Installation

1. If removed, install the return spring post (C, **Figure 46**). Apply threadlock to the threads before tightening the post.
2. Install the pin in the end of the shift drum.
3. Install the shift cam, engaging the bore in the shift cam with the pin (**Figure 53**).
4. Apply threadlock to the threads of the shift cam bolt. Install and tighten the bolt to 12 N•m (106 in.-lb.).
5. Install the gear positioning lever and torsion spring (A, **Figure 46**).
   a. Check that the spring is correctly installed around the lever (A, **Figure 54**) and against the crankcase (B). For 2011-on models, place the washer between the spring and lever.
   b. Check that the bolt shoulder is seated into the lever before tightening. Tighten the gear positioning lever shoulder bolt to 8.8 N•m (78 in.-lb.).
6. Insert the shift shaft assembly through the engine (**Figure 45**). Seat the return spring around the post (**Figure 55**).
7. Install the shift lever onto the left side of the engine. If necessary, get assistance to hold the shaft in place on the right side while the lever is installed.
8. Check the shifting action of the linkage.
   a. Turn the transmission shaft to aid in shifting.
   b. The lever roller should lock into each indention on the shift cam as the transmission is shifted. In neutral, the lever roller should rest in the neutral detent (**Figure 44**).
9. Install the clutch as described in this chapter.
10. Install the right crankcase cover as described in this chapter.

OIL PUMP

The engine is a wet-sump engine, and therefore stores the engine oil in the crankcase. The oil supply flows from the crankcase oil strainer (A, **Figure 56**) to the oil pump (B), where it is pumped under pressure through the oil filter and to the engine components. After oil passes through a lubrication point, it falls to the crankcase, where it again circulates to the oil pump. The oil pump is driven by a gear (C, **Figure 56**) on the end of the crankshaft.

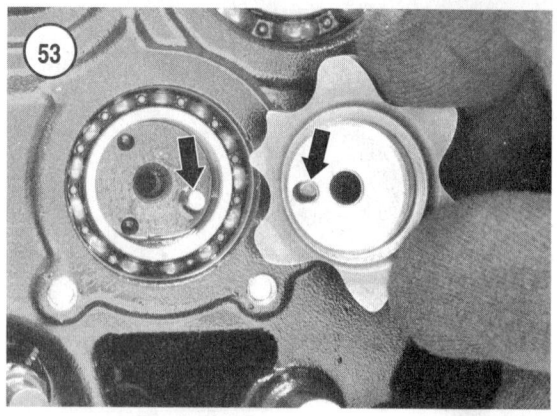
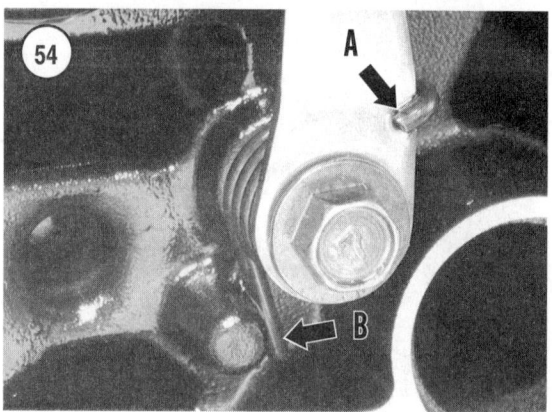
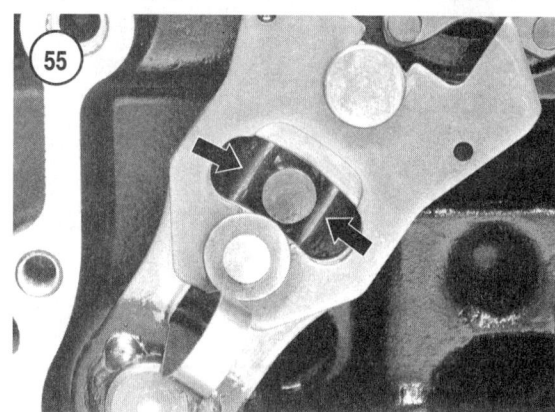

CLUTCH, GEARSHIFT MECHANISM AND LUBRICATION SYSTEM

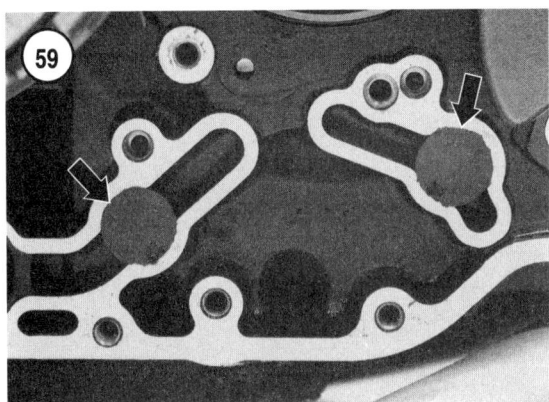

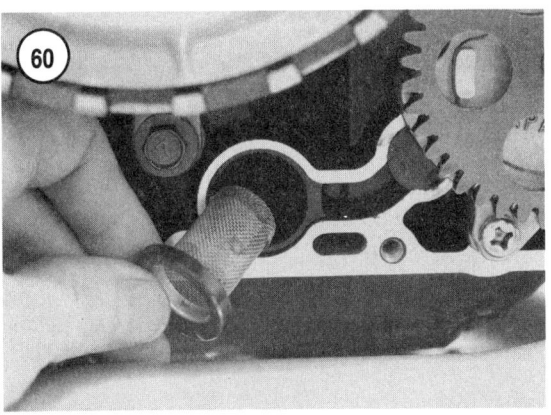

Removal/Installation

1. Remove the right crankcase cover as described in this chapter.
2. With the transmission in neutral, rotate the crankshaft and align the holes in the oil pump gear so the three pump mounting screws (A, **Figure 57**) are accessible. Fit an open-end wrench on the primary drive gear nut (B, **Figure 57**) to turn the crankshaft.
3. Remove the three mounting screws and the oil pump.
4. Account for the two dowels that are mounted in the holes shown in **Figure 58**. These dowels join the pump to the crankcase.
5. Remove the gasket.
6. Check that the plugs (**Figure 59**) are in place. Do not remove the plugs.
7. Disassemble, inspect and assemble the oil pump as described in this section.
8. Reverse these steps to install the oil pump. Note the following:
    a. Inspect and clean the crankcase oil strainer (**Figure 60**) and oil passage.
    b. Fill the pump with engine oil prior to mounting.
    c. Install a new oil pump gasket.
    d. Apply threadlock to the threads of the mounting screws before installing. Tighten the oil pump mounting screws to 4.4 N•m (39 in.-lb.).

Disassembly/Assembly

1. Remove the oil pump cover screw (**Figure 61**) from the pump body. Remove the rear plate.
2. Lift out the inner rotor (A, **Figure 62**) and outer rotor (B).
3. Remove the pin (**Figure 63**), then pull the gear out of the pump body.
4. Inspect the parts (**Figure 64**) as described in this section.
5. Reverse these steps to assemble the oil pump. Note the following:

CHAPTER SIX

a. Install the rotors into the pump body with the marks (**Figure 65**) facing down. The marks should not be visible when the rotors are installed.
b. Check that the rear plate is fully seated at its perimeter before screwing it into place.
c. Apply threadlock to the threads of the oil pump cover screw before installing. Tighten the oil pump cover screw to 4.2 N•m (37 in.-lb.).
d. Install the oil pump as described in this section.

Inspection

Visually inspect all parts for obvious wear or damage. Component specifications are not available for the oil pump.
1. Clean the parts in solvent.
2. Inspect the pump shaft (A, **Figure 66**), gear (B) and pin (C) for wear or scoring. The pin should firmly fit into the shaft. The pump shaft should fit into the pump body and rear plate with minimal perceptible play.
3. Inspect the rotors (**Figure 67**) for wear or scoring. When assembled, the inner rotor and pin should firmly fit onto the shaft.
4. Inspect the pump body and rear plate (**Figure 68**) for wear or scoring.
5. Assemble the oil pump as described in this section.

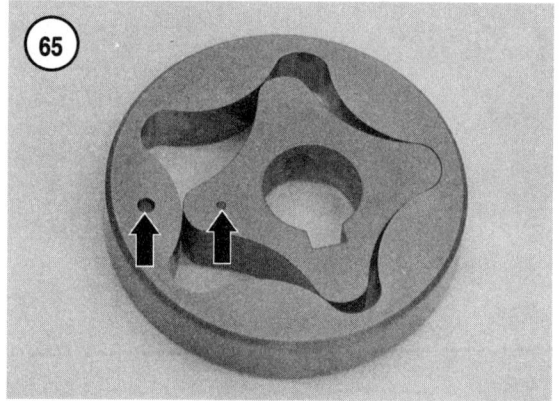

PRIMARY DRIVE GEAR

Removal/Inspection

Tools

The primary drive gear nut is very tight. The crankshaft must be held stable so the nut can be loosened. The following two methods can be used:
1. Use the rotor holder (Kawasaki part No. 57001-1184 or equivalent) to hold the rotor stable (**Figure 69**). The tool is placed against the top of the footpeg during removal, and against the bottom of the footpeg during installation.

CLUTCH, GEARSHIFT MECHANISM AND LUBRICATION SYSTEM

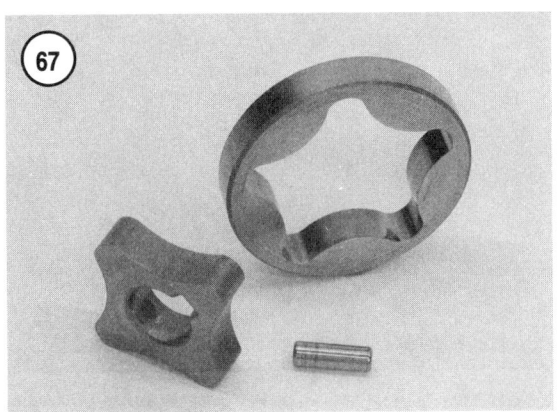

CAUTION
Do not jam the gears with screwdrivers or other tools. This could damage the gear.

2. Lock the primary drive gear and clutch housing gear together using a jam gear. This is typically a discarded drive gear. Place the gear above the primary and driven gears during removal (A, **Figure 70**), and below the gears during installation (B). The gear must completely mesh with both sets of gear teeth. Check with a dealership or motorcycle repair shop for a jam gear.

Procedure

1. Remove the right crankcase cover as described in this chapter.
2. Remove the oil pump as described in this chapter.
3A. If a rotor holder tool is used:
   a. Remove the alternator cover as described in Chapter Nine.
   b. Remove the clutch as described in this chapter.
   c. Flatten the perimeter of the lockwasher (**Figure 71**) so a socket fully seats on the nut.
   d. Fit the rotor holder tool onto the rotor.
   e. Loosen the nut.
3B. If a jam gear will be used:

CAUTION
Do not jam the gears with screwdrivers or other tools. This could damage the gear.

   a. Flatten the perimeter of the lockwasher (**Figure 71**) so a socket fully seats on the nut.
   b. Mesh the jam gear with the clutch housing gear and primary drive gear.
   c. Loosen the nut.
   d. Remove the clutch as described in this chapter.
4. Remove the primary drive gear nut and washer.
5. Remove the oil pump drive gear, primary drive gear, shaft key and spacer (**Figure 72**).
6. Inspect the parts (**Figure 73**).

a. Inspect the gears for worn or broken teeth.
b. Inspect the fit of the key in the gears and crankshaft (**Figure 74**). The key must fit in all parts with no play.
c. Inspect the spacer for visible damage.

Installation

1. Lubricate the crankshaft with engine oil, then install the spacer, shaft key, primary drive gear and oil pump drive gear.
2. Install a new lockwasher with the cupped side facing out. Make sure the tab on the backside of the washer fits into the keyway on the oil pump drive gear.
3. Apply engine oil to the crankshaft threads and primary drive gear nut. Finger-tighten the nut.
4A. If a rotor holder tool is used:
   a. Fit the rotor holder tool onto the rotor.
   b. Install and tighten the primary drive gear nut to 155 N•m (114 ft.-lb.).
   c. Flatten one side of the lockwasher (**Figure 75**) against the nut.
   d. Install the alternator cover as described in Chapter Nine.
   e. Install the clutch as described in this chapter.
4B. If a jam gear is used:
   a. Install the clutch as described in this chapter.
   b. Mesh the jam gear with the clutch housing gear and primary drive gear.

CAUTION
Do not jam the gears with screwdrivers or other tools. This could damage the gear.

   c. Install and tighten the primary drive gear nut to 155 N•m (114 ft.-lb.).
   d. Flatten one side of the lockwasher (**Figure 75**) against the nut.
5. Install the oil pump as described in this chapter.
6. Install the right crankcase cover as described in this chapter.

CLUTCH CABLE REPLACEMENT

1. Remove the clutch lever hand guard.
2. Loosen the clutch cable locknut (A, **Figure 76**), then turn the adjuster (B) in to increase cable slack.
3. Align the slots on the nut and adjuster, then detach the cable from the cable lever.

NOTE
It may be necessary to turn the adjustment nuts at the lower end of the clutch cable (A, Figure 77) to obtain sufficient cable slack to detach the cable from the hand lever.

CLUTCH, GEARSHIFT MECHANISM AND LUBRICATION SYSTEM

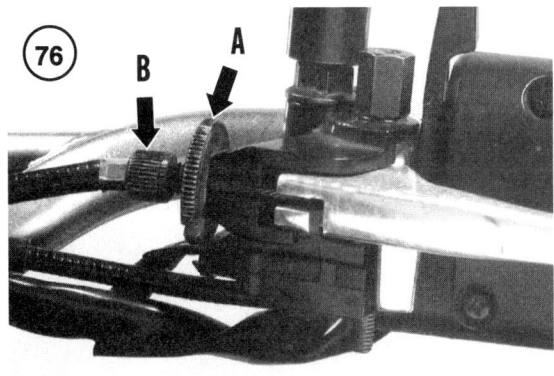

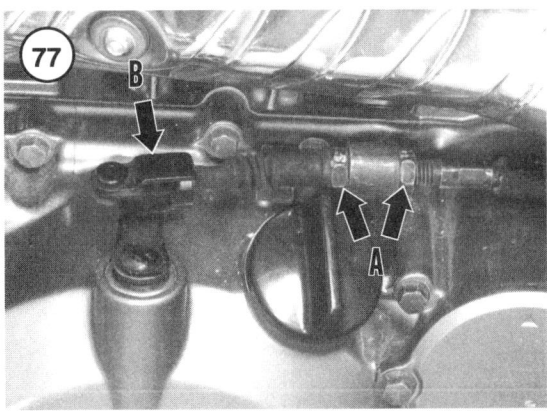

4. Remove the cable end from the release lever at the lower end of the cable (B, **Figure 77**).
5. Remove the cable from the motorcycle, noting the routing of the cable.
6. Clean the levers, pivot bolt and clutch lever housing.
7. Lubricate the new cable with an aerosol cable lubricant. Lubricate the lever, pivot bolt and cable ends with lithium grease.

8. Route the cable from the handlebar to the release lever.
9. Route the cable into the cable holder, then attach the cable to the release lever. Center the adjuster and locknuts in the cable holder.
10. At the handlebar, attach the cable to the clutch lever.
11. Adjust the clutch cable (Chapter Three).
12. Install the clutch lever hand guard.

Table 1 CLUTCH SPECIFICATIONS

Item	Standard mm (in.)	Service limit mm (in.)
Clutch spring free length	38.7 (1.52)	37.2 (1.46)
Friction plate		
Quantity	8	–
Thickness	2.90-3.10 (0.114-0.122)	2.7 (0.106)
Steel plate		
Quantity	7	–
Warp	–	0.30 (0.012)

Table 2 OIL PUMP SPECIFICATIONS

Lubrication system	Trochoid pump, forced pressure, wet sump
Oil pump pressure at 4000 rpm	78-147 kPa (11-21 psi)

Table 3 CLUTCH AND LUBRICATION SYSTEM TORQUE SPECIFICATIONS

Item	N•m	in.-lb.	ft.-lb.
Clutch locknut	135	–	100
Clutch spring bolts			
2008-2010 models	9.8	87	–
2011-on models	9.1	81	–
Front footpeg mounting bolts	25	–	18
Gear positioning lever shoulder bolt	8.8	78	–
Oil pressure relief valve	15	–	11
Oil pump cover screw	4.2	37	–
Oil pump mounting screws	4.4	39	–
Primary drive gear nut	155	–	114
Right crankcase cover oil seal			
retainer bolt	12.5	111	–
Shift cam bolt	12	106	–

CHAPTER SEVEN

TRANSMISSION AND SHIFT MECHANISM

This chapter provides service procedures for the transmission and internal shift mechanism. The external shift mechanism is covered in Chapter Six. Transmission and internal shift mechanism service requires crankcase disassembly as described in Chapter Five.

Transmission specifications are listed in **Table 1** and **Table 2**, located at the end of this chapter.

TRANSMISSION

Operation

The KLR650 is equipped with a five-speed constant-mesh transmission. The gears on the input shaft (A, **Figure 1**) are meshed with the gears on the output shaft (B). Each pair of meshed gears represents one gear ratio. For each pair of gears, one of the gears is splined to its shaft, while the other gear freewheels on its shaft.

Next to each freewheeling gear is a gear that is splined to the shaft. This locked gear can slide on the shaft and lock into the freewheeling gear, making that gear ratio active. Anytime the transmission is in gear one pair of meshed gears are locked to their shafts, and that gear ratio is selected. All other meshed gears have one freewheeling gear, making those ratios inoperative.

To engage and disengage the various gears, the splined gears are moved by shift forks. The shift forks are guided by the shift drum, which is operated by the shift lever. As the motorcycle is upshifted and downshifted, the shift drum rotates and guides the forks to engage and disengage pairs of gears on the transmission shafts.

Service

The engine crankcase must be split to remove the transmission gearshafts (**Figure 2**) and shift assembly. Remove and install the transmission assemblies as described in *Crankcase* (Chapter Five).

After the transmission is removed from the crankcase, disassembly, inspection and assembly can be performed. Careful inspection of the parts is required, as well as keeping the parts oriented so they can be reinstalled in the correct direction on the proper shafts. The gears, washers and snap rings must be installed in the same direction as they were before disassembly. If necessary, slide the parts onto a long dowel or screwdriver as they are removed, or make an identification mark on each part to indicate position and orientation.

Always install new snap rings. The snap rings fatigue and distort when they are removed. Do not reuse them, although they appear to be in good con-

TRANSMISSION AND SHIFT MECHANISM

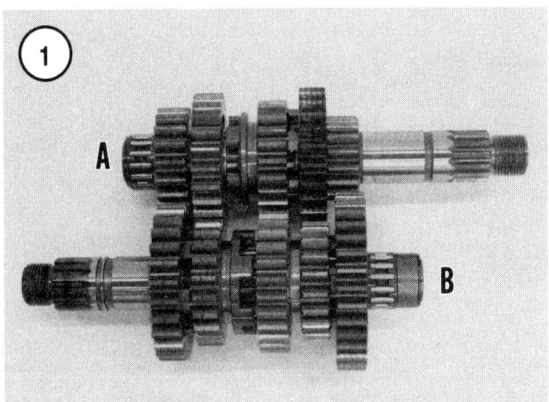

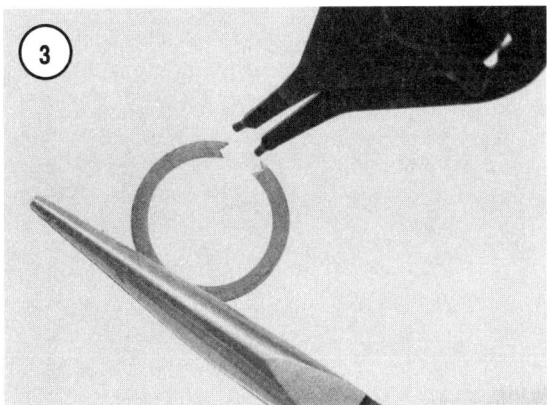

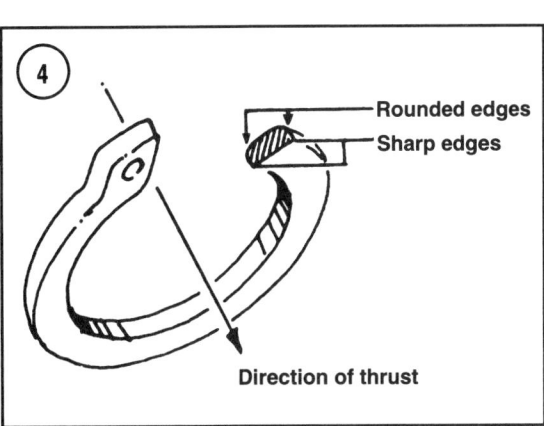

dition. To install a new snap ring without distorting it, hold the closed side of the snap ring with a pair of pliers while the open side is spread with snap ring pliers (**Figure 3**). While holding the spread ring with both tools, slide it over the shaft and into position. This technique is particularly useful when removing the notched-type snap ring shown in **Figure 3**. During removal, this type of snap ring tends to bind and grip the shaft.

Usually, snap rings have one rounded edge, while the other side has a sharp edge (**Figure 4**). The inner sharp edge prevents the snap ring from lifting out of the shaft groove when lateral pressure is applied to the snap ring. Always look at the inner and outer edges of the snap ring. Some snap rings are manufactured with the inner and outer sharp edge on opposite sides. If a snap ring has no identifiable sharp edge, the snap ring can be installed in either direction. In all cases, new snap rings must be installed at assembly, and when applicable, must be installed in the same direction as the removed snap rings.

When installed on a splined shaft, the snap ring gap should be positioned over a groove in the shaft (**Figure 5**). When a spline washer is used next to the snap ring, the teeth of the spline washer should be offset from the ends of the snap ring (**Figure 6**).

INPUT SHAFT ASSEMBLY

Figure 7

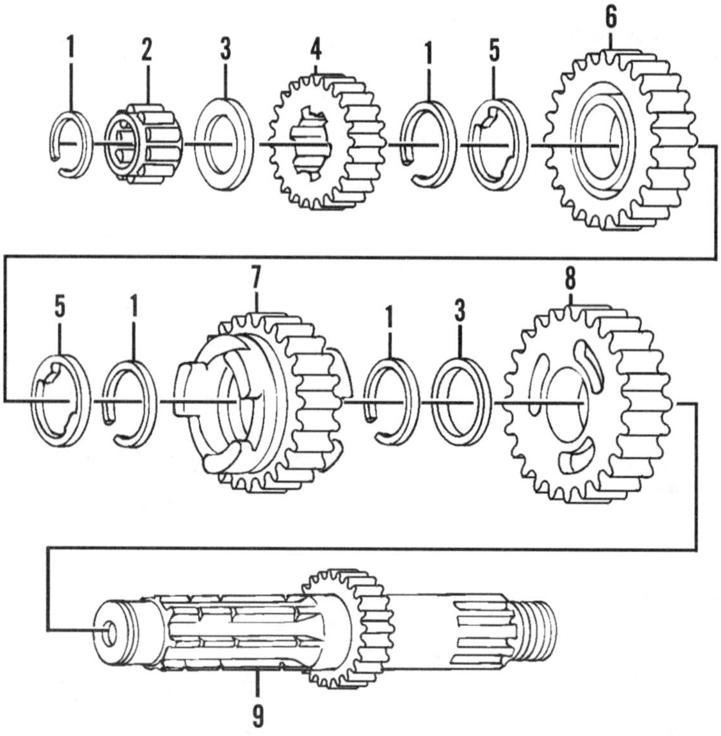

1. Snap ring
2. Bearing
3. Thrust washer
4. Second gear
5. Spline washer
6. Fourth gear
7. Third gear
8. Fifth gear
9. Input shaft

INPUT SHAFT

Disassembly

Refer to **Figure 7**.

> *CAUTION*
> *Keep parts oriented and note their direction and original location on the shaft. Preferably, mark the outer face of each part as it is removed from the shaft. Check all snap rings and note which direction the inner, sharp edge is facing. Some snap rings are identical on both edges, and therefore can be installed in either direction.*

1. Remove the parts from the input shaft (**Figure 8**) in the following order. Clean and organize the parts as they are removed.
    a. Snap ring.
    b. Bearing.
    c. Thrust washer.
    d. Second gear.
    e. Snap ring.
    f. Spline washer.
    g. Fourth gear.
    h. Spline washer.

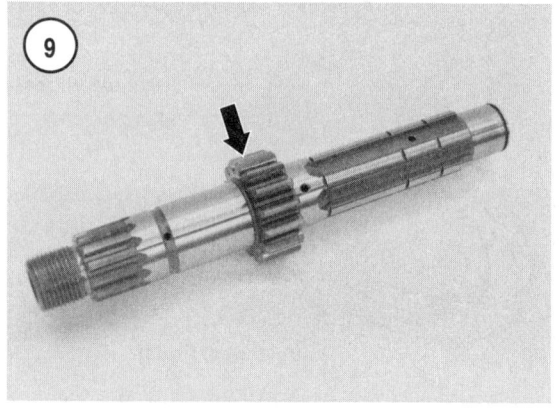

TRANSMISSION AND SHIFT MECHANISM

i. Snap ring.
j. Third gear.
k. Snap ring.
l. Thrust washer.
m. Fifth gear.

2. Inspect each part as described in this chapter. Then, return the part to its place until assembly.

Assembly

CAUTION
*Refer to **Transmission, Service** (this chapter) when installing the snap rings.*

Before beginning assembly, have new snap rings on hand. Throughout the procedure, the orientation of many parts is made in relation to first gear (**Figure 9**), on the input shaft. If desired, lock the lower portion of the shaft (below first gear) in a padded vise. With the shaft held stable and vertical, installation of the snap rings will be easier. Do not allow the vise to damage the shaft.

1. Clean and dry all parts before assembly. Lubricate all parts with engine oil.
2. Install fifth gear (**Figure 10**). The gear dog engagement slots must face out (away from first gear).
3. Install the thrust washer and snap ring (**Figure 11**). The snap ring must seat in the shaft groove.
4. Install third gear (**Figure 12**). The side of the gear with the shift fork groove must face out (away from first gear).
5. Install the snap ring and spline washer (**Figure 13**). The snap ring must seat in the shaft groove with the ends of the snap ring offset from the spline washer teeth.
6. Install fourth gear (**Figure 14**). The flat side, with the recesses, must face in (toward first gear).

7. Install the spline washer and snap ring (**Figure 15**). The snap ring must seat in the shaft groove with the ends of the snap ring offset from the spline washer teeth.

8. Install second gear (**Figure 16**). The chamfered, inner edge of the gear must face in (toward first gear).

9. Install the thrust washer and bearing (**Figure 17**).

10. Install the snap ring (**Figure 18**). The snap ring must seat in the shaft groove with the sharp edge of the snap ring facing out (away from first gear).

11. Check that all parts are secure and that the gears spin, slide and engage freely on the shaft. Wrap and store the assembly until it is ready to install into the crankcase. Install the complete transmission assembly as described in Chapter Five.

OUTPUT SHAFT

Disassembly

Remove the parts from the output shaft (**Figure 19**) in order. The parts are removed from both ends of the shaft. Clean and organize the parts as they are removed. Refer to **Figure 20**.

> *CAUTION*
> *Keep parts oriented and note their direction and original location on the shaft. Preferably, mark the outer face of each part as it is removed from the shaft. Check all snap rings and note which direction the inner, sharp edge is facing. Some snap rings are identical on both edges, and therefore can be installed in either direction.*

1. Beginning at the splined end of the shaft, disassemble the parts in the following order:
   a. Spacer.
   b. Second gear.
   c. Thrust washer.

TRANSMISSION AND SHIFT MECHANISM

OUTPUT SHAFT ASSEMBLY

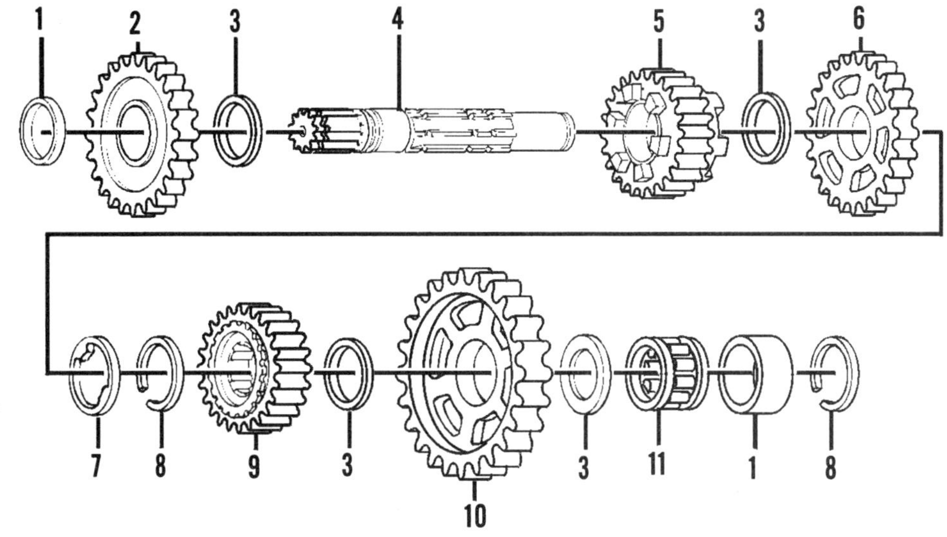

1. Spacer
2. Second gear
3. Thrust washer
4. Output shaft
5. Fourth gear
6. Third gear
7. Spline washer
8. Snap ring
9. Fifth gear
10. First gear
11. Bearing

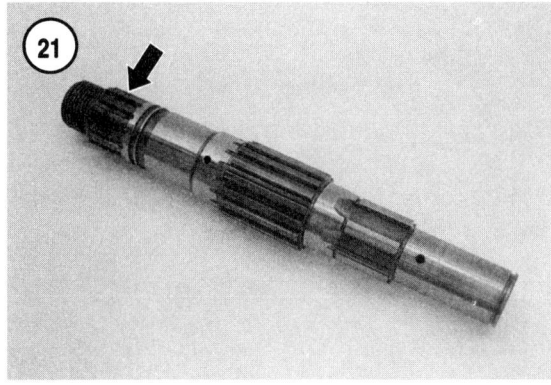

2. At the smooth end of the shaft, disassemble the parts in the following order:
   a. Snap ring.
   b. Spacer.
   c. Bearing.
   d. Thrust washer.
   e. First gear.
   f. Thrust washer.
   g. Fifth gear.
   h. Snap ring.
   i. Spline washer.
   j. Third gear.
   k. Thrust washer.
   l. Fourth gear.

3. Inspect each part as described in this chapter. Then, return the part to its place until assembly.

Assembly

CAUTION
*Refer to **Transmission, Service** (this chapter) when installing the snap rings.*

Before beginning assembly, have new snap rings on hand. Throughout the procedure, the orientation of many parts is made in relation to the splined end of the shaft (**Figure 21**). If desired, lock the splined end of the shaft in a padded vise. With the shaft held stable and vertical, installation of the snap rings will be easier. Do not allow the vise to damage the shaft.

For the model shown in this procedure, the notched snap rings were identical on both edges, and therefore could be installed in either direction. Refer to **Figure 20**.

1. Clean and dry all parts before assembly. Lubricate all parts with engine oil.

2. Install fourth gear (**Figure 22**). The side of the gear with the shift fork groove must face out (away from the splined end).

3. Install the thrust washer (**Figure 23**).

4. Install third gear (**Figure 24**). The side of the gear with the gear dog engagement slots must face in (toward the splined end).

5. Install the spline washer (**Figure 25**).

6. Install the snap ring (**Figure 26**). The snap ring must seat in the shaft groove with the ends of the snap ring offset from the spline washer teeth.

TRANSMISSION AND SHIFT MECHANISM

7. Install fifth gear (**Figure 27**). The side of the gear with the shift fork groove must face in (toward the splined end).
8. Install the thrust washer (**Figure 28**).
9. Install first gear (**Figure 29**). The side of the gear with the gear dog engagement slots must face in (toward the splined end).
10. Install the thrust washer (**Figure 30**).
11. Install the bearing and spacer (**Figure 31**).
12. Install the snap ring (**Figure 32**). The snap ring must seat in the shaft groove with the sharp edge of the snap ring facing out (away from the splined end).
13. At the splined end of the shaft, install the thrust washer (**Figure 33**).
14. Install second gear (**Figure 34**). The side of the gear with the gear dog engagement slots must face in (away from the splined end).
15. Install the spacer (**Figure 35**).
16. With the parts in their correct positions, wrap a strong rubber band around the end of the shaft.
17. Check that all parts are secure and that the gears spin, slide and engage freely on the shaft. Wrap and store the assembly until it is ready for installation into the crankcase. Install the complete transmission assembly as described in Chapter Five.

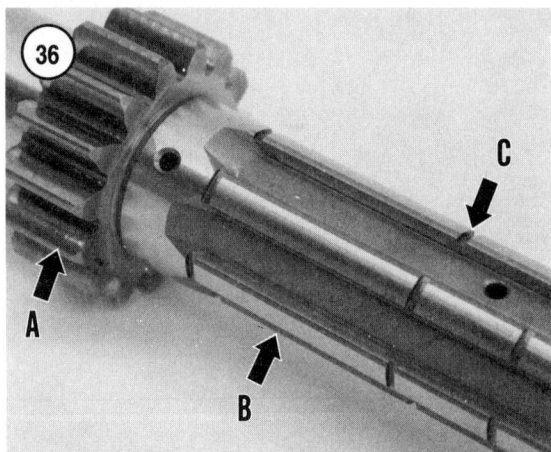

TRANSMISSION INSPECTION

Shaft Inspection

1. Inspect the shafts for the following:
   a. Broken or damaged gear teeth (A, **Figure 36**) on the input shaft.
   b. Worn or damaged splines (B, **Figure 36**).
   c. Rounded or damaged snap ring grooves (C, **Figure 36**).
   d. Clean oil holes (A, **Figure 37**).
   e. Wear, galling or other damage on the bearing/bushing surfaces (B, **Figure 37**). A blue discoloration indicates excessive heat.
   f. Damaged threads (C, **Figure 37**). Mildly damaged threads can be trued with a thread die.
2. Assemble the shafts as described in this chapter.

Component Inspection

1. Inspect the gears for the following:
   a. Broken or damaged teeth (A, **Figure 38**).
   b. Worn or damaged splines (B, **Figure 38**).
   c. Scored, galled or fractured bore (C, **Figure 38**). A blue discoloration indicates excessive heat.

   NOTE
   The side of the gear dogs that carries the engine load will wear and eventually become rounded. The unloaded side of the dogs will remain unworn. Rounded dogs will cause the transmission to jump out of gear.

   d. Worn, damaged or rounded gear dogs and engagement slots (D, **Figure 38**). Any wear on the dogs and mating slots should be uniform. If the dogs are not worn evenly, the remaining dogs will be overstressed and possibly fail. Check the engagement of the dogs by placing

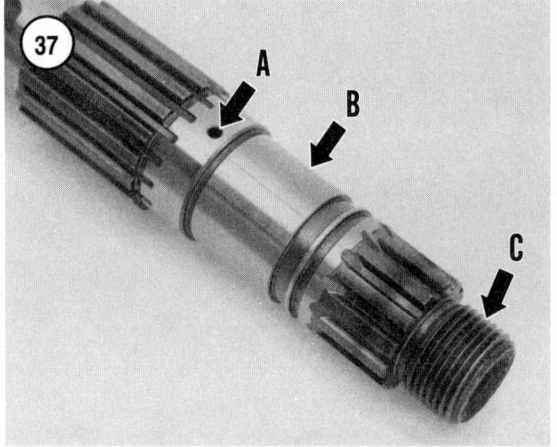

   the gears in their appropriate positions on the countershaft, and twisting the gears together. Check for positive engagement in both directions. If damage is evident, also check the condition of the shift forks, as described in this chapter.
   e. Worn or damaged shift fork groove. Measure the gear groove width (**Figure 39**). Compare the results to the specifications in **Table 2**.
   f. Smooth gear operation on the shafts. Bored gears should fit firmly on the shaft, yet spin smoothly and freely. Splined gears should fit snugly at their position on the shaft, yet slide smoothly and freely from side to side. If a gear is worn or damaged, also replace the mating gear on the other shaft.

2. Inspect the needle bearings for visible damage or heat discoloration. The bearings should rotate freely on the shaft and in their respective bushings in the crankcase.

3. Inspect the thrust washers, spacers and spline washers. The washers should be smooth and show no signs of wear or damage. The teeth on the spline washers should not be missing or damaged.

TRANSMISSION AND SHIFT MECHANISM

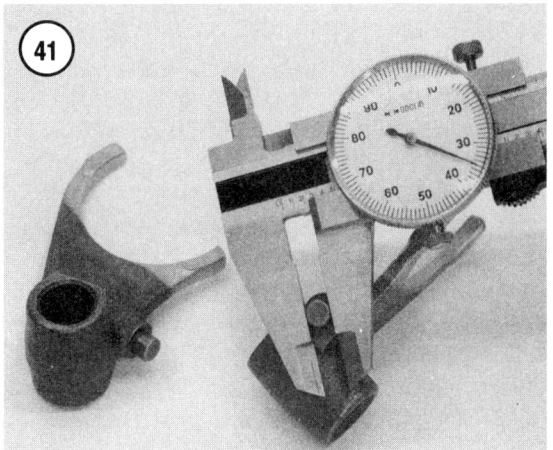

It is important that the shift drum grooves, shift forks and mating gear grooves are in good condition. Excessive wear between the parts will cause unreliable and poor engagement of the gears. This can lead to premature wear of the gear dogs and other parts.

Inspection

When inspecting the shift fork and drum assembly, replace parts that are worn or not within the specifications in **Table 2**.

1. Clean all parts in solvent and dry with compressed air.
2. Inspect the shift drum for the following:
   a. Worn shift drum grooves and cam points. The grooves should be a uniform width. Worn grooves can prevent complete gear engagement, which can cause rough shifting and allow the transmission to disengage. Measure the width (**Figure 40**) of each shift drum groove in several locations to determine wear.
   b. Worn or damaged bearing surfaces. Besides wear, look for overheating, discoloration, and a lack of lubrication. Fit the shift drum into the crankcase bearings and check for play. If necessary, replace the shift drum crankcase bearings as described in Chapter Five.
3. Inspect each shift fork for wear and damage. Inspect the:
   a. Guide pin. The pin should be symmetrical and not flat on the side. Measure the diameter of the guide pin (**Figure 41**).
   b. Shift fork claw thickness. Measure both claws at the end (**Figure 42**).
4. Inspect the shift fork shafts for wear and obvious damage.
5. Install the No. 1, No. 2 and No. 3 shift forks onto the fork shafts (**Figure 43**). The forks should slide and pivot smoothly with no excessive play or tight-

4. Install the gears and related components onto their respective shafts as described in this chapter.

SHIFT DRUM AND FORKS

As the machine is upshifted and downshifted, the shift drum and fork assembly engages and disengages pairs of gears on the transmission shafts. The shift forks move the gears for gear selection. The forks are guided by cam grooves in the shift drum.

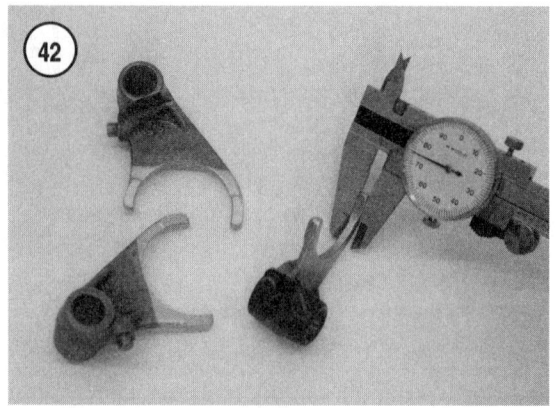

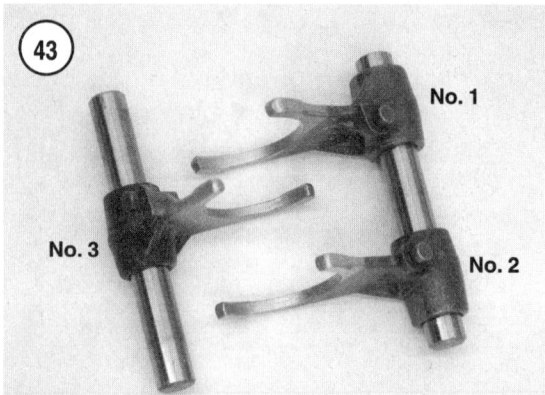

ness. If necessary, the forks can be identified as follows:
   a. Shift forks No. 1 and No. 2 can be identified by the casting around the guide pins (**Figure 44**). These forks mate with the output shaft gears. Shift fork No. 1 mates with fourth gear and shift fork No. 2 mates with fifth gear.
   b. Shift fork No. 3 has a smaller claw diameter and only mates with third gear on the input shaft.
6. Install the shift drum, forks and transmission assembly as described in Chapter Five.

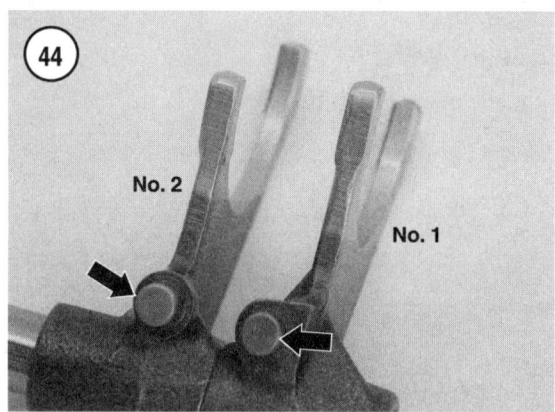

Table 1 GENERAL TRANSMISSION SPECIFICATIONS

Transmission type	Five-speed, constant mesh
Primary reduction ratio	2.272 (75/33)
Final reduction ratio	2.866 (43/15)
Overall drive ratio	5.157 (top gear)
Transmission gear ratios	
First gear	2.266 (34/15)
Second gear	1.444 (25/18)
Third gear	1.136 (25/22)
Fourth gear	0.954 (21/22)
Fifth gear	0.791 (19/24)

Table 2 TRANSMISSION INTERNAL SPECIFICATIONS

Item	Standard mm mm (in.)	Service limit mm (in.)
Gear groove width	4.55-4.65 (0.179-0.183)	4.8 (0.189)
Shift drum groove width	6.05-6.20 (0.238-0.244)	6.3 (0.248)
Shift fork claw thickness	4.4-4.5 (0.173-0.177)	4.3 (0.169)
Shift fork guide pin diameter	5.9-6.0 (0.232-0.236)	5.8 (0.228)

CHAPTER EIGHT

FUEL SYSTEM

This chapter provides service procedures for removing, disassembling, inspecting, repairing and assembling the carburetor. Also included is carburetor operation. **Table 1** at the end of this chapter provides standard carburetor specifications.

Refer to this chapter for fuel valve servicing, throttle and choke cable replacement and air filter housing removal. Also included is a schematic of the evaporative emission control system (California models only). Refer to Chapter Three for air filter service, cable adjustments and cable lubrication. Refer to *Safety* and *Service Methods* in Chapter One.

CARBURETOR

Operation

The Keihin CVK 40 is a vacuum-controlled, constant velocity carburetor. It uses both a throttle valve and diaphram-operated slide to regulate fuel to the engine. The throttle valve (**Figure 1**) is located on the outlet end of the carburetor and is connected to the throttle cables. The slide and diaphragm assembly, located at the center of the carburetor, regulates fuel by a jet needle at the bottom of the slide (**Figure 2**). The diaphragm is located at the top of the slide in the diaphragm chamber (**Figure 3**). The diaphragm divides and seals the large chamber into a lower and upper chamber.

During operation, when the throttle valve is opened, air demand and speed through the carburetor is increased. As air passes under the slide, air pressure drops in that area. This low air pressure is vented to the upper diaphragm chamber. The lower diaphragm chamber is vented to atmospheric pressure. This difference in pressure causes the slide and jet needle to rise, allowing fuel to pass into the carburetor throat. When the throttle valve is closed, the pressure differential lowers, allowing the slide and jet needle to return to a resting position. Refer to *Carburetor Operation* in this chapter for operational details of specific fuel circuits within the carburetor.

Removal/Installation

Refer to **Figure 4**.
1. Support the motorcycle so it is stable and secure.
2. Remove the starter relay as described in Chapter Nine.
3. Detach the clamp (A, **Figure 5**) securing the wires to the starter relay bracket.
4. Remove the bolt (B, **Figure 5**) and remove the bracket (C).

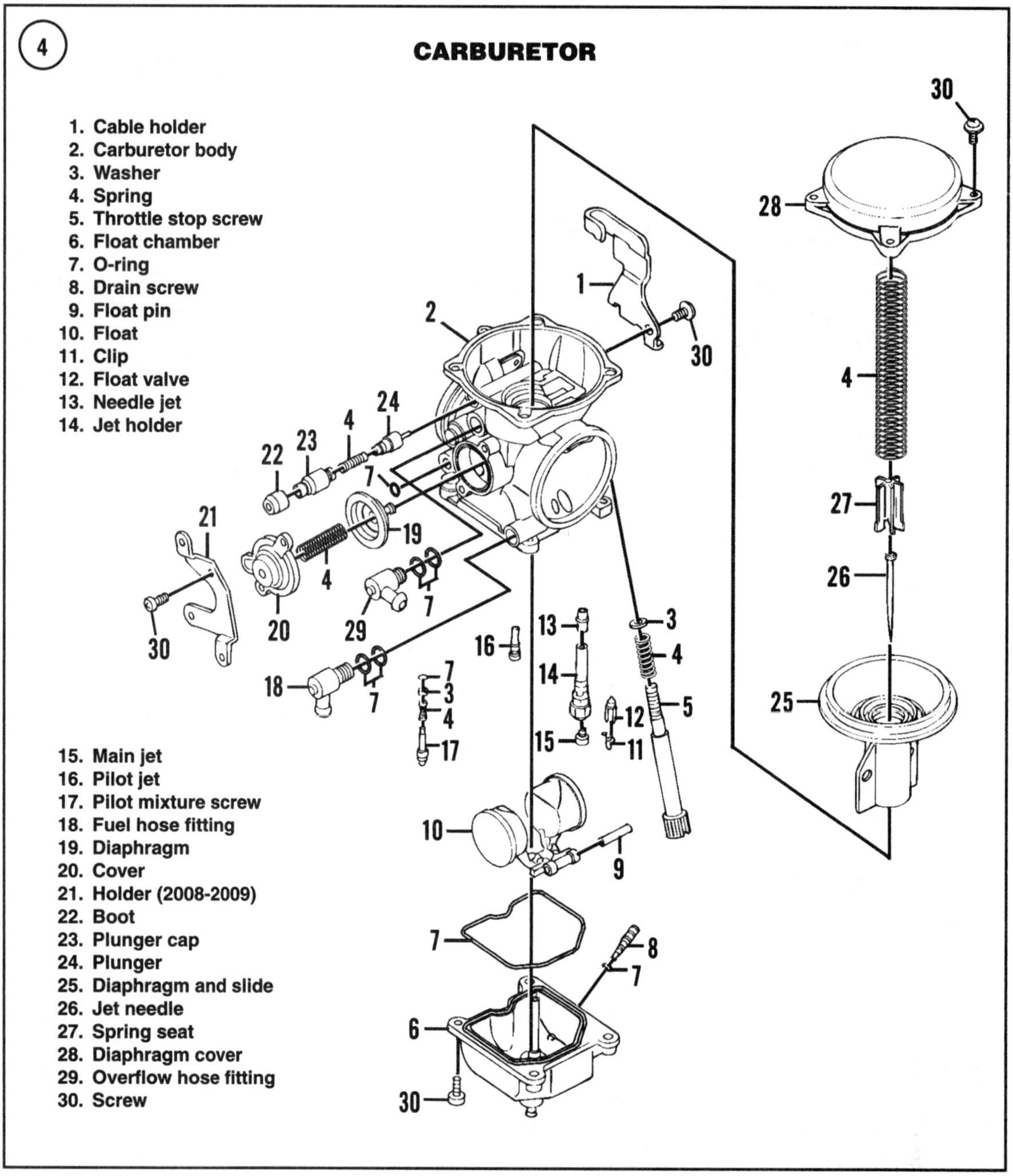

CHAPTER EIGHT

CARBURETOR

1. Cable holder
2. Carburetor body
3. Washer
4. Spring
5. Throttle stop screw
6. Float chamber
7. O-ring
8. Drain screw
9. Float pin
10. Float
11. Clip
12. Float valve
13. Needle jet
14. Jet holder
15. Main jet
16. Pilot jet
17. Pilot mixture screw
18. Fuel hose fitting
19. Diaphragm
20. Cover
21. Holder (2008-2009)
22. Boot
23. Plunger cap
24. Plunger
25. Diaphragm and slide
26. Jet needle
27. Spring seat
28. Diaphragm cover
29. Overflow hose fitting
30. Screw

FUEL SYSTEM

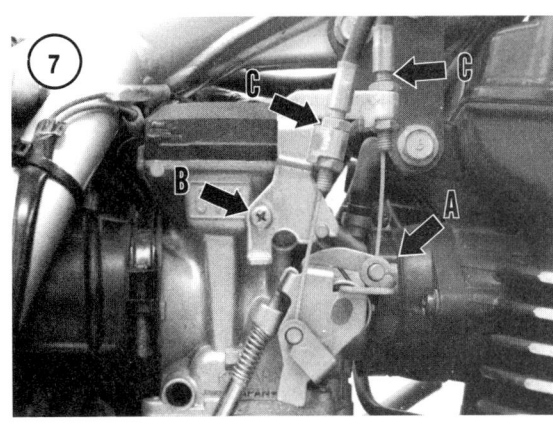

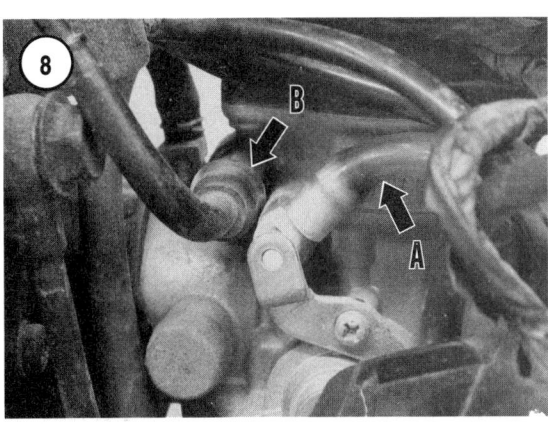

5. On California models, disconnect the vapor separator hose.
6. Remove the fuel tank as described in Chapter Fifteen.
7. Disconnect the vacuum switch hose (**Figure 6**) from the carburetor.
8. Remove the clamps from the air filter housing duct and intake duct (A, **Figure 7**).
9. Remove the cable holder screw (B, **Figure 7**). If the screw is too tight, disconnect the throttle cables (C, **Figure 7**) and leave the holder attached to the carburetor. If the cables are removed, mark the cables so they can be reinstalled in the correct position.
10. On the left side of the carburetor, remove the overflow hose (A, **Figure 8**) from the fitting.
11. Remove the carburetor from the ducts as follows:
   a. Pry up on the air filter housing duct to break it free from the carburetor. If necessary, lightly spray penetrating lubricant under the duct to reduce its grip on the carburetor. Pry the duct off the carburetor, keeping the carburetor upright.
   b. Push the carburetor back and pry the intake duct off the carburetor.
12. Tilt the carburetor to the left to access the choke plunger. Remove the choke plunger (B, **Figure 8**).
13. Remove the carburetor (**Figure 9**) out the right side of the motorcycle.
14. Open the drain on the bottom of the float chamber and drain any remaining fuel.
15. If necessary, disconnect the choke plunger (**Figure 10**) by pushing up on the spring and removing the cable from the plunger.
16. Reverse the preceding procedure to install the carburetor. Note the following:
   a. To ease carburetor installation, clean and lightly lubricate the inside edges of the ducts.
   b. Align and engage the tab on the carburetor with the slot in the intake duct. Although there

CHAPTER EIGHT

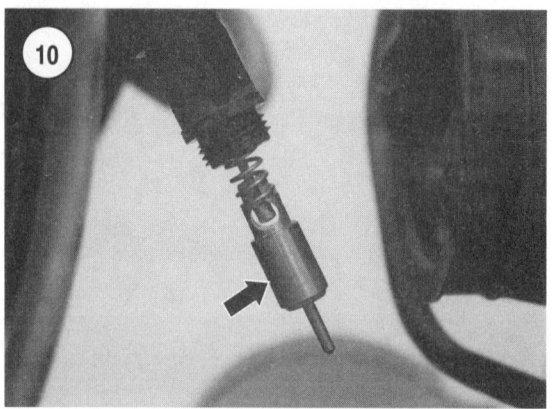

are slots (**Figure 11**) on both sides of the duct, there is only one tab on the carburetor.
  c. Check the fuel and overflow hose routing.
  d. Check/adjust the throttle and choke cables (Chapter Three).
  e. Check the throttle and choke for proper operation.
  f. Check the carburetor for leaks.
  g. If the carburetor was disassembled, adjust the carburetor (Chapter Three).

Disassembly/Assembly

Refer to **Figure 4**.
1. Remove the air cutoff valve assembly as follows:
  a. Remove the screws (**Figure 12**) from the holder/cover. The holder/cover is under spring pressure. Keep pressure on the holder/cover while removing the screws.
  b. Remove the holder/cover and spring (**Figure 13**).
  c. Remove the diaphragm (A, **Figure 14**) and O-ring (B).
2. Remove the hose fittings (**Figure 15**).
3. Remove the diaphragm cover and the slide assembly as follows:

FUEL SYSTEM

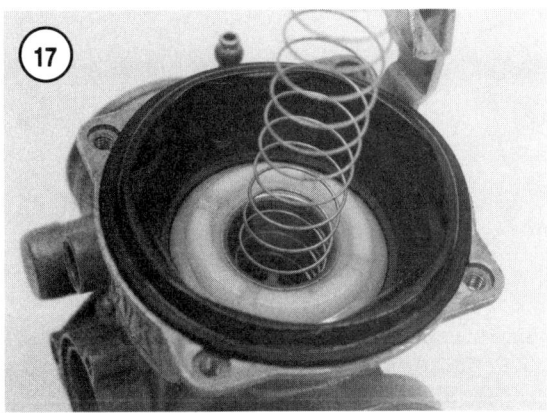

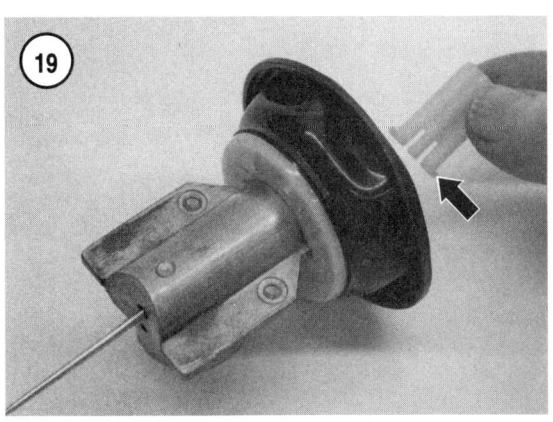

a. Remove the cover (**Figure 16**). The cover is under slight spring pressure. Hold the cover in place while removing the four screws. Lift off the cover.
b. Remove the spring (**Figure 17**).

CAUTION
Do not lift or hold the slide by the diaphragm. Do not damage the jet needle while raising it from the carburetor.

c. From the intake side, push up on the slide (**Figure 18**) so it can be lifted from the carburetor.
d. Remove the spring seat (**Figure 19**). Tilt the slide to remove the needle.

4. Remove the float chamber (**Figure 20**). Remove the drain screw and O-ring from the chamber.

5. Remove and disassemble the float assembly (**Figure 21**) as follows:
   a. Remove the pin (**Figure 22**) from the float.
   b. Carefully lift out the float (A, **Figure 23**) and float valve (B).
   c. Slide the clip (A, **Figure 24**) and float valve (B) off the float tab (C).

6. Remove the pilot mixture screw (**Figure 25**) as follows:

a. If a plug is installed over the screw, remove the plug by drilling through it with a small drill bit. The hole only needs to be large enough to insert a small sheet metal screw or pick tool. Using a large drill bit risks damaging the pilot mixture screw and the internal threads. When drilling, use a light touch so the bit does not contact the screw when the bit breaks through the plug. Carefully pry the plug after the hole is drilled.
b. Make a scratch on the edge of the bore, in line with the slot in the screw. This will be used as a reference point when installing the screw.
c. Turn the screw clockwise and accurately count the number of turns it takes to lightly seat the screw into the carburetor.
d. Record the number of turns.
e. Remove the pilot mixture screw, spring, washer and O-ring (**Figure 26**).

7. Remove the main jet assembly as follows:
   a. Remove the main jet (**Figure 27**).
   b. Remove the jet holder (**Figure 28**).
   c. Remove the needle jet (**Figure 29**). Unseat the jet from the carburetor venturi by hand. Note that the long end of the jet fits into the carburetor throat.
8. Remove the pilot jet (**Figure 30**).
9. Remove the throttle stop screw, spring and washer.
10. Clean and inspect the parts as described in this section.
11. Refer to *Carburetor Operation* in this chapter for the function of the jets and their effect on performance.
12. Reverse this procedure to assemble the carburetor. Note the following:
    a. Install new, lubricated O-rings. Install the small O-ring under the air cutoff valve with the round side facing out.
    b. Attach the float valve and clip to the float before installing the parts.

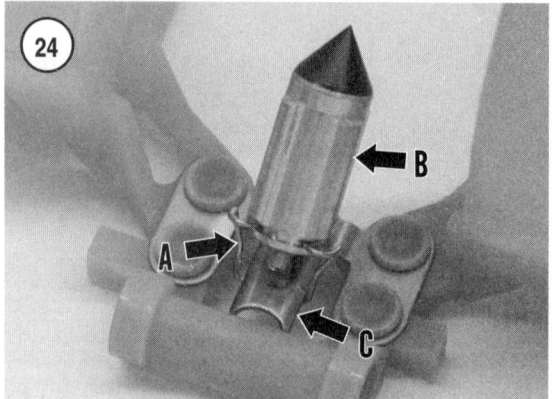

FUEL SYSTEM

c. Check and adjust the float height. Refer to *Float Adjustment* in this section.

d. When installing the pilot mixture screw, lightly seat the screw, and then turn it out the number of turns recorded during disassembly. Refer to the reference mark on the carburetor for the original setting. If the number of turns is not known, refer to **Table 1** for the basic setting.

e. It is easiest to install the spring, cover and holder over the air cutoff valve diaphragm as a single assembly (**Figure 13**). Check that the spring is seated in the cover and that the hose fittings are installed before assembling.

f. When installing the slide and diaphragm, or the diaphragm in the air cutoff valve, the diaphragm must be seated at its edge before installing the cover.

g. Install the carburetor as described in this section.

Cleaning and Inspection

Use the following procedure to clean and inspect the carburetor. Refer to *Carburetor Operation* in this chapter to gain an understanding of how the carburetor passages for each circuit are interconnected. When cleaning, this will help in verifying whether the entire length of a passage is clean. Always replace worn or damaged parts. Refer to **Figure 4** as needed.

It is recommended to use a commercial cleaner specifically for carburetors, since these cleaners contains agents for removing fuel residue and buildup. Use a cleaner that is harmless to rubber and plastic parts. Follow the manufacturer's instructions.

CAUTION
Do not clean the jet orifices or seats with wire or drill bits. These items can scratch the surfaces and alter flow rates, or cause leaking.

NOTE
Because of heat and age, O-rings eventually lose flexibility and do not seal properly. It is standard practice to replace all O-rings and gaskets when rebuilding a carburetor.

1. Clean all the parts in carburetor cleaner. Use compressed air to clean all passages, orifices and vents in the carburetor body.

2. Inspect the main jet assembly and pilot jet (**Figure 31**). Check that all holes in the ends and sides are clean and undamaged.

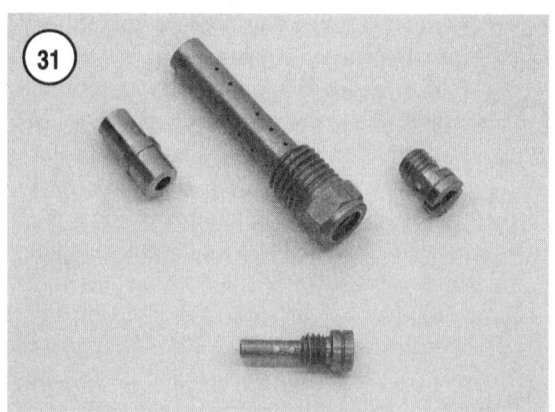

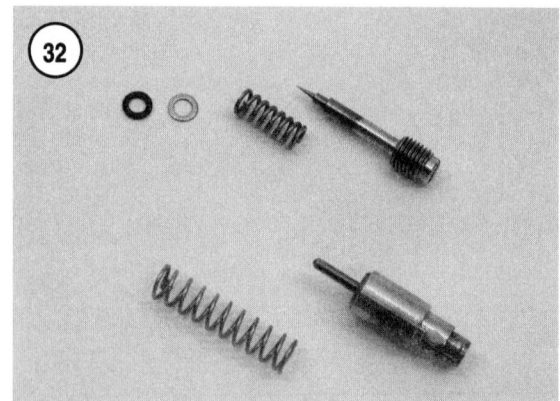

3. Inspect the pilot mixture screw assembly and choke plunger (**Figure 32**).
   a. Inspect the screw and plunger tips for dents or wear.
   b. The spring coils should be resilient and not be crushed.
   c. The plunger should move freely in its bore in the carburetor.
4. Inspect the throttle stop screw, spring and washer (**Figure 33**). Inspect the screw tip and threads for damage. The spring coils should be resilient and not be crushed.

5. Inspect the diaphragm and slide (**Figure 34**). If either part is damaged, the parts are only available together, as a single part number.
   a. Inspect the slide for wear and scratches. Fit the slide into the carburetor body and check for smooth operation. The slide should freely move vertically, but have minimal front to back play.
   b. Inspect the diaphragm for dryness, tears and holes. The diaphragm must be undamaged in order to isolate the pressure differences that are above and below the diaphragm. A leaking diaphragm prevents the slide from reaching or maintaining its normal level at any throttle position off idle. Engine performance will be noticeably diminished.

6. Inspect the diaphragm cover and needle assembly (**Figure 35**).
   a. The diaphragm cover must be undamaged in order to maintain low pressure in the upper chamber of the carburetor. A cracked or loose cover affects engine performance similarly to a damaged diaphragm.
   b. The jet needle (**Figure 36**) must be smooth and evenly tapered. If it is stepped, dented, worn or bent, replace the needle.
7. Inspect the float and float valve assembly (**Figure 37**).

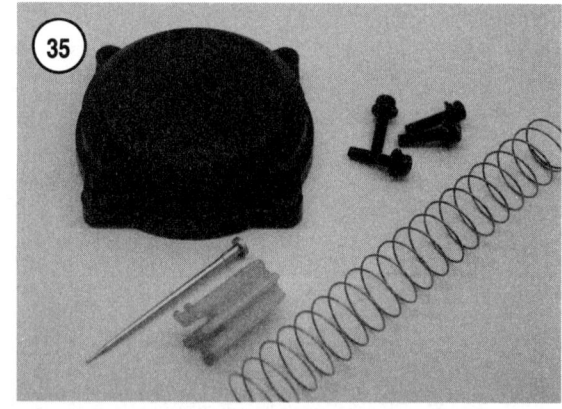

FUEL SYSTEM

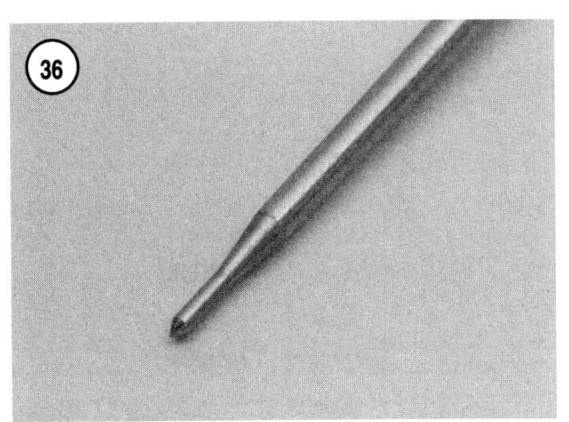

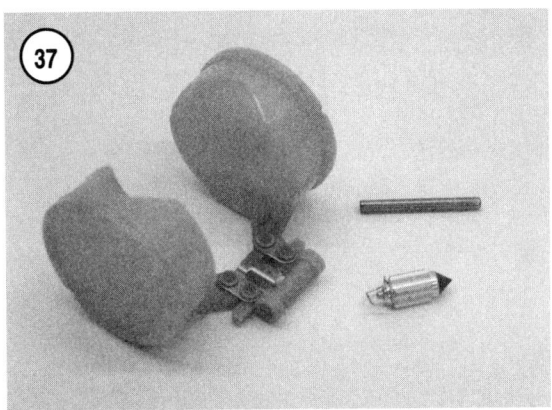

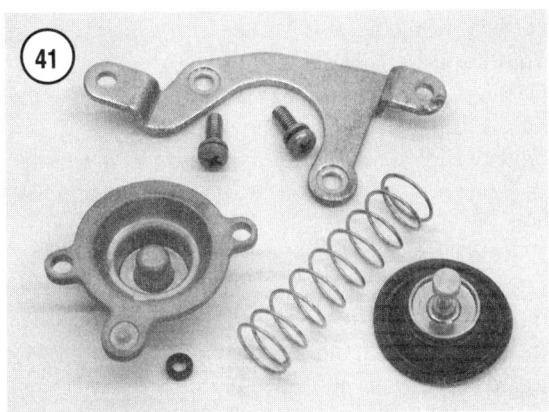

a. Inspect the tip of the float valve (**Figure 38**). If it is stepped or dented, replace the float valve.
b. Lightly press on the spring-loaded pin (**Figure 39**) in the float valve. The pin should easily move in and out of the valve. If it is varnished with fuel residue, replace the float valve.
c. Inspect the float valve seat in the carburetor body. The seat should be clean and scratch-free. If it is not, the float valve will not seat properly and the carburetor will overflow.
d. Inspect the float and pin. Submerge the float in water and check for leaks. Replace the float if water or fuel is detected inside the float. Check that the float pin is straight and smooth. It must be a slip-fit in the float.

8. Inspect the float bowl assembly (**Figure 40**).
   a. Check that all residue is removed from the interior of the bowl.
   b. Inspect threaded parts for damage.
   c. Replace the O-ring on the float bowl and drain screw.

9. Inspect the air cutoff valve assembly (**Figure 41**).
   a. The diaphragm must be free of damage in order to operate properly.

b. The plunger on the end of the diaphragm stem should move freely in its bore in the carburetor.

c. Inspect the small air hole at the edge of the cover for cleanliness.

10. Inspect the hose fittings (**Figure 42**) for damage. Replace the O-rings on both fittings.

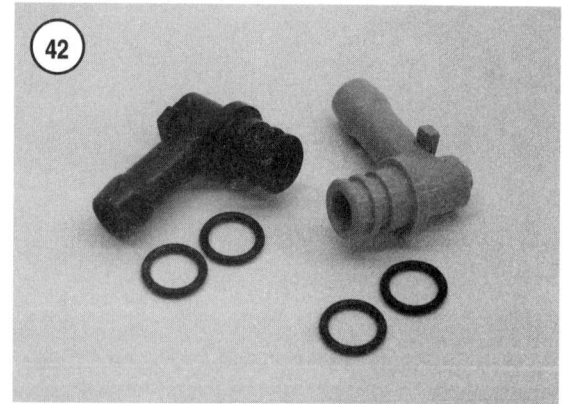

Float Adjustment

The float and float valve maintain a constant and measured fuel level in the float bowl. As fuel is used, the float lowers and allows more fuel past the valve. As the fuel level rises, the float closes the valve when the required fuel level is reached. If the float is out of adjustment, the fuel level will be too high or low. A low fuel level causes the engine to run as if the jetting is too lean. A high fuel level will cause the engine to run as if the jetting is too rich. It may also cause fuel overflow.

1. Remove the carburetor as described in this section.
2. Remove the float bowl.
3. Lightly touch the float to ensure the float valve is seated.
4. Hold the carburetor so the float valve remains seated, but the spring-loaded pin in the valve is not compressed by the tab on the float (**Figure 43**). The tab should only touch the pin.

5. Measure the distance from the carburetor body gasket surface to the highest point on the float (**Figure 43**). Refer to **Table 1** for the required float height.
6. If the float height is incorrect, do the following:
    a. Remove the float assembly from the carburetor.
    b. Remove the float valve and clip.
    c. Bend the float tab in the appropriate direction to raise or lower the float. Use care when bending the tab to prevent breaking the plastic lugs or float.
    d. Assemble the float and recheck the height. Adjust, if necessary.
7. Install the float bowl.
8. Install the carburetor as described in this section.

CARBURETOR OPERATION

Before disassembling the carburetor, understand the function of the pilot, needle and main jet circuits. When evaluating or troubleshooting these circuits, keep in mind that their operating ranges overlap during the transition from closed to fully open throttle.

Common factors that affect carburetor performance are altitude, temperature and engine load. If the engine is not running or performing up to expec-

FUEL SYSTEM

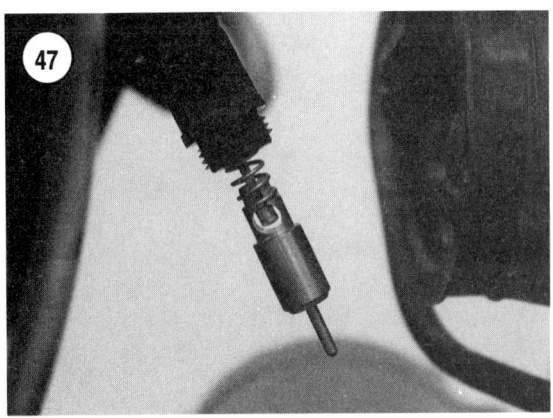

fuel mixture entering the engine, while turning the screw out will enrich the mixture.

The pilot hole and mixture screw affects idle and low engine speeds. As the throttle plate is opened, it uncovers the bypass pilot holes (B, **Figure 46**), which then become effective. These holes are connected to the passage between the pilot jet and pilot mixture screw. They are not affected by the mixture screw. As engine speed increases, fuel is drawn through these passages directly from the pilot jet.

For high altitudes, the pilot jet is interchangeable with a jet that provides a leaner air/fuel mixture. Refer to **Table 1** for the recommended pilot jet sizes.

Jet Needle Circuit

The jet needle is connected to the slide and controls the mixture from approximately 1/4 to 3/4 throttle. Air enters the main air jet (B, **Figure 44**), where it passes to the needle jet holder and needle jet. These parts are located above the main jet (C, **Figure 45**). The needle jet holder mixes fuel from the float chamber with the air from the main air jet. The atomized air/fuel mixture passes to the needle jet, where it is regulated by the jet needle into the throat of the carburetor. As the throttle is opened, the needle rises and fuel is regulated by the needle taper. The vertical position of the needle in the slide is not adjustable.

Main Jet Circuit

The main jet (C, **Figure 45**) is screwed to the bottom of the needle jet holder and controls the mixture from approximately 3/4 to full throttle. The main jet is numbered and is interchangeable with jets that provide a leaner or richer air/fuel mixture. Replacing the standard jet with a larger numbered jet will make the mixture richer. Jets with a smaller number will make the mixture leaner. Many of these jets are for off-road use only.

For high altitudes, the main jet is interchangeable with a jet that provides a leaner air/fuel mixture. Refer to **Table 1** for the standard recommended main jet sizes.

Choke Circuit

The choke circuit consists of a plunger assembly (**Figure 47**) and starter jet (D, **Figure 45**). The jet discharges fuel from the orifice in the plunger bore (A, **Figure 48**). The plunger bore also intersects an air vent (A, **Figure 49**), connecting the bottom of the slide diaphragm chamber and the throat of the carburetor.

When the choke is operated, the plunger opens the fuel and air passages. As the engine is cranked, air and fuel is drawn through these passages to the car-

tations, check the following before adjusting or replacing the components in the carburetor:
1. Throttle cables. Check that the cables are not dragging and are correctly adjusted.
2. Air filter. Check that the filter is clean.
3. Fuel flow. Check that fuel is adequately flowing from the fuel tank to the carburetor. Inspect in-line filter screens for plugging.
4. Ignition timing. Check that timing is correct.
5. Choke. Check that the choke fully opens and closes.
6. Muffler. Check that the muffler is not restricting flow.
7. Brakes. Check that the brake pads are not dragging on the discs.

Pilot Jet Circuit

The pilot circuit controls the air/fuel ratio from closed throttle to about 1/4 throttle. Air enters the pilot air jet (A, **Figure 44**), where it passes to the pilot jet (A, **Figure 45**). The pilot jet draws fuel from the float chamber and mixes it with the air from the pilot air jet. The atomized air/fuel mixture passes to the pilot mixture screw (B, **Figure 45**), where it is regulated into the throat of the carburetor. The mixture is discharged from the pilot hole (A, **Figure 46**). Turning the pilot mixture screw in will lean the air/

buretor throat. When the choke plunger is closed, the air and fuel passages are closed.

This type of choke is most effective if the throttle remains closed during startup, in order to maintain high vacuum at the air and fuel passages.

Air Cutoff Valve Circuit

The function of the air cutoff valve (**Figure 50**) is to richen the pilot jet system air/fuel mixture during compression braking, such as descending steep grades when the engine speed is high, but the throttle is closed. Without this valve, the engine will develop a lean air/fuel mixture in the pilot system, which will cause backfiring and possible engine damage. The air cutoff valve consists of a one-piece diaphragm with cylindrical plunger, spring and cover assembly (**Figure 41**). The function of the assembly is to open and close an air passage in the plunger bore.

During acceleration and steady running speeds, the diaphragm and plunger are in the down position. This allows air to vent from a passage in the slide diaphragm chamber (B, **Figure 49**) to the plunger bore (B, **Figure 48**). The air then passes to the pilot jet system. During deceleration, when the throttle valve is closed, engine vacuum vents through a passage (C, **Figure 46**) leading to the air cutoff valve cover. The vacuum pulls the diaphragm out, causing the plunger to block the air passage in the plunger bore. This reduces the amount of air going to the pilot jet system, and a rich fuel mixture is discharged from the pilot hole (A, **Figure 46**).

When acceleration resumes, the vacuum holding the diaphragm out is reduced, and the spring pushes the diaphragm and plunger down, again creating a normal fuel mixture in the pilot jet system.

FUEL VALVE

The fuel valve is equipped with a lever and diaphragm valve. The lever controls off, on and reserve fuel positions, while the diaphragm valve controls the flow of fuel out of the fuel valve. The diaphragm valve is vacuum-actuated and is connected by a hose to a fitting on the carburetor (C, **Figure 49**). During engine starting or operation, vacuum in the carburetor throat opens the diaphragm valve. In order for the diaphragm valve to operate properly, it must be kept clean and tight, in order to maintain vacuum. The vacuum hose must also be tight and in good condition.

Removal/Inspection/Installation

Refer to **Figure 51**.
1. Remove the fuel tank as described in Chapter Fifteen.

WARNING
Drain the fuel into an approved container. Perform the draining procedure a safe distance away from the work area.

2. Drain the fuel from the tank. Since the fuel valve does not allow fuel to pass without vacuum applied, the tank must be siphoned or emptied through the fill opening.
3. Place the fuel tank vertically on the workbench. Remove the bolts (A, **Figure 52**) securing the fuel valve assembly (B).
4. Remove the lever plate (A, **Figure 53**), wave washer (B), lever (C) and fuel gasket (D).

FUEL SYSTEM

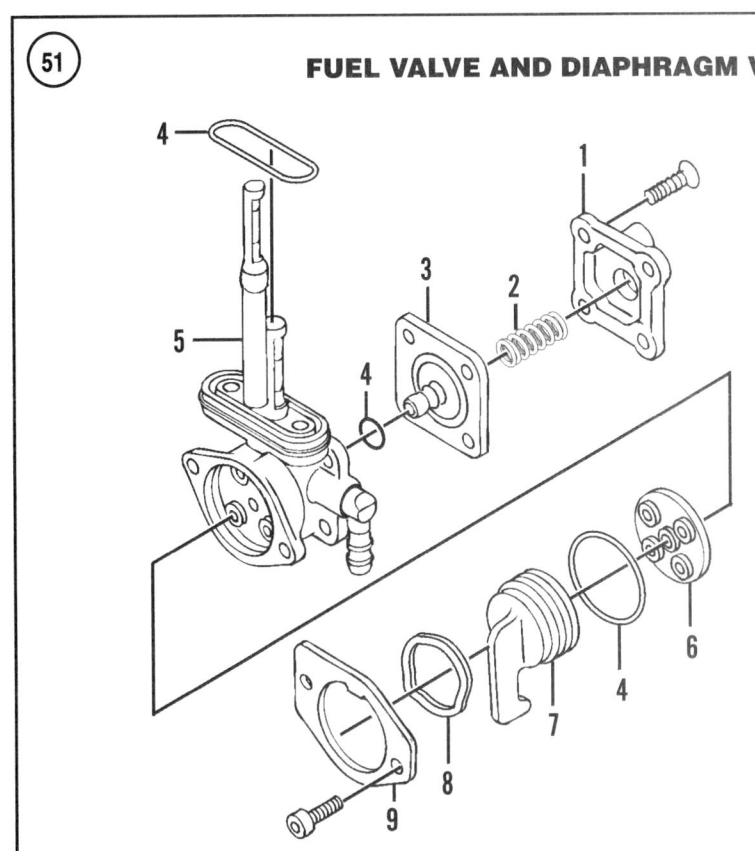

FUEL VALVE AND DIAPHRAGM VALVE

1. Vacuum cover
2. Spring
3. Diaphragm
4. O-ring
5. Fuel valve
6. Fuel gasket
7. Lever
8. Wave washer
9. Lever plate

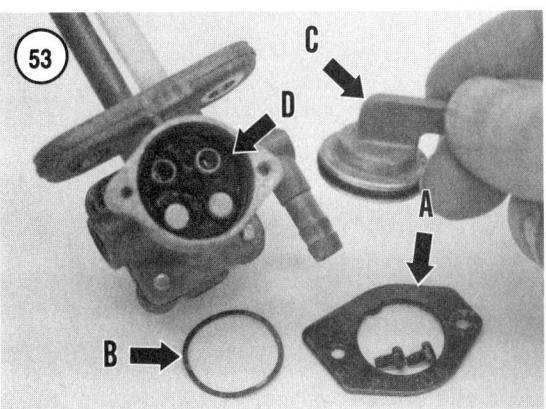

CAUTION
*Before removing the cover in Step 5, check that it is separated from the thin diaphragm (**Figure 54**) that contacts the cover. If necessary, use a small tool to gently separate the cover around its perimeter.*

5. Remove the vacuum cover (A, **Figure 55**) and spring (B).
6. Lift the diaphragm assembly from the fuel valve (**Figure 56**). Again, use a small tool to separate the inner diaphragm from the valve.
7. Clean the parts (**Figure 57**).

a. Wash the valve, fuel filters and other metal parts in solvent.
b. Gently wipe the diaphragm assembly.
8. Inspect the parts.
a. Check for buildup in the screen filters. If buildup is evident, lightly scrub the screens with a nylon brush and solvent. Carefully blow compressed air through the screen, from the inside to the outside.
b. Inspect the valve passages for buildup.
c. Inspect the vacuum holes (**Figure 58**) in the vacuum cover for cleanliness.
d. Make sure the diaphragm vent passage (**Figure 59**) is unobstructed.
e. Inspect the remaining parts for visible damage.
f. Replace all O-rings. If fuel has leaked past the fuel gasket, replace the gasket. Eventually, the gasket will wear on the face where it contacts the lever.
g. Inspect the vacuum hose connecting the fuel valve to the carburetor. The hose must be clean and tight on the fittings to hold vacuum.
9. Assemble the valve. Note the following:
a. Lightly lubricate the O-rings. Also, lubricate the fuel gasket.
b. Install the diaphragm assembly so the vent (**Figure 60**) faces the fuel fitting. Check that both diaphragms lay flat before installing the vacuum cover.
c. Install the vacuum cover with the vacuum fitting facing the fuel fitting. Tighten the cover screws evenly in several passes.
10. Install the fuel valve into the fuel tank and evenly tighten the bolts.
11. Install the fuel tank as described in Chapter Fifteen.
12. When filling the tank, start with a small amount of fuel and check for leaks. Operate the lever and check that all positions are leak-free.

EVAPORATIVE EMISSIONS CONTROL SYSTEM (CALIFORNIA MODELS ONLY)

No adjustments are required for the evaporative emissions control system. Visual inspection of the hoses and connections should be made as recommended in Chapter Three. If the system is suspected of causing poor running, or if obvious damage has occurred to the system, refer inspection and testing of the separator and canister to a dealership. Refer to **Figure 61** for parts identification and hose routing.

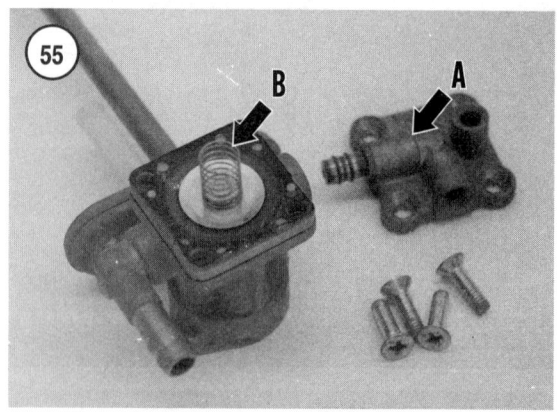

FUEL SYSTEM

59

60

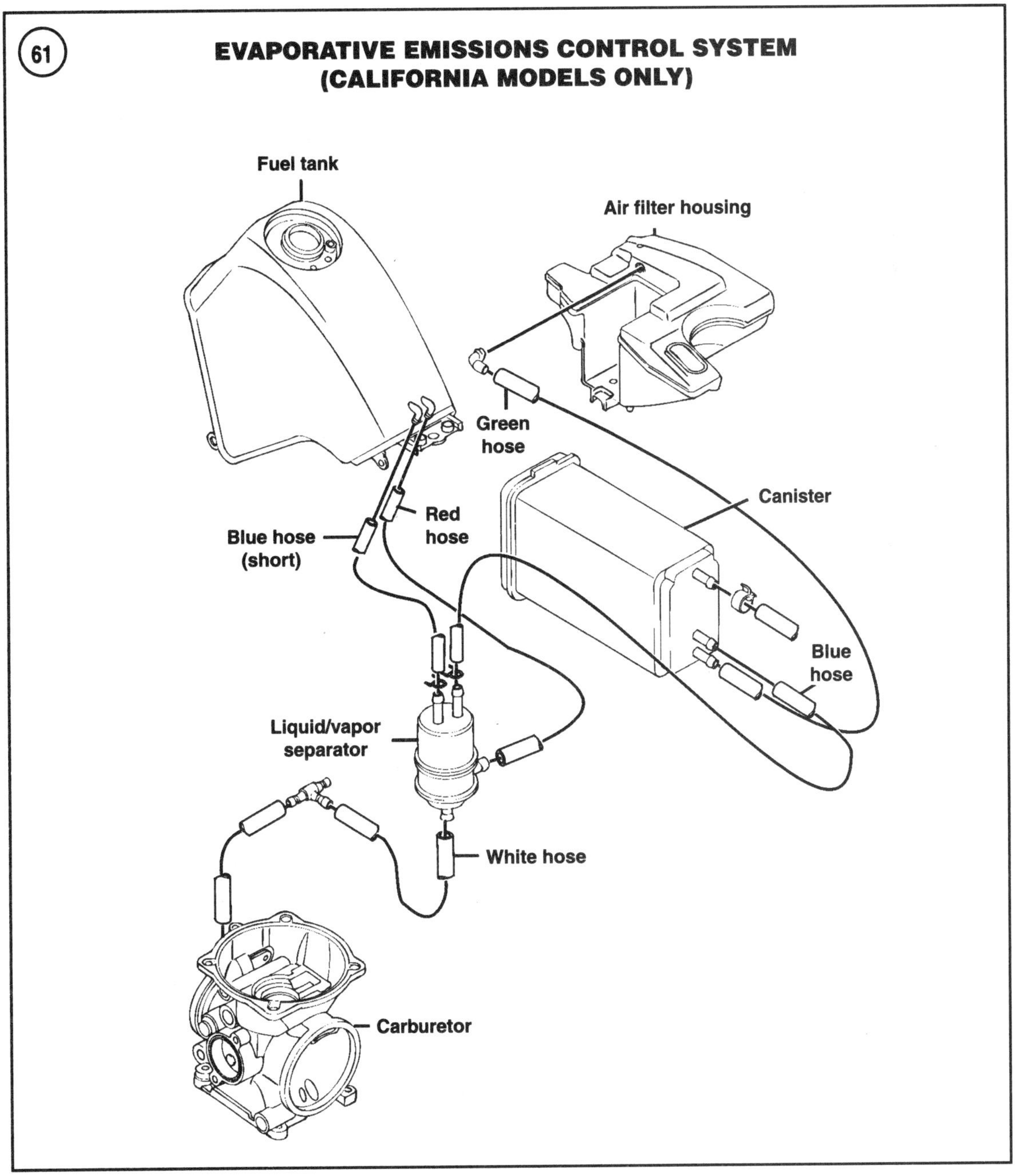

61

EVAPORATIVE EMISSIONS CONTROL SYSTEM
(CALIFORNIA MODELS ONLY)

- Fuel tank
- Air filter housing
- Green hose
- Blue hose (short)
- Red hose
- Canister
- Blue hose
- Liquid/vapor separator
- White hose
- Carburetor

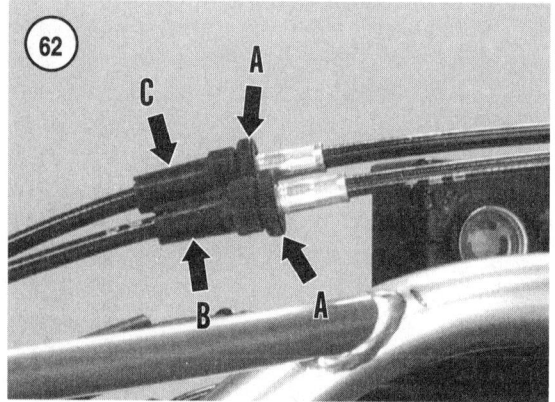

THROTTLE CABLE

Removal/Installation

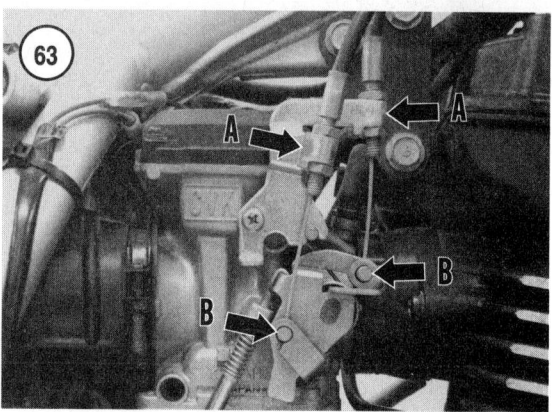

The throttle uses two cables. One cable pulls the throttle open during acceleration, while the other pulls the throttle closed during deceleration. In operation, the cables always move in opposite directions to one another. Use the following procedure to replace the throttle cables.

1. Remove the fuel tank as described in Chapter Fifteen.
2. At the handlebar, loosen the locknuts (A, **Figure 62**). Turn the adjuster on the accelerator cable (B, **Figure 62**) and decelerator cable (C) to obtain maximum cable slack.
3. At the carburetor, loosen the locknuts and remove the cables from the holders (A, **Figure 63**) and throttle valve (B). The left cable is the accelerator cable. Identify the cables so the new cables can be matched and installed in the correct position.
4. Note how the cables are routed. Pull the cables from the frame.
5. Remove the right hand guard.
6. Slide the rubber cable cover (A, **Figure 64**) off the throttle housing.
7. Move the rubber throttle housing cover (B, **Figure 64**) off the throttle housing by pushing it toward the cables. The cover must be pushed off the housing to allow housing disassembly.
8. Remove the screws (**Figure 65**) from the housing and separate the housing halves.

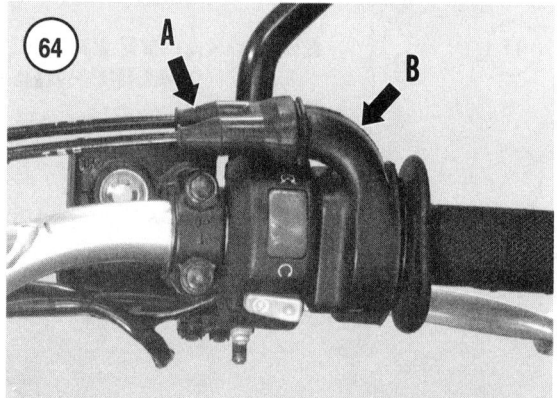

NOTE
The throttle cables are only available as a set. The cable guide at the upper end of each cable is molded onto the cable. Do not attempt removal.

9. Separate each cable guide (A, **Figure 66**) from its housing half (B). Note that each cable guide will only fit into its corresponding housing half.

FUEL SYSTEM

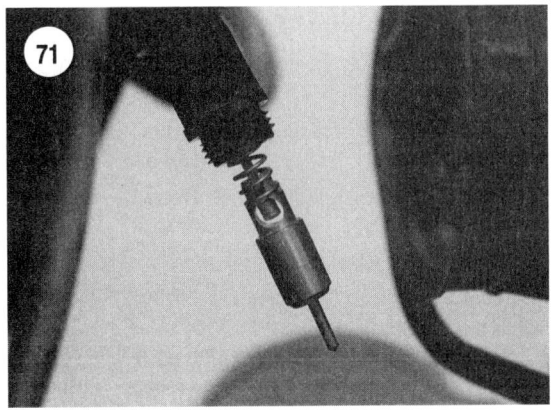

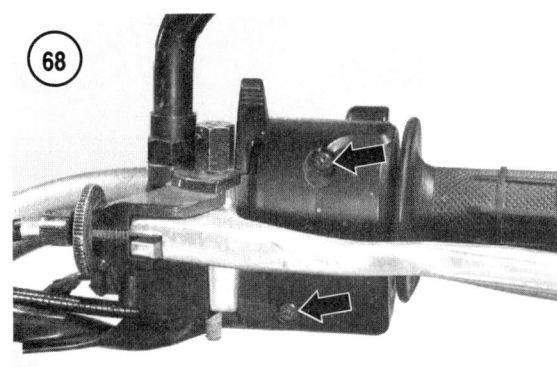

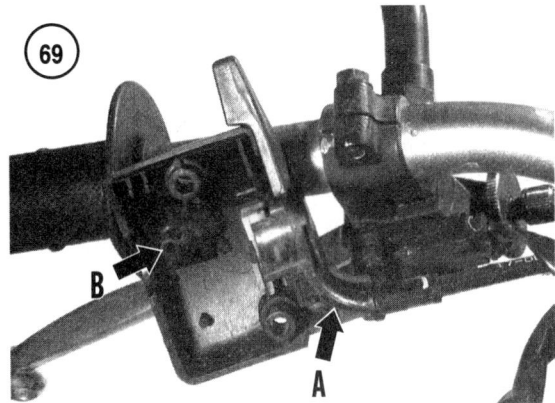

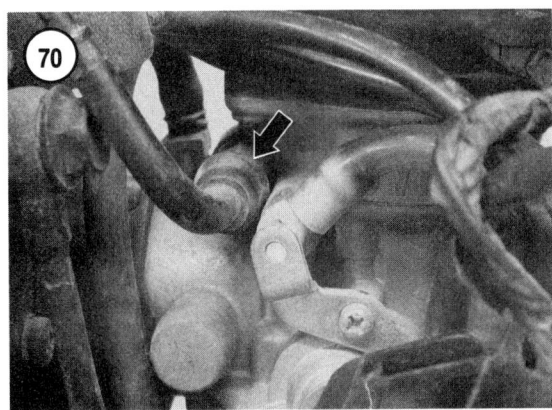

10. Detach the cable ends from the throttle pulley (**Figure 67**).
11. Clean the throttle assembly.
12. Lubricate the cables with an aerosol cable lubricant. Lubricate the throttle pulley and cable ends with lithium grease.
13. Install the new cables by reversing the removal procedure while noting the following:
   a. Pull all slack out of the cables, and then check that they move in the correct direction when the throttle is operated.
   b. Connect the cables to the carburetor. Adjust the throttle cables as described in Chapter Three.
   c. When throttle adjustment and proper operation are verified, install the fuel tank.

CHOKE CABLE

Removal/Installation

1. Remove the fuel tank as described in Chapter Fifteen.
2. Remove the left hand guard.
3. Remove the left handlebar switch screws (**Figure 68**) and separate the switch halves.
4. Dislodge the control lever and cable (A, **Figure 69**) from the switch half.
5. Detach the choke cable end from the control lever.
6. Remove the carburetor sufficiently for access to the choke plunger (**Figure 70**) on the carburetor.
7. If necessary, disconnect the choke plunger (**Figure 71**) by pushing up on the spring and removing the cable from the plunger.
8. Note the cable routing and remove the choke cable from the frame.
9. Reverse the removal procedure to install the choke cable while noting the following:
   a. Make sure the pin in the switch housing (B, **Figure 69**) fits into the hole in the handlebar.
   b. Adjust the choke as described in Chapter Three.

AIR FILTER HOUSING

Removal/Installation

1. Remove the subframe as described in Chapter Fifteen.
2. Disconnect the breather hose from the air filter housing (**Figure 72**).
3. Loosen the duct clamp screw.
4. Separate the housing from the carburetor and remove the housing.
5. Reverse the removal procedure to install the air filter housing.

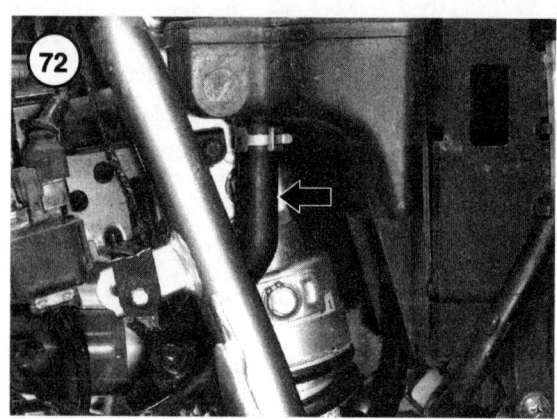

Table 1 CARBURETOR SPECIFICATIONS

Type	Keihin constant velocity
Throttle bore size	40 mm
Identification number	CVK40
Main jet	145
Pilot jet	40
Idle speed	1200-1400 rpm
Pilot screw adjustment*	1 5/8 turns out
Main air jet	50
Needle jet	6
Jet needle	N6NJ
Starter jet	52
Float height*	17.3-17.7 mm (0.61-0.77 in.)

*Refer to text.

CHAPTER NINE

ELECTRICAL SYSTEM

This chapter contains service and test procedures for the following systems and components:
1. Charging system.
2. Ignition system.
3. Starting system.
4. Lighting system.
5. Electrical components.
6. Switches.
7. Fuses.

Refer to **Tables 1-3** at the end of this chapter for specifications.

ELECTRICAL COMPONENT REPLACEMENT

Most dealerships and parts suppliers will not accept the return of any electrical part. If the exact cause of an electrical system malfunction cannot be determined, have a dealership retest that specific system to verify the test results. This may help avert the possibilty of purchasing an expensive, unreturnable part that does not fix the problem.

Consider any test results carefully before replacing a component that tests only slightly out of specification, especially for resistance. A number of variables can affect test results dramatically. These include the testing meter's internal circuitry, ambient temperature and conditions under which the machine has been operated. All instructions and specifications have been checked for accuracy; however, successful test results depend to a great extent upon individual accuracy.

CONTINUITY TESTING GUIDELINES

Circuits, switches, light bulbs and fuses can be checked for continuity (a completed circuit) using an ohmmeter connected to the appropriate color-coded wires in the circuit. Tests can be made at the connector or at the part. Use the following procedure as a guide to performing general continuity tests.

CAUTION
When performing continuity checks, do not turn on the ignition switch. Damage to parts and test equipment could occur. Also, verify that power from the battery is not routed directly into the test circuit, regardless of ignition switch position.

1. Refer to the wiring diagram at the back of this manual and find the part to be checked.
2. Identify the wire colors leading to the part and determine which pairs of wires should be checked. For

any check, the circuit should begin at the connector, pass through the part, then return to the connector.
3. Determine when continuity should exist.
   a. Typically, whenever a switch or button is turned on, it closes the circuit, and the meter should indicate continuity.
   b. When the switch or button is turned off, it opens the circuit, and the meter should not indicate continuity.
4. Trace the wires from the part to the nearest connector. Separate the connector.
5. Connect an ohmmeter to the connector half that leads to the part being checked. If the test is being made at the terminals on the part, remove all other wires connected to the terminals so they do not influence the meter reading.
6. Operate the switch or button and check for continuity.

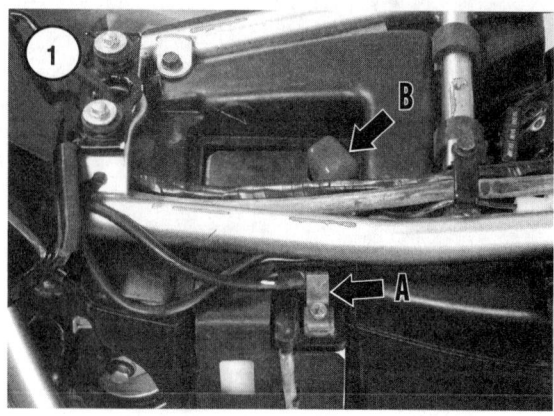

3. Remove the bolt and disconnect the cable from the negative battery terminal (A, **Figure 1**).
4. Move the cable out of the way and secure it so it cannot accidentally touch the battery terminal.
5. Reconnect the cable to the negative battery terminal and tighten the bolt securely.
6. Install the left side cover and seat as described in Chapter Fifteen.

ELECTRICAL CONNECTORS

All models are equipped with numerous electrical components, connectors and wires. Corrosion-causing moisture can enter these electrical connectors and cause poor electrical connections, leading to component failure. Troubleshooting an electrical circuit with one or more corroded electrical connectors can be time-consuming and frustrating.

When reconnecting electrical connectors, pack them in a dielectric grease compound. Dielectric grease is specially formulated for sealing and waterproofing electrical connections without interfering with current flow. Use only this compound or an equivalent designed for this specific purpose. Do not use a substitute that may interfere with the current flow within the electrical connector. Do not use silicone sealant.

After cleaning both the male and female connectors, make sure they are thoroughly dry. Apply dielectric grease to the interior of one of the connectors prior to connecting the connector halves. For best results, the compound should fill the entire inner area of the connector. On multi-pin connectors, also pack the backside of both the male and female side with the compound to prevent moisture from entering the connector. After the connector is fully packed, wipe all excess compound from the exterior.

NEGATIVE BATTERY TERMINAL

Some service procedures require disconnection of the battery cable from the negative battery terminal.
1. Turn the ignition switch to the off position.
2. Remove the seat and left side cover as described in Chapter Fifteen.

BATTERY

When new, the motorcycle is equipped with a 12 volt, 14 amp-hour battery. If the motorcycle has not been used for at least two weeks, the battery should be charged to prevent sulfation of the battery plates.

To prevent accidental shorts that could blow a fuse when working on the electrical system, always disconnect the negative battery cable from the battery as described in this chapter.

WARNING
Protect eyes, skin and clothing when servicing the battery; electrolyte is corrosive and can cause severe burns and permanent injury. The battery case may be cracked and leaking electrolyte. If electrolyte gets into the eyes, flush both eyes thoroughly with clean, running water and get immediate medical attention. Always wear safety goggles when servicing the battery.

WARNING
While batteries are being charged, highly explosive hydrogen gas forms in each cell. Some of this gas escapes through filler cap openings and may form an explosive atmosphere in and around the battery. This condition can persist for several hours. Sparks, an open flame or a lighted cigarette can ignite the gas, causing an internal bat-

ELECTRICAL SYSTEM

4. Remove the vent tube (A, **Figure 2**). Remove the screw (B, **Figure 2**) securing the battery holder.
5. Clean and check the components for damage.
6. Reverse the removal procedure to install the battery while noting the following:
   a. Check that the battery terminals face the rear of the motorcycle.
   b. To prevent corrosion, apply a thin coating of dielectric grease to the battery terminals and cable ends.
   c. Tighten the terminal bolts securely. Do not apply excessive force.

Cleaning/Inspection

1. Read *Safety Precautions* in this section.
2. Remove the battery as described in this section. Do not clean the battery while it is mounted in the motorcycle.
3. Clean the battery exterior with a solution of warm water and baking soda. Rinse thoroughly with clean water.
4. Perform the electrolyte check as described in this section.
5. Inspect the physical condition of the battery. Look for bulges or cracks in the case, leaking electrolyte or corrosion buildup.
6. Check the battery terminal bolts and nuts for corrosion and damage. Clean parts with a solution of baking soda and water, and rinse thoroughly. Replace the parts if damaged.
7. Check the battery cable clamps for corrosion and damage. If corrosion is minor, clean the battery cable clamps with a stiff brush. Replace excessively worn or damaged cables.

tery explosion and possible serious personal injury.

NOTE
Recycle the old battery. When replacing the old battery, be sure to turn in the old battery at that time. The lead plates and the plastic case can be recycled. Most dealerships accept old batteries in trade when purchasing a new one. Never place an old battery in household trash; it is illegal, in most states, to place any acid or lead (heavy metal) contents in landfills.

Safety Precautions

Follow these basic precautions to prevent an explosion.
1. Do not smoke or permit open flame near any battery being charged or which has been recently charged.
2. Do not disconnect live circuits at the battery. A spark usually occurs when a live circuit is broken.
3. Take care when connecting or disconnecting a battery charger. Turn the power switch OFF before making or breaking connections. Poor connections are a common cause of electrical arcs, which cause explosions.
4. Keep children and pets away from the charging equipment and the battery.

Removal/Installation

1. Check that the ignition switch is off.
2. Disconnect the negative battery terminal as described in this chapter.
3. Remove the insulator cover (B, **Figure 1**) from the positive cable, then remove the cable from the battery terminal.

Electrolyte Check

The battery electrolyte level for each cell must be maintained between the upper and lower level marks, indicated on the front of the battery. The battery should be removed from the motorcycle so the level of each cell can be viewed. The upper and lower level indicator on the battery holder only shows the condition of the cell at the left end of the battery. This should not be relied upon for the condition of all cells.

If the electrolyte level of any cell is too low, remove the cap above that cell, and then add distilled water to raise the level to the upper mark. Do not over fill the battery. Replace the cap.

Battery Voltage Test Unloaded

For a conventional (original equipment) battery, check the unloaded voltage using a hydrometer or voltmeter. An unloaded test will indicate the basic state of charge. To determine whether the battery is adequate to operate the motorcycle, perform a battery load test, as described in this section.

1. Connect a voltmeter to the negative and positive terminals. If a voltmeter is not available, use a syringe hydrometer (**Figure 3**) and measure the specific gravity of the electrolyte.
2. Measure the voltage.
    a. A fully charged battery will have a minimum of 12.6 volts (1.265 hydrometer reading).
    b. A battery that is approximately 75 percent charged will have a minimum of 12.4 volts (1.210 hydrometer reading).
    c. A battery that is approximately 50 percent charged will have a minimum of 12.1 volts (1.160 hydrometer reading).
3. If battery charging or replacement is required, refer to the procedures in this section.

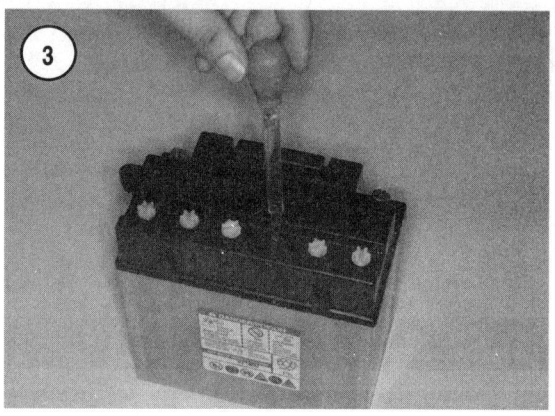

Battery Voltage Load Test

For a conventional (original equipment) battery, check the loaded voltage using a voltmeter. A load test requires the battery to discharge current. A load test indicates whether the battery is adequate to operate the motorcycle.

1. Connect a voltmeter to the negative and positive terminals as shown in **Figure 4**.
2. Turn on the headlight to the high beam.
3. Measure the voltage.
    a. A battery in good condition will have a minimum of 11.5 volts.
    b. If the battery needs charging or replacing, refer to the procedures in this section.

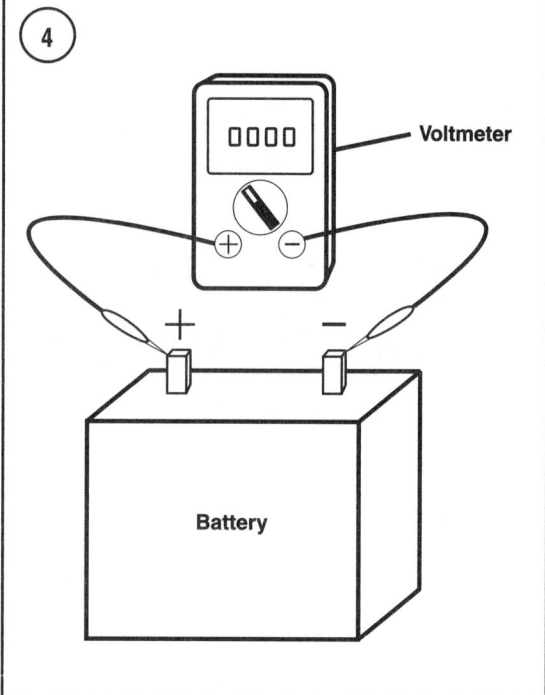

Battery Current Draw Test

If the battery is in good condition, but it discharges at a rapid rate when the motorcycle is not used, check the electrical system for a current draw. Machines that have a clock or some other type of aftermarket accessory (such as an alarm) will have a continuous parasitic current loss to operate these types of devices. This will show up as a current draw on the battery. However, on the KLR650 any current draw present when all electrical devices are shut off indicates a problem.

A short in a wire or component can allow the battery to discharge to ground. Dirt and moisture can also create a path to ground. To isolate the problem, an ammeter is connected to the battery and various circuits/components disconnected while observing the current reading.

1. Remove the fuel tank as described in Chapter Fifteen.
2. Turn the ignition switch off.
3. Disconnect the negative battery cable.
4. Make sure the battery is fully charged.

CAUTION
Before connecting the ammeter, set the amperage range to the highest setting. If there is an excessive amount of current flow, the meter may be damaged.

5. Connect the ammeter to the negative battery cable and terminal as shown in **Figure 5**.
    a. The meter should indicate no current draw.
    b. If a current draw is indicated, continue the test.

ELECTRICAL SYSTEM

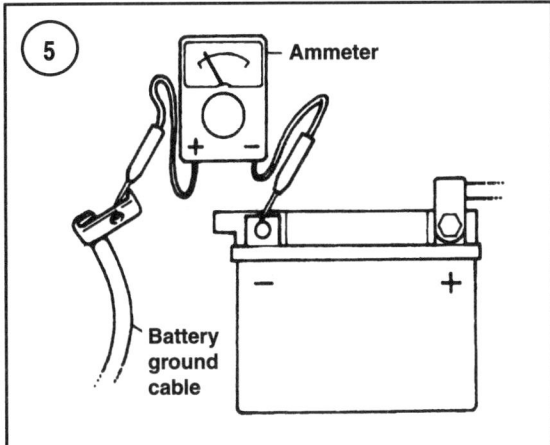

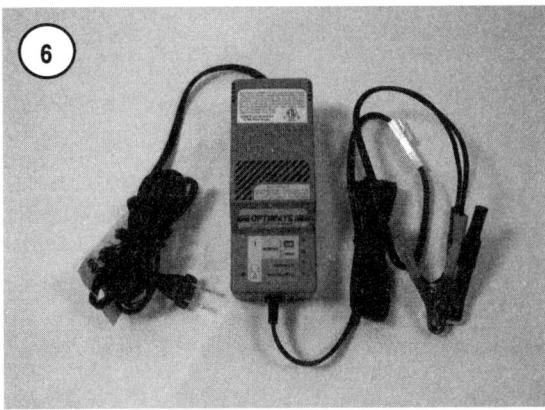

output. Also, do not use an automotive-type charger. The charge rates are too high and will overheat the battery and damage the battery plates.

CAUTION
To prevent possible electrical system damage, always remove the cables from the battery before charging the battery.

1. Remove the battery from the motorcycle as described in this section.
2. Make sure the battery is properly filled. Wait 30 minutes after filling the battery before charging the battery.
3. Connect the positive and negative leads of the charger to the positive and negative terminals on the battery.
4. Set the charger to 12 volts. If the charger has a variable charge rate, select a low setting. Using a 1-amp, constant-current charger, the suggested charge rates for a conventional battery are:
   a. 75% charge: 1 amp for 4 hours.
   b. 50% charge: 1 amp for 9 hours
5. Turn on the charger and allow the battery to charge for the specified time.
6. After the battery is charged, turn off the charger and remove the leads from the terminals.
7. If necessary, add distilled water to any cells that are below the upper level mark.
8. Check battery voltage as described in this section. If battery voltage does not remain stable for at least one hour, or the battery continues to be undercharged, replace the battery.

New Battery Set-Up

A new battery must be fully charged before installation. Failure to do so reduces the life of the battery. Using a new battery without an initial charge causes permanent battery damage. That is, the battery will never be able to hold more than an 80% charge. Charging a new battery after it has been used will not bring its charge to 100%. When purchasing a new battery from a dealership or parts store, verify its charge status. If necessary, have them perform the initial or booster charge before accepting the battery.

6. Remove the fuses from the headlight/taillight circuit and fan circuit. Observe the meter.
   a. If the current draw lessens, there is a problem indicated in one of the fused circuits. Install the fuse(s) and continue to isolate the problem by separating the connectors in the circuit.
   b. If the current draw remains the same, there is a problem indicated in the main circuit.
7. Check the connector as follows:
   a. Refer to any system diagrams in this chapter, and if necessary, to the wiring diagram at the back of the manual for additional circuits and part identifications.
   b. Separate the individual connectors of the appropriate parts. Work with one connector at a time, disconnecting and connecting the connectors until the meter indicates no current draw. When this occurs, the shorted circuit has been isolated.

Charging

When recharging the battery, a charger (**Figure 6**) with a variable amperage output is recommended. Do not use a charger that is rated higher than 1.4 amps

CHARGING SYSTEM

The charging system consists of the battery, alternator and a voltage regulator/rectifier. A 20-amp main fuse protects the circuit. Refer to the wiring diagram at the end of this manual.

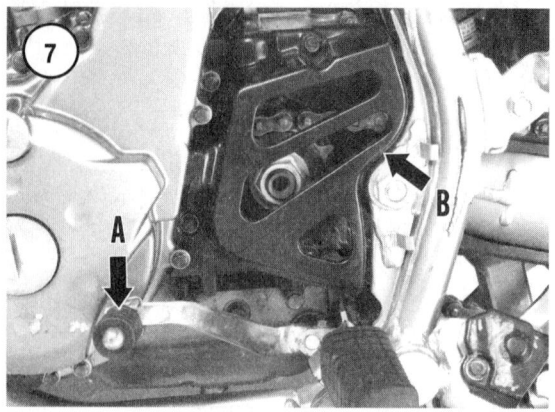

Alternating current generated by the alternator is rectified to direct current. The voltage regulator maintains constant voltage to the battery and additional electrical loads (such as lights or ignition) despite variations in engine speed and load.

Regulated Voltage Test

This procedure tests charging system operation. It does not measure maximum charging system output. **Table 2** lists charging system test specifications.

To obtain accurate test results, the battery must be fully charged (13.0 volts or higher).
1. Start and run the engine until it reaches normal operating temperature, then turn the engine off.
2. Connect a digital voltmeter to the battery terminals.

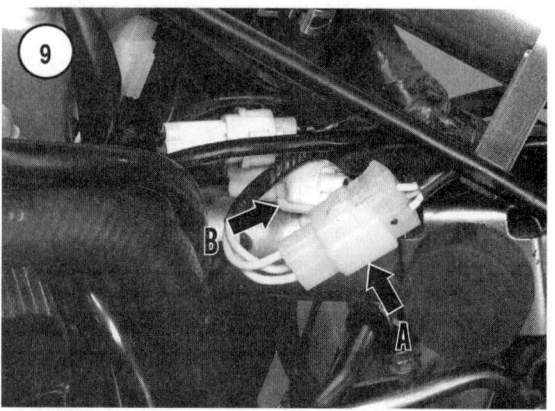

NOTE
Do not disconnect either battery cable when making this test.

3. Start the engine and allow it to idle. Turn the headlight switch to high beam.

NOTE
If the battery is often discharged, but charging voltage tests normal, the battery may be damaged.

4. Gradually increase engine speed to 3000 rpm and read the voltage indicated on the voltmeter. Compare this with the regulated voltage reading in **Table 2**.
5. If the regulated voltage is too low, check for an open or short circuit in the charging system wiring harness, an open or short in the stator or a damaged regulator/rectifier.
6. If the regulated voltage is too high, check for a poor regulator/rectifier ground, a damaged regulator/rectifier or a damaged battery.

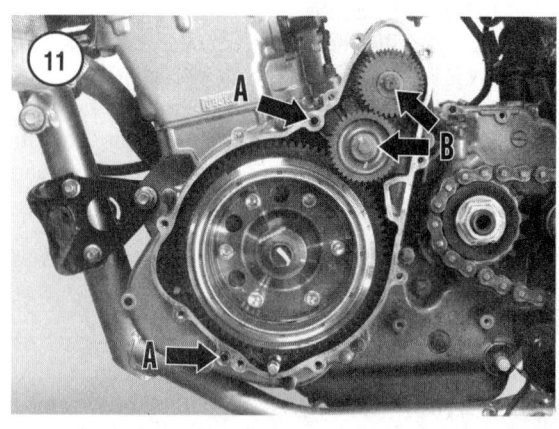

ELECTRICAL SYSTEM

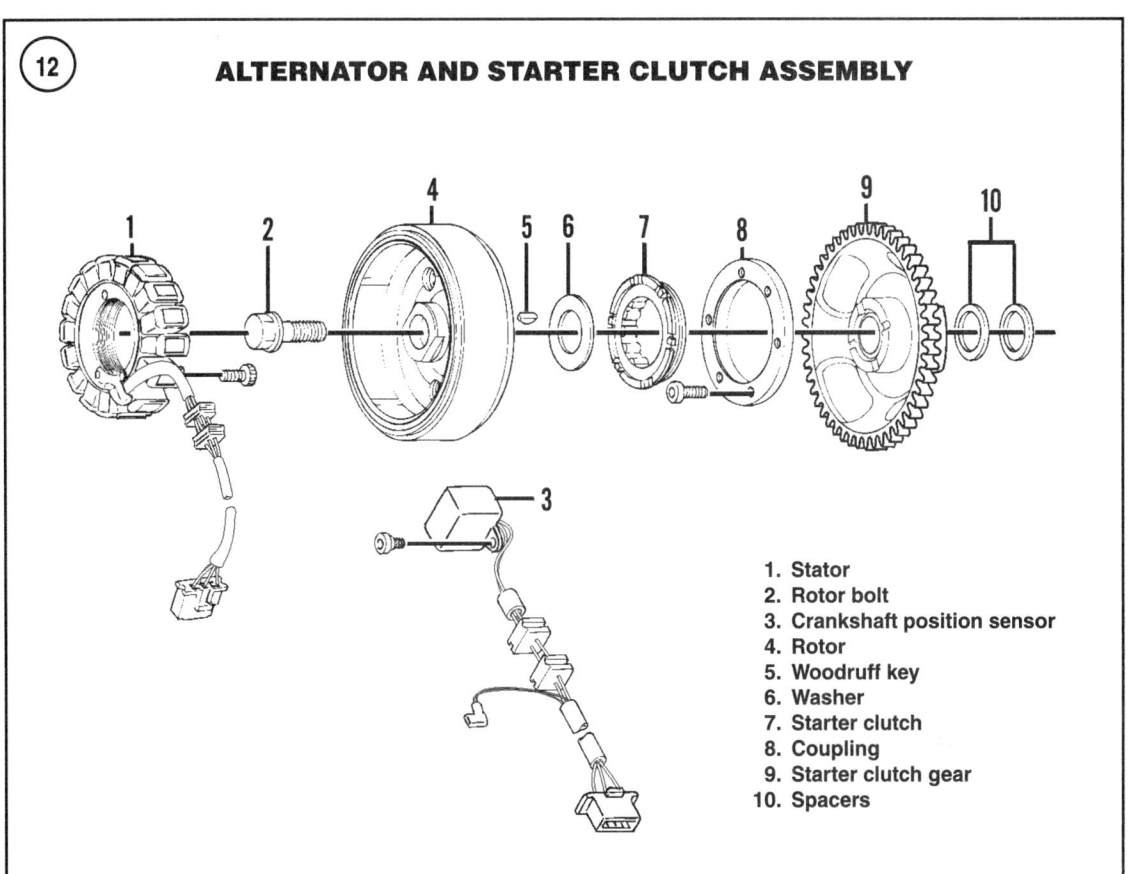

ALTERNATOR AND STARTER CLUTCH ASSEMBLY

1. Stator
2. Rotor bolt
3. Crankshaft position sensor
4. Rotor
5. Woodruff key
6. Washer
7. Starter clutch
8. Coupling
9. Starter clutch gear
10. Spacers

ALTERNATOR COVER

Removal/Installation

The alternator cover must be removed for access to the rotor, stator and crankshaft position sensor. The stator and crankshaft position sensor are mounted on the inside of the alternator cover.

1. Remove the skid plate as described in Chapter Fifteen.
2. Remove the clamp bolt; then, remove the shift lever (A, **Figure 7**).
3. Remove the chain sprocket guard (B, **Figure 7**).
4. Disconnect the neutral switch wire (**Figure 8**).
5. If the stator will be tested, remove the fuel tank (Chapter Fifteen) and disconnect the stator connector (A, **Figure 9**) and crankshaft position sensor connector (B), located on the left side of the frame.
6. Disengage the neutral, stator and crankshaft position sensor wires from the wire guides.
7. Remove the 10 bolts from the perimeter of the alternator cover.

WARNING
Keep fingers away from the edge of the cover to avoid possible pinching.

8. Pull the cover (**Figure 10**) away from the engine. Magnetic resistance will be felt as the cover is unseated.
9. Remove the cover gasket. Account for the two cover dowels (A, **Figure 11**) and the washer (B) on each starter gear shaft.
10. Remove and/or test the stator and crankshaft position sensor (**Figure 12**) as described in this chapter.
11. Reverse the removal procedure to install the stator and alternator cover. Note the following:
    a. Apply silicone sealer to the sealing surface of the wire grommets.
    b. Install a new cover gasket.
    c. Tighten the alternator cover bolts to 8.8 N•m (78 in.-lb.).
    d. Check that all wires are routed and secured.
    e. Clean all electrical connections, and then apply dielectric grease when assembling.

STATOR

The stator is mounted on the inside of the alternator cover. The stator can be tested without removing it from the cover.

Stator Resistance Test

1. Remove the fuel tank as described in Chapter Fifteen.
2. Disconnect the 3-wire stator connector (A, **Figure 9**) located on the left side of the frame.
3. Identify the half of the connector that leads to the stator.
4. Measure the stator coil resistance between the terminals of the yellow wires. Check all three combinations of the yellow wires. The resistance between all pairs of yellow wires should be within the specification listed in **Table 2**.
5. Ground one of the meter probes to the engine (or the alternator cover, if removed). Touch the other probe to the connector terminals. The resistance should be infinity. Any other reading indicates a short, and the stator should be replaced.
6. If the tests are not within specification, check the plug and wiring harness for visible damage and shorting.
7. If necessary, remove the alternator cover aad check the wiring harness and coils for damage. Replace the stator as necessary.

Stator Output Voltage Test

1. Remove the fuel tank.
2. Disconnect the 3-wire connector (A, **Figure 9**) located on the left side of the frame.
3. Identify the half of the connector that leads to the stator.
4. Connect an AC voltmeter to the connector terminals.
5. Start the engine and slowly increase engine speed while observing the voltmeter.
6. The voltmeter should indicate a voltage increase to at least 43 volts at 4000 rpm. Repeat the test at another pair of connector terminals.
7. If the voltage is below 43 volts, the stator or rotor is faulty.

Removal/Installation

Refer to **Figure 12**.

1. Remove the alternator cover as described in this chapter.
2. Remove the wiring harness holder (A, **Figure 13**).
3. Dislodge the grommets securing the crankshaft position sensor and stator wires from the alternator cover.
4. Remove the three bolts (B, **Figure 13**) from the stator.
5. Remove the stator assembly.

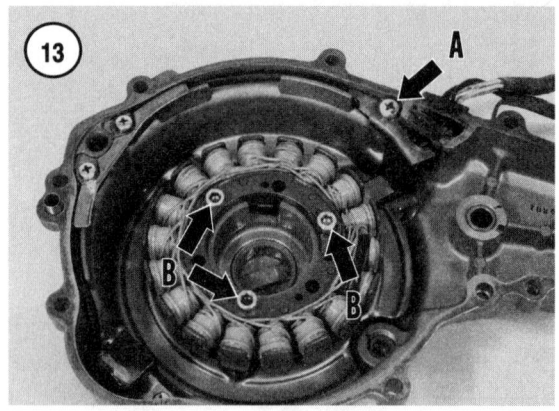

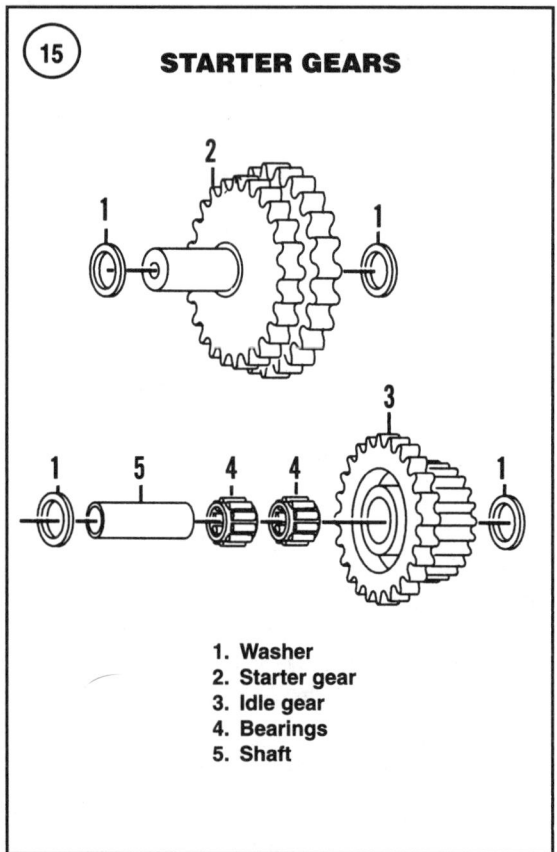

STARTER GEARS

1. Washer
2. Starter gear
3. Idle gear
4. Bearings
5. Shaft

ELECTRICAL SYSTEM

6. Reverse this procedure to install the stator while noting the following:
   a. Note that the stator wire grommet is located under the grommet securing the crankshaft position sensor wires.
   b. Apply a thin coat of silicone sealer to the grommet to prevent oil leakage.
   c. Push down the wire holder near the grommet before tightening the holder screw.

ROTOR AND STARTER CLUTCH

The starter clutch is mounted on the back of the rotor. The starter gears and rotor must be removed to access the clutch. To remove the rotor, hold it with the rotor holder tool (Kawasaki part No. 57001-1184 or equivalent), and then remove it with a rotor puller (Kawasaki part No. 57001-1216 or equivalent). The special tools are shown being used in the following procedure.

NOTE
*If troubleshooting the starter clutch, the clutch can be checked for free-wheel and lockup without removing the rotor. Turn the clutch gear clockwise (**Figure 14**). The clutch gear should turn freely and smoothly in that direction. Attempt to turn the gear counterclockwise. The gear should not turn. If the gear turns in both directions or is always locked, disassemble and inspect the clutch assembly.*

Removal/Installation

Refer to **Figure 15**.

1. Remove the alternator cover as described in this chapter.
2. Remove the starter gears as follows:
   a. Remove the outer washer (A, **Figure 16**) and idle gear (B).
   b. Remove the idle gear shaft, bearings and inner washer (**Figure 17**).
   c. Remove the starter gear and washers (**Figure 18**).
3. Remove the rotor bolt as follows:

NOTE
*The rotor holder tool (Kawasaki part No. 57001-1184 [A, **Figure 19**]) or a universal tool (A, **Figure 20**) may be used to hold the rotor. Because of the force required to loosen or tighten the rotor bolt, brace the holder handle to prevent holder rotation.*

a. Hold the rotor stationary with the rotor holder tool.
b. Remove the rotor bolt (B, **Figure 19**).
4. Loosen the rotor and starter clutch as follows:
   a. To aid in removal, spray penetrating lubricant into the rotor bore and Woodruff key area. Apply grease to the end and threads of the rotor puller.
   b. Thread the puller (B, **Figure 20**) into the crankshaft and hold the rotor stationary with the rotor holder tool.
   c. Tighten the rotor puller until the rotor breaks free from the crankshaft taper. The rotor is tight and requires a wrench that provides high leverage.
   d. Remove the rotor puller from the crankshaft.

5. Remove the rotor and starter clutch from the crankshaft. Hold the starter clutch (**Figure 21**) to prevent it from falling from the rotor.
6. Remove the Woodruff key (A, **Figure 22**) and spacers (B) from the crankshaft.
7. Inspect and lubricate the parts as described in this section.
8. Reverse this procedure to install the rotor/starter clutch assembly and the starter gears. Note the following:
   a. Install a new rotor bolt.
   b. Tighten the rotor bolt to 20 N•m (15 ft.-lb.) to seat the rotor. Then, loosen the bolt and remove it.
   c. Clean and dry the threads of the rotor bolt.
   d. Install and tighten the rotor bolt to 195 N•m (144 ft.-lb.).
   e. Lubricate the starter clutch gear bearing, starter gear shafts and bores with molydisulfide grease. Lubricate all other parts with engine oil.
   f. Install the alternator cover as described in this chapter.

Inspection

1. Inspect the clutch for proper operation as follows:
   a. With the clutch gear facing up, turn the gear counterclockwise (**Figure 23**). The gear should turn freely and smoothly in that direction.
   b. Attempt to turn the gear clockwise. The gear should not turn.
   c. If the gear turns in both directions or is always locked up, disassemble and inspect the clutch assembly.

2. Remove the clutch sprocket from the rotor. Turn the sprocket counterclockwise and twist it squarely away from the rotor. Remove the washer from the clutch.
3. Clean and inspect the clutch assembly (**Figure 24**).

ELECTRICAL SYSTEM

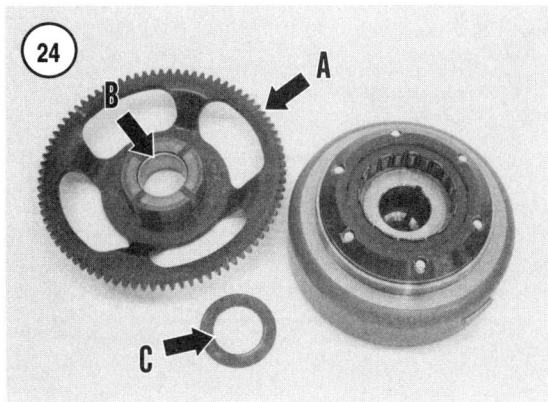

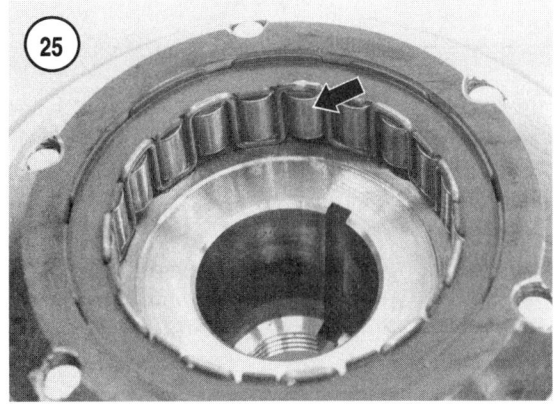

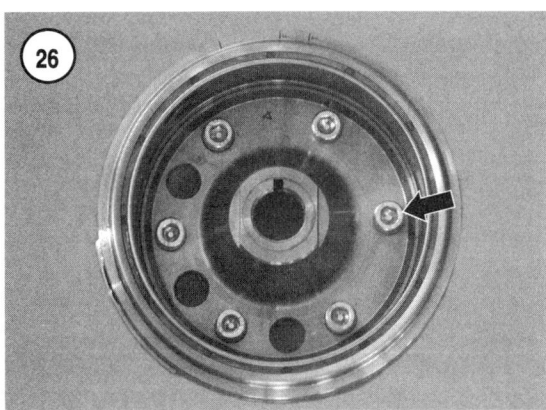

a. Inspect the clutch gear teeth (A, **Figure 24**) for wear or damage.
b. Inspect the clutch gear bearing (B, **Figure 24**) for wear or scoring.
c. Inspect the washer (C, **Figure 24**) for damage.
d. Inspect the clutch rollers (**Figure 25**). The rollers should be undamaged and operate smoothly.

4. If the clutch is damaged, remove the clutch from the rotor as follows:
   a. Remove the six bolts (**Figure 26**). Remove the clutch and coupling from the rotor.
   b. Install a new clutch and the coupling.
   c. Apply threadlock to the bolts. Tighten the starter bolts evenly in several steps to 34 N•m (25 ft.-lb.).

5. Lubricate the clutch rollers and washer with engine oil.

6. Install the washer and clutch sprocket into the rotor. Turn the sprocket counterclockwise and twist it squarely into the rotor. When the sprocket is fully seated, check that it turns only in the counterclockwise direction.

7. Clean and inspect the rotor components.

WARNING
Replace the rotor if damaged. The rotor can fly apart at high crankshaft speeds, causing severe injury and damage to the engine.

   a. Inspect the rotor for cracks and damage.
   b. Inspect the taper in the bore of the rotor and on the crankshaft for damage.

NOTE
If the Woodruff key is bent or sheared, the rotor will not properly align on the crankshaft, which causes the engine to be out of time.

   c. Inspect the Woodruff key, slot and spacers for damage (**Figure 22**).

8. Install the parts as described in this section.

REGULATOR/RECTIFIER

Removal/Installation

1. Disconnect the cable from the negative battery terminal as described in this chapter.
2. Disconnect the regulator/rectifier electrical connector (A, **Figure 27**).
3. Remove the bolts (B, **Figure 27**) securing the regulator/rectifier (C) to the frame bracket and remove it.

4. Install by reversing the preceding removal steps. Install the wire clamp (D, **Figure 27**) on the left mounting bolt. Make sure the electrical connector is secure and corrosion-free.

Testing

To check for a faulty regulator/rectifier, perform the *Regulated Voltage Test* in this chapter. The following resistance test checks for directional resistance in the regulator/rectifier.

Use an analog ohmmeter so meter deflection may be observed. For some checks, the result should be an infinity reading on the meter. For other checks, the result should be a meter reading from zero to approximately one-half of the meter scale. There is no specific resistance reading required. Each regulator/rectifier, as well as the ohmmeter used for the test, will produce slightly different results. However, the purpose of the test is to check for low resistance in one direction and infinite resistance in the other direction. For each of the following checks, the required result is indicated.

Refer to **Figure 28** for test points.

1. Disconnect the wire connector from the regulator/rectifier.
2. Connect the positive meter probe to the B terminal.
    a. Keep the probe on the B terminal, then touch the negative probe to terminals 1, 2 and 3.
    b. The meter should read zero to approximately one-half of the meter scale at all terminals.
3. Connect the negative meter probe to the B terminal.
    a. Keep the probe on the B terminal, then touch the positive probe to terminals 1, 2 and 3.
    b. The meter should read infinity at all terminals.
4. Connect the positive meter probe to the G terminal.
    a. Keep the probe on the G terminal, then touch the negative probe to terminals 1, 2 and 3.
    b. The meter should read infinity at all terminals.
5. Connect the negative meter probe to the G terminal.
    a. Keep the probe on the G terminal, then touch the positive probe to terminals 1, 2 and 3.
    b. The meter should read zero to approximately one-half of the meter scale at all terminals.
6. If any test results in a reading that is high or low in both directions, the regulator/rectifier is faulty.

STARTING SYSTEM

The starting system consists of the starter motor, starter relay, clutch switch, sidestand switch, starter

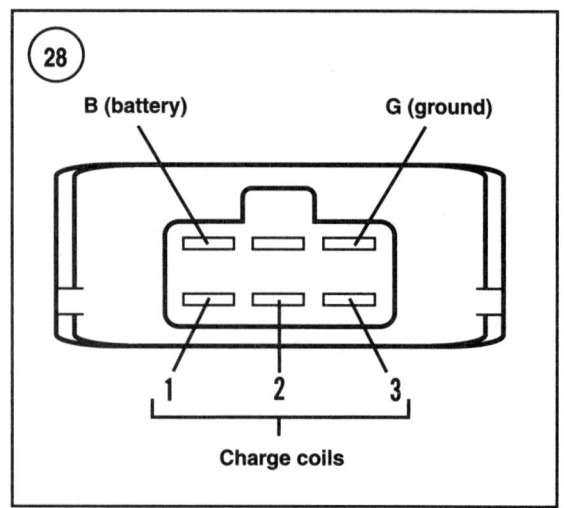

circuit relay, neutral switch, engine stop switch and the starter button. When the starter button is pressed, it engages the starter relay and completes the circuit allowing electricity to flow from the battery to the starter motor.

The starter motor rotates the engine crankshaft through the starter motor gears and the starter clutch. Refer to this chapter for service information related to those components.

CAUTION
Do not operate the starter for more than 5 seconds at a time. Let it cool approximately 10 seconds before operating it again.

STARTER

Removal/Installation

Refer to **Figure 29**.

1. Remove the exhaust pipe (Chapter Four).
2. Disconnect the ground (negative) cable from the battery and from the starter (A, **Figure 30**).
3. Disconnect the positive cable (B, **Figure 30**) from the starter.
4. Remove the remaining mounting bolt, then twist the starter out of the left crankcase cover. The starter is sealed to the cover by an O-ring, which causes resistance during removal.
5. Disassemble, inspect and test the starter as described in this section.
6. Reverse this procedure to install the starter. Note the following:
    a. Lubricate the O-ring on the front end cover (A, **Figure 31**) before inserting it into the crankcase cover.

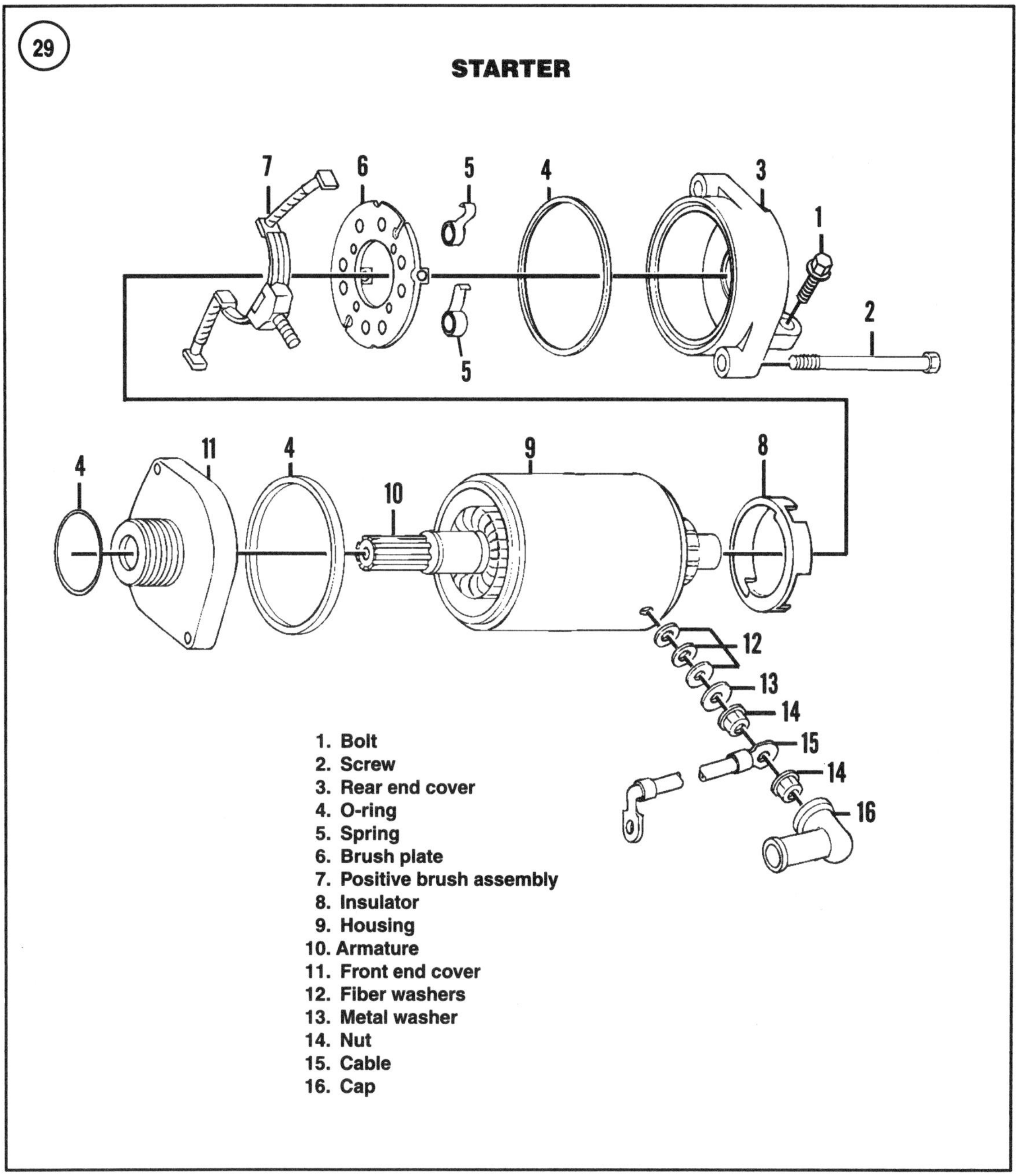

ELECTRICAL SYSTEM

㉙ STARTER

1. Bolt
2. Screw
3. Rear end cover
4. O-ring
5. Spring
6. Brush plate
7. Positive brush assembly
8. Insulator
9. Housing
10. Armature
11. Front end cover
12. Fiber washers
13. Metal washer
14. Nut
15. Cable
16. Cap

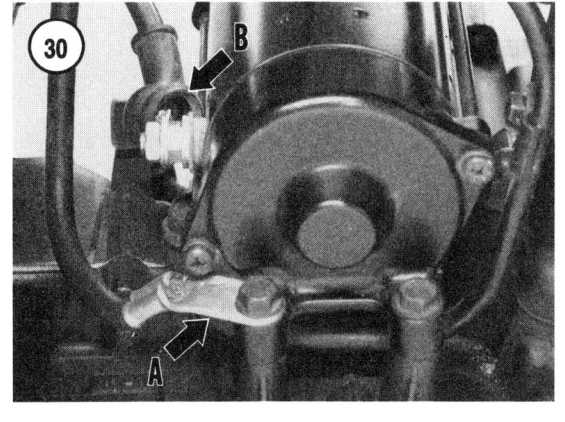

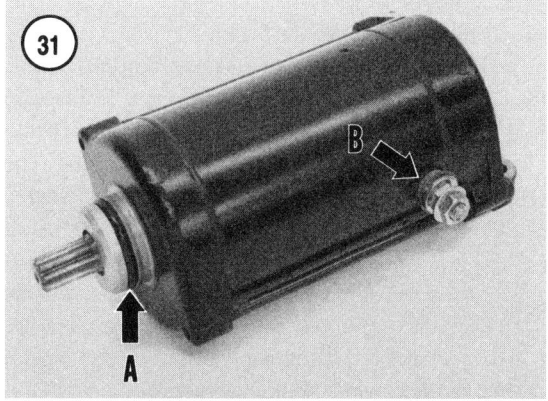

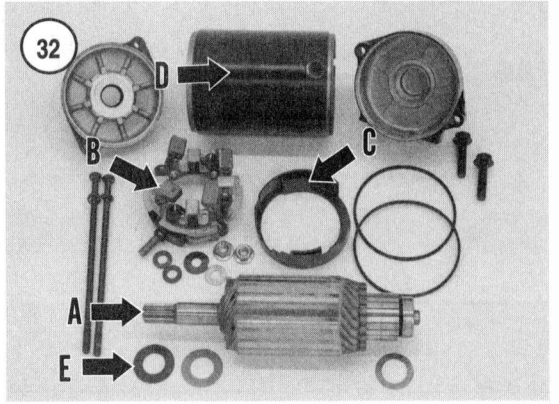
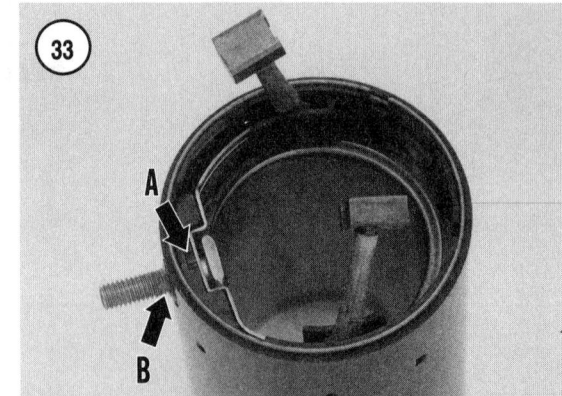

b. Check that the fiber washers (B, **Figure 31**) on the cable post are in good condition. The washers must insulate the cable from the housing.
c. Clean all cable connections, then apply dielectric grease to fittings and connectors before tightening.
d. Tighten the starter mounting bolts to 8.8 N•m (78 in.-lb.).

Disassembly and Assembly

Refer to **Figure 29**.
1. Remove the two housing screws, rear end cover and O-ring.

NOTE
If disassembling the starter to only check brush condition, remove only the rear end cover. The brushes can be inspected and the cover reinstalled if further disassembly is not required.

2. Remove the front end cover and O-ring.
3. Remove the armature (A, **Figure 32**), brush plate assembly (B) and insulator (C) from the housing (D). Make note of any shims (E, **Figure 32**) and their location on the armature shaft.
4. Inspect and test the starter components as described in this section.
5. Assemble the starter as follows:
   a. Install the insulator and positive brush plate. Check that the small projection (A, **Figure 33**) on the insulator faces up and that the O-ring (B) fits between the terminal and housing. The terminal must be insulated from the housing.
   b. Fit the positive brushes into the insulated brush plate slots, then seat the plate into the housing. Lock the positive brushes into the slots. The tabs (**Figure 34**) on the brush plate are not spaced symmetrically. Therefore, the plate only fits correctly in one position.

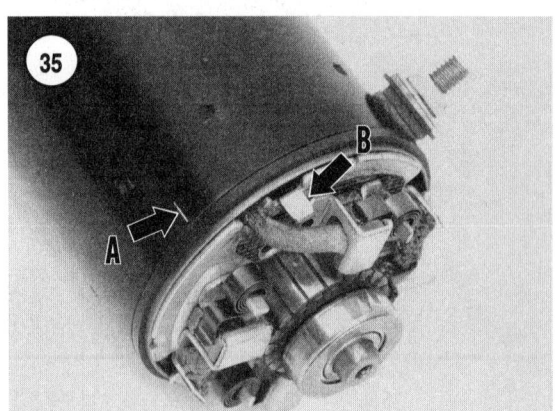
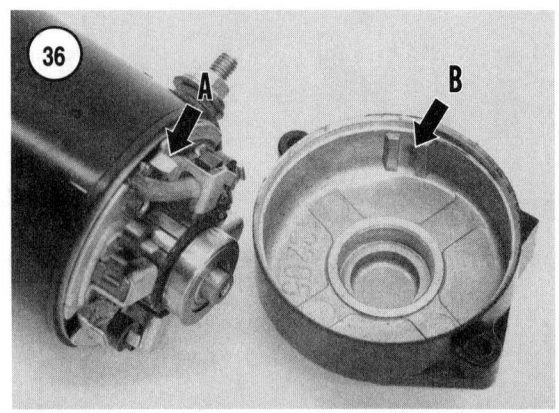

ELECTRICAL SYSTEM

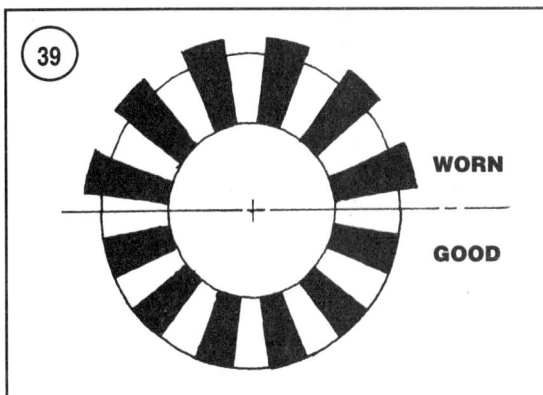

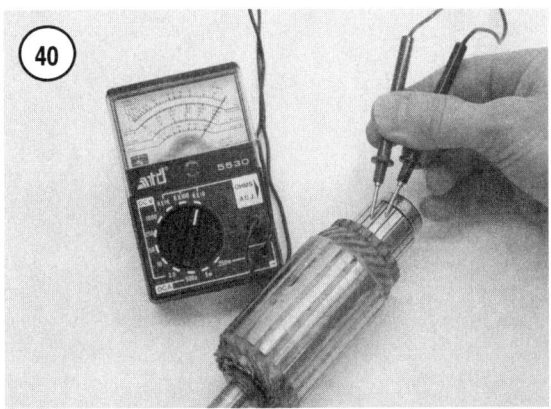

c. Install the armature. Use small plastic ties, or another method, to hold back the brushes so the commutator can pass under the brushes.
d. Check that the alignment mark (A, **Figure 35**) on the housing and the vertical tab (B) on the brush plate are oriented as shown.
e. Install a new O-ring on the housing, then align the vertical tab (A, **Figure 36**) on the brush plate with the slot (B) in the rear end cover. Seat the cover onto the housing. The alignment marks (**Figure 37**) on the exterior of the housing and cover should be aligned.
f. Install a new O-ring on the housing, then align and install the front end cover. Again, the alignment marks on the exterior of the housing and cover should be aligned.
g. Install and tighten the housing screws.
h. Install the fiber washers onto the cable terminal, followed by the metal washer and nut. The fiber washers must be in good condition so they insulate the cable from the starter housing.
i. Install a new, lubricated O-ring onto the front end cover.

Inspection/Testing

Use an ohmmeter for all electrical tests in this procedure. If the result for any test is incorrect, the part is either shorted, or there is an open circuit between the test points. Replace or recondition parts that are worn or damaged. Refer to **Figure 29**.

1. Clean the parts as required. Use a solvent specifically for electric motors to remove buildup and contamination, particularly between the commutator bars.
2. Inspect the condition of the housing and end covers. The armature should fit in the covers with little or no play.
3. Inspect the armature.
    a. The bearing should turn smoothly and freely.
    b. Inspect any shims for cracks or damage.
    c. Inspect the windings for obvious shorts or damage.
4. Inspect and test the commutator.
    a. Measure the outside diameter (**Figure 38**). Refer to **Table 2** for specifications.
    b. Inspect the bar height. The commutator bars should be taller than the insulation between the bars (**Figure 39**).
    c. Inspect the bars for discoloration. If a pair of bars is discolored, this indicates grounded armature coils.
    d. Inspect the bars for scoring. Mild scoring can be repaired with fine emery cloth.
    e. Check for continuity across all adjacent pairs of commutator bars (**Figure 40**). There should be continuity across all pairs of bars.

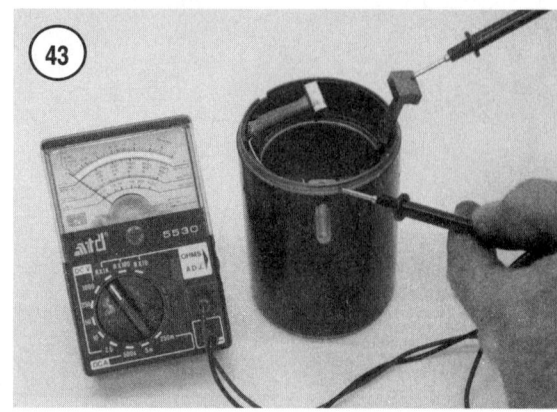

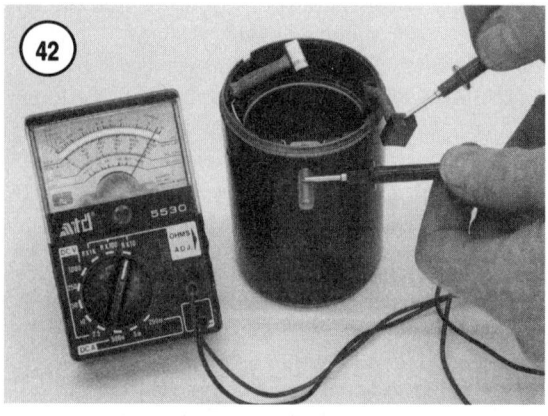

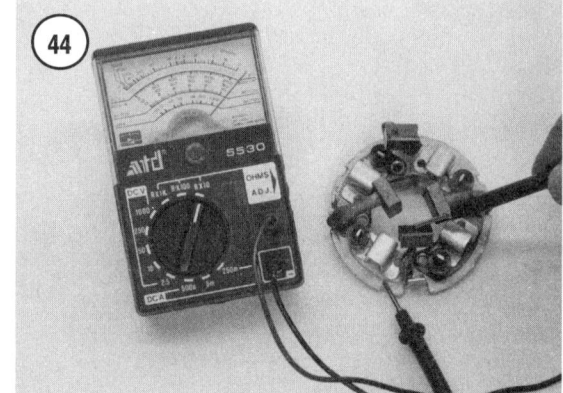

  f. Check for continuity between each commutator bar and the armature shaft (**Figure 41**). There should be no continuity.
5. Inspect and test the brush assembly. The positive brushes have insulated leads.
  a. Check for continuity between the positive brush and the cable terminal (**Figure 42**). There should be continuity between the parts.
  b. Check for continuity between the cable terminal and the starter housing. There should be no continuity between the parts.
  c. Check for continuity between the positive brush and the starter housing (**Figure 43**). There should be no continuity between the parts.
  d. Check for continuity between the grounded brush and the brush plate (**Figure 44**). There should be continuity between the parts.
  e. Check for continuity between the brush plate and the positive brush holders. There should be no continuity between the parts.
  f. Measure the length of each brush (**Figure 45**). Refer to **Table 2** for specifications.
  g. Inspect the condition of the brush springs.
6. Assemble the starter as described in this section.

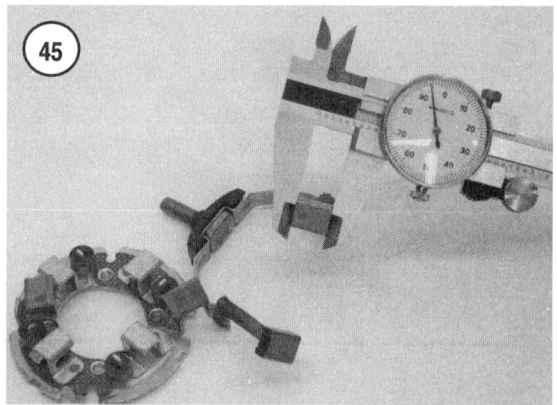

ELECTRICAL SYSTEM

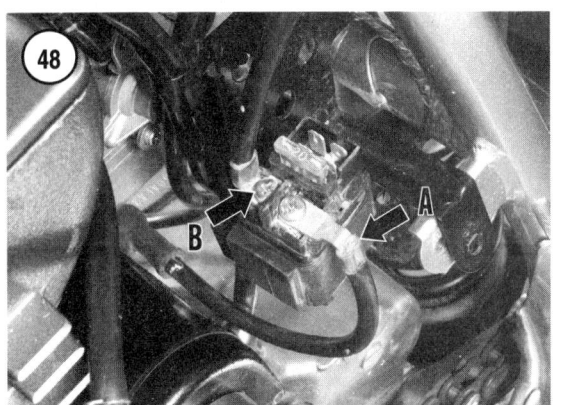

4. Disconnect the starter motor lead (A, **Figure 48**) and the positive battery cable (B) from the starter relay.
5. Remove the starter relay.
6. Install by reversing the removal steps while noting the following:
   a. Install both red and black electrical cables to the relay and tighten the nuts securely.
   b. Make sure the electrical connectors are tight.

Testing

1. Remove the starter relay as described in this chapter.
2. Connect a 12-volt battery to the positive terminal (**Figure 49**) and negative terminal on the relay.
3. Connect an ohmmeter to the relay terminals shown in **Figure 49**. There should be continuity (indicated resistance) indicating the relay is operating correctly. Replace the relay if there is no continuity (infinity).
4. Disconnect the 12-volt test battery from the relay.
5. There should be no continuity (infinity) when the battery is disconnected from the relay. Replace the relay if there is continuity.

STARTER CIRCUIT RELAY

The starter circuit relay (**Figure 50**) is located behind the upper fairing below the meter unit. The starter circuit relay passes current to the starter relay, which activates the starter. In order for the starter circuit relay to pass current, it requires that the starter lockout switch or neutral switch be in its safe startup position. When either or both of these switches are in their safe positions, the switch in the starter circuit relay closes and completes the circuit.

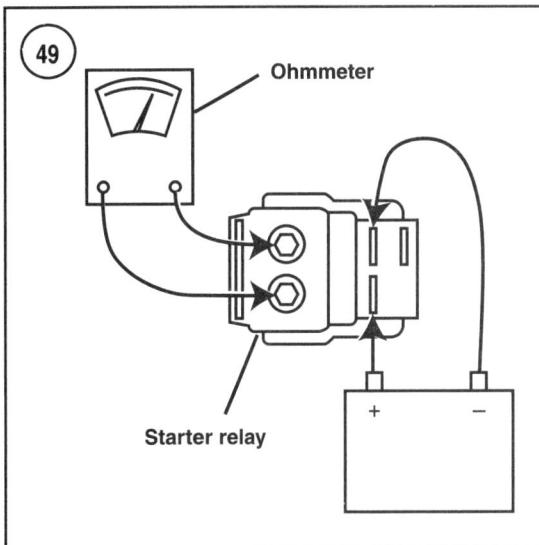

STARTER RELAY

Removal/Installation

1. Disconnect the negative battery cable as described in this chapter.
2. Remove the starter relay cover (**Figure 46**).
3. Disconnect the starter relay primary connector (**Figure 47**).

Removal/Installation

1. Remove the upper fairing as described in Chapter Fifteen.
2. Remove the relay from the mount, then unplug the relay (**Figure 50**).
3. Reverse the removal steps to install the relay.

Testing

1. Remove the starter circuit relay as described in this section.
2. Connect a 12-volt battery and ohmmeter to the relay terminals as shown in **Figure 51**. Note that terminals 1 (blue/red) and 2 (yellow/red) are connected to the relay coil and terminals 3 (black) and 4 (yellow/red) are connected to the starter circuit relay.
3. Make the following checks:
   a. With the battery and ohmmeter connected as shown in **Figure 51**, check for continuity through the starter circuit relay (terminals 3 and 4). There should be continuity.
   b. Disconnect the battery and check for continuity through the starter circuit relay (terminals 3 and 4). There should be no continuity.
4. Replace the relay if it fails any of the tests.

IGNITION SYSTEM

The engine is equipped with an electronic ignition system. The system consists of a crankshaft position sensor, igniter unit, ignition coil and spark plug. The crankshaft position sensor is mounted inside the alternator cover.

As the crankshaft rotates, the projections on the alternator rotor pass the crankshaft position sensor, which sends a signal to the igniter unit. The CPU (part of the igniter) uses this signal and a stored digital data map to determine the optimum ignition timing for the operating conditions.

The igniter unit also monitors the position of the gear shifter and sidestand through respective switches. The igniter stops ignition if the sidestand is down and the transmission is in any gear other than neutral, or if the transmission is shifted out of neutral with the sidestand down.

Precautions and Inspections

Ignition system components can be damaged if precautions are not taken during testing and troubleshooting. Note the following:
1. Never disconnect electrical connections while the engine is running or cranking.
2. Turn off the ignition switch before disconnecting or connecting electrical components.

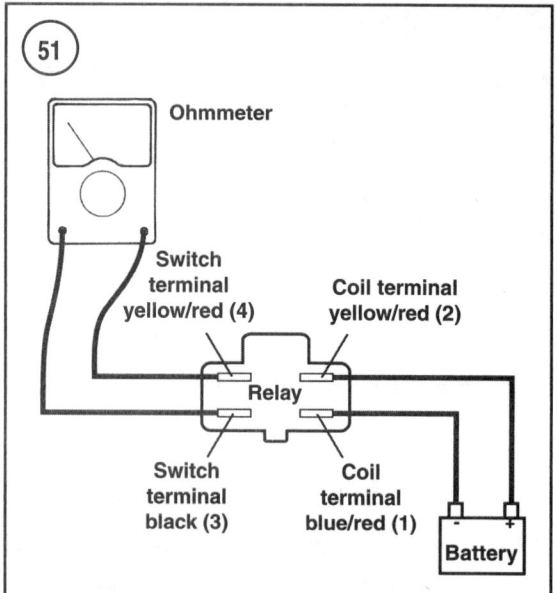

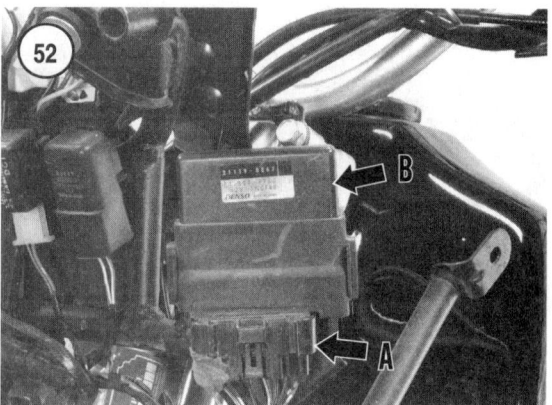

3. Handle the parts with care.
4. Check wiring for poor connections, corrosion and shorts before replacing components connected to the wiring.
5. Before testing components, check that the battery and spark plug are in good condition, and are not the cause of poor performance.

Igniter Unit

Testing

If all other ignition system components have been tested and the igniter unit is suspect, have the unit tested by a dealership before replacing the igniter unit.

NOTE
Many ignition problems are caused by faulty wiring and connections. Be sure to check all wires and connections before presuming the ignitor unit is faulty.

ELECTRICAL SYSTEM

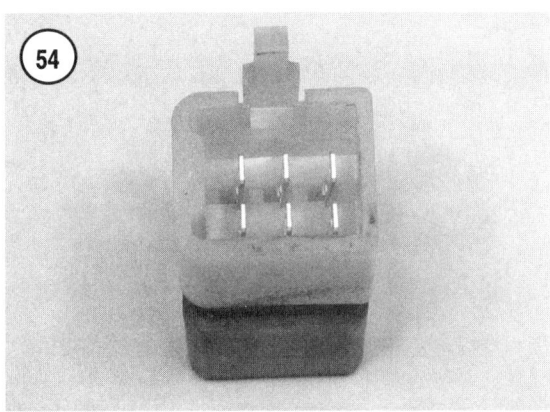

NOTE
Because electrical components are not returnable, if possible, install a good igniter unit for testing purposes and check operation before purchasing a new unit. A Kawasaki dealership may have a used igniter that is used for testing.

Removal/installation

1. Remove the upper fairing as described in Chapter Fifteen.
2. Disconnect the igniter connector (A, **Figure 52**).
3. Remove the igniter (B, **Figure 52**) from the rubber mount.
4. Reverse the removal steps to install the igniter unit.

Interlock Diode Unit

Removal/installation

1. Remove the upper fairing as described in Chapter Fifteen.
2. Disconnect the diode connector. Note that the diode unit and upper connector (**Figure 53**) are one assembly. The lower connector remains in the mounting bracket.

3. Reverse the removal steps to install the diode unit.

Testing

The three diode circuits act as one-way valves and allow power to enter one side of the unit and exit the opposite side of the unit. The purpose of this test is to check for low resistance in one direction and infinite resistance in the other direction.

1. Remove the unit. Note the three pairs of terminals (**Figure 54**).
2. Using an ohmmeter measure the resistance between a pair of terminals. Then reverse the ohmmeter leads and measure the resistance on the same pair of terminals.
3. The resistance should be infinite in one direction and low in the other direction. If any pair of terminals has low or high resistance in both directions, the diode unit is faulty.

Ignition Coil

Removal/installation

1. Remove the fuel tank as described in Chapter Fifteen.
2. Remove the coolant reserve tank as described in Chapter Ten.
3. Disconnect the brown/white wire (A, **Figure 55**) and black wire (B) from the coil terminals.
4. Disconnect the spark plug cap from the plug.
5. Remove the ignition coil mounting bolts (C, **Figure 55**) and remove the ignition coil.
6. Reverse the removal steps to install the ignition coil. Tighten the mounting bolts to 5.9 N•m (52 in.-lb.).

Testing

NOTE
If the coil and spark plug lead pass all tests, the spark plug cap may be faulty.

Replace with a new or good cap and check operation.

1. Check primary coil resistance as follows:
   a. Connect the meter probes to the terminals on the coil.
   b. Measure the resistance. Refer to **Table 2** for the specification.
2. Check secondary coil resistance as follows:
   a. Remove the spark plug cap from the spark plug lead.
   b. Connect one meter probe to the spark plug lead and the other meter probe to the terminal for the brown/white wire.
   c. Measure the resistance. Refer to **Table 2** for the specification.

Crankshaft Position Sensor

Peak voltage test

A hand tester (Kawasaki part No. 57001-1394 or equivalent) and peak voltage adapter (Kawasaki part No. 57001-1415 or equivalent) are required for accurate peak voltage testing of the crankshaft position sensor.

Refer to *Ignition System Precautions and Inspections* in this section.

> **WARNING**
> *High voltage is present during ignition system operation. Do not touch ignition components, wires or test leads while the engine is running or cranking.*

> **NOTE**
> *All peak voltage specifications are minimum values. If the measured voltage meets or exceeds the specifications, the test results are acceptable.*

1. Remove the fuel tank as described in Chapter Fifteen.
2. Disconnect the spark plug wire cap from the spark plug.
3. Disconnect the crankshaft position sensor connector (**Figure 56**).
4. Connect the tester to the following terminals: negative test lead to black/yellow wire terminal; positive test lead to black wire terminal.
5. Shift the transmission into neutral and turn the ignition switch on.
6. Press the starter button and crank the engine for a few seconds. Note the peak voltage reading achieved on the meter. Repeat the test several times and compare the readings with the specifications in **Table 2**.
7. If the peak voltage is less than specified, replace the crankshaft position sensor.

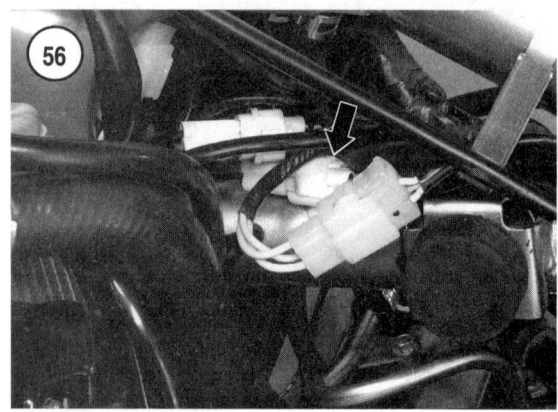

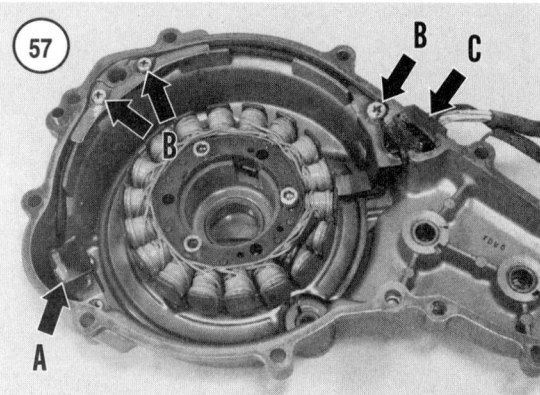

8. If all tests are acceptable, reconnect the electrical connector. Make sure the electrical connector is free of corrosion and tight.
9. Connect the spark plug wire.
10. Install the fuel tank as described in Chapter Fifteen.

Resistance test

A hand tester (Kawasaki part No. 57001-1394 or equivalvent) is required for accurate resistance testing of the ignition coil.

Refer to *Ignition System Precautions and Inspections* in this section.

ELECTRICAL SYSTEM

1. Remove the fuel tank as described in Chapter Fifteen.
2. Disconnect the crankshaft position sensor connector (**Figure 56**).
3. Connect the tester to the black wire terminal and black/yellow wire terminal.
4. Measure the resistance and compare the readings with the specifications in **Table 2**.
5. If the resistance is not as specified, replace the crankshaft position sensor.
6. Connect the test leads to each terminal of the sensor and to a chassis ground. If any reading is less than infinity, replace the crankshaft position sensor.
7. If all tests are acceptable, reconnect the electrical connector. Make sure the electrical connector is free of corrosion and tight.
8. Install the fuel tank as described in Chapter Fifteen.

Removal/installation

The crankshaft position sensor is located inside the alternator cover (A, **Figure 57**).
1. Remove the alternator cover as described in this chapter.
2. Remove the crankshaft position sensor wire holder retaining screws (B, **Figure 57**).

3. Remove the crankshaft position sensor mounting screws.
4. Dislodge the wire grommet (C, **Figure 57**), then remove the crankshaft position sensor.
5. Reverse the removal steps for installation while noting the following:
   a. Apply a thin coat of silicone sealer to the grommet to prevent oil leakage.
   b. Push down on the wire holder nearest the grommet before tightening the holder screw.

Ignition Timing

The ignition timing is electronically controlled by the igniter unit. No adjustment is possible to the ignition timing. The timing is checked to verify that the igniter unit is functioning properly.
1. Warm up the engine to operating temperature.
2. Remove the cap (**Figure 58**) from the timing hole.
3. Connect a timing light following the manufacturer's instructions.
4. Start the engine and allow it to idle at 1300 rpm.
5. Direct the timing light into the timing hole and observe the timing mark. The F mark should be aligned with the index mark in the hole (**Figure 59**).
6. Raise the engine speed and check that the F mark moves clockwise. When the engine speed reaches 4000 rpm, the timing is advanced. A single line should be visible in the timing hole.
7. If the timing check is incorrect:
   a. Test the igniter unit.
   b. If the igniter unit is good, inspect the Woodruff key (**Figure 60**), securing the rotor to the crankshaft. If the key is bent or sheared, the rotor will not be properly aligned on the crankshaft, causing the engine to be out of time. This slight change may not be obvious when checking ignition timing; however, the timing will be off enough to cause poor engine performance.
8. Turn off the engine and disconnect the test equipment.
9. Lubricate the O-ring on the cap, then screw the cap into the timing hole. Tighten the cap to 2.5 N•m (22 in.-lb.).

FAN SYSTEM

When the coolant temperature reaches a set point, an electric fan (**Figure 61**) turns on to increase airflow through the radiator fins. The fan circuit consists of the fan, fan switch, battery and fuse. The fan is turned on and off by the fan switch (**Figure 62**), located at the bottom of the radiator. The fan switch is thermally sensitive and controls the electrical grounding of the fan circuit. When the engine coolant is cold, the fan switch has an open circuit to ground and the fan relay and fan are inoperative. As coolant temperature rises and begins to exceed normal operating temperature, resistance in the fan switch lowers and the switch closes. When the switch is closed, current is passed to the fan and the fan turns on. As coolant temperature falls, resistance in the fan switch increases, until the switch opens and the fan stops.

When testing or troubleshooting the fan system, it is important that all connections are clean and tight. During assembly, apply dielectric grease to connections to prevent corrosion and the entry of moisture.

NOTE
Check the condition of the fan system fuse before testing individual components.

Fan Testing

In the following steps, two tests are performed to determine if the fan is faulty.
1. If the fan does not turn on at high temperature, perform the following simple check:
   a. Remove the connector from the switch terminal (**Figure 62**).
   b. Ground the connector to an engine fin, or other unpainted ground.
   c. If the fan turns on, test the fan switch.
   d. If the fan does not turn on, continue to check the fan as described in the following steps.
2. Remove the fuel tank as described in Chapter Fifteen.
3. Separate the connector (**Figure 63**).
4. Identify the half of the connector that leads to the fan.
5. Connect a 12-volt battery to the motor leads. Connect the positive test lead to the blue wire terminal and the negative test lead to the black wire terminal.
6. If the fan does not turn on, replace the fan. Replacement parts are not available for the fan.

Fan Switch Testing

The following test requires that the switch be placed in heated water, to simulate actual operating conditions. Read and understand the procedure so the proper equipment is on hand to safely perform the test.

Refer to **Table 2** for the temperature and resistance specifications.
1. Drain the cooling system (Chapter Three).
2. Remove the connector from the switch terminal. Remove the switch from the radiator.
3. Clean and inspect the switch for visible damage.
4. Test the switch at ambient temperature as follows:

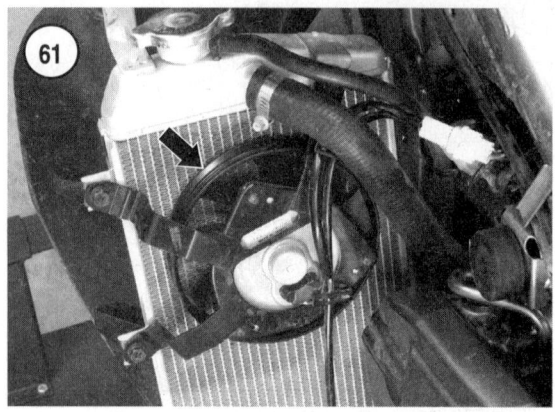

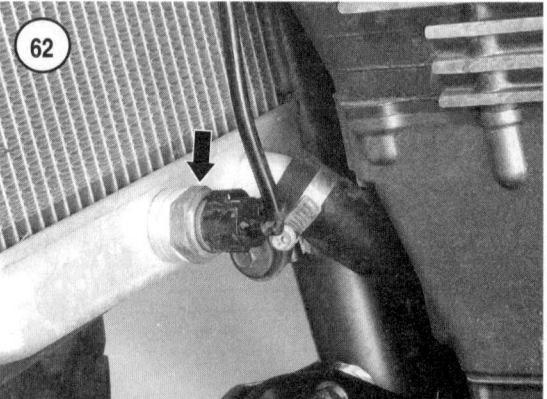

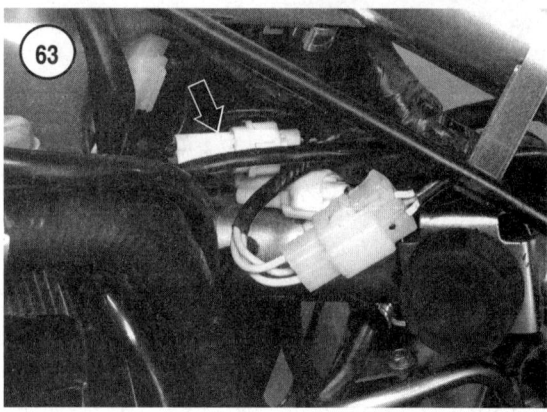

   a. Connect an ohmmeter to the switch terminals.
   b. If the reading is anything other than infinity, the switch is faulty. Low resistance in the switch could cause the fan to come on too soon and/or not turn off.
5. Test the switch at operating temperature as follows:
   a. Remove the fan switch as described in Chapter Ten.
   b. Connect an ohmmeter to the switch terminals.
   c. Suspend the switch (A, **Figure 64**) and an accurate thermometer (B) in a container of water. The temperature sensor and threads must be

ELECTRICAL SYSTEM

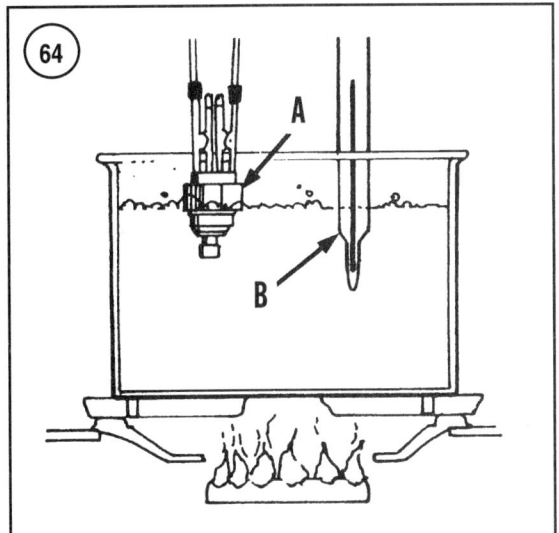

submerged. Do not allow the parts to touch the bottom or side of the container.
   d. Slowly heat the water and observe the thermometer and ohmmeter readings. Do not excessively overheat the switch.
   e. Replace the switch if it does not operate within the specifications.
6. Install the switch into the radiator. Tighten the fan switch to 18 N•m (13 ft.-lb.).

7. Fill and bleed the cooling system (Chapter Three).

COOLANT TEMPERATURE GAUGE AND SENDING UNIT

The coolant temperature sending unit is located on top of the cylinder head (**Figure 65**). The unit sends an electrical signal to the coolant temperature gauge, which reacts with a corresponding temperature reading. At low coolant temperatures, the sending unit has high resistance and the temperature gauge indicates a cold reading. As coolant temperature rises, the resistance of the sending unit lowers and the temperature gauge indicates a hotter reading.

Coolant Temperature Gauge Circuit Test

Use the following procedure to determine if the gauge or the sending unit should be tested.
1. Remove the fuel tank.
2. Disconnect the yellow wire from the terminal on the sending unit. Do not allow the loose wire to contact the engine or any other grounded surface.
3. Check the coolant temperature gauge circuit as follows:
   a. Turn on the ignition key and observe the gauge. The needle should indicate C.
   b. While observing the gauge, momentarily touch the yellow wire to the engine or another grounded (unpainted) surface on the motorcycle. The needle should should move toward H when the wire is grounded.

CAUTION
Ground the wire only long enough to verify the action of the gauge needle. Damage to the gauge can occur with excessive grounding.

   c. If the gauge passes the check, test the coolant temperature sending unit as described in this section.
   d. If the gauge does not pass the check, inspect the wiring harness for damaged or poor connections. If all wiring is in good condition, test the gauge as described in this section.

Coolant Temperature Gauge Testing

1. Remove the upper fairing as described in Chapter Fifteen.
2. Disconnect the meter connector (**Figure 66**).

CAUTION
Exercise care to prevent damage due to incorrect or accidental connections.

3. Refer to **Figure 67** and connect a 12-volt battery and 30-ohm resistor to the meter connector terminals.

4. When the battery is connected, the temperature gauge needle should move to and stay at the midpoint on the gauge scale.

Coolant Temperature Sending Unit Testing

The following test requires that the sending unit be placed in heated water to simulate actual operating conditions. Read and understand the procedure so the proper equipment is on hand to safely perform the test.

Refer to **Table 2** for the temperature and resistance specifications.

1. Remove the sending unit from the cylinder head (Chapter Ten).
2. Clean and inspect the sending for visible damage.
3. Test the sending unit as follows:
    a. Connect an ohmmeter to the sending unit terminal and to the threads.
    b. Suspend the unit (A, **Figure 68**) and an accurate thermometer (B) in a container of water. The sensor portion of the sending unit and threads must be submerged. Do not allow the parts to touch the bottom or side of the container.
    c. Slowly heat the water and observe the thermometer and ohmmeter readings. Do not excessively overheat the sending unit.
    d. Replace the sending unit if it does not operate within the specifications.
4. Install the sending unit (Chapter Ten).

METER UNIT

The meter unit includes a speedometer, tachometer, odometer, trip meter, coolant temperature gauge, neutral light, high beam light and turn signal light. The only parts available separately are the indicator light bulbs and the upper and lower covers. The meters and coolant temperature gauge are only available as part of the meter panel unit assembly.

Removal/Installation

1. Disconnect the negative battery cable as described in this chapter.
2. Remove the upper fairing as described in Chapter Fifteen.
3. Unscrew and disconnect the speedometer fitting (A, **Figure 69**) from the meter.

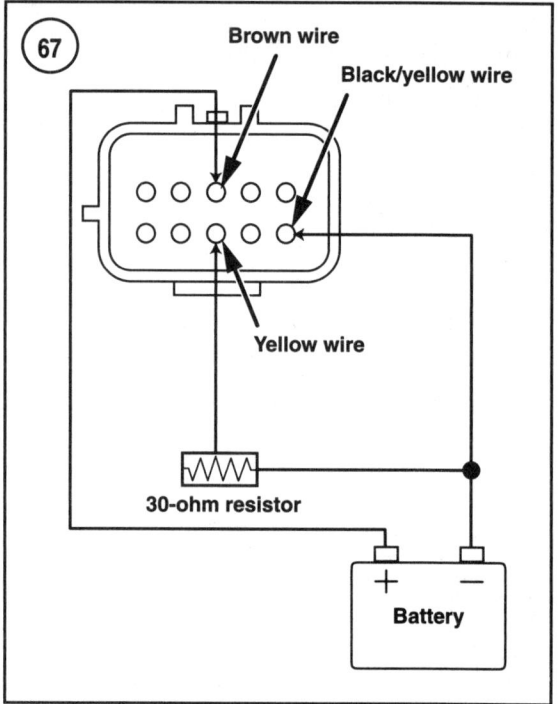

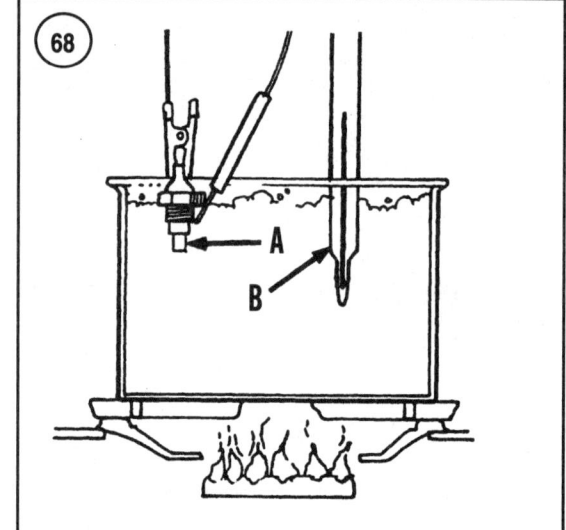

ELECTRICAL SYSTEM

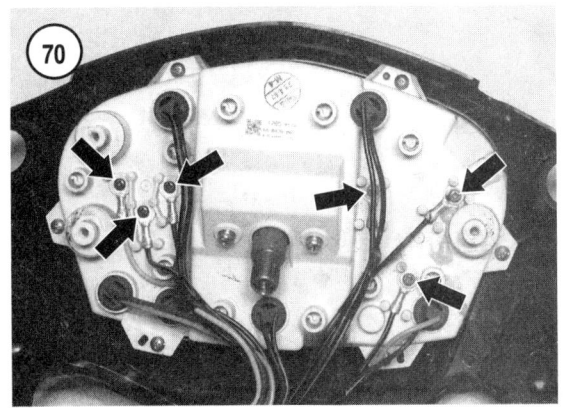

CAUTION
Handle the meter unit carefully. Do not position the unit so the face is down for an extended period. Doing so may cause a meter malfunction.

4. Disconnect the meter connector (B, **Figure 69**).
5. Remove the meter unit retaining screws and washers (C, **Figure 69**), and then remove the meter unit.
6. Inspect the mounting grommets and replace if damaged.
7. Reverse the removal steps to install the meter unit.

Disassembly/Reassembly

NOTE
Note that the wire color for each wire terminal and indicator bulb holder wire is embossed on the lower cover.

1. Extract the six indicator light bulb holders from the back of the lower meter cover.
2. Unscrew the six wire terminal connectors (**Figure 70**) from the back of the lower meter cover.

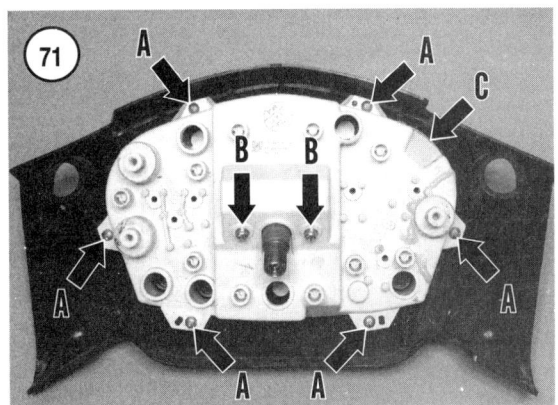

3. Remove the six peripheral mounting screws (A, **Figure 71**).
4. Remove the speedometer fitting mounting screws (B, **Figure 71**).
5. Remove the lower cover (C, **Figure 71**).

CAUTION
*Do not bend the odometer reset rod (**Figure 72**) when handling the meter panel.*

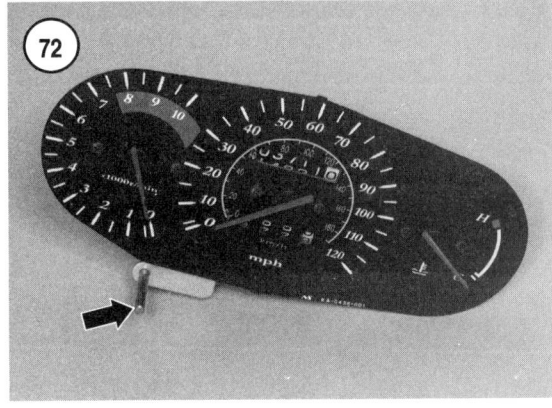

6. Lift the meter panel assembly (**Figure 73**) out of the upper cover.
7. Reverse the disassembly steps to reassemble the meter unit. Carefully insert the odometer reset rod into the button hole in the upper cover.

Tachometer Testing

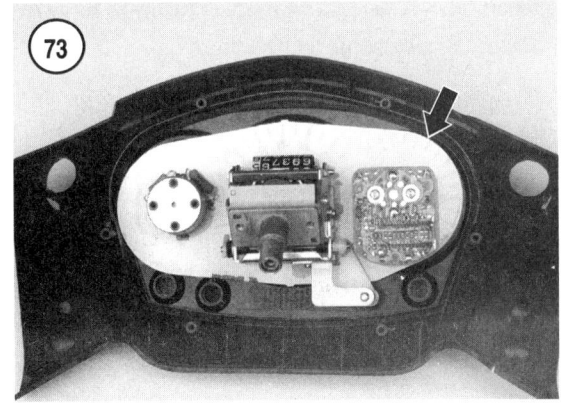

1. Remove the upper fairing as described in Chapter Fifteen.
2. Disconnect the meter connector (**Figure 66**).

CAUTION
Exercise care to prevent possible damage due to incorrect or accidental connections.

3. Refer to **Figure 74** and connect a 12-volt battery to the brown wire and black/yellow wire meter connector terminals.

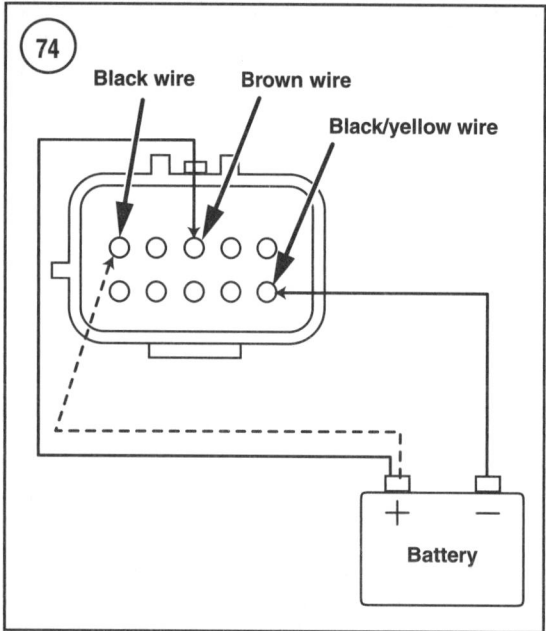

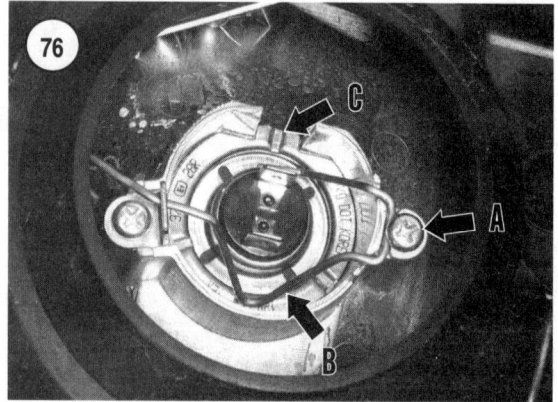

CAUTION
In the following step, contact the black wire just long enough to detect needle movement.

4. Momentarily connect the positive battery terminal to the black wire terminal in the meter connector while watching the tachometer needle. The needle should move each time a connection is made. If not, the tachometer is faulty.

Coolant Temperature Gauge Testing

Refer to the *Coolant Temperature Gauge And Sending Unit* section in this chapter.

LIGHTING SYSTEM

The lighting system consists of the headlights, taillight/brake light, turn signals, indicator lights and a fuse. **Table 1** lists replacement bulbs for these components.

Always use the correct wattage bulb as indicated in this section. A larger wattage bulb provides a dim light, and a smaller wattage bulb will burn out prematurely.

Headlight Bulb Replacement

1. Remove the upper fairing as described in Chapter Fifteen.
2. Remove the connector and rubber cover (A, **Figure 75**) from the back of the headlight lens unit.

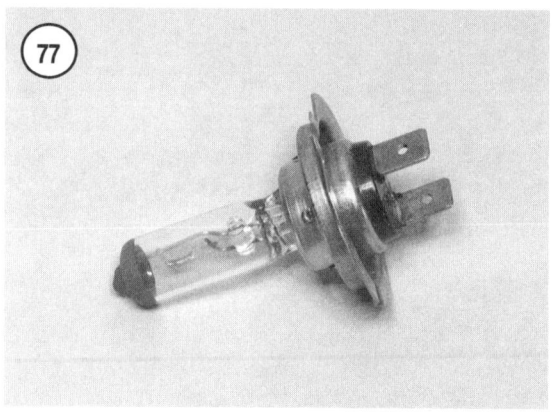

3. Remove the screw (A, **Figure 76**) from the wire retainer (B) that holds the headlight bulb.

CAUTION
Carefully read all instructions shipped with the replacement quartz bulb. Do not touch the bulb glass because traces of skin oil on the quartz halogen bulb will reduce bulb life. Clean oil or other contaminates from the bulb with a cloth moistened in alcohol or lacquer thinner.

ELECTRICAL SYSTEM

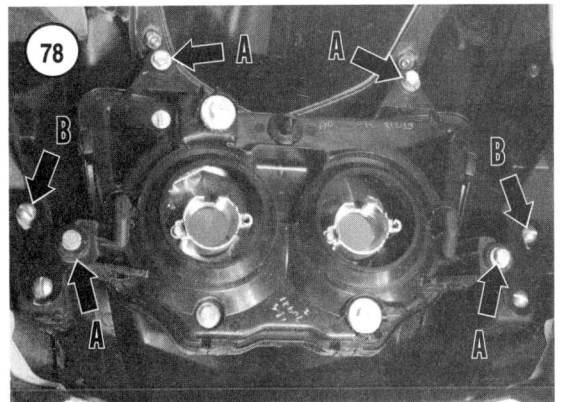

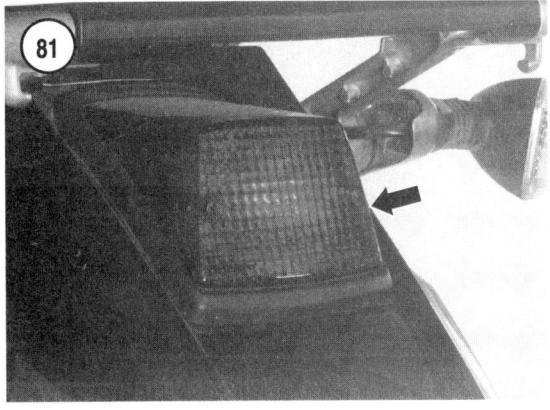

4. Remove the wire retainer, and then remove the bulb (**Figure 77**).

5. Reverse the removal steps to install the bulb while noting the following:
   a. Insert the bulb so the tab fits into the notch in the headlight housing (C, **Figure 76**).
   b. Install the rubber cover so one of the tabs (B, **Figure 75**) is on top. Make sure to push the cover and connector fully onto the bulb and headlight housing.
   c. Adjust the headlight as described in this section.

Headlight Housing
Removal/Installation

1. Remove the upper fairing as described in Chapter Fifteen.
2. Remove the headlight housing mounting bolts (A, **Figure 78**).
3. Remove the clamps (B, **Figure 78**), then remove the headlight housing.
4. Reverse the removal steps to install the headlight housing.

Headlight Adjustment

Adjust the headlight horizontally and vertically according to Department of Motor Vehicle regulations.

Horizontal headlight adjustment

1. Remove the right lower fairing as described in Chapter Fifteen.
2. Turn the adjuster (**Figure 79**) to relocate the headlight.
3. Install the right lower fairing as described in Chapter Fifteen.

Vertical headlight adjustment

1. Remove the windshield.
2. Turn the adjuster (**Figure 80**) to relocate the headlight.
3. Install the windshield.

Taillight/Brakelight Bulb Replacement

1. Remove the screws securing the lens (**Figure 81**) and remove the lens and gasket.
2. Wash out the inside and outside of the lens with a mild detergent and wipe dry.
3. Inspect the lens gasket and replace it if damaged or deteriorated.

4. Push in and turn the bulb counterclockwise and remove the bulb.
5. Carefully wipe off the reflector surface behind the bulb with a soft cloth.
6. Replace the bulb and install the lens and gasket; do not overtighten the screws as the lens may crack.

Turn Signal Light Bulb Replacement

1. The lens is secured by plastic prongs. Turn the lens counterclockwise and remove.
2. Push in and turn the bulb counterclockwise and remove the bulb.
3. Wash out the inside and outside of the lens with a mild detergent and wipe dry.
4. Inspect the lens gasket and replace it if damaged or deteriorated.
5. Carefully wipe off the reflector surface behind the bulb with a soft cloth.
6. Replace the bulb and install the lens.

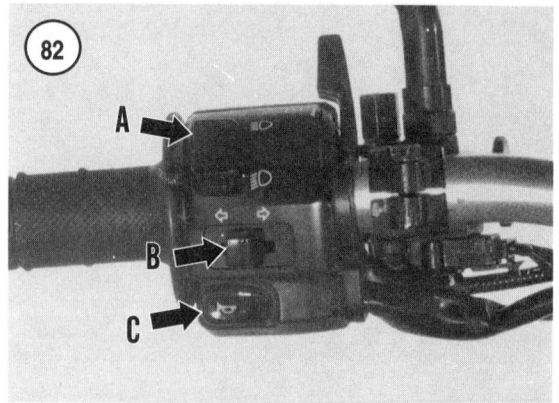

SWITCHES

Left Handlebar Switch Assembly

The left handlebar switch assembly houses the headlight dimmer switch (A, **Figure 82**), turn signal switch (B) and horn button (C). The switch housing also contains the choke control lever assembly. The switches can be checked for continuity using an ohmmeter connected to the appropriate color-coded wires in the connector plug. Refer to *Continuity Testing Guidelines* in this chapter for the test procedure.

NOTE
The switches mounted in the left handlebar switch housing are not available separately. If one switch is damaged, the entire housing must be replaced as an assembly.

Replacement

1. Remove the hand guard.
2. Remove the fuel tank as described in Chapter Fifteen.
3. Remove the upper fairing as described in Chapter Fifteen.
4. Remove the left handlebar switch screws (**Figure 83**) and separate the switch halves.
5. Dislodge the choke control lever and cable (A, **Figure 84**) from the switch half.
6. Remove the wire holder bracket (**Figure 85**).
7. Disconnect the switch connector (A, **Figure 86**) located below the top frame tube.

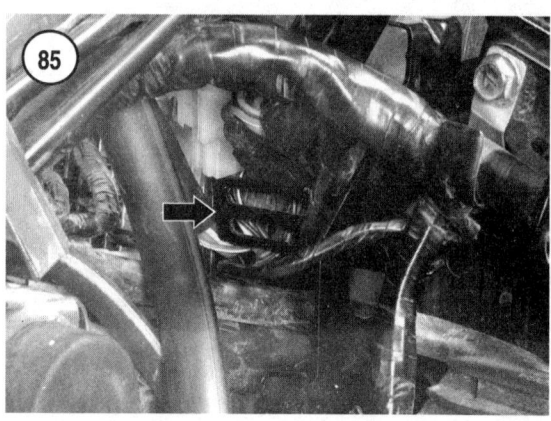

ELECTRICAL SYSTEM

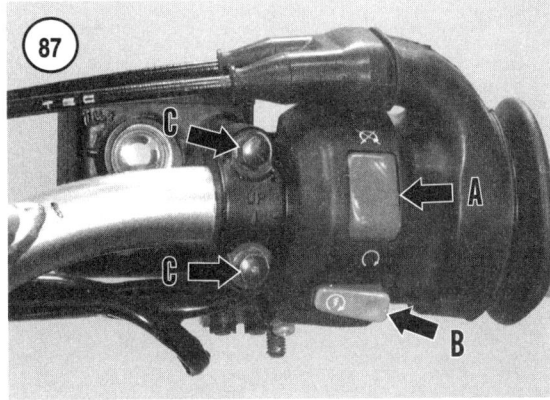

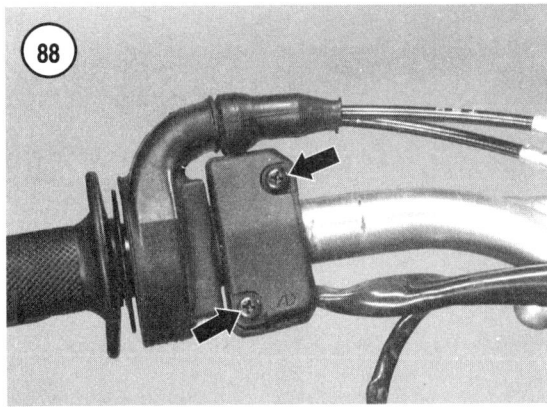

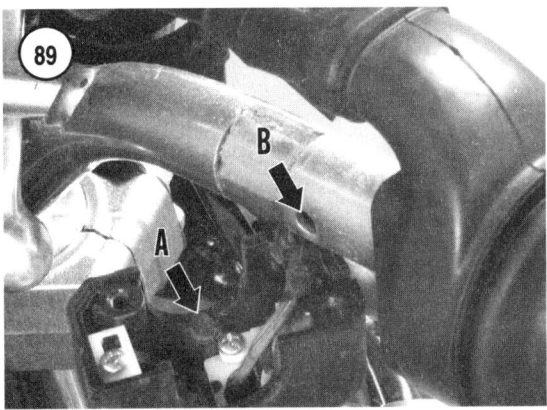

8. Reverse the removal procedure to install the switch housing while noting the following:
   a. Make sure the pin in the switch housing (B, **Figure 84**) fits into the hole in the handlebar.
   b. Adjust the choke as described in Chapter Three.

Right Handlebar Switch Assembly

The right handlebar switch assembly houses the engine stop switch (A, **Figure 87**) and starter button (B). The switches can be checked for continuity using an ohmmeter connected to the appropriate color-coded wires in the connector plug. Refer to *Continuity Testing Guidelines* in this chapter for the test procedure.

> *NOTE*
> *The switches mounted in the right handlebar switch housing are not available separately. If one switch is damaged, the entire housing must be replaced as an assembly.*

Replacement

1. Remove the hand guard.
2. Remove the fuel tank as described in Chapter Fifteen.
3. Remove the upper fairing as described in Chapter Fifteen.

> *CAUTION*
> *Do not allow the master cylinder to hang by its hose. Keep the master cylinder in an upright position so fluid cannot leak out of the cap. This also prevents air from getting into the system. Wrap the master cylinder with a clean shop cloth, and secure it to the motorcycle until after handlebar reassembly.*

4. Remove the bolts (C, **Figure 87**) securing the master cylinder assembly. Separate the master cylinder from the handlebar.
5. Remove the right handlebar switch screws (**Figure 88**) and separate the switch halves.
6. Remove the wire holder bracket (**Figure 85**).
7. Disconnect the switch connector (B, **Figure 86**) located below the top frame tube.
8. Reverse the removal procedure to install the switch housing. Make sure the pin (A, **Figure 89**) in the switch housing fits into the hole (B) in the handlebar.

Neutral Switch

The neutral switch is mounted on the left crankcase (**Figure 90**).

Testing

1. Shift the transmission into neutral.
2. Remove the sprocket guard (**Figure 91**).
3. Disconnect the connector from the switch.
4. Connect one lead of an ohmmeter to the neutral switch terminal and the other ohmmeter lead to a good engine ground.
5. Read the ohmmeter scale with the transmission in neutral, and then in gear. Note the following:
   a. The ohmmeter must read continuity with the transmission in neutral.
   b. The ohmmeter must read infinity with the transmission in gear.
   c. If either reading is incorrect, check the wiring harness for damage or dirty or loose-fitting terminals. If the wiring harness is good, replace the neutral switch.
6. Reconnect the switch connector.
7. Start the engine and check the operation of the neutral switch indicator light with the transmission in neutral and in gear.

Replacement

1. Shift the transmission into neutral.
2. Remove the sprocket guard (**Figure 91**).
3. Disconnect the electrical connector from the neutral switch.
4. Unscrew the neutral switch and washer from the crankcase.
5. Make sure the sealing washer is installed on the neutral switch. Install the neutral switch into the left crankcase and tighten to 15 N•m (11 ft.-lb.).

6. Connect the electrical connector to the neutral switch. Push it on and make sure it is seated correctly.

Front Brake Light Switch

The front brake switch is mounted on the front master cylinder assembly.

Testing

The switch can be checked for continuity using an ohmmeter connected to the appropriate color-coded wires in the connector plug. Refer to *Continuity Testing Guidelines* in this chapter for the test procedure.

Removal/installation

1. Disconnect the two electrical connectors (A, **Figure 92**) from the front brake light switch.
2. Remove the mounting screw (B, **Figure 92**) and brake switch.
3. Reverse the removal steps to install the switch.
4. Check brake light operation.

ELECTRICAL SYSTEM

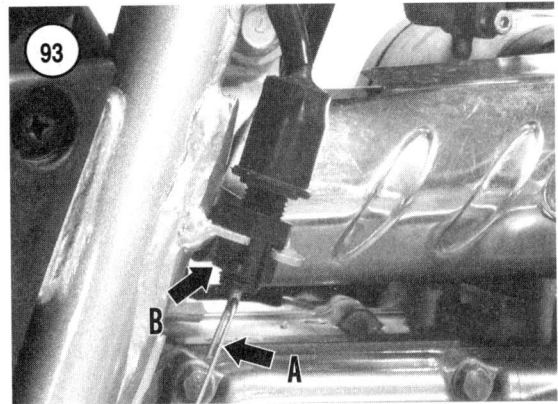

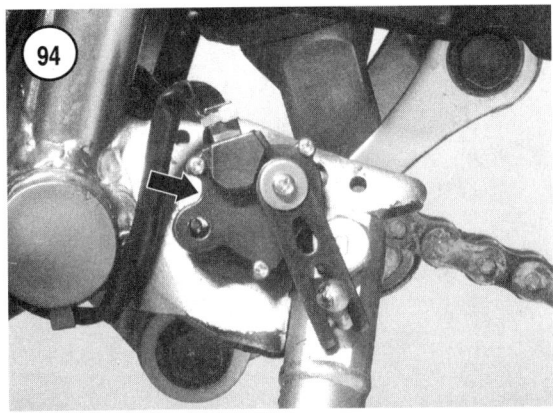

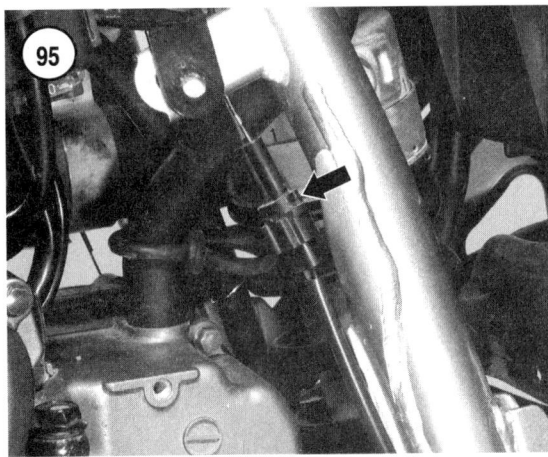

Rear Brake Light Switch

Testing

1. Disconnect the brake light switch wires at the electrical connector above the rear of the engine.
2. Connect the leads of an ohmmeter or continuity tester between the connector terminals. The tester should indicate continuity when the rear brake pedal is depressed and infinity when the pedal is released.
3. If necessary, replace the rear brake light switch if it fails to operate as described.

Removal/installation

1. Disconnect the brake light switch wires at the electrical connector above the rear of the engine.
2. Detach the spring (A, **Figure 93**) from the brake light switch.
3. Unscrew the brake light switch from the mounting nut (B, **Figure 93**).
4. Note the routing of the switch wires and remove the switch.
5. Reverse the removal steps to install the brake light switch.
6. Adjust the rear brake light switch as described in Chapter Three.

Sidestand Switch Testing/Replacement

The sidestand switch (**Figure 94**) is mounted behind the plastic cover at the sidestand pivot.

1. Support the motorcycle securely so it is not supported by the sidestand.
2. Disconnect the switch connector (**Figure 95**).
3. Connect an ohmmeter or continuity tester to the sidestand switch terminals in the connector.
4. Operate the sidestand in its up and down positions while reading the ohmmeter. Note the following:
   a. The ohmmeter must read continuity with the sidestand up.
   b. The ohmmeter must read infinity with the sidestand down.
   c. If either reading is incorrect, check the wiring harness for damage or dirty or loose-fitting terminals. If the wiring harness is good, replace the sidestand switch.
5. Remove the bolt securing the cover and switch. Remove the sidestand switch (**Figure 94**).
6. When installing the switch and cover, apply threadlock to the mounting bolt threads. Tighten the bolt to 8.8 N•m (78 in.-lb.).

Clutch Switch (Starter Interlock Switch)

The clutch switch, also named the starter interlock switch, is mounted on the clutch lever base.

Testing

The switch can be checked for continuity using an ohmmeter connected to the appropriate color-coded wires in the connector plug. Refer to *Continuity Testing Guidelines* in this chapter for the test procedure.

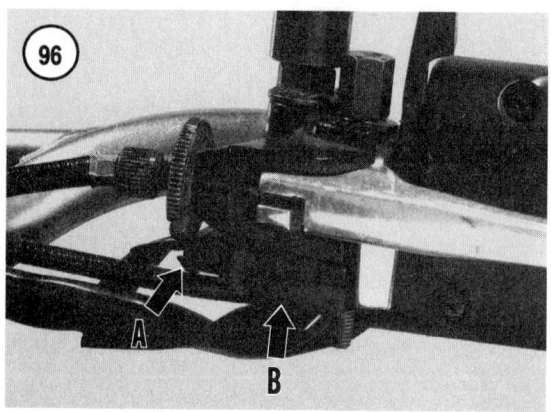
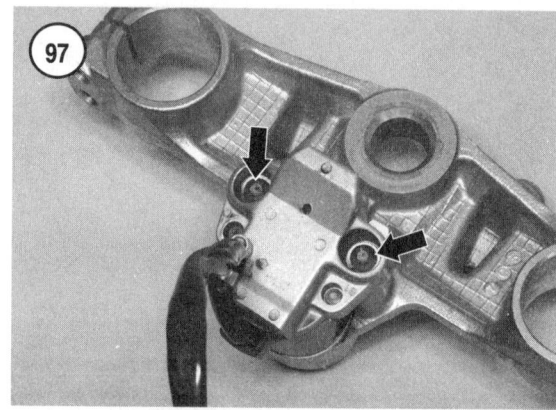

Removal/installation

1. Disconnect the electrical connector (A, **Figure 96**) from the switch.
2. Remove the mounting screws, then remove the switch (B, **Figure 96**).
3. Reverse the removal steps to install the switch.
4. Check starting system operation.

Ignition Switch Replacement

1. Remove the upper steering bracket as described in *Steering Stem And Head* (Chapter Twelve).
2. Drill out and remove the shear bolts (**Figure 97**) securing the ignition switch to the bottom surface of the upper steering bracket.
3. Remove the ignition switch and wiring harness.
4. Install *new* shear bolts securing the ignition switch. Tighten the bolts until the heads shear off.
5. Install the upper steering bracket as described in Chapter Twelve.
6. Check the operation of the ignition switch.

FUSES

Whenever a fuse blows, determine the cause before replacing the fuse. Usually, the trouble is a short circuit in the wiring. Worn-through insulation or a short to ground from a disconnected wire may cause this.

> **CAUTION**
> *If replacing a fuse, make sure the ignition switch is turned to the off position. This lessens the chance of a short circuit.*

> **CAUTION**
> *Never substitute any metal object for a fuse. Never use a higher amperage fuse than specified. An overload could*

ELECTRICAL SYSTEM

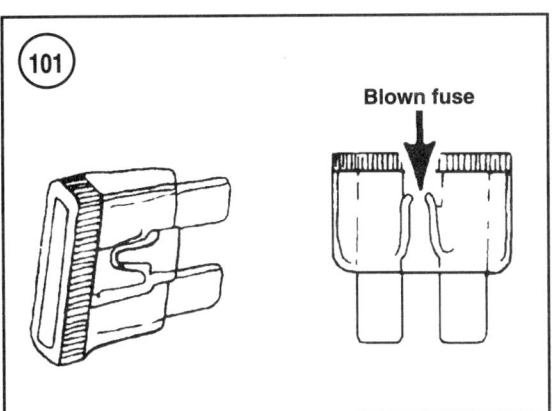

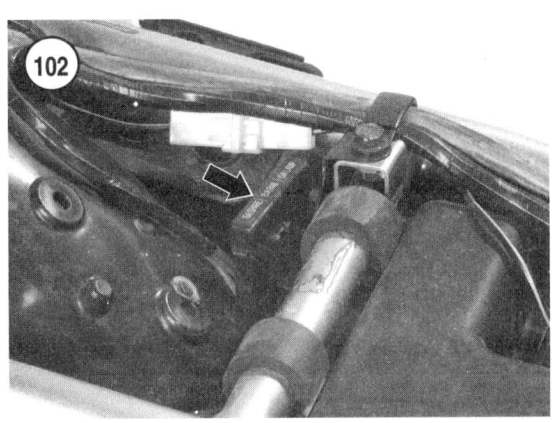

cause a fire and the complete loss of the motorcycle.

Main Fuse

The 20-amp main fuse is mounted on the starter relay. To check or replace the main fuse, perform the following:
1. Make sure the ignition switch is turned to the off position.
2. Remove the starter relay cover (**Figure 98**).
3. Disconnect the starter relay connector (**Figure 99**).
4. Remove the main fuse (**Figure 100**).
5. Inspect the fuse. Replace the fuse if it has blown (**Figure 101**).
6. Reverse the removal steps to install the main fuse.

Fuses

Fuses for the headlights and coolant fan are located in the fuse box (**Figure 102**) mounted underneath the seat. The current rating for each fuse is 15 amps.

NOTE
There is a spare fuse in the fuse box.

If a fuse in the fuse box blows, perform the following:
1. Turn the main switch to the off position.
2. Remove the seat as described in Chapter Fifteen.
3. Open the fuse box cover.
4. Remove and inspect the fuse. Replace the fuse if it has blown (**Figure 101**).
5. Close the fuse box cover.
6. Install the seat as described in Chapter Fifteen.

Table 1 ELECTRICAL SYSTEM GENERAL SPECIFICATIONS

Alternator	
Type	Three-phase AC
Output	
Regulated	
2008-2010	14 volts/17 amps at 7000 rpm
2011-on	14.5 volts/17 amps at 7000 rpm
Unregulated	43 volts or more at 4000 rpm (min)
Battery	12 volts/14 amp-hour
Ignition timing	
Idle	10° BTDC @ 1300 rpm
Advanced	30° BTDC @ 4000 rpm
Light bulbs	
Headlights	12 volt, 55/55 watts
Taillight/brake light	12 volt, 21/5 watts
Turn signal	12 volt, 21 watts
Spark plug	
Type	NGK DPR8EA-9 or ND X24EPR-U9
Gap	0.8-0.9 mm (0.031-0.035 in.)

Table 2 ELECTRICAL SYSTEM TEST SPECIFICATIONS

Charging system voltage (regulated)	13.8-14.8 volts
Coolant fan switch	
Off resistance	Infinity
On resistance	Less than 0.5 ohms
Off to on temperature	95-101° C (203-214° F)
On to off temperature	87° C (189° F) or less
Coolant temperature sending unit resistance	
At 80° C (176° F)	47-57 ohms
At 100° C (212° F)	26-30 ohms
Crankshaft position sensor	
Peak voltage	2 volts or more
Resistance	101-151 ohms
Ignition coil resistance	
Primary coil	1.8-2.6 ohms
Secondary coil (spark plug cap removed)	8.8k-13.2k ohms
Starter	
Brush length	
Standard	12 mm (0.47 in.)
Service limit	6.5 mm (0.26 in.)
Commutator	
Standard OD	28 mm (1.10 in.)
Service limit	27 mm (1.06 in.)
Stator coil resistance	0.1-0.8 ohms

Table 3 ELECTRICAL SYSTEM TORQUE SPECIFICATIONS

	N•m	in.-lb.	ft.-lb.
Alternator cover bolts	8.8	78	–
Coolant fan switch	18	–	13
Coolant temperature sending unit	15	–	11
Ignition coil mounting bolts	5.9	52	–
Neutral switch	15	–	11
Rotor bolt*	195	–	144
Sidestand cover bolt	8.8	78	–
Starter clutch bolt	34	–	25
Starter mounting bolts	8.8	78	–
Stator coil bolts	4.4	39	–
Timing hole cap	2.5	22	–
*Refer to text			

CHAPTER TEN

COOLING SYSTEM

This chapter provides service procedures for the radiator, fan, fan switch, thermostat, coolant temperature sending unit and water pump.

SAFETY PRECAUTIONS

WARNING
*Do not remove the radiator cap (**Figure 1**) immediately after or during engine operation. When the engine has been operated, the liquid in the cooling system is scalding hot and under pressure. Removing the cap while the engine is hot can cause the coolant to spray violently from the radiator opening, possibly causing injury.*

Wait for the engine to cool, then place a shop cloth over the cap. Slowly turn the cap to relieve any pressure. Turn the cap to the safety stop and check that all pressure is relieved. To remove the cap from the radiator, press down on the cap, then twist it free.

To prevent potential damage to the engine, change the coolant regularly as described in Chapter Three. Always use an antifreeze solution. Antifreeze contains lubricants and rust inhibitors that protect the components of the cooling system. Always dispose of coolant in an environmentally-safe manner.

RADIATOR AND FAN

The motorcycle is equipped with a radiator and a thermostatically-controlled fan. The fan is turned on and off by the fan switch. During engine operation, hot coolant from the engine enters the radiator from the upper hose. The coolant loses heat as it circulates to the bottom of the radiator. The coolant then returns to the engine by the lower hose. If the coolant returning to the engine is too hot, the radiator fan switch, located at the bottom of the radiator, turns on the fan. The fan draws air through the radiator to aid in lowering coolant temperature. The switch is set to turn on the fan when coolant temperature is 95-101° C (203-214° F). The fan shuts off when coolant temperature drops below 87° C (189° F).

Fan Removal/Installation

WARNING
Make sure the ignition switch is off when working on or around the cooling fan.

1. Remove the fuel tank as described in Chapter Fifteen.
2. Disconnect the battery.
3. Disconnect the fan motor wires at the connector (A, **Figure 2**).
4. Remove the wires from the retainers.
5. Remove the three bolts securing the fan (B, **Figure 2**) to the radiator.
6. If necessary, refer to Chapter Nine to test the fan.
7. Reverse the removal procedure to install the fan.

Radiator and Fan Switch Removal/Installation

1. Drain the cooling system as described in Chapter Three.
2. Remove the fuel tank as described in Chapter Fifteen.
3. Remove the radiator screen (**Figure 3**).
4. Remove the fan as described in this section.
5. Remove the connector (**Figure 4**) from the fan switch. If necessary, remove the fan switch.
6. Remove the hoses from the radiator. If the hoses are seized to the fittings, cut and split the hoses so they can be peeled from the fittings. Avoid scoring the fittings. Replace the hoses.
7. Remove the two bolts (**Figure 5**) at the front of the radiator.
8. Inspect the radiator as described in this chapter.
9. If necessary, refer to Chapter Nine to test the fan switch.
10. Reverse the removal procedure to install the radiator. Note the following:
    a. Tighten the radiator mounting bolts to 8.8 N•m (78 in.-lb.).
    b. Replace hoses that are hard, cracked or show signs of deterioration, both internally and externally. Hold each hose and flex it in several directions to check for damage. For a hose that is difficult to install on a fitting, dip the hose end in hot water until the rubber has softened, and then install the hose.
    c. Install clamps in their original positions.
    d. If removed, install and tighten the fan switch to 18 N•m (13 ft.-lb.).
    e. Fill and bleed the cooling system as described in Chapter Three.
    f. Start the engine and allow it to warm up. Check for leaks.

Inspection

1. Clean the exterior of the radiator with a low-pressure water spray. Allow the radiator to dry.

COOLING SYSTEM

2. Check for damaged cooling fins. Straighten bent fins with a screwdriver. If more than 20 percent of the cooling area is damaged, replace the radiator.
3. Check the seams and other soldered connections for corrosion (green residue). If corrosion is evident, there could be a leak in that spot. Perform a cooling system pressure check as described in *Cooling System Inspection* in Chapter Three. If the equipment is not available, take the radiator to a radiator repair shop to have it flushed and pressure checked.
4. Fill the radiator with water and check the flow rate out of the radiator. If the flow rate is slow, or if there is corrosion or other buildup, take the radiator to a radiator repair shop to have it flushed and pressure checked.

THERMOSTAT

The engine thermostat is located in a housing (A, **Figure 6**) on the right side of the cylinder head.

Removal/Inspection/Installation

1. Drain the cooling system as described in Chapter Three.
2. Remove the three bolts (B, **Figure 6**) securing the thermostat housing (A) to the cylinder head.
3. Remove the thermostat (**Figure 7**).
4. Visually inspect the valve in the thermostat. The valve should be closed when the thermostat is cold. If the valve is cold and it is open, replace the thermostat.
5. Wash the thermostat in cool water. If necessary, use a soft brush to scrub accumulation off the thermostat. If an accumulation of rubber particles is evident, inspect the radiator hoses for internal deterioration. Replace if necessary
6. Inspect the condition of the thermostat gasket.
7. If desired, open the drain bolt at the water pump and flush the cylinder head and cylinder.
8. Clean the bolts and threaded bores.
9. Test the thermostat as follows:
   a. Suspend the thermostat and an accurate thermometer in a container of water (**Figure 8**). Do not allow the parts to touch the bottom or side of the container.
   b. Slowly heat the water and observe the thermostat valve.
   c. When the thermostat begins to open, observe the temperature on the thermometer. The thermostat should start to open between 69.5-72.5° C (157-163° F).
   d. Continue to raise the temperature to 85° C (185° F). At this temperature, the thermostat

valve should reach full lift, which is 3 mm (0.12 in.) or greater.

e. Replace the thermostat if it does meet the conditions of these tests.

10. Install the thermostat with the air bleed hole (**Figure 9**) at the top of the opening. Seat the gasket in the bore.

11. Align and seat the housing, and then bolt it into place. Tighten the thermostat housing bolts to 8.8 N•m (78 in.-lb.).

12. Fill and bleed the cooling system as described in Chapter Three).

COOLANT TEMPERATURE SENDING UNIT

The coolant temperature sending unit (**Figure 10**) is located on top of the cylinder head.

Removal/Installation

1. Remove the wire from the sending unit connector.
2. Remove the sending unit from the cylinder head.
3. Clean the sending unit and the threads in the cylinder head.
4. Test the sending unit as described in Chapter Nine.
5. Apply waterproof sealant to the sending unit threads.
6. Tighten the sending unit to 15 N•m (11 ft.-lb.).

WATER PUMP

The water pump is located in the right crankcase cover. To inspect the condition of the impeller (A, **Figure 11**), mechanical seal, or water pump cover, the cover can be removed without removing the right crankcase cover. The cooling system must be drained before removing the water pump cover (B, **Figure 11**).

An inspection hole (**Figure 12**) for the water pump is located at the bottom of the case. If water leaks from this hole, the pump mechanical seal is leaking. If oil leaks from this point, the oil seal is leaking. Removal of the right crankcase cover is necessary to replace the seals.

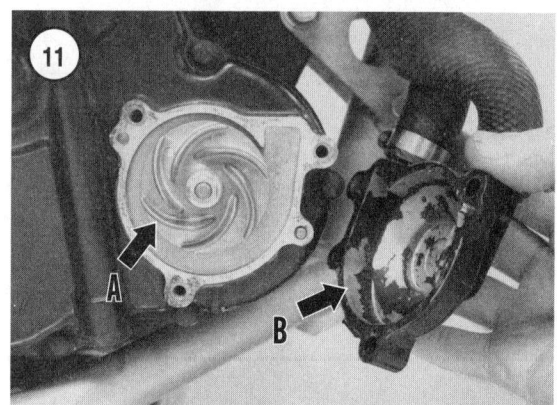

Removal/Inspection/Installation

Remove and install the water pump cover and right crankcase cover as follows. Inspect and repair the water pump as described in this section.

1. Drain the cooling system as described in Chapter Three.
2. If necessary, remove the hoses from the water pump cover.

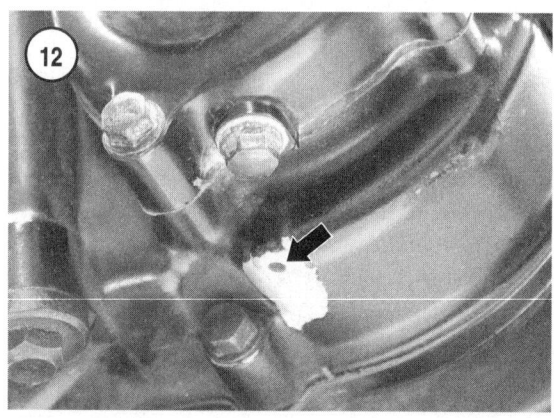

COOLING SYSTEM

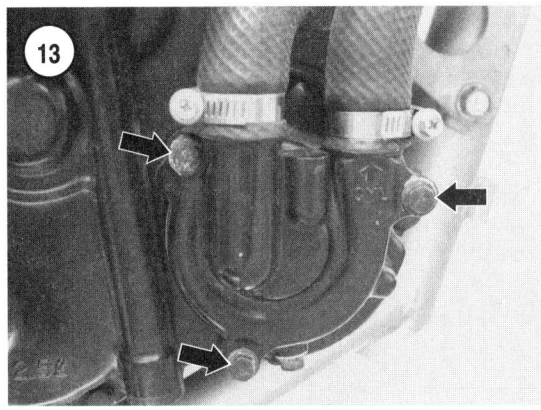

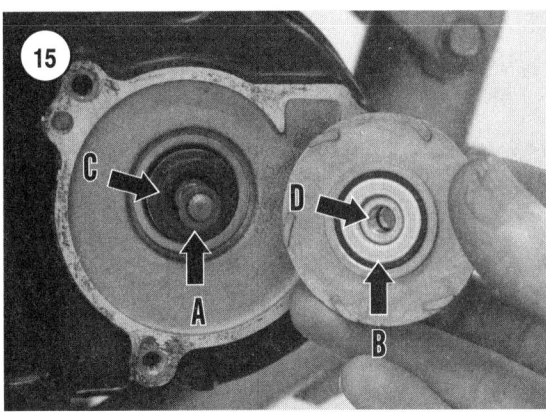

3. Remove the water pump cover as follows:
   a. Remove the three bolts (**Figure 13**) securing the water pump cover.
   b. Lightly tap the cover to loosen it from the crankcase cover.
   c. Pull the cover straight out. Remove the gasket and two dowels beneath the cover.
4. Remove the nut (**Figure 14**) and washer from the impeller.
5. Remove the impeller and the washer (A, **Figure 15**) behind the impeller.
6. Inspect the parts.
   a. Inspect the impeller and cover for obvious damage.
   b. Inspect the face of the mechanical seal on the impeller (B, **Figure 15**) and in the right crankcase cover (C). In order to seal properly, both faces must be smooth and free of scoring or damage. When installed, the impeller seal should fit firmly against the seal in the crankcase cover. Since the seal in the crankcase cover is spring loaded, it maintains pressure on the seals and compensates for wear. If necessary, replace the mechanical seal and oil seal as described in this section.
   c. Install a new O-ring inside the impeller (D, **Figure 15**). Lubricate the O-ring with waterproof grease.
7. If necessary, remove the right crankcase cover as described in Chapter Six.
8. Reverse the removal steps to install the impeller assembly and water pump cover. Note the following:
   a. Apply waterproof grease to the impeller shaft.
   b. Tighten the impeller nut to 10 N•m (89 in.-lb.).
   c. Install both dowels and a new gasket before installing the water pump cover.
   d. Fill and bleed the cooling system as described in Chapter Three.
   e. Start the engine and allow it to warm up. Check for leaks.

Seal Replacement

The water pump has a two-piece mechanical seal (A, **Figure 16**) and an oil seal (B). The mechanical seal prevents coolant in the pump chamber from passing into the right crankcase cover, which contains oil. Likewise, the oil seal prevents oil in the right crankcase cover from passing into the pump chamber, which contains coolant. A drain hole (**Figure 12**) is located between the seals to allow any leaking water or oil to drain to the outside of the engine. Whenever there are leaks at the drain hole, replace the seals. The mechanical seal must be removed from the right crankcase cover in order to remove the oil seal.

1. Replace the mechanical seal in the impeller as follows:
    a. Lift the impeller seal from the impeller (**Figure 17**). Clean the seal bore.
    b. Lightly lubricate the rubber edge of the new seal with waterproof grease.
    c. Seat the new seal into the impeller by hand.
2. In the right crankcase cover, replace the remaining half of the mechanical seal and the oil seal as follows:
    a. Place a narrow drift under the oil seal and onto the back of the mechanical seal (**Figure 18**). Work around the seal and drive it from the bore. Avoid any contact with the surface of the bore. Do not pry the seal from the front side of the crankcase cover.
    b. Place a driver on the oil seal and drive it from the bore.
    c. Turn over the crankcase cover and clean the bore and drain hole.
    d. Pack molydisulfide grease into the lip of the oil seal.
    e. Place the oil seal over the crankcase cover bore, with the closed side of the seal facing up.
    f. Drive the seal into the cover using a driver that fits on the perimeter of the seal. Check that the seal is fully seated and the drain hole is visible.
    g. Lightly lubricate the exterior of the mechanical seal.
    h. Place the mechanical seal into the crankcase cover bore, then drive it into place. Use a driver that fits on the flange at the perimeter (**Figure 19**) of the seal.

COOLANT RESERVE TANK

Removal/Installation

1. Remove the skid plate as described in Chapter Fifteen.
2. Support the motorcycle so it is vertical and level.
3. Remove the right, lower fairing as described in Chapter Fifteen.
4. Remove the reserve tank cover.
5. Detach the reserve tank overflow hose (A, **Figure 20**) from the tank.
6. Remove the bolts from the corners of the reserve tank (B, **Figure 20**), then invert the tank and pour out the contents.
7. Detach the radiator overflow hose from the tank, then remove the tank.
8. Reverse the removal steps for installation. Tighten the reserve tank bolts to 8.8 N•m (78 in.-lb.).
9. Fill the reserve tank as described in Chapter Three.

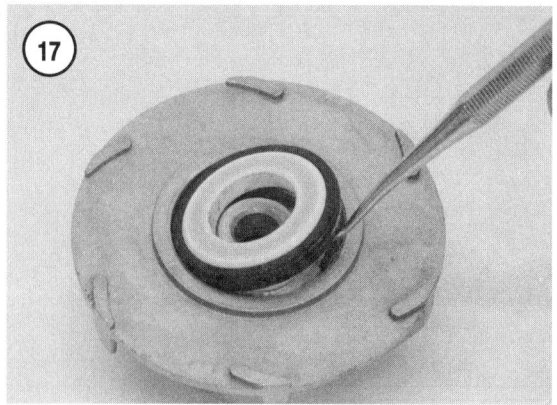
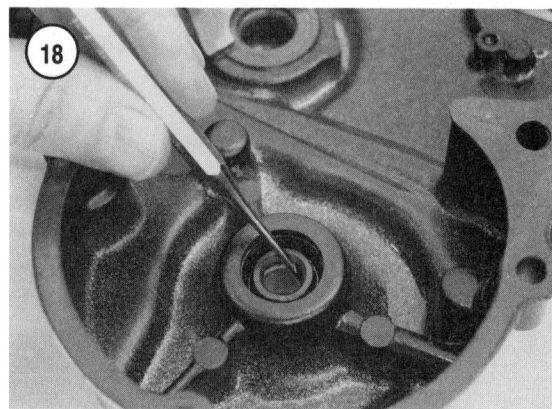

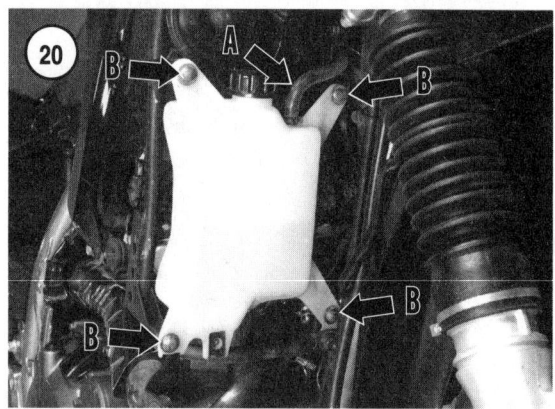

COOLING SYSTEM

Table 1 COOLING SYSTEM SPECIFICATIONS

Antifreeze type	Ethylene glycol containing anti-corrosion inhibitors for aluminum engines
Coolant mixture	50:50 (antifreeze/distilled water)
Cooling system capacity	1.55 liters (1.64 quarts)
Radiator cap relief pressure	
2008-2014 models	93-123 kPa (13.5-17.8 psi)
2015-on models	107.9-137.3 kPa (15.6-19.9 psi)
Thermostat opening temperature	69.5-72.5° C (157-163° F)
Thermostat minimum full open lift	3 mm (0.12 in.) at 85° C (185° F)

Table 2 COOLING SYSTEM TORQUE SPECIFICATIONS

	N•m	in.-lb.	ft.-lb.
Coolant reserve tank mounting bolts	8.8	78	–
Coolant temperature sending unit	15	–	11
Impeller nut	10	89	–
Radiator fan switch	18	–	13
Radiator mounting bolts	8.8	78	–
Thermostat housing bolts	8.8	78	–
Water pump drain bolt	8.8	78	–

CHAPTER ELEVEN

WHEELS, TIRES AND DRIVE CHAIN

This chapter provides service procedures for the wheels, speedometer drive unit, drive chain, sprockets and tires. Routine maintenance procedures for these components are found in Chapter Three. Refer to the tables at the end of this chapter for specifications.

FRONT WHEEL AND SPEEDOMETER DRIVE UNIT

Removal

1. Support the motorcycle so it is stable and the front wheel is off the ground.
2. Disconnect the speedometer cable (**Figure 1**) from the right side of the hub.
3. Remove the axle nut (A, **Figure 2**).
4. Loosen the axle clamp bolts (B, **Figure 2**) on both sides of the wheel.
5. Pull up on the wheel to take the weight off the axle, and then extract the axle from the right side.

NOTE
Do not operate the front brake lever while the wheel is removed. Insert a wooden block between the pads until the wheel is installed. This prevents the caliper pistons from extending if the lever is operated.

6. Remove the front wheel.
7. Remove the speedometer drive unit (**Figure 3**) from the right side of the hub. As the unit is removed,

tilt it upward to prevent parts from falling from the housing.
8. Remove the axle spacer (**Figure 4**) from the left side of the hub.
9. Inspect and/or repair the wheel, axle assembly and speedometer drive unit as described in this chapter.

Installation

1. Clean the axle contact surfaces on the fork tube and axle holders.
2. Apply waterproof grease to the axle, bearing seals, spacer, speedometer cable end, speedometer drive unit seal and speedometer drive unit tabbed washer. Do not apply grease to the threads on the axle or axle nut.
3. Install the axle spacer (**Figure 4**) onto the left side of the hub.

WHEELS, TIRES AND DRIVE CHAIN

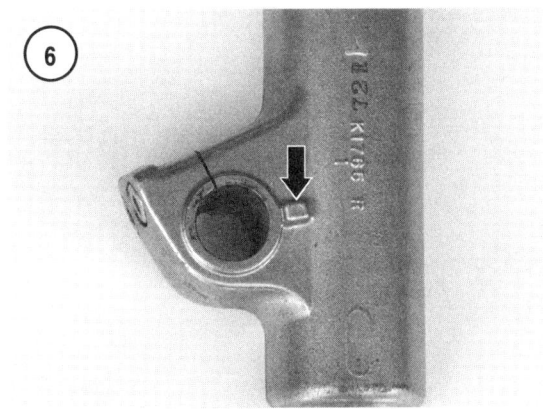

NOTE
The tabbed washer can become damaged when installing the wheel and axle assembly. The tabs on the washer will bend if the washer is not seated properly before tightening the axle.

4. Install the speedometer unit onto the right side of the hub. Make sure the tabbed washer engages the slots (**Figure 5**) in the hub.
5. Remove the spacer block from between the brake pads.
6. If necessary, carefully spread the brake pads so the brake disc can enter the brake assembly.
7. Place the front wheel between the fork legs while carefully inserting the brake disc between the brake pads
8. Check that the bosses on the speedometer housing fit around the boss (**Figure 6**) on the fork tube.
9. Install the front axle from the left side.
10. Tighten the axle nut finger-tight.

CAUTION
The front axle and pinch bolt tightening sequence in Steps 11-14 correctly seats the front axle so that the fork legs are parallel. Fork misalignment can cause premature fork seal and bushing wear, increased wear against the fork tube and reduced fork performance and operation.

11. Hold the right end of the axle and tighten the front axle nut (A, **Figure 2**) to 88 N•m (65 ft.-lb.).
12. Tighten the left axle pinch bolts (B, **Figure 2**) to 20 N•m (15 ft.-lb.).
13. Center the axle in the fork tube axle bores as follows:
   a. Lower the motorcycled so the front wheel is on the ground.
   b. Apply the front brake.

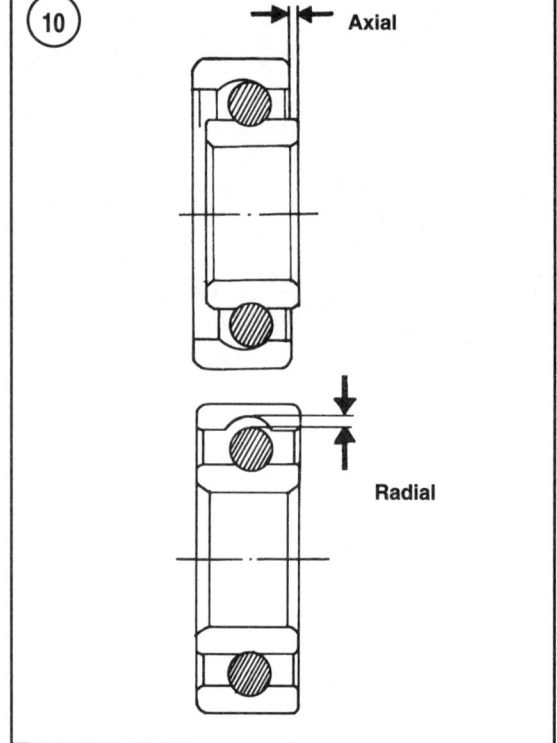

    c. Compresse and release the suspension several times to reposition the pads against the disc. Compress the fork as far as possible.

    d. Check that the fork legs are parallel.

14. Tighten the right axle pinch bolts to 20 N•m (15 ft.-lb.).

15. Install the speedometer cable so the slot in the cable end (**Figure 7**) engages the tab in the drive unit. If necessary, slowly rotate the front wheel until the cable housing fully seats (**Figure 8**) in the drive unit. Tighten the cable nut.

16. Check that the front wheel spins freely and the brake operates properly.

Inspection

Sealed bearings are installed in the wheel hub. If either the bearing or seal is damaged, replace the bearing.

1. Inspect the seal (**Figure 9**) on both sides of the wheel. Check seals for:

    a. Nicked, damaged or missing rubber.

    b. Grease or water seepage from the seal.

2. Inspect the bearing on both sides of the wheel. Check bearings for:

    a. Roughness. Turn each bearing by hand and check for smooth, quiet operation.

    b. Axial play (**Figure 10**). Try to push the bearing in and out to check for axial play.

    c. Radial play (**Figure 10**). Try to push the bearing up and down to check for radial play.

    d. Any play should be difficult to feel. If play is easily felt, the bearing is worn out. Always replace bearings as a pair.

3. If seal or bearing damage is evident, refer to *Front and Rear Hubs* in this chapter for replacement procedures.

4. Clean the axle assembly and speedometer drive unit. Inspect for:

    a. Axle straightness.

    b. Damaged threads on the axle and nut.

    c. Damaged spacer or washer.

WHEELS, TIRES AND DRIVE CHAIN

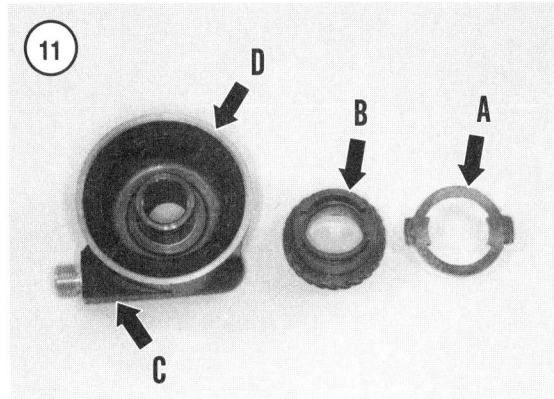

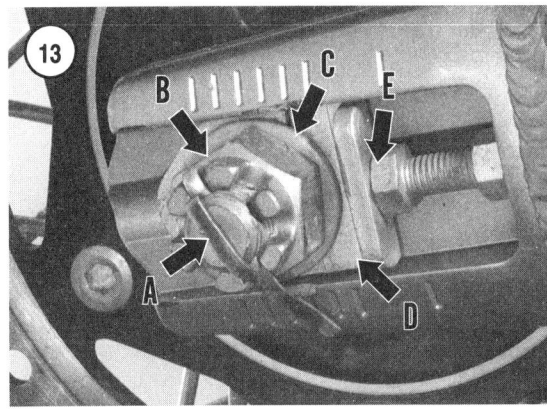

d. Damaged speedometer drive unit seal.

NOTE
If the speedometer drive unit contains water, dirt or dry grease, it should be disassembled and inspected as described in Step 5.

5. If necessary, service the speedometer drive unit as follows:
   a. Remove the tabbed washer (A, **Figure 11**) and drive gear (B) from the housing (C).
   b. If there are leaks around the seal (D, **Figure 11**), install a new seal after cleaning the housing.
   c. Clean all components in solvent. Inspect for visible component damage.

NOTE
The tabbed washer can become damaged when installing the wheel and axle assembly. The tabs on the washer will bend if the washer is not seated properly before tightening the axle.

   d. Inspect the driven gear in the housing for smooth operation.
   e. Pack waterproof grease into the housing and driven gear. Insert and engage the drive gear.
   f. Pack waterproof grease around the drive gear, and then install the tabbed washer.

6. Refer to *Rim and Spoke Service* in this chapter for inspecting and truing the rim.

REAR WHEEL

Removal/Installation

1. Support the motorcycle so it is stable and the rear wheel is off the ground.
2. Remove the brake hose guide mounting bolt (A, **Figure 12**).
3. Remove the two bolts (B, **Figure 12**) securing the brake caliper to the caliper holder.
4. Remove the caliper (C, **Figure 12**) and secure it with a length of wire. Do not allow the caliper to hang by the brake hose.
5. Remove the cotter pin (A, **Figure 13**), nut (B), washer (C), and chain adjuster plate (D) from the axle.
6. Pull up on the rear wheel to take the weight off the axle, and then remove the axle.

NOTE
Do not operate the rear brake pedal while the wheel is removed. Insert a wooden block between the pads until the wheel is installed. This prevents the caliper pistons from extending the pedal is operated.

7. Lower the wheel and remove the chain from the sprocket. Roll the wheel out of the swing arm.
8. Remove the spacer from the right side (**Figure 14**) and left side of the hub (**Figure 15**).
9. If necessary, remove the caliper holder (**Figure 16**) from the swing arm.
10. Inspect and/or repair the wheel and axle assembly as described in this chapter.
11. Reverse the removal procedure to install the wheel. Note the following:
    a. If removed, install the caliper holder.

b. If necessary, loosen the chain adjusters (E, **Figure 13**) so the chain and wheel can be mounted.
c. Apply waterproof grease to the axle, spacers, bearing seals and bores.
d. Install the axle nut and tighten it finger-tight.
e. If necessary, carefully spread the brake pads so the brake disc can enter the brake assembly.
f. Tighten the caliper mounting bolts to 25 N•m (18 ft.-lb.).
g. Adjust the chain (Chapter Three).
h. Check that the wheel spins freely and the brake operates properly.
i. Tighten the rear axle nut to 98 N•m (72 ft.-lb.).

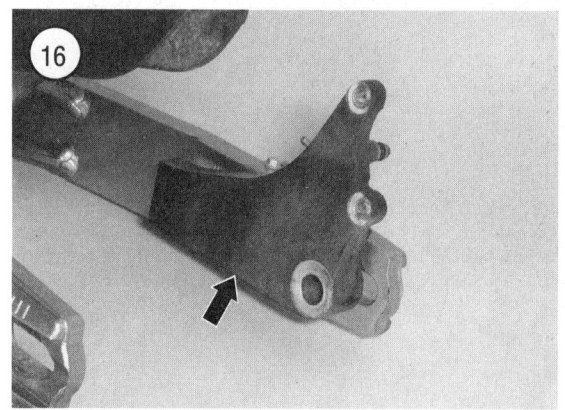

Inspection

1. Pull the sprocket hub from the wheel. Account for the spacer (**Figure 17**) in the back of the sprocket hub. Note that the small diameter of the spacer seats into the sprocket hub.
2. Inspect the seal on the right side of the wheel and on the outer face of the sprocket hub (**Figure 18**). Check seals for:
   a. Nicked, damaged or missing rubber.
   b. Grease or water seepage from the seal.

> *CAUTION*
> *Do not remove bearings to check their condition or to lubricate. Bearing damage is likely to occur. If the bearings are removed, they should be replaced.*

3. Inspect the bearings on both sides of the wheel, as well as the bearing in the sprocket hub. Check bearings for:
   a. Roughness. Turn each bearing by hand and check for smooth, quiet operation.
   b. Axial play (**Figure 10**). Try to push the bearing in and out to check for axial play.
   c. Radial play (**Figure 10**). Try to push the bearing up and down to check for radial play.

WHEELS, TIRES AND DRIVE CHAIN

  d. Any play should be difficult to feel. If play is easily felt, the bearing is worn out. Always replace bearings as a set.
4. If seal or bearing damage is evident, refer to *Front and Rear Hubs* in this chapter for replacement procedures.
5. Inspect the grease in the left hub bearing (A, **Figure 19**) and in the sprocket hub bearing (**Figure 20**). If the grease is dirty or dry, clean the bearings and repack with waterproof grease.
6. Inspect the rubber damper (B, **Figure 19**) in the wheel hub. The sprocket hub should fit firmly in the damper, with little or no play. A damaged damper creates excessive lash in the driveline, which can be felt during acceleration and deceleration.
7. Clean the axle assembly. Inspect the following:
  a. Axle straightness.
  b. Damaged threads on the axle, adjusters and locknuts.
  c. Damaged bores in the spacers and adjusters.
8. Refer to *Rim and Spoke Service* in this chapter for inspecting and truing the rim.

FRONT AND REAR HUBS

The wheel hubs contain bearings and a hub spacer. The bearings should be inspected anytime the wheel(s) are removed from the motorcycle. This section describes the removal and installation of bearings.

Bearing Inspection

CAUTION
Do not remove bearings to check their condition or to lubricate. Bearing damage is likely to occur. If the bearings are removed, replace them.

The bearings can be inspected with the wheels mounted on the motorcycle. With the wheels mounted, a high amount of leverage can be applied to the bearings to detect wear. Also, the wheels can be spun to listen for roughness in the bearings. Use the following procedure to check the bearings while the wheels are mounted. If the wheels are dismounted, make the additional checks described in the wheel removal and inspection procedures in this chapter.
1. Support the motorcycle with the wheel to be inspected off the ground. The axle nut must be tight. If inspecting the rear wheel, remove the chain from the sprocket.
2. Grasp the wheel, placing the hands 180° apart. Lever the wheel up and down, and side to side, to check for radial and axial play. Have an assistant apply the brake while repeating the test. Play will be detected in excessively worn bearings, even though the wheel is locked.

NOTE
If the disc brake drags and the bearing cannot be heard, remove the wheel. Place the axle in the wheel, and support the axle so the wheel spins freely.

3. Spin the wheel and listen for bearing noise. A damaged bearing inconsistently sounds rough and smooth. An excessively worn bearing sounds consistently rough. In either case, replace the bearing.
4. If damage is evident, replace the bearings as a set.

Seal Inspection

Seals prevent the entry of moisture and dirt into the bearings. The seals on the wheel bearings and sprocket hub are permanent and cannot be replaced. If a seal is damaged, the bearing must be replaced.

Bearing Replacement

Two methods for removing bearings from the wheel hub are provided in the following procedure. The first method uses a wheel bearing removal set and the second method uses common shop tools.

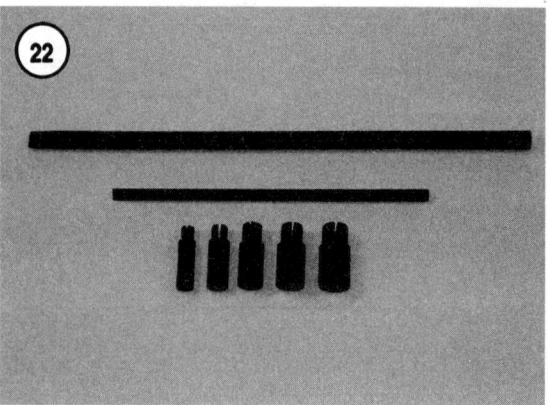
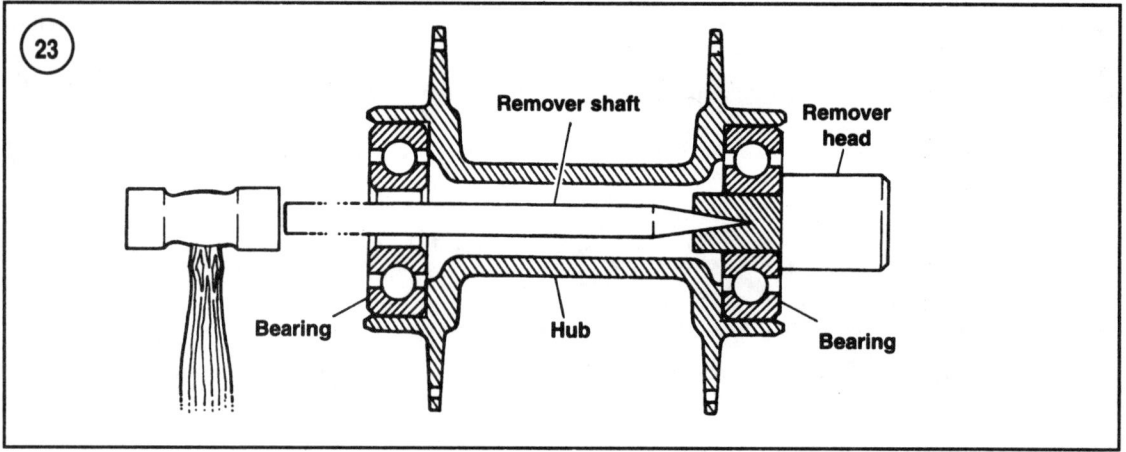

CAUTION
In the following procedure, do not allow the wheel to rest on the brake disc. Support the wheel to prevent pressure being applied to the disc.

1. Where used, remove any snap rings from the hub (**Figure 21**).
2. Examine the bearings. Note the following:
    a. Make note of any visible manufacturer's marks on the sides of the bearings. The new bearings must be installed with the marks in the same direction. Mark each bearing, indicating its original location in the hub. The replacement bearings can then be oriented correctly during installation.
    b. If the bearing is damaged, determine which bearing is damaged the least. Remove this bearing first.

3A. Remove the bearings using the wheel bearing removal set as follows:

NOTE
*The tools (**Figure 22**) used in this procedure are part of the Kowa Seiki Wheel Bearing Remover Set. The set is distributed by K & L Supply Co., (www.klsupply.com). The set is designed so a proper-size remover head can be wedged against the inner bearing race. The bearing can then be driven from the hub (**Figure 23**).*

a. Select the appropriate size remover head. The small, split end of the remover must fit inside the bearing race.
b. Insert the split end of the remover head into the bearing (**Figure 24**). Seat the remover head against the bearing.
c. Insert the tapered end of the driver through the back side of the hub. Fit the tapered end into the slot of the remover head.
d. Position the hub so the remover head is against a solid surface, such as a concrete floor.
e. Strike the end of the driver so it wedges firmly in the remover head. The remover head should now be jammed tight against the inner bearing race.
f. Reposition the assembly so the remover head is free to move and the driver can be struck again.
g. Strike the driver, forcing the bearing (**Figure 25**) and hub spacer from the hub.

WHEELS, TIRES AND DRIVE CHAIN

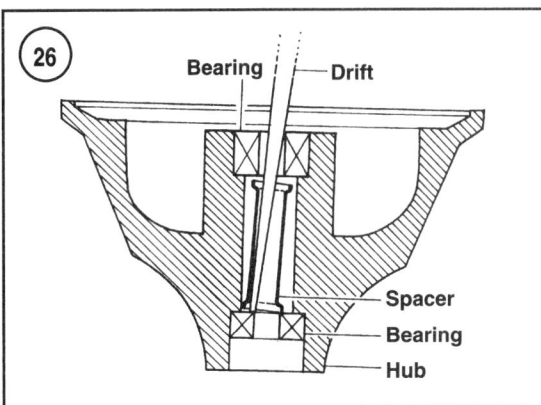

WARNING
When using a heat gun or propane torch to heat the hub, care must be taken to prevent burning finished or combustible surfaces. Work in a well-ventilated area and away from combustible materials. Wear protective clothing, including eye protection and insulated gloves.

   c. Heat the hub around the bearing to be removed. Keep the heat source moving at a steady rate and avoid heating the bearing. A large washer placed over the bearing helps insulate the bearing from the heat.
   d. Turn the wheel over and use the drift to tap around the inner bearing race. Make several passes until the bearing is removed from the hub.
   e. Remove the hub spacer.
   f. Heat the hub around the remaining bearing. Drive out the remaining bearing using a large socket or bearing driver that fits on the outer bearing race.

4. Clean and dry the interior of the hub. Inspect the hub for:
   a. Cracks, corrosion or other damage.
   b. Fit of the new bearings. If a bearing fits loosely in the hub bore, replace the hub. The bearings must be a snug, interference-fit in the bore.

5. Inspect the hub spacer for:
   a. Cracks, corrosion or other damage.
   b. Fit. Check the fit of the spacer against the back side of the bearings. It should fit flat against the bearings. Repair minor nicks and flaring with a file. Do not alter the length of the spacer. The spacer must remain its original length to prevent binding of the bearings when the axle is tightened.

6. Before installing the new bearings, note the following:
   a. Inspect the new bearings and determine which side faces out. This is usually the side with the manufacturer's marks and numbers. Bearings that are sealed on one side should be installed with the sealed side facing out.
   b. Apply waterproof grease to bearings that are not lubricated by the manufacturer, or that are not sealed on both sides. Work the grease into the cavities between the balls and races.
   c. Always support the bottom side of the hub, near the bore, when installing bearings.
   d. To aid in driving the bearings, chill them in a freezer to temporarily reduce their diameter.

7. Heat the hub around the bearing bore.
8. Place a bearing squarely over the bearing bore.

   h. Remove the driver from the remover head.
   i. Repeat the procedure to remove the remaining bearing(s).

3B. Remove the bearings using a hammer, drift and heat gun, or propane torch. The purpose for using heat is to slightly expand the hub bores so the bearings can removed with minimal resistance. Remove the bearings as follows:
   a. Clean all lubricants from the wheel. For the rear wheel, remove the rubber damper.
   b. Insert a long drift into the hub and tilt the hub spacer away from the bearing to be removed (**Figure 26**).

9. Place a suitable-size driver or socket over the bearing. The driver should seat against the outside diameter of the bearing (**Figure 27**).

CAUTION
Do not press or strike the bearing directly. Bearing damage will occur.

10. Hold the driver, and squarely drive in the bearing, seating it in the hub (**Figure 28**).
11. Where used, install the snap ring.
12. Turn the hub over and install the hub spacer.
13. Drive in the remaining bearing, seating it in the hub.

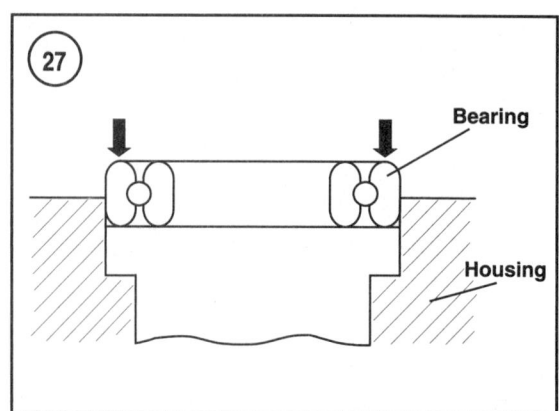

RIM AND SPOKE SERVICE

The rim and hub must be concentric to ensure good handling and prevent damage to the parts. When the motorcycle is new, all spokes are tensioned equally and the rim and hub are aligned and concentric. As the motorcycle is used, the spoke tensions become unequal and the rim may become damaged. When this occurs the wheel develops radial (up and down) and lateral (side to side) runout. Wheel truing is the procedure that retensions the spokes, aligns the rim and hub, and makes the parts concentric. Regularly inspect and correct any problems with the wheel assembly.

Rim Inspection

Inspect the rims for flat spots, dents and warping. Also check the spoke holes for enlargement. Wheel dents are common to this type of motorcycle and cause the wheel to have excessive runout. Attempting to true a wheel with large dents can cause hub and rim damage, due to the overtightened spokes. If the dent is minor and runout is minimal, the rider may find it acceptable to continue to use the rim.

Spoke Inspection

Inspect the spokes for damage and proper tightness. For new wheels, or wheels that have been rebuilt, check the spokes frequently. After the tensions stabilize, check the spokes as recommended in the *Maintenance Schedule* (Chapter Three).

When tightening spokes, always use the correct size spoke wrench and do not exceed 2-4 N•m (17-35 in.-lb.) of torque. Use spoke wrenches (**Figure 29**) that grip the spoke on three sides. The spoke nipples can be rounded off or crushed if other types of tools are used. Do not true a wheel that has broken, bent or damaged spokes. Also, do not straighten bent spokes by excessive tightening. The spoke can crack the hub fitting and enlarge the rim hole.

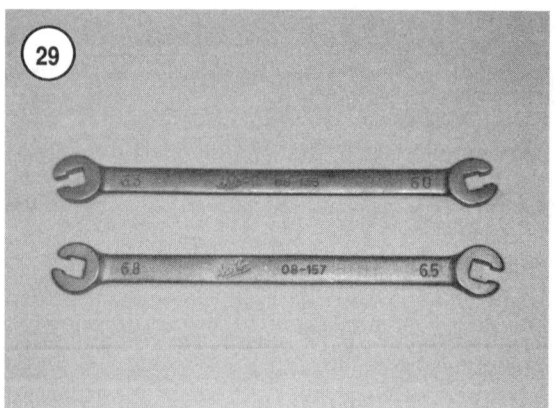

To change spoke tension, spokes must be able to turn easily in the spoke nipples. If a spoke is seized in its nipple, apply penetrating lubricant to the threads. If the spoke does not free itself or turn smoothly, replace the spoke and nipple.

Wheel Truing

Wheels can be trued with the wheel on or off the motorcycle. Before truing a wheel, check the condition of the wheel bearings. Accurate wheel truing is not possible with worn wheel bearings. Refer to

WHEELS, TIRES AND DRIVE CHAIN

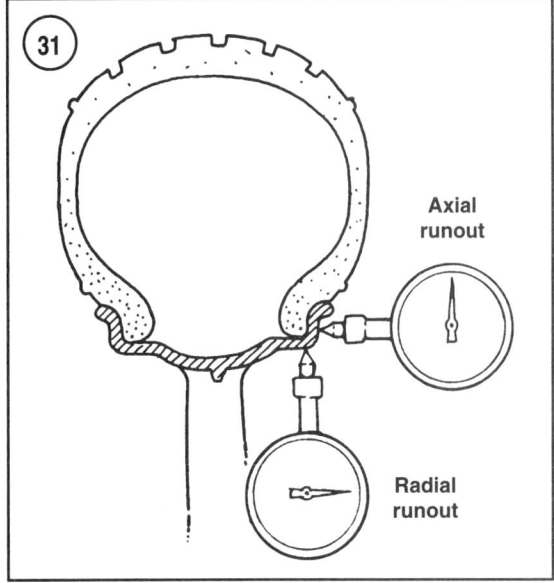

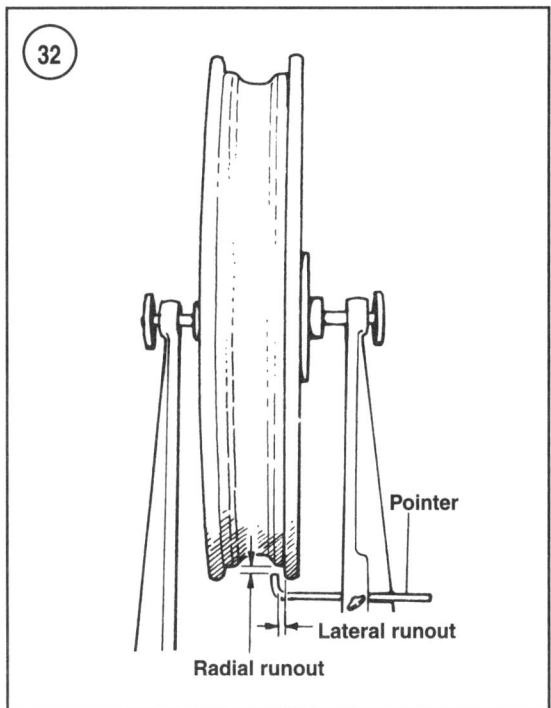

NOTE
Always loosen and tighten spokes equally. Loosen a minimum of three spokes, and then tighten the opposite three spokes. If runout is over a large area, loosen and tighten a larger number of spokes.

Correcting radial runout

To make the rim concentric with the hub, loosen and tighten the spokes, as shown in **Figure 34**. The rim will move in the direction of the tightened spokes.

NOTE
Always loosen and tighten spokes equally. Loosen a minimum of three spokes, and then tighten the opposite three spokes. If runout is over a large area, loosen and tighten a larger number of spokes.

DRIVE CHAIN

Refer to Chapter Three for drive chain cleaning, lubrication, adjustment and measurement. Refer to **Table 2** in this chapter for chain specifications.

When checking the condition of the chain, also check the condition of the sprockets, as described in Chapter Three. If either the chain or sprockets are worn, replace all drive components. Using new

Table 2 for wheel runout specifications. A wheel truing stand (**Figure 30**) is used to measure runout. However, if runout appears minimal, the wheel can be left on the motorcycle to make the check. Raise the wheel so it is level and free to spin. Solidly hold a pointer against the fork or swing arm. While the wheel is turned, move the pointer toward/away from the rim until maximum runout is determined. Measure the gap from the rim to the pointer. A more accurate check is to mount a dial indicator in the positions shown in **Figure 31**.

If the wheel needs major truing, mount the rim (tire and tube removed) on a truing stand and measure runout (**Figure 32**) in both directions.

Correcting lateral runout

To move the rim to the left or right of the hub, loosen and tighten spokes as shown in **Figure 33**. The rim will move in the direction of the tightened spokes.

sprockets with a worn chain, or a new chain on worn sprockets, will shorten the life of the new part.

The motorcycle was originally equipped with an endless O-ring type chain. To remove the chain, the swing arm must be removed so the chain can pass by the swing arm pivot.

The following procedure describes the removal and installation of the chain. The original chain is the endless type with no master link. A replacement chain may have been installed that uses a master link and spring clip (**Figure 35**), or a staked-pin master link (**Figure 36**) that is pressed on during assembly. Refer to the appropriate following procedure for chain service.

Chain With No Master Link Removal/Installation

1. Remove the swing arm as described in Chapter Thirteen.
2. Remove the sprocket guard so the chain can be removed from the drive sprocket (**Figure 37**).
3. Disengage the chain from the drive sprocket. Remove the chain.
4. Reverse the removal procedure to install the chain. Note the following:
    a. Clean and inspect the swing arm before assembly. Apply waterproof grease to the parts before installing.
    b. Adjust the chain (Chapter Three).

Clip Type Master Link Drive Chain Removal/Installation

1. Support the motorcycle on a workstand with its rear wheel off the ground and shift the transmission into neutral.
2. Find the master link on the chain. Remove the spring clip (**Figure 38**) with a pair of pliers, and then remove the link from the chain (**Figure 35**).
3. Remove the drive chain.
4. Clean and inspect the chain as described in Chapter Three.
5. Clean the drive and driven sprockets.
6. Check the drive chain sliders for worn or damaged parts.
7. Reverse the removal procedure to install the chain. Note the following:
    a. Install the chain and reassemble a new master link (**Figure 35**).
    b. Install the spring clip on the master link with the closed end of the clip pointing toward the direction of travel (**Figure 38**).
    c. Adjust the chain as described in Chapter Three.

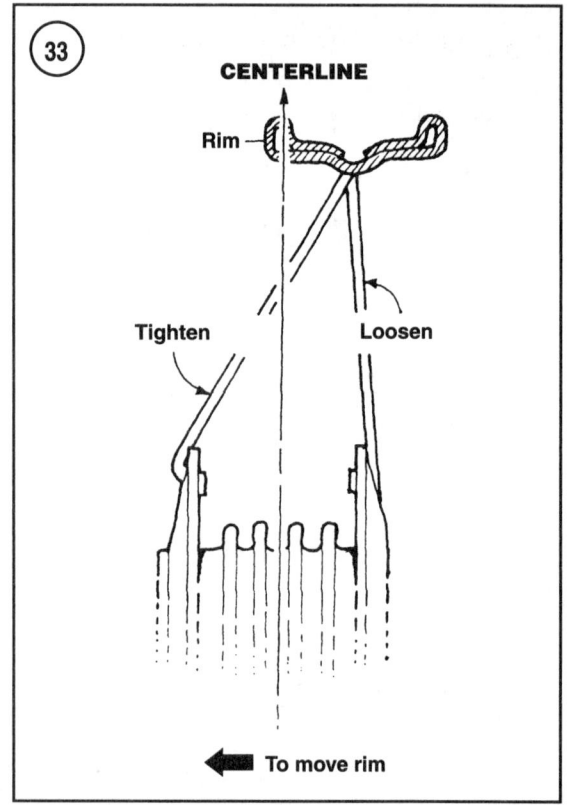

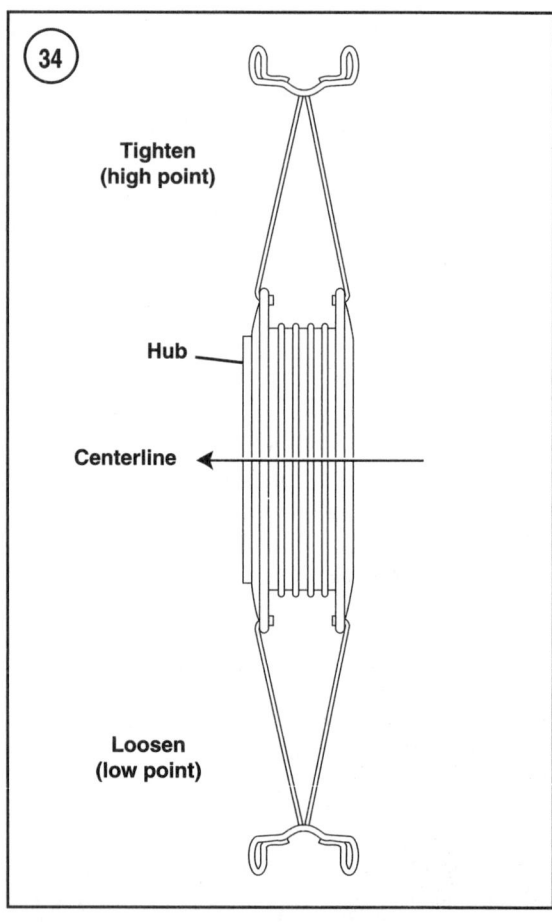

WHEELS, TIRES AND DRIVE CHAIN

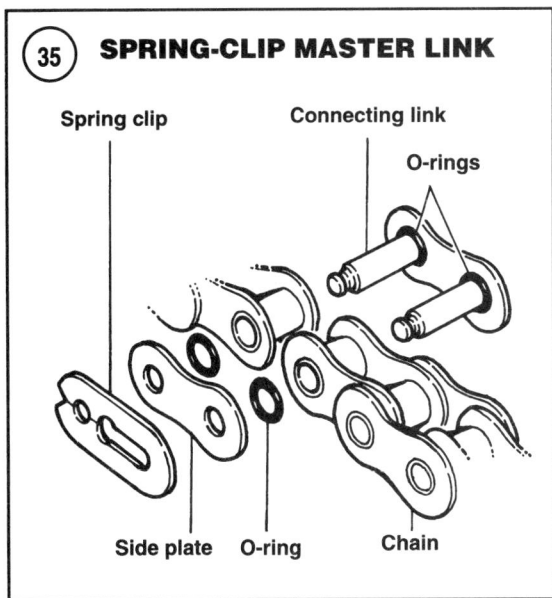

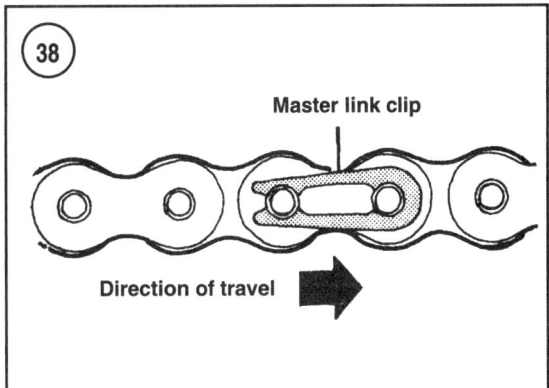

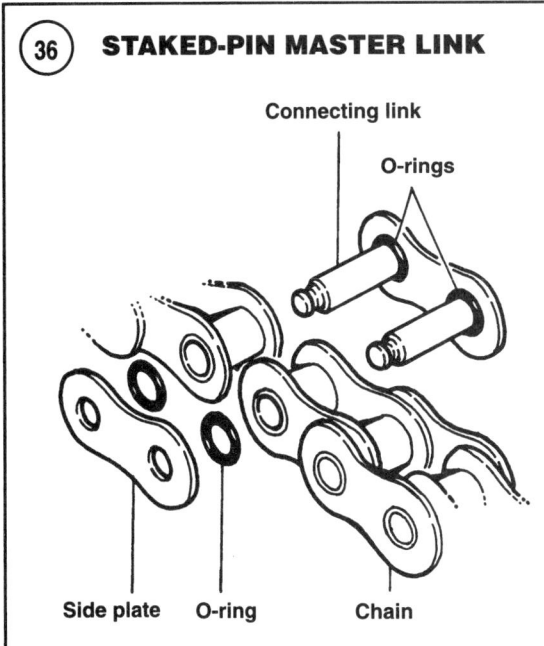

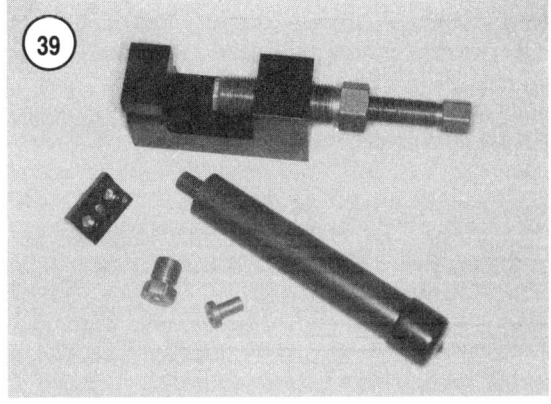

Staked Type Master Link Drive Chain Removal/Installation

The drive chain uses a staked-pin master link (**Figure 36**). It can be removed/replaced with the swing arm mounted on the motorcycle by breaking the chain at the master link. The following section describes chain removal and installation using the Jumbo Chain Tool (Motion Pro part no. 08-0135). The Jumbo Chain Tool (**Figure 39**) can be used to break roller chains up to No. 630 and can be used to rivet chain sizes up to No. 530. Always follow the tool manufacturer's instructions provided with the tool. Use the following steps to supplement the instructions provided with the chain tool.

1. Support the motorcycle with the rear wheel off the ground.

2. Loosen the rear axle nut and the chain adjusters. Push the rear wheel forward until maximum chain slack is obtained.

3. Assemble the extractor bolt onto the body bolt. Then, turn the extractor bolt until its pin is withdrawn into the pin guide chain tool, following the manufacturer's instructions.

4. Turn the chain to locate the crimped pin ends (**Figure 40**) on the master link. Break the chain at this point.

WARNING
Discard the connecting link, side plate and O-rings after removing them. Never reuse these parts as they could break and cause the chain to separate. Reusing a staked master link may cause the chain to come apart and lock the rear wheel, causing a serious accident.

5. Install the chain tool across the master link, and then operate the tool and push the connecting link out of the side plate to break the chain. Remove and discard the side plate, connecting link and O-rings (**Figure 36**).

6. If installing a new drive chain, count the links of the new chain. If necessary, cut the chain to length as described under *Cutting A Drive Chain to Length* in this section. See **Table 2** for the original equipment chain sizes and lengths.

NOTE
Always install the drive chain around the swing arm before connecting and staking the master link.

7. Install the chain around the drive sprocket, swing arm and driven sprocket.

8. Assemble the new master link as follows:
   a. Install an O-ring on each connecting link pin (**Figure 36**).
   b. Insert the connecting link through the inside of the chain and connect both chain ends together.
   c. Install the remaining two O-rings (**Figure 36**) onto the connecting link pins.
   d. Install the side plate (**Figure 36**) so the identification mark faces out (away from chain).

9. Stake each connecting link pin as follows:

NOTE
Refer to the drive chain manufacturer's specifications when pressing on the master link.

   a. Measure the height of the connecting link from the outer side plate surface to the top of the connecting link (**Figure 41**). The height measurement is specified by the chain manufacturer. If the height measurement is incorrect, confirm that the correct master link is being installed. If so, readjust the side plate height position on the connecting link.

NOTE
If the diameter of one pin end is out of specification, remove and discard the master link. Then, install a new master link assembly.

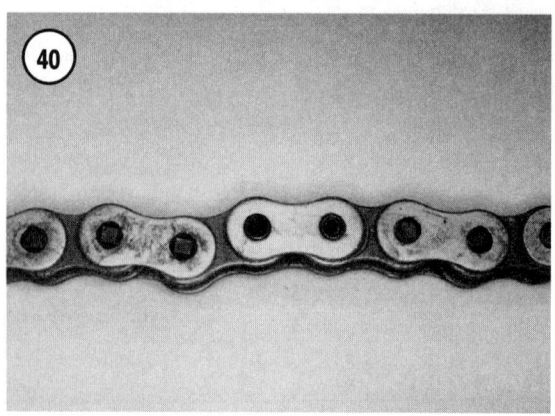

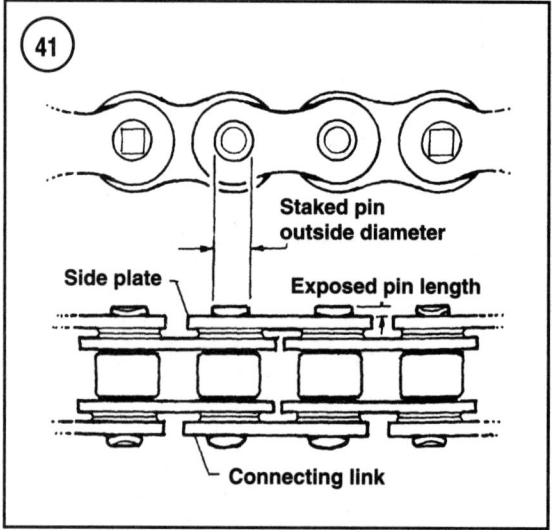

   b. Assemble the chain tool onto the master link and carefully stake each connecting link pin until its outside diameter (**Figure 41**) is as specified by the drive chain manufacturer. Work carefully and do not exceed the specified outside diameter measurement. Measure with a vernier caliper (**Figure 42**) in two places on each pin, 90° apart.

10. Remove the chain tool and inspect the master link for any cracks or other damage. Check the staked area for cracks (**Figure 43**). Make sure the master link O-rings were not crushed. If there are cracks on the staked link surfaces or other damage, remove the master link and install a new one.

11. If there are no cracks, pivot the chain ends where they hook onto the master link. Each chain end must pivot freely. Compare by pivoting other links of the chain. If one or both drive chain ends cannot pivot on the master link, the chain is too tight. Remove and install a new master link assembly.

WHEELS, TIRES AND DRIVE CHAIN

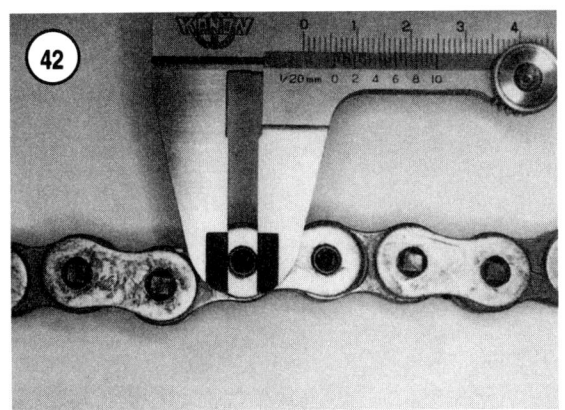

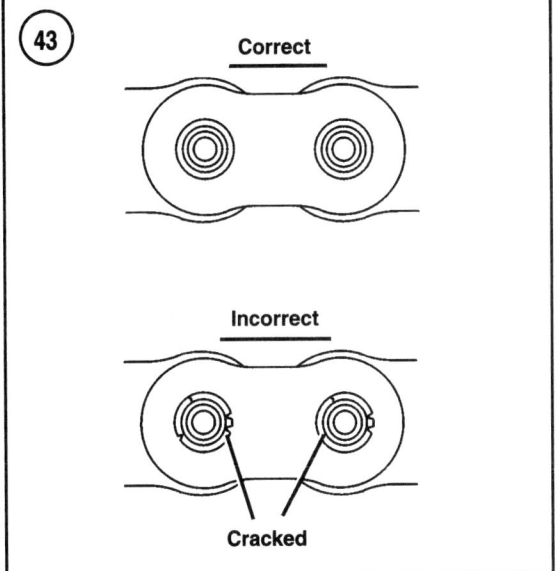

WARNING
An incorrectly installed master link may cause the chain to come apart and lock the rear wheel, causing a serious accident. If the tools to safely rivet the chain together are not available, take it to a dealership. Do not ride the motorcycle unless absolutely certain the master link is installed correctly.

12. Adjust the drive chain and tighten the rear axle nut as described in Chapter Three.

Cutting A Drive Chain To Length

Table 2 lists the correct number of chain links required for original equipment gearing. If the replacement drive chain is too long, cut it to length as follows.

1. Stretch the new chain on a workbench.
2A. If installing a new chain over stock gearing, refer to **Table 2** for the correct number of links.
2B. If sprocket sizes were changed, determine the correct number of links as follows:
   a. Move the rear wheel forward.
   b. Install the new chain over both sprockets (**Figure 44**).
   c. Make a chalf mark on the two pins to cut.
   d. Count the chain links one more time or check the chain length before cutting.
   e. Include the master link when counting the drive chain links.

WARNING
Using a hand or bench grinder will cause flying particles. Do not operate a grinding tool without proper eye protection.

3A. If using a chain breaker, use it to break the drive chain.
3B. To break the drive chain with a grinder, perform the following:
   a. Grind the head of two pins flush with the face of the side plate with a grinder or suitable grinding tool.
   b. Press the side plate out of the chain with a chain breaker; support the chain carefully while doing this. If the pins are still tight, grind more material from the end of the pins and then try again.
   c. Remove the side plate and push out the connecting link.
4. Install the new drive chain as described in this section.

Service and Inspection

For routine service and inspection of the drive chain, refer to Chapter Three.

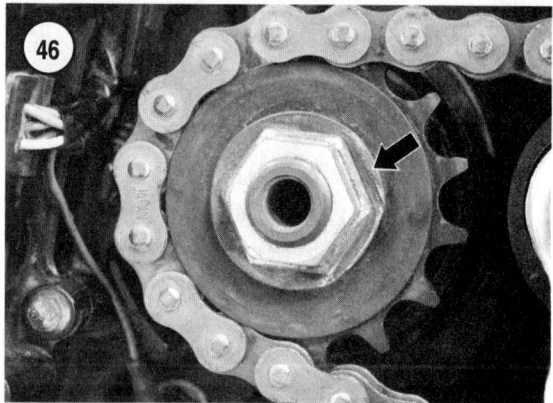

SPROCKETS

Check the condition of both sprockets and the drive chain, as described in Chapter Three. If either the chain or sprockets are worn, replace all drive components. Using new sprockets with a worn chain, or a new chain on worn sprockets, will shorten the life of the new part.

Drive Sprocket Removal/Installation

1. Support the motorcycle so it is stable and secure. Keep the rear wheel on the ground.
2. Put the transmission in gear.
3. Remove the sprocket guard (**Figure 45**).
4. Flatten the lockwasher (**Figure 46**).

NOTE
If the rear wheel turns, have an assistant lock the rear brake while loosening the nut.

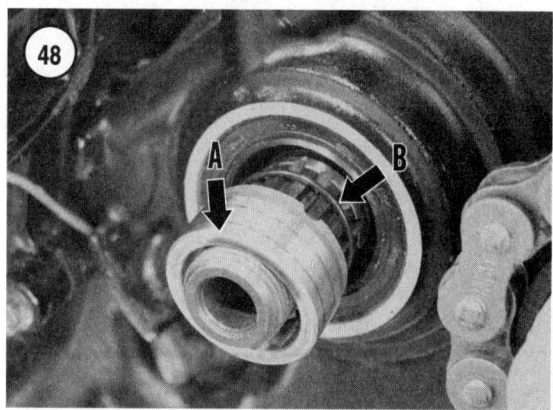

5. Loosen the locknut securing the sprocket to the shaft.
6. After loosening the locknut, raise the rear wheel and loosen the rear axle nut and chain adjusters. Remove the chain from the rear sprocket.
7. Remove the locknut and lockwasher from the output shaft.
8. Pull the chain forward, and then lift it from the sprocket while removing the sprocket.
9. Clean and inspect the output shaft spacer and seal (**Figure 47**). If there is damage or leakage, remove the spacer (A, **Figure 48**) and internal O-ring (B) as follows:
    a. With the transmission in gear, twist the spacer from the shaft. If necessary, warm the seal with a heat gun. Then, use locking pliers to grip the spacer near its outer edge, away from the seal surface.
    b. Remove the O-ring from the groove located past the seal lip.

WHEELS, TIRES AND DRIVE CHAIN

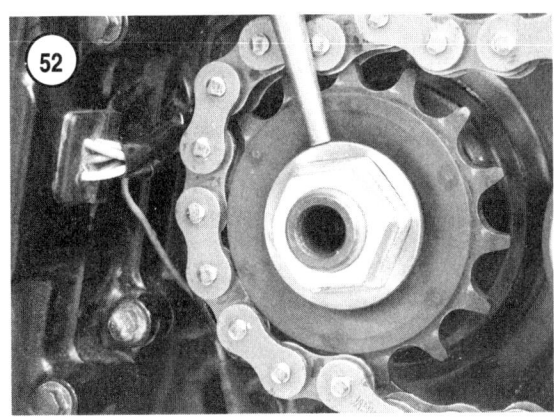

10. Inspect the drive sprocket as described in Chapter Three.
11. Inspect the sprocket guard assembly (**Figure 49**) for damage.
12. Clean and inspect the output shaft and seal area.
13. Reverse the removal procedure to install the drive sprocket while noting the following:
   a. If removed, install a new, lubricated O-ring onto the output shaft. The O-ring must seat in the groove (A, **Figure 50**), located past the seal lip.
   b. If removed, install the output shaft spacer with the notched edge (B, **Figure 50**) facing in.
   c. Install the sprocket with the cupped side facing out.
   d. Fit the sprocket into the chain before sliding the sprocket into position.
   e. Install a new lockwasher (**Figure 51**) with the cupped side facing out. Install the locknut with the small diameter facing out.
   f. Tighten the locknut to 98 N•m (72 ft.-lb.).
   g. Flatten two sides of the lockwasher against the locknut (**Figure 52**).
   h. Adjust the chain as described in Chapter Three.

Driven Sprocket Removal/Installation

1. Remove the rear wheel as described in this chapter.
2. Support the wheel so it does not rest directly on the brake disc, or remove the sprocket and hub from the wheel (**Figure 53**). It may be easier to leave the sprocket hub in the wheel until the sprocket nuts are loosened.
3. Remove the nuts securing the sprocket to the hub.
4. Inspect the sprocket as described in Chapter Three.
5. Inspect the hub as described in *Rear Wheel, Inspection*.
6. Reverse the removal procedure to install the driven sprocket and rear wheel while noting the following:
   a. Mount the sprocket so the tooth identification number (**Figure 54**) faces out.

b. Using a crossing pattern, evenly tighten the driven sprocket bolts in several passes to 32 N•m (24 ft.-lb.).
c. Adjust the chain as described in Chapter Three.

TIRE CHANGING

Removal

When changing a tire, work over a pad to prevent damage to the wheel assembly. Do not allow the wheel to rest on the brake disc.

1. Remove the core from the valve stem and deflate the tire.
2. Press the entire bead on both sides of the tire into the rim.
3. Lubricate the beads with soapy water.
4. Insert a tire iron under the bead, next to the valve stem (**Figure 55**). Pry the bead over the rim, while forcing the bead on the opposite side of the tire into the rim.
5. Insert a second tire iron next to the first (**Figure 56**). While holding the tire with one iron, work around the perimeter of the rim with the second iron, prying the tire over the rim.

NOTE
If the inner tube must be reused, be careful to not pinch the tube as the tire is being removed from the rim. It is common practice to replace the tube.

6. Remove the nut from the valve stem and remove the inner tube from the tire.
7. Pry the second tire bead over the rim (**Figure 57**).

Inspection

1. If the tire must be reused, inspect the inside and outside of the tire for damage and objects that could cause a puncture.
2. Inspect the rim for damage.
3. Check that the spokes do not protrude through the spoke nipples.
4. Inspect the rim band for deterioration. If a new rim band is installed, place the roughest side of the band against the rim. If water is entering the rim, an alternative to the rim band is to wrap the rim with two revolutions of duct tape. Punch a hole for the valve stem.

Installation

NOTE
Installation is easier if the tire is warm and pliable. This can be achieved by placing the tire in the sun or an enclosed vehicle.

1. Sprinkle talcum powder around the interior of the tire casing. Distribute the powder so it is on all surfaces that will touch the inner tube. The powder minimizes chafing and helps the tube distribute itself when inflated.

WHEELS, TIRES AND DRIVE CHAIN

NOTE
Depending on the make and type of tire installed, check the sidewall and determine if it must be installed in a specific direction. A direction arrow is often embossed in the sidewall. Also check for a dot or mark that indicates the light side of the tire. This mark should align with the valve stem.

2. Lubricate one of the tire beads and push it onto the rim (**Figure 58**). Use a tire iron to lever the final section of bead onto the rim.

3. Install the core into the valve stem, and then insert the tube into the tire. Check that the tube is not twisted while tucking it into the tire. Install the valve stem nut loosely,

4. Inflate the tube until it is rounded and no longer wrinkled. Too much air makes tire installation difficult and too little air increases the chance of pinching the tube.

5. Lubricate the second tire bead, and start installation opposite the valve stem. Hand-fit as much of the tire into the rim as possible (**Figure 59**). Before final installation, check that the valve stem is straight and the inner tube is not pinched. If necessary, relubricate the bead. Use tire irons to hold and pry the remaining section of bead onto the rim (**Figure 60**).

6. Check the bead for uniform fit, on both sides of the tire.

7. Lubricate both beads and inflate the tire to seat the beads onto the rim. Check the sidewall for a recommended seating pressure. If none is indicated, inflate the tire to 172-207 kPa (25-30 psi).

WARNING
If the tire does not seat at the recommended pressure, do not continue to overinflate the tire. Deflate the tire and reinflate to the recommended seating pressure. Relubricate the beads, if necessary.

8. Finger-tighten the valve stem nut.
9. Bleed the tire pressure to the recommended setting in **Table 1**.
10. Install the valve stem cap.
11. Balance the wheel as described in this section.

Wheel Balancing

Whenever a new tire is installed it should be inspected for proper balance. An unbalanced wheel shortens tire life and puts avoidable wear on the wheel bearings. Ride quality is also diminished. For maximum tire life, check wheel balance whenever the wheel is removed from the motorcycle. Balance changes over the life of the tire. If the proper equipment is not available, have the wheel balanced by a dealership.

NOTE
Do not balance a wheel that has damaged bearings. Balance will not be accurate. Replace the bearings before balancing.

1. Place the wheel and axle assembly in a truing stand, or a similar fixture that allows the axle to be level and the wheel to freely spin (**Figure 61**). Install

the necessary spacers to keep the wheel from moving laterally.

2. Spin the wheel and allow it to come to a complete stop. Mark the sidewall at the top of the tire. This is the light side of the wheel. Repeat the step several times to ensure an accurate reading. If the wheel consistently stops at a different location, balance is acceptable and additional weight is not required.

NOTE
Adhesive-backed weights are not recommended for this type of motorcycle because the weights are more vulnerable to falling off in off-road conditions.

3. When the light side of the wheel is verified, lightly clamp a weight (**Figure 62**) to the spoke nearest the light mark. Start with the smallest increment of weight. Weights are available from a dealership.

4. Continue to spin and check the tire for balance. Continue to add/subtract weight to the spokes until the wheel consistently stops at a different location. When balance is achieved, tightly clamp the weight(s) to the spoke(s).

Table 1 TIRE SPECIFICATIONS

Item	Front	Rear
Tire type	Tube	Tube
Size	90/90-21	130/80-17
Manufacturer	Dunlop K750	Dunlop K750
Minimum tread depth	2.0 mm (0.08 in.)	2.0 mm (0.08 in.)
Inflation pressure (cold)[1]	150 kPa (22 psi)[2]	150 kPa (22 psi)[2]

1. Tire inflation pressure is for original equipment tires. Aftermarket tires may require different inflation pressure.
2. Up to maximum weight capacity.

Table 2 WHEEL AND DRIVE CHAIN SPECIFICATIONS

Item	Specification
Axle runout (max.)	0.2 mm (0.008 in.)
Drive chain	
2008-2010	Enuma EK520SR-O2X (106 links)
2011-on	DID520VP2 (106 links)
Drive chain slack	35-45 mm (1 3/8-1 3/4 in.)
Drive chain length service limit (20 links/21 pins)	317.5-318.2 mm (12.50-12.53 in.)
Sprocket sizes	
Drive (front)	15 teeth
Driven (rear)	43 teeth
Wheel rim axial runout (max.)	2.0 mm (0.08 in.)
Wheel rim radial runout (max.)	2.0 mm (0.08 in.)
Wheel rim size	
Front	21 × 1.60
Rear	17 × 2.50

Table 3 WHEELS, TIRES AND DRIVE CHAIN TORQUE SPECIFICATIONS

Item	N•m	in. lb.	ft.-lb.
Axle pinch bolts	20	–	15
Drive sprocket lock nut	98	–	72
Driven sprocket bolts	32	–	24
Front axle nut	88	–	65
Rear axle nut	98	–	72
Rear brake caliper mounting bolts	25	–	18
Wheel spoke nipple	2-4	18-35	–

CHAPTER TWELVE

FRONT SUSPENSION AND STEERING

This chapter provides service procedures for the front suspension and steering components. This includes the handlebar, steering head and fork. Refer to the tables at the end of this chapter for specifications, capacities and torque requirements.

HANDLEBAR

Removal/Installation

Use the following procedure to remove and install the handlebar into the holders. If the handlebar only needs to be repositioned, adjust by loosening the lower holder cap bolts. Tilt the handlebar to the desired position, and then retorque the bolts. If complete disassembly of the handlebar is necessary, do so before removing it from the holders.

1. Support the motorcycle so it is stable and secure.
2. Extract the plastic caps (**Figure 1**) from the holder bolts.
3. Remove the bolts (**Figure 2**) from the holders.
4. Secure the handlebar either forward or back from the holders. Keep the brake fluid reservoir upright.
5. Clean the handlebar and holders.
6. Reverse the removal procedure to install the handlebar. Note the following:

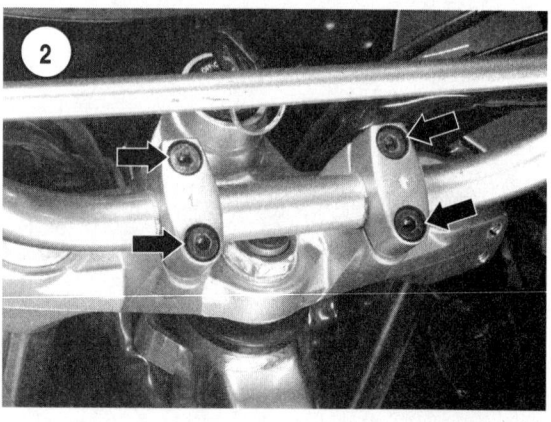

FRONT SUSPENSION AND STEERING

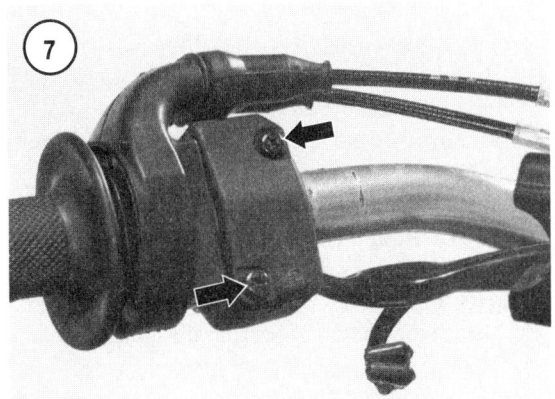

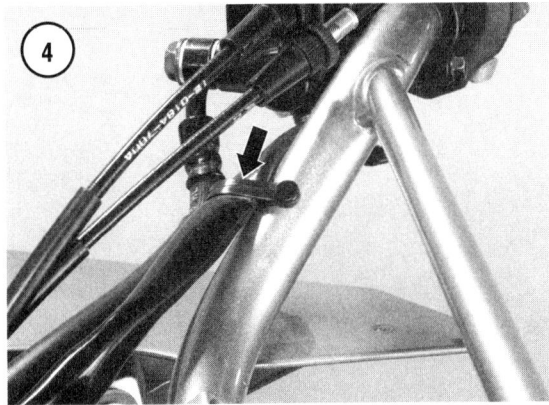

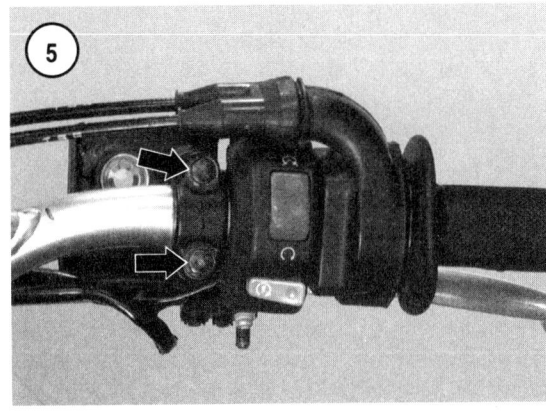

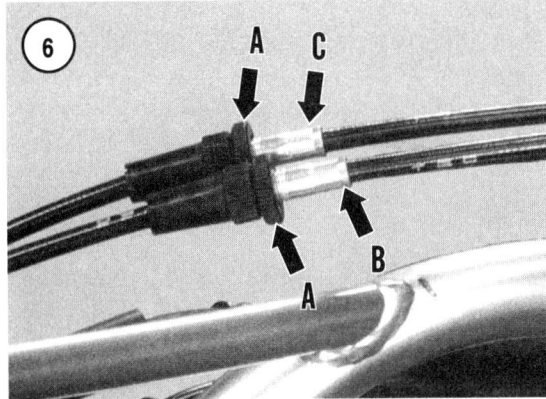

a. Position the holder caps so the arrows (**Figure 3**) on the caps point up.
b. Adjust the handlebar to the desired riding position. Finger-tighten the holder bolts.
c. Tighten the upper bolt on each cap first, and then tighten the lower bolt. Tighten the handlebar holder bolts to 25 N•m (18 ft.-lb.).

Disassembly/Assembly

1. Support the motorcycle so it is stable and secure.
2. Remove the hand guards.
3. Remove the mirrors.
4. Detach the wiring guide (**Figure 4**) from the right end of the handlebar.

CAUTION
Do not allow the master cylinder to hang by its hose. Keep the master cylinder in an upright position so fluid cannot leak out of the cap. This also prevents air from getting into the system. Wrap the master cylinder with a clean shop cloth, and secure it to the motorcycle until after handlebar reassembly.

5. Remove the bolts (**Figure 5**) securing the master cylinder assembly. Separate the master cylinder from the handlebar.
6. Loosen the throttle cable locknuts (A, **Figure 6**). Turn the adjuster on the accelerator cable (B, **Figure 6**) and decelerator cable (C) to obtain maximum cable slack.
7. Remove the right handlebar switch screws (**Figure 7**) and separate the switch halves.
8. Slide the rubber cable cover (A, **Figure 8**) off the throttle housing.
9. Move the rubber throttle housing cover (B, **Figure 8**) off the throttle housing by pushing it toward the cables. The cover must be pushed off the housing to allow housing disassembly.

10. Remove the screws (**Figure 9**) from the throttle housing. Separate and remove the housing halves.
11. Detach the wiring guide (A, **Figure 10**) from the left end of the handlebar.
12. Remove the left handlebar switch screws (**Figure 11**) and separate the switch halves.
13. Dislodge the choke control lever and cable (**Figure 12**) from the switch half.
14. Withdraw the choke control cable from the cable guide (B, **Figure 10**).
15. Detach the clutch cable from the clutch lever.
16. To remove the clutch lever, proceed as follows:
    a. Remove the left handlebar grip as described in this chapter.
    b. Loosen the clutch lever holder clamp bolt.
    c. Slide the clutch lever holder assembly off the handlebar.
17. To remove the throttle grip assembly, remove the balancer weight as described in this chapter.
18. Remove the handlebar as described in this section.
19. Note the following when installing handlebar-mounted components:
    a. Refer to *Throttle Cable* (Chapter Eight) and install the throttle cables and housing.
    b. Position the clutch lever holder so the gap aligns with the punch mark (**Figure 13**) on the handlebar. Tighten the clamp bolt securely.
    c. Refer to *Choke Cable* (Chapter Eight) and install the choke cable and left switch housing.
    d. Install the front brake master cylinder as described in Chapter Fourteen.

Inspection

> *WARNING*
> *Never straighten, weld or heat a damaged handlebar. The metal can weaken and possibly break when subjected to the shocks and stresses that occur when riding the motorcycle.*

1. Inspect the handlebar for cracks, bending or other damage. If the handlebar is made of aluminum, check closely where the handlebar is clamped to the fork, and at the clutch lever mount. If cracking, scoring or other damage is found, replace the handlebar. Damage in these areas may cause the handlebar to break.
2. Inspect the threads on the mounting bolts and the holders. Clean all residue from the threads. Replace damaged bolts.
3. Clean the handlebar, holders and caps with solvent or electrical contact cleaner. Use a stiff brush to clean

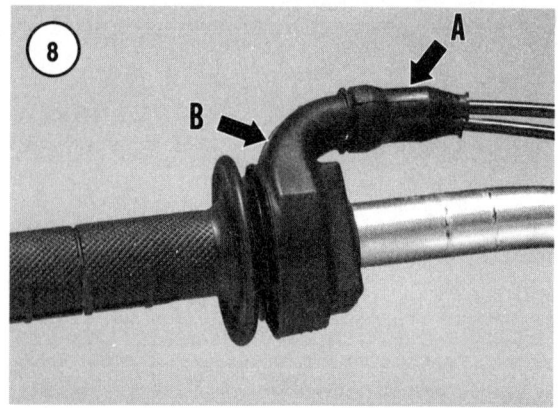

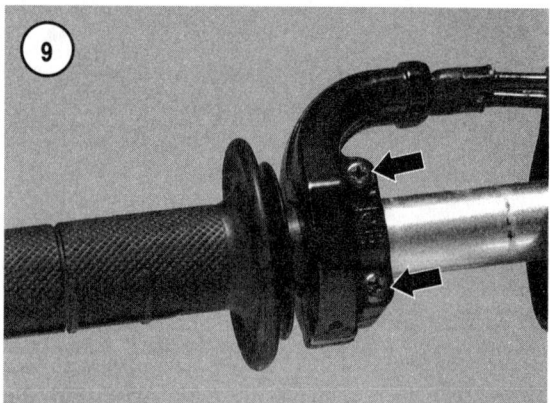

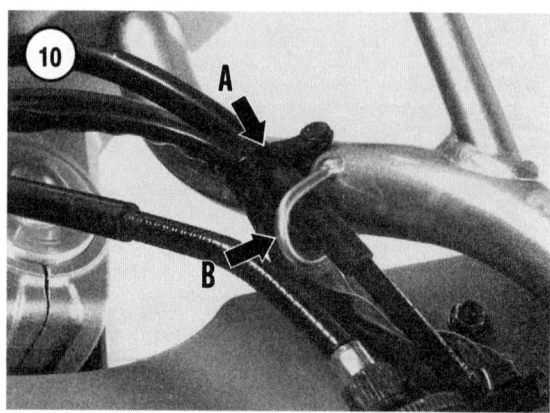

FRONT SUSPENSION AND STEERING

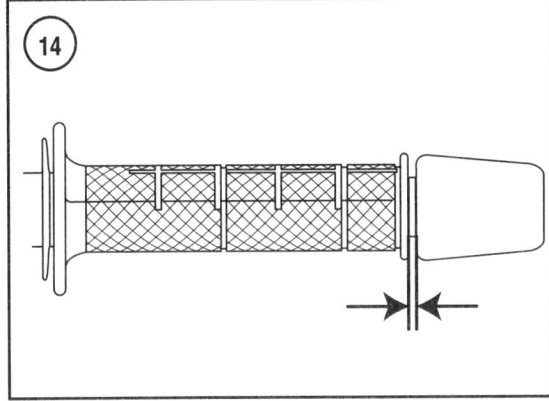

the residue from the knurled areas on the handlebar. Use a soft brush on aluminum handlebars.

HANDLEBAR LEFT HAND GRIP REPLACEMENT

NOTE
The factory-equipped right hand grip is part of the throttle grip assembly and cannot be replaced separately

1. Remove the balancer assembly from the end of the left handlebar as described in this chapter.
2. Slide a thin screwdriver between the left hand grip and handlebar. Spray electrical contact cleaner into the opening under the grip.
3. Pull the screwdriver out and quickly twist the grip to break its bond with the handlebar, then slide the grip off.
4. Clean the handlebar of all rubber or sealer residue.
5. Install the new grip following the manufacturer's directions. Note the following:
   a. For the left-hand grip, temporarily install the balancer weight and position the grip so the distance (**Figure 14**) between the weight and grip is 1 mm (0.4 in.) at the left handlebar end.
   b. For the right-hand grip, temporarily fit the throttle grip into the throttle housing and install the balancer weight. The distance between the weight and grip (**Figure 14**) should be 2.5 mm (0.1 in.) at the right handlebar end.
   c. Mark the position of the grip.
   d. Remove the balancer and new grip.
   e. Apply an adhesive, such as ThreeBond Griplock, between the grip and handlebar. When applying an adhesive, follow the manufacturer's directions regarding drying time before operating the motorcycle.
   f. Install the new grip so it is properly positioned.
   g. Install the balancer assembly onto the left end of the handlebar.

BALANCER WEIGHTS

A balancer weight (anti-vibration) assembly is located in each handlebar end. The weight assembly must be removed for access to the handlebar grips.

Removal/Installation

1. Remove the balancer weight mounting bolt (**Figure 15**) and remove the weight assembly.

234

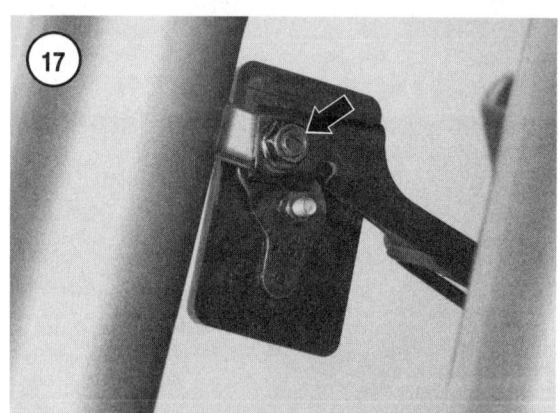

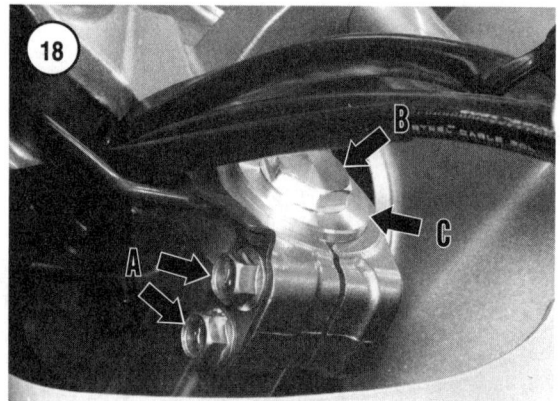

2. If necessary, remove the snap ring (**Figure 16**), then separate the inner rubber center from the end weight.
3. Inspect the rubber center. Replace if detiorated or otherwise damaged.
4. Assemble and install the weight assembly by reversing the removal procedure. Apply threadlock to the weight mounting bolt threads and tighten securely.

FORK SERVICE

To simplify fork service and to prevent mixing parts, service the fork legs individually.

Before presuming that an internal fork problem exists, drain the fork oil and refill with the proper type and quantity. If the problem persists, such as poor damping, a tendency to bottom out or top out, or leakage around the slider seal, follow the service procedures in this chapter.

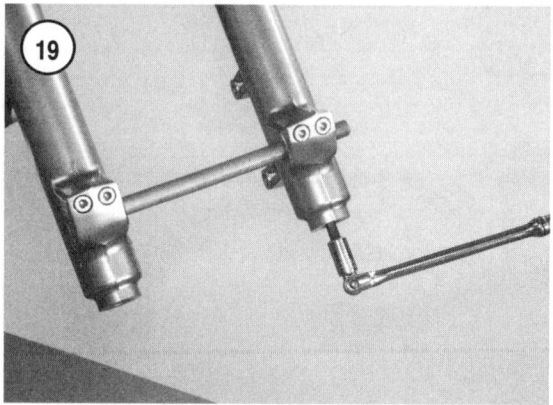

FRONT FORK

Removal/Installation

1. Remove the front brake caliper as described in Chapter Fourteen.
2. Remove the front wheel as described in Chapter Eleven.
3. Remove the reflector and hose/cable guide assembly (**Figure 17**) on each fork leg.
4. Loosen the upper clamp bolts (A, **Figure 18**).
5. If the fork leg(s) will be disassembled, loosen the cap(s) (B, **Figure 18**).
6. If the fork leg(s) will be disassembled, install the axle through both fork legs. Loosen the Allen bolt (**Figure 19**) in the bottom of each fork leg.
7. Loosen the lower fork tube clamp bolts (**Figure 20**).
8. Carefully pull each fork leg down and out of the upper and lower steering brackets. It may be neces-

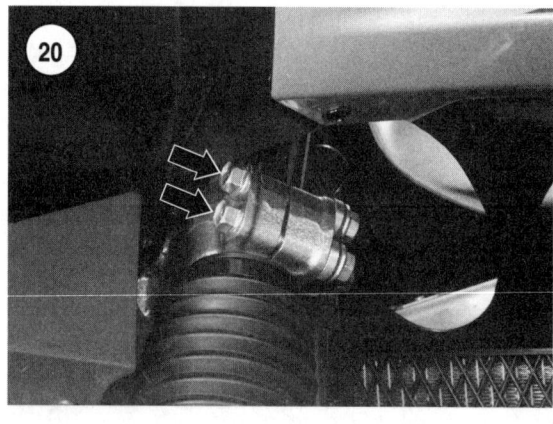

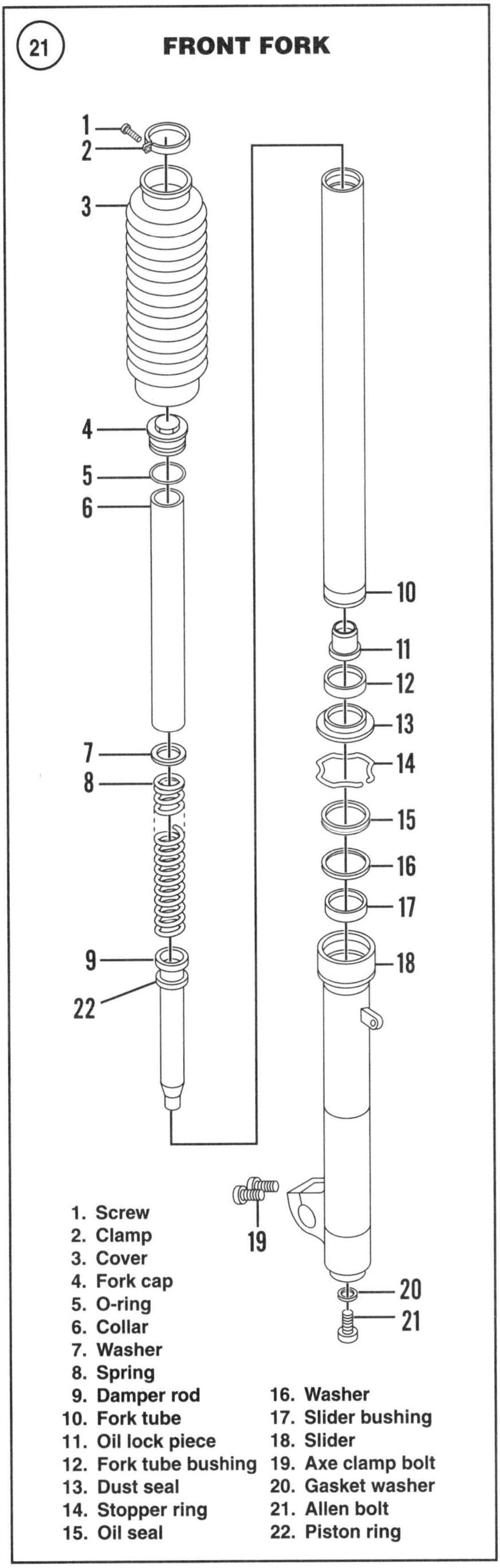

FRONT SUSPENSION AND STEERING

FRONT FORK (21)

1. Screw
2. Clamp
3. Cover
4. Fork cap
5. O-ring
6. Collar
7. Washer
8. Spring
9. Damper rod
10. Fork tube
11. Oil lock piece
12. Fork tube bushing
13. Dust seal
14. Stopper ring
15. Oil seal
16. Washer
17. Slider bushing
18. Slider
19. Axe clamp bolt
20. Gasket washer
21. Allen bolt
22. Piston ring

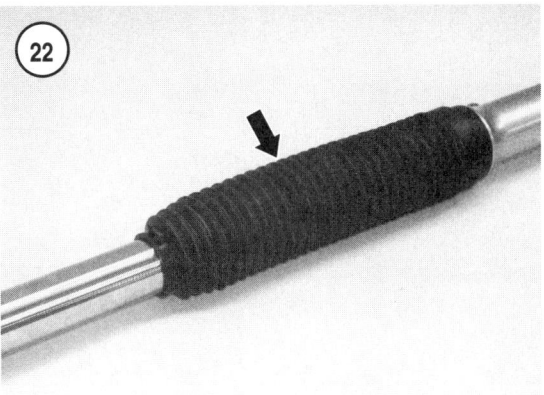

sary to rotate the fork tube slightly while pulling it down and out.

9. Install by reversing the removal steps while noting the following:
   a. Insert the fork upward until the upper end of the fork tube (C, **Figure 18**) is flush with the top surface of the upper steering bracket.
   b. Tighten the lower fork clamp bolts (**Figure 20**) to 20 N•m (15 ft.-lb.).
   c. If loosened or removed, tighten the fork cap (B, **Figure 18**) to 30 N•m (22 ft.-lb.).
   d. Tighten the upper fork clamp bolts (A, **Figure 18**) alternately in two steps to 20 N•m (15 ft.-lb.).

Disassembly

Refer to **Figure 21**.

1. Remove the front fork legs as described in this section.
2. Loosen the retaining clamps, and remove the fork cover (**Figure 22**).
3. If the Allen bolt in the bottom of the fork leg was not loosened prior to fork removal, use the following procedure:

NOTE
When loosening the Allen bolt in the bottom of the fork leg, leave the cap bolt and fork spring installed until the Allen bolt is loosened and removed. The internal spring pressure against the damper rod assembly will help hold it in place as the Allen bolt is being loosened and removed.

   a. Install the fork leg in a vise with soft jaws (**Figure 23**).
   b. Have an assistant compress the fork tube assembly as much as possible and hold it compressed against the damper rod.

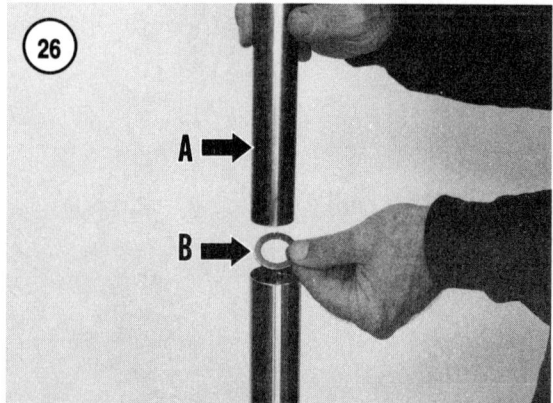

c. Loosen the Allen bolt at the base of the slider (**Figure 24**) with an Allen wrench and an impact tool. Do not remove the Allen bolt at this time.

WARNING
Be careful when removing the cap as the spring is under pressure. Protect your eyes accordingly.

NOTE
Keep the fork leg upright after removing the cap to prevent oil spills.

4. Slowly unscrew and remove the cap (**Figure 25**).
5. Remove the collar (A, **Figure 26**) and spring seat (B).
6. Remove the spring (**Figure 27**).
7. Turn the fork assembly upside down over a drain pan and completely drain the fork oil. Stroke the fork several times to pump out any oil that remains. Stand the fork tube upside-down in the drain pan and allow the oil to drain for several minutes.
8. Remove the dust seal (**Figure 28**) from the slider.
9. Remove the stopper ring (**Figure 29**) from the slider.
10. Remove the Allen bolt and washer from the bottom of the slider. If the Allen bolt was not loosened previously, use the holder tool and perform the following:

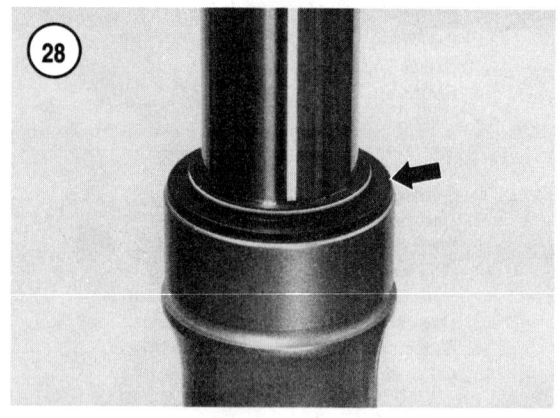

FRONT SUSPENSION AND STEERING

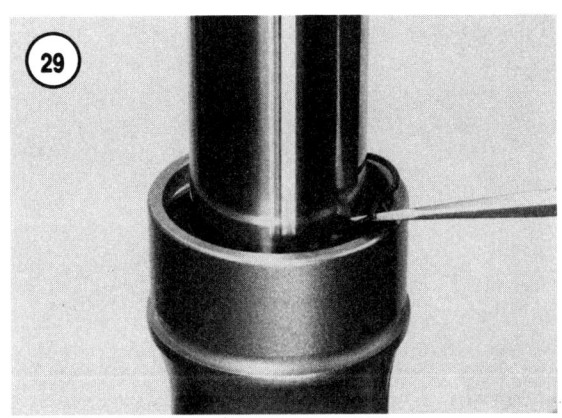

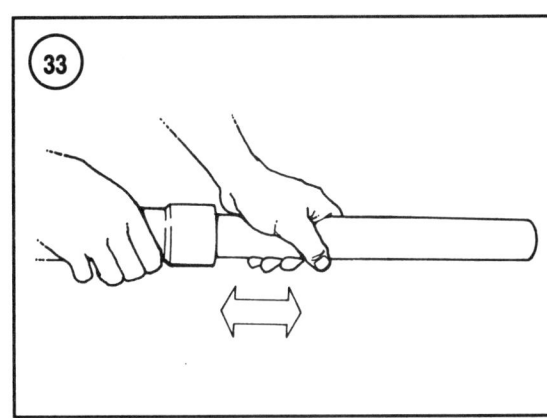

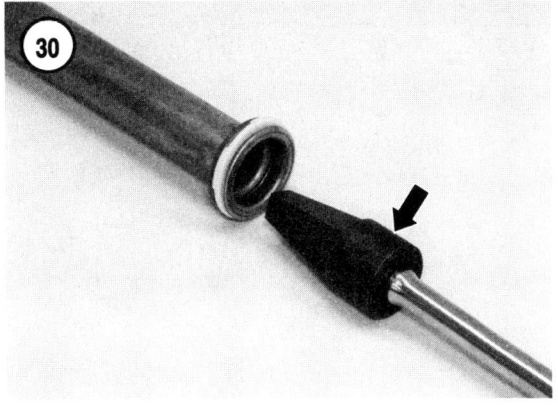

a. Install the holder tool (Kawasaki part No. 57001-1057) onto a wrench.
b. Insert this tool setup into the fork tube so the holder tool (**Figure 30**) fits into the top of the damper rod to hold the damper rod in place.
c. While holding the damper rod (A, **Figure 31**), use an Allen wrench to loosen the Allen bolt (B). Remove the Allen bolt and washer (**Figure 32**) from the base of the slider.

NOTE
The oil lock piece is often stuck to the bottom of the slider and may not come out with the damper rod. Do not lose the oil lock piece.

11. Turn the fork assembly upside down and slide out the damper rod assembly complete with the rebound spring and oil lock piece.

NOTE
On this type of fork, force is needed to remove the fork tube from the slider.

12. Install the slider in a vise with soft jaws.
13. There is an interference fit between the bushing in the fork slider and bushing in the fork tube. To remove the fork tube from the slider, pull hard on the fork tube using quick in-and-out strokes (**Figure 33**). Doing so will withdraw the slider bushing, oil seal retainer and oil seal from the slider (**Figure 34**).

NOTE
Do not remove the fork tube bushing unless it is going to be replaced. Inspect it as described in this section.

14. Withdraw the fork tube from the slider.
15. Remove the oil lock piece (A, **Figure 34**) from the slider if it did not come out in Step 11.
16. Slide off the oil seal (B, **Figure 34**), oil seal retainer (C) and bushing (D) from the fork tube.
17. Inspect all parts as described in this section.

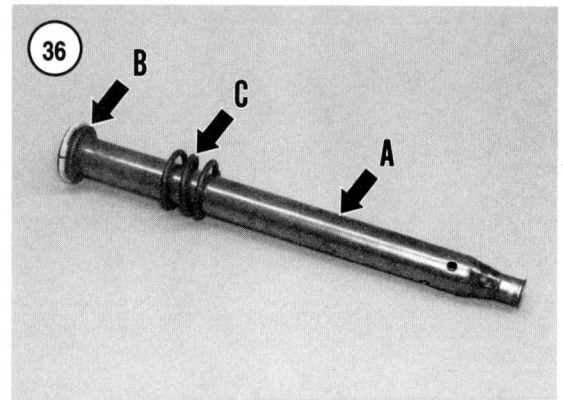

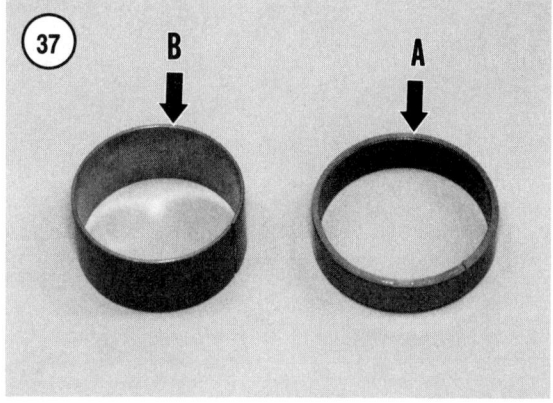

Inspection

1. Thoroughly clean all parts in solvent and dry them. Check the fork tube for signs of wear or scratches.
2. Check the damper rod for straightness (**Figure 35**). Replace a bent damper rod.
3. Make sure the oil holes in the damper rod are clear. Clean out if necessary.
4. Inspect the damper rod (A, **Figure 36**) and piston ring (B) for wear or damage. Replace if necessary.
5. Check the fork tube for straightness. If bent or severely scratched, replace it.
6. Inspect the slider for dents or exterior damage that may cause the upper fork tube to stick. Replace if necessary.
7. Inspect the brake caliper mounting bosses on the slider for cracks or other damage. If damaged, replace the slider.
8. Inspect the fork tube (A, **Figure 37**) and slider (B) bushings. If either is scratched or scored, replace them. If the Teflon coating is worn off so that the copper base material is showing on approximately 3/4 of the total surface, replace the bushing.
9. Check for a distorted washer; replace if necessary.
10. Inspect the fork cap bolt threads in the fork tube for wear or damage.
11. Inspect the fork cap bolt threads for wear or damage.
12. Inspect the oil seal seating area in the slider for damage or burrs. Clean up if necessary.
13. Inspect the gasket on the Allen bolt and replace it if damaged.

FRONT SUSPENSION AND STEERING

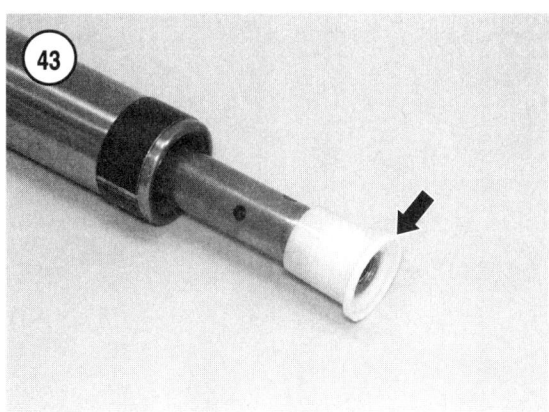

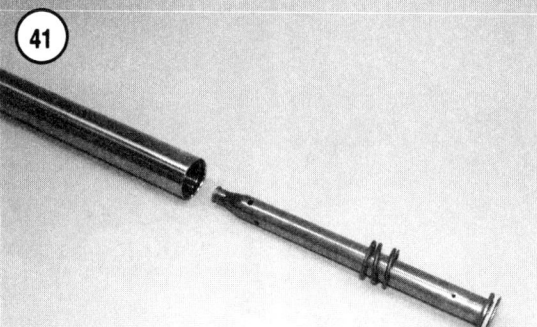

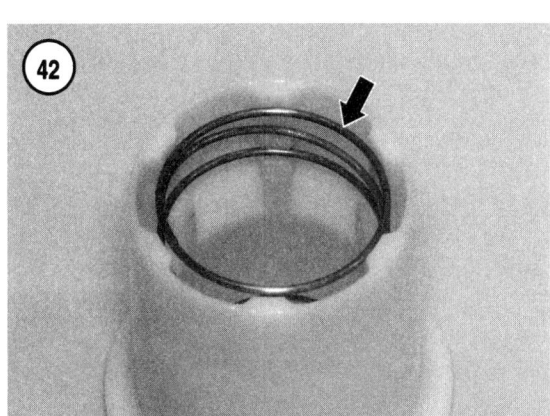

14. Clean the threads of the Allen bolt thoroughly with cleaning solvent or spray contact cleaner.

15. Measure the free length of the fork spring (not the rebound spring) as shown in **Figure 38**. If the spring free length is less than the service limit listed in **Table 1**, replace the spring.

16. Replace parts that are worn or damaged. Simply cleaning and reinstalling unserviceable components will not improve performance of the front suspension.

Assembly

1. Coat all parts with fresh fork oil prior to installation.
2. Carefully install the bushing onto the fork tube. Make sure the bushing fits properly in the groove on the tube (**Figure 39**).
3. If removed, install the piston ring (**Figure 40**) onto the damper rod. The notched side of the ring should be toward the tapered end of the damper rod.
4. Install the rebound spring (C, **Figure 36**) onto the damper rod (A). Lubricate the piston ring, then insert this assembly into the fork tube (**Figure 41**). Do not scratch the piston ring on the tube threads.
5. Temporarily install the fork spring, spring seat and collar to hold the damper rod in place.
6. Temporarily install the fork cap bolt and tighten securely.
7. Make sure the spring (**Figure 42**) is properly seated in the oil lock piece.
8. Install the oil lock piece (**Figure 43**) onto the damper rod.
9. Install the upper fork assembly into the slider.
10. Make sure the gasket washer is on the Allen bolt.
11. Apply a small amount of threadlock to the Allen bolt threads prior to installation. Install the Allen bolt and tighten to 30 N•m (22 ft.-lb.).

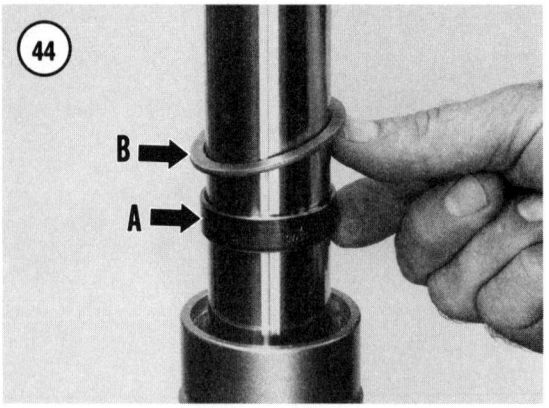

12. Push the fork slider bushing (A, **Figure 44**) and the washer (B) down the fork tube and rest them on top of the fork slider.

NOTE
*Place a plastic bag over the end of the fork tube and coat it with fork oil. This will avoid damage to the dust seal and the oil seal lips when installing them over the top of the fork tube (**Figure 45**).*

13. Install the new oil seal as follows:
   a. Coat the new seal with fresh fork oil.
   b. Position the seal with the open groove facing upward and slide the oil seal (**Figure 46**) down onto the fork tube.

NOTE
*A fork seal driver (**Figure 47**) is required to install the fork slider bushing and fork seal into the slider. A number of different aftermarket fork seal drivers are available that can be used for this purpose. Another method is to use a piece of pipe or metal collar with the correct dimensions to slide over the fork tube and seat against the seal. When selecting or fabricating a driver tool, it must have sufficient weight to drive the bushing and oil seal into the slider.*

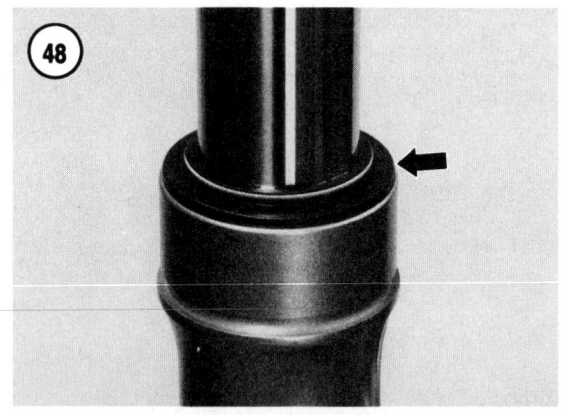

   c. Slide the fork seal driver down the fork tube and seat it against the seal.
   d. Operate the driver tool to drive the fork slider bushing and fork seal into the slider. Continue until the stopper ring groove in the slider is visible above the fork seal.
14. Slide the stopper ring down the fork tube.
15. Install the stopper ring and make sure it is completely seated in the groove in the fork slider.
16. Install the dust seal (**Figure 48**) into the slider. Press it in until it is completely seated.

FRONT SUSPENSION AND STEERING

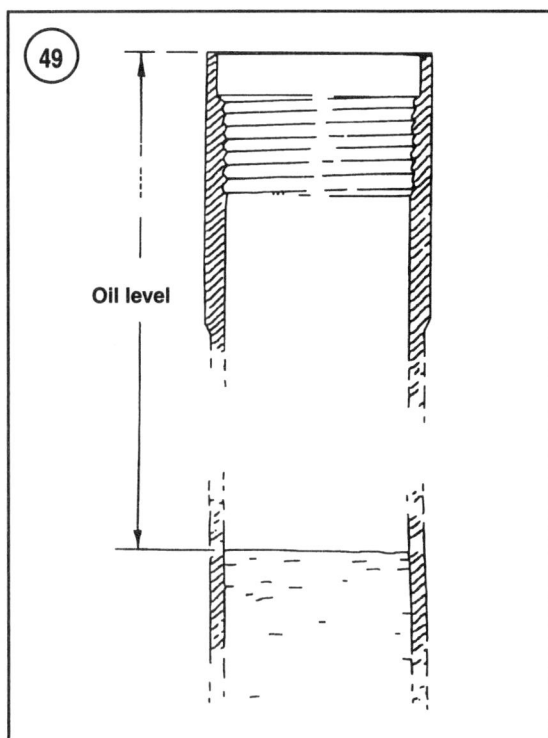

Oil level

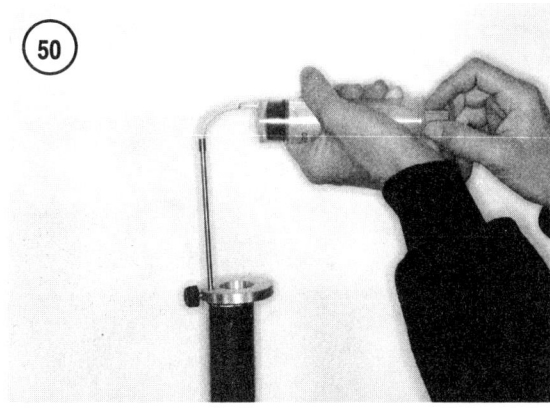

17. Unscrew the fork cap and remove the fork spring, spring seat and collar from the fork tube.

NOTE
The manufacturer recommends measurement of the fork oil level to ensure a more accurate filling.

NOTE
To measure the correct amount of fluid, use a plastic baby bottle. These bottles have measurements in milliliters (ml) on the side.

18. Compress the fork completely.
19. Add the recommended amount of SAE 10W fork oil, listed in **Table 3**, to the fork assembly.

NOTE
Make sure the tube is bottomed by pushing down slowly on the last stroke. Otherwise, hydraulic force may produce the feeling that the tube is bottomed.

20. Pump the fork leg several times to thoroughly distribute the oil. Bottom the fork tube in the fork slider and allow to stand in the vertical position for several minutes.
21. Hold the fork assembly as close to perfectly vertical as possible.
22. Use an accurate ruler (**Figure 49**) or an oil level gauge (Motion Pro part No. 08-121 [**Figure 50**] or equivalent) to achieve the correct oil level listed in **Table 2**.
23. Allow the oil to settle completely and recheck the oil level measurement. Adjust the oil level if necessary.
24. Install the fork spring, spring seat and collar.
25. Inspect the O-ring seal on the fork cap and replace it if necessary.
26. Install the fork cap. Tighten the cap after fork installation.
27. Install the fork cover and clamps.
28. Repeat this procedure for the other fork leg assembly.
29. Install the fork leg(s) as described in this section.

STEERING STEM AND HEAD

The steering stem pivots in the steering head on tapered roller bearings. The bearings are at the top and bottom of the steering stem. Do not remove the outer races (mounted in the frame) and the lower bearing (mounted on the steering stem) unless they require replacement. The bearings should be lubricated at the intervals specified in Chapter Three. Before disassembling the steering head, perform the *Steering Play Check and Adjustment* procedures in this section. This inspection will help determine if the bearings and races are worn, or if they only require adjustment.

Disassembly

1. Remove the lower fairings as described in Chapter Fifteen.
2. Remove the upper fairing as described in Chapter Fifteen.

NOTE
Although meter unit removal is not necessary, it is recommended to prevent possible damage to the unit. Refer to Chapter Nine for removal instructions.

3. Remove the front wheel as described in Chapter Eleven.
4. Remove the front fender (Chapter Fifteen).
5. Remove the fuel tank as described in Chapter Fifteen.
6. Disconnect the ignition switch connector (**Figure 51**) under the top frame tube. Remove the ignition switch wires from the cable guides.

NOTE
The handlebar may be disassembled and removed, or removed and suspended out of the way in the next step.

7. Remove the handlebar as described in this chapter.
8. Loosen the stem nut (A, **Figure 52**).
9. Remove the fork legs as described in this chapter.
10. Remove the cable, wire and brake hose guides from the upper steering bracket and the steering base.
11. Remove the retaining bolts (A, **Figure 53**). Remove the brake hose bracket (B, **Figure 53**) and lower cover (C).
12. Remove the stem nut and washer.
13. Remove the upper steering bracket (B, **Figure 52**).

NOTE
*If tight, loosen the adjust nut (**Figure 54**) using a spanner wrench or similar tool.*

14. Hold the steering base so it cannot fall, and remove the adjust nut (**Figure 54**).

CAUTION
The bottom bearing is pressed onto the steering stem. Do not remove the bearing unless it needs replacement. Damage will occur during removal.

15. Lower the steering stem assembly out of the steering head, then remove the bearing (**Figure 55**) at the top of the steering head.

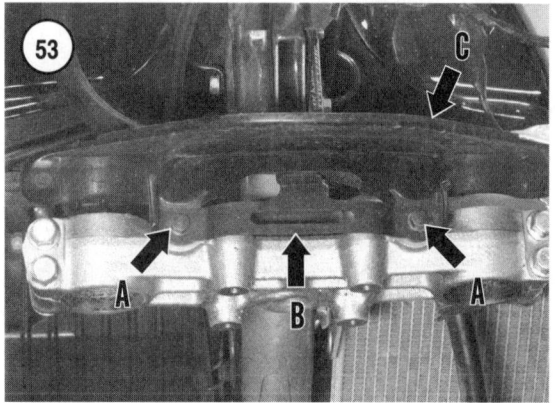

FRONT SUSPENSION AND STEERING 243

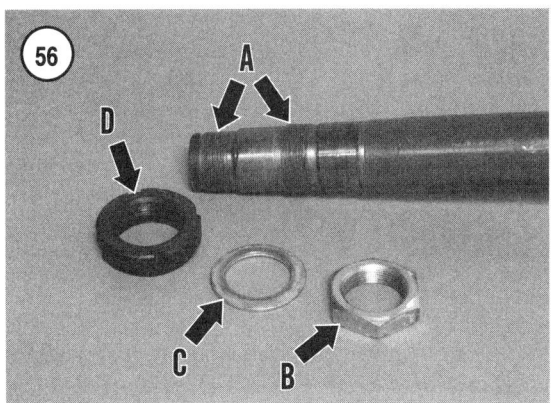

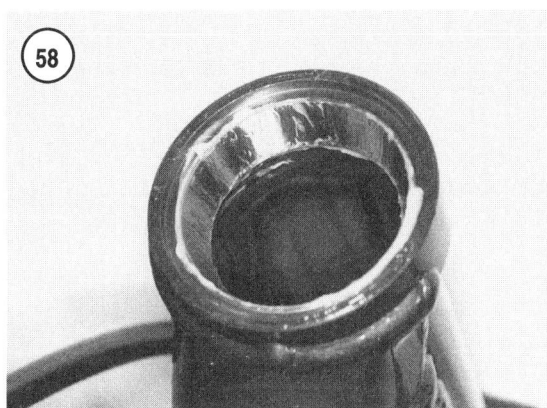

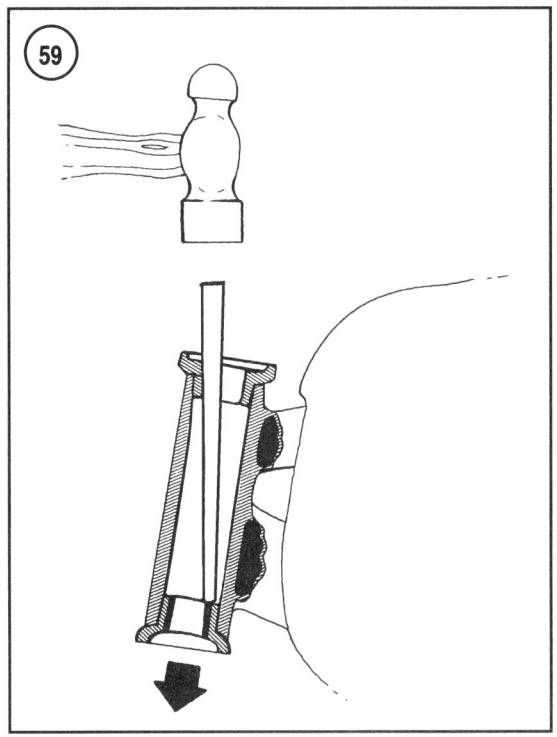

6. Inspect the bearings for pitting, scratches, corrosion or discoloration.

7. Inspect the bearing races (**Figure 58**) in the frame for pitting, galling or corrosion. If a race is worn or damaged, replace both races and bearings as described in this section.

8. If the bearings are to be reused, pack the bearings with waterproof grease.

Outer Bearing Race Replacement

Only remove the bearing races from the frame when installing new bearings. The bearing races are recessed in the bores, and installation requires drivers (Kawasaki part No. 57001-1076 and part No. 57001-1077 or equivalent) and a driver press shaft (Kawasaki part No. 57001-1075 or equivalent). The tool is a threaded rod with different sized disc drivers fitted to each end. A similar tool can be fabricated with common hardware. If this is done, the parts used as the drivers must fit at the outside edge of the races, and still be capable of entering the steering head bore. The drivers must not contact the surface of the races.

1. Insert an aluminum drift into the steering head and position it on the edge of the lower race (**Figure 59**). Carefully drive out the race. To prevent binding, make several passes around the perimeter of the race. Repeat the procedure to remove the upper race.

2. Clean the race bores and inspect them for damage.

Inspection

1. Clean the bearings and races with solvent.

2. Inspect the steering head (on the frame) for cracks or other damage. If damage is evident, have a qualified welding shop make the repairs.

3. Inspect the steering base assembly. Inspect the clamping and pivot areas for cracks or damage.

4. Inspect the steering stem threads (A, **Figure 56**), stem nut (B), washers (C), and adjust nut (D) for damage.

5. Inspect the seals for damage. If necessary, separate the top seal from the adjust nut (**Figure 57**).

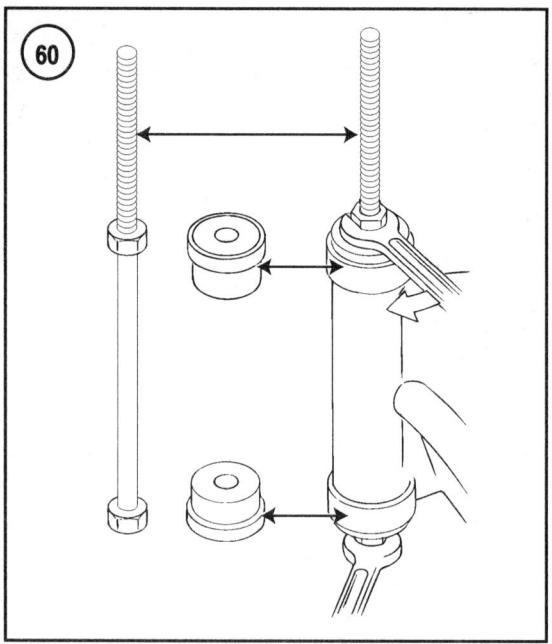

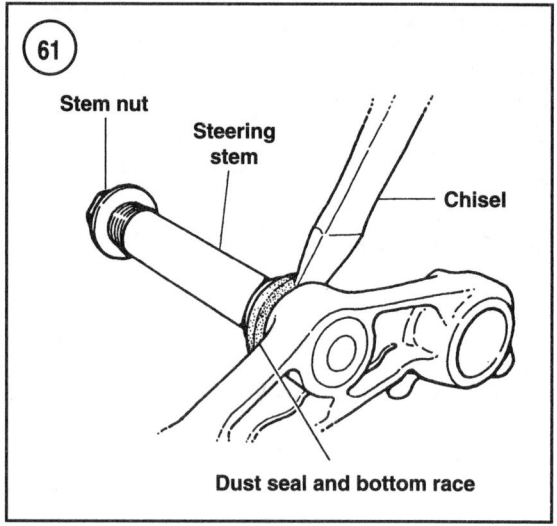

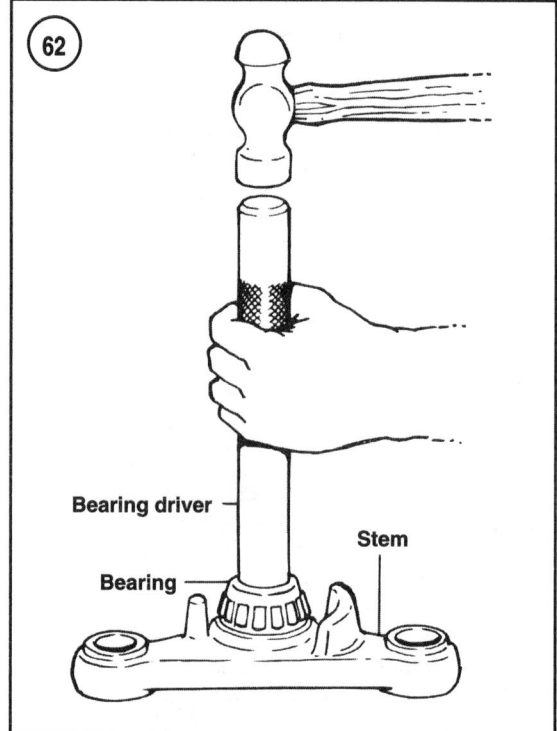

3. To install the upper race, do the following:
   a. Place a new, lubricated race squarely into the bore opening, with its wide side facing out.
   b. Assemble the tool (**Figure 60**), seating a driver at the outer edge of the race. The lower driver can rest on the perimeter of the steering head, or in the stepped bore.
   c. Hold the lower nut with a wrench and tighten the upper nut to seat the race.
   d. Remove the tool from the frame and check that the race is fully seated.
   e. Repeat the procedure to install the second race. During installation, do not allow the driver or shaft to contact the face of the first race. Damage will occur.
4. Lubricate the races with waterproof bearing grease.

Steering Stem Bearing Replacement

The steering stem bearing is a press fit. Perform the following steps to replace the bearing.

1. Thread the stem nut (**Figure 61**) onto the steering stem to protect the threads.

WARNING
Wear safety glasses when using the hammer and chisel.

2. Stabilize the steering stem, then remove the bearing and seal, using a hammer and chisel (**Figure 61**). To prevent binding, make several passes around the perimeter of the bearing.
3. Clean and inspect the steering stem.
4. Pack the new bearing and seal with waterproof grease.
5. Slide the new seal and bearing onto the steering stem.

NOTE
If available, a press can also be used to install the bearing and seal.

6. Drive the bearing into place as follows:
   a. Support the steering stem directly below the bearing.

FRONT SUSPENSION AND STEERING

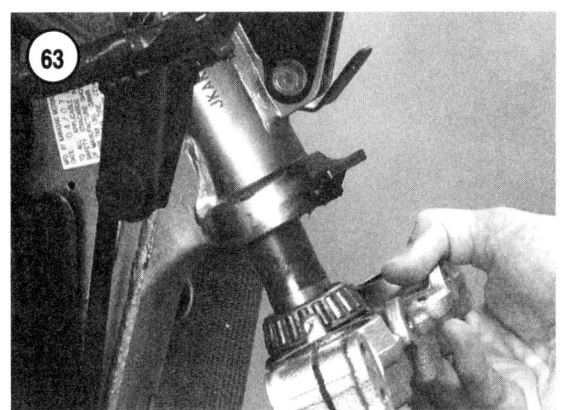

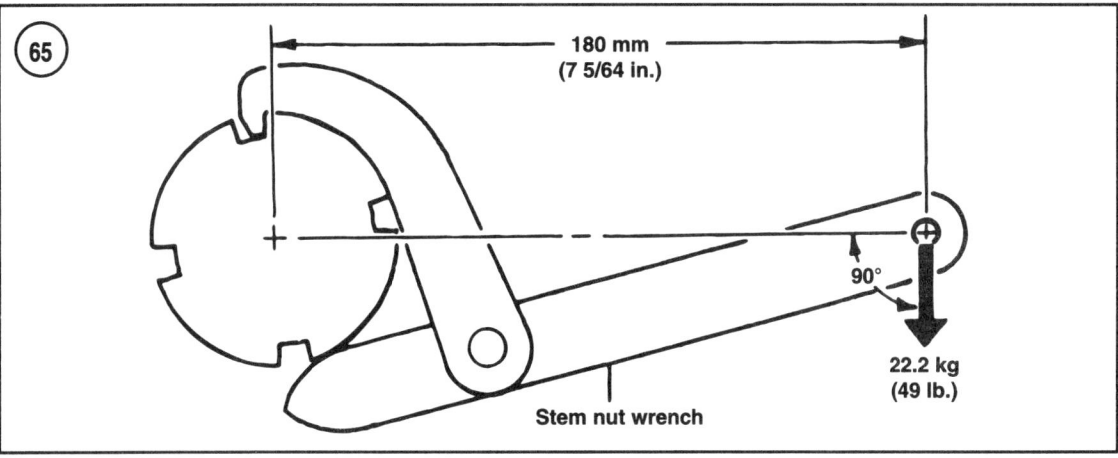

b. Slide a bearing driver or long pipe over the steering stem, seating the tool on the inner bearing race (**Figure 62**).

c. Drive the bearing onto the steering stem until it is seated.

Assembly and Adjustment

1. Check that the upper and lower bearing races are seated in the frame.
2. Check that bearings, races and seals are lubricated with waterproof grease.
3. If separated, install the adjust nut into the upper seal (**Figure 57**).
4. Guide the steering stem through the bottom of the frame (**Figure 63**).
5. Install the upper bearing into its race.
6. Install the bearing seal and adjust nut (**Figure 64**). Finger-tighten the adjust nut.

NOTE
The following step is best performed using an adjust nut wrench (Kawasaki part No. 57001-1100 or equivalent).

7. Seat the bearings as follows:

a. If using a wrench with the same dimensions shown in **Figure 65**, apply 22.2 kg (49 lb.) force (or weight) to the end of the wrench to obtain the desired 39 N•m (29 ft.-lb.) torque on the adjust nut.

NOTE
If a special adjust nut wrench is not available, tighten the adjust nut by feel using a spanner wrench or equivalent. Tighten the adjust nut until tight, then turn the steering stem back and forth to seat the bearings. Loosen the adjust nut 1/16 to 1/8 turn, then retighten it until the steering stem turns smoothly with no trace of play.

b. When the adjust nut is tightened properly, the steering stem should turn smoothly from side to side with no play.
c. Loosen the adjust nut a fraction of a turn until the steering stem turns lightly.
d. If using a wrench with the same dimensions shown in **Figure 65**, apply a 2.8 kg (1.3 lb.) force (or weight) to the end of the wrench to obtain the desired 4.9 N•m (43 in.-lb.) torque on the adjust nut. If the special adjust nut

wrench is not available, turn the steering stem nut lightly until the steering stem becomes hard to turn. Do not overtighten or the steering will be too tight.

e. Turn the steering stem by hand to make sure it turns freely and does not bind. Repeat if necessary.

8. Move the steering stem back and forth from side to side. The steering stem should move freely from side to side with no looseness or stiffness. If necessary, readjust the adjust nut.

9. Install the upper steering bracket, washer and stem nut. Finger-tighten the stem nut until the fork legs are installed.

10. Install the fork legs as described in this chapter. Tighten the bolts in order as follows:
    a. Tighten the upper fork clamp bolts alternately in two steps to 20 N•m (15 ft.-lb.).
    b. Tighten the stem nut to 49 N•m (36 ft.-lb.).
    c. Tighten the lower fork clamp bolts to 20 N•m (15 ft.-lb.).

11. Check bearing play again, as follows:
    a. Turn the steering stem from lock to lock. The steering stem should turn smoothly and freely. If binding occurs, the steering stem is too tight.
    b. Grasp the fork legs near the axle. Lever the fork legs in all directions and feel for play. If play is felt or heard, the steering stem is too loose. If necessary, remove the fork legs and readjust the bearing tension as described in this section to eliminate or add play.

12. Install the handlebar as described in this chapter.

13. Route the ignition switch wires through the cable guides and connect the ignition switch connector (**Figure 51**) under the top frame tube.

14. Install the fuel tank as described in Chapter Fifteen.

15. Install the front fender as described in Chapter Fifteen.

16. Install the front wheel as described in Chapter Eleven.

17. If removed, install the meter unit as described in Chapter Nine.

18. Install the upper fairing as described in Chapter Fifteen.

19. Install the lower fairings as described in Chapter Fifteen.

Steering Play Check and Adjustment

Steering adjustment takes up any play in the steering stem and bearings and allows the steering stem to operate freely. Excessive play or roughness in the steering stem makes steering imprecise and causes bearing damage. These conditions are usually caused

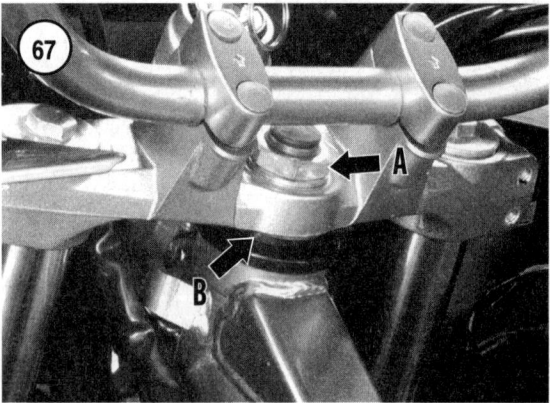

by improper bearing lubrication and steering adjustment. Improperly routed control cables can also affect steering operation.

1. Support the motorcycle so the front wheel is off the ground.

2. Turn the handlebar from lock to lock and check for roughness or binding. Movement should be smooth with no resistance.

3. Position the handlebar so the front wheel points straight ahead. Lightly push the end of the handlebar. The front end should fully turn to the side from the center position, under its own weight. Check in both directions. Note the following:
    a. If the steering stem moves roughly or stops before reaching the frame stop, check that all cables are routed properly.
    b. If cable routing is correct and the steering binds, the steering adjustment may be too tight. This condition can also occur if the bearings and races require lubrication or replacement. Perform the remaining checks before adjusting the steering.
    c. If the steering stem moves from side to side correctly, check for excessive looseness as described in this section.

4. Position the fork so it points straight ahead. Have an assistant hold the motorcycle, then grasp the fork

FRONT SUSPENSION AND STEERING

legs near the axle. Lever the fork legs in all directions and feel for play.

    a. If movement can be felt at the steering stem, adjust the steering as described in this section.

    b. If no excessive movement can be felt and the steering turns from side to side correctly, the steering is adjusted properly and in good condition.

5. To adjust the steering, proceed as follows:

    a. Remove the fuel tank as described in Chapter Fifteen.

NOTE
The handlebar may be removed and suspended out of the way without removing components on the handlebar.

    b. Remove the handlebar as described in this chapter.

    c. Loosen the upper fork clamp bolts (**Figure 66**).

    d. Loosen the steering stem nut (A, **Figure 67**).

    e. Loosen or tighten the adjust nut (B, **Figure 67**) using a spanner wrench.

    f. Tighten the upper fork clamp bolts alternately in two steps to 20 N•m (15 ft.-lb.).

    g. Tighten the stem nut to 49 N•m (36 ft.-lb.).

    h. Recheck bearing play. Adjust as necessary.

    i. Install the handlebar as described in this chapter.

    j. Install the fuel tank as described in Chapter Fifteen.

Table 1 STEERING AND FRONT SUSPENSION SPECIFICATIONS

Fork type	Telescopic, 41-mm, non-adjustable
Fork travel	200 mm (7.9 in.)
Fork spring free length	
2008-2014 (early models)	363.9 mm (14.33 in.)
2014 (later models)-on models	358.9 mm (14.13 in.)
Fork spring service length	
2008-2014 (early models)	357 mm (14.1 in.)
2014 (later models)-on models	352 mm (13.9 in.)
Steering caster	28 degree
Steering trail	112 mm (4.4 in.)

Table 2 FORK OIL LEVEL AND CAPACITY

Fork oil	Kayaba KHL34-G10 or equivalent
Fork oil capacity (each leg)	
Oil change	500 cc (16.9 U.S. oz.)
Fork rebuild (all parts dry)	581-589 cc (19.6-20.0 U.S. oz.)
Fork oil level (refer to text)	
2008-2014 (early models)	133-137 mm (5.24-5.39 in.)
2014 (later models)-on models	138-142 mm (5.42-5.58 in.)

Table 3 FRONT SUSPENSION TORQUE SPECIFICATIONS

Item	N•m	in.-lb.	ft.-lb.
Handlebar holder bolts	25	–	18
Fork clamp bolts	20	–	15
Fork cap	30	–	22
Fork lower Allen bolt	30	–	22
Steering adjust nut	Refer to text		
Steering stem nut	49	–	36

CHAPTER THIRTEEN

REAR SUSPENSION

This chapter contains repair and replacement procedures for the rear suspension. Rear suspension specifications and torque specifications are listed in tables at the end of this chapter.

SHOCK ABSORBER

The shock absorber is a spring-loaded, hydraulically damped unit with an integral oil/nitrogen reservoir. The shock absorber damper is not rebuildable. To adjust the shock absorber, refer to *Shock Absorber Adjustment* in this chapter.

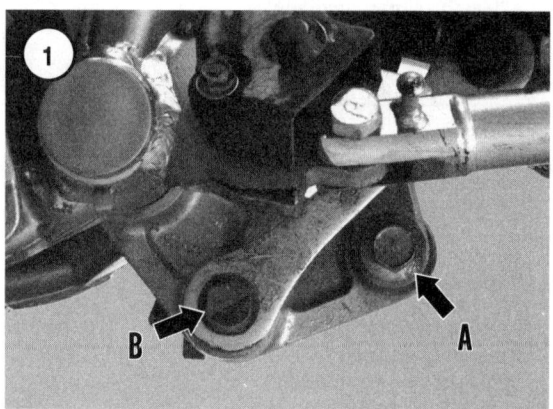

Removal/Installation

Read all procedures before removing the shock absorber. If the motorcycle has been modified, some disassembly procedures may not be necessary.

1. Raise the rear of the motorcycle so the rear wheel is just touching the ground.
2. Remove the lower shock absorber mounting bolt (A, **Figure 1**).
3. Remove the lower bolt (B, **Figure 1**) on the lever arms.
4. Remove the left side cover as described in Chapter Fifteen.
5. Remove the breather hose (**Figure 2**) near the top of the shock absorber. On California models, first remove the liquid/vapor separator.
6. Remove the upper mounting bolt (A, **Figure 3**), and then remove the shock absorber out the bottom of the motorcycle.
7. Inspect the shock absorber as described in this chapter.
8. Refer to **Table 2** for recommended shock absorber settings.
9. Reverse the removal procedure to install the shock absorber while noting the following:

REAR SUSPENSION

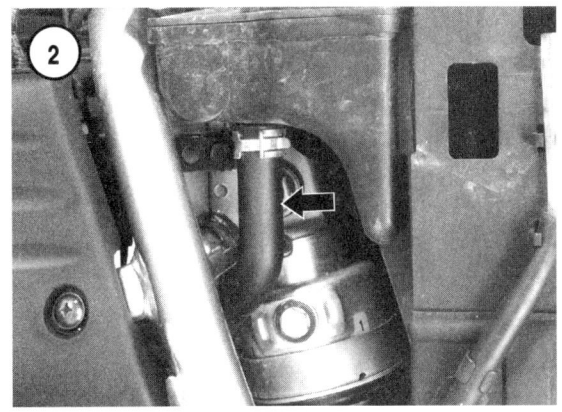

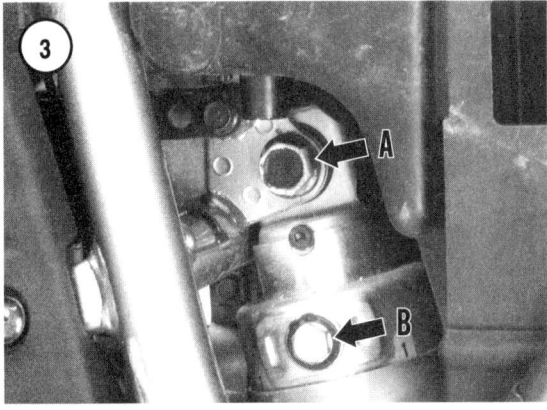

a. Lubricate the bores and mounting bolts with waterproof grease.
b. Install the shock absorber so the preload adjuster (B, **Figure 3**) is on the left side of the motorcycle.
c. Tighten the upper shock absorber mounting bolt to 59 N•m (43 ft.-lb.).
d. Tighten the lower shock absorber mounting bolt to 98 N•m (72 ft.-lb.).
e. Tighten the lower lever arm bolt to 98 N•m (72 ft.-lb.).

Inspection

Except for the upper mounting bushing, individual parts are not available from the manufacturer. If the shock absorber is damaged, replace the complete shock absorber, or take the unit to a shop that services motorcycle shock absorbers.

1. Inspect the upper bushing (**Figure 4**) and mounting bolt for wear or damage. The bolt must be a firm fit in the bore. The bushing must be tight in the rubber mounting. If the bushing is worn, press or drive out the bushing, and install a new one.
2. Check the shock absorber for signs of oil leakage. If the shock absorber is leaking, replace it.
3. Inspect the spring for cracks.
4. Check for proper operation of the spring preload adjuster and the rebound damper adjuster.
5. Inspect the lower clevis (**Figure 5**) and mounting bolt for wear or damage. The bolt must be a firm fit in the bore.

SHOCK ABSORBER LINKAGE

The shock linkage consists of the lever, lever arms, pivot bolts, seals, pivot spacers and needle bearings (**Figure 6**). The lever is joined to the swing arm by the lever arms. The linkage should be disassembled and lubricated at the intervals indicated in Chapter Three. If the linkage is often subjected to harsh riding conditions, service the linkage more frequently.

NOTE
In the following procedures, whenever grease is referenced, a molybdenum disulfide or waterproof grease should be used. The manufacturer recommends molydisulfide grease for all linkage bearings. This grease has excellent antiwear characteristics when subjected to extreme pressure. Waterproof grease, which is very durable, has a high tack and is very resistant to washout when subjected to wet conditions. The grease type used is a preference of the rider

SHOCK ABSORBER LINKAGE

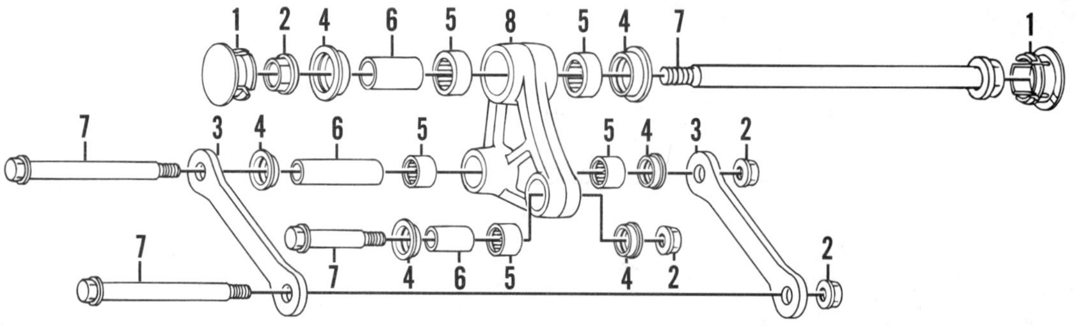

6

1. Cap
2. Nut
3. Lever arm
4. Seal
5. Needle bearing
6. Pivot spacer
7. Pivot bolt
8. Lever

and is determined by the conditions in which the motorcycle is operated. If the linkage is regularly maintained, either type of grease will perform well.

Lever and Lever Arms Removal and Installation

The lever and lever arms can be removed for service without removing the swing arm or rear wheel.

This procedure describes the removal and separation of the lever and lever arm assemblies. Note the direction of all bolts being removed. During assembly, install bolts in their original direction.

When disassembling the components, do not remove or allow the pivot spacers to slide out of the bearings. The original bearings have rollers that are locked into the bearing housing. However, if aftermarket replacement bearings have been installed, the needle bearings may be held in place only by the grease on the bearings. Keep any removed rollers with their respective bearing housing.

Refer to **Figure 6**.

1. Support the motorcycle so it is stable and secure. The rear wheel must just touch the ground, so the suspension is fully extended.
2. Remove the nuts and lever arm pivot bolts (A, **Figure 7**) connecting the lever arms to the swing arm

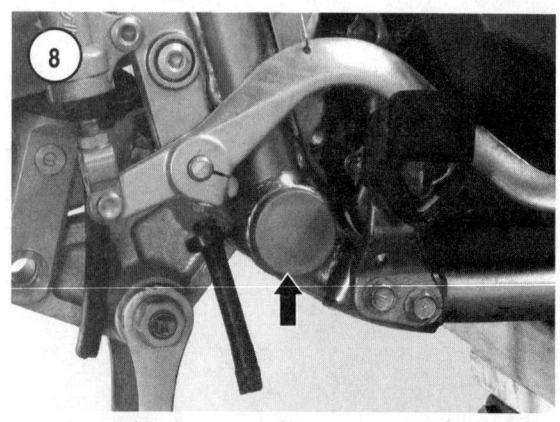

REAR SUSPENSION

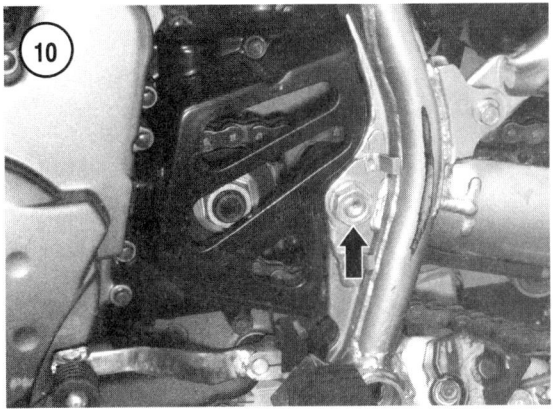

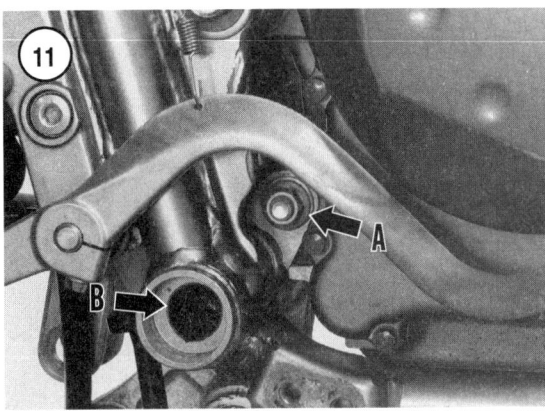

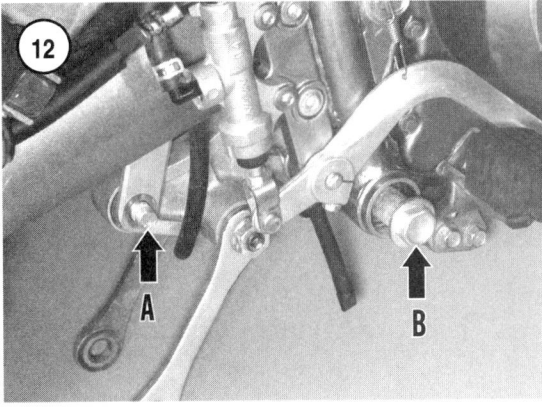

and lever. If desired, the lower pivot bolt connecting the lever arms to the lever can be removed at the workbench. However, the bolt is very tight and must be held stable in order to remove the nut.

3. Remove the nut and pivot bolt (B, **Figure 7**) from the shock absorber and lever.
4. Remove the cap (**Figure 8**) from both sides of the frame. Remove the nut and pivot bolt (**Figure 9**) from the frame.
5. Loosen the swing arm pivot shaft nut (**Figure 10**). Do not remove the nut.

NOTE
It may be necessary to remove the right front footpeg for access to the engine mounting nut.

6. Loosen the lower engine mounting nut (A, **Figure 11**). Do not remove the nut.
7. Move the shock absorber out of the way and tap the lever out of the frame.
8. Inspect and service the lever and lever arms as described in this section.
9. Reverse the removal steps to install the parts. Note the following:
    a. Lubricate all bearings, seals and pivot bolts with grease.
    b. Clean the frame mounting bores (B, **Figure 11**) and drain holes, and lubricate with grease.
    c. After the lever has been tapped into the frame, install the shock absorber mounting bolt (A, **Figure 12**). This holds the assembly in place while installing the pivot bolt (B, **Figure 12**) through the frame.
    d. Check that all pivot spacers are in place before installing the remaining components.
    e. Install and finger-tighten all bolts before final tightening.
    f. Tighten the lever-to-frame pivot bolt to 98 N•m (72 ft.-lb.).
    g. Tighten the swing arm pivot shaft bolt and nut to 88 N•m (65 ft.-lb.).
    h. Tighten the lower engine mounting bolt to 44 N•m (32 ft.-lb.).
    i. If removed, install the right front footpeg and tighten the mounting bolts to 25 N•m (18 ft.-lb.).
    j. Tighten the lever arm pivot bolts to 98 N•m (72 ft.-lb.).
    k. Tighten the lower shock absorber mounting bolt to 98 N•m (72 ft.-lb.).

Lever Arms Inspection

Refer to **Figure 6**.
1. Inspect for worn pivot bolts. Check the fit of the bolts in the lever arms. The bolts should be a snug

fit. Replace nuts and bolts that have rounded flats. Proper torquing may not be achieved if the nuts and bolts cannot be gripped securely.

2. Inspect the lever arms (A, **Figure 13**) for bends or twisting. The arms should lie flat.

3. Inspect the lever arm bores for damage and elongation. If worn or damaged, also replace the pivot bolts.

4. Inspect the contact point (B, **Figure 13**) where the lever arm and pivot spacer mate. If the area is worn or ground away, the pivot bolts have been inadequately torqued.

5. Install the lever arms as described in this section.

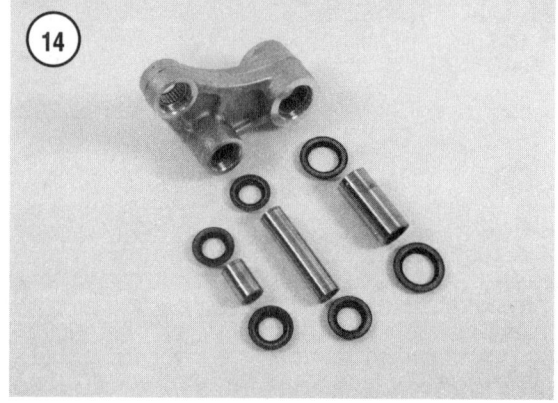

Lever Inspection and Repair

1. At each bearing, remove the pivot spacer and seals (**Figure 14**). Pry the seals at their outer edge.

NOTE
Inspect the bearing rollers to determine if they are removable. Original equipment bearings are not removable. Some aftermarket bearings may be removable. If the rollers can be removed, put the rollers in a marked container so they can be reinstalled in their original housing.

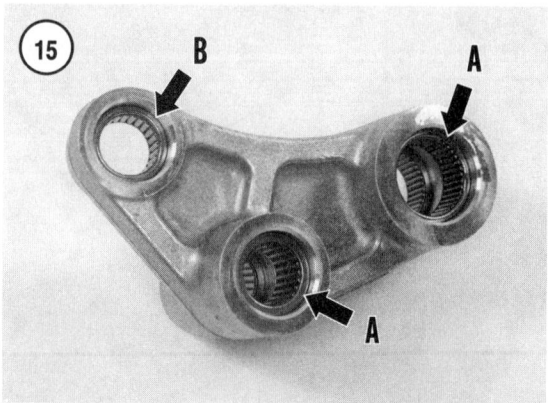

2. Clean the lever assembly in solvent. Carefully dry all parts.

3. Inspect the following:
   a. Inspect the lever for cracks, particularly around the bearing bores.
   b. Check the frame pivot bolt and nut for scoring, wear and other damage. Replace the nut and bolt if it has rounded flats. Proper torquing may not be achieved if the nut and bolt cannot be gripped securely.
   c. Check the seals for cracks, wear or other damage.
   d. Check the pivot spacers for scoring, wear or other damage.
   e. Check the needle bearings (**Figure 15**) for wear, flat spots, rust or discoloration. If the rollers are blue, overheating has occurred.
   f. Lightly lubricate the bearings and pivot spacers, and insert each spacer (**Figure 16**) into its respective bearing(s). The parts should turn freely and smoothly with no play. If play or roughness exists, replace the bearing(s) as described in this section For bores that contain two bearings, always replace both bearings and the pivot spacer.

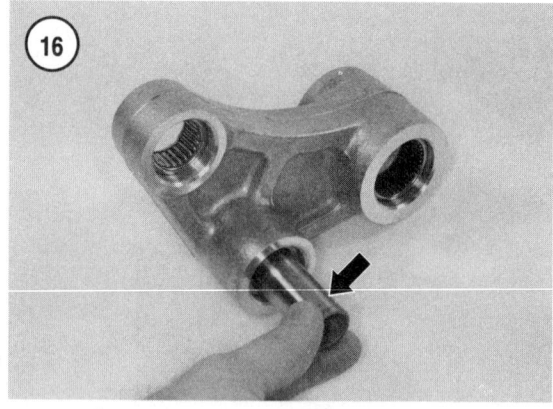

4. Replace the needle bearing(s) in the lever as follows:

REAR SUSPENSION

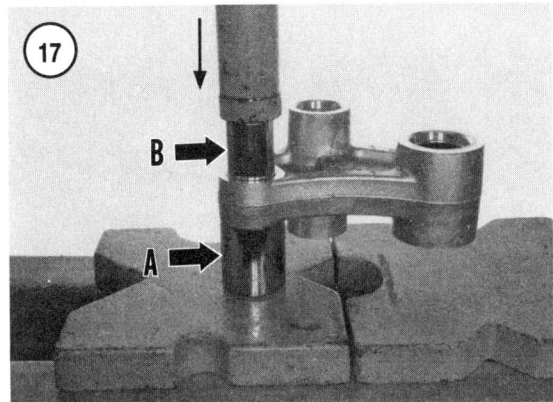

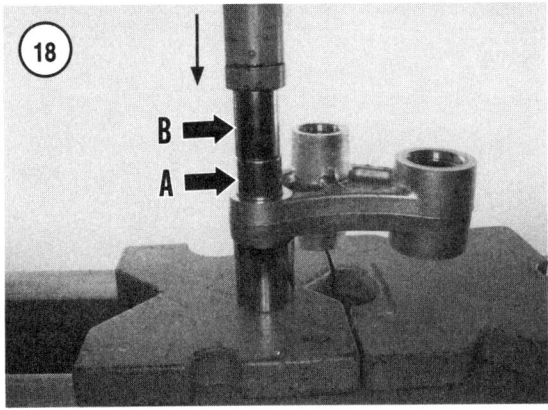

a. Apply penetrating oil to the bearing(s) and bore.

NOTE
The driver must be capable of passing through the bore and be longer than the bore depth. The lower socket must fit on the perimeter of the bore, but also be large enough to accept the removed bearing.

b. It is recommended to remove the bearing(s) with a press. If the bearing(s) and bore are not corroded, a drawbolt-type of bearing removal/installation tool can be used, as described in *Swing Arm Bearing Replacement* (this chapter). Whichever method is used, the lever is supported against the open side of a large socket (A, **Figure 17**), and a driver or appropriate-size socket (B) is used to drive the bearing(s) into the lower socket.
c. Clean and inspect the mounting bore.
d. Lubricate the new bearing(s) with grease.
e. Fit the bearing (A, **Figure 18**) squarely into the bore, with the manufacturer's marks facing out. Fit or assemble a driver tool (B, **Figure 18**) squarely against the end of the bearing. The lower socket only acts to support the lever around the bore.
f. Begin driving the bearing. After the bearing has entered the bore, frequently check the bearing depth (**Figure 19**). Bearings (A, **Figure 15**) that support the lever and lever arms should be driven 5 mm (0.20 in.) below the outer edge of the bore. The bearing (B, **Figure 15**) that supports the shock absorber should be driven 5.5 mm (0.22 in.) below the outer edge of the bore. These depths are required so the seals can be seated in the bore.
g. Repeat for any remaining bearings.

5. Pack the bearings, bearing bores and seals with grease. Also, apply grease to the pivot spacers and bolts.
6. Press the seals (**Figure 20**) into position by hand. If the seals do not seat, inspect the bearing depth. If necessary, adjust the depth of the bearing(s).
7. Install the pivot spacers into the lever. Check that all seals remain seated as the pivot spacers pass through the seals.
8. Install the lever as described in this section.

SWING ARM

Bearing Inspection

The swing arm bearings can be inspected with the swing arm mounted on the motorcycle. Periodically check the bearings for play, roughness or damage.

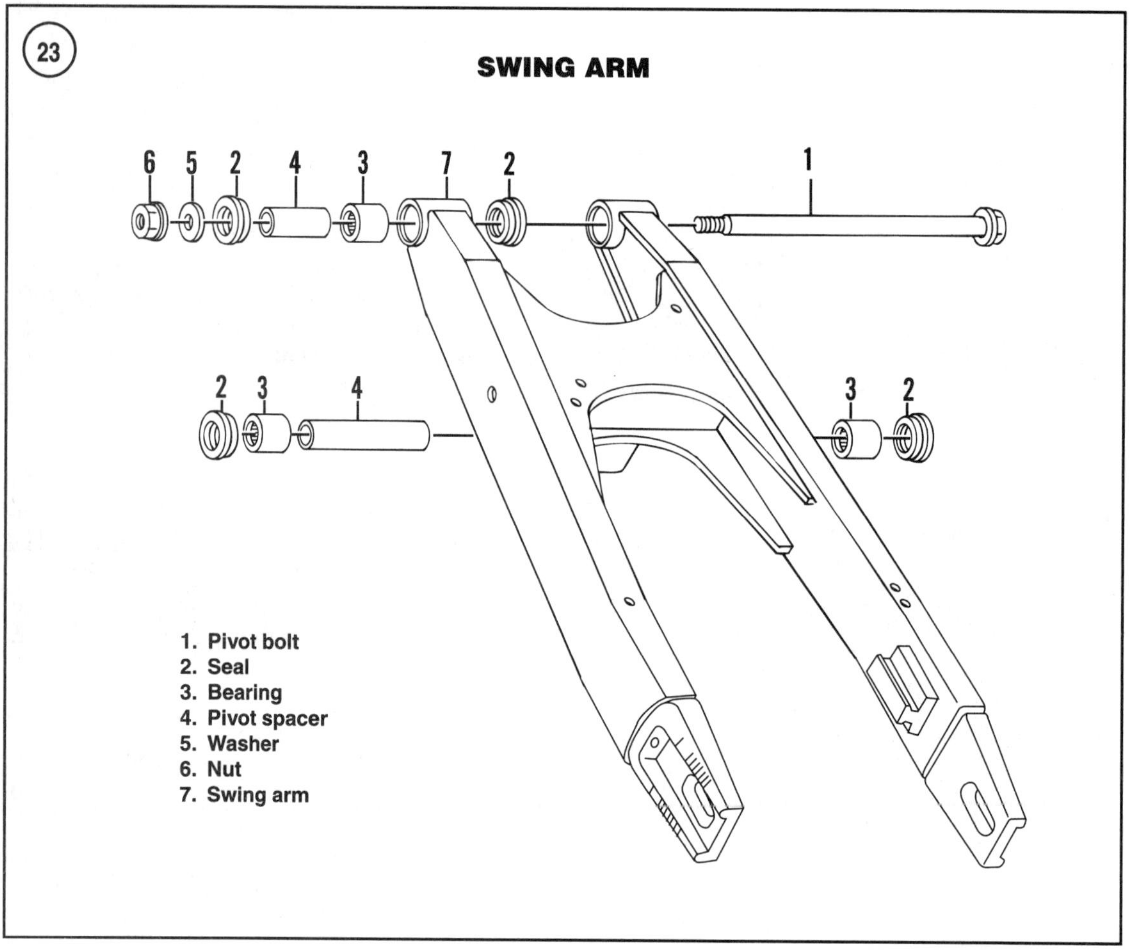

CHAPTER THIRTEEN

SWING ARM

1. Pivot bolt
2. Seal
3. Bearing
4. Pivot spacer
5. Washer
6. Nut
7. Swing arm

1. Remove the rear wheel as described in Chapter Eleven.
2. Loosen the swing arm pivot shaft nut (**Figure 21**), and then tighten it to 88 N•m (65 ft.-lb.).
3. Remove the upper lever arm pivot bolt (**Figure 22**) from the swing arm and lever arms.
4. Separate the linkage so the swing arm action is only influenced by the swing arm pivot bolt.
5. Check the bearings as follows:
   a. Have an assistant steady the motorcycle.
   b. Grasp the ends of the swing arm and leverage it from side to side. There should be no detectable play in the bearings.
   c. Pivot the swing arm up and down, through its full travel. The bearings must pivot smoothly.
   d. If there is play or roughness in the bearings, remove the swing arm and inspect the bearing and pivot assembly for wear.
6. Reinstall the lever arms and tighten the upper lever arm pivot bolt to 98 N•m (72 ft.-lb.).

REAR SUSPENSION

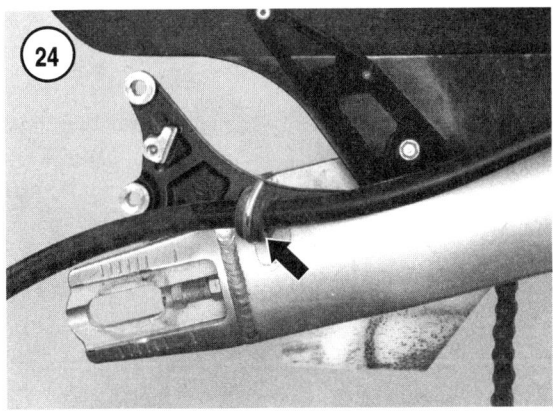

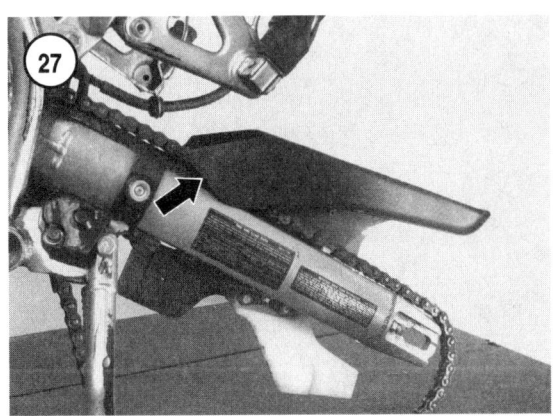

3. Remove the brake caliper bracket (**Figure 25**) from the swing arm.
4. Remove the hoses from the hose guide (**Figure 26**), or remove the hose guide and hoses.
5. Remove the lever arm pivot bolt (**Figure 22**).
6. Remove the nut and washer from the swing arm pivot shaft bolt (**Figure 21**).
7. Have an assistant hold the swing arm while the pivot shaft bolt is pulled from the swing arm. If using a drift to drive out the bolt, avoid damaging the bearing assemblies.
8. Pass the chain through the opening in the chain guard (**Figure 27**) so it is free of the swing arm.
9. Pull the swing arm out of the frame.
10. Inspect and service the swing arm as described in this chapter. If necessary, refer to *Shock Absorber Linkage* in this chapter for inspection and repair of the linkage.
11. Reverse the removal steps to install the swing arm while noting the following:
   a. Lubricate all bearings, seals and pivot bolts with grease.
   b. Check that the chain passes over and under the swing arm pivot shaft bolt.
   c. Install the pivot bolts in their correct direction.
   d. Tighten the swing arm pivot shaft bolt and nut to 88 N•m (65 ft.-lb.).
   e. Tighten the lever arm pivot bolt to 98 N•m (72 ft.-lb.).
   f. If the complete shock absorber linkage needs to be installed, raise the swing arm and wire it into position. This creates additional work space for installing the linkage. Optionally, install the linkage before installing the swing arm. Refer to *Shock Absorber Linkage* in this chapter for installation of the linkage.

Removal and Installation

If the components of the shock absorber linkage will be removed and inspected, remove or loosen all pivot bolts before removing the swing arm. The bolts are easier to loosen while the linkage is mounted on the motorcycle. Make note of the direction in which all pivot bolts are removed. Refer to **Figure 23**.

1. Remove the rear wheel as described in Chapter Eleven.
2. Disengage the brake hose from the guide (**Figure 24**) on the swing arm.

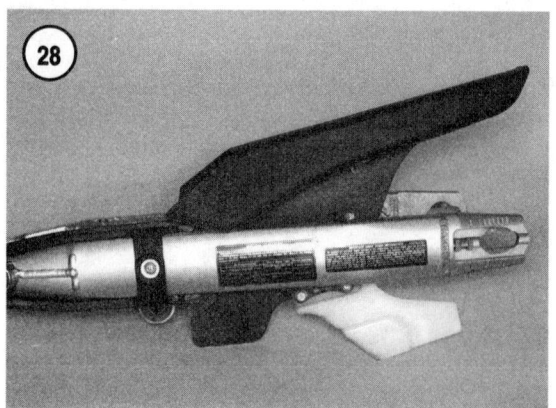

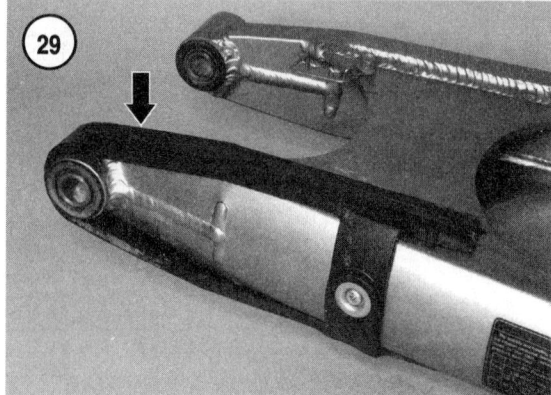

Inspection

When inspecting and cleaning the components, do not remove the bearing pivot spacers until the bearings will be inspected. The original bearings have rollers that are locked into the bearing housing. However, if aftermarket replacement bearings have been installed, the needle bearings may be held in place only by the grease on the bearings. Check that the spacers are firmly in place before inspecting. If necessary, tape the ends of the bearing bores.

Refer to **Figure 23**.

> *NOTE*
> *In the following procedures, whenever grease is referenced, a molybdenum disulfide or waterproof grease should be used. The manufacturer recommends molybdenum disulfide grease for all linkage bearings. This grease has excellent antiwear characteristics when subjected to extreme pressure. Waterproof grease, which is very durable, has a high tack and is very resistant to washout when subjected to wet conditions. The grease type used is a preference of the rider and is determined by the conditions in which the motorcycle is operated. If the linkage is regularly maintained, either type of grease will perform well.*

1. Clean the swing arm, particularly around all bearings.
2. Inspect the chain guard and chain guide (**Figure 28**).
    a. Check that all fasteners are tight.
    b. Check the chain guide for excessive wear.
3. Inspect the chain slider (**Figure 29**) and mounting bolts. Replace the slider if it is worn to more than half its thickness (**Figure 30**). Damage to the swing arm can occur if the slider wears through. Although not part of the swing arm, a small slider is located below the swing arm bolt, as the chain returns to the rear wheel. Check the condition of this slider.

> *NOTE*
> *Before servicing the bearings, removal of the chain guard and chain guide will make it easier to handle the swingarm.*

4. When working with each bearing(s), do the following:
    a. Remove the pivot spacer (**Figure 31**).
    b. Remove the seals (**Figure 32**). Pry the seals at their outer edge.

REAR SUSPENSION

c. Inspect the bearing rollers to determine if they are removable. Original equipment bearings are not removable. Some aftermarket bearings may be removable. If the rollers can be removed, put the rollers in a marked container so they can be reinstalled in their original housing.

5. Clean the bearings, spacers, seals and bores in solvent. Carefully dry all parts.
6. Inspect the following:
   a. Inspect the swing arm for cracks, particularly around the bearing bores.
   b. Check the swing arm pivot shaft bolt and nut for scoring, wear and other damage. Replace the nut and bolt if it has rounded flats. Proper torquing may not be achieved if the nut and bolt cannot be gripped securely.
   c. Check the fit of the pivot shaft bolt in the bushings, located at the back of the engine (**Figure 33**). If worn, use a drift to drive out both bushings. Replace with new bushings.
   d. Check the seals for cracks, wear or other damage.
   e. Check the pivot spacers for scoring, wear or other damage.
   f. Check the needle bearings for wear, flat spots, rust or discoloration. If the rollers are blue, overheating has occurred.
   g. Lightly lubricate the bearings and pivot spacers, and then insert each spacer into its respective bearing(s). The parts should turn freely and smoothly with no play. If play or roughness exists, replace the bearing set as described in *Swing Arm Bearing Replacement* (this section). When replacing bearing sets in the swing arm pivots, always replace the bushing (**Figure 34**) that fits into each side of the engine case.

7. Pack grease into the bearings and bores. Also apply grease to the seals, pivot spacers, swing arm bushings (at back of engine) and pivot bolts.
8. Press the seals into position by hand. If the seals do not seat, inspect the bearing depth. If necessary, adjust the depth of the bearing(s).
9. Install the pivot spacers. Grip the seals while twisting the pivot spacers into place.
10. If removed, install the chain guard and chain guide.
11. Install the swing arm as described in this section.

Bearing Replacement

Always replace both bearings if the bore contains two bearings. Replace both bearings in the swing arm. Mixing new and worn bearings on the same pivot bolt will shorten the life of the new part.

It is recommended to remove the bearings with a press. If the bearings and bores are not corroded, hand tools and a drawbolt can be used. The following procedures describe bearing removal and installation using both methods. Do not perform the following procedures until all seals, spacers and guards have been removed from the swing arm. Read both procedures to determine which method is most practical. If in doubt, take the swing arm to a dealership or machine shop to have the bearings replaced.

CHAPTER THIRTEEN

WARNING
If heat will be used to ease the removal of the bearings, take care to prevent burning finished or combustible surfaces. Refer to Chapter One for bearing removal and installation information.

Press method

1. Apply penetrating oil to the bearing(s) and bore.
2. If necessary, heat the immediate area around the bearing(s) to be removed.
3. Support the swing arm in a press. Place the bearing bore over a large socket or similar tool (A, **Figure 35**) so the bearing can be driven out of the bore. The lower socket fits on the perimeter of the bore, but is also large enough to accept the removed bearing.
4. Pass a driver (B, **Figure 35**) through the upper swing arm bore and to the lower bore.
5. Place a socket or driver (C, **Figure 35**) squarely against the bearing. The driver must be capable of passing through the bore, and be longer than the bore depth.
6. Press the bearing out of the arm. Turn the swing arm over and repeat for the other arm.
7. Clean and inspect the mounting bores.
8. Lubricate the new bearings with grease.
9. Support the swing arm bore on a flat stable surface. The lower socket is not required.
10. Fit the new bearing squarely over the bore with the manufacturer's marks facing out.
11. Place a socket or driver squarely against the bearing and drive the bearing into the swing arm. As the bearing driver begins to enter the bore (**Figure 36**), frequently check the bearing depth (**Figure 37**). All bearings in the swing arm should be driven 5 mm (0.20 in.) below the outer edge of the bore. The depth is required so the seals can be seated in the bore.
12. Drive in the remaining bearings.
13. Refer to *Swing Arm Inspection* in this section to complete the assembly.

Hand tool method

The following procedure requires a drawbolt-type of bearing removal/installation tool (Motion Pro Part No. 08-213 [**Figure 38**]). An equivalent tool can be made from a bolt, nut, washers, and sockets. The driver is a socket capable of passing through the bore, yet is longer than the bore depth. The larger socket fits on the perimeter of the bore, but is also large neough to accept the removed bearing(s).

1. Apply penetrating oil to the bearing(s) and bore.
2. If necessary, heat the immediate area around the bearing(s) to be removed.

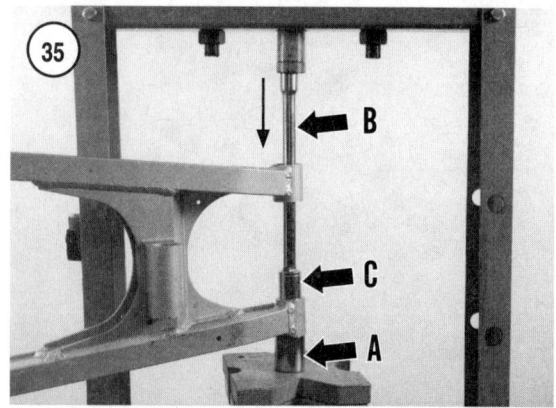

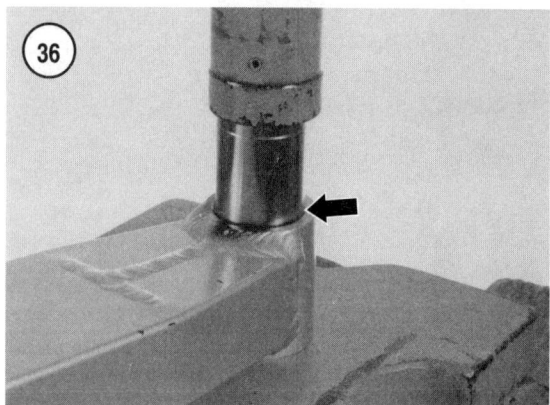

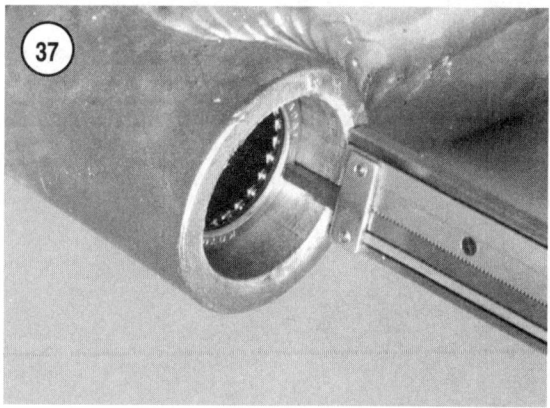

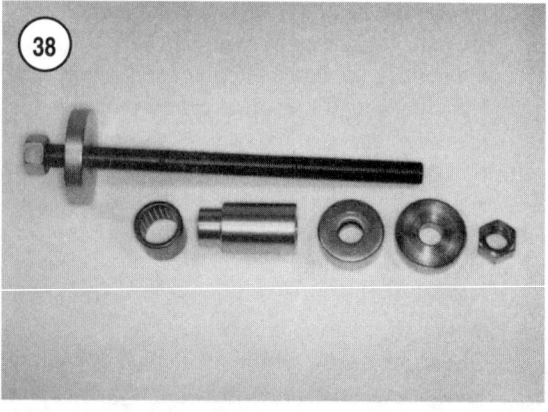

REAR SUSPENSION

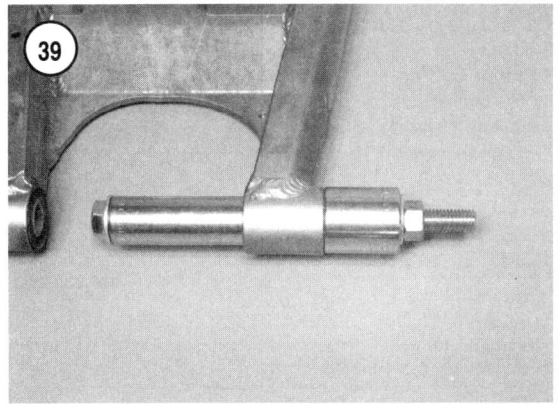

9. Reverse the direction of the tool and hand-tighten the nut until the tool and bearing are squarely positioned with the bore. Note that a large-diameter, thick washer can be substituted for the large socket to make handling the assembly easier.

10. Drive the bearing into the swing arm. As the bearing driver begins to enter the bore, frequently check the bearing depth (**Figure 37**). All bearings in the swing arm should be driven to 5 mm (0.20 in.) below the outer edge of the bore. The depth is required so the seals can be seated in the bore.

11. Drive the remaining bearings,

12. Refer to *Swing Arm Inspection* in this section to complete assembly.

SHOCK ABSORBER ADJUSTMENT

Shock Spring Preload Adjustment

Shock spring preload affects handling and ride quality, and should be adjusted to accommodate the load on the motorcycle. Spring preload can be adjusted with the shock absorber mounted on the motorcycle.

1. Refer to **Table 2** for the recommended settings. Higher settings increase preload.
2. To access the preload adjuster, near the top of the shock absorber, do the following:
   a. Remove the left side cover as described in Chapter Fifteen.
   b. On California models, remove the liquid/vapor separator.
3. Turn the adjuster (**Figure 40**) to the desired numerical setting.
4. Install the removed parts.

Rebound Damping Adjustment

Rebound damping controls the rate of extension of the shock absorber after it has been compressed. This setting has no effect on the compression rate of the shock. If rebound damping is set too high, the rear suspension will not extend quickly enough to prevent bottoming on subsequent bumps. Rebound damping that is set too low can cause unstable handling due to rear wheel kick-up.

1. Refer to **Table 2** for the recommended settings.
2. Turn the rebound damper adjuster (**Figure 41**) to the desired numerical setting. Turning the screw clockwise increases damping force. Standard setting for a 150-pound rider is one turn out (counterclockwise) from the full-in position.

3. Assemble the tool as shown in **Figure 39**.
4. Hand-tighten the nut until the assembly is squarely positioned against the bearing and swing arm contact points.
5. Turn the nut and drive the bearing(s) into the large socket.
6. Clean and inspect the bearing bore.
7. Lubricate the new bearings with grease.
8. Align the bearing squarely on the outside face of the bore. The manufacturer's marks on the bearing must face out. For bores that contain two bearings, install each bearing from its nearest end of the bore.

Table 1 REAR SUSPENSION SPECIFICATIONS

Suspension	Uni-Trak, link type
Suspension	185 mm (7.28 in.)
Shock absorber	Nitrogen-charged, adjustable for preload and rebound damping

Table 2 SHOCK ABSORBER SETTINGS*

Spring preload	1st position
Rebound damping	1 turn out

*Standard setting for a rider weighing 68 kg (150 lb.) with no passenger and no load.

Table 3 REAR SUSPENSION TORQUE SPECIFICATIONS

	N•m	in.-lb.	ft.-lb.
Front footpeg bolts	25	–	18
Lever arm pivot bolts	98	–	72
Lever-to-frame pivot bolt	98	–	72
Lower engine mounting bolt	44	–	32
Rear axle nut	98	–	72
Shock absorber mounting bolts			
Upper	59	–	43
Lower	98	–	72
Swing arm pivot shaft bolt and nut	88	–	65

CHAPTER FOURTEEN

BRAKES

This chapter covers service, repair and replacement procedures for the front and rear disc brake systems. Brake specifications are located in **Table 1** and **Table 2** at the end of this chapter.

> *WARNING*
> *After any brake service, make sure the brakes operate correctly before riding the motorcycle. Excessive brake lever travel or a spongy feeling may indicate the brake(s) must be bled as described in this chapter.*

BRAKE FLUID SELECTION

When adding brake fluid, use clean DOT 4 brake fluid from a sealed container. DOT 4 brake fluid is glycol-based and draws moisture, which greatly reduces its ability to perform correctly. Purchase brake fluid in small containers and discard small leftover quantities. Do not store a container of brake fluid with less than 1/4 of the fluid remaining.

Do not reuse drained fluid. Discard old fluid properly.

> *CAUTION*
> *Do not intermix silicone-based (DOT 5) brake fluid with glycol-based (DOT 4) brake fluid as it can cause brake system failure.*

BRAKE SERVICE

The disc brake system transmits hydraulic pressure from the master cylinder to the brake caliper. This pressure is transmitted from the caliper to the brake pads, which grip both sides of the brake disc and slow the motorcycle. As the pads wear, the caliper piston moves out of the caliper bore to automatically compensate for pad wear. As the piston moves the fluid level in the reservoir goes down. Additional fluid must be added to maintain the proper level.

Proper service includes carefully performed procedures and a clean work environment. Debris that enters the system can damage the components and cause poor brake performance. Do not use sharp tools while servicing the master cylinder, caliper or piston. Any damage to these components could cause a loss of hydraulic pressure in the system. If there is any doubt about having the ability to correctly and safely service the brake system, have a professional technician perform the task.

Consider the following when servicing the brake system:

1. When properly maintained, hydraulic components rarely require disassembly. Make sure it is necessary.
2. Keep the reservoir covers in place to prevent the entry of moisture and debris.
3. Clean parts with fresh DOT 4 brake fluid, an aerosol brake parts cleaner or denatured alcohol. Never use petroleum-based solvents on internal brake system components. They cause seals to swell and distort.

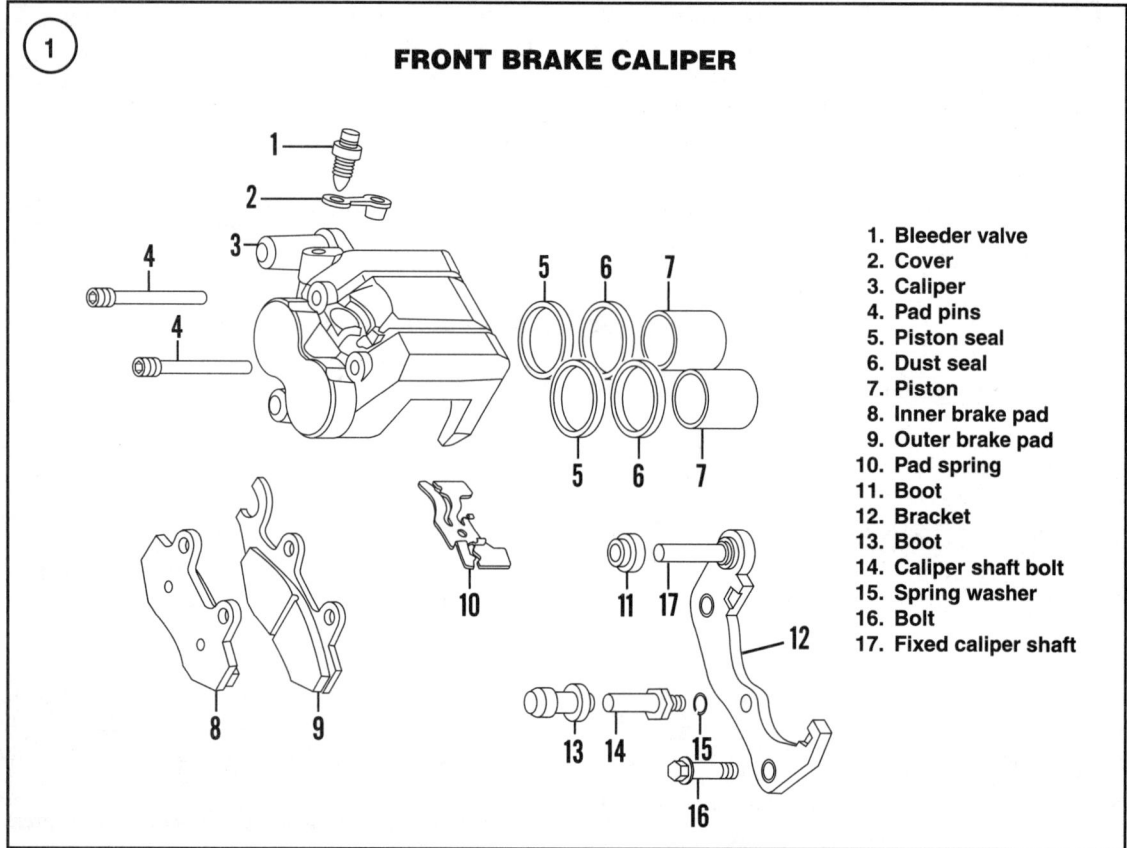

1. FRONT BRAKE CALIPER

1. Bleeder valve
2. Cover
3. Caliper
4. Pad pins
5. Piston seal
6. Dust seal
7. Piston
8. Inner brake pad
9. Outer brake pad
10. Pad spring
11. Boot
12. Bracket
13. Boot
14. Caliper shaft bolt
15. Spring washer
16. Bolt
17. Fixed caliper shaft

4. Do not allow brake fluid to contact plastic, painted or plated parts. It will damage the surface.
5. Dispose of brake fluid properly.
6. If the hydraulic system has been opened (not including the reservoir cover), it must be bled to remove air from the system. Refer to *Brake System Bleeding* in this chapter.

WARNING
Do not add to or replace the brake fluid with silicone-based (DOT 5) brake fluid. It is not compatible with the system and may cause brake failure.

WARNING
Whenever working on the brake system, do not inhale brake dust. It may contain asbestos, which can cause lung injury and cancer. Wear a facemask that meets OSHA requirements for trapping asbestos particles, and wash hands and forearms thoroughly after completing the work.

WARNING
NEVER use compressed air to clean any part of the brake system. This releases the harmful brake pad dust. Use an aerosol brake cleaner to clean parts when servicing any component still installed on the motorcycle.

FRONT BRAKE PADS

Brake pad life depends on the riding habits of the rider and the type of material used to manufacture the brake pads. Replace the pads when they are worn to within 1 mm (0.040 in.) of the backing plate, or if they have been contaminated with oil or other chemicals.

Removal/Installation

The brake pads can only be replaced by removing the caliper from the fork leg. Brake hose disconnection is not necessary. Keep the caliper supported and do not allow it to hang from the brake hose. When replacing brake pads, replace both pads as a set.

If the caliper will be rebuilt, or, if other damage is detected during this procedure, the pads can be removed when the caliper is at the workbench. Refer to *Front Brake Caliper* in this chapter for complete removal, repair and installation prodecures. Refer to **Figure 1**.

1. Loosen the pad pins (A, **Figure 2**).

BRAKES

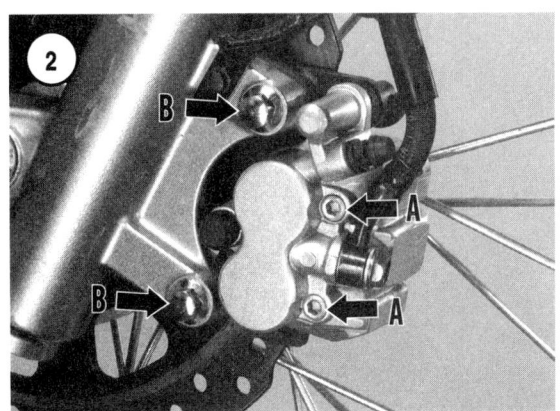

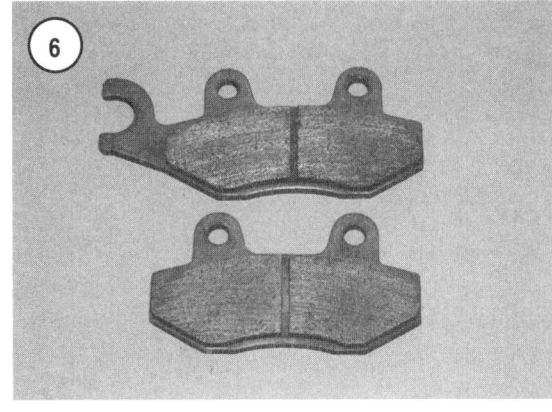

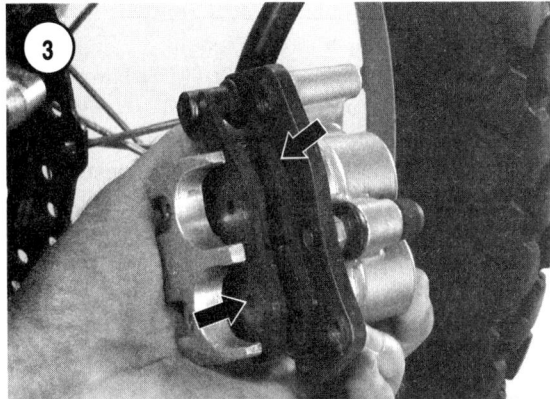

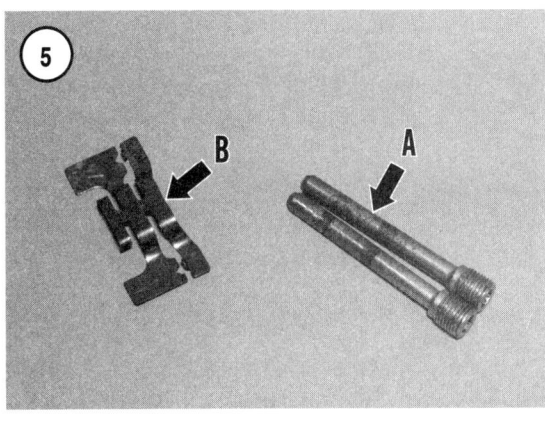

2. Remove the caliper mounting bolts (B, **Figure 2**). Remove the caliper from the disc. Avoid kinking the brake hose.

3. Remove the pad pins, and then remove the pads (**Figure 3**).

CAUTION
When pressing in the pistons, monitor the level of fluid in the master cylinder reservoir. Brake fluid will back flow to the reservoir when the caliper piston is pressed into the bore. Do not allow brake fluid to spill from the reservoir, or damage can occur to painted and plastic surfaces. Immediately clean up any spills, flooding the area with water.

NOTE
Do not operate the brake lever with the pads removed. Doing so may force the caliper piston out of the bore.

4. Press the caliper pistons back into the bore to create room for the new pads.

5. Remove the pad spring (A, **Figure 4**).

6. Clean the interior of the caliper and inspect for the following:
   a. Leaks or damage around the piston, bleeder valve and hose connection.
   b. Damaged or missing boots.
   c. Excessive drag of the caliper bracket when it is moved in and out of the caliper. If corrosion or water is detected around the rubber boots, clean the parts and lubricate with lithium-base grease.

7. Inspect the pad pins (A, **Figure 5**) and pad spring (B). The pins and spring must be in good condition to allow the inner pad to move slightly when installed. Check that both small tabs on the spring are not corroded or missing.

8. Inspect the pads (**Figure 6**) for wear and damage.

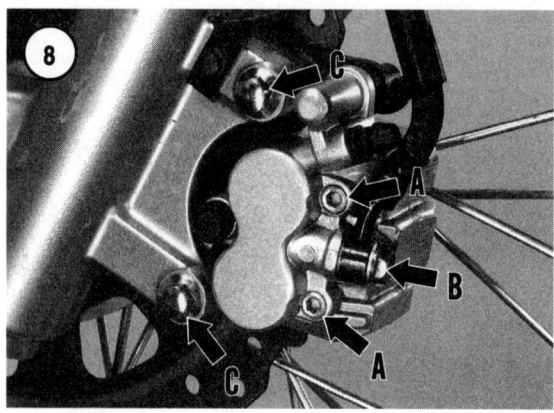

a. Replace the pads when they are worn to within 1 mm (0.040 in.) of the backing plate, as shown by the wear indicator (**Figure 7**). Always replace pads that are contaminated with oil or other chemicals.
b. If the pads are worn unevenly, the caliper is probably not sliding correctly on the caliper bracket. The caliper must be free to float on the slide pin and retainer bolt. Buildup or corrosion on the parts can hold the caliper in one position, causing brake drag and excessive pad wear.

9. Install the pad spring so the small tabs (B, **Figure 4**) are on the outer side.
10. Install the inner pad, seating the pad under the caliper bracket and against the piston.
11. Install the outer pad.
12. Align and install the pad pins. Do not tighten the pins completely until after the caliper is installed.
13. Spread the pads so there is clearance to fit the caliper over the brake disc.
14. Position the caliper over the brake disc and hub assembly, and then slide the caliper down around the brake disc.
15. Install and tighten the front caliper mounting bolts to 34 N•m (25 ft.-lb.).
16. Tighten the pad pins to 17 N•m (12.5 ft.-lb.).
17. Operate the front brake lever several times to seat the pads.
18. Check the brake fluid reservoir and replenish or remove fluid as necessary.

FRONT BRAKE CALIPER

Removal/Installation

1. If the brake pads will be removed, loosen the pad pins (A, **Figure 8**).
2. If the caliper will be disconnected from the brake hose, drain the system as described in this chapter. After draining, remove the brake hose banjo bolt (B, **Figure 8**) and both washers. Tie a plastic bag around the end of the hose.

3A. If the caliper will be removed from the motorcycle, remove the caliper mounting bolts (C, **Figure 8**).
3B. If the caliper will be left attached to the brake hose:
a. Remove the caliper mounting bolts (C, **Figure 8**) and secure the caliper with a length of wire. Do not allow the caliper to hang by the brake hose.

NOTE
Use a spacer block to prevent the pistons from being forced out of the caliper if the front brake lever is applied with the brake caliper removed.

b. Insert a spacer block between the brake pads.
4. Service the caliper as described in this section.
5. Reverse the removal procedure to install the caliper while noting the following:
a. Install and tighten the front caliper mounting bolts to 34 N•m (25 ft.-lb.).
b. Install new seal washers on the banjo bolt. Position the pin on the brake hose end against the boss on the caliper. Tighten the banjo bolt to 25 N•m (18 ft.-lb.).
c. If the caliper was rebuilt, or the brake hose disconnected from the caliper, fill and bleed the brake system as described in this chapter.
d. If removed, install the brake pads. Then, install the pad pins and tighten the pins to 17 N•m (12.5 ft.-lb.).
e. Operate the front brake lever several times to seat the pads.
f. Check the brake fluid reservoir and replenish or remove fluid, as necessary.

Disassembly

Refer to **Figure 1**.

Removing the pistons hydraulically

If the piston and dust seals are in good condition and there are no signs of brake fluid leaking from the

BRAKES

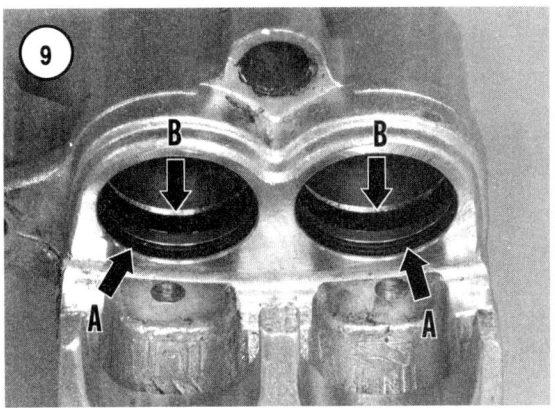

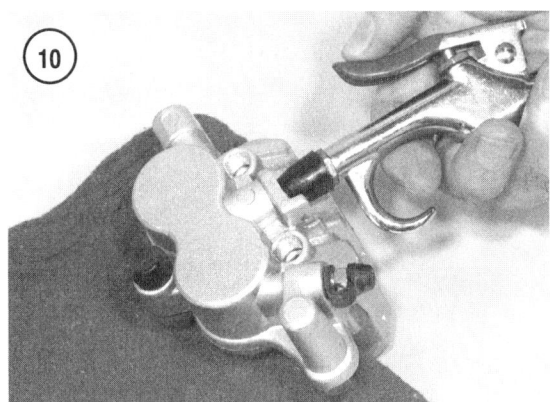

bores, it may be possible to remove the pistons hydraulically. However, note that brake fluid will spill from the caliper once the pistons are free.

Read this procedure through to understand the steps and tools required.

1. Remove the front brake caliper as described in this section. Do not loosen or remove the brake hose.
2. Remove the pads, pad spring and caliper bracket from the caliper.

NOTE
Have a supply of paper towels and a drain pan available to catch and wipe up spilled brake fluid.

3. Hold the caliper with the pistons facing down and slowly operate the brake lever to push the pistons out of their bores. If both pistons move evenly, continue until they extend far enough to be removed by hand.
4. If the pistons do not move evenly, perform the following:
   a. Stop and push the extended piston back into its bore by hand, so that both pistons are even.
   b. Operate the brake lever again. If the results are the same, reposition the extended piston again, and operate the brake lever while preventing the moving piston from extending. Install a strip of wood across the caliper to block the moving piston.
   c. If the other piston now starts to move, continue with this technique until both pistons move evenly and can be gripped and removed by hand.
   d. After removing the pistons, hold the caliper over the drain pan to catch the brake fluid draining through the caliper.
5. Remove the banjo bolt with an impact gun (air or electric), if available. Otherwise, hold the caliper in a secure manner and remove the banjo bolt with hand tools. If the caliper cannot be held securely to remove the bolt, stuff paper towels into the caliper bores to absorb brake fluid leaking from the hose and reservoir. Temporarily reinstall the caliper bracket and mount the caliper onto the slider with its mounting bolts to hold it in place. Then, remove the banjo bolt and both washers.
6. Use a small wooden or plastic tool and remove the dust seals (A, **Figure 9**) and piston seals (B) from the caliper bore grooves and discard them.
7. Remove the bleeder valve and its cover from the caliper.
8. Clean and inspect the brake caliper assembly as described in this section.

Removing the pistons with compressed air

1. Remove the brake caliper as described in this section.
2. Remove the pads, pad spring, and the caliper bracket from the caliper.
3. Remove the banjo bolt with an impact gun (air or electric), if available. Otherwise, hold the caliper in a secure manner and remove the banjo bolt with hand tools. If the caliper cannot be held securely to remove the bolt, stuff paper towels into the caliper bores to absorb brake fluid leaking from the hose and reservoir. Temporarily reinstall the caliper bracket and mount the caliper onto the slider with its mounting bolts to hold it in place, then remove the banjo bolt and both washers.
4. Make sure the bleeder valve is closed so air cannot escape.

WARNING
Wear eye protection when using compressed air to remove the pistons, and keep your fingers away from the piston.

CAUTION
Do not try to pry out the piston. This will damage the piston and caliper bore.

5. Cushion the caliper pistons with a shop rag and position the caliper with the piston bores facing down. Apply compressed air through the brake hose port (**Figure 10**) to pop the pistons out. If one piston sticks, block the other piston and reapply the compressed air.

6. Use a small wooden or plastic tool and remove the dust seals (A, **Figure 9**) and piston seals (B) from the caliper bore grooves and discard them.
7. Remove the bleeder valve and its cover from the caliper.
8. Clean and inspect the brake caliper assembly as described in this section.

Assembly

NOTE
Use clean DOT 4 brake fluid when lubricating the piston seals, pistons and caliper bores.

1. Install the bleeder valve and its cover into the caliper.
2. Soak the new piston seals and dust seals in brake fluid.
3. Lubricate the cylinder bores with brake fluid.

NOTE
*The piston seals (A, **Figure 11**) are thicker than the dust seals (B).*

4. Install a new piston seal (B, **Figure 9**) into each rear bore groove.

NOTE
Make sure each seal fits squarely inside its bore groove.

5. Install a new dust seal (A, **Figure 9**) into each front bore groove.
6. Lubricate the pistons with brake fluid.

CAUTION
The tight piston-to-seal fit can make piston installation difficult. Do not install the pistons by pushing them straight in as they may bind in their bores and tear the seals.

7. With the open side facing out, align a piston with the caliper bore. Rock the piston slightly to center it in the bore while at the same time pushing the lower end past the seals. When the lower end of the piston passes through both seals, push and bottom the piston (**Figure 12**) in the bore. After installing the other piston, clean spilled brake fluid from the area in front of the pistons to prevent brake pad contamination.

CAUTION
Use only lithium-base grease specified for brake use. Do not use brake fluid to lubricate the rubber boots or fixed shafts.

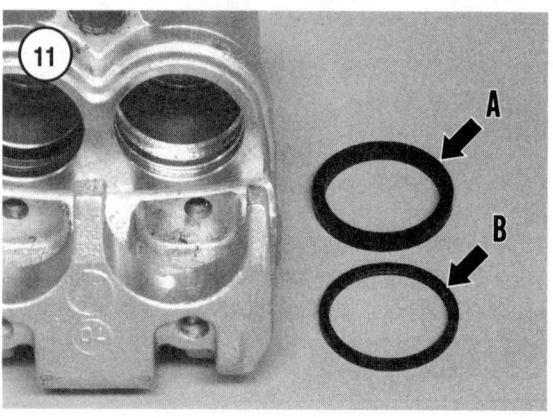

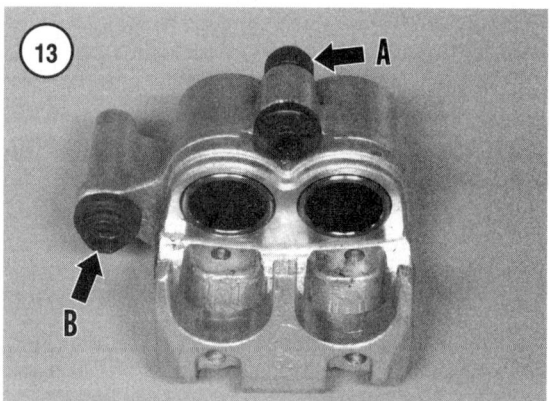

8. Pinch the open end of the large rubber boot (A, **Figure 13**) and push this end through the mounting hole in the caliper until its outer shoulder bottoms. Make sure the boot opening faces toward the inside of the caliper. Partially fill the boot with lithium-base grease.
9. Install the small boot (B, **Figure 13**) into the groove in the caliper. Partially fill the boot with lithium-base grease.
10. If removed, install the shaft bolt into the caliper bracket. Note the location of the short caliper shaft bolt (**Figure 14**) and lockwasher. Tighten the caliper shaft bolt to 17 N•m (12.5 ft.-lb.).

BRAKES

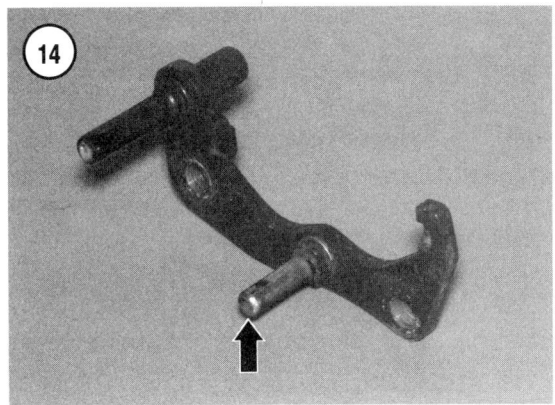

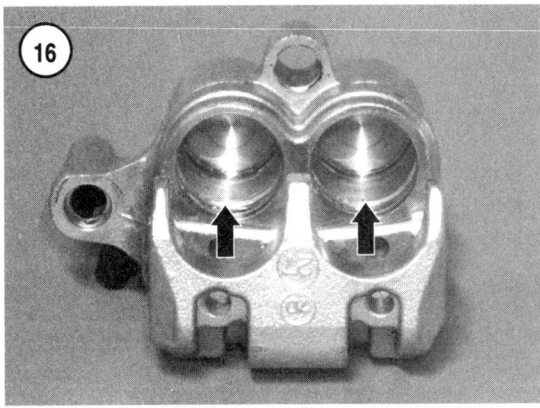

11. Lubricate the caliper bracket shafts with lithium-base grease.

12. Align and slide the mounting bracket (**Figure 15**) onto the caliper body. Hold the caliper and slide the caliper bracket in and out by hand. Make sure there is no roughness or binding.

13. Install the brake caliper assembly and brake pads as described in this chapter.

Inspection

The brake is a floating caliper design, where the caliper slides or floats on shafts mounted parallel with each other on the caliper and caliper bracket. One shaft is a bolt that threads into the caliper bracket, while the other shaft remains fixed. Rubber boots around each shaft prevent dirt from damaging the shafts. If the shafts are worn or damaged, the caliper can move out of alignment on the caliper bracket. This will cause brake drag, uneven pad wear and overheating. Inspect the rubber boots and shafts during caliper inspection as they play a vital role in brake performance.

Refer to **Figure 1** when servicing the front brake caliper assembly. Replace parts that are out of specification (**Table 1**) or damaged as described in this section.

WARNING
Do not allow oil or grease on the brake components. Do not clean the parts with kerosene or other petroleum products. These chemicals cause the rubber brake system components to swell, which may cause brake failure.

CAUTION
The caliper bore and seal grooves can be difficult to clean, especially if brake fluid was leaking past the seals. Clean the grooves carefully to avoid damaging the grooves and bore surfaces.

1. Clean and dry the caliper and the other metal parts. Clean the seal grooves carefully. If the contamination is difficult to remove, soak the caliper in a suitable solvent and reclean. If any of the rubber parts are to be reused, clean them with denatured alcohol or clean DOT 4 brake fluid. Do not use a petroleum-based solvent.

2. Inspect the caliper bracket, shafts and rubber boots as follows:
   a. Inspect the rubber boots for cracks, tearing, weakness or other damage.
   b. Inspect the shafts (**Figure 14**) on the caliper bracket for excessive or uneven wear. If the shaft is damaged, replace the shaft or caliper bracket as needed.

3. Inspect each cylinder bore (**Figure 16**) for corrosion, pitting, deep scratches or other wear.

4. Inspect the pistons for wear marks, scoring, cracks or other damage.

5. Check the bleeder valve and cap for wear or damage. Make sure air can pass through the bleeder valve.

6. Check the banjo bolt for wear or damage. Discard the washers.

7. Inspect the brake pads and pad spring as described in *Front Brake Pads* (this chapter).

FRONT MASTER CYLINDER

Removal/Installation

1. Remove the right hand guard.
2. Remove the mirror.

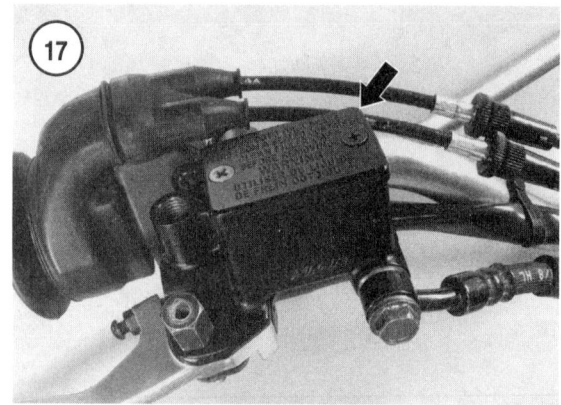

> *CAUTION*
> *Do not allow brake fluid to splash from the reservoir or hose. Brake fluid can damage painted and plastic surfaces. Immediately clean up any spills, flooding the area with water.*

3. Cover and protect the bodywork and area surrounding the master cylinder.
4. Drain the brake system as described in this chapter.
5. Remove the cap (**Figure 17**) and diaphragm and verify that the master cylinder is empty. Wipe the interior of the reservoir to absorb all remaining fluid.
6. Disconnect the two electrical connectors (A, **Figure 18**) from the front brake light switch.
7. If the master cylinder will be rebuilt, loosen the locknut (B, **Figure 18**) on the brake lever pivot bolt.
8. Disconnect the brake hose (C, **Figure 18**) from the master cylinder as follows:
    a. Remove the banjo bolt and seal washers from the brake hose. Have a shop cloth ready to absorb excess brake fluid that drips from the hose.
    b. Tie a plastic bag around the end of the hose.

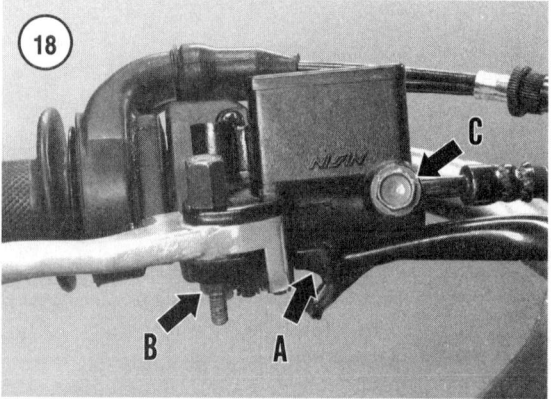

9. Remove the bolts (A, **Figure 19**) securing the master cylinder to the handlebar. Remove the master cylinder.
10. Disassemble and inspect the front master cylinder as described in this section.
11. Reverse the removal procedure to install the master cylinder. Note the following:
    a. The mounting bracket must be installed so UP and the arrow (B, **Figure 19**) are facing up.
    b. Position the master cylinder so the clamp joint aligns with the punch mark (**Figure 20**) on the handlebar.
    c. Tighten the upper clamp bolt first, and then the bottom clamp bolt. Tighten the clamp bolts to 8.8 N•m (78 in.-lb.).
    d. Install new seal washers on the banjo bolt. Tighten the banjo bolt to 25 N•m (18 ft.-lb.).
    e. Check that the brake light operates when the lever is operated.

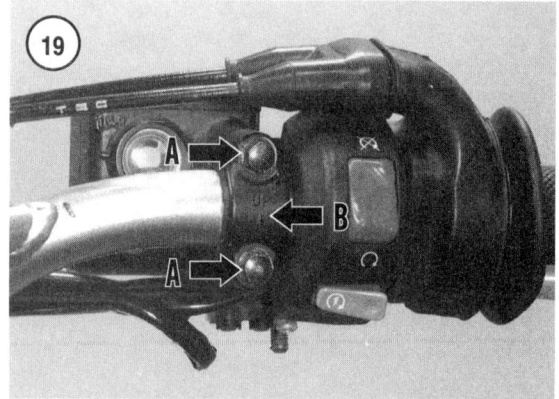

12. Fill the brake fluid reservoir and bleed the brake system as described in this chapter.

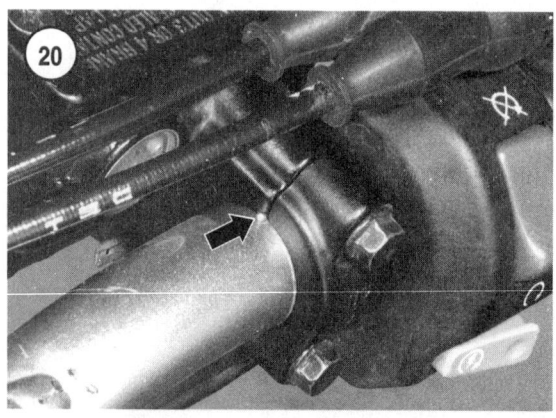

Disassembly/Reassembly/Inspection

Refer to **Figure 21**. Use the following procedure to disassemble, inspect and assemble the master cyl-

BRAKES

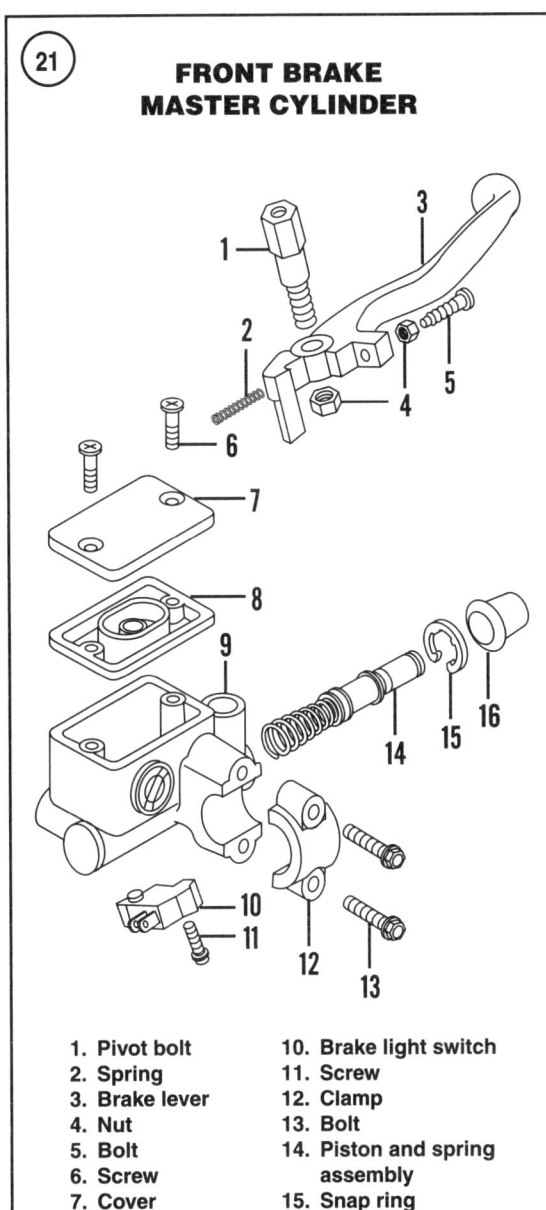

FRONT BRAKE MASTER CYLINDER

1. Pivot bolt
2. Spring
3. Brake lever
4. Nut
5. Bolt
6. Screw
7. Cover
8. Diaphragm
9. Master cylinder
10. Brake light switch
11. Screw
12. Clamp
13. Bolt
14. Piston and spring assembly
15. Snap ring
16. Boot

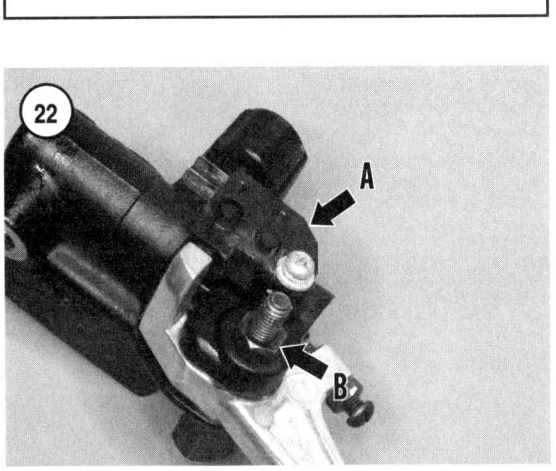

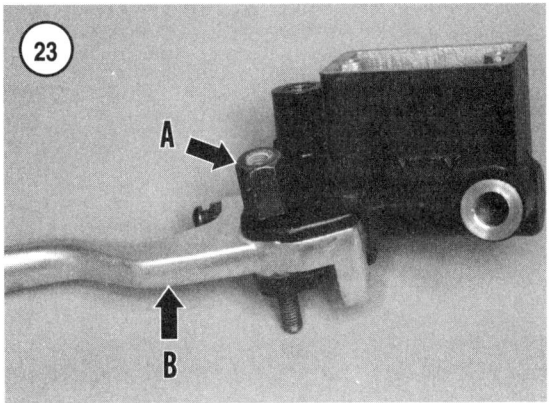

inder. The piston, seals and spring are only available as a complete assembly.

1. Remove the master cylinder as described in this section.
2. Remove the mounting screw and brake switch (A, **Figure 22**).
3. Remove the brake lever pivot bolt locknut (B, **Figure 22**).
4. Remove the pivot bolt (A, **Figure 23**) and brake lever (B).
5. Remove the lever spring (**Figure 24**) from the master cylinder.
6. Remove the boot (**Figure 25**) from the piston. The boot is a friction fit. To avoid damaging the boot

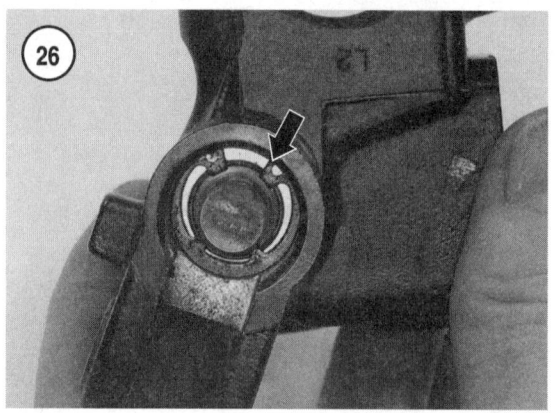

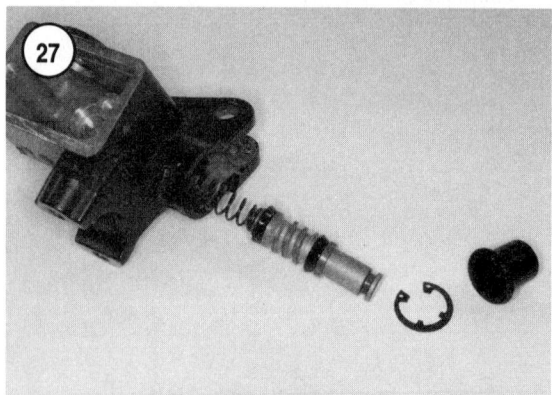

on removal, apply penetrating lubricant around the perimeter of the boot. Carefully pull the bottom edge back so the lubricant can loosen the boot.

7. Remove the snap ring (**Figure 26**) from the master cylinder as follows:
   a. Press down on the piston to relieve pressure on the snap ring, and then remove the snap ring.
   b. Slowly relieve the pressure on the piston.
8. Remove the piston assembly (**Figure 27**) from the bore.
9. Clean all parts that will be reused with fresh brake fluid or isopropyl (rubbing) alcohol.
10. Inspect the cylinder bore (**Figure 28**) for wear, pitting or corrosion.
11. Inspect and clean the threads and orifices in the reservoir. Clean with compressed air.
12. Inspect the diaphragm and reservoir cap for damage.
13. Inspect the brake lever pivot bolt hole and pivot bolt for wear or other damage.
14. Inspect the mounting hardware and banjo bolt for corrosion and damage. Install new seal washers on the banjo bolt.
15. Inspect the brake switch. Clean the switch with electrical contact cleaner by spraying into the holes (**Figure 29**) in the case. Operate the switch while flushing the contacts. If the switch condition is not known, attach an ohmmeter or continuity tester to the switch terminals. There should be continuity with the switch actuator out, and no continuity with the actuator depressed.
16. Assemble the piston, seals and spring (**Figure 30**) as follows:
   a. Soak the primary seal (A, **Figure 30**) and secondary seal (B) in fresh DOT 4 brake fluid for 15 minutes. This will soften and lubricate the seals.
   b. Apply brake fluid to the piston so the seals can slide over the ends.
   c. Mount the seals on the piston. Identify the wide (open) side of both seals. When installed, the wide side of the seals must face in the direction

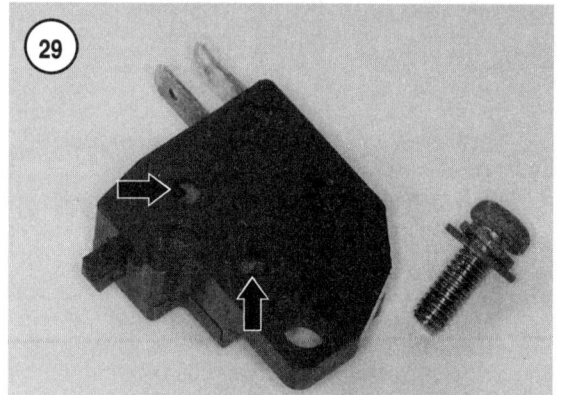

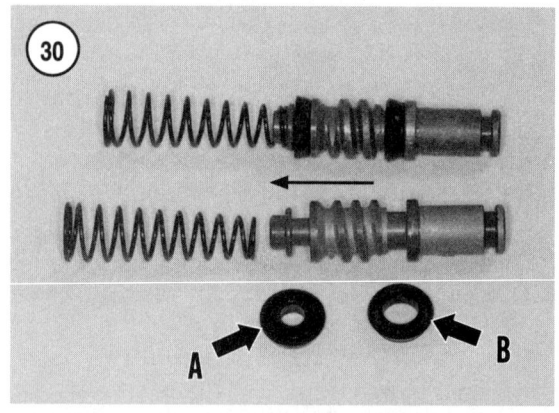

BRAKES

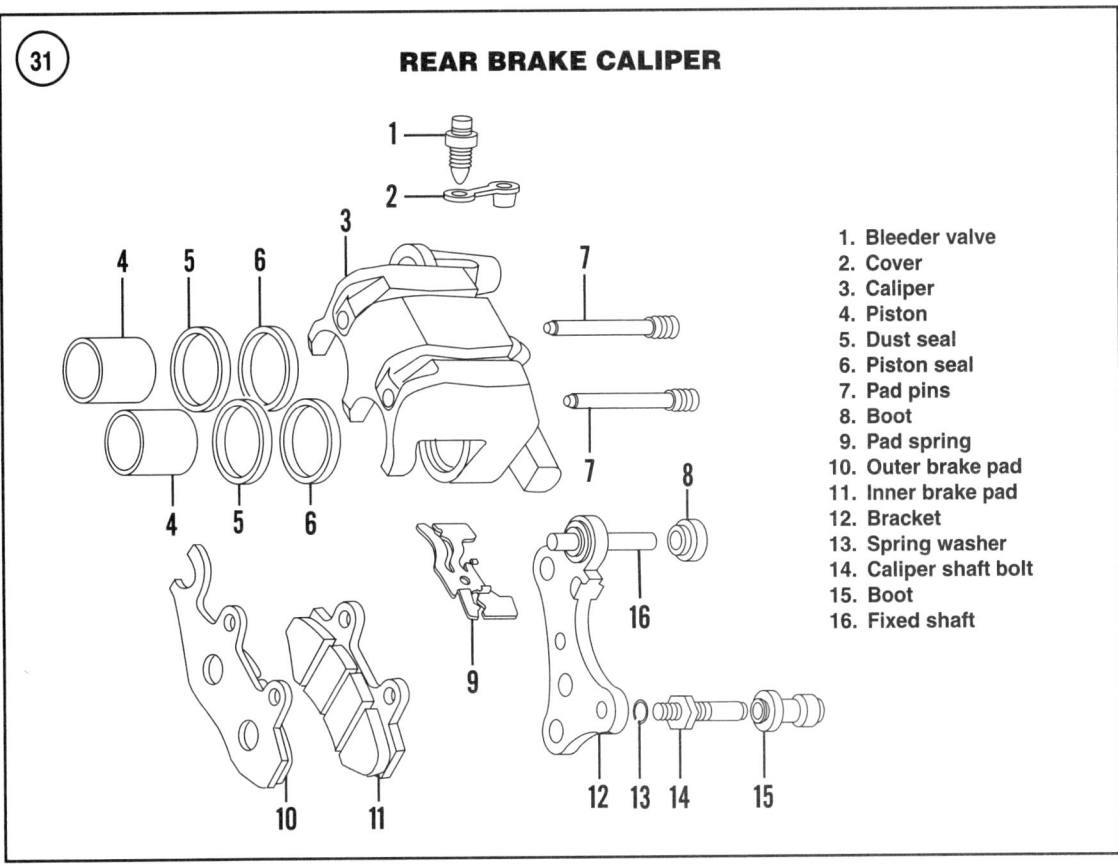

REAR BRAKE CALIPER

1. Bleeder valve
2. Cover
3. Caliper
4. Piston
5. Dust seal
6. Piston seal
7. Pad pins
8. Boot
9. Pad spring
10. Outer brake pad
11. Inner brake pad
12. Bracket
13. Spring washer
14. Caliper shaft bolt
15. Boot
16. Fixed shaft

of the arrow in **Figure 30**. Install the primary seal nearest the spring.

   d. Install and seat the spring onto the piston. The small spring end must contact the piston.

17. Install the piston and snap ring into the master cylinder as follows:

   a. Place the cylinder in a vise with soft jaws. Do not overtighten the vise or cylinder damage could occur.

   b. Lubricate the cylinder bore and piston assembly with clean brake fluid.

NOTE
After the piston cups have entered the cylinder, the piston should be held in place until the snap ring is installed. Anytime the cups come out of the cylinder there is a chance of damaging the cup lips during the reinsertion process. This should be avoided.

   c. Insert the piston assembly into the cylinder.

   d. While holding the piston in the cylinder, install the snap ring (**Figure 26**) so the flat side faces out.

18. Apply lithium-base grease to the inside of the boot. Seat the boot into the cylinder.

19. Install the lever and pivot bolt. Apply waterproof grease to the pivot bolt and lever contact point.

20. Install the diaphragm and cap onto the reservoir but do not tighten the screws.

21. Install the brake switch and mounting screw.

22. Install the master cylinder as described in this section.

REAR BRAKE PADS

Brake pad life depends on the riding habits of the rider and the type of material used to manufacture the brake pads. Replace the pads when they are worn to within 1 mm (0.040 in.) of the backing plate, or if they have been contaminated with oil or other chemicals.

Removal/Installation

The brake pads can only be replaced by removing the caliper from the swing arm. Brake hose disconnection is not necessary. Keep the caliper supported and do not allow it to hang from the brake hose. When replacing brake pads, replace both pads as a set.

If the caliper will be rebuilt, or if other damage is detected during this procedure, the pads can be removed when the caliper is at the workbench. Refer to *Rear Brake Caliper* in this chapter for complete removal, repair and installation procedures. Refer to **Figure 31**.

1. Loosen the pad pins (A, **Figure 32**).

2. Remove the hose guide mounting bolt (B, **Figure 32**) and guide.
3. Remove the caliper mounting bolts (C, **Figure 32**), and remove the caliper from the disc. Avoid kinking the brake hose.
4. Remove the pad pins, and then remove the pads (**Figure 33**).

CAUTION
When pressing in the pistons, monitor the level of fluid in the master cylinder reservoir. Brake fluid will back flow to the reservoir when the caliper piston is pressed into the bore. Do not allow brake fluid to spill from the reservoir, or damage can occur to painted and plastic surfaces. Immediately clean up any spills, flooding the area with water.

NOTE
Do not operate the brake pedal with the pads removed. Doing so may force the caliper pistons out of the bores.

5. Press the caliper pistons back in their bores to create room for the new pads.
6. Remove the pad spring (A, **Figure 34**).
7. Clean the interior of the caliper and inspect for the following:
   a. Leaks or damage around the piston, bleeder valve and hose connection.
   b. Damaged or missing boots.
   c. Excessive drag of the caliper bracket when it is moved in and out of the caliper. If corrosion or water is detected around the rubber boots, clean the parts and lubricate with lithium-base grease.
8. Inspect the pad pins (A, **Figure 35**) and pad spring (B). The pins and spring must be in good condition to allow the inner pad to move sightly when installed. Check that both small tabs on the spring are not corroded or missing.
9. Inspect the pads (**Figure 36**) for wear and damage.
   a. Replace the pads when they are worn to within 1 mm (0.040 in.) of the backing plate, as shown by the wear indicator (**Figure 37**). Always replace pads that are contaminated with oil or other chemicals.
   b. If the pads are worn unevenly, the caliper is probably not sliding correctly on the caliper bracket. The caliper must be free to float on the slide pin and retainer bolt. Buildup or corrosion on the parts can hold the caliper in one position, causing brake drag and excessive pad wear.
10. Install the pad spring so the small tabs (B, **Figure 34**) are on the outer side.
11. Install the inner pad, seating the pad under the caliper bracket and against the piston.

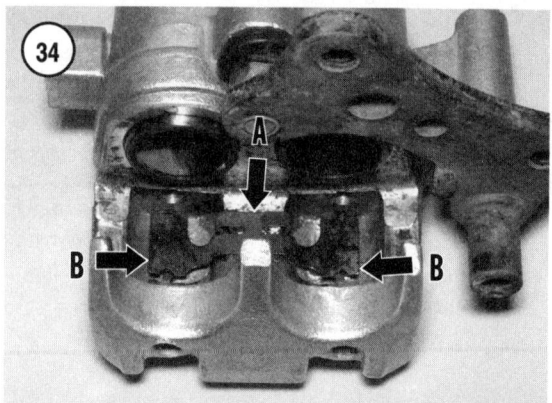

12. Install the outer pad.
13. Align and install the pad pins. Do not tighten the pins completely until after the caliper is installed.
14. Spread the pads so there is clearance to fit the caliper over the brake disc.
15. Position the caliper over the brake disc and hub assembly. Slide the caliper down around the brake disc.
16. Install and tighten the rear caliper mounting bolts to 25 N•m (18 ft.-lb.).
17. Tighten the pad pins to 17 N•m (12.5 ft.-lb.).
18. Install the hose guide and mounting bolt (B, **Figure 32**).

BRAKES

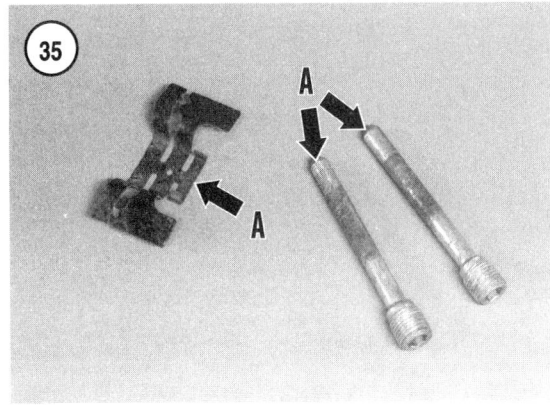

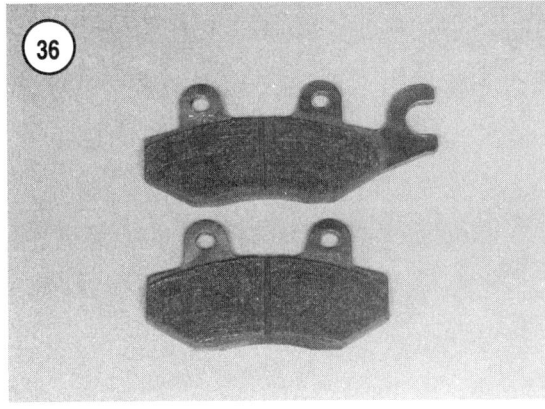

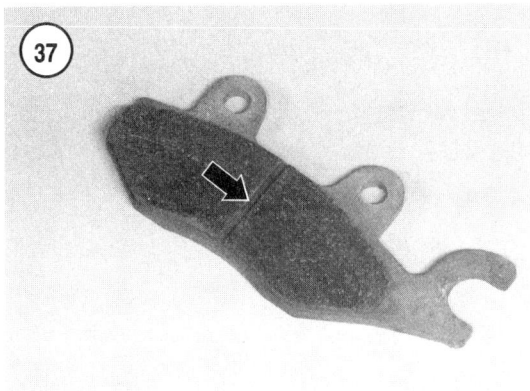

19. Operate the rear brake pedal several times to seat the pads.
20. Check the brake fluid reservoir and replenish or remove fluid as necessary.

REAR BRAKE CALIPER

Removal/Installation

1. If the brake pads will be removed, loosen the pad pins (A, **Figure 38**).
2. Remove the hose guide mounting bolt (B, **Figure 38**) and guide.
3. If the caliper will be disconnected from the brake hose, drain the system as described in this chapter. After draining, remove the brake hose banjo bolt (C, **Figure 38**) and both washers. Tie a plastic bag around the end of the hose.
4A. If the caliper will be removed from the motorcycle, remove the caliper mounting bolts (D, **Figure 38**).
4B. If the caliper will be left attached to the brake hose:
   a. Remove the caliper mounting bolts (D, **Figure 38**) and secure the caliper with a length of wire. Do not allow the caliper to hang by the brake hose.

NOTE
Use a spacer block to prevent the pistons from being forced out of the caliper if the rear brake pedal is applied with the brake caliper removed.

   b. Insert a spacer block between the brake pads.
5. Service the caliper as described in this chapter.
6. Reverse the removal procedure to install the caliper while noting the following:
   a. Install and tighten the rear caliper mounting bolts to 25 N•m (18 ft.-lb.).
   b. Install new seal washers on the banjo bolt. Position the pin on the brake hose end against the boss on the caliper, and tighten the banjo bolt to 25 N•m (18 ft.-lb.).
   c. If the caliper was rebuilt, or the brake hose disconnected from the caliper, fill and bleed the brake system as described in this chapter.
   d. If removed, install the brake pads. Install the pad pins and tighten the pins to 17 N•m (12.5 ft.-lb.).
   e. Operate the rear brake pedal several times to seat the pads.
   f. Check the brake fluid reservoir and replenish or remove fluid, as necessary.

Disassembly

Refer to **Figure 31**.

Removing the pistons hydraulically

If the piston and dust seals are in good condition and there are no signs of brake fluid leaking from the bores, it may be possible to remove the pistons hydraulically. However, note that brake fluid will spill from the caliper once the pistons are free.

Read this procedure through to understand the steps and tools required.

1. Remove the rear brake caliper as described in this section. Do not loosen or remove the brake hose.
2. Remove the pads, pad spring, and caliper bracket from the caliper.

NOTE
Have a supply of paper towels and a drain pan available to catch and wipe up spilled brake fluid.

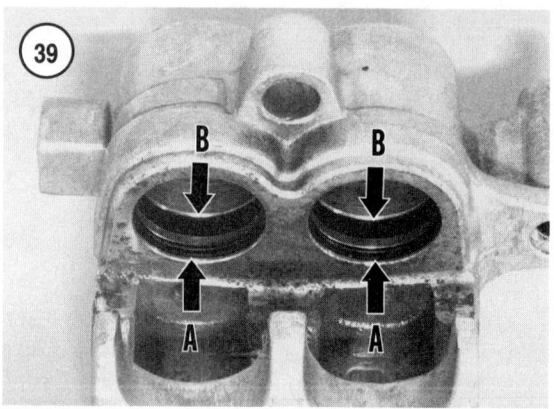

3. Hold the caliper with the pistons facing down and slowly operate the brake pedal to push the pistons out of their bores. If both pistons move evenly, continue until they extend far enough to be removed by hand.
4. If the pistons do not move evenly, perform the following:
   a. Stop and push the extended piston back into its bore by hand, so that both pistons are even.
   b. Operate the brake pedal again. If the results are the same, reposition the extended piston again, and operate the brake pedal while preventing the moving piston from extending. Install a strip of wood across the caliper to block the piston.
   c. If the other piston now starts to move, continue with this technique until both pistons move evenly and can be gripped and removed by hand.
   d. After removing the pistons, hold the caliper over the drain pan to catch the brake fluid draining through the caliper.

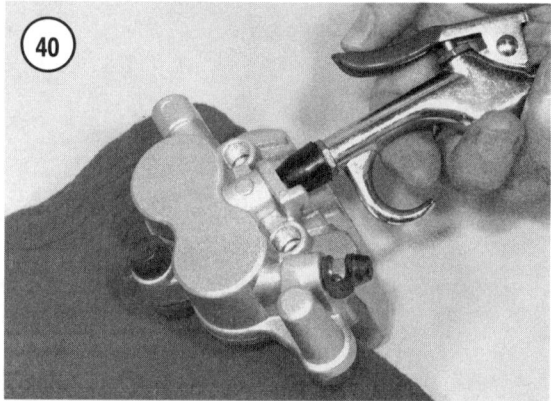

5. Remove the banjo bolt with an impact gun (air or electric), if available. Otherwise, hold the caliper in a secure manner and remove the banjo bolt with hand tools. If the caliper cannot be held securely to remove the bolt, stuff paper towels into the caliper bores to absorb brake fluid leaking from the hose and reservoir. Temporarily reinstall the caliper bracket and mount the caliper onto the swing arm with its mounting bolts to hold it in place. Remove the banjo bolt and both washers.
6. Use a small wooden or plastic tool and remove the dust seals (A, **Figure 39**) and piston seals (B) from the caliper bore grooves and discard them.
7. Remove the bleeder valve and its cover from the caliper.
8. Clean and inspect the brake caliper assembly as described in this section.

Removing the pistons with compressed air

1. Remove the brake caliper as described in this section.
2. Remove the pads, pad spring, and the caliper bracket from the caliper.
3. Remove the banjo bolt with an impact gun (air or electric), if available. Otherwise, hold the caliper in a secure manner and remove the banjo bolt with hand tools. If the caliper cannot be held securely to remove the bolt, stuff paper towels into the caliper bores to absorb brake fluid leaking from the hose and reservoir. Temporarily reinstall the caliper bracket and mount the

BRAKES

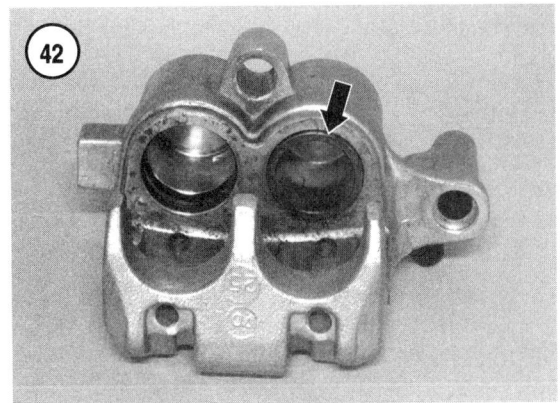

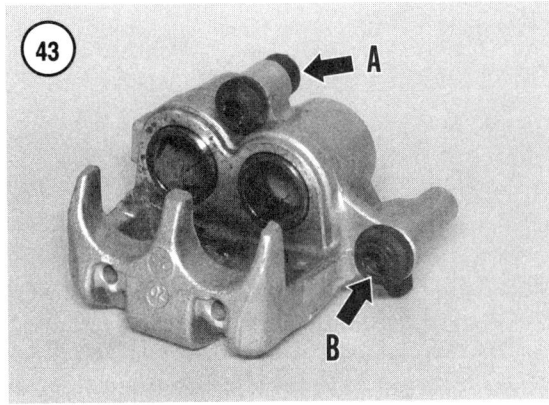

caliper onto the slider with its mounting bolts to hold it in place. Remove the banjo bolt and both washers.
4. Make sure the bleeder valve is closed so air cannot escape.

WARNING
Wear eye protection when using compressed air to remove the pistons, and keep your fingers away from the piston.

CAUTION
Do not try to pry out the piston. This will damage the piston and caliper bore.

5. Cushion the caliper pistons with a shop rag and position the caliper with the piston bores facing down. Apply compressed air through the brake hose port (**Figure 40**) to pop the pistons out. If one piston sticks, block the other piston and reapply the compressed air.
6. Use a small wooden or plastic tool and remove the dust seals (A, **Figure 39**) and piston seals (B) from the caliper bore grooves and discard them.
7. Remove the bleeder valve and its cover from the caliper.
8. Clean and inspect the brake caliper assembly as described in this section.

Assembly

NOTE
Use clean DOT 4 brake fluid when lubricating the piston seals, pistons and caliper bores.

1. Install the bleeder valve and its cover into the caliper.
2. Soak the new piston seals and dust seals in brake fluid.
3. Lubricate the cylinder bores with brake fluid.

NOTE
*The piston seals (A, **Figure 41**) are thicker than the dust seals (B).*

4. Install a new piston seal (B, **Figure 39**) into each rear bore groove.

NOTE
Make sure each seal fits securely inside its bore groove.

5. Install a new dust seal (A, **Figure 39**) into each front bore groove.
6. Lubricate the pistons with brake fluid.

CAUTION
The tight piston-to-seal fit can make piston installation difficult. Do not install the pistons by pushing them straight in as they may bind in their bores and tear the seals.

7. With the open side facing out, align a piston with the caliper bore. Rock the piston slightly to center it in the bore while at the same time pushing the lower end past the seals. When the lower end of the piston passes through both seals, push and bottom the piston (**Figure 42**) in the bore. After installing the other piston, clean spilled brake fluid from the area in front of the pistons to prevent brake pad contamination.

CAUTION
Use only lithium-base grease specified for brake use. Do not use brake fluid to lubricate the rubber boots or fixed shafts.

8. Pinch the open end of the large rubber boot (A, **Figure 43**) and push this end through the mounting hole in the caliper until its outer shoulder bottoms. Make sure the boot opening faces toward the inside of the caliper. Partially fill the boot with lithium-base grease.
9. Install the small boot (B, **Figure 43**) into the groove in the caliper. Partially fill the boot with lithium-base grease.

10. If removed, install the shaft bolt into the caliper bracket. Note the location of the short caliper shaft bolt (**Figure 44**) and lockwasher. Tighten the caliper shaft bolt to 17 N•m (12.5 ft.-lb.).
11. Lubricate the caliper bracket shafts with lithium-base grease.
12. Align and slide the mounting bracket (**Figure 45**) onto the caliper body. Hold the caliper and slide the caliper bracket in and out by hand. Make sure there is no roughness or binding.
13. Install the brake caliper assembly and brake pads as described in this chapter.

Inspection

The brake is a floating caliper design, where the caliper slides or floats on threaded shafts mounted parallel with each other on the caliper and caliper bracket. One shaft is a bolt that threads into the caliper bracket, while the other shaft remains fixed. Rubber boots around each shaft prevent dirt from damaging the shafts. If the shafts are worn or damaged, the caliper can move out of alignment on the caliper bracket. This will cause brake drag, uneven pad wear and overheating. Inspect the rubber boots and shafts during caliper inspection as they play a vital role in brake performance.

Refer to **Figure 31** when servicing the front brake caliper assembly. Replace parts that are out of specification (**Table 1**) or damaged as described in this section.

> **WARNING**
> *Do not allow oil or grease on the brake components. Do not clean the parts with kerosene or other petroleum products. These chemicals cause the rubber brake system components to swell, which may cause brake failure.*

> **CAUTION**
> *The caliper bore and seal grooves can be difficult to clean, especially if brake fluid was leaking past the seals. Clean the grooves carefully to avoid damaging the grooves and bore surfaces.*

1. Clean and dry the caliper and the other metal parts. Clean the seal grooves carefully. If the contamination is difficult to remove, soak the caliper in a suitable solvent and reclean. If any of the rubber parts are to be reused, clean them with denatured alcohol or clean DOT 4 brake fluid. Do not use a petroleum-based solvent.
2. Inspect the caliper bracket, shafts and rubber boots as follows:
   a. Inspect the rubber boots for cracks, tearing, weakness or other damage.
   b. Inspect the shafts (**Figure 44**) on the caliper bracket for excessive or uneven wear. If the shaft is damaged, replace the shaft or caliper bracket as needed.
3. Inspect each cylinder bore (**Figure 46**) for corrosion, pitting, deep scratches or other wear.
4. Inspect the pistons for wear marks, scoring, cracks or other damage.
5. Check the bleeder valve and cap for wear or damage. Make sure air can pass through the bleeder valve.
6. Check the banjo bolt for wear or damage. Discard the washers.
7. Inspect the brake pads and pad spring as described under *Rear Brake Pads* in this chapter.

BRAKES

47 REAR MASTER CYLINDER

1. Bolt
2. Master cylinder
3. Fitting
4. Snap ring
5. O-ring
6. Spring
7. Piston assembly
8. Snap ring
9. Push rod and clevis assembly
10. Clevis pin
11. Cotter pin

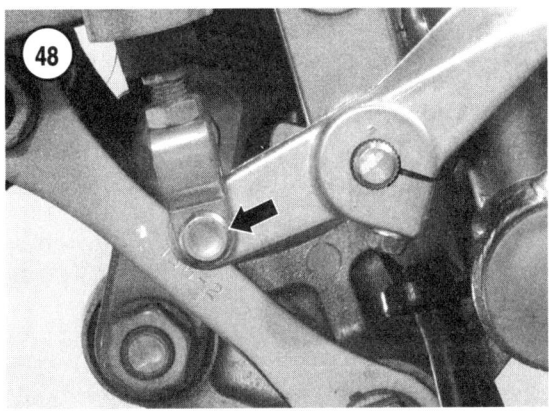

48

49

REAR MASTER CYLINDER

Removal/Installation

Refer to **Figure 47**.

1. Drain the brake system as described in this chapter.
2. Remove the cotter pin and clevis pin (**Figure 48**) that secure the master cylinder clevis to the brake pedal.
3. Be prepared to catch any remaining brake fluid. Detach the reservoir hose (A, **Figure 49**) from the master cylinder fitting.

4. Remove the banjo bolt (B, **Figure 49**) and seal washers from the brake hose. Have a shop cloth ready to absorb excess brake fluid that drips from the hose. Wrap the hose end in a plastic bag to prevent brake fluid from damaging other surfaces.
5. Remove the master cylinder mounting bolts (C, **Figure 49**). Remove the master cylinder.
6. Repair the master cylinder as described in this section.
7. Reverse the removal procedure to install the master cylinder and reservoir. Note the following:
   a. Tighten the master cylinder mounting bolts to 25 N•m (18 ft.-lb.).
   b. Install new seal washers on the banjo bolt. Tighten the bolt to 25 N•m (18 ft.-lb.).
   c. Install a new cotter pin on the clevis pin.
8. Fill the brake fluid reservoir and bleed the brake system as described in this chapter.

Disassembly/Reassembly/Inspection

Refer to **Figure 47**.

1. Remove the master cylinder as described in this section.
2. Remove the snap ring that retains the hose and fitting against the master cylinder (**Figure 50**). Remove the hose assembly and internal O-ring.

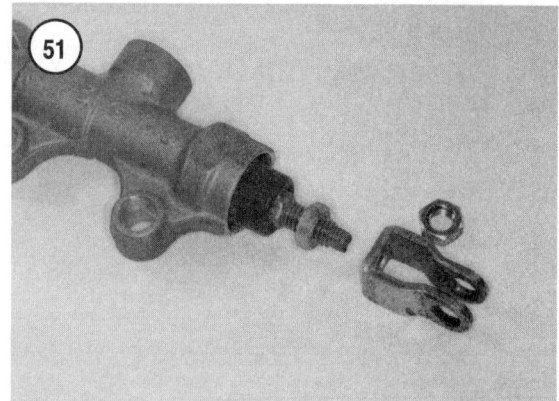

3. Remove the clevis and locknuts (**Figure 51**).
4. Remove the boot (**Figure 52**) from the pushrod. The boot is a friction fit. To avoid damaging the boot during removal, apply penetrating lubricant around the perimeter of the boot. Carefully pull the bottom edge back so the lubricant can loosen the boot.
5. Remove the snap ring from the master cylinder as follows:
   a. Lock the master cylinder in a vise with soft jaws.
   b. Thread a locknut onto the end of the pushrod (**Figure 53**). The locknut creates a larger and more comfortable area when depressing the pushrod.
   c. Press down on the pushrod to relieve pressure on the snap ring. Remove the snap ring with snap ring pliers.
   d. Slowly relieve the pressure on the piston.
6. Remove the piston and pushrod assembly (**Figure 54**) from the bore.
7. Inspect the master cylinder assembly as follows:
   a. Clean all parts that will be reused with fresh brake fluid or isopropyl (rubbing) alcohol.
   b. Inspect the cylinder bore (**Figure 55**) for wear, pitting or corrosion.
   c. Inspect and clean the threads and orifices (**Figure 56**) in the master cylinder. Clean with compressed air.
   d. Inspect the boot, snap ring and pushrod (**Figure 57**). Check the parts for corrosion and damage.
   e. Inspect the clevis and pin (**Figure 58**) for wear at their contact points.
8. Soak the seals (A, **Figure 59**) in clean DOT 4 brake fluid for 15 minutes. This softens and lubricates the seals. Install new seals so the open side is toward the spring (B, **Figure 59**).
9. Install the spring, piston, pushrod and snap ring into the master cylinder as follows:
   a. Lubricate the cylinder bore and piston assembly with clean brake fluid.

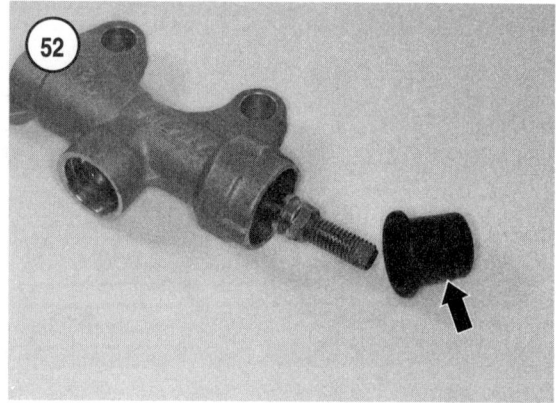

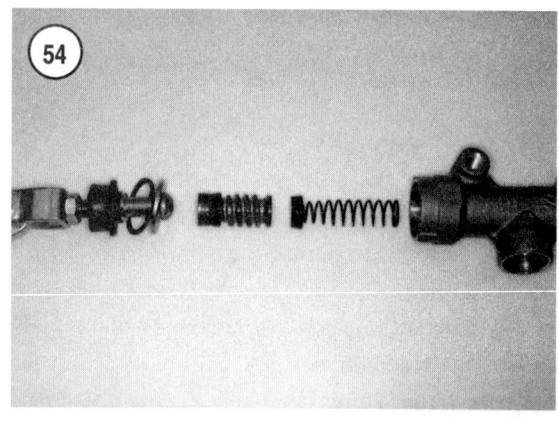

BRAKES

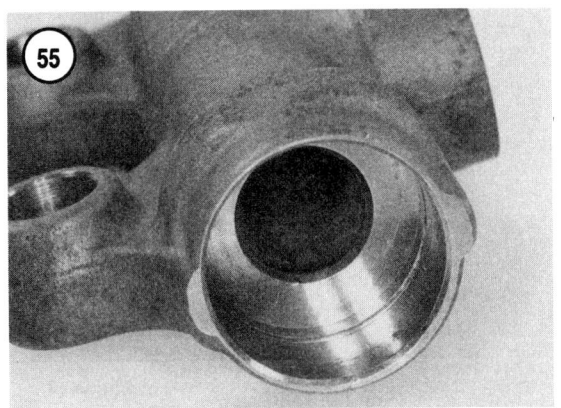

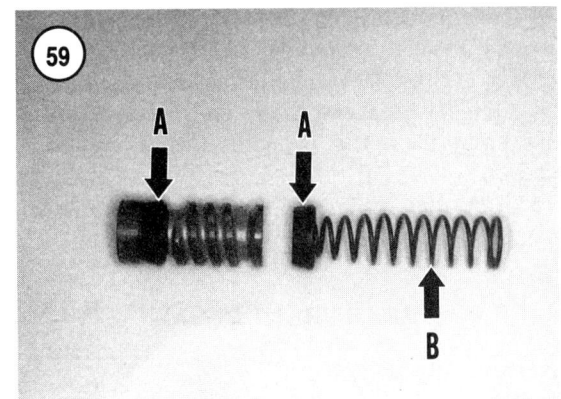

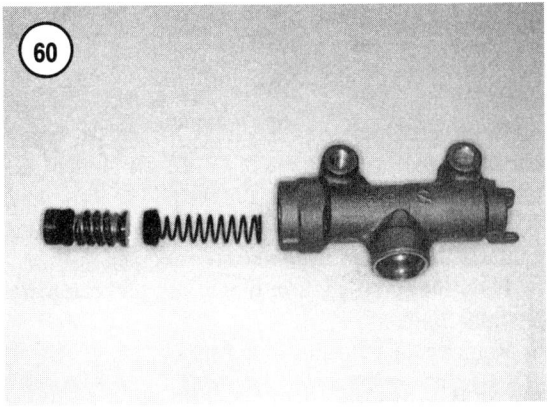

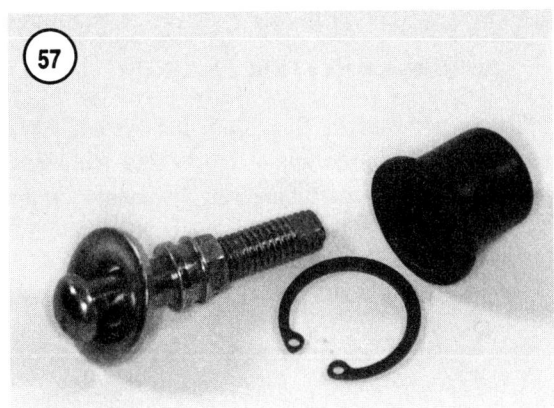

b. Apply a small amount of silicone brake grease to the contact area of the pushrod.
c. Insert the spring and piston (**Figure 60**) into the cylinder.
d. Lock the cylinder in a vise with soft jaws. Do not overtighten the vise or cylinder damage could occur.
e. Thread a nut onto the end of the pushrod. Rest the pushrod in the cylinder (**Figure 53**). The nut will provide a more comfortable surface when the pushrod is depressed.
f. Place the snap ring over the end of the pushrod, resting it on the edge of the bore. The flat side of the snap ring must face out.
g. Compress the snap ring with snap ring pliers.
h. Press the pushrod into the cylinder while guiding the snap ring into position. If the snap ring does not seat easily, release the snap ring and use the tip of the pliers to press it into the groove. Keep the pushrod compressed until the snap ring seats.

10. Remove the cylinder from the vise. Remove the nut from the pushrod.
11. Apply silicone brake grease to the inside the boot. Seat the boot into the cylinder.
12. Install the clevis and locknuts.

13. Install a new, lubricated O-ring (A, **Figure 61**) into the master cylinder. Lock the hose and fitting (B, **Figure 61**) into place with a new snap ring. Install the snap ring (C, **Figure 61**) so the flat side faces out.
14. Install the master cylinder as described in this section.
15. Adjust the brake pedal position as described in Chapter Three.

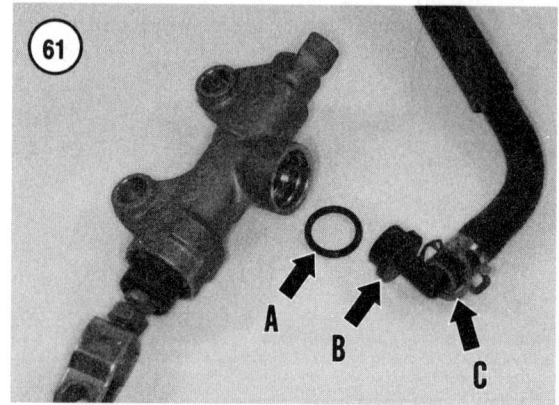

REAR BRAKE PEDAL

Removal/Installation

1. Disengage the brake light switch spring from the pedal.
2. Remove the cotter pin and clevis pin (A, **Figure 62**) that secure the master cylinder clevis to the brake pedal.
3. Completely remove the bolt (B, **Figure 62**) securing the pedal to the shaft. For 2011-on models, remove the bolt and washer from the end of the shaft.
4. Before removing the pedal, note how the spring contacts the post on the brake stay and pedal.
5. Hold the pedal shaft in place, and pull the pedal from the shaft.
6. Remove the pedal shaft and spring.
7. Clean and inspect the parts.
    a. Inspect the pedal shaft and bore bushing for scoring, damage or the entry of water and dirt. If the bushing is worn, replace it.
    b. Inspect the clevis pin and pedal bore. The pin must be a firm fit in the clevis and pedal.
    c. Inspect the spring and shaft bolt for corrosion and damage.
    d. Check that the brake stay is tightly fastened.
8. Install the pedal as follows:
    a. Apply waterproof grease to the bushing and pedal shaft.
    b. Install the spring, seating it against the brake stay. The straight end of the spring rests against the back of the brake stay post.
    c. Install the pedal shaft. Engage the hooked end of the spring with the narrow arm on the pedal shaft.
    d. Hold the shaft in place. Turn it forward to preload the spring.
    e. Install the pedal, guiding it into the clevis, and aligning the index marks (C, **Figure 62**) on the pedal and shaft.
    f. Bolt the pedal to the shaft.
    g. Install the clevis pin and a new cotter pin.
    h. Attach the brake light switch spring.
    i. Check pedal height and operation as described in Chapter Three.
    j. Check brake light operation. If necessary, adjust the switch as described in Chapter Three.

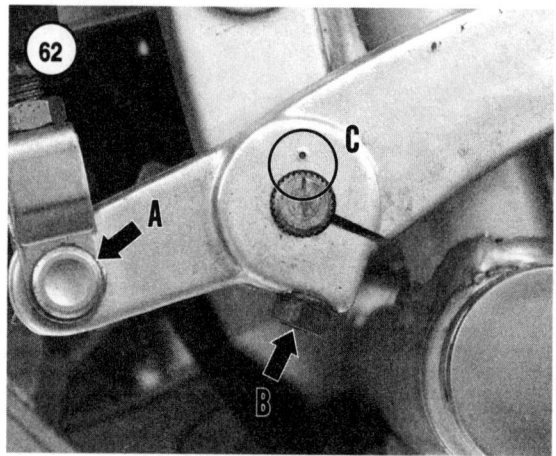

BRAKE SYSTEM DRAINING

To drain the brake fluid from the system, have available a 10-mm wrench, tip-resistant container and a length of clear tubing that fits snugly on the bleeder valve. Use the following procedure to drain either the front or rear brakes.

CAUTION
Brake fluid can damage painted and finished surfaces. Use water to immediately wash any surface that becomes contaminated with brake fluid.

1. Attach one end of the tubing to the bleeder valve and place the other end into the container (**Figure 63**).
2. Open the bleeder valve so fluid can pass into the tubing.
3. Pump the brake lever/pedal to force the fluid from the system.
4. When the system no longer drips fluid, close the bleeder valve.
5. Dispose of the brake fluid in an environmentally safe manner.

BRAKES

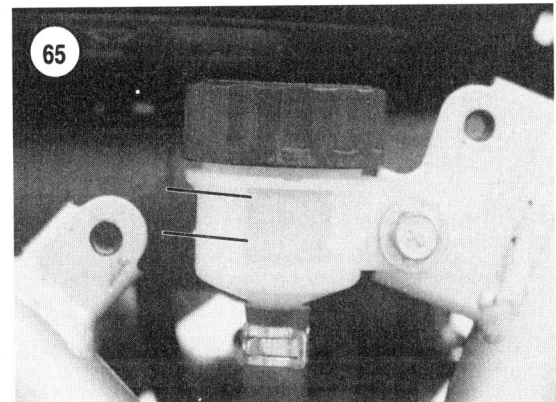

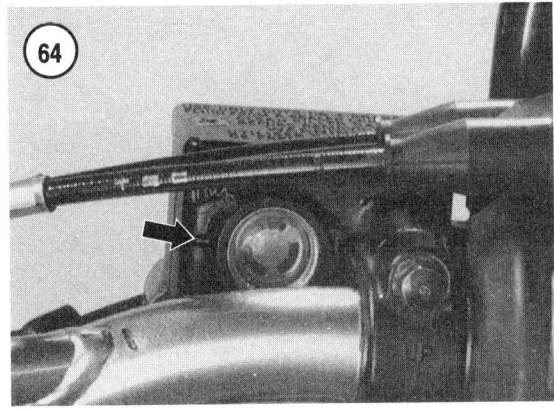

BRAKE SYSTEM BLEEDING

Whenever the brake fluid is replaced, or if the brake lever or pedal feels spongy, bleed the brakes to purge all air from the system. Before bleeding the brakes, determine where the air is entering the system. Check all brake components for leaks, and all fittings and hoses for deterioration, damage or looseness. The brake system can be bled manually or by using a vacuum pump. Both methods are described in this section.

> **CAUTION**
> *Before bleeding brakes, always secure the motorcycle so it is stable and locked in place, particularly the fork. This minimizes the chance of spilled fluid from an open reservoir.*

Brake Fluid Reservoirs

Regardless of the bleeding method used, the reservoir cap of the master cylinder being bled must be removed so the reservoir can be filled with brake fluid. The reservoirs must not be over or under filled. When working with each reservoir, note the following:
1. Front brake reservoir.
   a. After removing the cap, remove the diaphragm from the reservoir before filling with fluid.
   b. Keep the reservoir filled between the top of the sight glass and the lower mark (**Figure 64**) on the reservoir during the bleeding procedure.
   c. After bleeding, replenish the reservoir to the upper mark. Install the diaphragm and cap.
2. Rear brake reservoir.
   a. Remove the reservoir guard and backing plate. Remove the cap, diaphragm plate and diaphragm.
   b. Keep the reservoir filled between the upper and lower marks (**Figure 65**) on the reservoir during the bleeding procedure.
   c. After bleeding, replenish the reservoir to the upper mark. Install the diaphragm, diaphragm plate and cap.
   d. Install the backing plate and reservoir guard.

Manual Bleeding

To manually bleed the brake system, have available a 10-mm wrench, tip-resistant container and a length of clear tubing that fits snugly on the brake bleeder. Bleeding the system is much easier if two people are available to perform the procedure. One person can open and close the bleeder valve while the other person operates the brake lever or pedal. Use the following procedure to bleed either the front or rear brake.

> **CAUTION**
> *Brake fluid can damage painted and finished surfaces. Use water and immediately wash any surface that contacts brake fluid.*

1. Attach one end of the tubing to the bleeder valve and place the other end into the container (**Figure 63**).

CHAPTER FOURTEEN

> *CAUTION*
> *Do not use brake fluid from an unsealed container. It may be contaminated by moisture absorbed from the air. Use DOT 4 brake fluid from a sealed container.*

2. Fill the reservoir to the upper level with fresh DOT 4 brake fluid.

3. Apply pressure (do not pump) to the brake lever or pedal, and then open the bleeder valve. As the fluid is forced from the system, the lever/pedal travels its full length of operation. When the lever/pedal can move no farther, hold the lever/pedal in the down position and close the bleeder valve. Do not allow the lever or pedal to return to its up position before the bleeder valve is closed as air will be drawn into the system.

> *NOTE*
> *Release the lever/pedal slowly. This minimizes the chance of fluid splashing out of the reservoir as excess fluid in the brake line is returned to the reservoir.*

4. When the bleeder valve is closed, release the lever/pedal so it returns to its up position. Check the fluid level in the reservoir and replenish, if necessary.

> *NOTE*
> *During the bleeding process, the reservoir must contain fluid during the entire procedure. If the reservoir is allowed to empty, air will enter the system and the bleeding process must be repeated.*

5. Repeat Step 3 and Step 4 until bubble-free, clear fluid passes out of the bleeder valve. Unless the bleeder valve threads are wrapped with Teflon tape, or coated with silicone brake grease, a small amount of air will enter the system when the bleeder valve is opened.

> *NOTE*
> *If small bubbles (foam) remain in the system after several bleeding attempts, close the reservoir and allow the system to stand undisturbed for a few hours. The system will stabilize and the air can be purged as large bubbles.*

6. The bleeding procedure is completed when the lever/pedal feels firm at the bottom of the stroke.
7. Check the brake fluid reservoir and fill the reservoir to the upper level, if necessary.
8. Tighten the bleeder valve to 8 N•m (71 in.-lb.). Do not overtighten.
9. Dispose of the waste brake fluid in an environmentally-safe manner.

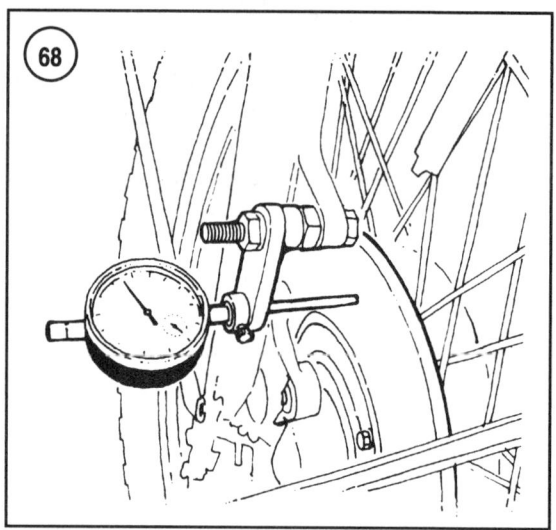

Vacuum Bleeding

To vacuum-bleed the brake system, have available a 10-mm wrench and a vacuum pump, such as the Mityvac pump shown in **Figure 66**. Use the following procedure to bleed either the front or rear brake.

> *CAUTION*
> *Brake fluid can damage painted and finished surfaces. Use water and imme-*

BRAKES

diately wash any surface that contacts brake fluid.

1. Check that the banjo bolts are tight at the master cylinder and caliper.
2. Attach the brake bleeder to the bleeder valve (**Figure 66**). Suspend the tool with wire. This allows the tool to be released when the fluid reservoir needs to be refilled.

CAUTION
Do not use brake fluid from an unsealed container. It may be contaminated by moisture absorbed from the air. Use DOT 4 brake fluid from a sealed container.

3. Fill the reservoir to the upper level with clean DOT 4 brake fluid.

NOTE
During the bleeding process, the reservoir must contain fluid during the entire procedure. If the reservoir is allowed to empty, air will enter the system and the bleeding process must be repeated.

4. Pump the handle on the brake bleeder to create a vacuum.
5. Open the bleeder valve and draw the air and fluid from the system. Close the valve before the fluid stops moving. If the vacuum pump is equipped with a gauge, close the bleeder before the gauge reaches 0 in.-Hg. Replenish the fluid level in the reservoir.
6. Repeat Step 4 and Step 5 until clear fluid (minimal air bubbles) is passing out of the bleeder. Unless the bleeder valve threads are wrapped with Teflon tape, or coated with silicone brake grease, a small amount of air will enter the system when the bleeder valve is opened. The bleeding procedure is completed when the feel of the lever/pedal is firm.
7. Check the brake fluid reservoir and fill the reservoir to the upper level, if necessary.

8. Tighten the bleeder valve to 8 N•m (70 in.-lb.). Do not overtighten.
9. Dispose of the waste brake fluid in an environmentally-safe manner.

BRAKE DISC

The condition of the brake discs and pads are often a reflection of one another. If disc scoring is evident, inspect the pads and disc as soon as possible. Visually inspect the discs and pads with the wheels mounted on the motorcycle (Chapter Three). If damage is detected, perform the inspections described in this section.

NOTE
Do not true a deeply scored or warped disc. Removing disc material causes the disc to overheat rapidly and warp. Maintain the discs by keeping them clean and corrosion-free. Use a solvent that is not oil-based to wipe off grit that accumulates on the discs and at the edge of the pads.

Thickness and Runout Inspection

1. Measure the thickness of each disc at several locations around its perimeter (**Figure 67**). Refer to **Table 1** for the service limit. Replace the disc if it is out of specification.
2. Measure disc runout as follows:
   a. Mount a dial indicator on a stable surface and in contact with the disc (**Figure 68**).
   b. Zero the gauge.
   c. Turn the wheel and watch the amount of runout measured on the gauge.

NOTE
If the disc runout is out of specification, check the condition of the wheel bearings before replacing the disc. Damaged bearings will affect disc runout.

   d. Refer to **Table 1** for the service-limit. Replace the disc if it is out of specification.

Removal and Installation

The discs are mounted to the hubs with bolts. Remove and install either disc as follows:
1. Remove the wheel from the motorcycle as described in Chapter Eleven.
2. Remove the bolts (**Figure 69**) that secure the disc to the hub.

3. Clean the bolts and mounting holes.
4. Reverse the removal procedure to install the discs. Note the following:

   a. Install the disc with the thickness marking (**Figure 70**) facing out.
   b. Apply nonpermanent threadlock to the bolt threads.
   c. Using a crossing pattern, evenly tighten the brake disc bolts in several passes to 27 N•m (20 ft.-lb.).
   e. Check the disc for runout as described in this section.

Table 1 BRAKE SERVICE SPECIFICATIONS

	New mm (in.)	Service limit mm (in.)
Brake disc thickness	4.8-5.1 (0.19-0.20)	4.5 (0.18)
Brake disc runout	0.15 (0.006)	0.30 (0.012)
Brake pad thickness		
Front	4.5 (0.18)	1.0 (0.039)
Rear	5.5 (0.22)	1.0 (0.039)

Table 2 BRAKE TORQUE SPECIFICATIONS

	N•m	in.-lb.	ft.-lb.
Banjo bolt	25	–	18
Bleeder valve	8	71	–
Brake caliper shaft bolt	17	–	12.5
Brake disc bolts	27	–	20
Brake pad pins	17	–	12.5
Front brake caliper mounting bolts	34	–	25
Front brake master cylinder clamp bolts	8.8	78	–
Rear brake caliper mounting bolts	25	–	18
Rear brake master cylinder mounting bolts	25	–	18

CHAPTER FIFTEEN

BODY

SIDE COVERS

Removal/Installation

1. Remove the bolts at the front and rear of the cover (**Figure 1**).
2. Pull out the bottom of the cover to detach the friction barb from the frame grommet.
3. Remove the cover.
4. To install the cover:
   a. Insert the rear edge of the cover first. The cover must fit under the rear fender.
   b. Align the friction barb with the grommet, and push the cover into place.
   c. Install and tighten the bolts.

SEAT

Removal/Installation

1. Remove the side covers as described in this chapter.
2. Remove the bolt (**Figure 2**) from both sides of the seat.
3. Pull the seat backward to disengage the seat brackets.
4. Remove the seat.
5. Reverse the removal steps to install the seat. Make sure the seat brackets (**Figure 3**) engage the frame and fuel tank.

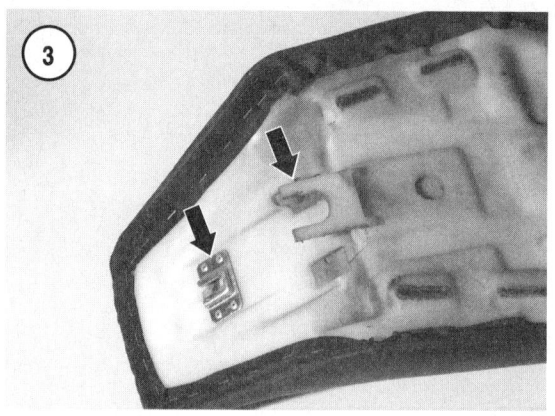

FUEL TANK

Removal/Installation

1. Remove the seat as described in this chapter.
2. Remove the lower fairings as described in this chapter.
3. Move the fuel tank valve to the off position.
4A. On all models, disconnect the fuel hose (A, **Figure 4**) and vacuum hose (B) from the fuel valve.
4B. On California models, also disconnect the fuel return hose next to the breather hose.
5. Disconnect the breather hose (A, **Figure 5**).
6. Remove the fuel tank retaining bolts (B, **Figure 5**).
7. Move the fuel tank toward the rear to disengage the inner mounting pads. Lift off the fuel tank.
8. Inspect the mounting pads (**Figure 6**) on the frame. Replace if deteriorated or damaged.
9. Make sure the fuel cap gasket (A, **Figure 7**) is in good condition and the cap vent (B) and breather pipe (C) are open.
10. Reverse the removal steps to install the fuel tank.

LOWER FAIRING

Removal/Installation

1. Remove the inner bolt on the left fairing (**Figure 8**) or right fairing (**Figure 9**).
2. Remove the upper mounting screw (**Figure 10**). Do not lose the spacer between the upper fairing and lower fairing.
3. Remove the lower mounting bolt (**Figure 11**).

> *NOTE*
> *The inner and lower mounting bolts for the right lower fairing also secure the radiator screen, which may fall out while removing the fairing.*

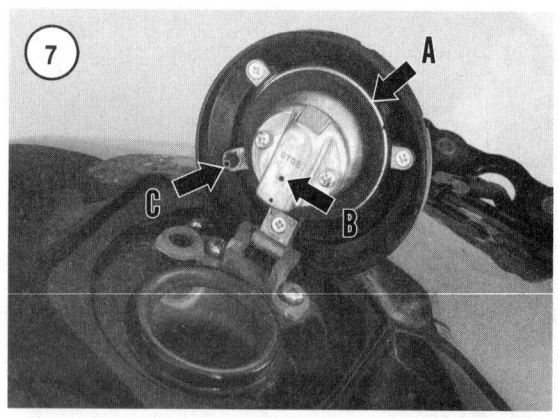

BODY

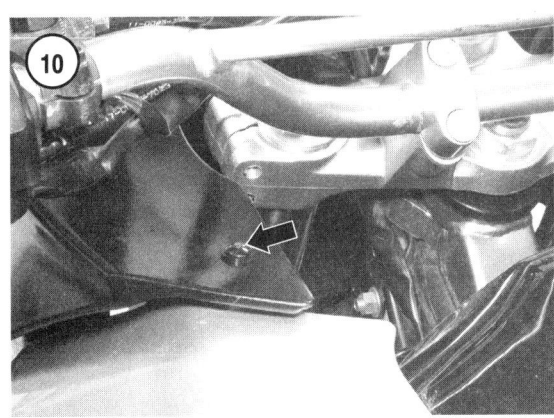

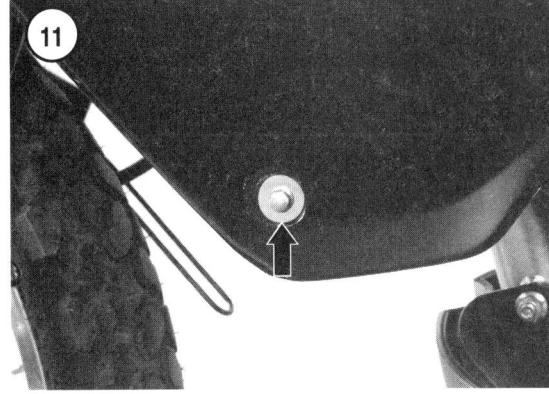

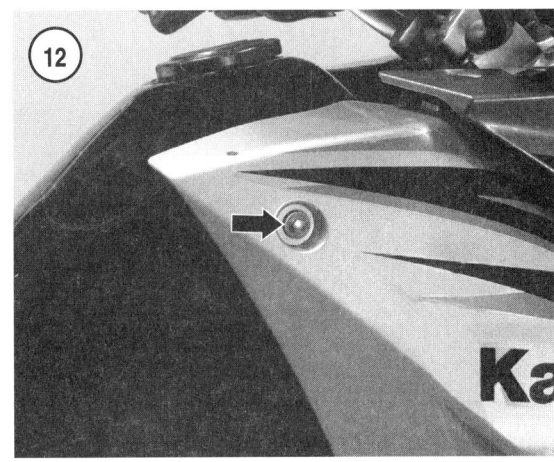

4. Support the fairing and remove the upper mounting bolt (**Figure 12**).

5. Pull out the fairing so the friction barb releases from the frame grommet, and remove the fairing.

6. Reverse the removal steps for installation and note the following:
   a. If the radiator screen was removed, make sure the bosses on the inner side fit into the holes in the radiator mounting bracket.
   b. Tighten the lower fairing mounting bolts to 8.8 N•m (78 in.-lb.).

UPPER FAIRING

Removal/Installation

NOTE
It is not necessary to remove the lower fairings to remove the upper fairing. However, doing so provides greater access and reduces the possibility of damage to the lower fairings.

1. Remove the lower fairings as described in this chapter.
2. Remove the rear mounting bolt (**Figure 13**) on each side.
3. Remove the mounting bolts in the upper corners of the instrument panel (**Figure 14**).
4. Disconnect the connectors for the turn signals.
5. Disconnect the connector from each headlight.
6. Remove the upper fairing.
7. If necessary, separate the side panels from the center section by removing the retaining screw and bolts. Disengage the bosses from the guide slots.
8. Reverse the removal procedure for installation.

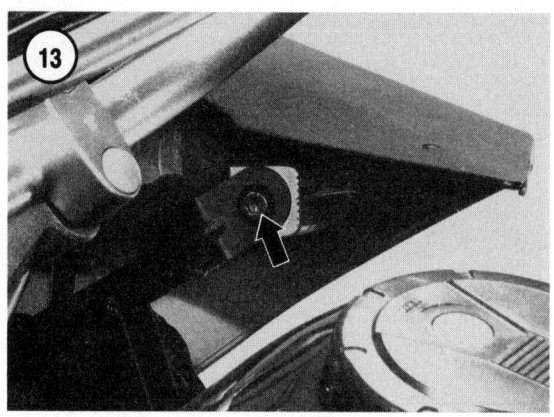

FRONT FENDER

Removal/Installation

1. Disconnect the speedometer cable (**Figure 15**) from the right side of the front hub.
2. Remove the fender retaining bolts (**Figure 16**).
3. Remove the fender while routing the speedometer cable through the cable guide on the fender.
4. Reverse the removal steps for installation. Install the speedometer cable so the slot (**Figure 17**) in the cable end engages the tab in the drive unit. If necessary, slowly rotate the front wheel until the cable housing fully seats (**Figure 18**) in the drive unit. Tighten the cable nut.

REAR CARRIER

Removal/Installation

1. Disconnect the rear turn signal and taillight connectors (A, **Figure 19**).
2. Remove the rear fender mounting screws (B, **Figure 19**).
3. Remove the front carrier mounting bolts (C, **Figure 19**).
4. Remove the carrier mounting bolts (D, **Figure 19**).
5. Remove the flap mounting bolts (**Figure 20**).
6. Invert the carrier and fender assembly.
7. Detach the turn signal wire, and then separate the carrier from the fender.
8. Reverse the removal procedure for installation.

REAR FENDER

Removal/Installation

1. Remove the rear carrier as described in this chapter. The rear portion of the rear fender is loose after separation from the carrier.
2. To remove the fender flap, proceed as follows:

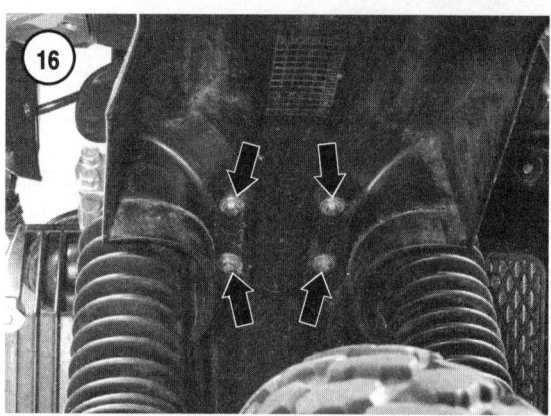

BODY

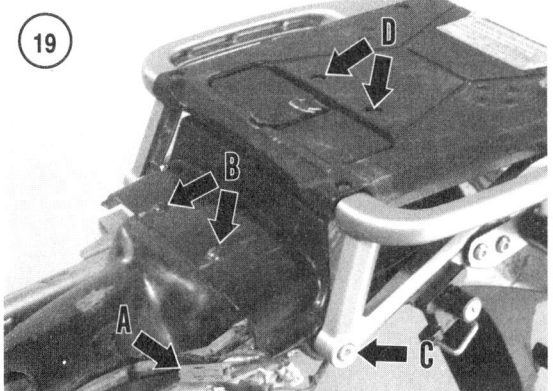

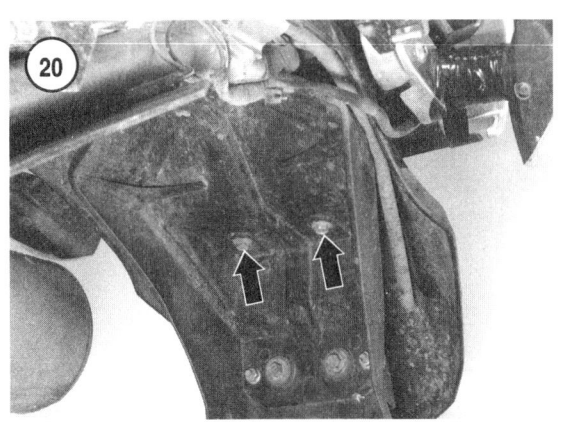

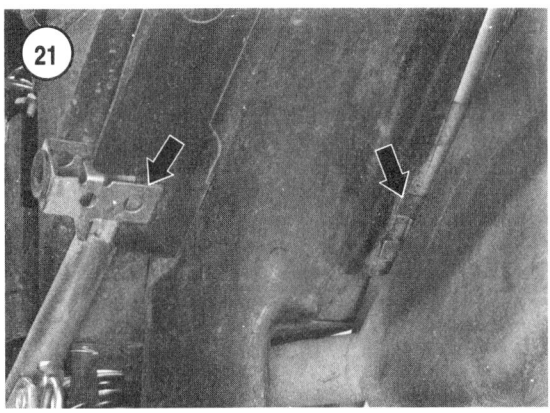

a. Disconnect the license plate light connector.
b. Remove the flap mounting bolts, and then remove the flap.

3. To remove the front portion of the rear fender, proceed as follows:
   a. Detach the battery vent hose.
   b. Pull the fender backward until it releases from the frame brackets (**Figure 21**).
4. Reverse the removal procedure for installation. Make sure the fender is fully seated in the frame brackets.

SUBFRAME

Removal/Installation

1. Remove the fuel tank as described in this chapter.
2. Remove the muffler from the exhaust pipe and frame as described in Chapter Four.
3. Remove the battery as described in Chapter Nine.
4. Remove the rear fender and flap as described in this chapter.
5. On California models, remove the vapor canister.
6. Remove the bolts (A, **Figure 22**) from the right rear footpeg. Then, remove the footpeg.
7. Note the location and routing of hoses and wires passing from the front to the rear of the motorcycle. Disconnect the hoses and wires and guide them out of the subframe.
8. Remove the bolt (**Figure 23**) securing the air filter housing to the subframe
9. Remove the bolt (**Figure 24**) securing the air filter housing support bracket to the subframe.
10. Remove the lower subframe bolts (B, **Figure 22**).

CAUTION
Have an assistant help with removal by holding the subframe and preventing it from falling when the upper subframe bolts are removed.

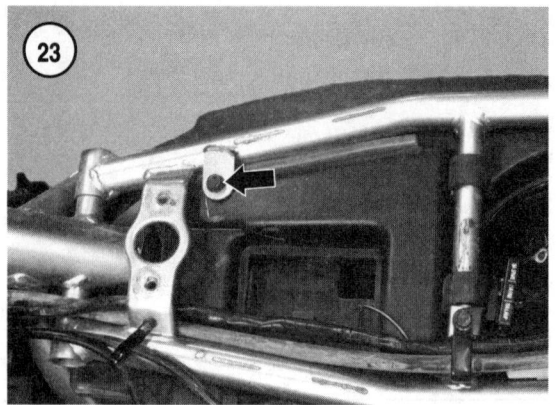

11. Remove the upper subframe bolts (**Figure 25**). Remove the subframe.
12. To install the subframe, reverse the removal procedure while noting the following:
    a. Inspect and replace subframe mounting bolts that are corroded or damaged.
    b. Have an assistant aid in installing the subframe.
    c. Finger-tighten all subframe mounting bolts before final tightening.
    d. Tighten the upper subframe bolts to 45 N•m (33 ft.-lb.).
    e. Tighten the lower subframe bolts to 25 N•m (18 ft.-lb.).
    f. Tighten the right rear footpeg bolts to 25 N•m (18 ft.-lb.).
    g. Tighten the air filter housing bolt (**Figure 23**) to 8.8 N•m (78 in.-lb.).
    h. Securely tighten the bolt (**Figure 24**) mounting the air filter housing support bracket to the subframe.

SKID PLATE

The skid plate is secured by two bolts and flanged collars at the front, and by two bolts and collars on the underside of the frame. An aftermarket skid plate may be installed for additional protection.

Table 1 BODY TORQUE SPECIFICATIONS

	N•m	in.-lb.	ft.-lb.
Air filter housing bolt	8.8	78	–
Lower fairing mounting bolts	8.8	78	–
Rear footpeg bolts	25	–	18
Subframe bolts			
Upper	45	–	33
Lower	25	–	18

INDEX

A

Air filter
  housing 168
    drain hose, maintenance 48
    lubrication 47-48
Alternator cover 175

B

Balancer chain tensioner adjustment 49
Battery 170-173
  negative terminal 170
Body
  carrier, rear 288
  fairing
    lower 286-287
    upper 287-288
  fender
    front 288
    rear 289
  fuel tank 286
  seat 285
  side covers 285
  skid plate 290
  specifications, torque 290
  subframe 289-290
Brakes
  bleeding 281-283
  caliper
    front 264-267
    rear 273-276
  disc 283-284
    troubleshooting 38
  draining 280
  fluid
    level inspection 58
    selection 261
  light switch adjustment, rear 57
  master cylinder
    front 267
    rear 277-280
  pads
    and disc inspection 58
    front 262-264
    rear 271-273
  pedal
    adjustment 56-57
    rear 280
  service 261-262
  specifications
    service 284
    torque 284
  troubleshooting 37

C

Cable lubrication 44-46
Caliper
  front 264-267
  rear 273-276
Cam chain and lower guide 105-106
Camshafts and cam chain tensioner 74-81

INDEX

Carburetor 151-157
  cleaning and inspection 157-160
  float
    adjustment 160
    chamber drain, maintenance 49
  idle speed and mixture adjustment 62
  operation 160-162
  specifications 168
Carrier, rear 288
Chain lubrication 42
Charging system 173-174
Choke cable 167
  adjustment 56
Clutch 126-131
  cable
    lubrication 44-45
    replacement 138-139
    lever adjustment 55-56
  primary drive gear 136-138
  troubleshooting 36-37
  specifications 139
  torque 139
Compression test 62-23
Conversion tables 26-27
Cooling system
  coolant
    level inspection 50
    reserve tank 208
    temperature gauge
      and sending unit 191-192, 206
  draining and replacement 51-52
  inspection 50-51
  radiator and fan 203-205
  safety precautions 203
  specifications 209
  torque 209
  thermostat 205-206
  water pump 206-208
Crankcase 113-118
  bearing replacement 119-120
  cover
    left 106
    right 123-125
Crankshaft 120-121
Cylinder 91-95
  head 81-86
  cover 71-74

D

Drive chain 219-223
  adjustment 53-54
  inspection, maintenance 52-53
  lubrication 46-47
  specifications 228
  torque 229
  sprockets 224-226
Drive gear, primary 136-138

E

Electrical system
  alternator cover 175
  battery 170-173
    negative terminal 170
  charging system 173-174
  component replacement 169
  connectors 170
  continuity testing guidelines 169-170
  coolant temperature gauge
    and sending unit 191-192
  fan system 189-191
  fundamentals 18
  fuses 200-201
  ignition system 186-189
  lighting system 194-196
  meter unit 192-194
  regulator/rectifier 179-180
  rotor and starter clutch 177-179
  specifications
    general 201
    testing 202
    torque 202
  starter 180-184
    circuit relay 185-186
    relay 185
  starting system 180
  stator 175-177
  switches 196-200
  wiring diagram 296-297
Engine
  balancer 106-113
  break-in 121-122
  compression test 62-63
  tune-up 60-63
  leakdown test, troubleshooting 35
  lower end 103-105
    cam chain and lower guide 105-106
    crankcase 113-118
      bearings 119-120
      cover, left 106
    crankshaft 120-121
    engine balancer 106-113
    seal replacement 118
    specifications 122
    torque 122
  lubrication, troubleshooting 34
  noise, troubleshooting 34
  oil and filter change 43-44
  oil level check 42-43
  performance, troubleshooting 31-33

INDEX

removal and installation 103-105
spark test, troubleshooting. 31
specifications
   general 100
   top end 100-101
   torque. 102
starting, troubleshooting. 29-31
top end
   camshafts and cam chain tensioner 74-81
   cylinder. 91-95
      head 81-86
      cover 71-74
   exhaust system 70-71
   piston and piston rings 95-100
   specifications. 100-101
   valves. 87-91
Evaporative emissions control system . . . 164-165
   inspection 48
Exhaust system 70-71

F

Fairing
   lower. 286-287
   upper. 287-288
Fan system 189-191
Fasteners 4-6
Fender
   front 288
   rear. 289
Float adjustment. 160
Front fork 234-241
   oil specifications. 247
   service 234
Fuel
   and lubricants 40-42
   system
      air filter housing 168
      carburetor 151-157
         cleaning and inspection 157-160
         systems 160-162
      choke cable. 167
      evaporative emissions control system . . 164-165
      float adjustment 160
      fuel valve. 162-164
      specifications, carburetor. 168
      throttle cable 166-167
Fuel
   lubricants and fluids, specifications 69
   tank. 286
   valve 162-164
Fuses 200-201

G

Gearshift linkage, external 132-134
   troubleshooting 37

H

Handlebar, ... 230-233
   balancer weights. 233-234
   left hand grip replacement. 233
Hubs, front and rear 215-218

I

Ignition system 186-189
Ignition timing 189

L

Lighting system 194-196
Lubrication
   air filter 47-48
   cable 44-46
   chain 42
   drive chain 46-47
   oil and filter change 43-44
   oil level check 42-43
   specifications and recommendations 69

M

Maintenance
   and inspection 48-60
   balancer chain tensioner adjustment. 49
   brakes
      fluid level inspection. 58
      light switch adjustment 57
      pad and disc inspection 58
      pedal adjustment 56-57
   carburetor, idle speed and mixture adjustment . 62
   choke cable adjustment 56
   clutch, lever adjustment 55-56
   coolant level inspection 50
   cooling system
      draining and replacement 51-52
      inspection 50-51
   drive chain and sprockets
      adjustment 53-54
      inspection 52-53
   ignition timing. 189
   muffler. 48
   routine checks and adjustments 69
   schedule 66-68
   spark plug
      cap 66
      gap and installation 64-66
      removal. 63
   steering head bearing inspection 58
   swing arm bearing inspection 59
   throttle free play adjustment. 54-55
   tires, tube alignment 59
   torque specifications. 69

valves, clearance. 60-62
Master cylinder
   front 267-271
   rear. 277-280
Meter unit 192-194
Metric
   tap drill size 28
   decimal and fractional equivalents 26
Muffler, maintenance 48

N

Noise, troubleshooting 34

O

Oil
   and filter change. 43-44
   level check. 42-43
   pump. 134-136
      specifications. 139
   pressure test specifications, troubleshooting . . 38

P

Periodic lubrication, maintenance. 42-48
Piston and piston rings 95-100
Pre-ride inspection 39

R

Radiator and fan. 203-205
Regulator/rectifier. 179-180
Right crankcase cover. 123-126
Rim and spoke service 218-219
Rotor and starter clutch 177-179

S

Safety 3-4
Seal replacement 118
Seat 285
Serial numbers 3
Shift
   clutch 126-131
   clutch cable replacement 138-139
   drum and forks. 149-150
   oil pump. 134-136
   primary drive gear. 136-138
   right crankcase cover 123-125
Shock absorber 248-249
   adjustment 259
   linkage 249-253
   settings, specifications. 260
Shop supplies 6-8
Side covers 285
Skid plate 290

Spark plugs 63-66
   cap. 66
   gap and installation 64-66
   plug, removal 63
Specifications
   carburetor 168
   clutch 139
   conversion tables 26-27
   cooling system. 209
   electrical system 201-202
   engine
      lower end. 122
      top end 100-101
   fork oil 247
   fuel, lubricants and fluids 69
   maintenance schedule 66-68
   metric
      tap drill size 28
      decimal and fractional equivalents. 26
   motorcycle dimensions and weight 26
   oil
      pressure test 38
      pump. 139
   routine checks and adjustments 69
   steering 247
   suspension
      front 247
         fork oil. 247
      rear. 260
      shock absorber settings 260
   tires 228
   torque
      body 290
      brakes 284
      clutch. 139
      cooling system 209
      electrical system 202
      engine
         lower end 122
         top end. 102
      general recommendations 27
      maintenance 69
      suspension
         front 247
         rear. 260
   wheels, tires and drive chain. 229
   transmission 150
   tune-up. 69
   wiring diagram. 296-297
   wheel and drive chain 228
Speedometer drive unit and front wheel . . 210-213
Sprockets 224-226
Starter 180-184
   circuit and relay 185-186
Starting system 180
   troubleshooting 34

INDEX

Stator 175-177
Steering
  balancer weights 233-234
  fork 234-241
    service 234
  handlebar 230-233
    left hand grip replacement 233
  head bearing inspection 58
  play check and adjustment 246-247
  stem and head 241-247
  specifications 247
  stem and head 241-247
  troubleshooting 37-38
Storage 24-25
Subframe 289-290
Suspension
  balancer weights 233-234
  fork 234
    oil, specifications 247
    service 234-241
  shock absorber, rear 248-249
    adjustment 259
    linkage 249-253
    settings, specifications 260
  specifications
    front 247
    rear 260
  steering stem and head 241-247
    specifications 247
  swing arm 253-259
    bearing inspection 59
Swing arm 253-259
Switches, electrical 196-200

T

Technical abbreviations 27-28
Thermostat 205-206
Throttle
  cable 166-167
    lubrication 45-46
  free play adjustment 54-55
Timing, ignition 189
Tires
  changing 226-228
  specifications 228
  torque 229
  tube alignment 59
Tools 8-14
  measuring 14-18
Torque specifications
  body 290
  brakes 284
  clutch 139
  cooling system 209

electrical system 202
engine
  lower end 122
  top end 102
general recommendations 27
maintenance 69
suspension
  front 247
  rear 260
wheels, tires and drive chain 229
Transmission 140-141
  input shaft 142-144
  inspection 148-149
  operation 140
  output shaft 144-147
  shift drum and forks 149-150
  specifications 150
  troubleshooting 37
Troubleshooting
  brakes 37
    disc 38
  clutch 36-37
  engine
    leakdown test 35
    lubrication 34
    noise 34
    performance 31-33
    spark test 31
    starting 29-31
  gear shift linkage and transmission 37
  noise 34
  oil pressure test specifications 38i
  starting system 34
  steering and handling 37-38
Tune-up
  service intervals 39-40
  specifications 69

V

Valves 87-91
  clearance 60-62

W

Water pump 206-208
Wiring diagram 296-297
Wheels
  front 210-213
  hubs 215-218
  rear 213-215
  rim and spoke service 218-219
  specifications 228
  torque 229

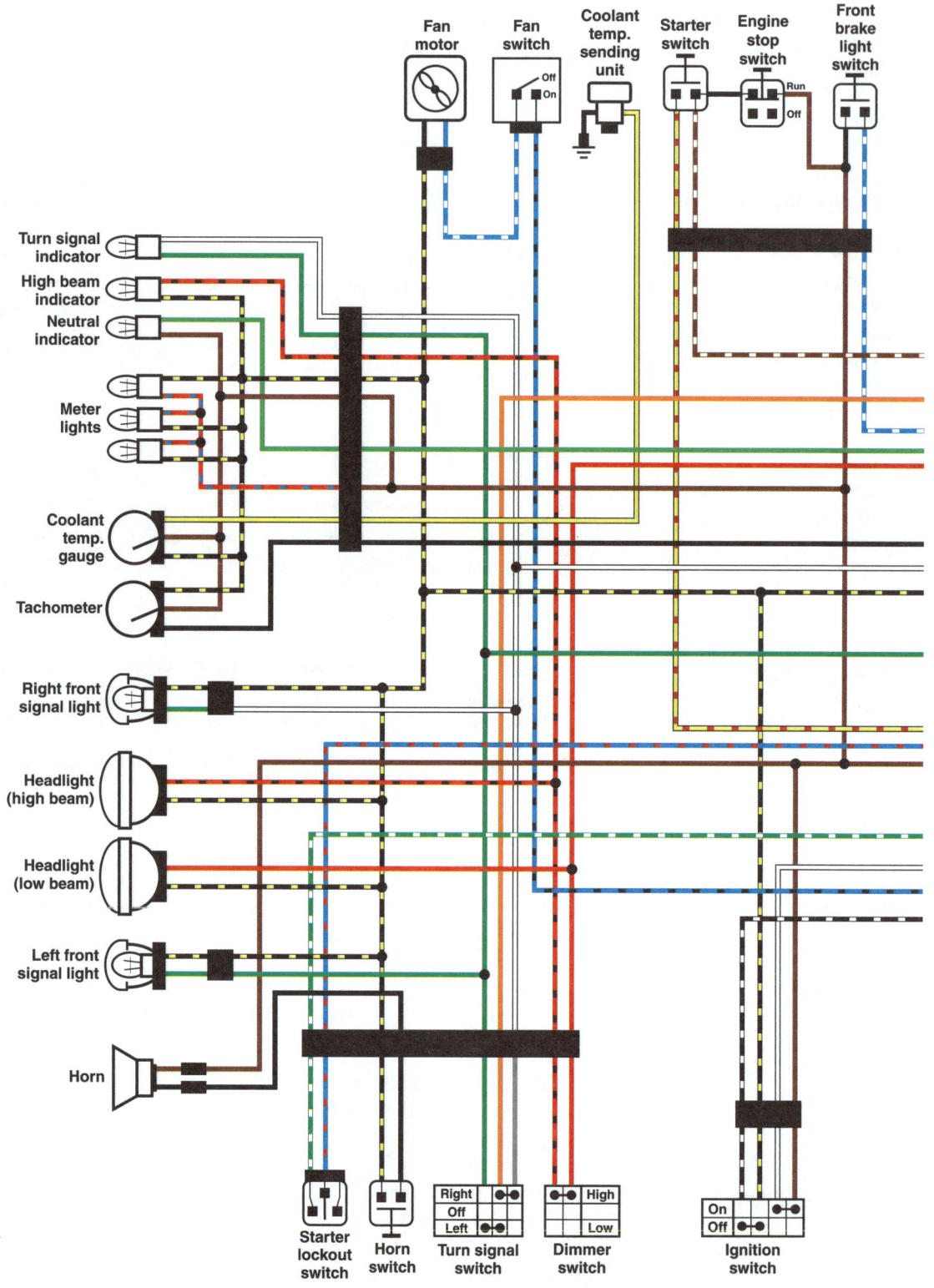

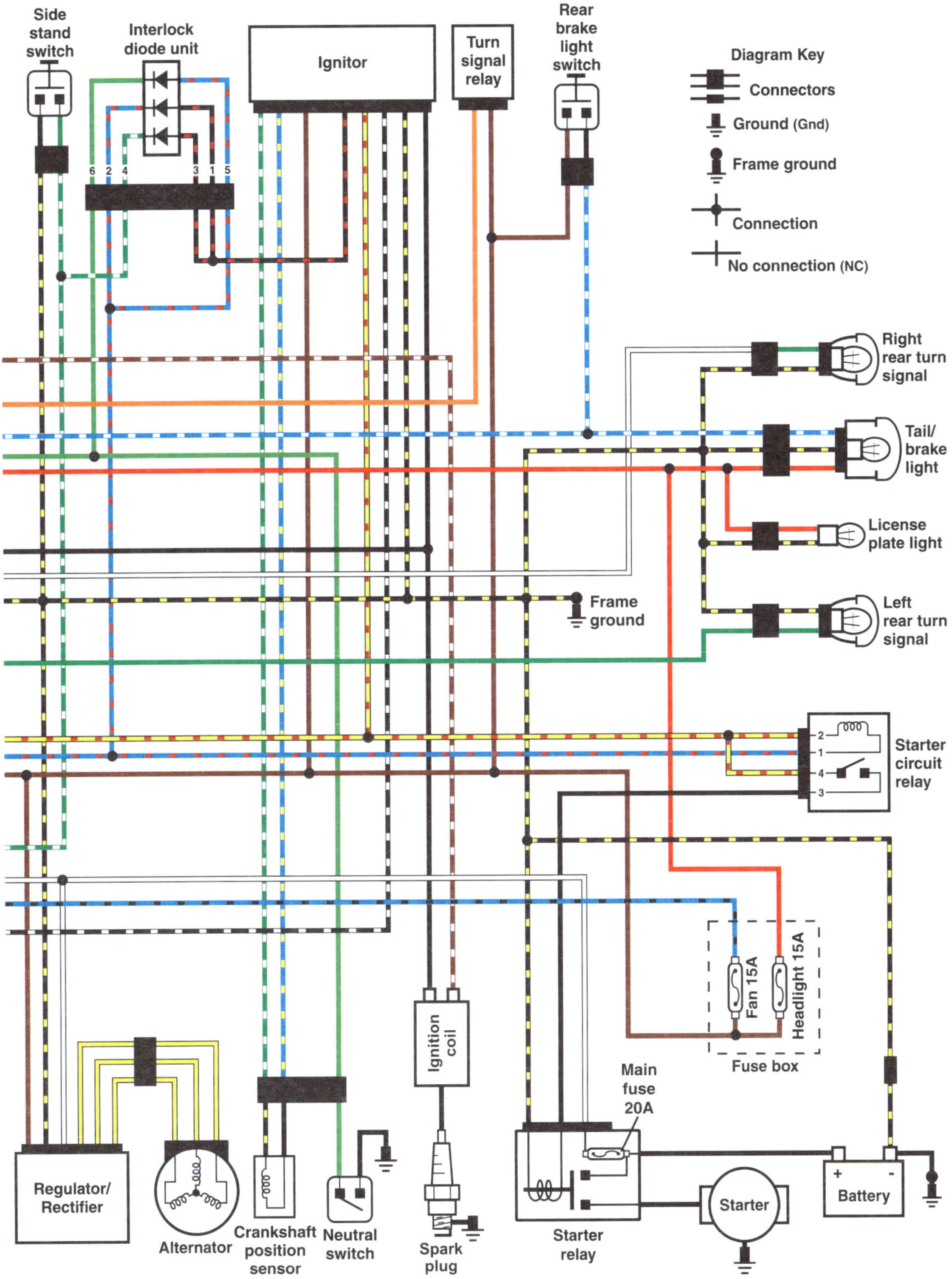

WIRING DIAGRAM

297

NOTES

NOTES

NOTES

MAINTENANCE LOG

Date	Miles	Type of Service

Check out *clymer.com* for our full line of powersport repair manuals.

M308	500 & 600cc Twins, 55-69
M502-3	BMW R50/5-R100GS PD, 70-96
M500-3	BMW K-Series, 85-97
M501-3	K1200RS, GT & LT, 98-10
M503-3	R850, R1100, R1150 & R1200C, 93-05
M309	F650, 1994-2000
M419	Sportsters, 59-85
M429-5	XL/XLH Sportster, 86-03
M427-3	XL Sportster, 04-11
M418	Panheads, 48-65
M420	Shovelheads, 66-84
M421-3	FLS/FXS Evolution, 84-99
M423-2	FLS/FXS Twin Cam, 00-05
M250	FLS/FXS/FXC Softail, 06-09
M422-3	FLH/FLT/FXR Evolution, 84-98
M430-4	FLH/FLT Twin Cam, 99-05
M252	FLH/FLT, 06-09
M426	VRSC Series, 02-07
M424-2	FXD Evolution, 91-98
M425-3	FXD Twin Cam, 99-05
M316	Odyssey FL250, 77-84
M311	ATC, TRX & Fourtrax 70-125, 70-87
M433	Fourtrax 90, 93-00
M326	ATC185 & 200, 80-86
M347	ATC200X & Fourtrax 200SX, 86-88
M455	ATC250 & Fourtrax 200/250, 84-87
M342	ATC250R, 81-84
M348	TRX250R/Fourtrax 250R & ATC250R, 85-89
M456-4	TRX250X 87-92; TRX300EX 93-06
M446-3	TRX250 Recon & Recon ES, 97-07
M215	TRX250EX, 01-05
M346-3	TRX300/Fourtrax 300 & TRX300FW/Fourtrax 4x4, 88-00
M200-2	TRX350 Rancher, 00-06
M459-3	TRX400 Foreman 95-03
M454-4	TRX400EX 99-07
M201	TRX450R & TRX450ER, 04-09
M205	TRX450 Foreman, 98-04
M210	TRX500 Rubicon, 01-04
M206	TRX500 Foreman, 05-11
M310-13	50-110cc OHC Singles, 65-99
M315	100-350cc OHC, 69-82
M317	125-250cc Elsinore, 73-80
M442	CR60-125R Pro-Link, 81-88
M431-2	CR80R, 89-95, CR125R, 89-91
M435	CR80R & CR80RB, 96-02
M457-2	CR125R, 92-97; CR250R, 92-96
M464	CR125R, 1998-2002
M443	CR250R-500R Pro-Link, 81-87
M432-3	CR250R, 88-91 & CR500R, 88-01
M437	CR250R, 97-01
M352	CRF250R, CRF250X, CRF450R & CRF450X, 02-05
M319-3	XR50R, CRF50F, XR70R & CRF70F, 97-09
M312-14	XR/XR75-100, 75-91
M222	XR80R, CRF80F, XR100R, & CRF100F, 92-09
M318-4	XL/XR/TLR 125-200, 79-03
M328-4	XL/XR250, 78-00; XL/XR350R 83-85; XR200R, 84-85; XR250L, 91-96
M320-2	XR400R, 96-04
M221	XR600R, 91-07; XR650L, 93-07
M339-8	XL/XR 500-600, 79-90
M225	XR650R, 00-07

M321	125-200cc Twins, 65-78
M322	250-350cc Twins, 64-74
M323	250-360cc Twins, 74-77
M324-5	Twinstar, Rebel 250 & Nighthawk 250, 78-03
M334	400-450cc Twins, 78-87
M333	450 & 500cc Twins, 65-76
M335	CX & GL500/650, 78-83
M344	VT500, 83-88
M313	VT700 & 750, 83-87
M314-3	VT750 Shadow Chain Drive, 98-06
M440	VT1100C Shadow, 85-96
M460-4	VT1100 Series, 95-07
M230	VTX1800 Series, 02-08
M231	VTX1300 Series, 03-09
M332	CB350-550, SOHC, 71-78
M345	CB550 & 650, 83-85
M336	CB650, 79-82
M341	CB750 SOHC, 69-78
M337	CB750 DOHC, 79-82
M436	CB750 Nighthawk, 91-93 & 95-99
M325	CB900, 1000 & 1100, 80-83
M439	600 Hurricane, 87-90
M441-2	CBR600F2 & F3, 91-98
M445-2	CBR600F4, 99-06
M220	CBR600RR, 03-06
M434-2	CBR900RR Fireblade, 93-99
M329	500cc V-Fours, 84-86
M349	700-1000cc Interceptor, 83-85
M458-2	VFR700F-750F, 86-97
M438	VFR800FI Interceptor, 98-00
M327	700-1100cc V-Fours, 82-88
M508	ST1100/Pan European, 90-02
M340	GL1000 & 1100, 75-83
M504	GL1200, 84-87
M505	GL1500 Gold Wing, 88-92
M506-2	GL1500 Gold Wing, 93-00
M507-3	GL1800 Gold Wing, 01-10
M462-2	GL1500C Valkyrie, 97-03
M465-3	Bayou KLF220 & KLF250, 88-10
M466-4	Bayou KLF300, 86-04
M467	Bayou KLF400, 93-99
M470	Lakota KEF300, 95-99
M385-2	Mojave KSF250, 87-04
M350-9	80-350cc Rotary Valve, 66-01
M444-2	KX60, 83-02; KX80 83-90
M448-2	KX80, 91-00; KX85, 01-10 & KX100, 89-09
M351	KDX200, 83-88
M447-3	KX125 & KX250, 82-91; KX500, 83-04
M472-2	KX125, 92-00
M473-2	KX250, 92-00
M474-3	KLR650, 87-07
M240-2	KLR650, 08-12
M355	KZ400, KZ/Z440, EN450 & EN500, 74-95
M360-3	EX500, GPZ500S, & Ninja 500R, 87-02
M356-5	Vulcan 700 & 750, 85-06
M354-3	Vulcan 800 & Vulcan 800 Classic, 95-05
M357-2	Vulcan 1500, 87-99
M471-3	Vulcan 1500 Series, 96-08
M245	Vulcan 1600 Series, 03-08

M449	KZ500/550 & ZX550, 79-85
M450	KZ, Z & ZX750, 80-85
M358	KZ650, 77-83
M359-3	Z & KZ 900-1000cc, 73-81
M451-3	KZ, ZX & ZN 1000 &1100cc, 81-02
M452-3	ZX500 & Ninja ZX600, 85-97
M468-2	Ninja ZX-6, 90-04
M469	Ninja ZX-7, ZX7R & ZX7RR, 91-98
M453-3	Ninja ZX900, ZX1000 & ZX1100, 84-01
M409	Concours, 86-04
M496	3-, 4- and 6-Wheel Models w/250-425cc Engines, 85-95
M362-2	Magnum & Big Boss, 96-99
M363	Scrambler 500 4X4, 97-00
M365-4	Sportsman/Xplorer, 96-10
M366	Sportsman 600/700/800 Twins, 02-10
M367	Predator 500, 03-07
M381	ALT/LT 125 & 185, 83-87
M475	LT230 & LT250, 85-90
M380-2	LT250R Quad Racer, 85-92
M483-2	LT-4WD, LT-F4WDX & LT-F250, 87-98
M270-2	LT-Z400, 03-08
M343-2	LT-F500F Quadrunner, 98-02
M369	125-400cc, 64-81
M371	RM50-400 Twin Shock, 75-81
M379	RM125-500 Single Shock, 81-88
M386	RM80-250, 89-95
M400	RM125, 96-00
M401	RM250, 96-02
M476	DR250-350, 90-94
M477-3	DR-Z400E, S & SM, 00-09
M384-4	LS650 Savage/S40, 86-07
M372	GS400-450 Chain Drive, 77-87
M484-3	GS500E Twins, 89-02
M361	SV650, 1999-2002
M481-5	VS700-800 Intruder/S50, 85-07
M261-2	1500 Intruder/C90, 98-09
M260-2	Volusia/Boulevard C50, 01-08
M482-3	VS1400 Intruder/S83, 87-07
M368	GT380, 550 & 750, 72-77
M373	GS550, 77-86
M364	GS650, 81-83
M370	GS750, 77-82
M376	GS850-1100 Shaft Drive, 79-84
M378	GS1100 Chain Drive, 80-81
M383-3	Katana 600, 88-96 GSX-R750-1100, 86-87
M331	GSX-R600, 97-00
M264	GSX-R600, 01-05
M478-2	GSX-R750, 88-92; GSX750F Katana, 89-96
M485	GSX-R750, 96-99
M377	GSX-R1000, 01-04
M266	GSX-R1000, 05-06
M265	GSX1300R Hayabusa, 99-07
M338	Bandit 600, 95-00
M353	GSF1200 Bandit, 96-03

M499-2	YFM80 Moto-4, Badger & Raptor, 85-08
M394	YTM200, 225 & YFM200, 83-86
M488-5	Blaster, 88-05
M489-2	Timberwolf, 89-00
M487-5	Warrior, 87-04
M486-6	Banshee, 87-06
M490-3	Moto-4 & Big Bear, 87-04
M493	Kodiak, 93-98
M287	YFZ450, 04-09
M285-2	Grizzly 660, 02-08
M280-2	Raptor 660R, 01-05
M290	Raptor 700R, 06-09
M492-2	PW50 & 80 Y-Zinger & BW80 Big Wheel 80, 81-02
M410	80-175 Piston Port, 68-76
M415	250-400 Piston Port, 68-76
M412	DT & MX Series, 77-83
M414	IT125-490, 76-86
M393	YZ50-80 Monoshock, 78-90
M413	YZ100-490 Monoshock, 76-84
M390	YZ125-250, 85-87 YZ490, 85-90
M391	YZ125-250, 88-93 & WR250Z, 91-93
M497-2	YZ125, 94-01
M498	YZ250, 94-98; WR250Z, 94-97
M406	YZ250F & WR250F, 01-03
M491-2	YZ400F, 98-99 & 426F, 00-02; WR400F, 98-00 & 426F, 00-01
M417	XT125-250, 80-84
M480-3	XT350, 85-00; TT350, 86-87
M405	XT/TT 500, 76-81
M416	XT/TT 600, 83-89
M403	650cc Twins, 70-82
M395-10	XV535-1100 Virago, 81-03
M495-6	V-Star 650, 98-09
M281-4	V-Star 1100, 99-09
M283	V-Star 1300, 07-10
M282-2	Road Star, 99-07
M404	XS750 & XS850, 77-81
M387	XJ550, XJ600 & FJ600, 81-92
M494	XJ600 Seca II/Diversion, 92-98
M388	YX600 Radian & FZ600, 86-90
M396	FZR600, 89-93
M392	FZ700-750 & Fazer, 85-87
M411	XS1100, 78-81
M461	YZF-R6, 99-04
M398	YZF-R1, 98-03
M399	FZ1, 01-05
M397	FJ1100 & 1200, 84-93
M375	V-Max, 85-03
M374-2	Royal Star, 96-10
M330	Vintage British Street Bikes, BSA 500–650cc Unit Twins; Norton 750 & 850cc Commandos; Triumph 500-750cc Twins
M300	Vintage Dirt Bikes, V. 1 Bultaco, 125-370cc Singles; Montesa, 123-360cc Singles; Ossa, 125-250cc Singles
M305	Vintage Japanese Street Bikes Honda, 250 & 305cc Twins; Kawasaki, 250-750cc Triples; Kawasaki, 900 & 1000cc Fours